THE CHOMSKY READER

The CHOMSKY READER

Noam Chomsky

Edited by James Peck

Pantheon books
NEW YORK

Library of Congress Cataloging-in-Publication Data

Chomsky, Noam.
The Chomsky reader.

Includes index.
1. United States—Foreign relations—1945–
I. Peck, James, 1944-   . II. Title.
E840.C47   1987   327.73   86-42975
ISBN 0-394-55956-8
ISBN 0-394-75173-6 (pbk.)

Manufactured in the United States of America

Book Design by Guenet Abraham

30 29 28 27 26 25 24 23 22

CONTENTS

INTRODUCTION

To confront a mind that radically alters our perception of the world is one of life's most unsettling yet liberating experiences. Unsettling because it can undercut carefully constructed rationales, liberating because at last the obvious is seen for what it is. However troubling reality may be, human dignity is not affirmed in fleeing it. Rather, dignity lies in seeing reality for what it is—and acting responsibly in the face of it.

In all American history, no one's writings are more unsettling than Noam Chomsky's. He is among our greatest dissenters. No intellectual tradition quite captures his voice; thinking within traditions is anathema to him. No party claims him; he is a spokesman for no ideology. His position is not a liberalism become radical, or a conservatism in revolt against the betrayal of claimed principles. It is an indication of the radical nature of his dissent that it fits nowhere.

Such a radical stance is hard to sustain. Even our most famous dissenters have often turned back from what they saw. Their insights became too painful. Many lapsed into despair, lamenting as did Mark Twain the follies of human nature, or as did Henry Adams the failure of the American promise.

But Chomsky does not turn back. He relentlessly pursues what he sees. No one has exposed more forcefully the self-righteous beliefs on which America's imperial role is based, or delineated more effectively the appalling actions which maintain it. No one has focused more compellingly on the violence of our world, or conveyed more directly the responsibility of the United States for much of it. Few have so carefully dissected how America's acclaimed freedoms mask its irresponsible power and unjustified privilege.

Chomsky's insights, though forbidding in their intensity, bring that sense of relief that comes when someone speaks the truth directly. That relief was palpable among Chomsky's readers in the 1960s and 1970s when the war raged in Vietnam. Bluntly, unsparingly, he marshaled the evidence and described the brutal realities of the war—American aggression, genocide, war crimes, mass murder. He showed us how these realities were carefully homogenized and sanitized on the evening news to make them acceptable to the powers that be. And he asked why this was so.

His answer is shocking at first: there is a pervasive, omnipresent ideological process of indoctrination that permeates American life, makes us immune to the suffering all around us, and blinds us to what is all too obvious. In these writings, Chomsky explores logically and methodically how the process works. As he looks at its workings in Vietnam, Central America, and the Middle East, he makes us confront the way in which the very foundations of American civilization and its economic life are at war with the prospects for human dignity and freedom—here and abroad.

His tenacity is extraordinary. It is there in the skillfully crafted logical character of his writings, the careful gathering of evidence, the undiminished ardor over the years to expose the mystifications so continually used to conceal the truth. It is there as well in his outpouring of writings for even the smallest journals, in his determination through countless speaking engagements to reach any audience willing to listen. In the early days of the antiwar movement, Chomsky willingly came and spoke with just a handful of people, with students in all disciplines—from physics to Asian studies—urging them to use their minds and not just their bodies to oppose the war; to not have illusions about America's aggression in Vietnam, or the long-term character of the struggle to end it; to not seek easy alternative faiths in other countries: not in Castro's Cuba, or Ho Chi Minh's Vietnam, or Mao's China.

Today Chomsky draws large audiences of college students never exposed to his writings about Vietnam. But his impact is comparable: his direct portrayal of U.S. policy around the world communicates a sense that people can see if they care to, if they step back just long enough to question the ideological milieu which shapes them.

Now as then, his is not the counsel of despair. True, Chomsky does not believe that the truth by itself will simply win out, given the realities of power he describes. But he refuses to turn from analyzing the reasons for the evils and horrors of our time, for they are neither unknowable nor intractable. They are all too understandable. Otherwise so many efforts would not be undertaken to deflect such realities, much as the psyche deflects painful truths deeply known within, but for that reason consciously denied all the more fervently as irrelevant.

Chomsky's achievement lies in the extraordinary and illuminating consistency with which he uses his rational intensity on any problem he analyzes. His use of science and reason is essentially the same everywhere. It connotes a unity of outlook and mind rare among intellectuals today, a conviction that reason, however limited, should examine everything—from global questions of war and peace to the most intricate questions of human intelligence, creativity, IQ, and language.

To ask the fundamental questions takes one outside prevailing assumptions. And Chomsky has an uncanny ability, as do many great thinkers, to make the unknown ultimately appear obvious. This is as true of his world-famous work in linguistics as of his political analyses. In linguistics, he began by challenging the field's reigning beliefs and ended up revolutionizing them. He started as an outsider, as the interview which opens this book suggests, and in many ways remains so to this day. But his work continues at the center of linguistic debates.

Elsewhere, the story is quite different. Chomsky's political writings are just as central to an understanding of our time as are his linguistic writings to our understanding of language. Yet they are often studiously ignored or angrily dismissed. His rational intensity, so applauded in linguistics, is derided when he turns it upon the United States.

Why this is so suggests something of the dimensions of Chomsky's intellectual achievement and the character of the questions he raises. Chomsky's consistent application of reason exposes the inconsistency of others—and their often active propagation of ideology under the guise of rational analysis and science. His laserlike rationality is so radical, as others' thinking is not, because of its intense anti-ideological ethos. Ideology and science are veritable opposites in Chomsky's thought. It is his acute awareness of this opposition that makes him such a remarkable demystifier of beliefs that cannot stand the light of reason.

Chomsky's writings from the mid-1960s to the present take us into one taboo subject after another. In "Psychology and Ideology," he dissects B. F. Skinner's popular behaviorism and portrays the near total bankruptcy of modern social science. Far from an accurate depiction of human nature, Chomsky finds in social science no scientific basis for the most widely held assumptions of contemporary thought. None for the argument that individuals labor only for gain and wealth, or the belief that people are inherently aggressive or egocentric, or the conviction that humans are so constituted as to feel deprived if others are particularly talented in certain areas and are acclaimed for their accomplishments. And his analysis of "meritocracy" reveals the crude and misleading assumptions about creativity and intelligence upon which it rests. Instead of the comforting rationale that merit breeds success and that the successful have merit, Chomsky suggests, a more rational approach would be to speculate that in our society "wealth and power tend to accrue to those who are ruthless, cunning, avaricious, self-seeking, lacking in sympathy and compassion, subservient to authority and willing to abandon principle for material gain, and so on."

Chomsky is not spelling out a specific theory of human freedom here. His sympathy for anarchist thinkers (he often speaks of himself as a "libertarian socialist") reflects his deep challenge to all comprehensive doctrines about human nature, all simplifying visions of humanity's potential diversity, all unjustifiable restraints. We still have, he writes, only glimmerings of insight into freedom and man's capacities in history and the sciences. Our awareness of them rests "one way or another on intuition and personal experience, extrapolations from particles of evidence." Yet he thinks it possible that there is a deep "instinct for freedom" in man, and he suggests that where ideology thrives, freedom is likely to be under attack. For ideology flourishes where there is a denial of human diversity and creativity. And it finds its most suitable home amid the rationales for the state's power and actions.

The United States has a long history of critical intellectuals, but Chomsky does not quite fit into any American tradition of protest. He is not part of that long line of critics—from Emerson and Thoreau to J. William Fulbright and Martin Luther King, Jr.—who bemoaned America's betrayal of its promise. He does not share the belief that America is a "city on a hill," a nation that operates according to principles radically different from others, or that this is a country in which ideas flow relatively freely and without discrimination, where the truth generally wins out over falsehood. Nor does he accept a vision of America as a well-intentioned, morally inclined power whose ideals embody the best aspirations of mankind. No American dream is part of his beliefs.

Chomsky's analysis of America's most popular and omnipresent self-images is thorough and devastating. His careful scrutiny reveals them to be neither accurate nor rational. Rather, they are part of an ideological ethos whose function is comparable with what all great powers require: an ideological rationale for their wealth and power, whether it be called Pax Romana, *mission civilisatrice,* or "the white man's burden." They manifest an adamant refusal to see that the United States secretes its own ways of seeing the world, shaped to the needs of quite specific, powerful interests. Often so noble and inspiring, the rhetoric of American life is quite compatible with an aggressive global policy. Lamentations about American "innocence" fit snugly with ruthless pursuit of self-interest by powerful institutions and individuals throughout U.S. history. The "free market" involves a freedom for some, inseparable from a global system of exploitation and injustice.

What is particular about Chomsky's perspective is that he does not merely ask why this is so, but why we should ever have expected otherwise given the world we live in. Why expect societies to expose their actual inner workings when suitable rationalizations serve powerful interests far more effectively? Why are we shocked that societies have castes of thinkers who propagate the faith, that great powers manufacture the rationales for their imperial and self-interested pursuits using the most noble-sounding rhetoric? Why are we surprised that nations themselves, rather than powerful, specific interests within them, are depicted as acting for the well-being of society in foreign affairs?

Much of the power of Chomsky's analysis flows from the detailed ways in which he shows how the United States is not exempt from what is so reasonably expected from others. A rational approach will begin by looking for what is reasonable to expect of all nations. Thus Chomsky expects to find great powers cloaking their aggressive self-interested quests in clouds of inspiring rhetoric, while all along a chorus of its supporters insist that it is uniquely exempt from the aggressive pursuits so easily depicted in its enemies. He suggests that a reasonable way to understand the foreign policy of any state begins by studying the domestic social structure. Who sets foreign policy? What interests do they represent? On what is their domestic power based? The policy that evolves can reasonably be expected to reflect the special interests of those who shape it.

Further, it is only reasonable to expect that the harsh facts of social and political life will be mystified, guarded, enshrouded in complexity if they threaten the faith. In every society, groups will emerge to disguise the obvious, to obfuscate the workings of power, to spin a web of mystification through transcendent goals and purposes, totally benign, that allegedly guide national policy. Quite understandably such people will not see themselves as a caste of propagandists or as indoctrinators. They prefer to think of themselves as educators, religious leaders, often as fervent apostles of truths which place them in conflict with the state. Yet to see just what the shared consensus is in a society, Chomsky suggests, look at what the "influential" critics do not challenge. There the extent to which they are submissive and obedient to the state can be expected to reveal itself.

Ferocious debates are not indications that consensus values are questioned. Doves and hawks can reasonably be expected to differ on the exact nature of the evil practices, real or imagined, of current enemies of the state, but the debates will go on within a quite expectable narrow set of patriotic premises. Both speak of "the nation" as the active agent in international affairs, not special groups within it. Both tend to argue that the "national interests" as articulated reflect such common interests as might be generally shared within society.

Chomsky skillfully demonstrates how this process works. Debates about Vietnam between hawks and doves (or on Nicaragua or El Salvador or numerous other countries) might heatedly dispute whether the war was a "costly mistake," an "error," even a great "tragedy." But "responsible" debate simply excludes from serious consideration that the war was wrong in principle or an act of aggression.

Like George Orwell, Chomsky has an uncanny ability to suggest the ideological message in all its blatancy just beneath the apparently objective façade of argument. At first, his statements startle—such as when he calls America's presence in South Vietnam an "invasion." But his masterful use of comparisons exposes the ideological character underlying our political debates. Thus Chomsky compares South Vietnam and Afghanistan to show how little difficulty U.S. observers have in spotting a Russian invasion of a country. If a puppet regime in Kabul "requests" Soviet military aid, there is no question that aggression is taking place. But when a puppet regime in South Vietnam "requests" U.S. military aid, no aggression or invasion is even at issue. Quite the contrary.

Or again, if the Soviet Union invades Hungary or Czechoslovakia, such acts are easily seen to involve questions about the basic character of the Soviet system. Yet explanations for America's role in Vietnam or Nicaragua or countless other lands invite no comparable questions about the basic character of the U.S. system. The focus is on the countless difficulties in Vietnam, the diabolic skills of the Communists, or misguided American idealism. It is acceptable to lament the failure of America's noble impulses that lead people astray. Or the cultural differences that limit effective action. Or even the corruption, brutality, and ignorance of the people being aided. But should someone focus on the nature of the capitalist system, for example, he will likely be dismissed as "simplistic," a "vulgar economic determinist." If U.S. government documents show a preoccupation with just such economic issues, this is explained away by being carefully set within "wider" parameters of concern. Speak of "power drives" of a nation rather than the needs of capital. Speak of them as distinct from specific social and economic organizations. And remind your audience that in the end America is different—a well-intentioned, uniquely nonimperial, nonexploitative power, ultimately benevolent, and attuned to the aspirations and strivings of individuals throughout the world. Then let the debate rage on: no fundamental level of the American faith will be deeply challenged, and the debate itself can be held up as an example of just how free America really is.

For Chomsky, these debates are shaped by a group he calls the "secular priesthood," the intellectuals, technocrats, and propagandists whose task it is to make the actions of the state palatable, its lofty, transcendent ideals believable. Chomsky's analysis of the secular priesthood is among the most suggestive examinations in our time of just how and why ideology and indoctrination are so pervasive in democratic societies. Again, his method is the same. If other societies generate an unchallengeable consensus, the question is not how the United States is exempt from the process, but how the process works here.

Perhaps no other theme of his so bewilders intellectuals or is greeted with such incredulity. That they, the most educated, are described as among the most ideological elements in a society is utterly unacceptable to them. However much they see other intellectuals as ideological, they cannot envision this of themselves. Though they attack intellectuals in other societies for endorsing state policies, they rarely see this as part of their function. Societies elsewhere can be seen as having rituals and faiths that constrict the range of debate, but a comparable process in the United States is inconceivable to them.

By examining both the faith and those who propagate it, Chomsky lets us see how the freedoms that do exist in the United States are used mainly to reinforce rather than challenge the prevailing consensus. He suggests why proliferating numbers of experts and specialists do not breed greater insight into the innermost workings of our society, but obfuscate it, making people feel passive and less able to effectively participate. He explores how our domestic freedoms not unexpectedly are interwoven with the dynamics of empire, instead of being at war with them; why our freedoms and a process of indoctrination can go hand in hand. What Chomsky offers is a radically different approach for thinking about the

United States, one in which our freedoms exist within an ideological consensus that limits debate and protects powerful interests in ways all too similar to those in which obviously repressive societies operate.

As Chomsky writes in "The Manufacture of Consent," the mechanisms of indoctrination in a totalitarian regime are relatively simple and transparent. Its official spokesmen and policy intellectuals are expected to parrot the official line. Overt expression of criticism is risky, but internally the critic often grasps quite well the propaganda message and rejects it.

In the United States, the mechanisms of indoctrination are different, but equally omnipresent. There are brutal acts of state violence (as those who have borne the brunt of them know only too well). But the absence of the kind of oppression and coercion that exist in other societies necessitates a particularly virulent ideological dynamic in American life. "Brainwashing under freedom" is a more apt way to understand America, Chomsky suggests, than the comforting shibboleths of "freedom."

Nor have some of the most perceptive establishment thinkers thought otherwise as they sought to ensure that the "farsighted" insights of the leadership will become palatable to the people. As Chomsky writes, it is what Walter Lippmann was referring to when he spoke of the "manufacture of consent," or Edward Bernays when he talked about the "engineering of consent," or Harold Lasswell when he wrote that with the rise of democracy, "propaganda attains eminence as the one means of mass mobilization which is cheaper than violence, bribery or other possible control techniques."

All these writers have noted the connection between the elitism of the priesthood and the consequent passivity of the people. Chomsky probes many of the actual costs and consequences—moral, political, cultural, and in terms of basic human decency. Indeed, the ways people are desensitized has been a notable theme in his writings beginning with Vietnam. Was it, he asked, a testament to our "free institutions" that some of our war crimes were so publicly displayed—or a graphic illustration of how we have become immune to suffering?

Why is this faith believed so intensely? Why is it necessary for the operations of our society? Why is it so pervasive in the media and in our history texts? Why are the basic facts about the role of corporations in foreign policy not known or, if investigated, relegated to an academic corner or the corporate boardroom, where they will be sure not to enter the mainstream of public debate?

The answer is simple. If the truth is told without ideological varnish, ideologists fear, people will not support them: people will not tolerate the way power operates if they see what is actually happening. Possibly they are wrong, Chomsky says, and people will support the policies anyway. But proponents of the faith do not act as though this is likely.

This is why the secular priesthood, beginning with Vietnam, so often ignores Chomsky's work. The truths he speaks are not admissible in the American terms of debate. The nature of the debate over Vietnam makes this graphically clear. Some people have never seen Vietnam as anything but an aberration; others forswore their earlier attacks on American policy and once again spoke of a more benign America committed to freedom and human rights. But there is none of this in Chomsky, no turning away from the nature of American imperialism or the genocidal character of the war in Vietnam. His analysis leaves no aspect of American history untouched. Vietnam, as Chomsky shows us, was no gross aberration in American life; to understand it fully is to face all-too-standard U.S. operating procedures. A confrontation ultimately with a nation whose foreign policy is a record of ruthless pursuits of its imperial self-interests as violent as any great power in history.

Chomsky's writings about Vietnam will long remain among the most valuable ever written precisely because they show so much of the war's reality at the time, far more than most of the current outpouring of books reassessing the war's meaning today. They suggest as well just how successfully the U.S. political system has worked to digest the war with barely a trace of its deepest implications, why the people who ran it still largely manage national affairs, and why so many critics have lapsed into silence or lack access to the national media.

In one area after another, as this book reveals, Chomsky's writings continue to challenge the orthodoxies of our time. In the Middle East, he has shown how the mystique of Israel as supported by America continues to thwart any resolution of the Israeli-Palestinian conflict. No one has more directly confronted the issues involved in Israel's dispossession of the Palestinians ("One land—two nations. That is the essence of the problem of Israel and the Palestinians"), or so well delineated the global interests the United States pursues in the region.

His writings on Central America today are comparable to his essays on Vietnam. Once again, there is the blunt description of the character of the regimes the United States supports, in Guatemala and El Salvador; the war against Nicaragua, and the assiduous pursuits of its imperial interests in the area.

Here, as elsewhere, there are no painless answers for Americans willing to confront what their nation is doing, no easy solution to the arms race, given the interests served by the Cold War and the Keynesian militarism that fuels the American economy; no reason to believe that America any more than the Soviet Union is interested in any peaceful solutions to the world's problems that would challenge its own power.

■ ■ ■

In dissecting the obfuscations it is reasonable to expect in the United States and other societies, Chomsky also focuses in his writings on the American attempt, particularly since 1945, to construct an integrated global economy dominated by U.S. capital. Its operating principle, he argues, is "economic freedom," meaning freedom for U.S. business to invest, to sell, and to repatriate profits. Its two essential prerequisites are a favorable investment climate and specific forms of local stability. Though such "freedom" is lauded (and largely believed compatible with all others by the secular priesthood), its actual consequences are studiously ignored. For the United States, nothing has been more ideologically useful than anticommunism to accomplish this task. In it is displayed the quite particular shape of the "official enemy" great powers can reasonably be expected to have.

Chomsky's dissection of U.S. anticommunism is among the most persuasive yet written. Part of its power comes from his lack of any illusions about the Soviet Union or communism. This is quite clear in his depiction of the Cold War as a system of global management in which each superpower invokes the danger of the other to justify terror, violence, subversion, and aggression in its own domains. It is effectively argued in "Objectivity and Liberal Scholarship," one of his most influential essays, where he reveals the shared elitism of bolshevism and liberalism, their similar attacks on any decentralized, self-organized processes of radical social change.

Precisely this lack of illusion about the Soviet Union adds to the lack of any illusion about the U.S. invocation of anticommunism to justify U.S. foreign policy. Anticommunism's actual understanding of communism is of limited value, but how it functions ideologically casts a great deal of light on the American faith.

How might we test what anticommunism's role is? Chomsky's work suggests various ways. Let's take official explanations of what the United States stands for at face value. Is the United States anticommunist because it is fighting for political democracy? No, political democracy counts for little if "economic freedom" is challenged. In a typically illuminating comparison, Chomsky shows how U.S. policy usually evolves when political democracy is destroyed in a country while U.S. investment is freed from restraints (as in Chile under Pinochet) and contrasts this with the reaction if American economic investments are threatened, whether or not political democracy is maintained in some fashion (as in Chile under Allende). Such results are startlingly consistent.

Does anticommunism accurately state the dangers the United States faces from rival great powers and explain why it intervened halfway around the world in Vietnam? No. As Chomsky reveals in "The Mentality of the Backroom Boys," there was little government evidence to substantiate the claim that Russia or China was responsible for "internal aggression." The truth is little different in Central America today.

Is it, then, that the United States opposes communism because it fears its victory will result in terrifying bloodbaths and massacres? Yet the United States does not blanch when they are in its own interests, as in Indonesia in 1965 or the decades-long support for South Africa's own diabolic forms of inhumanity.

Is it a commitment to development or to help the poor countries of the world? Again, the key is quite different—whether local practices are compatible with direct U.S. investment. It is unthinkable that Cuba might benefit from capital grants (though invasion, assassination attempts, and blockades are quite acceptable).

But anticommunism is not just a blind faith; Chomsky shows how functional it is. It mobilizes the domestic population for vast war expenditures. It justifies a highly covert, at times overt, interventionist policy, conveniently setting aside such principles as nonintervention in the internal affairs of another country. And it practically sorts out friends and foes by their role in maintaining an integrated global economy in which American capital can operate with relative freedom. Any nation's attempt to extricate itself from the global marketplace is anathema and is labeled "Communist."

No fate is worse for the anti-Communist than a nation opting out of such a "Free World" market. Should a nation try to opt out, or take significant steps to control its own resources for the native population, the U.S. reaction is swift and savage. Chomsky shows the remarkably consistent means the United States uses to undercut such revolutionary regimes—or even a potential for them. The goal is to create such harsh conditions—as in Vietnam during and after the war or in Nicaragua today—that by the time the conflict is over there will be little left of what is needed to build a better society. No shred of a radical democratic alternative can be tolerated.

The brutalization of the regimes that remain in power is then used to justify the brutalizing actions of the United States. And in the process, United States responsibility slips safely into the background. As in Cambodia, the United States can bomb a nation to pieces. Its population can be driven into a huge urban center, the economic order reduced to ruins. And when the war ends, the United States refuses all aid and trade, and tries to make others do the same. The barbarous contexts which shaped the Khmer Rouge are largely explained away, the reasons for their crimes and the mass suffering decisively shifted onto Communist iniquity. American crimes become "mistakes" by a well-intentioned power. The Khmer Rouge atrocities flow logically and naturally from demonic ideological Communist convictions. A more useful ideological explaining away of U.S. actions is hard to imagine.

Chomsky, in Cambodia as elsewhere, is not making the United States the source of all the crimes and horrors in the world. But he relentlessly insists upon asking just what responsibility the United States bears. He does so because it is our responsibility. He has no illusions about the prospects of revolutionary movements in the world today. Even without U.S. hostility and pressures, even without "capitalist encirclement," the truly democratic elements in revolutionary movements that he describes—in collectives, in soviets, in cooperative drives of various kinds—might well be undermined by an elite of bureaucrats and technical intelligentsia, by a Stalinist type of organization. Yet this becomes a near certainty considering the fact of capitalist encirclement which all revolutionary movements have had to face.

The odds against them are staggering. And it is the democratic elements in them that America is most at war with today, not the dictatorial shapes they succumb to. The United States can live with brutal regimes, far better than with a regime that might offer an alternative that would allow for mass participation, freedom, and radical social change. As with the Russians in Eastern Europe, neither superpower is in the slightest degree sympathetic to the emergence of democratic revolutionary forces.

Chomsky never averts his eyes from what happens to them—and why. Nor does his focus waver from the murderous violence and brutality in the world—and its victims. He does not expect the secular priesthood to accept the responsibility of intellectuals to speak the truth. But there is a deep sense of responsibility that pervades his writings—and a strong suggestion of what animates them.

> If we had the honesty and the moral courage, we would not let a day pass without hearing the cries of the victims. We would turn on the radio in the morning and listen to the voices of the people who escaped the massacres in Quiché province, and the Guazapa Mountains, and the daily press would carry front-page pictures of children dying of malnutrition and disease in the countries where order reigns and crops and beef are exported to the American market, with an explanation of why this is so. We would listen to the extensive and detailed record of terror and torture in our dependencies, compiled by Amnesty International, Americas Watch . . .

But the radios do not report this. The media are largely silent. And the reasons given, if given at all, are those comfortable to the ease of wealth and power. Chomsky does not provide answers for the world we live in.

His demystification draws on no alternative ideology. Yet his writings constitute a way of coming to understand the world without illusion. They offer a stark but not despairing view of the world—a vision without an ideology, a radicalness without blueprints or prescribed structural alternatives.

There is indeed something that resonates throughout these writings that in the end is uplifting. Chomsky is not a cynical man. Nor is he disillusioned. To become disillusioned is to have been illusioned—and this Chomsky is not. There is a deep affirmation in these writings which cuts through the bleakness, a certain nobility of humanity reaffirmed. This comes not just from the struggles of a single mind refusing to bend to a myriad of ideological pressures in our time, but from the way Chomsky's willingness to stand so outside prevailing beliefs makes him so central to a reaffirmation of a concern with human freedom and dignity, with creativity, and with the commitment to seek their multiple manifestations.

James Peck

PART ONE

ℐNTERVIEW

JP: You've rarely written much on the kinds of experiences that led to your politics, even though, it seems to me, they may have been deeply formed and influenced by your background.

NC: No. I've not thought about it a great deal. . . .

JP: For example, I am struck by how seldom you mention literature, culture, culture in the sense of a struggle to find alternative forms of life through artistic means; rarely a novel that has influenced you. Why is this so? Were there some works that did influence you?

NC: Of course there have been, but it is true that I rarely write about these matters. I am not writing about myself, and these matters don't seem particularly pertinent to the topics I am addressing. There are things that I resonate to when I read, but I have a feeling that my feelings and attitudes were largely formed prior to reading literature. In fact, I've been always resistant consciously to allowing literature to influence my beliefs and attitudes with regard to society and history.

JP: You once said, "It is not unlikely that literature will forever give far deeper insight into what is sometimes called 'the full human person' than any modes of scientific inquiry may hope to do."

NC: That's perfectly true and I believe that. I would go on to say it's not only not unlikely, but it's almost certain. But still, if I want to understand, let's say, the nature of China and its revolution, I ought to be cautious about literary renditions. Look, there's no question that as a child, when I read about China, this influenced my attitudes—*Rickshaw Boy,* for example. That had a powerful effect when I read it. It was so long ago I don't remember a thing about it, except the impact. And I don't doubt that, for me, personally, like anybody, lots of my perceptions were heightened and attitudes changed by literature over a broad range—Hebrew literature, Russian literature, and so on. But ultimately, you have to face the world as it is on the basis of other sources of evidence that you can evaluate. Literature can heighten your imagination and insight and understanding, but it surely doesn't provide the evidence that you need to draw conclusions and substantiate conclusions.

JP: But it might be very influential in making one sensitive to areas of human experience otherwise not even asked about.

NC: People certainly differ, as they should, in what kinds of things make their minds work.

JP: You seem a little reticent about it.

NC: Well, I'm reticent because I don't really feel that I can draw any tight connections. I can think of things that I read that had a powerful effect on me, but whether they changed my attitudes and understanding in any striking or crucial way, I can't really say.

JP: What kind of schools did you go to as a child?

NC: I was sent to an experimental progressive school from infancy, before I was two, until about twelve years old, until high school, at which point I went into the academic, college-oriented school in the city.

JP: In New York?

NC: In Philadelphia. That experience, both the early experience in the progressive school and the later experience in the academically oriented high school, elite high school, was very instructive. For example, it wasn't until I was in high school that I knew I was a good student. The question had never arisen. I was very surprised when I got into high school and discovered that I was getting all A's and that was supposed to be a big deal. That question had simply never arisen in my entire education. In fact, every student in the school I had previously attended was regarded as somehow being a very successful student. There was no sense of competition, no ranking of students. It was never anything even to think about. It just never came up that there was a question of how you were ranked relative to other students. Well, anyway, at this particular school, which was essentially a Deweyite school and I think a very good one, judging from my experience, there was a tremendous premium on individual creativity, not in the sense of slapping paints on paper, but doing the kind of work and thinking that you were interested in. Interests were encouraged and children were encouraged to pursue their interests. They worked jointly with others or by themselves. It was a lively atmosphere, and the sense was that everybody was doing something important.

It wasn't that they were a highly select group of students. In fact, it was the usual mixture in such a school, with some gifted students and some problem children who had dropped out of the public schools. But nevertheless, at least as a child, that was the sense that one had—that, if competing at all, you were competing with yourself. What can I do? But no sense of strain about it and certainly no sense of relative ranking. Very different from what I notice with my own children, who as far back as the second grade knew who was "smart" and who was "dumb," who was high-tracked and who was low-tracked. This was a big issue.

Well, then I got to high school, the academic high school in the public school system, which was supposed to be a very good high school, and it was a real shocker. For one thing, as I said, there was the shock of discovering that I was a good student, which had never occurred to me before. And then there was the whole system of prestige and value that went along with that. And the intense competitiveness and the regimentation. In fact, I can remember a lot about elementary school, the work I did, what I studied and so on. I remember virtually nothing about high school. It's almost an absolute blank in my memory apart from the emotional tone, which was quite negative.

If I think back about my experience, there's a dark spot there. That's what schooling generally is, I suppose. It's a period of regimentation and control, part of which involves direct indoctrination, providing a system of false beliefs. But more importantly, I think, is the manner and style of preventing and blocking independent and creative thinking and imposing hierarchies and competitiveness and the need to excel, not in the sense of doing as well as you can, but doing better than the next person. Schools vary, of course, but I think that those features are commonplace. I know that they're not necessary, because, for example, the school that I went to as a child wasn't like that at all.

I think schools could be run quite differently. That would be very important, but I really don't think that any society based on authoritarian hierarchic institutions would tolerate such a school system for very long. As Sam Bowles and Herb Gintis have pointed out, it might be tolerated for the elite, because they would have to learn how to think and create and so on, but not for the mass of the population. There are roles that the public schools play in society that can be very destructive.

JP: What was your college experience like?

NC: I was probably lucky in that respect. I really never went to college. I did finally get a Ph.D, and I did go through the first two years of college, but after that, I did not really attend college in the normal manner.

I attended the University of Pennsylvania, living at home, of course, which meant several hours commuting, and working, mainly teaching Hebrew school afternoons and Sunday, sometimes evenings as well. There was no thought in those days of attending college in any other way in our circles, and no financial means to do so. The first two years of college were pretty much an extension of high school, except in one respect. I entered with a good deal of enthusiasm and expectations that all sorts of fascinating prospects would open up, but these did not survive long, except in a few cases—an exciting freshman course with C. West Churchman in philosophy, for example, and courses in Arabic that I took and became quite immersed in, in part out of political interests, in part out of an interest in Semitic linguistics that derives from my father's work in that area, and in part through the influence of Giorgio Levi Della Vida, an antifascist exile from Italy who was a marvelous person as well as an outstanding scholar. At the end of two years, I was planning to drop out to pursue my own interests, which were then largely political. This was 1947, and I had just turned eighteen. I was deeply interested, as I had been for some years, in radical politics with an anarchist or left-wing (anti-Leninist) Marxist flavor, and even more deeply involved in Zionist affairs and activities—or what was then called "Zionist," though the same ideas and concerns are now called "anti-Zionist." I was interested in socialist, binationalist options for Palestine, and in the kibbutzim and the whole cooperative labor system that had developed in the Jewish settlement there (the Yishuv), but had never been able to become close to the Zionist youth groups that shared these interests because they were either Stalinist or Trotskyite and I had always been strongly anti-Bolshevik. We should bear in mind that in the latter stages of the Depression, when I was growing up, and even in subsequent years to an extent, these were very lively issues.

I intended to drop out of college and to pursue these interests. The vague ideas I had at the time were to go to Palestine, perhaps to a kibbutz, to try to become involved in efforts at Arab-Jewish cooperation within a socialist framework, opposed to the deeply antidemocratic concept of a Jewish state (a position that was considered well within the mainstream of Zionism). Through these interests, I happened to meet Zellig Harris, a really extraordinary person who had a great influence on many young people in those days. He had a coherent understanding of this whole range of issues, which I lacked, and I was immensely attracted by it, and by him personally as well, also by others who I met through him. He happened to be one of the leading figures in modern linguistics, teaching at the University of Pennsylvania. His interests were very broad, linguistics being only a small corner of them, and he was a person of unusual brilliance and originality. I began to take his graduate courses; in fact, the first reading I did in linguistics was the proofs of his book *Methods in Structural Linguistics,* which appeared several years later. At his suggestion, I also began to take graduate courses in philosophy—with Nelson Goodman, Morton White, and others—and mathematics—with Nathan Fine—fields in which I had no background at all, but which I found fascinating, in part, no doubt, thanks to unusually stimulating teachers. I suppose Harris had in mind to influence me to return to college, though I don't recall talking about it particularly, and it all seemed to happen without much planning.

Anyway, it worked, but I had a highly unconventional college experience. The linguistics department consisted of a small number of graduate students, and in Harris' close circle, a very small group who shared political and other interests apart from linguistics, and was quite alienated from the general college atmosphere. In fact, our "classes" were generally held either in the Horn & Hardart restaurant across the street or in Harris' apartment in Princeton or New York, all-day sessions that ranged widely over quite a variety of topics and were intellectually exciting as well as personally very meaningful experiences. I had almost no contact with the university, apart from these connections. I was by then very deeply immersed in linguistics, philosophy, and logic, and received (highly unconventional) B.A. and M.A. degrees.

Nelson Goodman recommended me for the Society of Fellows at Harvard, and I was admitted in 1951. That carried a stipend, and was the first time I could devote myself to study and research without working on the side. With the resources of Harvard available and no formal requirements, it was a wonderful opportunity. I did technically receive a Ph.D. from Penn in 1955, submitting a chapter of a book that I was then working on—it was quite unconventional, so much so that although pretty much completed in 1955–56, it wasn't published until 1975 as the *Logical Structure of Linguistic Theory,* and then only in part. But I hadn't actually been there since 1951 and had no contact with the university apart from Harris and Goodman. So my college experience was unusual to say the least.

JP: Was it after college that you went to live on a kibbutz in Israel?

NC: I went for a few months while I was at the Society of Fellows, in 1953. The kibbutz where we lived, which was about twenty years old, was then very poor. There was very little food, and work was hard. But I liked it very much in many ways. Abstracting it from context, this was a functioning and very successful libertarian community, so I felt. And I felt it would be possible for me to find some mixture of intellectual and physical work.

I came close to returning there to live, as my wife very much wanted to do at the time. I had nothing particularly attractive here. I didn't expect to be able to have an academic career, and was not particularly interested in one. There was no major drive to stay. On the other hand, I did have a lot of interest in the kibbutz and I liked it very much when I was there. But there were things I didn't like, too. In particular, the ideological conformity was appalling. I don't know if I could have survived long in that environment because I was very strongly opposed to the Leninist ideology, as well as the general conformism, and uneasy—less so than I should have been—about the exclusiveness and the racist institutional setting.

What I did not then face honestly was the fairly obvious fact that these are Jewish institutions and are so because of legal and administrative structures and practice. So, for example, I doubt if there's an Arab in any kibbutz, and there hardly could be, because of the land laws and the role the institution plays in the Israeli system. In fact, even the Oriental Jews, some of whom were marginally at the kibbutz or in the immigrant town nearby, were treated rather shabbily, with a good deal of contempt and fear. I also visited some Arab villages, and learned some unpleasant things, which I've never seen in print, about the military administration to which Arab citizens were subjected.

Now I had some fairly strong feelings about all of that at the time. In fact, as I mentioned, I was very strongly opposed to the idea of a Jewish state back in 1947–48. I felt sure that the socialist institutions of the Yishuv—the pre-state Jewish settlement in Palestine—would not survive the state system, as they would become integrated into a sort of state management and that would destroy the aspects of the Yishuv that I found most attractive.

But, if we abstract away from those factors, the external environment, it was a kind of anarchist community.

JP: What did you do on the kibbutz? Did you find the intellectual life stimulating? And why did you leave?

NC: Remember that I was only there for about six weeks. I was completely unskilled, so I was doing only unskilled agricultural work, under the guidance of kibbutz members. I actually enjoyed the work very much, though for how long I would have, I don't know.

As for the intellectual life, this kibbutz was Buberite in origin, mainly German Jews who were quite well educated, though one of the people I came to know best was a Christian immigrant who had left a large farm he owned in Rhodesia out of hatred for the racist society there, and who was really a first-class agronomist with many interesting ideas. There were very interesting people there, but it was surreal in some ways. This was 1953, at the time of the Slansky trials in Czechoslovakia and the last stages of Stalinist lunacy. These late Stalin purges also had a strong anti-Semitic element, but people there actually defended them. They even defended the trial of a fellow kibbutz member who was an emissary of the kibbutz movement there and was charged with being a spy, which they knew to be false. Not all did, of course. Those who thought about these things—many did not—were orthodox Marxist-Leninists, and I could discern no visible departure from a fairly rigid party line, though there may well have been much that I never saw.

It was a short visit, and I returned to Harvard, planning to come back, maybe to stay, in a few years. My term at the Society of Fellows was supposed to end in 1954, but I had no job prospects and asked for a year's extension, which I received. My wife, meanwhile, went back to the kibbutz for a longer visit. We planned then to return to stay, but by then I had obtained a research position at MIT and was very much involved in my own linguistic work. For one reason or another, without any particular conscious decision at any point, we never did return.

JP: Were you active in political organizations in earlier years in the United States?

NC: I didn't have any affiliation to any group, the Zionist left or elsewhere. Partly it was that I'm not much of a "joiner," I guess. Furthermore, every organization that I knew of, on the left at least, was Leninist, either Stalinist or Trotskyite. I was always very anti-Leninist, and I simply didn't know of any group at all that shared my views. This was true of the Zionist left, and of much of the American left at the time, as far as I knew. This was the early forties that we're talking about. Quite frankly I didn't see any significant difference between the Trotskyites and the Stalinists, except that the Trotskyites had lost. They of course saw a big difference. There are some differences, but basically I thought they were exaggerated. That's what I felt at the time, and I still do feel that essentially. So there was no group that I knew of that

I could have had any affiliation with. But I was personally very much involved in lots of things that were happening.

JP: Did you come out of a political family? Was politics something that was discussed within the family?

NC: Well, my immediate family, my parents, were normal Roosevelt Democrats, and very much involved with Jewish affairs, deeply Zionist and interested in Jewish culture, the revival of Hebrew, and generally the cultural Zionism that had its origins in the ideas of people like Ahad Ha-'am, but increasingly, in mainstream Zionism. The next range of family, uncles and cousins and so on, was in part Jewish working-class, or around that kind of social group. A number of them were Communists, or close to such circles, very much involved in the politics of the Depression period. In particular, one uncle who had a lot of influence on me in the late thirties and later, at that time had a newsstand in New York which was sort of a radical center. We'd hang out all night and have discussions and arguments, there or in his small apartment nearby. The great moments of my life in those years were when I could work at the newsstand at night and listen to all this.

JP: What part of the city was that in?

NC: That was at the kiosk at Seventy-second Street and Broadway, if it's still there. There used to be four newsstands there. There were two on the way that most people left the subway station, which was to Seventy-second Street. And there were two on the other side, where few people ever left. He had one of those. It was very exciting intellectually, but I guess they didn't make much money selling newspapers. In the late thirties, it became a center for some European émigrés and others, and it was quite lively. He had been through a lot of the Marxist sectarian politics—Stalinist, Trotskyite, non-Leninist sects of one sort or another. I was just beginning to learn about all of that. It was a very lively intellectual community.

The Jewish working-class culture in New York was very unusual. It was highly intellectual, very poor; a lot of people had no jobs at all and others lived in slums and so on. But it was a rich and lively intellectual culture: Freud, Marx, the Budapest String Quartet, literature, and so forth. That was, I think, the most influential intellectual culture during my early teens.

JP: Were you also brought up in certain aspects of the Jewish cultural tradition?

NC: I was deeply immersed in that. In fact, I probably did more reading in that area than any other until I was maybe fifteen or sixteen.

JP: You rarely draw on it in your public writings. Are there reasons for that?

NC: No, it didn't seem to be particularly relevant. It's there, I mean, it certainly had a good amount of influence on me. For example, the brilliant nineteenth-century Yiddish-Hebrew writer Mendele Mocher Sfarim, who wrote about Jewish life in Eastern Europe, had tremendous instinct and understanding. It cheapens it to call it proletarian literature, but it gave a kind of understanding of the lives of the poor with a mixture of humor and sympathy and cynicism that is quite remarkable. I also read fairly widely in works of the nineteenth-century Hebrew renaissance—novels, stories, poetry, essays. I can't say what long-term effect this reading had on me. It certainly had an emotional impact.

JP: There seem to be in your thinking certain insights about society and intellectuals that span the course of your adult life. So much so that you are not surprised by what often seems to shock others. You are not shocked when intellectuals perform certain ideological functions—you expect this of them. You are not surprised when American power operates by cloaking itself in an idealistic garb to conceal its pursuit of various interests—you expect it of such power. And so on. Your insights seem less derived initially from prolonged historical observation than a sense of how things can be expected to operate.

NC: I guess I just always assumed it. It seems to me to follow from the most simple and uncontroversial assumptions about motivation and interests and the structure of power.

JP: And yet in some ways those assumptions are at the heart of what outrages individuals about your thoughts and writing. They have to be dismissed because if people were to confront them, they'd have to write differently about the United States.

NC: Well, it's interesting that it doesn't enrage anyone when I say this about enemies of the United States. Then it's obvious. What outrages them is when I try to show how these patterns also are exhibited in our own society, as they are. If I were talking to a group of Russian intellectuals, they would be outraged that I failed to see the idealism and commitment to peace and brotherhood of the Russian state. That's the way propaganda systems function.

JP: But do you wonder why so many share such assumptions—and you do not?

NC: Well, maybe part of the reason is that in a certain sense I grew up in an alien culture, in the Jewish-Zionist cultural tradition, in an immigrant community in a sense, though of course others reacted to the same conditions quite differently. I suppose I am also a child of the Depression. Some of my earliest memories, which are very vivid, are of people selling rags at our door, of violent police strikebreaking, and other Depression scenes. Whatever the reason may be, I was very much affected by events of the 1930s, the Spanish Civil War, for example, though I was barely literate. The first article I wrote was an editorial in the school newspaper on the fall of Barcelona, a few weeks after my tenth birthday. The rise of nazism also made a deep impression, intensified perhaps because we were practically the only Jewish family in a bitterly anti-Semitic Irish and German Catholic neighborhood in which there was open support for the Nazis until December 1941.

JP: Yet the "New York intellectuals" have become prime exponents of a virulent anticommunism that denies almost all the insights you start with as "common sense."

NC: In part, I think, age maybe was a lucky accident in my case. I was just a little too young to have ever faced the temptation of being a committed Leninist, so I never had any faith to renounce, or any feeling of guilt or betrayal. I was always on the side of the losers—the Spanish anarchists, for example.

JP: Do you look back and see this as exceptional?

NC: Oh yes. I always felt completely out of tune with almost everything around me. As I mentioned, I never joined any organized group because of sharp disagreement and skepticism about them, though emotionally I was drawn to such youth groups as Hashomer Hatzair, which in those days professed a commitment to socialist binationalism in Palestine and kibbutz values, as well as the Hebraic culture that I was very much part of.

In fact, I was rather skeptical about the Second World War. I didn't know anybody who shared that skepticism, literally not a single person. But I used to go to the Philadelphia public library—this must have been about 1944 or 1945, when I was about fifteen or sixteen—to read sectarian leftist literature of a very strange nature. For example, groups like the Marlenites, who probably you've never heard of, who were trying to show that the war was a phony war, that it was simply a war designed by the capitalists of the West, acting in conjunction with the state capitalists of the Soviet system to try to destroy the proletarians of Europe. I never really believed the thesis, but I found it intriguing enough to try to figure out what they were talking about. Enough rang true to make me very skeptical about much of the patriotic interpretation of the war. I also recall being appalled by the treatment of German POWs. For some reason, there were some in a camp right next to my high school, and it was considered the red-blooded "thing to do" to taunt them across the barbed wire. That struck me as disgraceful at the time, though I was much more of a committed anti-Nazi than the kids engaging in this sport. I recall bitter arguments about it.

I remember on the day of the Hiroshima bombing, for example, I remember that I literally couldn't talk to anybody. There was nobody. I just walked off by myself. I was at a summer camp at the time, and I walked off into the woods and stayed alone for a couple of hours when I heard about it. I could never talk to anyone about it and never understood anyone's reaction. I felt completely isolated.

As for the things that I was involved in directly, like the Zionist issues again, the position that I held, while I wouldn't say I was the only person in the world to hold it, nevertheless it was very far from the mainstream. It was a position that did have some standing and some support in the Zionist movement. But it was also one that was distinct from those of any of the existing movements, except for ones that were Stalinist or Trotskyite, therefore out for me, so I couldn't join in. I don't know how far back it goes. But, anyway, ever since I had any political awareness, I've felt either alone or part of a tiny minority.

JP: If your work in linguistics often seems to generate intense debates shaped by your ideas, do you feel anything comparable happens in response to your writings on American imperialism, ideology, the role of intellectuals?

NC: Well, there are differences, surely, and they're complex. I've already mentioned something about my own early work in linguistics, in the 1950s, as a graduate student, when I in fact did a good deal of the basic work that I've been developing since. I didn't care very much, frankly, but I made a few efforts to do the natural things, to present some of this work to a professional public. I gave a paper at a summer institute of linguistics in 1953 or 1954, but never at the professional society meetings. The only paper I submitted to the main professional journal had little to do with my own work. It was a response to a critique of Harris that I thought was very unfair. I submitted an article to another journal at Roman Jakobson's suggestion, and got it back, rejected, by return mail. Except for a few reviews, I published outside the field, for example, in the *Proceedings of the Institute of Radio Engineers*. I submitted the book I was working on to one publisher, but it was rejected. It finally came out twenty years later when people were interested in resurrecting it. A monograph called *Syntactic Structures* appeared in 1957, published in Holland. It was actually a write-up of some course notes for undergraduate lectures at MIT, which the editor of the series had seen and asked me to let him publish at the recommendation of my friend and colleague Morris Halle. I saw little prospect of interesting professional linguists in this work, which I tended to regard as pretty much a personal interest. I presented some of this material at workshops in 1958 and 1959. A few linguists were interested, but not many. The 1959 paper has in fact never been published. Other work that I did in the late 1940s only appeared thirty years later.

    The reason I'm teaching at MIT is a direct reflection of this. I had no prospects in a university that had a tradition in any field related to linguistics, whether it was anthropology, or whatever, because the work that I was doing was simply not recognized as related to that field—maybe rightly. Furthermore, I didn't have real professional credentials in the field. I'm the first to admit that. And, therefore, I ended up in an electronics laboratory. I don't know how to handle anything more complicated than a tape recorder, and not even that, but I've been in an electronics laboratory for the last thirty years, largely because there were no vested interests there and the director, Jerome Wiesner, was willing to take a chance on some odd ideas that looked as if they

might be intriguing. It was several years, in fact, before there was
any public, any professional community with which I could have
an interchange of ideas in what I thought of as my own field, apart
from a few friends. The talks that I gave in the 1950s were usually
at computer centers, psychology seminars, and other groups outside of what was supposed to be my field. There were a few
professional linguists, Bernard Bloch at Yale, for example, who
were somewhat interested in this kind of work. Bloch put a copy
of my unpublished book in his department library, and invited me
to give some talks there in the late fifties. I was also invited to
commute down to Columbia and Penn for courses at about that
time. That's about it.

Now by the early sixties, things began to change. The main
reason is that we initiated our own graduate program at MIT, and
students were coming along, and it then proliferated. Not only
at MIT, but at a few other places, too. Within a few years, a rather
new field had emerged. Then there was a professional community with whom one could have interchange of the sort that is not
uncharacteristic of the sciences. There's irrationality, as everywhere, but the general assumptions of rational debate are widely
held. Someone publishes a book or an article, and others are
expected to look at the arguments and think about them, and see
if the facts are right, the arguments sound, and provide critical
analysis or improvements and modifications. And it's done, for
better or worse. But, at least, those are the assumptions in the
field.

JP: The assumptions—how common do you think they are?

NC: It's hard to make a quantitative judgment. I don't think it's different in principle in the physical sciences. Look, in the physical
sciences there's by now a history of success, there's an accumulated record of achievement which simply is an intrinsic part
of the field. You don't even have any right to enter the discussion
unless you've mastered that. You could challenge it, it's not given
by God, but nevertheless you have to at least understand it and
understand why the theories have developed the way they have
and what they're based on and so on. Otherwise, you're just not
part of the discussion, and that's quite right.

But that's only true in very small areas of human inquiry. Occasionally other areas join them like say, molecular biology thirty
to thirty-five years ago. But most fields, and linguistics is sort of
in that peripheral area, do not have that record of intellectual

achievement, of intellectual depth. Of course, there's a lot to know. In fact, the amount that you have to know in a field is not at all correlated with the success of the field. Maybe it's even inversely related because the more success there is, in a sense, the less you have to know. You just have to understand; you have to understand more, but maybe know less. Whereas in fields with less depth of insight and understanding, there's an enormous amount you have to know to control the facts. In fields of this sort, the kind of intellectual interchange that takes place is necessarily very different from the ideal of the sciences. It's hard to evaluate arguments because the arguments aren't very precise, they're not very far-reaching and also often only marginally supported by evidence. Now linguistics is somewhere in between.

Nevertheless, what I meant to say is that the assumptions of the field are that argument and evidence have to be evaluated. It's done more effectively or less effectively, in a better or worse way, but those are the assumptions that people are at least committed to. In other areas, say, in the area of trying to understand social processes, especially contemporary affairs, I don't think that those assumptions are accepted or even that there is much of a pretense of accepting them. Maybe they're professed, but I don't think they're internalized. So, for example, you ask about the reaction to, say, my work in these areas. Well, there is none. For example, I doubt that anything I write on these topics could even be reviewed in a professional journal in the United States.

JP: Have any of the books you wrote over the years been reviewed in the major professional journals?

NC: Well, here in this country, I don't recall offhand any case, ever. But just across the border in Canada, they are reviewed in professional journals. So, for example, I think just about every one of the books I wrote on Southeast Asia has been reviewed in *Pacific Affairs,* which is the Canadian professional Asia journal. Or in Australia, or say, even England. England is in a sense a very highly colonized country, intellectually. But still, say, a journal like *International Affairs* would review books of mine, or of my coauthor Edward Herman, for example. Not all of them, but some of them. On the other hand, I can't imagine that an American journal concerned with international affairs would do so. I don't recall any case.

I suppose the reason is largely that this work is critical not only of the United States and U.S. policy—that's not the main point—

but more crucially of the role of intellectuals in the United States. As a result, it's just beyond the pale. And when there are references, I think they are notable for their almost total lack of even a pretense of rational argument or concern for evidence.

The same is true pretty much of the media. My books on contemporary issues are generally reviewed quite widely in Canada, for example, or England or Australia and elsewhere, but only sporadically here. I also find easy access to national TV and radio outside the United States, as well as journals. Though I've been highly critical of Israeli policy, I've been asked to write in the mainstream Israeli press. That is virtually unthinkable here. Apart from the Soviet bloc, where I am under a total ban (including even linguistics), the United States is probably the country where I have least access to the media or journals of opinion. My experience in this respect is not at all unique. The same is true commonly for critics of U.S. policy and ideology. It is not a matter of a hundred percent versus zero, but the tendencies are apparent, and not very surprising in my opinion. There was a brief and partial opening in the late sixties and early seventies under the pressure of large popular movements, but those few windows quickly were closed as part of the process of ideological reconstruction in the seventies.

When there is some reference to what I or other critics have said, it seems often that the commentators are barely aware of what the argument is, or what position is actually being formulated. On the rare occasions in which I have an opportunity to discuss these issues, whether in print or in person with people in the media or the academic professions, I often find not so much disagreement as an inability to hear. I have found all sorts of strange illusions about what, say, my attitude was toward the Vietnam War, because elite intellectuals often simply cannot perceive that one could have the opinions that I do hold. For example, my basic attitude toward the American war in Vietnam was based on the principle that aggression is wrong, including the aggression of the United States against South Vietnam. There's only a small number of people in American academic circles who could even hear those words. They wouldn't know what I'm referring to when I talk about American aggression in South Vietnam. There is no such event in official history, though there clearly was in the real world. It seems difficult for elite intellectuals to believe that my opposition to the American attack against South Vietnam was based on the same principle that led me to oppose the Russian invasion of Czechoslovakia or Afghanistan, for example. That is impossible. They assume that it must be either that I was opposed to the costs of the war, maybe the cost to the Vietnamese, maybe the cost to us, or to the failure of the war, or else that I was a supporter of North Vietnam, the common assumption, as, for example, in a recent interchange I had with Joseph Nye of Harvard. It's got to be one of those alternatives. There's no other possibility. It's excluded in principle that one could be opposed to the use of force and violence by the United States against South Vietnam, since no such event took place as far as they are concerned and therefore one couldn't have any interpretation of events based on that fact. According to official history, the United States was *defending* South Vietnam, not attacking it—unwisely, the doves maintain. Perhaps there are Soviet doves who criticize "the defense of Afghanistan" in similar terms.

These are very hard barriers to overcome. There's a complicated system of illusions and self-deception that are the given framework for most discussion and debate. And if you don't happen to take part in that system of illusions and self-deception, what you say is incomprehensible.

JP: A great strength of the anarchist tradition seems to lie in its critique of the state and the role of intellectuals and in its vision of how to cope with complex, highly organized societies within the framework of free institutions and a genuinely cooperative ethos. One of Marxism's great strengths has been in its relatively consistent focus on the global structure of capitalism and empire in the last five hundred years. Why has the anarchist tradition seemed weaker on such questions?

NC: Well, one reason, I think, is that there has not been a very substantial anarchist intelligentsia. Anarchism is not a position that appeals to the intellectuals. For one thing, it does not answer to their class interests. In a modern industrial society, power lies in the state or in control of the private economy—two centers of power that are closely linked in a capitalist democracy. Those who take on a leadership role, or the role of propagandists, in the private economy are generally not accorded the honorific title of "intellectuals"—rather "managers," or "PR specialists," or the like. Those whom we call "intellectuals" have tended to see the state as the avenue to power, prestige, and influence. Leninism is a typical expression of this tendency. Its appeal to the intelligentsia is that it offers a justification for their rise to positions of power and manipulation in the course of popular struggles which they can exploit and subvert. When such hopes are seen to be illusory, it has been an easy transition to celebration of liberal state capitalism and association with or service to its dominant elites.

The organized intelligentsia, the people who would do analytic work of the kind you describe, have tended toward state socialist or state capitalist ideologies. Their natural ideology is one that gives a major role to state power, whether it's state socialism, or welfare-state capitalism, or military-state capitalism of the Reaganite variety. That's where the overwhelming majority of the intelligentsia have tended to find their place.

Now modern anarchism, after all, with Bakunin at least, began with a sharp critique of the technical intelligentsia—the Marxists in particular—and their class interests in serving as agents for oppressive state systems. They were Bakunin's "new class," the "Red bureaucracy" or their counterpart in emerging state-capitalist society.

There's been a good deal of antagonism between the anarchist movements and the intelligentsia, for quite understandable reasons. Anarchism offers no position of privilege or power to the intelligentsia. In fact, it undermines that position. As a result, it's not particularly attractive to many of them and in fact, the number of anarchist intellectuals, though there are some, has been quite limited as compared with those who associated themselves with one or another variety of so-called Marxism, or state socialism. So that's one reason.

Another reason is that many of the anarchist intellectuals basically accepted the Marxian analysis of capitalism. Marx was, after all, a theorist of capitalism. He had very little to say about socialism. And his decriptive and theoretical analysis of capitalism was pretty much accepted by many anarchists who opposed what they perceived as the antisocialist tendencies in his thought and actions—with justice, I think particularly in the Leninist variety, which was sharply condemned by left Marxists like Anton Pannekoek as well.

Take the case of Bakunin. He praised Marx as a historian and analyst who had a great deal of value to say about the rise and nature of capitalism. In this respect, many of the socialist-anarchist intellectuals felt that the Marxists had developed considerable insight and understanding of the development of capitalism and capitalist imperialism. But they felt that the Marxists totally misunderstood the prospects for the development of a freer society, or worse, that they would undermine these prospects in their own class interest as state managers and ideologists. That's where they really drew the issue.

They often tended to be more future-oriented than the Marxists. But not entirely. After all, Kropotkin wrote about the French Revolution, about mutual aid as a factor in evolution (perhaps the first major contribution to "sociobiology"), and so on. Rudolf Rocker wrote on nationalism and culture over a long period. But the Marxist literature is far more extensive.

JP: In an anarchist society, what would the intellectual's role be?

NC: That of intellectual worker. A person whose work happens to be more with the mind than with the hands. Although I would think that in a decent society there ought to be a mixture of the kinds of work that one does. Marx would agree in principle. An anarchist picture of society, or anarchist tendencies in society, offer no privileged role to the organized intelligentsia or to the professional intellectuals. And, in fact, it would tend to blur the distinctions between intellectual and worker, so that workers should take a direct, active role in the mental aspects of whatever work they're doing, its organization and planning, formation of its purposes, and so on. The people whose major professional concern is knowledge and the application of knowledge would have no special opportunity to manage the society, to gain any position of power and prestige by virtue of this special training and talent. And that's not a point of view that the intelligentsia are naturally drawn to.

I think Bakunin's remarks on this subject are perceptive: that the intelligentsia tend to associate themselves with the state-socialist and state-capitalist visions which would assign them a managerial role, including the role of ideological managers of "the engineering of consent," as democratic theorists call it. And, of course, modern societies have often offered intellectuals a good deal of just plain privilege as well.

JP: You have written that perhaps some day there can be a science of aspects of human nature that might give us insight into how we can go about creating a better society. In this effort, has not the relationship between science and anarchism historically often been an antagonistic one? Haven't many European anarchists been uneasy not simply with the uses of science, but with "science" itself?

NC: Well, again, it's mixed. Kropotkin, for example, was a natural scientist, not in one of the fancy fields of science, but he certainly regarded himself as having the mentality and background and concerns of a natural scientist. But I think you're right. Within the anarchist tradition, there's been a certain feeling that there's something regimented or oppressive about science itself, that we should break free of the oppressive structures of scientific thinking, and so on. I'm totally out of sympathy with that attitude. There are no arguments that I know of for irrationality. I don't think that the methods of science amount to anything more than being reasonable, and I don't see why anarchists shouldn't be reasonable. I don't think that being reasonable is to succumb to oppression or regimentation. I can sort of understand what lies behind such feelings, but I just don't have sympathy with them.

JP: What can scientific reasoning reveal to us today about the nature of human freedom?

NC: At the present, very little, as far as I am aware. One might imagine theoretical principles that could lead to some kinds of predictions about behavior under restricted conditions, but not to any serious understanding of choice of action.

    Here, even relaxing all ethical considerations, I don't think one could design meaningful experiments, because there's so little understanding of what's involved in free choice of action. In order to design experiments, you have to begin with some kind of tentative hypotheses, some partial understanding of what might, or what you propose might, underlie the phenomena. And in the case of free will and free choice, I don't think there are even glimmerings of such understanding. These are aspects of human thought and behavior which just elude our intellectual grasp at the moment and maybe in principle forever.

JP: You often refer to European, rarely to American, anarchists in your writings, though Rocker lived in this country.

NC: Well, in part that may be an accident of my own experience. But in part it probably reflects the fact that the American anarchist tradition, at least the more articulate part of it, is composed of writers in an individualist tradition, who are worth thinking about, but who I have not found very helpful for the problems that interest me. What attracts me about anarchism personally are the tendencies in it that try to come to grips with the problem of dealing with complex organized industrial societies within a framework of free institutions and structures. And the American anarchists rarely dealt with these questions.

JP: When you look for the people who have done that, who do you include?

NC: Well, among anarchists people like Rudolf Rocker, for example, or a number of Spanish anarchists. Some of them tried to plan a kind of libertarian society in some detail—for example, Diego Abad de Santillán, who wrote a book called *After the Revolution* in 1937, right in the middle of the Spanish revolution, and was quite unhappy about the way in which the anarchist revolution was developing. He did lay out an interesting program of anarchist development, specifically for Spain, which I picked up in the early 1940s when I was haunting anarchist bookstores and offices in New York, and read with interest at the time. There is also a substantial relevant literature on workers control, some of it Marxist in orientation.

JP: Do you think there is any significant research in anarchist thinking along this line in the Western world today?

NC: Well, I don't think there have been major contributions to that kind of thought in recent years. There have been expansions of anarchist thinking to other issues, like ecology, for example. There was a kind of sympathy for elements of anarchist thought in parts of the New Left. It's a complex matter, related in part to a salutary decline in the stranglehold of orthodox Marxism, in some circles of the left at least.

JP: Your focus on the global structures of power and empire *and* on "libertarian socialism" and anarchist traditions seems rather atypical. What has made it so difficult for anarchists in practice to confront both at once?

NC: Libertarians have often found it difficult to involve themselves actively in anti-imperialist and nationalist struggles. Unfortunately the fact is that in a world of tremendous concentrated power, which is determined to undermine any social experiment that might be beneficial to the mass of the population and harmful to privileged sectors of the powerful states, harmful to foreign investors, for example—in such a world there are very few options even for the most libertarian forces, if they were to exist. A real libertarian socialist revolution requires substantial preparation on the part of very large sectors of the population, which are prepared to take over management of production, distribution, and communities, to develop federal arrangements, and in general to create institutions of meaningful democracy that would offer the population at large means for controlling their own lives and communities and work and for participating in the formation of public policy in broader domains. Any such effort would at once be destroyed by outside force. Recall the fate of the Spanish anarchist revolution, crushed by the combined forces of communism, fascism, and the liberal democracies, which set about fighting one another once the threat of real freedom had been overcome.

Considering the actual situation in Third World countries, suppose some revolutionary leadership develops that is truly committed to directing meager resources to the poor majority, perhaps within an authoritarian state system. The first problem it will face is "capital strike" and capital flight on the part of those who control investment decisions and production in the private economy. The leadership may yield, restoring the old order. Or it may try to take over the private economy so that production can continue and expand, placing it under public control, which will probably lead to a harsh form of state socialism under existing conditions, with true libertarian alternatives too undeveloped to be realistic. The leadership might respond to popular efforts to take over land and production; it might facilitate or not stand in the way of popular mobilization in the social, economic, and political domains. But the unfortunate fact is that any such development, whether libertarian or authoritarian in tendency—more so in the former case—would lead to unremitting hostility on the part of the great powers—in the domains of our influence, to attack by the United States. The primary goal would be to prevent any infringement on private privilege linked to U.S. power, to abort these efforts by subversion or direct attack or economic pressures that no weak and underdeveloped country can withstand. Or, second best, to drive the perpetrators of this iniquity into the hands of the Soviet Union; then further attacks can be justified in terms of "defense" and the revolutionary leadership will be compelled to institute harsh and authoritarian measures under duress, so that popular discontent will mount and the endeavor will fail for that reason. Nicaragua today is a case in point. There are few realistic options, in the world as it exists, unless the population of the major powers reaches a level of civilization transcending anything we now see and restrains the violence of the states that dominate the international system.

In middle-level countries such as Chile, one might imagine trying the Allende way, which at least didn't work in that case and probably could not for very much the reasons just briefly indicated. One should be cautious about trying to draw historical lessons. Each situation is unlike every other one, though one can perhaps learn something. In general, options are very few. We are not in the eighteenth century, when American colonists, who lived in what was even then probably the richest country in the world, could proceed to eliminate the indigenous population, extend their borders through conquest, enslave a large work force when it was needed, absorb a flow of cheap labor and needed capital while developing the unparalleled resources of the region they occupied, quite safe from the depredations of the great powers of Europe that were immersed in their own conflicts, and becoming after a century the world's richest and most powerful state. Such luxuries are not available to developing countries today.

Given these realities, it is hard for people with libertarian commitments to support Third World struggles. I am not saying that the reluctance is justified, but it is understandable. What they will properly ask is whether there are libertarian options and alternatives. Is it possible for the popular institutions that always arise in incipient form in a revolutionary struggle actually to prevail, to continue to exist and create a framework solid and stable enough to withstand foreign attack and subversion, or internal subversion of the Lenin-Trotsky variety, as after the Bolshevik coup in 1917? I don't think the prospects are very good, in the real world as it exists. It is easy to say yes, but hard to sketch out realistic possibilities. It is easy, for example, to say that what is needed is democracy, but harder to face the fact that meaningful democracy is limited at best when resources are narrowly concentrated and crucial investment decisions are in private hands, with all of the consequences that follow for political action and ideological influence and control. In this respect, classical Marxism may well be right in believing that any real advance toward a more free and democratic society, a socialist society in the real sense of the word, could only take place in the more advanced industrial societies. When anarchists or other libertarians are critical of Third World revolutionary societies, as they have every right to be, that criticism ought to engage these questions, engage the specific problems that are faced in the real world of state terrorism and violence.

JP: There was a hope at least in the sixties that people in the capitalist world could learn something from the Third World beyond how the United States operated globally. Do you think that is so today?

NC: Well, we can learn from all sorts of people. For example, I think we can learn a good deal from the peasants and workers of revolutionary Spain, in large part a Third World society in the 1930s. As for the Third World liberation movements of the sixties, I never thought that they were likely to provide any useful lessons for Western socialists. They were confronted with all kinds of problems that we do not face, even apart from the problems of foreign attack and domestic national consolidation. We do not confront the problem of developing an industrial society under the onerous conditions that hold throughout most of the Third World. Again, honest libertarians should recognize these facts.

Take the Vietnam War. It was clear by the end of the sixties that the United States had achieved its primary objectives. It had effectively destroyed the National Liberation Front of South Vietnam and the Pathet Lao in Laos, ensuring, as I wrote at the time, that only the harshest and most authoritarian elements in Indochina would survive, if any would. This was a major victory for U.S. aggression. Principled opponents of the U.S. war were therefore in the position of, in effect, helping to defend the only surviving resistance in Vietnam, which happened to be highly authoritarian state-socialist groups. Now I don't think that that was a reason for not opposing the American war in Vietnam, but I think it's a reason why many anarchists could not throw themselves into that struggle with the energy and sympathy that they might have. Some did, but others were reluctant because they were highly critical of the regime that was going to emerge, as I was. Within peace movement groups, I tried to dissociate opposition to the American war from support for state socialism in Vietnam, as many will recall. But it was not easy to undertake serious opposition to imperial aggression, with the very real personal costs that this entailed, on such a basis. This was easy enough for bystanders who were satisfied to cluck their tongues in dismay, but it was quite a different matter for those—primarily young—people who were really trying to do something to end these atrocities.

In fact, the American movement tended to become quite pro–North Vietnamese, segments of it, at least. They felt that they were not simply opposing the American war, but they were defending the North Vietnamese vision of a future society.

JP: I think there was the wish on the part of some to see a genuinely humane alternative society.

NC: Yes. And many felt that this is what the North Vietnamese, the state-socialist bureaucrats would create, which was highly unlikely, particularly as the war progressed with mounting terror and destruction.

It's worth trying to come to grips with these questions, but that is a very difficult thing to do, for one reason because we're not doing it in outer space. We're doing it in the United States, in the midst of a society which is devoting every effort to enhancing the most harsh and authoritarian and oppressive elements in that regime, or to destroy the country outright. We are doing it in a society which will use our very critique for these destructive purposes. Those are facts which no honest person will suppress or fail to attend to. And this remains true today, just as it was during the war. The United States has never terminated its effort to win the war in Vietnam. It's still trying to win it, and in many ways it is winning. One of the ways it's winning is by imposing conditions which will bring out and emphasize the repressive elements which were present in the Vietnamese Communist movement. American dissidents face a dilemma. They have to face the fact that they are living in a state with enormous power, used for murderous and destructive ends. And what we do, the very acts that we perform, will be exploited where possible for those ends. Honest people will have to face the fact that they are morally responsible for the predictable human consequences of their acts. One of those acts is accurate criticism, accurate critical analysis of authoritarian state socialism in North Vietnam or in Cuba or in other countries that the United States is trying to undermine and subvert. The consequences of accurate critical analysis will be to buttress these efforts, thus contributing to suffering and oppression. These are dilemmas which are hard to deal with. They are not unique to the United States. Should an honest Russian dissident, for example, publicly denounce the atrocities and oppressive character of the Afghan resistance, knowing that such accurate criticism will be exploited in support of Soviet aggression?

Suppose that we could somehow manage to conduct this inquiry and discussion without contributing to the designs of imperialist power. Well, then really hard questions would arise. For example, it's cheap and easy to say that these are repressive state-socialist societies. That's true. But then serious questions arise as to what one can do, say, in Indochina, in a society that has been so severely, almost lethally damaged by destructive war and by a legacy of colonialism with horrifying effects, virtually unknown in the West. Nobody much cares what happened to the natives.

Even apart from such colossal man-made disasters, what really are the prospects for development for such societies? There are cheap and easy answers, but they are not very helpful.

JP: Do you see much thought about such problems?

NC: There is very little constructive thinking about them. I mean, for example, I think there's very little effort to come to grips with the fact that the Third World societies as a whole today are at a lower level of development than were the industrializing societies of Europe and the United States in the eighteenth century. And, furthermore, the industrializing societies of Europe and the United States were not faced with a hostile environment in which the major resources had already been preempted. These are really important things to think about. They raise the question whether development is even possible in the Third World.

JP: You once wrote that if by some quirk of history the advanced Western powers should actually decide to genuinely give assistance to Third World countries, it wouldn't be all that easy to know what should be done or how to do it.

NC: That's correct. These countries could become subsidiaries of Western capitalism. We have a good deal of experience with the consequences of that option. What other models of development are there? Well, there's the authoritarian state-capitalist model of South Korea, or the authoritarian state-socialist model. Not very pretty, in many respects. But is there really a libertarian model of development that's meaningful? Maybe there is, but it requires some real work and thought to show that. It's not enough just to mouth slogans. And those are questions that anarchists have not faced with sufficient seriousness.

JP: In what ways was Marx significant for the development of your
      views? Have you read extensively in the "Marxist tradition"?

NC: Not very much. I find much of the Marxist literature rather bor-
      ing, frankly, and I am far from a Marx scholar. I've been much
      interested in the left Marxist tradition: Pannekoek, Korsch, Lux-
      emburg, Mattick. And I have read Marx selectively. I don't try
      to keep up with the current literature, with Marxology. Some-
      times there are things written by particular people that I find
      interesting, but as an intellectual tradition, I don't find it very
      exciting.

JP: Intellectuals are often deeply involved with "traditions," the
      "Marxist tradition," the "Freudian tradition." Is one of the as-
      pects of the anarchist an uneasiness with any doctrine?

NC: Well, anarchism isn't a doctrine. It's at most a historical ten-
      dency, a tendency of thought and action, which has many differ-
      ent ways of developing and progressing and which, I would
      think, will continue as a permanent strand of human history.
      Take the most optimistic assumptions. What we can expect is
      that in some new and better form of society in which certain
      oppressive structures have been overcome, we will simply dis-
      cover new problems that haven't been obvious before. And the
      anarchists will then be revolutionaries trying to overcome these
      new kinds of oppression and unfairness and constraint that we
      weren't aware of before. Looking back over the past, that's
      pretty much what has happened. Just take our own lifetimes.
      Sexism, for example. Twenty years ago it was not in the con-
      sciousness of most people as a form of oppression. Now it is a
      live issue, which has reached a general level of consciousness
      and concern. The problems are still there, but at least they are
      on the agenda. And others will enter our awareness if the ones
      we now face are addressed.

JP: What do you think of speaking in terms of a Marxist or
      Freudian tradition?

NC: I think it's a bad idea. The whole concept of Marxist or
      Freudian or anything like that is very odd. These concepts be-
      long to the history of organized religion. Any living person, no
      matter how gifted, will make some contributions intermingled
      with error and partial understanding. We try to understand and

improve on their contributions and eliminate the errors. But how can you identify yourself as a Marxist, or a Freudian, or an X-ist, whoever X may be? That would be to treat the person as a God to be revered, not a human being whose contributions are to be assimilated and transcended. It's a crazy idea, a kind of idolatry. I would be very suspicious of . . .

JP: And yet one to which many intellectuals have been drawn.

NC: Well, because in subjects that really don't have a great deal of intellectual depth, that are not living intellectual disciplines that confront problems and try to overcome them and honestly try to make progress and so on, what you can do is accept the faith and repeat it. I don't mean to suggest that this is a fair characterization of the work of those individuals who call themselves "Marxists" or "Freudians." But the fact that such concepts persist and are taken seriously is a sign of the intellectual inadequacy of the traditions, and probably hampers their further development. We should not be worshiping at shrines, but learning what we can from people who had something serious to say, or who did something valuable in their lives, while trying to overcome the inevitable errors and flaws.

JP: How does this compare with how you see the professional guild structure in the social sciences?

NC: The professional guild structure in the social sciences, I think, has often served as a marvelous device for protecting them from insight and understanding, for filtering out people who raise unacceptable questions, for limiting research—not by force, but by all sorts of more subtle means—to questions that are not threatening. Take a look at any society, I'm convinced, and you'll find that where there is a more or less professionalized guild of people who inquire into the social process, there will be certain topics that they will be very reluctant to investigate. There will be striking taboos on what they will study. In particular, one of the things that they are very unlikely to study is the way power is actually exercised in their own society, or their own relationship to that power. These are topics that won't be understood, won't be studied.

JP: Do you think Marxists have presented any viable alternative ways of organizing industrial societies?

NC: Now thinking of Marxism as a theory of social change, not as a theory of capitalism. For the most part, Marx was a theorist of capitalism and the evolution of capitalism. Then there is the revolutionary strand aimed toward a future society that is supposed to develop pretty much by virtue of alleged historical laws. That's the thinnest part. There isn't much there. Marx had very little to say about a future society. One striking difference between Marx and the anarchists was expressed in Bakunin's remark about how a revolutionary would try to build the structures of a future society within the present society. And in much of the anarchist tradition, at least, the most lively parts, there was a good deal of thought about what kind of society we are trying to achieve, along with efforts to construct at least some of its elements, or to develop some consciousness of how people could be more free. As an activist, Marx's behavior also left much to be desired, in the politics of the First International, for example.

JP: It was very difficult to find even a notion of alternative values?

NC: There was a famous remark about hunting in the morning, fishing in the afternoon, criticizing in the evening, and so on—a fully integrated way of life. You can find hints of ideas about workers' self-management and producers' control of production and so on. But it's obviously not where his heart is. I think he was primarily interested in other questions. He thought socialism would emerge when the capitalist system had run its course. Inexorable historical processes will create the basic structures of the new society and its institutions. Well, that doesn't really give you a very serious vision of social change and what it is aiming to accomplish.

       Marx was, in a sense, you might say, an opportunist. I don't mean this critically. Rather, he rightly felt that different approaches were necessary in different circumstances as a means for social change. Parliamentarian measures in some cases, revolutionary efforts in others. I don't think he had a very clear picture of what could be done, or if he did, it was largely a matter of historical contingency.

JP: And what of Marxism in the Third World?

NC: Well, in Third World countries, I think Marxism has a different meaning. In Third World countries, I think Marxism is largely the ideology of the radical intelligentsia who hope to take state power riding the wave of popular struggles. That's a perfectly understandable motivation on their part. I don't think it's particularly attractive. Whatever Marx's intentions may have been, Marxism lends itself to these conceptions. You can find some support for this in the writings of the master, and in his own actions. Lenin's primary contribution was to fashion this doctrine out of elements of Marxist thought. It's a doctrine that merges readily with radical nationalist currents.

JP:　Are there any particular movements toward building alternative structures today within Western capitalist societies that you find hopeful?

NC:　It's a complicated matter. Take the moves toward workers' self-management that you can detect with a sufficiently powerful microscope in Europe, and sometimes here. On the one hand, these integrate the work force into the system. They might lead to class harmony, suppression of industrial strife, to acceptance of lower wages and higher profits. In this sense they serve as a device for socializing the work force within the existing system of oppression. On the other hand, they also have the possibility of developing the awareness and understanding that it is perfectly possible for workers to manage without authoritarian structures; that bosses are not needed; that there's no God-given necessity to have hierarchical structure of authority and organizational structures in the workplace of a kind that we would call fascist in the political domain. It can lead to that. The question is, how do these tendencies play themselves out? From the point of view of the capitalists themselves or the managerial elite or the state management, of course any such forms of worker participation would be used to the extent possible as a technique of subordinating the work force. And the question is, to what extent can self-conscious working-class groups struggle against this and try to turn these efforts into something else?

As long as a complex social system is more or less working, satisfying at least basic needs, and sometimes considerably better than basic needs, to substantial parts of the population, and is not creating totally intolerable conditions for large numbers, I would imagine that it would persist. That has been true generally in industrial capitalism.

JP:　You've written about the way that professional ideologists and the mandarins obfuscate reality. And you have spoken—in some places you call it a "Cartesian common sense"—of the common-sense capacities of people. Indeed, you place a significant emphasis on this common sense when you reveal the ideological aspects of arguments, especially in contemporary social science. What do you mean by common sense? What does it mean in a society like ours? For example, you've written that within a highly competitive, fragmented society, it's very difficult for people to become aware of what their interests are. If you are not able to participate in the political system in meaningful ways, if you are reduced to the role of a passive spectator, then what kind of knowledge do you have? How can common sense emerge in this context?

NC: Well, let me give an example. When I'm driving, I sometimes turn on the radio and I find very often that what I'm listening to is a discussion of sports. These are telephone conversations. People call in and have long and intricate discussions, and it's plain that quite a high degree of thought and analysis is going into that. People know a tremendous amount. They know all sorts of complicated details and enter into far-reaching discussion about whether the coach made the right decision yesterday and so on. These are ordinary people, not professionals, who are applying their intelligence and analytic skills in these areas and accumulating quite a lot of knowledge and, for all I know, understanding. On the other hand, when I hear people talk about, say, international affairs or domestic problems, it's at a level of superficiality which is beyond belief.

In part, this reaction may be due to my own areas of interest, but I think it's quite accurate, basically. And I think that this concentration on such topics as sports makes a certain degree of sense. The way the system is set up, there is virtually nothing people can do anyway, without a degree of organization that's far beyond anything that exists now, to influence the real world. They might as well live in a fantasy world, and that's in fact what they do. I'm sure they are using their common sense and intellectual skills, but in an area which has no meaning and probably thrives because it has no meaning, as a displacement from the serious problems which one cannot influence and affect because the power happens to lie elsewhere.

Now it seems to me that the same intellectual skill and capacity for understanding and for accumulating evidence and gaining information and thinking through problems could be used—would be used—under different systems of governance which involve popular participation in important decision-making, in areas that really matter to human life.

There are questions that are hard. There are areas where you need specialized knowledge. I'm not suggesting a kind of anti-intellectualism. But the point is that many things can be understood quite well without a very far-reaching, specialized knowledge. And in fact, even a specialized knowledge in these areas is not beyond the reach of people who happen to be interested.

So take simple cases. Take the Russian invasion of Afghanistan—a simple case. Everybody understands immediately without any specialized knowledge that the Soviet Union invaded Afghanistan. That's exactly what it is. You don't debate it; it's not a deep point that is difficult to understand. It isn't necessary to know the history of Afghanistan to understand the point. All right. Now let's take the American invasion of South Vietnam. The phrase itself is very strange. I don't think you will ever find that phrase—I doubt if you'll find one case in which that phrase was used in any mainstream journal, or for the most part, even in journals of the left, while the war was going on. Yet it was just as much an American invasion of South Vietnam as it is a Russian invasion of Afghanistan. By 1962, when nobody was paying any attention, American pilots—not just mercenaries but actual American pilots—were conducting murderous bombing raids against Vietnamese villages. That's an American invasion of South Vietnam. The purpose of that attack was to destroy the social fabric of rural South Vietnam so as to undermine a resistance which the American-imposed client regime had evoked by its repression and was unable to control, though they had already killed perhaps eighty thousand South Vietnamese since blocking the political settlement called for in the 1954 Geneva Accords.

So there was a U.S. attack against South Vietnam in the early sixties, not to speak of later years when the United States sent an expeditionary force to occupy the country and destroy the indigenous resistance. But it was never referred to or thought of as an American invasion of South Vietnam.

I don't know much about Russian public opinion, but I imagine if you picked a man off the street, he would be surprised to hear a reference to the Russian invasion of Afghanistan. They're defending Afghanistan against capitalist plots and bandits supported by the CIA and so on. But I don't think he would find it difficult to understand that the United States invaded Vietnam.

Well, these are very different societies; the mechanisms of control and indoctrination work in a totally different fashion. There's a vast difference in the use of force versus other techniques. But

the effects are very similar, and the effects extend to the intellectual elite themselves. In fact, my guess is that you would find that
the intellectual elite is the most heavily indoctrinated sector, for
good reasons. It's their role as a secular priesthood to really
believe the nonsense that they put forth. Other people can repeat
it, but it's not that crucial that they really believe it. But for the
intellectual eilte themselves, it's crucial that they believe it because, after all, they are the guardians of the faith. Except for a
very rare person who's just an outright liar, it's hard to be a
convincing exponent of the faith unless you've internalized it and
come to believe it. I find that intellectuals just look at me with
blank stares of incomprehension when I talk about the American
invasion of South Vietnam. On the other hand, when I speak to
general audiences, they don't seem to have much difficulty in
perceiving the essential points, once the facts are made accessible. And that's perfectly reasonable—that's what should be expected in a society set up the way ours is.

When I talk about, say, Cartesian common sense, what I mean
is that it does not require very far-reaching, specialized knowledge to perceive that the United States was invading South Vietnam. And, in fact, to take apart the system of illusions and
deception which functions to prevent understanding of contemporary reality, that's not a task that requires extraordinary skill
or understanding. It requires the kind of normal skepticism and
willingness to apply one's analytical skills that almost all people
have and that they can exercise. It just happens that they exercise
them in analyzing what the New England Patriots ought to do
next Sunday instead of questions that really matter for human
life, their own included.

JP: Do you think people are inhibited by expertise?

NC: There are also experts about football, but these people don't
defer to them. The people who call in talk with complete confidence. They don't care if they disagree with the coach or whoever
the local expert is. They have their own opinion and they conduct
intelligent discussions. I think it's an interesting phenomenon.
Now I don't think that international or domestic affairs are much
more complicated. And what passes for serious intellectual discourse on these matters does not reflect any deeper level of
understanding or knowledge.

One finds something similar in the case of so-called primitive
cultures. What you find very often is that certain intellectual

systems have been constructed of considerable intricacy, with specialized experts who know all about it and other people who don't quite understand and so on. For example, kinship systems are elaborated to enormous complexity. Many anthropologists have tried to show that this has some kind of functional utility in the society. But one function may be just intellectual. It's a kind of mathematics. These are areas where you can use your intelligence to create complex and intricate systems and elaborate their properties pretty much the way we do mathematics. They don't have mathematics and technology; they have other systems of cultural richness and complexity. I don't want to overdraw the analogy, but something similar may be happening here.

The gas station attendant who wants to use his mind isn't going to waste his time on international affairs, because that's useless; he can't do anything about it anyhow, and he might learn unpleasant things and even get into trouble. So he might as well do it where it's fun, and not threatening—professional football or basketball or something like that. But the skills are being used and the understanding is there and the intelligence is there. One of the functions that things like professional sports play in our society and others is to offer an area to deflect people's attention from things that matter, so that the people in power can do what matters without public interference.

JP: I asked a while ago whether people are inhibited by the aura of expertise. Can one turn this around—are experts and intellectuals afraid of people who could apply the intelligence of sport to their own areas of competency in foreign affairs, social sciences, and so on?

NC: I suspect that this is rather common. Those areas of inquiry that have to do with problems of immediate human concern do not happen to be particularly profound or inaccessible to the ordinary person lacking any special training who takes the trouble to learn something about them. Commentary on public affairs in the mainstream literature is often shallow and uninformed. Everyone who writes or speaks about these matters knows how much you can get away with as long as you keep close to received doctrine. I'm sure just about everyone exploits these privileges. I know I do. When I refer to Nazi crimes or Soviet atrocities, for example, I know that I will not be called upon to back up what I say, but a detailed scholarly apparatus is necessary if I say anything critical about the practice of one of the Holy States: the United States itself, or Israel, since it was enshrined by the intelligentsia after its 1967 victory. This freedom from the requirements of evidence or even rationality is quite a convenience, as any informed reader of the media and journals of opinion, or even much of the scholarly literature, will quickly discover. It makes life easy, and permits expression of a good deal of nonsense or ignorant bias with impunity, also sheer slander. Evidence is unnecessary, argument beside the point. Thus a standard charge against American dissidents or even American liberals—I've cited quite a few cases in print and have collected many others—is that they claim that the United States is the sole source of evil in the world or other similar idiocies; the convention is that such charges are entirely legitimate when the target is someone who does not march in the appropriate parades, and they are therefore produced without even a pretense of evidence. Adherence to the party line confers the right to act in ways that would properly be regarded as scandalous on the part of any critic of received orthodoxies. Too much public awareness might lead to a demand that standards of integrity should be met, which would certainly save a lot of forests from destruction, and would send many a reputation tumbling.

The right to lie in the service of power is guarded with considerable vigor and passion. This becomes evident whenever anyone takes the trouble to demonstrate that charges against some official enemy are inaccurate or, sometimes, pure invention. The immediate reaction among the commissars is that the person is an apologist for the real crimes of official enemies. The case of Cambodia is a striking example. That the Khmer Rouge were guilty of gruesome atrocities was doubted by no one, apart from a few marginal Maoist sects. It is also true, and easily documented, that Western propaganda seized upon these crimes with great relish, exploiting them to provide a retrospective justification for Western atrocities, and since standards are nonexistent in such a noble cause, they also produced a record of fabrication and deceit that is quite remarkable. Demonstration of this fact, and fact it is, elicited enormous outrage, along with a stream of new and quite spectacular lies, as Edward Herman and I, among others, have documented. The point is that the right to lie in the service of the state was being challenged, and that is an unspeakable crime. Similarly, anyone who points out that some charge against Cuba, Nicaragua, Vietnam, or some other official enemy is dubious or false will immediately be labeled an apologist for real or alleged crimes, a useful technique to ensure that rational standards will not be imposed upon the commissars and that there will be no impediment to their loyal service to power. The critic typically has little access to the media, and the personal consequences for the critic are sufficiently annoying to deter many from taking this course, particularly because some journals—the *New Republic,* for example—sink to the ultimate level of dishonesty and cowardice, regularly refusing to permit even the right of response to slanders they publish. Hence the sacred right to lie is likely to be preserved without too serious a threat. But matters might be different if unreliable sectors of the public were admitted into the arena of discussion and debate.

The aura of alleged expertise also provides a way for the indoctrination system to provide its services to power while maintaining a useful image of indifference and objectivity. The media, for example, can turn to academic experts to provide the perspective that is required by the centers of power, and the university system is sufficiently obedient to external power so that appropriate experts will generally be available to lend the prestige of scholarship to the narrow range of opinion permitted broad expression. Or when this method fails—as in the current case of Latin America, for example, or in the emerging discipline of terrorology—a new category of "experts" can be established who can be trusted to provide the approved opinions that the media cannot express directly without abandoning the pretense of objectivity that serves to legitimate their propaganda function. I've documented many examples, as have others.

The guild structure of the professions concerned with public affairs also helps to preserve doctrinal purity. In fact, it is guarded with much diligence. My own personal experience is perhaps relevant. As I mentioned earlier, I do not really have the usual professional credentials in any field, and my own work has ranged fairly widely. Some years ago, for example, I did some work in mathematical linguistics and automata theory, and occasionally gave invited lectures at mathematics or engineering colloquia. No one would have dreamed of challenging my credentials to speak on these topics—which were zero, as everyone knew; that would have been laughable. The participants were concerned with what I had to say, not my right to say it. But when I speak, say, about international affairs, I'm constantly challenged to present the credentials that authorize me to enter this august arena, in the United States, at least—elsewhere not. It's a fair generalization, I think, that the more a discipline has intellectual substance, the less it has to protect itself from scrutiny, by means of a guild structure. The consequences with regard to your question are pretty obvious.

JP: You have said that most intellectuals end up obfuscating reality. Do they understand the reality they are obfuscating? Do they understand the social processes they mystify?

NC: Most people are not liars. They can't tolerate too much cognitive dissonance. I don't want to deny that there are outright liars, just brazen propagandists. You can find them in journalism and in the academic professions as well. But I don't think that's the norm. The norm is obedience, adoption of uncritical attitudes, taking the easy path of self-deception. I think there's also a selective process in the academic professions and journalism. That is, people who are independent-minded and cannot be trusted to be obedient don't make it, by and large. They're often filtered out along the way.

JP: You wrote somewhere that Israel has served since 1967 for American intellectuals or a segment of American intellectuals in a similar way to which the Soviet Union did in the 1930s. Could you talk a little about this?

NC: Well, I think that there are some striking similarities in the attitudes of the American intelligentsia toward Israel and the attitudes of similar segments toward the Soviet Union in the 1930s. These cases are not precisely comparable, of course, but I think that there are instructive similarities. The protective attitude, the defensive attitude toward the Holy State and the effort to downplay its repression and violence, to provide apologetics for it, and to interpret events of the world in terms of how they affect its interests, for example. Or the tunnel vision of the awed visitor, who returns home to proclaim the glories of what he has witnessed. Also the commitment to discredit and undermine any critical analysis of the Holy State. All of these things are very similar. I don't think that they originate from exactly the same sources, but they are very similar in style, and they reflect the strong tendency of much of the intelligentsia to commit themselves to one or another form of state worship, generally of one's own state, the source of power and privilege, but on occasion some favored foreign state. Here we find differences. We have to ask why a particular state is selected as an object of worship at particular moments—apart from one's own, the norm, too common even to be noticed, the reasons in this case being obvious.

The Stalinist commitments of large sections of the American intelligentsia of the 1930s were, I believe, related to the fact that they saw opportunities for power and privilege for themselves through something like the Leninist model, a phenomenon that we observe in much of the Third World today. It may look unrealistic in retrospect, but during the Depression many felt that there were prospects for a Leninist-style state in the United States which would relate itself to the glorious revolution. And these elements would, they assumed, take on the managerial and leadership role in such a society. They would be the Lenins, they would be the revolutionary vanguard who would become the Red bureaucracy in this state. Now, of course, it was never internalized in that crass form. Rather they were fighting for justice and all sorts of marvelous things, and some of them indeed were.

JP: Do you think that mentality was different from the Trotskyites?

NC: Well, I'm a little reluctant to generalize too far. Even with regard to the Stalinists, what I'm saying is an overgeneralization. There were many deeply committed Stalinists who really didn't know or probably didn't care very much about what was happening in Russia. They cared about the suffering of oppressed people in the United States and they were going to help them. Some of those people committed themselves to crazy and unbelievable positions with regard to the Soviet Union. But the sphere of their concern was primarily at home, and much of what they did was quite respectable, very admirable in fact, within the sphere of their primary concern. In defense of civil rights of blacks, for example, or in union organizing. We probably wouldn't have the CIO without the courageous efforts of these organizers.

But recognizing that there's a degree of overgeneralization here, it still makes sense to identify some leading factors, putting aside important nuances. I think what I've said about the appeal of Stalinism is basically correct.

As far as Trotskyism is concerned, in part it involved a recognition of very ugly things that were happening in the Soviet Union. But it never, by definition, involved any really critical analysis of those developments. After all, who was Trotsky? Trotsky was Lenin's associate. Whatever he may have said during periods when he didn't have power, either prior to the revolution or after he was kicked out, when it was easy to be a libertarian critic, it was when he did have power that the real Trotsky emerged. That

Trotsky was the one who labored to destroy and undermine the popular organizations of workers in the Soviet Union, the factory councils and soviets, who wanted to subordinate the working class to the will of the maximum leader and to institute a program of militarization of labor in the totalitarian society that he and Lenin were constructing. That was the real Trotsky—not only the Trotsky who sent his troops to Kronstadt and wiped out Makhno's peasant forces once they were no longer needed to fend off the Whites, but the Trotsky who, from the very first moment of access to power, moved to undermine popular organizations and to institute highly coercive structures in which he and his associates would have absolute authority, with absolute submission of the working population to these leaders. That was the essential doctrine of Trotskyism in power, whatever he may have said before or after.

Now for people to identify themselves as Trotskyists, to adopt that label in the 1930s and 1940s, that simply indicated either appalling ignorance, the kind of ignorance that one could plead in the defense of Stalinists who just didn't know or didn't want to know what was happening, or else it meant a real commitment to these Leninist ideas. And I think that basically it was such a commitment, a commitment that's not fundamentally different from that of the Stalinists. That's what I felt at the time. It was essentially for this reason that I could never associate at all with any Trotskyite organization as a young radical. Remember that these were live issues in those years. And I think that was correct. So it's in this respect, at the level that we're now discussing, that I wouldn't differentiate the Stalinists from the Trotskyites. The crucial element is the Leninist concept of a revolutionary vanguard, an attractive idea for the radical intelligentsia who hope to assume state power at a time of revolutionary ferment. True, the Trotskyites did not have the same element of state worship, because there wasn't any state around that they could worship. But had there been one, they would have.

Now as far as Israel is concerned, I don't think that the motives are at all the same. It's the style and the technique that are the same. So, say, the *New Republic* will deal with a critic of Israel today in exactly the style with which a Stalinist journal of the thirties—in some cases, the *New Republic* itself—would deal with a critic of the Soviet Union then. It is easy enough to give examples. And the regular stream of apologetics for Israeli repression and atrocities have a very familiar ring to anyone familiar with the Stalinist literature of the thirties, with the very similar productions of the American commissars today who, in the familiar style, serve as apologists for the atrocities of their own state while vilifying those who do not meet their standards of servility.

As for the sources of the love affair of the intellectuals with Israel, that is an interesting matter. There was a qualitative shift in this regard in 1967, when Israel demonstrated its military prowess. I won't elaborate here—I've written about this elsewhere several times—except to say that the basic reasons for Israel's great appeal at this particular moment have to do, I think, with its successful use of violence at a moment when there seemed to be a real challenge to privilege and authority, both at home in the United States itself, and abroad. Israel was able to combine the image of a victim with effective use of the mailed fist to teach Third World upstarts their proper place. That's an irresistible combination, particularly in the context of the developing strategic alliance with U.S. power.

JP: You wrote that Henry Kissinger's memoirs "give the impression of a middle-level manager who has learned to conceal vacuity with pretentious verbiage." You doubt that he has any subtle "conceptual framework" or global design. Why do such individuals gain such extraordinary reputations, given what you say about his actual abilities? What does this say about how our society operates?

NC: Our society is not really based on public participation in decision-making in any significant sense. Rather, it is a system of elite decision and periodic public ratification. Certainly people would like to think that there's somebody up there who knows what he's doing. Since we don't participate, we don't control and we don't even think about questions of crucial importance, we hope somebody is paying attention who has some competence. Let's hope the ship has a captain, in other words, since we're not taking part in deciding what's going on. I think that's a factor. But also, it is an important feature of the ideological system to impose on people the feeling that they really are incompetent to deal with these complex and important issues; they'd better leave it to the captain. One device is to develop a star system, an array of figures who are often media creations or creations of the academic propaganda establishment, whose deep insights we are supposed to admire and to whom we must happily and confidently assign the right to control our lives and control international affairs. In fact, power is very highly concentrated, decision-making is highly concentrated in small interpenetrating elites, ultimately based on ownership of the private economy in large measure, but also in related ideological and political and managerial elites. Since that's the way the society effectively functions, it has to have political theology that explains that that's the way it ought to function, which means that you have to establish the pretense that the participants of that elite know what they are doing, in our interest, and have the kind of understanding and access to information that is denied the rest of us, so that we poor slobs ought to just watch, not interfere. Maybe we can choose one or another of them every few years, but it's their job to manage things, not ours. It's in this context that we can understand the Kissinger phenomenon. His ignorance and foolishness really are a phenomenon. I've written about this in some detail. But he did have a marvelous talent, namely, of playing the role of the philosopher who understands profound things in ways that are beyond the capacity of the ordinary person. He played that role quite elegantly. That's one reason why I think he was so attractive to the people who actually have power. That's just the kind of person they need.

JP: Does the business elite have an accurate perception of how our system operates?

NC: Yes, quite commonly. For example, in business schools and in business journals, one often finds a fairly clear perception of what the world is really like. On the other hand, in the more ideological circles, like the academic social sciences, I think you find much more deep-seated illusion and misunderstanding, which is quite natural. In the business school, they have to deal with the real world and they'd better know what the facts are, what the real properties of the world are. They are training the real managers, not the ideological managers, so the commitment to propaganda is less intense. Across the river from the business school in Cambridge, you have a different story. You have people one of whose functions is to prevent understanding on the part of others. Again, I don't want to overdraw the lines, but I think there are tendencies in these directions. There are some cases where it has even been investigated, though this is naturally not a very popular topic in the ideological disciplines. For example, some years ago, there was a review in the *Annals of the American Academy of Political and Social Science,* which I have quoted now and then, of research into the relation of corporations and foreign policy.

This was not done by any radicals. It was done by a mainstream political scientist named Dennis Ray. It wasn't a very far-reaching study, but some of the remarks that he makes are quite correct and to the point. He reports a survey of some two hundred works drawn from what he calls "the respectable literature on international relations and U.S. foreign policy." In this "respectable literature," he found no reference at all to the role of corporations in U.S. foreign relations in over 95 percent of the books surveyed, while in less than 5 percent he found passing mention. This was in 1972—there may have been a slight shift since as a result of the challenge to strict orthodoxy in the 1960s. This is quite remarkable. This is a marvelous example of the way the taboo system operates. Anyone with even the slightest knowledge of these matters knows that there's a very significant relation between corporations and foreign policy. It's perfectly obvious, and for good reasons. How strong corporate influence is and how it is manifested, one could debate. But that it's a strong and major influence, no serious person could deny. Nevertheless, the academic profession had succeeded in essentially eliminating this central topic from consideration.

Now the relevant point is this. Ray said he was excluding from his study two categories: one, what he called "radical and often neo-Marxist analyses," which presumably means anything critical of the corporate role, anything dissenting from the standard religious doctrines; and two, statements of corporate executives and business school professors. In both of these categories, there is discussion of the role of corporations in U.S. foreign policy. Ray concludes from his own investigation that the role is significant, as of course it is, but those who point out these obvious and important facts are not admitted into the "respectable literature," just as those who avoid the obvious do not lose "respectability" thereby.

I think this illustrates something which is fairly standard; that the real world is much more easily understood among people who really have to deal with the facts than among those one of whose functions is the creation of ideological cover and support for the doctrines of the faith.

JP: Yet the business community can turn out an enormous literature about development and modernizing other lands—not to speak of the good life here at home.

NC: That is certainly correct. The business community in the United States has demonstrated a high degree of class consciousness and an understanding of the importance of controlling what they call "the public mind." The rise of the public relations industry is one manifestation of this concern for "the engineering of consent," the essence of democracy according to Edward Bernays, the leading figure in this system of business propaganda. Part of this effort has been to create a certain conception of "the good life" at home, as you say, a conception that happens to conform to the needs of the wealthy and privileged sectors that dominate the economy as well as the political and ideological systems. They have also favored a particular form of "development and modernization" which happens to conform to the interests of American investors. These are very important matters, which merit much more attention than they receive.

But there are other elements of the picture that are worth considering, too, apart from the vast stream of propaganda aimed directly at control of the public mind and ensuring that public policy will conform to the needs of the privileged. The favored conception of development, for example, is commonly presented in terms of the alleged benefits to the indigenous population, not the interests of American investors and corporations or their local clients and associates. The belief that what you are doing is helpful to the peasants of northeastern Brazil doesn't harm your business operations, but just makes it psychologically easier to continue to act in your own interest. But a failure to recognize how state policy is and must be determined, fantasies about pluralist interactions and popular sovereignty—these could be an impediment to real world operations. It is important to keep a firm grasp on reality in this domain. The propaganda may be what it is, but dominant elites must have a clearer understanding among themselves. We can see what this understanding is from documents that are not intended for the general public, for example, the very illuminating report on the "Crisis of Democracy" to the Trilateral Commission—liberal elites in this case—explaining the need to return the general population to passivity and obedience, reversing the threat of democratization posed during the 1960s as normally irrelevant sectors of the population actually attempted to become organized for political action and to enter the political arena, threatening the domination of business-based elites.

But alongside of such frank internal discussion of the need to reverse the democratic thrust of the sixties, to ensure that there is no tampering with the institutions responsible for "the indoctrination of the young," to muzzle potentially dissident elements of the media, and so on—alongside of this we commonly find the construction of a system of beliefs that justifies what one is doing as right and good. That is natural enough, and is just as common in business circles as elsewhere.

JP: What kind of awareness do you think people in the CIA have of our world? And how does it compare with academic scholarship?

NC: Well, from the fragments available to us, it seems possible that the CIA is more honest than a good deal of academic writing in the ideological disciplines, less concerned with ideological purity and control and more concerned with the facts, just as the business press often turns out to be more honest than the mass media because it's more concerned with various facts which businessmen have to know, and less concerned with ideological control.

JP: Of course, there can certainly be CIA operations that are very interested in ideological control.

NC: That is certainly another aspect of their operations, as we know from many sources: leaking fabricated stories in the expectation that they will be picked up by the media, for example. Furthermore, I wouldn't suggest that the CIA escapes ideological controls itself. It's interesting to see the extent to which U.S. intelligence itself is controlled by the ideological framework that also governs the media and academic scholarship to a large degree. There are some dramatic examples of this. For example, take the Pentagon Papers, which covered a record of about twenty-five years, with a fair degree of access to reports by intelligence. One of the most interesting revelations in the Pentagon Papers is that the analysts found only one staff paper in this twenty-five-year period which even raised the question of whether Hanoi was acting on its own, rather than acting simply as a puppet of Moscow or "Peiping," as they used to call it. This was apparently the only time in twenty-five years that U.S. intelligence was even able to face what was the obvious truth and reality. One expects this on the part of people like Dean Acheson and Dean Rusk, and on the part of "respectable" academic scholarship and journalism. But it's intriguing that even intelligence analysts who, after all, are paid to find out the truth, were unable to face the fact that the Vietnamese might be acting in terms of their own perceived interests. It was just crucially necessary to make them puppets of somebody. It didn't much matter who. Russia would do, or China, or a Sino-Soviet conspiracy would be even better. That would then justify American aggression, whereas if they were acting on their own, it would be harder to justify the American aggression, since Vietnam itself can hardly be presented as a threat to our security. It is very intriguing to see the extent to which the intelligence apparatus was trapped in these religious doctrines.

JP: What do you think of the CIA's role in American universities?

NC: Well, it's something that I've never gotten much exercised about, frankly. For example, take MIT. I imagine that the MIT Press at one time was publishing some books with a CIA subsidy. I was actually the reader for one book—Douglas Pike's *Viet Cong*—which was published on my recommendation though I assumed at the time that there was probably a secret subsidy somewhere, and if I recall correctly, some information later surfaced about that. Up until, I think, the early sixties, the CIA was openly funding the Center for International Studies. Since that time, as far as I know, they're not. But I don't see that it matters much one way or another. People do essentially the same kind of work. The institution pretty much serves the interests of the state where it can. Whether it's being directly funded by the CIA or in some other fashion seems to me a marginal question. Frankly, I think it might be better to have direct, open funding by the CIA. At least, everything would be open and aboveboard. I once suggested that the universities should establish a Department of Death, which would incorporate all work concerned with weapons systems, policy studies oriented to international affairs, ideological contributions in these areas, and so on. Insofar as all of this goes on, it should be visible, not concealed.

JP: What do you think of Harvard's attempt to deal with the CIA?

NC: Well, they didn't want to keep any official connections with the CIA. But does that mean, for example, that work on international affairs at Harvard will be directed toward the needs of liberation movements? Hardly. As long as the work in fact will be what it always has been over many years, namely, committed to the needs of the powers that dominate these institutions, primarily the government, the major corporations, and so on, as long as that's the case, I'd just as soon see the connections made overt.

JP: Do you have a deep faith in reason?

NC: I don't have a faith in that or anything else.

JP: Not even in reason?

NC: I wouldn't say "faith." I think . . . it's all we have. I don't have faith that the truth will prevail if it becomes known, but we have no alternative to proceeding on that assumption, whatever its credibility may be. It's of more than a little interest that ideological managers act in ways that indicate that they share this belief. This is shown, for example, by the substantial efforts to conceal the obvious. After all, it would be easier just to tell the truth.

Why is it that the propaganda system is geared to suppressing any inquiry into such questions as the role of corporations in foreign policy? Or let's take contemporary history. Why isn't the terrible history of U.S. intervention in Central America and the Caribbean a staple of the curriculum, so that everyone learns, for example, that there are people living under conditions of virtual slavery in Guatemala because land reform was stopped by a CIA coup in 1954, and subsequent interventions under Kennedy and Johnson helped maintain a terror-and-torture state with few counterparts in the modern world? Why isn't it a staple of modern history that in Greece in the late 1940s the United States, with a degree of fanaticism, organized a murderous counterinsurgency campaign, putting tens of thousands of people into reeducation camps where they were tortured and killed, backing the expulsion of tens of thousands of others, destroying the unions and the political system and carrying on massacres? Why doesn't everybody know that? It's really important to know. Look at Vietnam. What about that? Why is so much effort undertaken to ensure that the basic facts about the U.S. attack against South Vietnam will not be known, will not be investigated, or if investigated, will be dismissed or swept into a corner, and certainly won't enter the mainstream of academic interpretation or education? Why such efforts to conceal the real history with fables about the awesome nobility of our intentions, flawed only by blunders arising from our naiveté and simpleminded goodness, which is unique in history?

I think there's good reason why the propaganda system works that way. It recognizes that the public will not support the actual policies. Therefore, it's important to prevent any knowledge or understanding of them. Correspondingly, the other side of the coin is that it's extremely important to try to bring out the truth about these matters, as best we can.

Maybe if people knew the truth, they would still support the same policies. Well, that could be. Certainly the ideologists of the propaganda system do not believe that. Why is the history of the Vietnam War being so completely rewritten and so distorted in the media and popular books? Well, again, the same thing. It's very recent, after all, but there has been quite an effort to construct a purified history of the war, to conceal and suppress what too many people had come to understand when they escaped the control of the ideological system temporarily. Not that much rewriting had to be done, actually, because, contrary to many illusions, the intellectual community remained quite loyal to official doctrine throughout. But much of the public did not. Recently I reviewed some of the popular historical literature and the media retrospectives. It's an interesting case of "the engineering of consent," or thought control, to put it bluntly. It's also interesting that the general servility, readily documented, is denounced as "antiestablishment" and "hypercritical," unfair to our noble efforts. It all amounts to an impressive commitment to suppress the kind of understanding that was achieved by many people and to ensure that it doesn't persist or proliferate.

JP: At times it's a system that seems to have extraordinary strength and other moments there's a question of vulnerabilities that are evident in the unease, fear . . .

NC: Well, it's extremely unstable because of the reliance on lies. Any system that's based on lying and deceit is inherently unstable. But, on the other hand, it does have enormous resilience and very little challenge, limited enough and sufficiently marginalized so that the impact of the propaganda system is powerful and pervasive.

JP: Is not debate limited by a general lack of belief in alternatives to how we live?

NC: Well, it's very hard to get to the point where you can even discuss alternatives until you first peel away layer after layer of myth and illusion. Friends who share my interests and concerns have often criticized the work I do, maybe rightly, because they say it's much too critical of superficial phenomena, in a sense. A lot of what I have written and what I speak about has been devoted to particular atrocities in Vietnam, in Latin America, in the Middle East, in East Timor, things like that, and to the web of deceit that has been constructed about them. Now these are matters that have enormous human significance, but they're superficial in a sort of technical sense; that is, they are the end result of much deeper, central factors in our society and culture. The criticism is that I ought to pay more attention to the central factors and to ways of changing them, to revolutionary strategy, for example. Well, I've been resistant to that, rightly or wrongly, but I see the point, certainly. I mean, suppose that we could, say, induce the United States to stop supporting massacre and repression in East Timor. It would be very important for the Timorese, if they survive. But it would be like putting a Band-Aid on a cancer. It's just going to show up somewhere else.

To the extent that one can reach the general public on these issues—it's very limited because the media and journals don't really permit it—but to the extent that one can, well, East Timor or Vietnam are topics that you can talk to people about in a way that is meaningful to them, whereas talking to them about institutional change and the possibility that they might play a role in changing the institutions is like talking to them about Mars. I don't know how you get to the point where those kinds of questions can be raised. Certainly not just by talk. Those are things that people have to live; aspirations and understanding have to grow out of experience and struggle and conflict.

For example, take a runaway plant. At the time when the plant is being removed from Connecticut to Taiwan, it's quite possible that questions about, say, workers' decision-making, worker control, can be raised in a way which would seem exotic and academic when the system is functioning. I have a lot of respect for the people who are doing it. There are plenty of opportunities to raise issues for thinking and consideration that are somehow related to the actual options that people have, that are not just abstract and esoteric, like, could an alternative society work? It's very hard to think about abstractly. It's just too remote from the options that people actually have for them to even pay any attention to that. But I think these are the kinds of questions that ultimately have to become central to the concerns of the great mass of the population if we are going to be able to do anything more than put Band-Aids on cancers.

JP: So what is most needed is some mass popular base within which dissent and alternatives could take root?

NC: That much is clear enough. What we don't have and should have is mass popular organization. Then critical discussion and analysis, and serious thought about social issues, can become significant. During the Vietnam War, it was possible for dissident intellectuals to have a useful role in raising questions and helping to expand the horizons of understanding. A big, popular mass movement developed. One could write for a mass audience, a reasonably large audience in the sixties. What you said could be picked up, criticized, disseminated, and so on. That's what happened to a significant extent, thanks to very substantial and quite successful efforts at low-level grass-roots organizing, which reached quite a substantial scale. The appropriate role for intellectuals, I guess, is to try to contribute to the work of mass, popular, democratic libertarian movements. But right now they barely exist.

    Sometimes there is a detectable effect, even in the absence of such popular organization. Well, take the Timor case. There weren't more than half a dozen people in the United States who were devoting real effort and energy to trying to lift the curtain of silence on the topic during the worst period of the slaughter. But there were a few, and after several years they actually did succeed in breaking through to the point where a few people in Congress became quite upset about the issue, there were occasional articles and editorials, and some limited news-reporting. Well, you might say that's a pretty small achievement after a hundred thousand people have been massacred, maybe more. But it is certainly better than nothing. And there was an effect. The Red Cross was finally allowed in sporadically and some aid flowed to the victims. Tens of thousand of lives were saved. That's not a small achievement for a small group of mainly young people.

JP: What do you think are the most important insights that should be preserved from the 1960s? What will prove most lasting about the civil rights movement and the antiwar movement?

NC: Here we have to make a distinction between the real popular movements and the elements that have passed through the filter of the media and popular history. The constructed image of the New Left, and the sixties generally, is far from the reality, or

rather, is a carefully selected choice from a much more complex
reality, a choice that as usual reflects the needs of privileged
groups who, in this case, felt threatened by the rise of popular
movements and the notable improvement in the moral and intellectual climate that took place as a result of their activities. This
rise in the moral and cultural level was a matter of real significance, as is shown rather clearly by the fears and anguish it
elicited: for example, the fears over the "crisis of democracy"
that threatened to bring an end to the good old days when the
president could run the country "with the cooperation of a relatively small number of Wall Street lawyers and bankers," as Harvard professor Samuel Huntington put it with a trace of nostalgia
in the Trilateral Commission report; or the concern about the
"Vietnam syndrome," a dread disease that spread over much of
the population with such symptoms as distaste for torture and
massacre and sympathy for the victims; or the "malaise" noted
by Henry Kissinger in his memoirs, illustrated for example by the
challenge to "the hitherto almost unanimous conviction that the
Cold War had been caused by Soviet intransigence" alone, a
dangerous departure from the doctrines of the faith. A look at
what was written on these topics in the early sixties, before the
New Left and the student movement made it impossible to suppress the challenge to comfortable orthodoxies, is most instructive with regard to the notable improvement in the general
cultural climate.

The movement against the war in Vietnam had long-lasting, I
hope permanent, effects in raising the general level of insight and
understanding among the general public, with an impact on
scholarship and journalism as well. The civil rights movement
also had significant and I presume permanent effects, as did the
feminist movement, the ecological movements, and many other
offshoots of the organizing and educational efforts of the 1960s.
The universities were opened up quite markedly to ideas and
thinking that had been effectively marginalized and suppressed.
This is a phenomenon that can hardly escape notice. Despite the
intense efforts undertaken in the 1970s to reverse this general
cultural progress and enlightenment, much of it remains.

One can see the change in general consciousness and culture,
for example, by comparing the reaction when Kennedy sent U.S.
forces to attack South Vietnam in 1962 to the reaction when
Reagan made moves toward direct military intervention in Central America a few weeks after coming to office. The U.S. Air
Force began its direct participation in bombing and defoliation
in Vietnam in 1962, as part of the effort to drive several million

peasants into concentration camps where they could be "protected" from the guerrillas who, the government conceded, they were willingly supporting, after tens of thousands had been slaughtered and the United States had effectively blocked any political settlement, including the offer of the NLF (the "Vietcong," in the terms of U.S. propaganda) to neutralize South Vietnam, Cambodia, and Laos. The public reaction was virtually nil; all of this was regarded as entirely legitimate, even praiseworthy. Even when a huge American expeditionary force was sent to invade South Vietnam and the United States expanded its war to the North and to Laos, protest was very limited. We sometimes forget that as late as 1966 it was impossible to have an outdoor public meeting in Boston—probably the most liberal city in the United States—to protest the war, because it would be broken up with considerable violence. In the spring of 1966, even meetings in churches were physically attacked by counterdemonstrators. Compare all of this to what happened in 1981, when Ronald Reagan moved to escalate Carter's war of torture and massacre in El Salvador with measures that threatened to lead to the direct use of U.S. military forces. The February 1981 white paper, which laid the basis for this escalation, elicited virtually no critical comment in the media, reflecting the subordination of the intellectual community to the state propaganda system, but there was a spontaneous popular reaction, unanticipated by people who had assumed that the Vietnam syndrome had been laid to rest by the ideological campaigns of the seventies. This public reaction led the government to back away from its provocative rhetoric for fear that more central programs would be threatened, particularly the programs of military Keynesianism and transfer of resources from the poor to the wealthy. Afterward, the media began to criticize the white paper and, for a period, to report on the U.S.-backed massacres in El Salvador that were designed to abort the threat of meaningful democracy there, as they have.

The comparison between 1962 and 1981 is instructive. It reflects the substantial change in popular awareness and concern, and popular understanding of political realities, a result of the ferment of the 1960s. I do not want to exaggerate the difference, but it is nevertheless quite real.

The change in the cultural climate is illustrated in many other ways. It is, for example, an astonishing fact that for almost two hundred years after the establishment of the United States, it was impossible to face honestly what had been done to the indigenous population. This, too, changed, rather dramatically, as a result of the improvement in the moral and cultural climate in the

1960s. There are many other illustrations ranging from conditions of personal life and interaction, to scholarship, and beyond.

The accomplishments, which were very real, can be credited largely to young people, most of them nameless and forgotten, who devoted themselves to organizing, education, civil disobedience, and resistance. Few people can remember the names of the SNCC activists who were on the front lines during the hardest days of the civil rights movement, or the people who worked to create and sustain the mass-based antiwar movement, or others who did the real and important work that laid the basis for the significant achievements of the period. Naturally all of this is suppressed in official history, which offers a quite different picture, helped, in this case, by self-proclaimed "leaders" and "activists" who understand that prestige and privilege will be accorded those willing to pander to the needs of dominant elites by concocting generally fanciful tales about what was happening in those years of turmoil and struggle. The insight that should be preserved is a simple one: honest commitment, though it often carries severe personal cost, can achieve a great deal and, if it can be sustained, might make it possible for us to come to grips in a serious way with essential problems of modern society, not the least of them being a permanent threat of global destruction.

JP: In looking back on those years, did you find yourself significantly changed by them? Were they essential for you to develop the entire range of your work in areas outside of linguistics?

NC: Sure, my life and activities changed quite a lot, in ways that I have mixed feelings about. I faced a serious and uncomfortable decision about this in 1964—much too late, I think. I was deeply immersed in the work I was doing. It was intellectually exciting, and all sorts of fascinating avenues of research were opening up. Furthermore, I was pretty well settled then into a comfortable academic life, with very satisfying work, security, young kids growing up, everything that one could ask from a personal standpoint. The question I had to face was whether to become actively engaged in protest against the war, that is, engaged beyond signing petitions, sending money, and other peripheral contributions. I knew very well that once I set forth along that path, there would be no end. For better or worse, that is what I decided to do, with considerable reluctance. In those days, protest against the war meant speaking several nights a week at a church to an audience of half a dozen people, mostly bored or hostile, or at someone's home where a few people might be gathered, or at a meeting at a college that included the topics of Vietnam, Iran, Central America, and nuclear arms, in the hope that maybe the participants would outnumber the organizers. Soon after, it meant participation in demonstrations, lobbying, organizing resistance, civil disobedience and arrests, endless speaking and travel, and the expected concomitants: threats of a fairly serious nature that were quite real by the late 1960s, which I don't particularly want to enter into, and so on. As I knew would happen, the issues in which I became involved rapidly proliferated. Political demands tend to fill every vacuum, and to displace other commitments, since they are often urgent and very few people are available to answer to the demand for speakers, participants in civil disobedience, and other activities that are constantly on the agenda. I had to give up many things, personal and professional, that I very much wanted to do, and to take on many obligations that I often found far from pleasant.

On the other had, there are numerous compensations, even apart from the fact that it is possible to look at oneself in the mirror without too much shame—there is always more than enough, since what should be done is so vastly beyond what one can do or chooses to do. I met wonderful people whom I would never have come to know, and experienced aspects of life here and abroad that I would never have seen directly. And while I expect that any worthwhile cause will achieve at best very limited success, and will quite probably largely fail, nevertheless there are accomplishments that give much satisfaction, however small they may be in the face of what one would like to see.

A look at the record will answer your question about range of work. I began to write about topics that had long been of intense interest to me, but that I never would have thought of writing about. Actually a large part of what I have published consists of expanded versions of talks, which I've been giving for the past twenty years or more at a rate that I'd prefer not to think about.

So it is a mixed story, but I think in retrospect that it was the right decision.

You asked whether I was significantly changed personally? Not really, I think, in any fundamental way. I've learned a lot, experienced a lot that I never would have seen or lived through, but I cannot honestly say that my beliefs or attitudes have changed in any significant ways.

the RESPONSIBILITY of INTELLECTUALS

The Responsibility of
Intellectuals

(1966)

───────────────

*T*WENTY YEARS AGO, DWIGHT MACDONALD PUBLISHED A SERIES
of articles in *Politics* on the responsibilities of peoples and,
specifically, the responsibility of intellectuals. I read them as an
undergraduate, in the years just after the war, and had occasion to read
them again a few months ago. They seem to me to have lost none of their
power or persuasiveness. Macdonald is concerned with the question of
war guilt. He asks the question: to what extent were the German or
Japanese people responsible for the atrocities committed by their governments? And, quite properly, he turns the question back to us: to what
extent are the British or American people responsible for the vicious
terror bombings of civilians, perfected as a technique of warfare by the
Western democracies and reaching their culmination in Hiroshima and

Nagasaki, surely among the most unspeakable crimes in history? To an undergraduate in 1945–1946—to anyone whose political and moral consciousness had been formed by the horrors of the 1930s, by the war in Ethiopia, the Russian purge, the "China incident," the Spanish Civil War, the Nazi atrocities, the Western reaction to these events and, in part, complicity in them—these questions had particular significance and poignancy.

With respect to the responsibility of intellectuals, there are still other, equally disturbing questions. Intellectuals are in a position to expose the lies of governments, to analyze actions according to their causes and motives and often hidden intentions. In the Western world at least, they have the power that comes from political liberty, from access to information and freedom of expression. For a privileged minority, Western democracy provides the leisure, the facilities, and the training to seek the truth lying hidden behind the veil of distortion and misrepresentation, ideology, and class interest through which the events of current history are presented to us. The responsibilities of intellectuals, then, are much deeper than what Macdonald calls the "responsibility of peoples," given the unique privileges that intellectuals enjoy.

The issues that Macdonald raised are as pertinent today as they were twenty years ago. We can hardly avoid asking ourselves to what extent the American people bear responsibility for the savage American assault on a largely helpless rural population in Vietnam, still another atrocity in what Asians see as the "Vasco da Gama era" of world history. As for those of us who stood by in silence and apathy as this catastrophe slowly took shape over the past dozen years, on what page of history do we find our proper place? Only the most insensible can escape these questions. I want to return to them, later on, after a few scattered remarks about the responsibility of intellectuals and how, in practice, they go about meeting this responsibility in the mid-1960s.

It is the responsibility of intellectuals to speak the truth and to expose lies. This, at least, may seem enough of a truism to pass without comment. Not so, however. For the modern intellectual, it is not at all obvious. Thus we have Martin Heidegger writing, in a pro-Hitler declaration of 1933, that "truth is the revelation of that which makes a people certain, clear, and strong in its action and knowledge"; it is only this kind of "truth" that one has a responsibility to speak. Americans tend to be more forthright. When Arthur Schlesinger was asked by the *New York Times,* in November 1965, to explain the contradiction between his published account of the Bay of Pigs incident and the story he had given the press at the time of the attack, he simply remarked that he had lied; and a few days later, he went on to compliment the *Times* for also having suppressed information on the planned invasion, in "the national interest," as this was defined by the group of arrogant and deluded men of whom Schlesinger gives such a flattering portrait in his recent account of the Kennedy administration. It is of no particular interest that one man is quite happy to lie in behalf of a cause which he knows to be unjust; but it is significant that such events provoke so little response in the intellectual community—no feeling, for example, that there is something strange in the offer of a major chair in humanities to a historian who feels it to be his duty to persuade the world that an American-sponsored invasion of a nearby country is nothing of the sort. And what of the incredible sequence of lies on the part of our government and its spokesmen concerning such matters as negotiations in Vietnam? The facts are known to all who care to know. The press, foreign and domestic, has presented documentation to refute each falsehood as it appears. But the power of the government propaganda apparatus is such that the citizen who does not undertake a research project on the subject can hardly hope to confront government pronouncements with fact.[1]

The deceit and distortion surrounding the American invasion of Vietnam are by now so familiar that they have lost their power to shock. It is therefore well to recall that although new levels of cynicism are constantly being reached, their clear antecedents were accepted at home with quiet toleration. It is a useful exercise to compare government statements at the time of the invasion of Guatemala in 1954 with Eisenhower's admission—to be more accurate, his boast—a decade later that American planes were sent "to help the invaders."[2] Nor is it only in moments of crisis that duplicity is considered perfectly in order. "New Frontiersmen," for example, have scarcely distinguished themselves by a passionate concern for historical accuracy, even when they are not being called upon to provide a "propaganda cover" for ongoing actions. For example, Arthur Schlesinger describes the bombing of North Vietnam and the massive escalation of military commitment in early 1965 as based on a "perfectly rational argument": ". . . so long as the Vietcong thought they were going to win the war, they obviously would not be interested in any kind of negotiated settlement."[3] The date is important. Had the statement been made six months earlier, one could attribute it to ignorance. But this statement appeared after months of front-page news reports detailing the United Nations, North Vietnamese, and Soviet initiatives that preceded the February 1965 escalation and that, in fact, continued for several weeks after the bombing began, after months of soul-searching by Washington correspondents who were trying desperately to find some mitigating circumstances for the startling deception that had been revealed. (Chalmers Roberts, for example, wrote with unconscious irony that late February 1965 "hardly seemed to Washington to be a propitious moment for negotiations [since] Mr. Johnson . . . had just ordered the first bombing of North Vietnam in an effort to bring Hanoi to a conference table where bargaining chips on both sides would be more closely matched."[4]) Coming at this moment, Schlesinger's statement is less an example of deceit than of contempt—contempt for an audience that can be expected to tolerate such behavior with silence, if not approval.[5]

To turn to someone closer to the actual formation and implementation of policy, consider some of the reflections of Walt Rostow, a man who, according to Schlesinger, brought a "spacious historical view" to the conduct of foreign affairs in the Kennedy administration.[6] According to his analysis, the guerrilla warfare in Indochina in 1946 was launched by Stalin,[7] and Hanoi initiated the guerrilla war against South Vietnam in 1958 (*The View from the Seventh Floor,* pp. 39 and 152). Similarly, the Communist planners probed the "free world spectrum of defense" in Northern Azerbaijan and Greece (where Stalin "supported substantial guerrilla warfare"—pp. 36 and 148), operating from plans carefully laid in 1945. And in Central Europe, the Soviet Union was not "prepared to accept a solution which would remove the dangerous tensions from Central Europe at the risk of even slowly staged corrosion of communism in East Germany" (p. 156).

It is interesting to compare these observations with studies by scholars actually concerned with historical events. The remark about Stalin's initiating the first Vietnamese war in 1946 does not even merit refutation. As to Hanoi's purported initiative of 1958, the situation is more clouded. But even government sources[8] concede that in 1959 Hanoi received the first direct reports of what Diem referred to[9] as his own Algerian war, and that only after this did they lay their plans to involve themselves in this struggle. In fact, in December 1958, Hanoi made another of its many attempts—rebuffed once again by Saigon and the United States—to establish diplomatic and commercial relations with the Saigon government on the basis of the status quo.[10] Rostow offers no evidence of Stalin's support for the Greek guerrillas; in fact, though the historical record is far from clear, it seems that Stalin was by no means pleased with the adventurism of the Greek guerrillas, who, from his point of view, were upsetting the satisfactory postwar imperialist settlement.[11]

Rostow's remarks about Germany are more interesting still. He does not see fit to mention, for example, the Russian notes of March–April 1952, which proposed unification of Germany under internationally supervised elections, with withdrawal of all troops within a year, *if* there was a guarantee that a reunified Germany would not be permitted to join a Western military alliance.[12] And he has also momentarily forgotten his own characterization of the strategy of the Truman and Eisenhower administrations: "to avoid any serious negotiation with the Soviet Union until the West could confront Moscow with German rearmament within an organized European framework, as a *fait accompli*"[13]—to be sure, in defiance of the Potsdam agreements.

But most interesting of all is Rostow's reference to Iran. The facts are that there was a Russian attempt to impose by force a pro-Soviet government in Northern Azerbaijan that would grant the Soviet Union access to Iranian oil. This was rebuffed by superior Anglo-American force in 1946, at which point the more powerful imperialism obtained full rights to Iranian oil for itself, with the installation of a pro-Western government. We recall what happened when, for a brief period in the early 1950s, the only Iranian government with something of a popular base experimented with the curious idea that Iranian oil should belong to the Iranians. What is interesting, however, is the description of Northern Azerbaijan as part of "the free world spectrum of defense." It is pointless, by now, to comment on the debasement of the phrase "Free World." But by what law of nature does Iran, with its resources, fall within Western dominion? The bland assumption that it does is most revealing of deep-seated attitudes towards the conduct of foreign affairs.

In addition to this growing lack of concern for truth, we find in recent statements a real or feigned naiveté with regard to American actions that reaches startling proportions. For example, Arthur Schlesinger has recently characterized our Vietnamese policies of 1954 as "part of our general program of international goodwill."[14] Unless intended as irony, this remark shows either a colossal cynicism or an inability, on a scale that defies comment, to comprehend elementary phenomena of contemporary history. Similarly, what is one to make of the testimony of Thomas Schelling before the House Foreign Affairs Committee, January 27, 1966, in which he discusses the two great dangers if all Asia "goes Communist"?[15] First, this would exclude "the United States and what we call Western civilization from a large part of the world that is poor and colored and potentially hostile." Second, "a country like the United States probably cannot maintain self-confidence if just about the greatest thing it ever attempted, namely to create the basis for decency and prosperity and democratic government in the underdeveloped world, had to be acknowledged as a failure or as an attempt that we wouldn't try again." It surpasses belief that a person with even minimal acquaintance with the record of American foreign policy could produce such statements.

It surpasses belief, that is, unless we look at the matter from a more historical point of view, and place such statements in the context of the hypocritical moralism of the past; for example, of Woodrow Wilson, who was going to teach the Latin Americans the art of good government, and who wrote (1902) that it is "our peculiar duty" to teach colonial peoples "order and self-control . . . [and] . . . the drill and habit of law and obedience." Or of the missionaries of the 1840s, who described the hideous and degrading opium wars as "the result of a great design of Providence to make the wickedness of men subserve his purposes of mercy toward China, in breaking through her wall of exclusion, and bringing the empire into more immediate contact with western and Christian nations." Or, to approach the present, of A. A. Berle, who, in commenting on the Dominican intervention, has the impertinence to attribute the problems of the Caribbean countries to imperialism—*Russian* imperialism.[16]

As a final example of this failure of skepticism, consider the remarks of Henry Kissinger in concluding his presentation in a Harvard-Oxford television debate on American Vietnam policies. He observed, rather sadly, that what disturbs him most is that others question not our judgment but our motives—a remarkable comment on the part of one whose professional concern is political analysis, that is, analysis of the actions of governments in terms of motives that are unexpressed in official propaganda and perhaps only dimly perceived by those whose acts they govern. No one would be disturbed by an analysis of the political behavior of Russians, French, or Tanzanians, questioning their motives and interpreting their actions in terms of long-range interests, perhaps well concealed behind official rhetoric. But it is an article of faith that American motives are pure and not subject to analysis (see note 1). Although it is nothing new in American intellectual history—or, for that matter, in the general history of imperialist apologia—this innocence becomes increasingly distasteful as the power it serves grows more dominant in world affairs and more capable, therefore, of the unconstrained viciousness that the mass media present to us each day. We are hardly the first power in history to combine material interests, great technological capacity, and an utter disregard for the suffering and misery of the lower orders. The long tradition of naiveté and self-righteousness that disfigures our intellectual history, however, must serve as a warning to the Third World, if such a warning is needed, as to how our protestations of sincerity and benign intent are to be interpreted.

The basic assumptions of the "New Frontiersmen" should be pondered carefully by those who look forward to the involvement of academic intellectuals in politics. For example, I have referred to Arthur Schlesinger's objections to the Bay of Pigs invasion, but the reference was imprecise. True, he felt that it was a "terrible idea," but "not because the notion of sponsoring an exile attempt to overthrow Castro seemed intolerable in itself." Such a reaction would be the merest sentimentality, unthinkable to a tough-minded realist. The difficulty, rather, was that it seemed unlikely that the deception could succeed. The operation, in his view, was ill-conceived but not otherwise objectionable.[17] In a similar vein, Schlesinger quotes with approval Kennedy's "realistic" assessment of the situation resulting from Trujillo's assassination: "There are three possibilities in descending order of preference: a decent democratic regime, a continuation of the Trujillo regime or a Castro regime. We ought to aim at the first, but we really can't renounce the second until we are sure that we can avoid the third."[18] The reason why the third possibility is so intolerable is explained a few pages later: "Communist success in Latin America would deal a much harder blow to the power and influence of the United States." Of course, we can never really be sure of avoiding the third possibility; therefore, in practice, we will always settle for the second, as we are now doing in Brazil and Argentina, for example.[19]

Or consider Walt Rostow's views on American policy in Asia.[20] The basis on which we must build this policy is that "we are openly threatened and we feel menaced by Communist China." To prove that we are menaced is of course unnecessary, and the matter receives no attention; it is enough that we feel menaced. Our policy must be based on our national heritage and our national interests. Our national heritage is briefly outlined in the following terms: "Throughout the nineteenth century, in good conscience Americans could devote themselves to the extension of both their principles and their power on this continent," making use of "the somewhat elastic concept of the Monroe doctrine" and, of course, extending "the American interest to Alaska and the mid-Pacific islands. . . . Both our insistence on unconditional surrender and the idea of post-war occupation . . . represented the formulation of American security interests in Europe and Asia." So much for our heritage. As to our interests, the matter is equally simple. Fundamental is our "profound interest that societies abroad develop and strengthen those elements in their respective cultures that elevate and protect the dignity of the individual against the state." At the same time, we must counter the "ideological threat," namely, "the possibility that the Chinese Communists can prove to Asians by progress in China that Communist methods are better and faster than democratic methods." Nothing is said about those people in Asian cultures to whom our "conception of the proper relation of the individual to the state" may not be the uniquely important value, people who might, for example, be concerned with preserving the "dignity of the individual" against concentrations of foreign or domestic capital, or against semifeudal structures (such as Trujillo-type dictatorships) introduced or kept in power by American arms. All of this is flavored with allusions to "our religious and ethical value systems" and to our "diffuse and complex concepts" which are to the Asian mind "so much more difficult to grasp" than Marxist dogma, and are so "disturbing to some Asians" because of "their very lack of dogmatism."

Such intellectual contributions as these suggest the need for a correction to De Gaulle's remark, in his memoirs, about the American "will to power, cloaking itself in idealism." By now, this will to power is not so much cloaked in idealism as it is drowned in fatuity. And academic intellectuals have made their unique contribution to this sorry picture.

Let us, however, return to the war in Vietnam and the response that it has aroused among American intellectuals. A striking feature of the recent debate on Southeast Asian policy has been the distinction that is commonly drawn between "responsible criticism" on the one hand, and "sentimental" or "emotional" or "hysterical" criticism on the other. There is much to be learned from a careful study of the terms in which this distinction is drawn. The "hysterical critics" are to be identified, apparently, by their irrational refusal to accept one fundamental political axiom, namely, that the United States has the right to extend its power and control without limit, insofar as is feasible. Responsible criticism does not challenge this assumption, but argues, rather, that we probably can't "get away with it" at this particular time and place.

A distinction of this sort seems to be what Irving Kristol has in mind, for example, in his analysis of the protest over Vietnam policy, in *Encounter*, August 1965. He contrasts the responsible critics, such as Walter Lippmann, the *New York Times*, and Senator Fulbright, with the "teach-in movement." "Unlike the university protesters," he maintains, "Mr. Lippmann engages in no presumptuous suppositions as to 'what the Vietnamese people really want'—he obviously doesn't much care—or in legalistic exegesis as to whether, or to what extent, there is 'aggression' or 'revolution' in South Vietnam. His is a *realpolitik* point of view; and he will apparently even contemplate the possibility of a *nuclear* war against China in extreme circumstances." This is commendable, and contrasts favorably, for Kristol, with the talk of the "unreasonable, ideological types" in the teach-in movement, who often seem to be motivated by such absurdities as "simple, virtuous 'anti-imperialism,' " who deliver "harangues on 'the power structure,' " and who even sometimes stoop so low as to read "articles and reports from the foreign press on the American presence in Vietnam." Furthermore, these nasty types are often psychologists, mathematicians, chemists, or philosophers (just as, incidentally, those most vocal in protest in the Soviet Union are generally physicists, literary intellectuals, and others remote from the exercise of power), rather than people with Washington contacts, who of course realize that "had they a new, good idea about Vietnam, they would get a prompt and respectful hearing" in Washington.

I am not interested here in whether Kristol's characterization of protest and dissent is accurate, but rather in the assumptions that it expresses with respect to such questions as these: Is the purity of American motives a matter that is beyond discussion, or that is irrelevant to discussion? Should decisions be left to "experts" with Washington contacts—that is, even if we assume that they command the necessary knowledge and principles to make the "best" decision, will they invariably do so? And, a logically prior question, is "expertise" applicable—that is, is there a body of theory and of relevant information, not in the public domain, that can be applied to the analysis of foreign policy or that demonstrates the correctness of present actions in some way that the psychologists, mathematicians, chemists, and philosophers are incapable of comprehending? Although Kristol does not examine these questions directly, his attitudes presuppose answers, answers which are wrong in all cases. American aggressiveness, however it may be masked in pious rhetoric, is a dominant force in world affairs and must be analyzed in terms of its causes and motives. There is no body of theory or significant body of relevant information, beyond the comprehension of the layman, which makes policy immune from criticism. To the extent that "expert knowledge" is applied to world affairs, it is surely appropriate—for a person of any integrity, quite necessary—to question its quality and the goals that it serves. These facts seem too obvious to require extended discussion.

A corrective to Kristol's curious belief in the administration's openness to new thinking about Vietnam is provided by McGeorge Bundy in a recent article.[21] As Bundy correctly observes, "On the main stage . . . the argument on Viet Nam turns on tactics, not fundamentals," although, he adds, "there are wild men in the wings." On stage center are, of course, the president (who in his recent trip to Asia had just "magisterially reaffirmed" our interest "in the progress of the people across the Pacific") and his advisers, who deserve "the understanding support of those who want restraint." It is these men who deserve the credit for the fact that "the bombing of the North has been the most accurate and the most restrained in modern warfare"—a solicitude which will be appreciated by the inhabitants, or former inhabitants, of Nam Dinh and Phu Ly and Vinh. It is these men, too, who deserve the credit for what was reported by Malcolm Browne as long ago as May 1965: "In the South, huge sectors of the nation have been declared 'free bombing zones,' in which anything that moves is a legitimate target. Tens of thousands of tons of bombs, rockets, napalm and cannon fire are poured into these vast areas each week. If only by the laws of chance, bloodshed is believed to be heavy in these raids."

Fortunately for the developing countries, Bundy assures us, "American democracy has no enduring taste for imperialism," and "taken as a whole, the stock of American experience, understanding, sympathy and simple knowledge is now much the most impressive in the world." It is true that "four-fifths of all the foreign investing in the world is now done by Americans" and that "the most admired plans and policies . . . are no better than their demonstrable relation to the American interest"—just as it is true, so we read in the same issue of *Foreign Affairs,* that the plans for armed action against Cuba were put into motion a few weeks after Mikoyan visited Havana, "invading what had so long been an almost exclusively American sphere of influence." Unfortunately such facts as these are often taken by unsophisticated Asian intellectuals as indicating a "taste for imperialism." For example, a number of Indians have expressed their "near exasperation" at the fact that "we have done everything we can to attract foreign capital for fertilizer plants, but the American and the other Western private companies know we are over a barrel, so they demand stringent terms which we just cannot meet,"[22] while "Washington . . . doggedly insists that deals be made in the private sector with private enterprise."[23] But this reaction, no doubt, simply reveals once again how the Asian mind fails to comprehend the "diffuse and complex concepts" of Western thought.

It may be useful to study carefully the "new, good ideas about Vietnam" that are receiving a "prompt and respectful hearing" in Washington these days. The United States Government Printing Office is an endless source of insight into the moral and intellectual level of this expert advice. In its publications one can read, for example, the testimony of Professor David N. Rowe, director of graduate studies in international relations at Yale University, before the House Committee on Foreign Affairs (see note 15). Professor Rowe proposes (p. 266) that the United States buy all surplus Canadian and Australian wheat, so that there will be mass starvation in China. These are his words: "Mind you, I am not talking about this as a weapon against the Chinese people. It will be. But that is only incidental. The weapon will be a weapon against the Government because the internal stability of that country cannot be sustained by an unfriendly Government in the face of general starvation." Professor Rowe will have none of the sentimental moralism that might lead one to compare this suggestion with, say, the *Ostpolitik* of Hitler's Germany.[24] Nor does he fear the impact of such policies on other Asian nations, for example Japan. He assures us, from his "very long acquaintance with Japanese questions," that "the Japanese above all are people who respect power and determination." Hence "they will not be so much alarmed by American policy in Vietnam that takes off from a position of power and intends to seek a solution based upon the imposition of our power upon local people that we are in opposition to." What would disturb the Japanese is "a policy of indecision, a policy of refusal to face up to the problems [in China and Vietnam] and to meet our responsibilities there in a positive way," such as the way just cited. A conviction that we were "unwilling to use the power that they know we have" might "alarm the Japanese people very intensely and shake the degree of their friendly relations with us." In fact, a full use of American power would be particularly reassuring to the Japanese, because they have had a demonstration "of the tremendous power in action of the United States . . . because they have felt our power directly." This is surely a prime example of the healthy *"realpolitik* point of view" that Irving Kristol so much admires.

But, one may ask, why restrict ourselves to such indirect means as mass starvation? Why not bombing? No doubt this message is implicit in the remarks to the same committee of the Reverend R. J. de Jaegher, regent of the Institute of Far Eastern Studies, Seton Hall University, who explains that like all people who have lived under communism, the North Vietnamese "would be perfectly happy to be bombed to be free" (p. 345).

Of course, there must be those who support the Communists. But this is really a matter of small concern, as the Honorable Walter Robertson, assistant secretary of state for far eastern affairs from 1953 to 1959, points out in his testimony before the same committee. He assures us that "the Peiping regime . . . represents something less than 3 percent of the population" (p. 402).

Consider, then, how fortunate the Chinese Communist leaders are, compared to the leaders of the Vietcong, who, according to Arthur Goldberg, represent about "one-half of one percent of the population of South Vietnam," that is, about one half the number of new southern recruits for the Vietcong during 1965, if we can credit Pentagon statistics.[25]

In the face of such experts as these, the scientists and philosophers of whom Kristol speaks would clearly do well to continue to draw their circles in the sand.

Having settled the issue of the political irrelevance of the protest movement, Kristol turns to the question of what motivates it—more generally, what has made students and junior faculty "go left," as he sees it, amid general prosperity and under liberal, welfare-state administrations. This, he notes, "is a riddle to which no sociologist has as yet come up with an answer." Since these young people are well off, have good futures, etc., their protest must be irrational. It must be the result of boredom, of too much security, or something of this sort.

Other possibilities come to mind. It might be, for example, that as honest men the students and junior faculty are attempting to find out the truth for themselves rather than ceding the responsibility to "experts" or to government; and it might be that they react with indignation to what they discover. These possibilities Kristol does not reject. They are simply unthinkable, unworthy of consideration. More accurately, these possibilities are inexpressible; the categories in which they are formulated (honesty, indignation) simply do not exist for the tough-minded social scientist.

In this implicit disparagement of traditional intellectual values, Kristol reflects attitudes that are fairly widespread in academic circles. I do not doubt that these attitudes are in part a consequence of the desperate attempt of the social and behavioral sciences to imitate the surface features of sciences that really have significant intellectual content. But they have other sources as well. Anyone can be a moral individual, concerned with human rights and problems; but only a college professor, a trained expert, can solve technical problems by "sophisticated" methods. Ergo, it is only problems of the latter sort that are important or real. Responsible, nonideological experts will give advice on tactical questions; irresponsible "ideological types" will "harangue" about principle and trouble themselves over moral issues and human rights, or over the traditional problems of man and society, concerning which "social and behavioral science" have nothing to offer beyond trivialities. Obviously, these emotional, ideological types are irrational, since, being well off and having power in their grasp, they shouldn't worry about such matters.

At times this pseudoscientific posing reaches levels that are almost pathological. Consider the phenomenon of Herman Kahn, for example. Kahn has been both denounced as immoral and lauded for his courage. By people who should know better, his *On Thermonuclear War* has been described "without qualification . . . [as] . . . one of the great works of our time" (Stuart Hughes). The fact of the matter is that this is surely one of the emptiest works of our time, as can be seen by applying to it the intellectual standards of any existing discipline, by tracing some of its "well-documented conclusions" to the "objective studies" from which they derive, and by following the line of argument, where detectable. Kahn proposes no theories, no explanations, no empirical assumptions that can be tested against their consequences, as do the sciences he is attempting to mimic. He simply suggests a terminology and provides a façade of rationality. When particular policy conclusions are drawn, they are supported only by *ex cathedra* remarks for which no support is even suggested (e.g., "The civil defense line probably should be drawn somewhere below $5 billion annually" to keep from provoking the Russians—why not $50 billion, or $5?). What is more, Kahn is quite aware of this vacuity; in his more judicious moments, he claims only that "there is no reason to believe that relatively sophisticated models are more likely to be misleading than the simpler models and analogies frequently used as an aid to judgment." For those whose humor tends towards the macabre, it is easy to play the game of "strategic thinking" à la Kahn, and to prove what one wishes. For example, one of Kahn's basic assumptions is that "an all-out surprise attack in which all resources are devoted to counter-value targets would be so irrational that, barring an incredible lack of sophistication or actual insanity among Soviet decision-makers, such an attack is highly unlikely." A simple argument proves the opposite. Premise 1: American decision-makers think along the lines outlined by Herman Kahn. Premise 2: Kahn thinks it would be better for everyone to be red than for everyone to be dead. Premise 3: If the Americans were to respond to an all-out counter-value attack, then everyone would be dead. Conclusion: The Americans will not respond to an all-out countervalue attack, and therefore it should be launched without delay. Of course, one can carry the argument a step further. Fact: The Russians have not carried out an all-out countervalue attack. It follows that they are not rational. If they are not rational, there is no point in "strategic thinking." Therefore . . .

Of course, this is all nonsense, but nonsense that differs from Kahn's only in the respect that the argument is of slightly greater complexity than anything to be discovered in his work. What is remarkable is that serious people actually pay attention to these absurdities, no doubt because of the façade of tough-mindedness and pseudoscience.

It is a curious and depressing fact that the "antiwar movement" falls prey all too often to similar confusions. In the fall of 1965, for example, there was an International Conference on Alternative Perspectives on Vietnam, which circulated a pamphlet to potential participants stating its assumptions. The plan was to set up study groups in which three "types of intellectual tradition" will be represented: (1) area specialists; (2) "social theory, with special emphasis on theories of the international system, of social change and development, of conflict and conflict resolu-tion, or of revolution"; (3) "the analysis of public policy in terms of basic human values, rooted in various theological, philosophical and humanist traditions." The second intellectual tradition will provide "general propositions, derived from social theory and tested against historical, comparative, or experimental data"; the third "will provide the frame-work out of which fundamental value questions can be raised and in terms of which the moral implications of societal actions can be analyzed." The hope was that "by approaching the questions [of Vietnam policy] from the moral perspectives of all great religions and philosophical systems, we may find solutions that are more consistent with fundamental human values than current American policy in Vietnam has turned out to be."

In short, the experts on values (i.e., spokesmen for the great religions and philosophical systems) will provide fundamental insights on moral perspectives, and the experts on social theory will provide general em-pirically validated propositions and "general models of conflict." From this interplay, new policies will emerge, presumably from application of the canons of scientific method. The only debatable issue, it seems to me, is whether it is more ridiculous to turn to experts in social theory for general well-confirmed propositions, or to the specialists in the great religions and philosophical systems for insights into fundamental human values.

There is much more that can be said about this topic, but without continuing, I would simply like to emphasize that, as is no doubt obvious, the cult of the expert is both self-serving, for those who propound it, and fraudulent. Obviously, one must learn from social and behavioral science whatever one can; obviously, these fields should be pursued in as serious a way as is possible. But it will be quite unfortunate, and highly dangerous, if they are not accepted and judged on their merits and according to their actual, not pretended, accomplishments. In particular, if there is a body of theory, well tested and verified, that applies to the conduct of foreign affairs or the resolution of domestic or international conflict, its existence has been kept a well-guarded secret. In the case of Vietnam, if those who feel themselves to be experts have access to principles or information that would justify what the American government is doing in that unfortunate country, they have been singularly ineffective in making this fact known. To anyone who has any familiarity with the social and behavioral sciences (or the "policy sciences"), the claim that there are certain considerations and principles too deep for the outsider to comprehend is simply an absurdity, unworthy of comment.

When we consider the responsibility of intellectuals, our basic concern must be their role in the creation and analysis of ideology. And in fact, Kristol's contrast between the unreasonable ideological types and the responsible experts is formulated in terms that immediately bring to mind Daniel Bell's interesting and influential essay on the "end of ideology,"[26] an essay which is as important for what it leaves unsaid as for its actual content. Bell presents and discusses the Marxist analysis of ideology as a mask for class interest, in particular quoting Marx's well-known description of the belief of the bourgeoisie "that the *special* conditions of its emancipation are the *general* conditions through which alone modern society can be saved and the class struggle avoided." He then argues that the age of ideology is ended, supplanted, at least in the West, by a general agreement that each issue must be settled on its own individual terms, within the framework of a welfare state in which, presumably, experts in the conduct of public affairs will have a prominent role. Bell is quite careful, however, to characterize the precise sense of "ideology" in which "ideologies are exhausted." He is referring only to ideology as "the conversion of ideas into social levers," to ideology as "a set of beliefs, infused with passion, . . . [which] . . . seeks to transform the whole of a way of life." The crucial words are "transform" and "convert into social levers." Intellectuals in the West, he argues, have lost interest in converting ideas into social levers for the radical transformation of society. Now that we have achieved the pluralistic society of the welfare state, they see no further need for a radical transformation of society; we may tinker with our way of life here and there, but it would be wrong to try to modify it in any significant way. With this consensus of intellectuals, ideology is dead.

There are several striking facts about Bell's essay. First, he does not point out the extent to which this consensus of the intellectuals is self-serving. He does not relate his observation that, by and large, intellectuals have lost interest in "transforming the whole way of life" to the fact that they play an increasingly prominent role in running the welfare state; he does not relate their general satisfaction with the welfare state to the fact that, as he observes elsewhere, "America has become an affluent society, offering place . . . and prestige . . . to the onetime radicals." Secondly, he offers no serious argument to show that intellectuals are somehow "right" or "objectively justified" in reaching the consensus to which he alludes, with its rejection of the notion that society should be transformed. Indeed, although Bell is fairly sharp about the empty rhetoric of the "New Left," he seems to have a quite utopian faith that technical experts will be able to come to grips with the few problems that still remain; for example, the fact that labor is treated as a commodity, and the problems of "alienation."

It seems fairly obvious that the classical problems are very much with us; one might plausibly argue that they have even been enhanced in severity and scale. For example, the classical paradox of poverty in the midst of plenty is now an ever increasing problem on an international scale. Whereas one might conceive, at least in principle, of a solution within national boundaries, a sensible idea as to how to transform international society in such a way as to cope with the vast and perhaps increasing human misery is hardly likely to develop within the framework of the intellectual consensus that Bell describes.

Thus it would seem natural to describe the consensus of Bell's intellectuals in somewhat different terms than his. Using the terminology of the first part of his essay, we might say that the welfare-state technician finds justification for his special and prominent social status in his "science," specifically, in the claim that social science can support a technology of social tinkering on a domestic or international scale. He then takes a further step, proceeding, in a familiar way, to claim universal validity for what is in fact a class interest: he argues that the special conditions on which his claims to power and authority are based are, in fact, the general conditions through which alone modern society can be saved; that social tinkering within a welfare-state framework must replace the commitment to the "total ideologies" of the past, ideologies which were concerned with a transformation of society. Having found his position of power, having achieved security and affluence, he has no further need for ideologies that look to radical change. The scholar-expert replaces the "free-floating intellectual" who "felt that the wrong values were being honored, and rejected the society," and who has now lost his political role (now, that is, that the right values are being honored).

Conceivably it is correct that the technical experts who will (or hope to) manage the "postindustrial society" will be able to cope with the classic problems without a radical transformation of society. Just so, it is conceivably true that the bourgeoisie was right in regarding the special conditions of its emancipation as the general conditions through which alone modern society would be saved. In either case, an argument is in order, and skepticism is justified where none appears.

Within the same framework of general utopianism, Bell goes on to pose the issue between welfare-state scholar-experts and Third World ideologists in a rather curious way. He points out, quite correctly, that there is no issue of communism, the content of that doctrine having been "long forgotten by friends and foes alike." Rather, he says, "the question is an older one: whether new societies can grow by building democratic institutions and allowing people to make choices—and sacrifices—voluntarily, or whether the new elites, heady with power, will impose totalitarian means to transform their countries." The question is an interesting one; it is odd, however, to see it referred to as "an older one." Surely he cannot be suggesting that the West chose the democratic way—for example, that in England during the industrial revolution, the farmers voluntarily made the choice of leaving the land, giving up cottage industry, becoming an industrial proletariat, and voluntarily decided, within the framework of the existing democratic institutions, to make the sacrifices that are graphically described in the classic literature on nineteenth-century industrial society. One may debate the question whether authoritarian control is necessary to permit capital accumulation in the underdeveloped world, but the Western model of development is hardly one that we can point to with any pride. It is perhaps not surprising to find a Walt Rostow referring to "the more humane processes [of industrialization] that Western values would suggest."[27] Those who have a serious concern for the problems that face backward countries and for the role that advanced industrial societies might, in principle, play in development and modernization must use somewhat more care in interpreting the significance of the Western experience.

Returning to the quite appropriate question of whether "new societies can grow by building democratic institutions" or only by totalitarian means, I think that honesty requires us to recognize that this question must be directed more to American intellectuals than to Third World ideologists. The backward countries have incredible, perhaps insurmountable problems, and few available options; the United States has a wide range of options, and has the economic and technological resources, though evidently neither the intellectual nor the moral resources, to confront at least some of these problems. It is easy for an American intellectual to deliver homilies on the virtues of freedom and liberty, but if he is really concerned about, say, Chinese totalitarianism or the burdens imposed on the Chinese peasantry in forced industrialization, then he should face a task that is infinitely more significant and challenging—the task of creating, in the United States, the intellectual and moral climate, as well as the social and economic conditions, that would permit this country to participate in modernization and development in a way commensurate with its material wealth and technical capacity. Massive capital gifts to Cuba and China might not succeed in alleviating the authoritarianism and terror that tend to accompany early stages of capital accumulation, but they are far more likely to have this effect than lectures on democratic values. It is possible that even without "capitalist encirclement" in its varying manifestations, the truly democratic elements in revolutionary movements—in some instances soviets and collectives, for example—might be undermined by an "elite" of bureaucrats and technical intelligentsia; but it is a near certainty that the fact of capitalist encirclement, which all revolutionary movements now have to face, will guarantee this result. The lesson, for those who are concerned to strengthen the democratic, spontaneous, and popular elements in developing societies, is quite clear. Lectures on the two-party system, or even the really substantial democratic values that have been in part realized in Western society, are a monstrous irrelevance in the face of the effort that is required to raise the level of culture in Western society to the point where it can provide a "social lever" for both economic development and the development of true democratic institutions in the Third World—and for that matter, at home as well.

A good case can be made for the conclusion that there is indeed something of a consensus among intellectuals who have already achieved power and affluence, or who sense that they can achieve them by "accepting society" as it is and promoting the values that are "being honored" in this society. And it is also true that this consensus is most noticeable among the scholar-experts who are replacing the free-floating intellectuals of the past. In the university, these scholar-experts construct a "value-free technology" for the solution of technical problems that arise in contemporary society,[28] taking a "responsible stance" toward these problems, in the sense noted earlier. This consensus among the responsible scholar-experts is the domestic analogue to that proposed, in the international arena, by those who justify the application of American power in Asia, whatever the human cost, on the grounds that it is necessary to contain the "expansion of China" (an "expansion" which is, to be sure, hypothetical for the time being)[29]—to translate from State Department Newspeak, on the grounds that it is essential to reverse the Asian nationalist revolutions, or at least to prevent them from spreading. The analogy becomes clear when we look carefully at the ways in which this proposal is formulated. With his usual lucidity, Churchill outlined the general position in a remark to his colleague of the moment, Joseph Stalin, at Teheran in 1943: ". . . the government of the world must be entrusted to satisfied nations, who wished nothing more for themselves than what they had. If the world-government were in the hands of hungry nations, there would always be danger. But none of us had any reason to seek for anything more. The peace would be kept by peoples who lived in their own way and were not ambitious. Our power placed us above the rest. We were like rich men dwelling at peace within their habitations."[30]

For a translation of Churchill's biblical rhetoric into the jargon of contemporary social science, one may turn to the testimony of Charles Wolf, senior economist of the RAND Corporation, at the congressional committee hearings cited earlier:

> I am dubious that China's fears of encirclement are going to be abated, eased, relaxed in the long-term future. But I would hope that what we do in Southeast Asia would help to develop within the Chinese body politic more of a realism and willingness to live with this fear than to indulge it by support for liberation movements, which admittedly depend on a great deal more than external support . . . the operational question for American foreign policy is not whether that fear can be eliminated or substantially alleviated, but whether China can be faced with a structure of incentives, of penalties and rewards, of inducements that will make it willing to live with this fear.[31]

The point is further clarified by Thomas Schelling: "There is growing experience which the Chinese can profit from, that although the United States may be interested in encircling them, may be interested in defending nearby areas from them, it is, nevertheless, prepared to behave peaceably if they are."[32]

In short, we are prepared to live peaceably within our—to be sure, rather extensive—habitations. And quite naturally, we are offended by the undignified noises from the servants' quarters. If, let us say, a peasant-based revolutionary movement tries to achieve independence from foreign domination or to overthrow semifeudal structures supported by foreign powers, or if the Chinese irrationally refuse to respond properly to the schedule of reinforcement that we have prepared for them, if they object to being encircled by the benign and peace-loving "rich men" who control the territories on their borders as a natural right, then, evidently, we must respond to this belligerence with appropriate force.

It is this mentality that explains the frankness with which the United States government and its academic apologists defend the American refusal to permit a political settlement in Vietnam at a local level, a settlement based on the actual distribution of political forces. Even government experts freely admit that the National Liberation Front is the only "truly mass-based political party in South Vietnam";[33] that the NLF had "made a conscious and massive effort to extend political participation, even if it was manipulated, on the local level so as to involve the people in a self-contained, self-supporting revolution" (p. 374); and that this effort had been so successful that no political groups, "with the possible exception of the Buddhists, thought themselves equal in size and power to risk entering into a coalition, fearing that if they did the whale would swallow the minnow" (p. 362). Moreover, they concede that until the introduction of overwhelming American force, the NLF had insisted that the struggle "should be fought out at the political level and that the use of massed military might was in itself illegitimate. . . . The battleground was to be the minds and loyalties of the rural Vietnamese, the weapons were to be ideas" (pp. 91–92; cf. also pp. 93, 99–108, 155ff.); and correspondingly, that until mid-1964, aid from Hanoi "was largely confined to two areas—doctrinal know-how and leadership personnel" (p. 321). Captured NLF documents contrast the enemy's "military superiority" with their own "political superiority" (p. 106), thus fully confirming the analysis of American military spokesmen who define our problem as how, "with considerable armed force but little political power, [to] contain an adversary who has enormous political force but only modest military power."[34]

Similarly, the most striking outcome of both the Honolulu conference in February and the Manila conference in October was the frank admission by high officials of the Saigon government that as Charles Mohr says, "they could not survive a 'peaceful settlement' that left the Vietcong *political* structure in place even if the Vietcong guerrilla units were disbanded," that "they are not able to compete *politically* with the Vietnamese Communists."[35] Thus, Mohr continues, the Vietnamese demand a "pacification program" which will have as "its core . . . the destruction of the clandestine Vietcong political structure and the creation of an iron-like system of government political control over the population." And from Manila, the same correspondent, on October 23, quotes a high South Vietnamese official as saying: "Frankly, we are not strong enough now to compete with the Communists on a purely political basis. They are organized and disciplined. The non-Communist nationalists are not—we do not have any large, well-organized political parties and we do not yet have unity. We cannot leave the Vietcong in existence." Officials in Washington understand the situation very well. Thus Secretary Rusk has pointed out that "if the Vietcong come to the conference table as full partners they will, in a sense, have been victorious in the very aims that South Vietnam and the United States are pledged to prevent" (January 28, 1966). Similarly, Max Frankel reported from Washington: "Compromise has had no appeal here because the Administration concluded long ago that the non-Communist forces of South Vietnam could not long survive in a Saigon coalition with Communists. It is for that reason—and not because of an excessively rigid sense of protocol—that Washington has steadfastly refused to deal with the Vietcong or recognize them as an independent political force."[36]

In short, we will—magnanimously—permit Vietcong representatives to attend negotiations, but only if they will agree to identify themselves as agents of a foreign power and thus forfeit the right to participate in a coalition government, a right which they have now been demanding for a half dozen years. We know well that in any representative coalition, our chosen delegates could not last a day without the support of American arms. Therefore, we must increase American force and resist meaningful negotiations, until the day when a client government can exert both military and political control over its own population—a day which may never dawn, for as William Bundy has pointed out, we could never be sure of the security of a Southeast Asia "from which the Western presence was effectively withdrawn." Thus if we were to "negotiate in the direction of solutions that are put under the label of neutralization," this would amount to capitulation to the Communists.[37] According to this reasoning, then, South Vietnam must remain, permanently, an American military base.

All of this is reasonable, of course, so long as we accept the fundamental political axiom that the United States, with its traditional concern for the rights of the weak and downtrodden, and with its unique insight into the proper mode of development for backward countries, must have the courage and the persistence to impose its will by force until such time as other nations are prepared to accept these truths—or simply to abandon hope.

If it is the responsibility of the intellectual to insist upon the truth, it is also his duty to see events in their historical perspective. Thus one must applaud the insistence of the secretary of state on the importance of historical analogies, the Munich analogy, for example. As Munich showed, a powerful and aggressive nation with a fanatic belief in its manifest destiny will regard each victory, each extension of its power and authority, as a prelude to the next step. The matter was very well put by Adlai Stevenson, when he spoke of "the old, old route whereby expansive powers push at more and more doors, believing they will open, until, at the ultimate door, resistance is unavoidable and major war breaks out."

Herein lies the danger of appeasement, as the Chinese tirelessly point out to the Soviet Union, which they claim is playing Chamberlain to our Hitler in Vietnam. Of course, the aggressiveness of liberal imperialism is not that of Nazi Germany, though the distinction may seem rather academic to a Vietnamese peasant who is being gassed or incinerated. We do not want to occupy Asia; we merely wish, to return to Mr. Wolf, "to help the Asian countries progress toward economic modernization, as relatively 'open' and stable societies, to which our access, as a country and as individual citizens, is free and comfortable."[38] The formulation is appropriate. Recent history shows that it makes little difference to us what form of government a country has as long as it remains an "open society," in our peculiar sense of this term—a society, that is, which remains open to American economic penetration or political control. If it is necessary to approach genocide in Vietnam to achieve this objective, then this is the price we must pay in defense of freedom and the rights of man.

It is no doubt superfluous to discuss at length the ways in which we assist other countries to progress toward open societies "to which our access is free and comfortable." One enlightening example is discussed in the recent congressional hearings from which I have now quoted several times, in the testimony of Willem Holst and Robert Meagher, representing the Standing Committee on India of the Business Council for International Understanding.[39] As Mr. Meagher points out: "If it was possible, India would probably prefer to import technicians and know-how rather than foreign corporations. Such is not possible; therefore India accepts foreign capital as a necessary evil." Of course, "the question of private capital investment in India . . . would be no more than a theoretical exercise" had the groundwork for such investment not been laid by foreign aid, and were it not that "necessity has forced a modification in India's approach to private foreign capital." But now, "India's attitude toward private foreign investment is undergoing a substantial change. From a position of resentment and ambivalence, it is evolving toward an acceptance of its necessity. As the necessity becomes more and more evident, the ambivalence will probably be replaced by a more accommodating attitude." Mr. Holst contributes what is "perhaps a typical case history," namely, "the plan under which it was proposed that the Indian Government in partnership with a United States private consortium was to have increased fertilizer production by a million tons per year, which is just double presently installed capacity in all of India. The unfortunate demise of this ambitious plan may be attributed in large part to the failure of both Government and business to find a workable and mutually acceptable solution within the framework of the well-publicized 10 business incentives." The difficulty here was in connection with the percentage of equity ownership. Obviously, "fertilizers are desperately needed in India." Equally obviously, the consortium "insisted that to get the proper kind of control majority ownership was in fact needed." But "the Indian Government officially insisted that they shall have majority ownership," and "in something so complex it was felt that it would be a self-defeating thing."

Fortunately, this particular story has a happy ending. The remarks just quoted were made in February 1966, and within a few weeks, the Indian government had seen the light, as we read in a series of reports in the *New York Times*. The criticism, inside India, that "the American Government and the World Bank would like to arrogate to themselves the right to lay down the framework in which our economy must function," was stilled (April 24); and the Indian government accepted the conditions for resumed economic aid, namely, "that India provide easier terms for foreign private investment in fertilizer plants" and that the American investors "have substantial management rights" (May 14). The development is summarized in a dispatch datelined April 28, from New Delhi, in these terms:

> There are signs of change. The Government has granted easy terms to private foreign investors in the fertilizer industry, is thinking about decontrolling several more industries and is ready to liberal-ize import policy if it gets sufficient foreign aid. . . . Much of what is happening now is a result of steady pressure from the United States and the International Bank for Reconstruction and Develop-ment, which for the last year have been urging a substantial freeing of the Indian economy and a greater scope for private enterprise. The United States pressure, in particular, has been highly effective here because the United States provides by far the largest part of the foreign exchange needed to finance India's development and keep the wheels of industry turning. Call them "strings," call them "conditions" or whatever one likes, India has little choice now but to agree to many of the terms that the United States, through the World Bank, is putting on its aid. For India simply has nowhere else to turn.

The heading of the article refers to this development as India's "drift from socialism to pragmatism."

Even this was not enough, however. Thus we read a few months later, in the *Christian Science Monitor* (December 5), that American entre-preneurs insist "on importing all equipment and machinery when India has a tested capacity to meet some of their requirements. They have insisted on importing liquid ammonia, a basic raw material, rather than using indigenous naphtha which is abundantly available. They have laid down restrictions about pricing, distribution, profits, and management control." The Indian reaction, I have already cited (see p. 68).

In such ways as these, we help India develop toward an open society, one which, in Walt Rostow's words, has a proper understanding of "the core of the American ideology," namely, "the sanctity of the individual in relation to the state." And in this way, too, we refute the simpleminded view of those Asians who, to continue with Rostow's phrasing, "believe or half-believe that the West has been driven to create and then to cling to its imperial holdings by the inevitable workings of capitalist economies."[40]

In fact, a major postwar scandal is developing in India as the United States, cynically capitalizing on India's current torture, applies its economic power to implement India's "drift from socialism to pragmatism."

In pursuing the aim of helping other countries to progress toward open societies, with no thought of territorial aggrandizement, we are breaking no new ground. Hans Morgenthau has aptly described our traditional policy toward China as one of favoring "what you might call freedom of competition with regard to the exploitation of China."[41] In fact, few imperialist powers have had explicit territorial ambitions. Thus in 1784, the British Parliament announced that "to pursue schemes of conquest and extension of dominion in India are measures repugnant to the wish, honor, and policy of this nation." Shortly after, the conquest of India was in full swing. A century later, Britain announced its intentions in Egypt under the slogan "Intervention, Reform, Withdrawal." It is unnecessary to comment on which parts of this promise were fulfilled, within the next half century. In 1936, on the eve of hostilities in North China, the Japanese stated their Basic Principles of National Policy. These included the use of moderate and peaceful means to extend her strength, to promote social and economic development, to eradicate the menace of communism, to correct the aggressive policies of the great powers, and to secure her position as the stabilizing power in East Asia. Even in 1937, the Japanese government had "no territorial designs upon China." In short, we follow a well-trodden path.

It is useful to remember, incidentally, that the United States was apparently quite willing, as late as 1939, to negotiate a commercial treaty with Japan and arrive at a modus vivendi if Japan would "change her attitude and practice towards our rights and interests in China," as Secretary Hull put it. The bombing of Chungking and the rape of Nanking were rather unpleasant, it is true, but what was really important was our rights and interests in China, as the responsible, unhysterical men of the day saw quite clearly. It was the closing of the Open Door by Japan that led inevitably to the Pacific war, just as it is the closing of the Open Door by

"Communist" China itself that may very well lead to the next, and no doubt last, Pacific war.

Quite often, the statements of sincere and devoted technical experts give surprising insight into the intellectual attitudes that lie in the background of the latest savagery. Consider, for example, the following comment by economist Richard Lindholm, in 1959, expressing his frustration over the failure of economic development in "free Vietnam": ". . . the use of American aid is determined by how the Vietnamese use their incomes and their savings. The fact that a large portion of the Vietnamese imports financed with American aid are either consumer goods or raw materials used rather directly to meet consumer demands is an indication that the Vietnamese people desire these goods, for they have shown their desire by their willingness to use their piasters to purchase them."[42]

In short, the Vietnamese *people* desire Buicks and air conditioners, rather than sugar-refining equipment or road-building machinery, as they have shown by their behavior in a free market. And however much we may deplore their free choice, we must allow the people to have their way. Of course, there are also those two-legged beasts of burden that one stumbles on in the countryside, but as any graduate student of political science can explain, they are not part of a responsible modernizing elite, and therefore have only a superficial biological resemblance to the human race.

In no small measure, it is attitudes like this that lie behind the butchery in Vietnam, and we had better face up to them with candor, or we will find our government leading us toward a "final solution" in Vietnam, and in the many Vietnams that inevitably lie ahead.

Let me finally return to Macdonald and the responsibility of intellectuals. Macdonald quotes an interview with a death-camp paymaster who bursts into tears when told that the Russians would hang him. "Why should they? What have I done?" he asked. Macdonald concludes: "Only those who are willing to resist authority themselves when it conflicts too intolerably with their personal moral code, only they have the right to condemn the death-camp paymaster." The question "What have I done?" is one that we may well ask ourselves, as we read, each day, of fresh atrocities in Vietnam—as we create, or mouth, or tolerate the deceptions that will be used to justify the next defense of freedom.

Objectivity and Liberal
Scholarship

(1968)

*I*F IT IS PLAUSIBLE THAT IDEOLOGY WILL IN GENERAL SERVE AS
a mask for self-interest, then it is a natural presumption that
intellectuals, in interpreting history or formulating policy, will
tend to adopt an elitist position, condemning popular movements and
mass participation in decision-making, and emphasizing rather the necessity for supervision by those who possess the knowledge and understanding that is required (so they claim) to manage society and control social
change. This is hardly a novel thought. One major element in the anarchist critique of Marxism a century ago was the prediction that, as Bakunin formulated it:

According to the theory of Mr. Marx, the people not only must not destroy [the state] but must strengthen it and place it at the complete disposal of their benefactors, guardians, and teachers—the leaders of the Communist party, namely Mr. Marx and his friends, who will proceed to liberate [mankind] in their own way. They will concentrate the reins of government in a strong hand, because the ignorant people require an exceedingly firm guardianship; they will establish a single state bank, concentrating in its hands all commercial, industrial, agricultural and even scientific production, and then divide the masses into two armies—industrial and agricultural—under the direct command of the state engineers, who will constitute a new privileged scientific-political estate.[1]

One cannot fail to be struck by the parallel between this prediction and that of Daniel Bell—the prediction that in the new postindustrial society, "not only the best talents, but eventually the entire complex of social prestige and social status, will be rooted in the intellectual and scientific communities." Pursuing the parallel for a moment, it might be asked whether the left-wing critique of Leninist elitism can be applied, under very different conditions, to the liberal ideology of the intellectual elite that aspires to a dominant role in managing the welfare state.[2]

Rosa Luxemburg, in 1918, argued that Bolshevik elitism would lead to a state of society in which the bureaucracy alone would remain an active element in social life—though now it would be the "Red bureaucracy" of that state socialism that Bakunin had long before described as "the most vile and terrible lie that our century has created."[3] A true social revolution requires a "spiritual transformation in the masses degraded by centuries of bourgeois class rule";[4] "it is only by extirpating the habits of obedience and servility to the last root that the working class can acquire the understanding of a new form of discipline, self-discipline arising from free consent."[5] Writing in 1904, she predicted that Lenin's organizational concepts would "enslave a young labor movement to an intellectual elite hungry for power . . . and turn it into an automaton manipulated by a Central Committee."[6] In the Bolshevik elitist doctrine of 1918, she saw a disparagement of the creative, spontaneous, self-correcting force of mass action, which alone, she argued, could solve the thousand problems of social reconstruction and produce the spiritual transformation that is the essence of a true social revolution. As Bolshevik practice hardened into dogma, the fear of popular initiative and spontaneous mass action, not under the direction and control of the properly designated vanguard, became a dominant element of so-called "Communist" ideology.

Antagonism to mass movements and to social change that escapes the control of privileged elites is also a prominent feature of contemporary liberal ideology.[7] I would like to investigate how, in one rather crucial case, this particular bias in American liberal ideology can be detected even in the interpretation of events of the past in which American involvement was rather slight, and in historical work of very high caliber.

In 1966, the American Historical Association gave its biennial award for the most outstanding work on European history to Gabriel Jackson, for his study of Spain in the 1930s.[8] There is no question that of the dozens of books on this period, Jackson's is among the best, and I do not doubt that the award was well deserved. The Spanish Civil War is one of the crucial events of modern history, and one of the most extensively studied as well. In it, we find the interplay of forces and ideas that have dominated European history since the industrial revolution. What is more, the relationship of Spain to the great powers was in many respects like that of the countries of what is now called the Third World. In some ways, then, the events of the Spanish Civil War give a foretaste of what the future may hold, as Third World revolutions uproot traditional societies, threaten imperial dominance, exacerbate great-power rivalries, and bring the world perilously close to a war which, if not averted, will surely be the final catastrophe of modern history. My reason for wanting to investigate an outstanding liberal analysis of the Spanish Civil War is therefore twofold: first, because of the intrinsic interest of these events; and second, because of the insight that this analysis may provide with respect to the underlying elitist bias which I believe to be at the root of the phenomenon of counterrevolutionary subordination.

In his study of the Spanish Republic, Jackson makes no attempt to hide his own commitment in favor of liberal democracy, as represented by such figures as Azaña, Casares Quiroga, Martínez Barrio,[9] and the other "responsible national leaders." In taking this position, he speaks for much of liberal scholarship; it is fair to say that figures similar to those just mentioned would be supported by American liberals, were this possible, in Latin America, Asia, or Africa. Furthermore, Jackson makes little attempt to disguise his antipathy toward the forces of popular revolution in Spain, or their goals.

It is no criticism of Jackson's study that his point of view and sympathies are expressed with such clarity. On the contrary, the value of this work as an interpretation of historical events is enhanced by the fact that the author's commitments are made so clear and explicit. But I think it can be shown that Jackson's account of the popular revolution that took place in Spain is misleading and in part quite unfair, and that the failure of objectivity it reveals is highly significant in that it is characteristic of the attitude taken by liberal (and Communist) intellectuals toward revolutionary movements that are largely spontaneous and only loosely organized, while rooted in deeply felt needs and ideals of dispossessed masses. It is a convention of scholarship that the use of such terms as those of the preceding phrase demonstrates naiveté and muddle-headed sentimentality. The convention, however, is supported by ideological conviction rather than history or investigation of the phenomena of social life. This conviction is, I think, belied by such events as the revolution that swept over much of Spain in the summer of 1936.

The circumstances of Spain in the 1930s are not duplicated elsewhere in the underdeveloped world today, to be sure. Nevertheless, the limited information that we have about popular movements in Asia, specifically, suggests certain similar features that deserve much more serious and sympathetic study than they have so far received.[10] Inadequate information makes it hazardous to try to develop any such parallel, but I think it is quite possible to note long-standing tendencies in the response of liberal as well as Communist intellectuals to such mass movements.

As I have already remarked, the Spanish Civil War is not only one of the critical events of modern history but one of the most intensively studied as well. Yet there are surprising gaps. During the months following the Franco insurrection in July 1936, a social revolution of unprecedented scope took place throughout much of Spain. It had no "revolutionary vanguard" and appears to have been largely spontaneous, involving masses of urban and rural laborers in a radical transformation of social and economic conditions that persisted, with remarkable success, until it was crushed by force. This predominantly anarchist revolution and the massive social transformation to which it gave rise are treated, in recent historical studies, as a kind of aberration, a nuisance that stood in the way of successful prosecution of the war to save the bourgeois regime from the Franco rebellion. Many historians would probably agree with Eric Hobsbawm[11] that the *failure* of social revolution in Spain "was due to the anarchists," that anarchism was "a disaster," a kind of "moral gymnastics" with no "concrete results," at best "a profoundly moving spectacle for the student of popular religion." The most extensive historical study of the anarchist revolution[12] is relatively inaccessible, and neither its author, now living in southern France, nor the many refugees who will never write memoirs but who might provide invaluable personal testimony have been consulted, apparently, by writers of the major historical works.[13] The one published collection of documents dealing with collectivization[14] has been published only by an anarchist press and hence is barely accessible to the general reader, and has also rarely been consulted—it does not, for example, appear in Jackson's bibliography, though Jackson's account is intended to be a social and political, not merely a military, history. In fact, this astonishing social upheaval seems to have largely passed from memory. The drama and pathos of the Spanish Civil War have by no means faded; witness the impact a few years ago of the film *To Die in Madrid.* Yet in this film (as Daniel Guérin points out) one finds no reference to the popular revolution that had transformed much of Spanish society.

I will be concerned here with the events of 1936–37,[15] and with one particular aspect of the complex struggle involving Franco Nationalists, Republicans (including the Communist party), anarchists, and socialist workers' groups. The Franco insurrection in July 1936 came against a background of several months of strikes, expropriations, and battles between peasants and Civil Guards. The left-wing socialist leader Largo Caballero had demanded in June that the workers be armed, but was refused by Azaña. When the coup came, the Republican government was paralyzed. Workers armed themselves in Madrid and Barcelona, robbing government armories and even ships in the harbor, and put down the insurrection while the government vacillated, torn between the twin dangers of submitting to Franco and arming the working classes. In large areas of Spain, effective authority passed into the hands of the anarchist and socialist workers who had played a substantial, generally dominant role in putting down the insurrection.

The next few months have frequently been described as a period of "dual power." In Barcelona, industry and commerce were largely collectivized, and a wave of collectivization spread through rural areas, as well as towns and villages, in Aragon, Castile, and the Levante, and to a lesser but still significant extent in many parts of Catalonia, Asturias, Estremadura, and Andalusia. Military power was exercised by defense committees; social and economic organization took many forms, following in main outlines the program of the Saragossa Congress of the anarchist CNT (Confederación Nacional del Trabajo) in May 1936. The revolution was "apolitical," in the sense that its organs of power and administration remained separate from the central Republican government and, even after several anarchist leaders entered the government in the autumn of 1936, continued to function fairly independently until the revolution was finally crushed between the fascist and Communist-led Republican forces. The success of collectivization of industry and commerce in Barcelona impressed even highly unsympathetic observers such as Franz Borkenau. The scale of rural collectivization is indicated by these data from anarchist sources: in Aragon, 450 collectives with 500,000 members; in the Levante, 900 collectives accounting for about half the agricultural production and 70 percent of marketing in this, the richest agricultural region of Spain; in Castile, 300 collectives with about 100,-000 members.[16] In Catalonia, the bourgeois government headed by Luis Companys retained nominal authority, but real power was in the hands of the anarchist-dominated committees.

The period of July through September may be characterized as one of spontaneous, widespread, but unconsummated social revolution.[17] A number of anarchist leaders joined the government; the reason, as stated by Federica Montseny on January 3, 1937, was this: ". . . the anarchists have entered the government to prevent the Revolution from deviating and in order to carry it further beyond the war, and also to oppose any dictatorial tendency, from wherever it might come."[18] The central government fell increasingly under Communist control—in Catalonia, under the control of the Communist-dominated PSUC (Partit Socialista Unificat de Catalunya)—largely as a result of the valuable Russian military assistance. Communist success was greatest in the rich farming areas of the Levante (the government moved to Valencia, capital of one of the provinces), where prosperous farm owners flocked to the Peasant Federation that the party had organized to protect the wealthy farmers; this federation "served as a powerful instrument in checking the rural collectivization promoted by the agricultural workers of the province."[19] Elsewhere as well, counterrevolutionary successes reflected increasing Communist dominance of the Republic.

The first phase of the counterrevolution was the legalization and regulation of those accomplishments of the revolution that appeared irreversible. A decree of October 7 by the Communist minister of agriculture, Vicente Uribe, legalized certain expropriations—namely, of lands belonging to participants in the Franco revolt. Of course, these expropriations had already taken place, a fact that did not prevent the Communist press from describing the decree as "the most profoundly revolutionary measure that has been taken since the military uprising."[20] In fact, by exempting the estates of landowners who had not directly participated in the Franco rebellion, the decree represented a step backward, from the standpoint of the revolutionaries, and it was criticized not only by the CNT but also by the socialist Federation of Land Workers, affiliated with the UGT (Unión General de Trabajadores). The demand for a much broader decree was unacceptable to the Communist-led ministry, since the Communist party was "seeking support among the propertied classes in the anti-Franco coup" and hence "could not afford to repel the small and medium proprietors who had been hostile to the working class movement before the civil war."[21] These "small proprietors," in fact, seem to have included owners of substantial estates. The decree compelled tenants to continue paying rent unless the landowners had supported Franco, and by guaranteeing former landholdings, it prevented distribution of land to the village poor. Ricardo Zabalza, general secretary of the Federation of Land Workers, described the resulting situation as one of "galling injustice"; "the sycophants of the former political bosses still enjoy a privileged position at the expense of those persons who were unable to rent even the smallest parcel of land, because they were revolutionaries."[22]

To complete the stage of legalization and restriction of what had already been achieved, a decree of October 24, 1936, promulgated by a CNT member who had become councilor for economy in the Catalonian Generalitat, gave legal sanction to the collectivization of industry in Catalonia. In this case, too, the step was regressive, from the revolutionary point of view. Collectivization was limited to enterprises employing more than a hundred workers, and a variety of conditions were established that removed control from the workers' committees to the state bureaucracy.[23]

The second stage of the counterrevolution, from October 1936 through May 1937, involved the destruction of the local committees, the replacement of the militia by a conventional army, and the reestablishment of the prerevolutionary social and economic system, wherever this was possible. Finally in May 1937 came a direct attack on the working class in Barcelona (the May Days).[24] Following the success of this attack, the process of liquidation of the revolution was completed. The collectivization decree of October 24 was rescinded and industries were "freed" from workers' control. Communist-led armies swept through Aragon, destroying many collectives and dismantling their organizations and, generally, bringing the area under the control of the central government. Throughout the Republican-held territories, the government, now under Communist domination, acted in accordance with the plan announced in *Pravda* on December 17, 1936: "So far as Catalonia is concerned, the cleaning up of Trotzkyist and Anarcho-Syndicalist elements there has already begun, and it will be carried out there with the same energy as in the U.S.S.R."[25]—and, we may add, in much the same manner.

In brief, the period from the summer of 1936 to 1937 was one of revolution and counterrevolution: the revolution was largely spontaneous with mass participation of anarchist and socialist industrial and agricultural workers; the counterrevolution was under Communist direction, the Communist party increasingly coming to represent the right wing of the Republic. During this period and after the success of the counterrevolution, the Republic was waging a war against the Franco insurrection; this has been described in great detail in numerous publications, and I will say little about it here. The Communist-led counterrevolutionary struggle must, of course, be understood against the background of the ongoing antifascist war and the more general attempt of the Soviet Union to construct a broad antifascist alliance with the Western democracies. One reason for the vigorous counterrevolutionary policy of the Communists was their belief that England would never tolerate a revolutionary triumph in Spain, where England had substantial commercial interests, as did France and to a lesser extent the United States.[26] I will return to this matter below. However, I think it is important to bear in mind that there were undoubtedly other factors as well. Rudolf Rocker's comments are, I believe, quite to the point:

> . . . the Spanish people have been engaged in a desperate struggle against a pitiless foe and have been exposed besides to the secret intrigues of the great imperialist powers of Europe. Despite this the Spanish revolutionaries have not grasped at the disastrous expedient of dictatorship, but have respected all honest convictions. Everyone who visited Barcelona after the July battles, whether friend or foe of the C.N.T., was surprised at the freedom of public life and the absence of any arrangements for suppressing the free expression of opinion.
>
> For two decades the supporters of Bolshevism have been hammering it into the masses that dictatorship is a vital necessity for the defense of the so-called proletarian interests against the assaults of the counter-revolution and for paving the way for Socialism. They have not advanced the cause of Socialism by this propaganda, but have merely smoothed the way for Fascism in Italy, Germany and Austria by causing millions of people to forget that dictatorship, the most extreme form of tyranny, can never lead to social liberation. In Russia, the so-called dictatorship of the proletariat has not led to Socialism, but to the domination of a new bureaucracy over the proletariat and the whole people. . . .
>
> What the Russian autocrats and their supporters fear most is that the success of libertarian Socialism in Spain might prove to their blind followers that the much vaunted "necessity of a dictatorship" is nothing but one vast fraud which in Russia has led to the despotism of Stalin and is to serve today in Spain to help the counter-revolution to a victory over the revolution of the workers and peasants.[27]

After decades of anti-Communist indoctrination, it is difficult to achieve a perspective that makes possible a serious evaluation of the extent to which Bolshevism and Western liberalism have been united in their opposition to popular revolution. However, I do not think that one can comprehend the events in Spain without attaining this perspective.

With this brief sketch—partisan, but I think accurate—for background, I would like to turn to Jackson's account of this aspect of the Spanish Civil War (see note 8).

Jackson presumes (p. 259) that Soviet support for the Republican cause in Spain was guided by two factors: first, concern for Soviet security;

second, the hope that a Republican victory would advance "the cause of the world-wide 'people's revolution' with which Soviet leaders hoped to identify themselves." They did not press their revolutionary aims, he feels, because "for the moment it was essential not to frighten the middle classes or the Western governments."

As to the concern for Soviet security, Jackson is no doubt correct. It is clear that Soviet support of the Republic was one aspect of the attempt to make common cause with the Western democracies against the fascist threat. However, Jackson's conception of the Soviet Union as a revolutionary power—hopeful that a Republican victory would advance "the interrupted movement toward world revolution" and seeking to identify itself with "the cause of the world-wide 'people's revolution' "—seems to me entirely mistaken. Jackson presents no evidence to support this interpretation of Soviet policy, nor do I know of any. It is interesting to see how differently the events were interpreted at the time of the Spanish Civil War, not only by anarchists like Rocker but also by such commentators as Gerald Brenan and Franz Borkenau, who were intimately acquainted with the situation in Spain. Brenan observes that the counterrevolutionary policy of the Communists (which he thinks was "extremely sensible") was

> the policy most suited to the Communists themselves. Russia is a totalitarian regime ruled by a bureaucracy: the frame of mind of its leaders, who have come through the most terrible upheaval in history, is cynical and opportunist: the whole fabric of the state is dogmatic and authoritarian. To expect such men to lead a social revolution in a country like Spain, where the wildest idealism is combined with great independence of character, was out of the question. The Russians could, it is true, command plenty of idealism among their foreign admirers, but they could only harness it to the creation of a cast-iron bureaucratic state, where everyone thinks alike and obeys the orders of the chief above him.[28]

He sees nothing in Russian conduct in Spain to indicate any interest in a "people's revolution." Rather, the Communist policy was to oppose "even such rural and industrial collectives as had risen spontaneously and flood the country with police who, like the Russian OGPU, acted on the orders of their party rather than those of the Ministry of the Interior." The Communists were concerned to suppress altogether the impulses toward "spontaneity of speech or action," since "their whole nature and history made them distrust the local and spontaneous and put their faith in order, discipline and bureaucratic uniformity"—hence placed them in opposition to the revolutionary forces in Spain. As Brenan also notes, the

Russians withdrew their support once it became clear that the British would not be swayed from the policy of appeasement, a fact which gives additional confirmation to the thesis that only considerations of Russian foreign policy led the Soviet Union to support the Republic.

Borkenau's analysis is similar. He approves of the Communist policy, because of its "efficiency," but he points out that the Communists "put an end to revolutionary social activity, and enforced their view that this ought not to be a revolution but simply the defence of a legal government. . . . communist policy in Spain was mainly dictated not by the necessities of the Spanish fight but by the interests of the intervening foreign power, Russia," a country "with a revolutionary past, not a revolutionary present." The Communists acted "not with the aim of transforming chaotic enthusiasm into disciplined enthusiasm [which Borkenau feels to have been necessary], but with the aim of substituting disciplined military and administrative action for the action of the masses and getting rid of the latter entirely." This policy, he points out, went "directly against the interests and claims of the masses" and thus weakened popular support. The now apathetic masses would not commit themselves to the defense of a Communist-run dictatorship, which restored former authority and even "showed a definite preference for the police forces of the old regime, so hated by the masses." It seems to me that the record strongly supports this interpretation of Communist policy and its effects, though Borkenau's assumption that Communist "efficiency" was necessary to win the anti-Franco struggle is much more dubious—a question to which I return below.[29]

It is relevant to observe, at this point, that a number of the Spanish Communist leaders were reluctantly forced to similar conclusions. Burnett Bolloten cites several examples,[30] specifically, the military commander "El Campesino" and Jesús Hernández, a minister in the Caballero government. The former, after his escape from the Soviet Union in 1949, stated that he had taken for granted the "revolutionary solidarity" of the Soviet Union during the Civil War—a most remarkable degree of innocence—and realized only later "that the Kremlin does not serve the interests of the peoples of the world, but makes them serve its own interests; that, with a treachery and hypocrisy without parallel, it makes use of the international working class as a mere pawn in its political intrigues." Hernández, in a speech given shortly after the Civil War, admits that the Spanish Communist leaders "acted more like Soviet subjects than sons of the Spanish people." "It may seem absurd, incredible," he adds, "but our education under Soviet tutelage had deformed us to such an extent that we were completely denationalized; our national soul was torn out of us and replaced by a rabidly chauvinistic internationalism, which began and ended with the towers of the Kremlin."

Shortly after the Third World Congress of the Communist International in 1921, the Dutch "ultra-leftist" Hermann Gorter wrote that the congress "has decided the fate of the world revolution for the present. The trend of opinion that seriously desired world revolution . . . has been expelled from the Russian International. The Communist Parties in western Europe and throughout the world that retain their membership of the Russian International will become nothing more than a means to preserve the Russian Revolution and the Soviet Republic."[31] This forecast has proved quite accurate. Jackson's conception that the Soviet Union was a revolutionary power in the late 1930s, or even that the Soviet leaders truly regarded themselves as identified with world revolution, is without factual support. It is a misinterpretation that runs parallel to the American Cold War mythology that has invented an "international Communist conspiracy" directed from Moscow (now Peking) to justify its own interventionist policies.

Turning to events in revolutionary Spain, Jackson describes the first stages of collectivization as follows: the unions in Madrid, "as in Barcelona and Valencia, abused their sudden authority to place the sign *incautado* [placed under workers' control] on all manner of buildings and vehicles" (p. 279). Why was this an *abuse* of authority? This Jackson does not explain. The choice of words indicates a reluctance on Jackson's part to recognize the reality of the revolutionary situation, despite his account of the breakdown of Republican authority. The statement that the workers "abused their sudden authority" by carrying out collectivization rests on a moral judgment that recalls that of Ithiel Pool, when he characterizes land reform in Vietnam as a matter of "despoiling one's neighbors," or of Franz Borkenau, when he speaks of expropriation in the Soviet Union as "robbery," demonstrating "a streak of moral indifference."

Within a few months, Jackson informs us, "the revolutionary tide began to ebb in Catalonia" after "accumulating food and supply problems, and the experience of administering villages, frontier posts, and public utilities, had rapidly shown the anarchists the unsuspected complexity of modern society" (pp. 313–14). In Barcelona, "the naïve optimism of the revolutionary conquests of the previous August had given way to feelings of resentment and of somehow having been cheated," as the cost of living doubled, bread was in short supply, and police brutality reached the levels of the monarchy. "The POUM [Partido Obrero de Unificación Marxista] and the anarchist press simultaneously extolled the collectivizations and explained the failures of production as due to Valencia policies of boycotting the Catalan economy and favoring the *bourgeoisie.* They explained the loss of Málaga as due in large measure to the low morale and the disorientation of the Andalusian proletariat, which saw the Valencia government evolving steadily toward the right" (p. 368). Jackson evidently believes that this left-wing interpretation of events was nonsensical, and that in fact it was anarchist incompetence or treachery that was responsible for the difficulties: "In Catalonia, the CNT factory committees dragged their heels on war production, claiming that the government deprived them of raw materials and was favoring the *bourgeoisie*" (p. 365).

In fact, "the revolutionary tide began to ebb in Catalonia" under a middle-class attack led by the Communist party, not because of a recognition of the "complexity of modern society." And it was, moreover, quite true that the Communist-dominated central government attempted, with much success, to hamper collectivized industry and agriculture and to disrupt the collectivization of commerce. I have already referred to the early stages of counterrevolution. Further investigation of the sources to which Jackson refers and others shows that the anarchist charges were not baseless, as Jackson implies. Bolloten cites a good deal of evidence in support of his conclusion that

> in the countryside the Communists undertook a spirited defence of the small and medium proprietor and tenant farmer against the collectivizing drive of the rural wage-workers, against the policy of the labour unions prohibiting the farmer from holding more land than he could cultivate with his own hands, and against the practices of revolutionary committees, which requisitioned harvests, interfered with private trade, and collected rents from tenant farmers.[32]

The policy of the government was clearly enunciated by the Communist minister of agriculture: "We say that the property of the small farmer is sacred and that those who attack or attempt to attack this property must be regarded as enemies of the regime."[33] Gerald Brenan, no sympathizer with collectivization, explains the failure of collectivization as follows (p. 321):

> The Central Government, and especially the Communist and Socialist members of it, desired to bring [the collectives] under the direct control of the State: they therefore failed to provide them with the credit required for buying raw materials: as soon as the supply of raw cotton was exhausted the mills stopped working. . . . even [the munitions industry in Catalonia] were harassed by the new bureaucratic organs of the Ministry of Supply.[34]

He quotes the bourgeois president of Catalonia, Companys, as saying that "workers in the arms factories in Barcelona had been working 56 hours and more each week and that no cases of sabotage or indiscipline

had taken place," until the workers were demoralized by the bureaucrati-
zation—later, militarization—imposed by the central government and the
Communist party.[35] His own conclusion is that "the Valencia Government was now using the P.S.U.C. against the C.N.T.—but not . . . because
the Catalan workers were giving trouble, but because the Communists
wished to weaken them before destroying them."

The cited correspondence from Companys to Indalecio Prieto, according to Vernon Richards (p. 47), presents evidence showing the success
of Catalonian war industry under collectivization and demonstrating how
"much more could have been achieved had the means for expanding the
industry not been denied them by the Central Government." Richards
also cites testimony by a spokesman for the Subsecretariat of Munitions
and Armament of the Valencia government admitting that "the war industry of Catalonia had produced ten times more than the rest of Spanish
industry put together and [agreeing] . . . that this output could have been
quadrupled as from beginning of September* if Catalonia had had access
to the necessary means for purchasing raw materials that were unobtain-
able in Spanish territory." It is important to recall that the central government had enormous gold reserves (soon to be transmitted to the Soviet
Union), so that raw materials for Catalan industry could probably have
been purchased, despite the hostility of the Western democracies to the
Republic during the revolutionary period (see below). Furthermore, raw
materials had repeatedly been requested. On September 24, 1936, Juan
Fabregas, the CNT delegate to the Economic Council of Catalonia who
was in part responsible for the collectivization decree cited earlier, reported that the financial difficulties of Catalonia were created by the
refusal of the central government to "give any assistance in economic and
financial questions, presumably because it has little sympathy with the
work of a practical order which is being carried out in Catalonia"[36]—that
is, collectivization. He "went on to recount that a Commission which went
to Madrid to ask for credits to purchase war materials and raw materials,
offering 1,000 million pesetas in securities lodged in the Bank of Spain,
met with a blank refusal. It was sufficient that the new war industry in
Catalonia was controlled by the workers of the C.N.T. for the Madrid
Government to refuse any unconditional aid. Only in exchange for government control would they give financial assistance."[37]

Pierre Broué and Émile Témime take a rather similar position. Commenting on the charge of "incompetence" leveled against the collectivized industries, they point out that "one must not neglect the terrible

---

*The quoted testimony is from September 1, 1937; presumably, the reference is
to September 1936.

burden of the war." Despite this burden, they observe, "new techniques of management and elimination of dividends had permitted a lowering of prices" and "mechanisation and rationalisation, introduced in numerous enterprises . . . had considerably augmented production. The workers accepted the enormous sacrifices with enthusiasm because, in most cases, they had the conviction that the factory belonged to them and that at last they were working for themselves and their class brothers. A truly new spirit had come over the economy of Spain with the concentration of scattered enterprises, the simplification of commercial patterns, a significant structure of social projects for aged workers, children, disabled, sick and the personnel in general" (pp. 150–51). The great weakness of the revolution, they argue, was the fact that it was not carried through to completion. In part this was because of the war; in part, a consequence of the policies of the central government. They too emphasize the refusal of the Madrid government, in the early stages of collectivization, to grant credits or supply funds to collectivized industry or agriculture—in the case of Catalonia, even when substantial guarantees were offered by the Catalonian government. Thus the collectivized enterprises were forced to exist on what assets had been seized at the time of the revolution. The control of gold and credit "permitted the government to restrict and prevent the function of collective enterprises at will" (p. 144).

According to Broué and Témime, it was the restriction of credit that finally destroyed collectivized industry. The Companys government in Catalonia refused to create a bank for industry and credit, as demanded by the CNT and POUM, and the central government (relying, in this case, on control of the banks by the socialist UGT) was able to control the flow of capital and "to reserve credit for private enterprise." All attempts to obtain credit for collectivized industry were unsuccessful, they maintain, and "the movement of collectivization was restricted, then halted, the government remaining in control of industry through the medium of the banks . . . [and later] through its control of the choice of managers and directors," who often turned out to be the former owners and managers, under new titles. The situation was similar in the case of collectivized agriculture (pp. 204ff.).

The situation was duly recognized in the West. The *New York Times,* in February 1938, observed: "The principle of State intervention and control of business and industry, as against workers' control of them in the guise of collectivization, is gradually being established in loyalist Spain by a series of decrees now appearing. Coincidentally there is to be established the principle of private ownership and the rights of corporations and companies to what is lawfully theirs under the Constitution."[38]

Morrow cites (pp. 64–65) a series of acts by the Catalonian government restricting collectivization, once power had shifted away from the new institutions set up by the workers' revolution of July 1936. On February 3, the collectivization of the dairy trade was declared illegal.[39] In April, "the Generalidad annulled workers' control over the customs by refusing to certify workers' ownership of material that had been exported and was being tied up in foreign courts by suits of former owners; henceforth the factories and agricultural collectives exporting goods were at the mercy of the government." In May, as has already been noted, the collectivization decree of October 24 was rescinded, with the argument that the decree "was dictated without competency by the Generalidad," because "there was not, nor is there yet, legislation of the [Spanish] state to apply" and "article 44 of the Constitution declares expropriation and socialization are functions of the State." A decree of August 28 "gave the government the right to intervene in or take over any mining or metallurgical plant." The anarchist newspaper *Solidaridad Obrera* reported in October a decision of the department of purchases of the Ministry of Defense that it would make contracts for purchases only with enterprises functioning "on the basis of their old owners" or "under the corresponding intervention controlled by the Ministry of Finance and Economy."[40]

Returning to Jackson's statement that "in Catalonia, the CNT factory committees dragged their heels on war production, claiming that the government deprived them of raw materials and was favoring the *bourgeoisie*," I believe one must conclude that this statement is more an expression of Jackson's bias in favor of capitalist democracy than a description of the historical facts. At the very least, we can say this much: Jackson presents no evidence to support his conclusion; there is a factual basis for questioning it. I have cited a number of sources that the liberal historian would regard, quite correctly, as biased in favor of the revolution. My point is that the failure of objectivity, the deep-seated bias of liberal historians, is a matter much less normally taken for granted, and that there are good grounds for supposing that this failure of objectivity has seriously distorted the judgments that are rather brashly handed down about the nature of the Spanish revolution.

Continuing with the analysis of Jackson's judgments, unsupported by any cited evidence, consider his remark, quoted above, that in Barcelona "the naïve optimism of the revolutionary conquests of the previous August had given way to feelings of resentment and of somehow having been cheated." It is a fact that by January 1937 there was great disaffection in Barcelona. But was this simply a consequence of "the unsuspected complexity of modern society"? Looking into the matter a bit more closely, we see a rather different picture. Under Russian pressure, the PSUC was given substantial control of the Catalonian government, "putting into the Food Ministry [in December 1936] the man most to the Right in present Catalan politics, Comorera"[41]—by virtue of his political views, the most willing collaborator with the general Communist party position. According to Jackson, Comorera "immediately took steps to end barter and requisitioning, and became a defender of the peasants against the revolution" (p. 314); he "ended requisition, restored money payments, and protected the Catalan peasants against further collectivization" (p. 361). This is all that Jackson has to say about Juan Comorera.

We learn more from other sources: for example, Borkenau, who was in Barcelona for the second time in January 1937—and is universally recognized as a highly knowledgeable and expert observer, with strong antianarchist sentiments. According to Borkenau, Comorera represented "a political attitude which can best be compared with that of the extreme right wing of the German social-democracy. He had always regarded the fight against anarchism as the chief aim of socialist policy in Spain. . . . To his surprise, he found unexpected allies for his dislike [of anarchist policies] in the communists."[42] It was impossible to reverse collectivization of industry at that stage in the process of counterrevolution; Comorera did succeed, however, in abolishing the system by which the provisioning of Barcelona had been organized, namely, the village committees, mostly under CNT influence, which had cooperated (perhaps, Borkenau suggests, unwillingly) in delivering flour to the towns. Continuing, Borkenau describes the situation as follows:

> . . . Comorera, starting from those principles of abstract liberalism which no administration has followed during the war, but of which right-wing socialists are the last and most religious admirers, did not substitute for the chaotic bread committees a centralized administration. He restored private commerce in bread, simply and completely. There was, in January, not even a system of rationing in Barcelona. Workers were simply left to get their bread, with wages which had hardly changed since May, at increased prices, as well as they could. In practice it meant that the women had to form queues from four o'clock in the morning onwards. The resentment in the working-class districts was naturally acute, the more so as the scarcity of bread rapidly increased after Comorera had taken office.[43]

In short, the workers of Barcelona were not merely giving way to "feelings of resentment and of somehow having been cheated" when they learned of "the unsuspected complexity of modern society." Rather, they had good reason to believe that they *were* being cheated, by the old dog with the new collar.

George Orwell's observations are also highly relevant:

Everyone who has made two visits, at intervals of months, to Barcelona during the war has remarked upon the extraordinary
changes that took place in it. And curiously enough, whether they
went there first in August and again in January, or, like myself, first
in December and again in April, the thing they said was always the
same: that the revolutionary atmosphere had vanished. No doubt to
anyone who had been there in August, when the blood was scarcely
dry in the streets and militia were quartered in the small hotels,
Barcelona in December would have seemed bourgeois; to me, fresh
from England, it was liker to a workers' city than anything I had
conceived possible. Now [in April] the tide had rolled back. Once
again it was an ordinary city, a little pinched and chipped by war,
but with no outward sign of working-class predominance. . . . Fat
prosperous men, elegant women, and sleek cars were everywhere.
. . . The officers of the new Popular Army, a type that had scarcely
existed when I left Barcelona, swarmed in surprising numbers
. . . [wearing] an elegant khaki uniform with a tight waist, like a
British Army officer's uniform, only a little more so. I do not suppose that more than one in twenty of them had yet been to the front,
but all of them had automatic pistols strapped to their belts; we, at
the front, could not get pistols for love or money. . . .* A deep
change had come over the town. There were two facts that were the
keynote of all else. One was that the people—the civil population—
had lost much of their interest in the war; the other was that the
normal division of society into rich and poor, upper class and lower
class, was reasserting itself.[44]

Whereas Jackson attributes the ebbing of the revolutionary tide to the
discovery of the unsuspected complexity of modern society, Orwell's
firsthand observations, like those of Borkenau, suggest a far simpler
explanation. What calls for explanation is not the disaffection of the
workers of Barcelona but the curious constructions of the historian.

Let me repeat, at this point, Jackson's comments regarding Juan Comorera: Comorera "immediately took steps to end barter and requisitioning, and became a defender of the peasants against the revolution";
he "ended requisitions, restored money payments, and protected the
Catalan peasants against further collectivization." These comments
imply that the peasantry of Catalonia was, as a body, opposed to the
revolution and that Comorera put a stop to the collectivization that they

---

*Orwell had just returned from the Aragon front, where he had been serving with
the POUM militia in an area heavily dominated by left-wing (POUM and anarchist) troops.

feared. Jackson nowhere indicates any divisions among the peasantry on this issue and offers no support for the implied claim that collectivization was in process at the period of Comorera's access to power. In fact, it is questionable that Comorera's rise to power affected the course of collectivization in Catalonia. Evidence is difficult to come by, but it seems that collectivization of agriculture in Catalonia was not, in any event, extensive, and that it was not extending in December, when Comorera took office. We know from anarchist sources that there had been instances of forced collectivization in Catalonia,[45] but I can find no evidence that Comorera "protected the peasantry" from forced collectivization. Furthermore, it is misleading, at best, to imply that the peasantry *as a whole* was opposed to collectivization. A more accurate picture is presented by Bolloten (p. 56), who points out that "if the individual farmer viewed with dismay the swift and widespread development of collectivized agriculture, the farm workers of the Anarchosyndicalist CNT and the Socialist UGT saw in it, on the contrary, the commencement of a new era." In short, there was a complex class struggle in the countryside, though one learns little about it from Jackson's oversimplified and misleading account. It would seem fair to suppose that this distortion again reflects Jackson's antipathy toward the revolution and its goals. I will return to this question directly, with reference to areas where agricultural collectivization was much more extensive than in Catalonia.

The complexities of modern society that baffled and confounded the unsuspecting anarchist workers of Barcelona, as Jackson enumerates them, were the following: the accumulating food and supply problems and the administration of frontier posts, villages, and public utilities. As just noted, the food and supply problems seem to have accumulated most rapidly under the brilliant leadership of Juan Comorera. So far as the frontier posts are concerned, the situation, as Jackson elsewhere describes it (p. 368), was basically as follows: "In Catalonia the anarchists had, ever since July 18, controlled the customs stations at the French border. On April 17, 1937, the reorganized carabineros, acting on orders of the Finance Minister, Juan Negrín, began to reoccupy the frontier. At least eight anarchists were killed in clashes with the carabineros." Apart from this difficulty, admittedly serious, there seems little reason to suppose that the problem of manning frontier posts contributed to the ebbing of the revolutionary tide. The available records do not indicate that the problems of administering villages or public utilities were either "unsuspected" or too complex for the Catalonian workers—a remarkable and unsuspected development, but one which nevertheless appears to be borne out by the evidence available to us. I want to emphasize again that Jackson presents no evidence to support his conclusions about the ebbing of the revolutionary tide and the reasons for the disaffection of the Catalonian workers.

Once again, I think it fair to attribute his conclusions to the elitist bias of the liberal intellectual rather than to the historical record.

Consider next Jackson's comment that the anarchists "explained the loss of Málaga as due in large measure to the low morale and the disorientation of the Andalusian proletariat, which saw the Valencia government evolving steadily toward the right." Again, it seems that Jackson regards this as just another indication of the naiveté and unreasonableness of the Spanish anarchists. However, here again there is more to the story. One of the primary sources that Jackson cites is Borkenau, quite naturally, since Borkenau spent several days in the area just prior to the fall of Málaga on February 8, 1937. But Borkenau's detailed observations tend to bear out the anarchist "explanation," at least in part. He believed that Málaga might have been saved, but only by a "fight of despair" with mass involvement, of a sort that "the anarchists might have led." But two factors prevented such a defense: First, the officer assigned to lead the defense, Lieutenant Colonel Villalba, "interpreted this task as a purely military one, whereas in reality he had no military means at his disposal but only the forces of a popular movement"; he was a professional officer, "who in the secrecy of his heart hated the spirit of the militia" and was incapable of comprehending the "political factor."[46] A second factor was the significant decline, by February, of political consciousness and mass involvement. The anarchist committees were no longer functioning, and the authority of the police and Civil Guards had been restored. "The nuisance of hundreds of independent village police bodies had disappeared, but with it the passionate interest of the village in the civil war. . . . The short interlude of the Spanish Soviet system was at an end" (p. 212). After reviewing the local situation in Málaga and the conflicts in the Valencia government (which failed to provide support or arms for the militia defending Málaga), Borkenau concludes (p. 228): "The Spanish republic paid with the fall of Málaga for the decision of the Right wing of its camp to make an end of social revolution and of its Left wing not to allow that." Jackson's discussion of the fall of Málaga refers to the terror and political rivalries within the town but makes no reference to the fact that Borkenau's description, and the accompanying interpretation, do support the belief that the defeat was due in large measure to low morale and to the incapacity, or unwillingness, of the Valencia government to fight a popular war. On the contrary, he concludes that Colonel Villalba's lack of means for "controlling the bitter political rivalries" was one factor that prevented him from carrying out the essential military tasks. Thus he seems to adopt the view that Borkenau condemns, that the task was a "purely military one." Borkenau's eyewitness account appears to me much more convincing.

In this case, too, Jackson has described the situation in a somewhat

misleading fashion, perhaps again because of the elitist bias that dominates the liberal-Communist interpretation of the Civil War. Like Lieutenant Colonel Villalba, liberal historians often reveal a strong distaste
for "the forces of a popular movement" and "the spirit of the militia."
And an argument can be given that they correspondingly fail to comprehend the "political factor."

In the May Days of 1937, the revolution in Catalonia received the final
blow. On May 3, the councilor for public order, PSUC member Ro-
dríguez Salas, appeared at the central telephone building with a detachment of police, without prior warning or consultation with the anarchist
ministers in the government, to take over the telephone exchange. The
exchange, formerly the property of IT&T, had been captured by Barcelona workers in July and had since functioned under the control of a
UGT-CNT committee, with a governmental delegate, quite in accord
with the collectivization decree of October 24, 1936. According to the
London *Daily Worker* (May 11, 1937), "Salas sent the armed republican
police to disarm the employees there, most of them members of the CNT
unions." The motive, according to Juan Comorera, was "to put a stop to
an abnormal situation," namely, that no one could speak over the telephone "without the indiscreet ear of the controller knowing it."[47] Armed
resistance in the telephone building prevented its occupation. Local defense committees erected barricades throughout Barcelona. Companys
and the anarchist leaders pleaded with the workers to disarm. An uneasy
truce continued until May 6, when the first detachments of Assault
Guards arrived, violating the promises of the government that the truce
would be observed and military forces withdrawn. The troops were under
the command of General Pozas, formerly commander of the hated Civil
Guard and now a member of the Communist party. In the fighting that
followed, there were some five hundred killed and over a thousand
wounded. "The May Days in reality sounded the death-knell of the revolution, announcing political defeat for all and death for certain of the
revolutionary leaders."[48]

These events—of enormous significance in the history of the Spanish
revolution—Jackson sketches in bare outline as a marginal incident. Obviously, the historian's account must be selective; from the left-liberal
point of view that Jackson shares with Hugh Thomas and many others,
the liquidation of the revolution in Catalonia was a minor event, as the
revolution itself was merely a kind of irrelevant nuisance, a minor irritant
diverting energy from the struggle to save the bourgeois government.
The decision to crush the revolution by force is described as follows:

> On May 5, Companys obtained a fragile truce, on the basis of which
> the PSUC councilors were to retire from the regional government,
> and the question of the Telephone Company was left to future

negotiation. That very night, however, Antonio Sesé, a UGT official who was about to enter the reorganized cabinet, was murdered. In any event, the Valencia authorities were in no mood to temporize further with the Catalan Left. On May 6 several thousand *asaltos* arrived in the city, and the Republican Navy demonstrated in the port.[49]

What is interesting about this description is what is left unsaid. For example, there is no comment on the fact that the dispatch of the *asaltos* violated the "fragile truce" that had been accepted by the Barcelona workers and the anarchist and the POUM troops nearby, and barely a mention of the bloody consequences or the political meaning of this unwillingness "to temporize further with the Catalan Left." There is no mention of the fact that along with Sesé, Berneri and other anarchist leaders were murdered, not only during the May Days but in the weeks preceding.[50] Jackson does not refer to the fact that along with the Republican navy, British ships also "demonstrated" in the port.[51] Nor does he refer to Orwell's telling observations about the Assault Guards, as compared to the troops at the front, where he had spent the preceding months. The Assault Guards "were splendid troops, much the best I had seen in Spain. . . . I was used to the ragged, scarcely-armed militia on the Aragon front, and I had not known that the Republic possessed troops like these. . . . The Civil Guards and Carabineros, who were not intended for the front at all, were better armed and far better clad than ourselves. I suspect it is the same in all wars—always the same contrast between the sleek police in the rear and the ragged soldiers in the line."[52] (See p. 105 below.)

The contrast reveals a good deal about the nature of the war, as it was understood by the Valencia government. Later, Orwell was to make this conclusion explicit: "A government which sends boys of fifteen to the front with rifles forty years old and keeps its biggest men and newest weapons in the rear is manifestly more afraid of the revolution than of the fascists. Hence the feeble war policy of the past six months, and hence the compromise with which the war will almost certainly end."[53] Jackson's account of these events, with its omissions and assumptions, suggests that he perhaps shares the view that the greatest danger in Spain would have been a victory of the revolution.

Jackson apparently discounts Orwell's testimony, to some extent, commenting that "the readers should bear in mind Orwell's own honest statement that he knew very little about the political complexities of the struggle." This is a strange comment. For one thing, Orwell's analysis of the "political complexities of the struggle" bears up rather well after thirty years; if it is defective, it is probably in his tendency to give too much prominence to the POUM in comparison with the anarchists—not surprising, in view of the fact that he was with the POUM militia. His exposure of the fatuous nonsense that was appearing at the time in the Stalinist and liberal presses appears quite accurate, and later discoveries have given little reason to challenge the basic facts that he reported or the interpretation that he proposed in the heat of the conflict. Orwell does, in fact, refer to his own "political ignorance." Commenting on the final defeat of the revolution in May, he states: "I realized—though owing to my political ignorance, not so clearly as I ought to have done—that when the Government felt more sure of itself there would be reprisals." But this form of "political ignorance" has simply been compounded in more recent historical work.

Shortly after the May Days, the Caballero government fell and Juan Negrín became premier of Republican Spain. Negrín is described as follows by Broué and Témime: ". . . he is an unconditional defender of capitalist property and resolute adversary of collectivization, whom the CNT ministers find blocking all of their proposals. He is the one who solidly reorganized the carabineros and presided over the transfer of the gold reserves of the Republic to the USSR. He enjoyed the confidence of the moderates . . . [and] was on excellent terms with the Communists."

The first major act of the Negrín government was the suppression of the POUM and the consolidation of central control over Catalonia. The government next turned to Aragon, which had been under largely anarchist control since the first days of the revolution, and where agricultural collectivization was quite extensive and Communist elements very weak. The municipal councils of Aragon were coordinated by the Council of Aragon, headed by Joaquín Ascaso, a well-known CNT militant, one of whose brothers had been killed during the May Days. Under the Caballero government, the anarchists had agreed to give representation to other antifascist parties, including the Communists, but the majority remained anarchist. In August, the Negrín government announced the dissolution of the Council of Aragon and dispatched a division of the Spanish army, commanded by the Communist officer Enrique Lister, to enforce the dissolution of the local committees, dismantle the collectives, and establish central government control. Ascaso was arrested on the charge of having been responsible for the robbery of jewelry—namely, the jewelry "robbed" by the Council for its own use in the fall of 1936. The local anarchist press was suppressed in favor of a Communist journal, and, in general, local anarchist centers were forcefully occupied and closed. The last anarchist stronghold was captured, with tanks and artillery, on September 21. Because of government-imposed censorship, there is very little of a direct record of these events, and the major histories pass over them quickly.[54] According to Felix Morrow, "the official CNT press . . . compared the assault on Aragon with the subjection of Asturias by Lopez Ochoa in October 1934"—the latter, one of the bloodiest acts of repression in modern Spanish history. Although this is an exaggeration, it is a fact that the popular organs of administration were wiped out by Lister's legions, and the revolution was now over, so far as Aragon was concerned.

About these events, Jackson has the following comments:

> On August 11 the government announced the dissolution of the *Consejo de Aragón,* the anarchist-dominated administration which had been recognized by Largo Caballero in December, 1936. The peasants were known to hate the Consejo, the anarchists had deserted the front during the Barcelona fighting, and the very existence of the Consejo was a standing challenge to the authority of the central government. For all these reasons Negrín did not hesitate to send in troops, and to arrest the anarchist officials. Once their authority had been broken, however, they were released.[55]

These remarks are most interesting. Consider first the charge that the anarchists had deserted the front during the May Days. It is true that elements of certain anarchist and POUM divisions were prepared to march on Barcelona, but after the "fragile truce" was established on May 5, they did not do so; no anarchist forces even approached Barcelona to defend the Barcelona proletariat and its institutions from attack. However, a motorized column of 5,000 Assault Guards was sent from the front by the government to break the "fragile truce."[56] Hence the only forces to "desert the front" during the Barcelona fighting were those dispatched by the government to complete the job of dismantling the revolution, by force. Recall Orwell's observations quoted above, page 103.

What about Jackson's statement that "the peasants were known to hate the Consejo"? As in the other cases I have cited, Jackson gives no indication of any evidence on which such a judgment might be based. The most detailed investigation of the collectives is from anarchist sources, and they indicate that Aragon was one of the areas where collectivization was most widespread and successful.[57] Both the CNT and the UGT Federation of Land Workers were vigorous in their support for collectivization, and there is no doubt that both were mass organizations. A number of nonanarchists, observing collectivization in Aragon firsthand, gave very favorable reports and stressed the voluntary character of collectivization.[58] According to Gaston Leval, an anarchist observer who carried out detailed investigation of rural collectivization, "In Aragon 75 percent of small proprietors have voluntarily adhered to the new order of things," and others were not forced to involve themselves in collectives.[59] Other anarchist observers—Augustin Souchy in particular—gave detailed observations of the functioning of the Aragon collectives. Unless one is willing to assume a fantastic degree of falsification, it is impossible to reconcile their descriptions with the claim that "the peasants were known to hate the Consejo"—unless, of course, one restricts the term "peasant" to "individual farm owner," in which case it might very well be true, but would justify disbanding the council only on the assumption that the rights of the individual farm owner must predominate, not those of the landless worker. There is little doubt that the collectives were economically successful,[60] hardly likely if collectivization were forced and hated by the peasantry.

I have already cited Bolloten's general conclusion, based on very extensive documentary evidence, that while the individual farmer may have viewed the development of collectivized agriculture with dismay, "the farm workers of the Anarchosyndicalist CNT and the Socialist UGT saw in it, on the contrary, the commencement of a new era." This conclusion seems quite reasonable, on the basis of the materials that are available. With respect to Aragon, specifically, he remarks that the "debt-ridden peasants were strongly affected by the ideas of the CNT and FAI [Federación Anarquista Ibérica], a factor that gave a powerful spontaneous impulse to collective farming," though difficulties are cited by anarchist sources, which in general appear to be quite honest about failures. Bolloten cites two Communist sources, among others, to the effect that about 70 percent of the population in rural areas of Aragon lived in collectives (p. 71); he adds that "many of the region's 450 collectives were largely voluntary," although "the presence of militiamen from the neighbouring region of Catalonia, the immense majority of whom were members of the CNT and FAI" was "in some measure" responsible for the extensive collectivization. He also points out that in many instances peasant proprietors who were not compelled to adhere to the collective system did so for other reasons: ". . . not only were they prevented from employing hired labour and disposing freely of their crops . . . but they were often denied all benefits enjoyed by members" (p. 72). Bolloten cites the attempt of the Communists in April 1937 to cause dissension in "areas where the CNT and UGT had established collective farms by mutual agreement" (p. 195), leading in some cases to pitched battles and dozens of assassinations, according to CNT sources.[61]

Bolloten's detailed analysis of the events of the summer of 1937 sheds considerable light on the question of peasant attitudes toward collectivization:

> It was inevitable that the attacks on the collectives should have had an unfavorable effect upon rural economy and upon morale, for while it is true that in some areas collectivization was anathema to the majority of peasants, it is no less true that in others collective

farms were organized spontaneously by the bulk of the peasant population. In Toledo province, for example, where even before the war rural collectives existed, 83 per cent of the peasants, according to a source friendly to the Communists, decided in favour of the collective cultivation of the soil. As the campaign against the collective farms reached its height just before the summer harvest [1937] . . . a pall of dismay and apprehension descended upon the agricultural labourers. Work in the fields was abandoned in many places or only carried on apathetically, and there was danger that a substantial portion of the harvest, vital for the war effort, would be left to rot. [P. 196]

It was under these circumstances, he points out, that the Communists were forced to change their policy and—temporarily—to tolerate the collectives. A decree was passed legalizing collectives *"during the current agricultural year"* (his italics) and offering them some aid. This "produced a sense of relief in the countryside during the vital period of the harvest." Immediately after the crops had been gathered, the policy changed again to one of harsh repression. Bolloten cites Communist sources to the effect that "a short though fierce campaign at the beginning of August" prepared the way for the dissolution of the Council of Aragon. Following the dissolution decree, "the newly appointed Governor General, José Ignacio Mantecón, a member of the Left Republican Party, but a secret Communist sympathizer [who joined the party in exile, after the war], . . . ordered the break-up of the collective farms." The means: Lister's division, which restored the old order by force and terror. Bolloten cites Communist sources conceding the excessive harshness of Lister's methods. He quotes the Communist general secretary of the Institute of Agrarian Reform, who admits that the measures taken to dissolve the collectives were "a very grave mistake, and produced tremendous disorganization in the countryside," as "those persons who were discontented with the collectives . . . took them by assault, carrying away and dividing up the harvest and farm implements without respecting the collectives that had been formed without violence or pressure, that were prosperous, and that were a model of organization. . . . As a result, labour in the fields was suspended almost entirely, and a quarter of the land had not been prepared at the time for sowing" (p. 200). Once again, it was necessary to ameliorate the harsh repression of the collectives, to prevent disaster. Summarizing these events, Bolloten describes the resulting situation as follows:

But although the situation in Aragon improved in some degree, the hatreds and resentments generated by the break-up of the collectives and by the repression that followed were never wholly dispelled. Nor was the resultant disillusionment that sapped the spirit of the Anarchosyndicalist forces on the Aragon front ever entirely removed, a disillusionment that no doubt contributed to the collapse of that front a few months later. . . . after the destruction of the collective farms in Aragon, the Communist Party was compelled to modify its policy, and support collectives also in other regions against former owners who sought the return of confiscated land. . . . [Pp. 200–201]

Returning to Jackson's remarks, I think we must conclude that they seriously misrepresent the situation.[62] The dissolution of the Council of Aragon and the large-scale destruction of the collectives by military force was simply another stage in the eradication of the popular revolution and the restoration of the old order. Let me emphasize that I am not criticizing Jackson for his negative attitude toward the social revolution, but rather for the failure of objectivity when he deals with the revolution and the ensuing repression.

Among historians of the Spanish Civil War, the dominant view is that the Communist policy was in essentials the correct one—that in order to consolidate domestic and international support for the Republic it was necessary to block and then reverse the social revolution. Jackson, for example, states that Caballero "realized that it was absolutely necessary to rebuild the authority of the Republican state and to work in close cooperation with the middle-class liberals." The anarchist leaders who entered the government shared this view, putting their trust in the good faith of liberals such as Companys and believing—naively, as events were to show—that the Western democracies would come to their aid.

A policy diametrically opposed to this was advocated by Camillo Berneri. In his open letter to the anarchist minister Federica Montseny,[63] he summarizes his views in the following way: "The dilemma, war or revolution, no longer has meaning. *The only dilemma is this: either victory over Franco through revolutionary war, or defeat*" (his italics). He argued that Morocco should be granted independence and that an attempt should be made to stir up rebellion throughout North Africa. Thus a revolutionary struggle should be undertaken against Western capitalism in North Africa and, simultaneously, against the bourgeois regime in Spain, which was gradually dismantling the accomplishments of the July revolution. The primary front should be political. Franco relied heavily on Moorish contingents, including a substantial number from French Morocco. The Republic might exploit this fact, demoralizing the Nationalist forces and perhaps even winning them to the revolutionary cause by political agitation based on the concrete alternative of pan-Islamic—specifically, Moroccan—revolution. Writing in April 1937, Berneri urged that the army of the Republic be reorganized for the defense of the revolution, so that it might recover the spirit of popular participation of the early days of the revolution. He quotes the words of his compatriot Louis Bertoni, writing from the Huesca front:

> The Spanish war, deprived of all new faith, of any idea of a social transformation, of all revolutionary grandeur, of any universal meaning, is now merely a national war of independence that must be carried on to avoid the extermination that the international plutocracy demands. There remains a terrible question of life or death, but no longer a war to build a new society and a new humanity.

In such a war, the human element that might bring victory over fascism is lost.

In retrospect, Berneri's ideas seem quite reasonable. Delegations of Moroccan nationalists did in fact approach the Valencia government asking for arms and matériel, but were refused by Caballero, who actually proposed territorial concessions in North Africa to France and England to try to win their support. Commenting on these facts, Broué and Témime observe that these policies deprived the Republic of "the instrument of revolutionary defeatism in the enemy army," and even of a possible weapon against Italian intervention. Jackson, on the other hand, dismisses Berneri's suggestion with the remark that independence for Morocco (as for that matter, even aid to the Moroccan nationalists) was "a gesture that would have been highly appreciated in Paris and London." Of course, it is correct that France and Britain would hardly have appreciated this development. As Berneri points out, "it goes without saying that one cannot simultaneously guarantee French and British interests in Morocco and carry out an insurrection." But Jackson's comment does not touch on the central issue, namely, whether the Spanish revolution could have been preserved, both from the fascists at the front and from the bourgeois-Communist coalition within the Republic, by a revolutionary war of the sort that the left proposed—or, for that matter, whether the Republic might not have been saved by a political struggle that involved Franco's invading Moorish troops, or at least eroded their morale. It is easy to see why Caballero was not attracted by this bold scheme, given his reliance on the eventual backing of the Western democracies. On the basis of what we know today, however, Jackson's summary dismissal of revolutionary war is much too abrupt.

Furthermore, Bertoni's observations from the Huesca front are borne out by much other evidence, some of it cited earlier. Even those who accepted the Communist strategy of discipline and central control as necessary concede that the repressions that formed an ineliminable part of this strategy "tended to break the fighting spirit of the people."[64] One can only speculate, but it seems to me that many commentators have seriously underestimated the significance of the political factor, the potential strength of a popular struggle to defend the achievements of the revolution. It is perhaps relevant that Asturias, the one area of Spain where the system of CNT-UGT committees was not eliminated in favor of central control, is also the one area where guerrilla warfare continued well after Franco's victory. Broué and Témime observe[65] that the resistance of the partisans of Asturias "demonstrates the depth of the revolutionary élan, which had not been shattered by the reinstitution of state authority, conducted here with greater prudence." There can be no doubt that the revolution was both widespread and deeply rooted in the Spanish masses. It seems quite possible that a revolutionary war of the sort advocated by Berneri would have been successful, despite the greater military force of the fascist armies. The idea that men can overcome machines no longer seems as romantic or naive as it may have a few years ago.

Furthermore, the trust placed in the bourgeois government by the anarchist leaders was not honored, as the history of the counterrevolution clearly shows. In retrospect, it seems that Berneri was correct in arguing that they should not have taken part in the bourgeois government, but should rather have sought to replace this government with the institutions created by the revolution.[66] The anarchist minister Juan García Oliver stated that "we had confidence in the word and in the person of a Catalan democrat and retained and supported Companys as President of the Generalitat,"[67] at a time when in Catalonia, at least, the workers' organizations could easily have replaced the state apparatus and dispensed with the former political parties, as they had replaced the old economy with an entirely new structure. Companys recognized fully that there were limits beyond which he could not cooperate with the anarchists. In an interview with H. E. Kaminski, he refused to specify these limits, but merely expressed his hope that "the anarchist masses will not oppose the good sense of their leaders," who have "accepted the responsibilities incumbent upon them"; he saw his task as "directing these responsibilities in the proper path," not further specified in the interview, but shown by the events leading up to the May Days.[68] Probably, Companys' attitude toward this willingness of the anarchist leaders to cooperate was expressed accurately in his reaction to the suggestion of a correspondent of the *New Statesman and Nation,* who predicted that the assassination of the anarchist mayor of Puigcerdá would lead to a revolt: "[Companys] laughed scornfully and said the anarchists would capitulate as they always had before."[69] As has already been pointed out in some detail, the liberal-Communist party coalition had no intention of letting the war against Franco take precedence over the crushing of the revolution. A spokesman for Comorera put the matter clearly: "This slogan has been attributed to the P.S.U.C.: 'Before taking Saragossa, it is necessary to take Barcelona.' This reflects the situation exactly. . . ."[70] Comorera himself had, from the beginning, pressed Companys to resist the CNT.[71] The first task of the antifascist coalition, he maintained, was to dissolve the revolutionary committees.[72] I have already cited a good deal of evidence indicating that the repression conducted by the Popular Front seriously weakened popular commitment and involvement in the antifascist war. What was evident to George Orwell was also clear to the Barcelona workers and the peasants in the collectivized villages of Aragon: the liberal-Communist coalition would not tolerate a revolutionary transformation of Spanish society; it would commit itself fully to the anti-Franco struggle only after the old order was firmly reestablished, by force, if necessary.[73]

There is little doubt that farm workers in the collectives understood quite well the social content of the drive toward consolidation and central control. We learn this not only from anarchist sources but also from the socialist press in the spring of 1937. On May 1, the Socialist party newspaper *Adelante* had the following to say:

> At the outbreak of the Fascist revolt the labor organizations and the democratic elements in the country were in agreement that the so-called Nationalist Revolution, which threatened to plunge our people into an abyss of deepest misery, could be halted only by a Social Revolution. The Communist Party, however, opposed this view with all its might. It had apparently completely forgotten its old theories of a "workers' and peasants' republic" and a "dictatorship of the proletariat." From its constant repetition of its new slogan of the parliamentary democratic republic it is clear that it has lost all sense of reality. When the Catholic and conservative sections of the Spanish bourgeoisie saw their old system smashed and could find no way out, the Communist Party instilled new hope into them. It assured them that the democratic bourgeois republic for which it was pleading put no obstacles in the way of Catholic propaganda and, above all, that it stood ready to defend the class interests of the bourgeoisie.[74]

That this realization was widespread in the rural areas was underscored dramatically by a questionnaire sent by *Adelante* to secretaries of the UGT Federation of Land Workers, published in June 1937.[75] The results are summarized as follows:

> The replies to these questions revealed an astounding unanimity. Everywhere the same story. The peasant collectives are today most

vigorously opposed by the Communist Party. The Communists organize the well-to-do farmers who are on the lookout for cheap labor and are, for this reason, outspokenly hostile to the cooperative undertakings of the poor peasants.

It is the element which before the revolution sympathized with the Fascists and Monarchists which, according to the testimony of the trade-union representatives, is now flocking into the ranks of the Communist Party. As to the general effect of Communist activity on the country, the secretaries of the U.G.T. had only one opinion, which the representative of the Valencia organization put in these words: "It is a misfortune in the fullest sense of the word."[76]

It is not difficult to imagine how the recognition of this "misfortune" must have affected the willingness of the land workers to take part in the antifascist war, with all the sacrifices that this entailed.

The attitude of the central government to the revolution was brutally revealed by its acts and is attested as well in its propaganda. A former minister describes the situation as follows:

> The fact that is concealed by the coalition of the Spanish Communist Party with the left Republicans and right wing Socialists is that there has been a successful social revolution in half of Spain. Successful, that is, in the collectivization of factories and farms which are operated under trade union control, and operated quite efficiently. During the three months that I was director of propaganda for the United States and England under Alvarez del Vayo, then Foreign Minister for the Valencia Government, I was instructed not to send out one word about this revolution in the economic system of loyalist Spain. Nor are any foreign correspondents in Valencia permitted to write freely of the revolution that has taken place.[77]

In short, there is much reason to believe that the will to fight Franco was significantly diminished, perhaps destroyed, by the policy of authoritarian centralization undertaken by the liberal-Communist coalition, carried through by force, and disguised in the propaganda that was disseminated among Western intellectuals[78] and that still dominates the writing of history. To the extent that this is a correct judgment, the alternative proposed by Berneri and the left "extremists" gains in plausibility.

As noted earlier, Caballero and the anarchist ministers accepted the policy of counterrevolution because of their trust in the Western democracies, which they felt sure would sooner or later come to their aid. This feeling was perhaps understandable in 1937. It is strange, however, that a historian writing in the 1960s should dismiss the proposal to strike at

Franco's rear by extending the revolutionary war to Morocco, on grounds that this would have displeased Western capitalism (see p. 109 above).

Berneri was quite right in his belief that the Western democracies would not take part in an antifascist struggle in Spain. In fact, their complicity in the fascist insurrection was not slight. French bankers, who were generally pro-Franco, blocked the release of Spanish gold to the loyalist government, thus hindering the purchase of arms and, incidentally, increasing the reliance of the Republic on the Soviet Union.[79] The policy of "nonintervention," which effectively blocked Western aid for the loyalist government while Hitler and Mussolini in effect won the war for Franco, was also technically initiated by the French government— though apparently under heavy British pressure.[80]

As far as Great Britain is concerned, the hope that it would come to the aid of the Republic was always unrealistic. A few days after the Franco coup, the foreign editor of *Paris-Soir* wrote: "At least four countries are already taking active interest in the battle—France, which is supporting the Madrid Government, and Britain, Germany and Italy, each of which is giving discreet but nevertheless effective assistance to one group or another among the insurgents."[81] In fact, British support for Franco took a fairly concrete form at the very earliest stages of the insurrection. The Spanish navy remained loyal to the Republic,* and made some attempt to prevent Franco from ferrying troops from Morocco to Spain. Italian and German involvement in overcoming these efforts is well documented;[82] the British role has received less attention, but can be determined from contemporary reports. On August 11, 1936, the *New York Times* carried a front-page report on British naval actions in the Straits of Gibraltar, commenting that "this action helps the Rebels by preventing attacks on Algeciras, where troops from Morocco land." (A few days earlier, loyalist warships had bombarded Algeciras, damaging the British consulate.) An accompanying dispatch from Gibraltar describes the situation as it appeared from there:

> Angered by the Spanish factions' endangering of shipping and neutral Gibraltar territory in their fighting, Great Britain virtually blockaded Gibraltar Harbor last night with the huge battleship Queen Elizabeth in the center of the entrance, constantly playing searchlights on near-by waters.
>
> Many British warships patrolled the entire Strait today, determined to prevent interference with Britain's control over the en-

---

*To be more precise, pro-Franco officers were killed, and the seamen remained loyal to the Republic, in many instances.

trance to the Mediterranean, a vital place in the British "lifeline to the East."

This action followed repeated warnings to the Spanish Government and yesterday's decree that no more fighting would be permitted in Gibraltar Harbor. The British at Gibraltar had become increasingly nervous after the shelling of Algeciras by the Loyalist battleship Jaime I.

Although British neutrality is still maintained, the patrol of the Strait and the closing of the harbor will aid the military Rebels because Loyalist warships cannot attempt to take Algeciras, now in Rebel hands, and completely isolate the Rebels from Morocco. The Rebels now can release some troops, who were rushed back to Algeciras, for duty further north in the drive for Madrid.

It was reported in Gibraltar tonight that the Rebels had sent a transport across the Strait and had landed more troops from Morocco for use in the columns that are marching northward from headquarters at Seville.

This was the second time this year that Britain warned a power when she believed her measure of Mediterranean control was threatened, and it remains to be seen whether the Madrid Government will flout the British as the Italians did. If it attempts to do so, the British gunners of the Gibraltar fort have authority to fire warning shots. What will happen if such shots go unheeded is obvious.

All the British here refer to the Madrid Government as the "Communists" and there is no doubt where British sympathies now lie, encouraged by the statement of General Francisco Franco, leader of the Rebels, that he is not especially cooperating with Italy.

The British Government has ordered Spaniards here to cease plotting or be expelled and has asked Britons "loyally to refrain from either acting or speaking publicly in such a manner as to display marked partiality or partisanship."

The warning, issued in the official Gibraltar Gazette, was signed by the British Colonial Secretary here.

The warning was issued after reports of possible Communist troubles here had reached official ears and after strong complaints that Spanish Rebels were in Gibraltar. It was said Rebels were making headquarters here and entering La Linea to fight. [My italics]

I have quoted this dispatch in full because it conveys rather accurately the character of British "neutrality" in the early stages of the war and thenceforth. In May 1938, the British ambassador to Spain, Sir Henry Chilton, "expressed the conviction that a Franco victory was necessary for peace in Spain; that there was not the slightest chance that Italy and/or Germany would dominate Spain; and that even if it were possible for the

Spanish Government to win (which he did not believe) he was convinced that a victory for Franco would be better for Great Britain."[83] Churchill, who was at first violently opposed to the Republic, modified his position somewhat after the crushing of the revolution in the summer of 1937. What particularly pleased him was the forceful repression of the anarchists and the militarization of the Republic (necessary when "the entire structure of civilization and social life is destroyed," as it had been by the revolution, now happily subdued).[84] However, his good feelings toward the Republic remained qualified. In an interview of August 14, 1938, he expressed himself as follows: "Franco has all the right on his side because he loves his country. Also Franco is defending Europe against the Communist danger—if you wish to put it in those terms. But I, I am English, and I prefer the triumph of the wrong cause. I prefer that the other side wins, because Franco could be an upset or a threat to British interests, and the others no."[85]

The Germans were quite aware of British sentiments, naturally, and therefore were much concerned that the supervisory committee for the nonintervention agreement be located in London rather than Paris. The German Foreign Ministry official responsible for this matter expressed his view on August 29, 1936, as follows: "Naturally, we have to count on complaints of all kinds being brought up in London regarding failure to observe the obligation not to intervene, but we cannot avoid such complaints in any case. It can, in fact, only be agreeable to us if the center of gravity, which after all has thus far been in Paris because of the French initiative, is transferred to London."[86] They were not disappointed. In November, Foreign Secretary Anthony Eden stated in the House of Commons: "So far as breaches [of the nonintervention agreement] are concerned, I wish to state categorically that I think there are other Governments more to blame than those of Germany and Italy."[87] There was no factual basis for this statement, but it did reflect British attitudes. It is interesting that, according to German sources, England was at that time supplying Franco with munitions through Gibraltar and, at the same time, providing information to Germany about Russian arms deliveries to the Republic.[88]

The British left was for the most part in support of the liberal-Communist coalition, regarding Caballero as an "infantile leftist" and the anarchists as generally unspeakable.

The British policy of mild support for Franco was to be successful in preserving British interests in Spain, as the Germans soon discovered. A German Foreign Ministry note of October 1937 to the embassy in Nationalist Spain included the following observation: "That England cannot permanently be kept from the Spanish market as in the past is a fact with which we have to reckon. England's old relations with the Spanish mines

and the Generalissimo's desire, based on political and economic considerations, to come to an understanding with England place certain
limits on our chances of reserving Spanish raw materials to ourselves
permanently."[89]

One can only speculate as to what might have been the effects of
British support for the Republic. A discussion of this matter would take
us far afield, into a consideration of British diplomacy during the late
1930s. It is perhaps worth mention, now that the "Munich analogy" is
being bandied about in utter disregard for the historical facts by Secretary Rusk and a number of his academic supporters, that "containment
of Communism" was not a policy invented by George Kennan in 1947.
Specifically it was a dominant theme in the diplomacy of the 1930s. In
1934, Lloyd George stated that "in a very short time, perhaps in a year,
perhaps in two, the conservative elements in this country will be looking to Germany as the bulwark against Communism in Europe. . . . Do
not let us be in a hurry to condemn Germany. We shall be welcoming
Germany as our friend."[90] In September 1938, the Munich agreement
was concluded; shortly after, both France and Britain did welcome Germany as "our friend." As noted earlier (see note 53), even Churchill's
role at this time is subject to some question. Of course, the Munich
agreement was the death knell for the Spanish Republic, exactly as the
necessity to rely on the Soviet Union signaled the end of the Spanish
revolution in 1937.

The United States, like France, exhibited less initiative in these events
than Great Britain, which had far more substantial economic interests in
Spain and was more of an independent force in European affairs.
Nevertheless, the American record is hardly one to inspire pride. Technically the United States adhered to a position of strict neutrality. However, a careful look raises some doubts. According to information
obtained by Jackson, "the American colonel who headed the Telephone
Company had placed private lines at the disposal of the Madrid plotters
for their conversations with Generals Mola and Franco,"[91] just prior to
the insurrection on July 17. In August, the American government urged
the Martin Aircraft Company not to honor an agreement made prior to
the insurrection to supply aircraft to the Republic, and it also pressured
the Mexican government not to reship to Spain war materials purchased in the United States.[92] An American arms exporter, Robert
Cuse, insisted on his legal right to ship airplanes and aircraft engines to
the Republic in December 1936, and the State Department was forced
to grant authorization. Cuse was denounced by Roosevelt as unpatriotic, though Roosevelt was forced to admit that the request was quite
legal. Roosevelt contrasted the attitude of other businessmen to that of
Cuse as follows:

Well, these companies went along with the request of the Government. There is the 90 percent of business that is honest, I mean ethically honest. There is the 90 percent we are always pointing at with pride. And then one man does what amounts to a perfectly legal but thoroughly unpatriotic act. He represents the 10 percent of business that does not live up to the best standards. Excuse the homily, but I feel quite deeply about it.[93]

Among the businesses that remained "ethically honest" and therefore did not incur Roosevelt's wrath was the Texas Company (now Texaco), which violated its contracts with the Spanish Republic and shipped oil instead to Franco. (Five tankers that were on the high seas in July 1936 were diverted to Franco, who received six million dollars worth of oil on credit during the Civil War.) Apparently, neither the press nor the American government was able to discover this fact, though it was reported in left-wing journals at the time.[94] There is evidence that the American government shared the fears of Churchill and others about the dangerous forces on the Republican side. Secretary of State Cordell Hull, for example, informed Roosevelt on July 23, 1936, that "one of the most serious factors in this situation lies in the fact that the [Spanish] Government has distributed large quantities of arms and ammunition into the hands of irresponsible members of left-wing political organizations."[95]

Like Churchill, many responsible Americans began to rethink their attitude toward the Republic after the social revolution had been crushed.[96] However, relations with Franco continued cordial. In 1957, President Eisenhower congratulated Franco on the "happy anniversary" of his rebellion,[97] and Secretary Rusk added his tribute in 1961. Upon criticism, Rusk was defended by the American ambassador to Madrid, who observed that Spain is "a nation which understands the implacable nature of the communist threat,"[98] like Thailand, South Korea, Taiwan, and selected other countries of the Free World.[99]

In the light of such facts as these, it seems to me that Jackson is not treating the historical record seriously when he dismisses the proposals of the Spanish left as absurd. Quite possibly Berneri's strategy would have failed, as did that of the liberal-Communist coalition that took over the Republic. It was far from senseless, however. I think that the failure of historians to consider it more seriously follows, once again, from the elitist bias that dominates the writing of history—and, in this case, from a certain sentimentality about the Western democracies.

The study of collectivization published by the CNT in 1937[100] concludes with a description of the village of Membrilla. "In its miserable huts live the poor inhabitants of a poor province; eight thousand people, but the streets are not paved, the town has no newspaper, no cinema, neither a café nor a library. On the other hand, it has many churches that have been burned." Immediately after the Franco insurrection, the land was expropriated and village life collectivized. "Food, clothing, and tools were distributed equitably to the whole population. Money was abolished, work collectivized, all goods passed to the community, consumption was socialized. It was, however, not a socialization of wealth but of poverty." Work continued as before. An elected council appointed committees to organize the life of the commune and its relations to the outside world. The necessities of life were distributed freely, insofar as they were available. A large number of refugees were accommodated. A small library was established, and a small school of design.

The document closes with these words:

> The whole population lived as in a large family; functionaries, delegates, the secretary of the syndicates, the members of the municipal council, all elected, acted as heads of a family. But they were controlled, because special privilege or corruption would not be tolerated. Membrilla is perhaps the poorest village of Spain, but it is the most just.

An account such as this, with its concern for human relations and the ideal of a just society, must appear very strange to the consciousness of the sophisticated intellectual, and it is therefore treated with scorn, or taken to be naive or primitive or otherwise irrational. Only when such prejudice is abandoned will it be possible for historians to undertake a serious study of the popular movement that transformed Republican Spain in one of the most remarkable social revolutions that history records.

Franz Borkenau, in commenting on the demoralization caused by the authoritarian practices of the central government, observes (p. 295) that "newspapers are written by Europeanized editors, and the popular movement is inarticulate as to its deepest impulses . . . [which are shown only] . . . by acts." The objectivity of scholarship will remain a delusion as long as these inarticulate impulses remain beyond its grasp. As far as the Spanish revolution is concerned, its history is yet to be written.

I have concentrated on one theme—the interpretation of the social revolution in Spain—in one work of history, a work that is an excellent example of liberal scholarship. It seems to me that there is more than enough evidence to show that a deep bias against social revolution and a commitment to the values and social order of liberal bourgeois democracy has led the author to misrepresent crucial events and to overlook major historical currents. My intention has not been to bring into question the commitment to these values—that is another matter entirely. Rather, it has been to show how this commitment has led to a striking failure of objectivity, providing a particularly subtle and interesting example of "counterrevolutionary subordination."*

In opening this discussion of the Spanish revolution, I referred to the classical left-wing critique of the social role of intellectuals, Marxist or otherwise, in modern society, and to Luxemburg's reservations regarding Bolshevism. Western sociologists have repeatedly emphasized the relevance of this analysis to developments in the Soviet Union,[101] with much justice. The same sociologists formulate "the world revolution of the epoch" in the following terms: "The major transformation is the decline of business (and of earlier social formations) and the rise of intellectuals and semi-intellectuals to effective power."[102] The "ultra-left" critic foresaw in these developments a new attack on human freedom and a more efficient system of exploitation. The Western sociologist sees in the rise of intellectuals to effective power the hope for a more humane and smoothly functioning society, in which problems can be solved by "piecemeal technology." Who has the sharper eye? At least this much is plain: there are dangerous tendencies in the ideology of the welfare-state intelligentsia who claim to possess the technique and understanding required to manage our "postindustrial society" and to organize an international society dominated by American superpower. Many of these dangers are revealed, at a purely ideological level, in the study of the counterrevolutionary subordination of scholarship. The dangers exist both insofar as the claim to knowledge is real and insofar as it is fraudulent. Insofar as the technique of management and control exists, it can be used to consolidate the authority of those who exercise it and to diminish spontaneous and free experimentation with new social forms, as it can limit the possibilities for reconstruction of society in the interests of those who are now, to a greater or lesser extent, dispossessed. Where the techniques fail, they will be supplemented by all of the methods of coercion that modern technology provides, to preserve order and stability.

For a glimpse of what may lie ahead, consider the Godkin lectures of McGeorge Bundy, recently delivered at Harvard.[103] Bundy urges that more power be concentrated in the executive branch of the government, now "dangerously weak in relation to its present tasks." That the powerful executive will act with justice and wisdom—this presumably needs no

---

*The term "counterrevolutionary subordination" is borrowed from Conor Cruise O'Brien, who edited the volume in which the article appeared from which this material is excerpted. See the opening paragraph of the original in *American Power and the New Mandarins.*

argument. As an example of the superior executive who should be attracted to government and given still greater power, Bundy cites Robert McNamara. Nothing could reveal more clearly the dangers inherent in the "new society" than the role that McNamara's Pentagon has played for the past half dozen years. No doubt McNamara succeeded in doing with utmost efficiency that which should not be done at all. No doubt he has shown an unparalleled mastery of the logistics of coercion and repression, combined with the most astonishing inability to comprehend political and human factors. The efficiency of the Pentagon is no less remarkable than its pratfalls.[104] When understanding fails, there is always more force in reserve. As the "experiments in material and human resources control" collapse and "revolutionary development" grinds to a halt, we simply resort more openly to the Gestapo tactics that are barely concealed behind the facade of "pacification."[105] When American cities explode, we can expect the same. The technique of "limited warfare" translates neatly into a system of domestic repression—far more humane, as will quickly be explained, than massacring those who are unwilling to wait for the inevitable victory of the war on poverty.

Why should a liberal intellectual be so persuaded of the virtues of a political system of four-year dictatorship? The answer seems all too plain.

The Manufacture of Consent

(1984)

*D*URING THE THANKSGIVING HOLIDAY A FEW WEEKS AGO, I took a walk with some friends and family in a national park. We came across a gravestone, which had on it the following inscription: "Here lies an Indian woman, a Wampanoag, whose family and tribe gave of themselves and their land that this great nation might be born and grow."

Of course, it is not quite accurate to say that the indigenous population gave of themselves and their land for that noble purpose. Rather, they were slaughtered, decimated, and dispersed in the course of one of the greatest exercises in genocide in human history. Current estimates suggest that there may have been about 80 million Native Americans in Latin America when Columbus "discovered" the continent—as we say—and about 12 to 15 million more north of the Rio Grande. By 1650, about 95 percent of the population of Latin America had been wiped out, and by the time the continental borders of the United States had been established, some 200,000 were left of the indigenous population. In short, mass genocide, on a colossal scale, which we celebrate each October when we honor Columbus—a notable mass murderer himself—on Columbus Day.

Hundreds of American citizens, well-meaning and decent people, troop by that gravestone regularly and read it, apparently without reaction; except, perhaps, a feeling of satisfaction that at last we are giving some due recognition to the sacrifices of the native peoples, presumably the reason why it was placed there. They might react differently if they were to visit Auschwitz or Dachau and find a gravestone reading: "Here lies a woman, a Jew, whose family and people gave of themselves and their possessions that this great nation might grow and prosper."

The truth is not entirely suppressed. The distinguished Harvard historian and Columbus biographer Samuel Eliot Morrison does comment that "the cruel policy initiated by Columbus and pursued by his successors resulted in complete genocide." This statement is "buried halfway into the telling of a grand romance," Howard Zinn observes in his *People's History of the United States,* noting that in the book's last paragraph, Morrison sums up his view of Columbus as follows:

> He had his faults and his defects, but they were largely the defects of the qualities that made him great—his indomitable will, his superb faith in God and in his own mission as the Christ-bearer to lands beyond the seas, his stubborn persistence despite neglect, poverty and discouragement. But there was no flaw, no dark side to the most outstanding and essential of all his qualities—his seamanship.

I omit the corresponding paragraph that some acolyte might compose about other practitioners of "complete genocide" or even lesser crimes, or the reaction that this would arouse among us if such examples existed.

The sentiment on the gravestone of the Wampanoag woman is not original. One hundred sixty years ago, John Quincy Adams explained in a Fourth of July address that our government is superior to all others because it was based upon consent, not conquest:

> The first settlers . . . immediately after landing, purchased from the Indian natives the right of settlement upon the soil. Thus was a social compact formed upon the elementary principles of civil soci-

ety, in which conquest and servitude had no part. The slough of brutal force was entirely cast off: all was voluntary: all was unbiased consent: all was the agreement of soul with soul.

Citing these remarks by a president known as a legalist who respected Indian treaties, T. D. Allman observes that "the American national experience of genocidal slaughter of the Indian" is "nearly nonexistent." "They were not human beings; they were only obstacles to the inexorable triumph of American virtue, who must be swept away to make room for a new reality of American freedom." The consensus has been that "our own solemnly proclaimed rights to life, liberty and the pursuit of happiness totally superseded the rights of the peoples whose lives, liberties and happiness we were expunging from the face of the earth." The Indians were the first "aggressors" who had to be faced in our celebration of freedom, the definition of "aggressor" being "that we have attacked them," to be followed by Mexicans, Filipinos, Vietnamese, Nicaraguans and many others. It may be added that U.S. history is hardly unique in this respect, down to the present day.

The sense in which the native population had given "unbiased consent" in this "agreement of soul with soul" was explained further by one of the early American sociologists, Franklin Henry Giddings, at the time when we were obtaining the consent of the Filipinos at the turn of the century. He coined the phrase "consent without consent" to deal with the achievement of the British in extending the "English sacredness of life" and the "requirement of social order" to "racially inferior types." "If in later years," he wrote, the colonized "see and admit that the disputed relation was for the highest interest, it may be reasonably held that authority has been imposed with the consent of the governed"—just as we may say that a young child gives "consent without consent" when its parents prevent it from running into the street.

During a visit to a fine and much-respected college some months ago, I was taken on a tour of the college cathedral and shown the series of stained-glass windows recording the history of the college from the days when it was attacked by Union soldiers to the present. One panel was devoted to the founding of the air force ROTC chapter shortly after the Second World War. It showed a man sitting at a desk signing some document, with an air force officer standing nearby. An American bomber was shown in the background and on a blackboard we read: $E = mc^2$. Though it is difficult to believe at first, the stained-glass window in this cathedral is celebrating the atomic bombing of Hiroshima and Nagasaki, what Truman described at the time as "the greatest thing in history."

Not everyone, incidentally, felt quite that way. The distinguished Indian jurist Radhabinod Pal, in his dissenting opinion at the Tokyo Tribunal that assessed Japanese war guilt, wrote that "if any indiscriminate destruction of civilian life and property is still illegitimate in warfare, then in the Pacific war, this decision to use the atom bomb is the only near approach to the directives . . . of the Nazi leaders during the Second World War. Nothing like this could be traced to the credit of the present accused." He did not expand on what it implies with regard to war-crimes trials. But such perceptions are remote from the consciousness of the victors, and perhaps we should not be surprised that "the greatest thing in history" merits a stained-glass window in the cathedral of a college dedicated to humane values and religious devotion.

The process of creating and entrenching highly selective, reshaped or completely fabricated memories of the past is what we call "indoctrination" or "propaganda" when it is conducted by official enemies, and "education," "moral instruction" or "character building," when we do it ourselves. It is a valuable mechanism of control, since it effectively blocks any understanding of what is happening in the world. One crucial goal of successful education is to deflect attention elsewhere—say, to Vietnam, or Central America, or the Middle East, where our problems allegedly lie—and away from our own institutions and their systematic functioning and behavior, the real source of a great deal of the violence and suffering in the world. It is crucially important to prevent understanding and to divert attention from the sources of our own conduct, so that elite groups can act without popular constraints to achieve their goals—which are called "the national interest" in academic theology.

The importance of blocking understanding, and the great successes that have been achieved, are very well illustrated in current affairs. A few days ago, the World Court rejected the American contention that it had no jurisdiction with regard to the Nicaraguan complaint concerning U.S. aggression against Nicaragua. The issue arose last April, when Nicaragua brought to the Court its charge that the United States was mining its harbors and attacking its territory. With exquisite timing, President Reagan chose that very day to issue a Presidential Proclamation designating May 1 as "Law Day 1984." He hailed our "200-year-old partnership between law and liberty," adding that without law, there can be only "chaos and disorder." The day before, as part of his tribute to the rule of law, he had announced that the United States would not recognize any decision of the World Court.

These events aroused much anger. In the *New York Times,* Anthony Lewis decried Reagan's "failure to understand what the rule of law has meant to this country." He observed that Senator Moynihan had "made the point with great power" in a law school address in which he criticized the Reagan administration for "forsaking our centuries-old commitment to the idea of law in the conduct of nations" and for its "mysterious collective amnesia," its "losing the memory that there once was such a commitment." Our U.N. delegation, Moynihan said, "does not know the history of our country."

Unfortunately it is Ronald Reagan and Jeane Kirkpatrick who understand what the rule of law has meant to this country, and it is Anthony Lewis and Senator Moynihan who are suffering from a mysterious collective amnesia. The case they are discussing is a good example. It happened before, in almost exactly the same way. The story is told by Walter LaFeber, in his valuable book *Inevitable Revolutions.* In 1907, a Central American Court of Justice was established at the initiative of Washington to adjudicate conflicts among the states of the region. "Within nine years," LaFeber observes, "the institution was hollow because twice—in 1912 and 1916—the United States refused to recognize Court decisions that went against its interests in Nicaragua." In 1912, the court condemned U.S. military intervention in Nicaragua; Washington simply ignored the ruling. In 1916, the Court upheld a Costa Rican claim that U.S. actions in Nicaragua infringed its rights, and again the United States simply disregarded the decision, effectively destroying the Court. "In establishing its control over Central America," LaFeber comments, "the United States killed the institution it had helped create to bring Central America together." A final blow was administered in 1922 when Secretary of State Charles Evans Hughes convened a conference of Central American states in Washington. LaFeber comments:

> The occasion was not to be a replay of the 1907 conference, when the Central Americans had come to their own conclusions. Now the United States, with the help of faithful (and marine occupied) Nicaragua, set the agenda, which included the admonition that no one mention the late, unlamented Central American Court.

There are, to be sure, differences between the earlier case and today's, though not those that our current historical amnesia would suggest. Now Nicaragua is not under marine occupation—merely under military attack by a U.S. mercenary army called "freedom fighters"; and the United States is not powerful enough simply to disband the World Court.

It is, incidentally, a little difficult to believe that Senator Moynihan was serious in his reference to our commitment to the rule of law; more likely these remarks were produced with tongue in cheek, or intended as an example of his Irish wit. In his memoir of his tenure as U.N. ambassador, Moynihan gives graphic examples of this commitment to the rule of law, particularly to the United Nations charter, which forbids the use of force in international affairs. Thus when Indonesia invaded East Timor in

1975, illegally using U.S. arms and obviously with the blessing of the United States, Moynihan dedicated his efforts to blocking any moves by the United Nations to deter the crime of aggression—for which people were hanged at Nuremberg—and takes great pride in his success in this endeavor, which, as he observes, led to a huge massacre. It is of some interest that his pride in his complicity in war crimes does not affect his reputation as a leading advocate of the sanctity of the rule of law among American liberals.

The World Court incident provides some lessons concerning the system of indoctrination. It is easy enough to make fun of Ronald Reagan, but that is itself a diversion from the main point. Violence, deceit, and lawlessness are natural functions of the state, any state. What is important in the present context is the contribution of the harshest critics (within the mainstream) to reinforcing the system of indoctrination, of which they themselves are victims—as is the norm for the educated classes, who are typically the most profoundly indoctrinated and in a deep sense the most ignorant group, the victims as well as the purveyors of the doctrines of the faith. The great achievement of the critics is to prevent the realization that what is happening today is not some departure from our historical ideals and practice, to be attributed to the personal failings of this or that individual. Rather, it is the systematic expression of the way our institutions function and will continue to function unless impeded by an aroused public that comes to understand their nature and their true history—exactly what our educational institutions must prevent if they are to fulfill *their* function, namely, to serve power and privilege.

A useful rule of thumb is this: If you want to learn something about the propaganda system, have a close look at the critics and their tacit assumptions. These typically constitute the doctrines of the state religion.

Let's take another current case. The justification for our attack against Nicaragua is that Nicaragua is a Soviet proxy, threatening Mexico, ultimately the United States itself. It is worth emphasizing that the basic assumptions of this doctrinal system extend across the political spectrum. Consider the tale of the Russian MIGs allegedly sent to Nicaragua, a fable nicely timed to divert attention from the Nicaraguan elections that we had sought to undermine and from the fact that we are sending advanced aircraft to El Salvador to facilitate the massacre of peasants; this is now conducted with improved efficiency thanks to the direct participation of U.S. military forces based in our Honduran and Panamanian sanctuaries, who coordinate bombing strikes on villages and fleeing peasants while we debate the profound question whether Nicaragua is obtaining aircraft that might enable it to defend itself against an attack by our mercenary army, not "guerrillas," but rather a well-equipped military force that in some respects outmatches the army of Nicaragua in the level and quality of its armaments.

When the neatly timed MIG story was leaked by the administration, thus setting the framework for further discussion of the issues within the ideological system, senatorial doves made it clear that if MIGs were indeed sent, then we have a right to bomb Nicaragua because of the threat they pose to us. Senator Dodd stated that the United States would "have to go in and take (them) out—you'd have to bomb the crates." Senator Tsongas added:

> You just could not allow them to put those MIGs together, because the MIGs are not only capable vis-à-vis El Salvador and Honduras, they're also capable against the United States and Nicaraguans knew for a long time that they could not do this without violating a clear sense of the sort of U.S. sphere of influence. [*Boston Globe,* November 9, 1984]

Let us put aside the quaint idea that the Nicaraguans would be "escalating" illegitimately by obtaining aircraft to defend themselves against our military attacks or that they might attack Honduras and El Salvador—while the United States stands by, a pitiful helpless giant, as Nixon once whined. Consider the threat that Nicaragua poses to us. By these standards, the USSR has a right to bomb Denmark, which is no less a threat to them than Nicaragua is to us—a far greater threat, in fact, because it is part of a hostile military alliance of great power—and it surely has the right to bomb Turkey, on its border, with its major NATO bases threatening the security of the Soviet Union. Fifty years ago, Hitler warned that Czechoslovakia was a dagger pointed at the heart of Germany, an intolerable threat to its security. By our standards, Hitler appears to have been rather sane. Again, it is the contribution of the critics that is noteworthy.

But let us return to the claim that Nicaragua is a Soviet proxy, threatening Mexico. In 1926, the marines were sent back to Nicaragua, which they had occupied through much of the century, to combat a Bolshevik threat. Then Mexico was a Soviet proxy, threatening Nicaragua, ultimately the United States itself. "Mexico was on trial before the world," President Coolidge proclaimed as he sent the marines to Nicaragua once again, an intervention that led to the establishment of the Somoza dictatorship with its terrorist U.S.-trained National Guard and the killing of the authentic Nicaraguan nationalist Sandino. Note that though the cast of characters has changed, the bottom line remains the same: kill Nicaraguans.

What did we do before we could appeal to the Bolshevik threat? Woodrow Wilson, the great apostle of self-determination, celebrated this doctrine by sending his warriors to invade Haiti and the Dominican Republic, where they reestablished slavery, burned and destroyed villages, tortured and murdered, leaving in Haiti a legacy that remains today in one of the most miserable corners of one of the most miserable parts of the world, and in the Dominican Republic setting the stage for the Trujillo dictatorship, established after a brutal war of counterinsurgency that has virtually disappeared from American history; the first book dealing with it has just appeared, after sixty years. There were no Bolsheviks then to justify these actions, so we were defending ourselves from the Huns. Marine Commander Thorpe described how he told new marine arrivals "that they were serving their country just as valuably as were their fortunate comrades across the seas, and the war would last long enough to give every man a chance against the Hun in Europe as against the Hun in Santo Domingo." The hand of the Huns was particularly evident in Haiti. Thorpe explained: "Whoever is running this revolution is a wise man; he certainly is getting a lot out of the niggers. . . . It shows the handwork of the German." "If I do a good job of clearing these . . . provinces of insurgents and kill a lot," he added, "it ought to demonstrate I'd be a good German-killer."

In earlier years, we were defending ourselves against other aggressors. When Polk stole a third of Mexico, we were defending ourselves against Mexican "aggression" (initiated well inside Mexican territory); we had to take California to protect ourselves from a possible British threat to do so. The Indian wars were also defensive; the Indians were attacking us from their British and Spanish sanctuaries, so we were compelled to take Florida and the West, with consequences for the native population that are, or should be, well-known. Before that, the doctrine of moralist Cotton Mather sufficed: he expressed his pleasure that "the woods were almost cleared of those pernicious creatures, to make room for a better growth." These, incidentally, were the pernicious creatures who "gave of themselves and their land that this great nation might be born and grow." The job was done so well that we no longer slaughter Indians here, though in areas where the task has not yet been successfully consummated, as in Guatemala, we continue to support massacres that the conservative Church hierarchy calls "genocide," within the "sphere of influence" that we must "defend," according to senatorial doves, just as we have "defended" it—from its own population—so effectively in past years.

Looking at the real history, we see the current attack on Nicaragua in a perspective different from the conventional one and we can come to understand its causes in the normal and essentially invariant functioning of our own institutions. And we can also come to understand the brainwashing techniques employed to conceal what is happening before our eyes. It is a relatively simple exercise to refute the administration case, though one that must be constantly undertaken in a highly indoctrinated society where elementary truths are easily buried. What is more to the point is to recognize that this case is just another contribution to familiar historical fraud, while the events themselves are just another chapter in a shameful and sordid history, concealed from us by a contrived history framed in terms of such ideals as the rule of law, Wilsonian principles of self-determination, democracy and human rights, and others like them, which bear to American history the relation of irrelevance, under an interpretation that is rather too charitable.*

In their important study *Demonstration Elections*, Edward Herman and Frank Brodhead include a photograph of Notre Dame President Theodore Hesburgh contemplating a ballot box while he was serving as an observer during the 1982 election in El Salvador, much heralded as a step toward something that we call "democracy." The caption reads: "The Rev. Theodore Hesburgh, 'observing' the Salvadoran election, but not 'seeing' the transparent voting box," plainly shown in the photograph. One of the central tasks of a successful educational system is to endow its victims with the capacity to observe, but not to see, a capacity that is the hallmark of the "responsible intellectual."

There did, of course, develop a kind of opposition to the Vietnam War in the mainstream, but it was overwhelmingly "pragmatic," as the critics characterized it with considerable self-adulation, distinguishing themselves from the "emotional" or "irresponsible" opponents who objected to the war on principled grounds. The "pragmatic" opponents argued that the war could not be won at an acceptable cost, or that there was unclarity about goals, or duplicity, or errors in execution. On similar grounds, the German general staff was no doubt critical of Hitler after Stalingrad. Public attitudes, incidentally, were rather different. As recently as 1982, over 70 percent of the population held that the war was "fundamentally wrong and immoral," not merely a "mistake," a position held by far fewer "opinion leaders" and by virtually none of the articulate intelligentsia, even at the height of opposition to the war in 1970.

How has this remarkable subservience to the doctrinal system been achieved? It is not that the facts were unavailable, as is sometimes the case. The devastating bombing of northern Laos and the 1969 bombing and other attacks against Cambodia were suppressed by the media, a fact that is suppressed within the mainstream until today (these are called "secret wars," meaning that the government kept the attack secret—as it did, with the complicity of the media). But in the case of the American attack against South Vietnam, sufficient facts were always available. They were observed, but not seen.

---

*Following this paragraph, material has been deleted from the original text.

American scholarship is particularly remarkable. The official historian of the Kennedy administration, Arthur Schlesinger, regarded as a leading dove, does indeed refer to aggression in 1962: "1962 had not been a bad year," he writes in his history *A Thousand Days*; "aggression [was] checked in Vietnam." That is, the year in which the United States undertook direct aggression against South Vietnam was the year in which aggression was *checked* in Vietnam. Orwell would have been impressed. Another respected figure in the liberal pantheon, Adlai Stevenson, intoned at the United Nations that in Vietnam we were combating "internal aggression," another phrase that Orwell would have admired; that is, we were combating aggression by the Vietnamese against us in Vietnam, just as we had combated aggression by the Mexicans against us in Mexico a century earlier. We had done the same in Greece in the late 1940s, Stevenson went on to explain, intervening to protect Greece from "the aggressors" who had "gained control of most of the country," these "aggressors" being the Greeks who had led the anti-Nazi resistance and who we succeeded in removing with an impressive display of massacre, torture, expulsion, and general violence, in favor of the Nazi collaborators of our choice. The analogy was, in fact, more apt than Stevenson— apparently a very ignorant man—was likely to have known. As always, the American posture is defensive, even as we invade a country halfway around the world after having failed to destroy the political opposition by large-scale violence and terror.

A closer look at the debate that did develop over the Vietnam War provides some lessons about the mechanisms of indoctrination. The debate pitted the hawks against the doves. The hawks were those, like journalist Joseph Alsop, who felt that with a sufficient exercise of violence we could succeed in our aims. The doves felt that this was unlikely, although, as Arthur Schlesinger explained, "We all pray that Mr. Alsop will be right," and "we may all be saluting the wisdom and statesmanship of the American government" if the U.S. succeeds (contrary to his expectations) in a war policy that was turning Vietnam into "a land of ruin and wreck." It was this book that established Schlesinger as a leading war opponent, in the words of Leslie Gelb.

It is, of course, immediately evident that there is a possible position omitted from the fierce debate between the hawks and the doves, which allegedly tore the country apart during these trying years: namely, the position of the peace movement, a position in fact shared by the large majority of citizens as recently as 1982: the war was not merely a "mistake," as the official doves allege, but was "fundamentally wrong and immoral." To put it plainly: war crimes, including the crime of launching aggressive war, are wrong, even if they succeed in their "noble" aims. This position does not enter the debate, even to be refuted; it is unthinkable, within the ideological mainstream.

It should be emphasized that departures from orthodoxy were very rare among the articulate intelligentsia. Few journalists were more critical of the war than Anthony Lewis, who summed up his attitude in 1975 by explaining that the war began with "blundering efforts to do good," though by 1969 (1969!) it was clear that it was a "disastrous mistake." In mainstream academic circles, it would have been difficult to find a more committed critic of the war than John King Fairbank of Harvard, the dean of American Asian scholars, who was considered so extreme as to be a "Comsymp" or worse in McCarthyite terminology. Fairbank gave the presidential address to the American Historical Association in December 1968, a year after the Tet offensive had converted most of the corporate elite and other top planning circles to dovedom. He was predictably critical of the Vietnam War, in these terms: this is "an age when we get our power politics overextended into foreign disasters like Vietnam mainly through an excess of righteousness and disinterested benevolence"; "Our role in defending the South after 1965" was based on analytic errors, so that "we had great trouble in convincing ourselves that it had a purpose worthy of the effort." The doves felt that the war was "a hopeless cause," we learn from Anthony Lake, a leading dove who resigned from the government in protest against the Cambodia invasion. All agree that it was a "failed crusade," "noble" but "illusory," and undertaken with the "loftiest intentions," as Stanley Karnow puts it in his best-selling companion volume to the Public Broadcasting System television series, highly regarded for its critical candor. Those who do not appreciate these self-evident truths, or who maintain the curious view that they should be supported by some evidence, simply demonstrate thereby that they are emotional and irresponsible ideologues, or perhaps outright Communists. Or more accurately, their odd views cannot be heard; they are outside the spectrum of thinkable thought. Few dictators can boast of such utter conformity to Higher Truths.

All of this illustrates very well the genius of democratic systems of thought control, which differ markedly from totalitarian practice. Those who rule by violence tend to be "behaviorist" in their outlook. What people may think is not terribly important; what counts is what they do. They must obey, and this obedience is secured by force. The penalties for disobedience vary depending on the characteristics of the state. In the USSR today, the penalties may be psychiatric torture, or exile, or prison, under harsh and grim conditions. In a typical U.S. dependency such as El Salvador, the dissident is likely to be found in a ditch, decapitated after hideous torture; and when a sufficient number are dispatched, we can even have elections in which people march toward democracy by rejecting the Nazi-like D'Aubuisson in favor of Duarte, who presided over one of the great mass murders of the modern period (the necessary prerequisite to democratic elections, which obviously cannot proceed while popular organizations still function), and his minister of defense, Vides Casanova, who explained in 1980 that the country had survived the massacre of 30,000 peasants in the 1932 *Matanza,* and "today, the armed forces are prepared to kill 200,000–300,000, if that's what it takes to stop a Communist takeover."

Democratic systems are quite different. It is necessary to control not only what people do, but also what they think. Since the state lacks the capacity to ensure obedience by force, thought can lead to action and therefore the threat to order must be excised at the source. It is necessary to establish a framework for possible thought that is constrained within the principles of the state religion. These need not be asserted; it is better that they be presupposed, as the unstated framework for thinkable thought. The critics reinforce this system by tacitly accepting these doctrines, and confining their critique to tactical questions that arise within them. To achieve respectability, to be admitted to the debate, they must accept without question or inquiry the fundamental doctrine that the state is benevolent, governed by the loftiest intentions, adopting a defensive stance, not an actor in world affairs but only reacting to the crimes of others, sometimes unwisely because of personal failures, naiveté, the complexity of history or an inability to comprehend the evil nature of our enemies. If even the harshest critics tacitly adopt these premises, then, the ordinary person may ask, who am I to disagree? The more intensely the debate rages between hawks and doves, the more firmly and effectively the doctrines of the state religion are established. It is because of their notable contribution to thought control that the critics are tolerated, indeed honored—that is, those who play by the rules.

This is a system of thought control that was not perceived by Orwell, and is never understood by dictators who fail to comprehend the utility for indoctrination of permitting a class of critics who denounce the errors and failings of the leadership while tacitly adopting the crucial premises of the state religion.

These distinctions between totalitarian and democratic systems of thought control are only rough first approximations. In fact, even a totalitarian state must be concerned about popular attitudes and understanding, and in a democracy, it is the politically active segments of the population, the more educated and privileged, who are of prime concern. This is obvious in the United States, where the poor tend not even to vote, and more significant forms of political participation—the design and formulation of political programs, candidate selection, the requisite material support, educational efforts or propaganda—are the domain of relatively narrow privileged elites. Three-quarters of the population may support a nuclear freeze, and some of them may even know that this is official Soviet policy as well, but that has no impact on the policy of massive government intervention to subsidize high-technology industry through a state-guaranteed market for armaments, since no serious alternative is available in the system of political economy. Mass popular resistance to military aggression does serve as an impediment to the planners, as has been evident in the last few years with regard to Central America. Just this morning, the press reported a memorandum written by Secretary of Defense McNamara in May 1967, warning that escalation of the Vietnam War might "polarize opinion to the extent that 'doves' in the U.S. will get out of hand—massive refusals to serve, or to fight, or to cooperate, or worse?" The "doves" that concerned him here are not the official "doves" of the doctrinal system, few of whom were doves of any stripe at the time, but rather the general population. But such resistance, while sometimes effective in raising the costs of state violence, is of limited efficacy as long as it is not based on understanding of the forces at work and the reasons for their systematic behavior, and it tends to dissipate as quickly as it arises. At the same time, a frightened and insecure populace, trained to believe that Russian demons and Third World hordes are poised to take everything they have, is susceptible to jingoist fanaticism. This was shown dramatically by the popular response to the Grenada invasion. The United States is again "standing tall," Reagan proclaimed, after 6,000 elite troops managed to overcome the resistance of a handful of Cuban military men and a few Grenadan militiamen, winning 8,700 medals for their valor, and eliciting a reaction here that cannot fail to awaken memories of other great powers that won cheap victories not too many years ago.

The more subtle methods of indoctrination just illustrated, are considerably more significant than outright lying or suppression of unwanted fact, though the latter are also common enough. Examples are legion.

Consider, for example, the current debate as to whether there is a "symmetry" between El Salvador and Nicaragua in that in each case rebels supported from abroad are attempting to overthrow the government. The administration claims that in one case the rebels are "freedom fighters" and the government is an illegitimate tyranny, while in the other case the rebels are terrorists and the government is a still somewhat flawed democracy. The critics question whether Nicaragua is really supporting the guerrillas in El Salvador or whether Nicaragua has already succumbed to totalitarianism.

Lost in the debate is a more striking symmetry. In each country, there is a terrorist military force that is massacring civilians, and in each country we support that force: the government of El Salvador, and the contras. That this has been true in El Salvador, particularly since the Carter administration undertook to destroy the popular organizations that had developed during the 1970s, is not in doubt. That the same is true in Nicaragua is also evident, though here we must turn to the foreign press, where we can read of "the contras' litany of destruction" as they murder, rape, mutilate, torture and brutalize the civilian population that falls within their clutches, primary targets being health and education workers and peasants in cooperatives (Jonathan Steele and Tony Jenkins, in the London *Guardian*; Marian Wilkinson, in the *National Times,* Australia; and many other sources where ample details are provided). The top commander of the "Democratic Force," Adolfo Calero, is quoted in the *New York Times* as saying that "there is no line at all, not even a fine line, between a civilian farm owned by the Government and a Sandinista military outpost," and an occasional report indicates the consequences of these assumptions, but press coverage here is muted and sporadic, devoted to more significant matters, such as opposition to the draft (in Nicaragua).

This is the real "symmetry" between Nicaragua and El Salvador. Its significance is lost as we debate the accuracy of the government case, meanwhile continuing to labor under the mysterious collective amnesia that prevents us from seeing that there is little here that is new, and from understanding why this should be so.

Or to turn to another part of the world, consider what is universally called the "peace process" in the Middle East, referring to the Camp David agreements. Israeli-run polls reveal that the population of the territories under Israeli military occupation overwhelmingly oppose the "peace process," regarding it as detrimental to their interests. Why should this be so? Surely of all the people in the region, they are among those who must be yearning the most for peace. But no journalist seems to have inquired into this strange paradox.

The problem is easily solved. The "peace process," as was evident at the time and should be transparent in retrospect, was designed in such a way as to remove the major Arab military force, Egypt, from the conflict, so that Israel would then be free, with a huge and rapidly-expanding U.S. subsidy, to intensify settlement and repression in the conquered territories and to attack its northern neighbor—exactly as it did, at once and unremittingly since. It is hardly a cause for wonder that the victims of the "peace process" overwhelmingly condemn and reject it, though it is perhaps a little surprising that such elementary truths, obvious enough at the outset, cannot be seen even today. Meanwhile, we must continue to support the "peace process." Who can be opposed to peace?

In this case, too, it would be salutary to overcome our mysterious collective amnesia about the facts of recent history. There is no time here to review the diplomatic record, but anyone who troubles to do so will quickly learn that there have been possibilities for peace with a modicum of justice for about fifteen years, blocked in every instance by U.S.-Israeli rejectionism. In the early 1970s, this rejectionist stance was so extreme as to block even Arab initiatives (by Egypt and Jordan) to attain a general peace settlement that entirely ignored Palestinian national rights. Since the international consensus shifted to adherence to a two-state settlement a decade ago, any such possibility has consistently been barred by the United States and Israel, which persist in rejecting any claim by the indigenous population to the rights that are accorded without question to the Jewish settlers who largely displaced them, including the right to national self-determination somewhere within their former home. Articulate American opinion lauds this stance, urging the Palestinians to accept the Labor party program that denies them any national rights and regards them as having "no role to play" in any settlement (Labor dove Abba Eban). There is no protest here, or even mere reporting of the facts, when the U.S. government blocks a U.N. peace initiative, stating that it will accept only negotiations "among the parties directly concerned with the Arab-Israeli dispute," crucially excluding the Palestinians, who are not one of these parties (January 1984). Analogous rejectionist attitudes on the part of Libya and the minority PLO Rejection Front are condemned here as racist and extremist; the quite comparable U.S.-Israeli stance, obviously racist in essence, is considered the soul of moderation.

The actual record has been obscured, denied, even inverted here in one of the most successful exercises in agitprop in modern history. I reviewed the record up to mid-1983 in a recent book (*The Fateful Triangle*). It continues since, without change. To mention only one recent case, last April and May Yasser Arafat made a series of proposals in statements published in France and England in the mainstream press and in speeches in Greece and Asia. He called explicitly for direct negotiations with Israel under U.N. auspices and for "mutual recognition of two states," Israel and a Palestinian state; this has long been the basic form of the international consensus, though it is excluded by the rejectionist "peace process." Israel immediately rejected the offer, and the United States simply ignored it. Media coverage in the United States followed an interesting pattern. The national press—the *New York Times* and the *Washington Post*— did not report the facts at all. The local "quality press" (the *Boston Globe, Los Angeles Times, Philadelphia Inquirer*) did report the basic facts, though they were obscured and quickly forgotten, to be replaced by familiar diatribes about Palestinian extremism. In the *San Francisco Examiner,* reputed to be one of the worst papers in any major city, a UPI story giving the basic facts appeared on the front page, under a full-page inch-high headline reading "Arafat to Israel: Let's Talk." A rational conclusion would be that the less sophisticated press simply does not understand what facts must be suppressed as inconsistent with the party line.*

---

*Following this paragraph, material has been deleted from the original essay.

I will not proceed with further examples. The crucial point is that the pattern is pervasive, persistent, and overwhelmingly effective in establishing a framework of thinkable thought.

Over sixty years ago, Walter Lippmann discussed the concept of "the manufacture of consent," an art that is "capable of great refinements" and that may lead to a "revolution" in "the practice of democracy." The idea was taken up with much enthusiasm in business circles—it is a main preoccupation of the public relations industry, whose leading figure, Edward Bernays, described "the engineering of consent" as the very essence of democracy. In fact, as Gabriel Kolko notes, "from the turn of the century until this day, [the public mind] was the object of a cultural and ideological industry that was as unrelenting as it was diverse: ranging from the school to the press to mass culture in its multitudinous dimensions." The reason, as an AT&T vice president put it in 1909, is that "the public mind . . . is in my judgment the only serious danger confronting the company." The idea was also taken up with vigor in the social sciences. The leading political scientist Harold Lasswell wrote in 1933 that we must avoid "democratic dogmatisms," such as the belief that people are "the best judges of their own interests." Democracy permits the voice of the people to be heard, and it is the task of the intellectual to ensure that this voice endorses what far-sighted leaders know to be the right course. Propaganda is to democracy what violence is to totalitarianism. The techniques have been honed to a high art, far beyond anything that Orwell dreamt of. The device of feigned dissent, incorporating the doctrines of the state religion and eliminating rational critical discussion, is one of the more subtle means, though more crude techniques are also widely used and are highly effective in protecting us from seeing what we observe, from knowledge and understanding of the world in which we live.

It should be stressed again that what the Communists call agitprop is far more important in the democracies than in states that rule by violence, for reasons already discussed, and is therefore more refined, and possibly more effective. There are no Danchevs* here, except at the remote margins of political debate.

For those who stubbornly seek freedom, there can be no more urgent task than to come to understand the mechanisms and practices of indoctrination. These are easy to perceive in the totalitarian societies, much less so in the system of "brainwashing under freedom" to which we are subjected and which all too often we serve as willing or unwitting instruments.

---

*On the courageous Soviet journalist Vladimir Danchev, see page 223, below.

$\mathscr{I}$NTERPRETING *the* $\mathscr{W}$ORLD

Language and Freedom

(1970)

W̶HEN I WAS INVITED TO SPEAK ON THE TOPIC "LANGUAGE and freedom," I was puzzled and intrigued. Most of my professional life has been devoted to the study of language. There would be no great difficulty in finding a topic to discuss in that domain. And there is much to say about the problems of freedom and liberation as they pose themselves to us and to others in the mid-twentieth century. What is troublesome in the title of this lecture is the conjunction. In what way are language and freedom to be interconnected?

As a preliminary, let me say just a word about the contemporary study of language, as I see it. There are many aspects of language and language use that raise intriguing questions, but—in my judgment—only a few have so far led to productive theoretical work. In particular, our deepest insights are in the area of formal grammatical structure. A person who knows a language has acquired a system of rules and principles—a "generative grammar," in technical terms—that associates sound and meaning in some specific fashion. There are many reasonably well-founded and, I think, rather enlightening hypotheses as to the character of such grammars, for quite a number of languages. Furthermore, there has been a renewal of interest in "universal grammar," interpreted now as the theory that tries to specify the general properties of those languages that can be learned in the normal way by humans. Here, too, significant progress has been achieved. The subject is of particular importance. It is appropriate to regard universal grammar as the study of one of the essential faculties of mind. It is, therefore, extremely interesting to discover, as I believe we do, that the principles of universal grammar are rich, abstract, and restrictive, and can be used to construct principled explanations for a variety of phenomena. At the present stage of our understanding, if language is to provide a springboard for the investigation of other problems of human nature, it is these aspects of language to which we will have to turn our attention, for the simple reason that it is only these aspects that are reasonably well understood. In another sense, the study of formal properties of language reveals something of the nature of humans in a negative way: it underscores, with great clarity, the limits of our understanding of those qualities of mind that are apparently unique to humans and that must enter into their cultural achievements in an intimate, if still quite obscure, manner.

In searching for a point of departure, one turns naturally to a period in the history of Western thought when it was possible to believe that "the thought of making freedom the sum and substance of philosophy has emancipated the human spirit in all its relationships, and . . . has given to science in all its parts a more powerful reorientation than any earlier revolution."[1] The word "revolution" bears multiple associations in this passage, for Schelling also proclaims that "man is born to act and not to speculate"; and when he writes that "the time has come to proclaim to a nobler humanity the freedom of the spirit, and no longer to have patience with men's tearful regrets for their lost chains," we hear the echoes of the libertarian thought and revolutionary acts of the late eighteenth century. Schelling writes that "the beginning and end of all philosophy is—Freedom." These words are invested with meaning and urgency at a time when people are struggling to cast off their chains, to resist authority that has lost its claim to legitimacy, to construct more humane and more democratic social institutions. It is at such a time that the philosopher may be driven to inquire into the nature of human freedom and its limits, and perhaps to conclude, with Schelling, that with respect to the human ego, "its essence is freedom"; and with respect to philosophy, "the highest dignity of Philosophy consists precisely therein, that it stakes all on human freedom."

We are living, once again, at such a time. A revolutionary ferment is sweeping the so-called Third World, awakening enormous masses from torpor and acquiescence in traditional authority. There are those who feel that the industrial societies as well are ripe for revolutionary change—and I do not refer only to representatives of the New Left.

The threat of revolutionary change brings forth repression and reaction. Its signs are evident in varying forms, in France, in the Soviet Union, in the United States—not least, in the city where we are meeting. It is natural, then, that we should consider, abstractly, the problems of human freedom, and turn with interest and serious attention to the thinking of an earlier period when archaic social institutions were subjected to critical analysis and sustained attack. It is natural and appropriate, so long as we bear in mind Schelling's admonition that man is born not merely to speculate but also to act.

One of the earliest and most remarkable of the eighteenth-century investigations of freedom and servitude is Rousseau's *Discourse on Inequality* (1755), in many ways a revolutionary tract. In it, he seeks to "set forth the origin and progress of inequality, the establishment and abuse of political societies, insofar as these things can be deduced from the nature of man by the light of reason alone." His conclusions were sufficiently shocking that the judges of the prize competition of the Academy of Dijon, to whom the work was originally submitted, refused to hear the manuscript through.[2] In it, Rousseau challenges the legitimacy of virtually every social institution, as well as individual control of property and wealth. These are "usurpations . . . established only on a precarious and abusive right . . . having been acquired only by force, force could take them away without [the rich] having grounds for complaint." Not even property acquired by personal industry is held "upon better titles." Against such a claim, one might object: "Do you not know that a multitude of your brethren die or suffer from need of what you have in excess, and that you needed express and unanimous consent of the human race to appropriate for yourself anything from common subsistence that exceeded your own?" It is contrary to the law of nature that "a handful of men be glutted with superfluities while the starving multitude lacks necessities."

Rousseau argues that civil society is hardly more than a conspiracy by the rich to guarantee their plunder. Hypocritically, the rich call upon their neighbors to "institute regulations of justice and peace to which all are obliged to conform, which make an exception of no one, and which compensate in some way for the caprices of fortune by equally subjecting the powerful and the weak to mutual duties"—those laws which, as Anatole France was to say, in their majesty deny to the rich and the poor equally the right to sleep under the bridge at night. By such arguments, the poor and weak were seduced: "All ran to meet their chains thinking they secured their freedom. . . ." Thus society and laws "gave new fetters to the weak and new forces to the rich, destroyed natural freedom for all time, established forever the law of property and inequality, changed a clever usurpation into an irrevocable right, and for the profit of a few ambitious men henceforth subjected the whole human race to work, servitude and misery." Governments inevitably tend toward arbitrary power, as "their corruption and extreme limit." This power is "by its nature illegitimate," and new revolutions must

> dissolve the government altogether or bring it closer to its legitimate institution. . . . The uprising that ends by strangling or dethroning a sultan is as lawful an act as those by which he disposed, the day before, of the lives and goods of his subjects. Force alone maintained him, force alone overthrows him.

What is interesting, in the present connection, is the path that Rousseau follows to reach these conclusions "by the light of reason alone," beginning with his ideas about human nature. He wants to see man "as nature formed him." It is from human nature that the principles of natural right and the foundations of social existence must be deduced.

> This same study of original man, of his true needs, and of the principles underlying his duties, is also the only good means one could use to remove those crowds of difficulties which present themselves concerning the origin of moral inequality, the true foundation of the body politic, the reciprocal rights of its members, and a thousand similar questions as important as they are ill explained.

To determine the nature of man, Rousseau proceeds to compare man and animal. Man is "intelligent, free . . . the sole animal endowed with reason." Animals are "devoid of intellect and freedom."

> In every animal I see only an ingenious machine to which nature has given senses in order to revitalize itself and guarantee itself, to a certain point, from all that tends to destroy or upset it. I perceive precisely the same things in the human machine, with the difference that nature alone does everything in the operations of a beast, whereas man contributes to his operations by being a free agent. The former chooses or rejects by instinct and the latter by an act

of freedom, so that a beast cannot deviate from the rule that is prescribed to it even when it would be advantageous for it to do so, and a man deviates from it often to his detriment. . . . it is not so much understanding which constitutes the distinction of man among the animals as it is his being a free agent. Nature commands every animal, and the beast obeys. Man feels the same impetus, but he realizes that he is free to acquiesce or resist; and it is above all in the consciousness of this freedom that the spirituality of his soul is shown. For physics explains in some way the mechanism of the senses and the formation of ideas; but in the power of willing, or rather of choosing, and in the sentiment of this power are found only purely spiritual acts about which the laws of mechanics explain nothing.

Thus the essence of human nature is human freedom and the consciousness of this freedom. So Rousseau can say that "the jurists, who have gravely pronounced that the child of a slave would be born a slave, have decided in other terms that a man would not be born a man."[3]

Sophistic politicians and intellectuals search for ways to obscure the fact that the essential and defining property of man is his freedom: "They attribute to men a natural inclination to servitude, without thinking that it is the same for freedom as for innocence and virtue—their value is felt only as long as one enjoys them oneself and the taste for them is lost as soon as one has lost them." In contrast, Rousseau asks rhetorically "whether, freedom being the most noble of man's faculties, it is not degrading one's nature, putting oneself on the level of beasts enslaved by instinct, even offending the author of one's being, to renounce without reservation the most precious of all his gifts and subject ourselves to committing all the crimes he forbids us in order to please a ferocious or insane master"—a question that has been asked, in similar terms, by many an American draft resister in the last few years, and by many others who are beginning to recover from the catastrophe of twentieth-century Western civilization, which has so tragically confirmed Rousseau's judgment:

Hence arose the national wars, battles, murders, and reprisals which make nature tremble and shock reason, and all those horrible prejudices which rank the honor of shedding human blood among the virtues. The most decent men learned to consider it one of their duties to murder their fellowmen; at length men were seen to massacre each other by the thousands without knowing why; more murders were committed on a single day of fighting and more horrors in the capture of a single city than were committed in the state of nature during whole centuries over the entire face of the earth.

The proof of his doctrine that the struggle for freedom is an essential human attribute, that the value of freedom is felt only as long as one enjoys it, Rousseau sees in "the marvels done by all free peoples to guard themselves from oppression." True, those who have abandoned the life of a free man

> do nothing but boast incessantly of the peace and repose they enjoy in their chains. . . . But when I see the others sacrifice pleasures, repose, wealth, power, and life itself for the preservation of this sole good which is so disdained by those who have lost it; when I see animals born free and despising captivity break their heads against the bars of their prison; when I see multitudes of entirely naked savages scorn European voluptousness and endure hunger, fire, the sword, and death to preserve only their independence, I feel that it does not behoove slaves to reason about freedom.

Rather similar thoughts were expressed by Kant, forty years later. He cannot, he says, accept the proposition that certain people "are not ripe for freedom," for example, the serfs of some landlord:

> If one accepts this assumption, freedom will never be achieved; for one can not arrive at the maturity for freedom without having already acquired it; one must be free to learn how to make use of one's powers freely and usefully. The first attempts will surely be brutal and will lead to a state of affairs more painful and dangerous than the former condition under the dominance but also the protection of an external authority. However, one can achieve reason only through one's own experiences and one must be free to be able to undertake them. . . . To accept the principle that freedom is worthless for those under one's control and that one has the right to refuse it to them forever, is an infringement on the rights of God himself, who has created man to be free.[4]

The remark is particularly interesting because of its context. Kant was defending the French Revolution, during the Terror, against those who claimed that it showed the masses to be unready for the privilege of freedom. Kant's remarks have contemporary relevance. No rational person will approve of violence and terror. In particular, the terror of the postrevolutionary state, fallen into the hands of a grim autocracy, has more than once reached indescribable levels of savagery. Yet no person of understanding or humanity will too quickly condemn the violence that often occurs when long-subdued masses rise against their oppressors, or take their first steps toward liberty and social reconstruction.

Let me return now to Rousseau's argument against the legitimacy of established authority, whether that of political power or of wealth. It is striking that his argument, up to this point, follows a familiar Cartesian model. Man is uniquely beyond the bounds of physical explanation; the beast, on the other hand, is merely an ingenious machine, commanded by natural law. Man's freedom and his consciousness of this freedom distinguish him from the beast-machine. The principles of mechanical explanation are incapable of accounting for these human properties, though they can account for sensation and even the combination of ideas, in which regard "man differs from a beast only in degree."

To Descartes and his followers, such as Cordemoy, the only sure sign that another organism has a mind, and hence also lies beyond the bounds of mechanical explanation, is its use of language in the normal, creative human fashion, free from control by identifiable stimuli, novel and innovative, appropriate to situations, coherent, and engendering in our minds new thoughts and ideas.[5] To the Cartesians, it is obvious by introspection that each man possesses a mind, a substance whose essence is thought; his creative use of language reflects this freedom of thought and conception. When we have evidence that another organism, too, uses language in this free and creative fashion, we are led to attribute to it as well a mind like ours. From similar assumptions regarding the intrinsic limits of mechanical explanation, its inability to account for man's freedom and consciousness of his freedom, Rousseau proceeds to develop his critique of authoritarian institutions, which deny to man his essential attribute of freedom, in varying degree.

Were we to combine these speculations, we might develop an interesting connection between language and freedom. Language, in its essential properties and the manner of its use, provides the basic criterion for determining that another organism is a being with a human mind and the human capacity for free thought and self-expression, and with the essential human need for freedom from the external constraints of repressive authority. Furthermore, we might try to proceed from the detailed investigation of language and its use to a deeper and more specific understanding of the human mind. Proceeding on this model, we might further attempt to study other aspects of that human nature which, as Rousseau rightly observes, must be correctly conceived if we are to be able to develop, in theory, the foundations for a rational social order.

I will return to this problem, but first I would like to trace further Rousseau's thinking about the matter. Rousseau diverges from the Cartesian tradition in several respects. He defines the "specific characteristic of the human species" as man's "faculty of self-perfection," which, "with the aid of circumstances, successively develops all the others, and resides among us as much in the species as in the individual." The faculty of self-perfection and of perfection of the human species through cultural transmission is not, to my knowledge, discussed in any similar terms by the Cartesians. However, I think that Rousseau's remarks might be interpreted as a development of the Cartesian tradition in an unexplored direction, rather than as a denial and rejection of it. There is no inconsistency in the notion that the restrictive attributes of mind underlie a historically evolving human nature that develops within the limits that they set; or that these attributes of mind provide the possibility for self-perfection; or that, by providing the consciousness of freedom, these essential attributes of human nature give man the opportunity to create social conditions and social forms to maximize the possibilities for freedom, diversity, and individual self-realization. To use an arithmetical analogy, the integers do not fail to be an infinite set merely because they do not exhaust the rational numbers. Analogously, it is no denial of man's capacity for infinite "self-perfection" to hold that there are intrinsic properties of mind that constrain his development. I would like to argue that in a sense the opposite is true, that without a system of formal constraints there are no creative acts; specifically, in the absence of intrinsic and restrictive properties of mind, there can be only "shaping of behavior" but no creative acts of self-perfection. Furthermore, Rousseau's concern for the evolutionary character of self-perfection brings us back, from another point of view, to a concern for human language, which would appear to be a prerequisite for such evolution of society and culture, for Rousseau's perfection of the species, beyond the most rudimentary forms.

Rousseau holds that "although the organ of speech is natural to man, speech itself is nonetheless not natural to him." Again, I see no inconsistency between this observation and the typical Cartesian view that innate abilities are "dispositional," faculties that lead us to produce ideas (specifically, innate ideas) in a particular manner under given conditions of external stimulation, but that also provide us with the ability to proceed in our thinking without such external factors. Language too, then, is natural to man only in a specific way. This is an important and, I believe, quite fundamental insight of the rationalist linguists that was disregarded, very largely, under the impact of empiricist psychology in the eighteenth century and since.[6]

Rousseau discusses the origin of language at some length, though he confesses himself to be unable to come to grips with the problem in a satisfactory way. Thus

> if men needed speech in order to learn to think, they had even greater need of knowing how to think in order to discover the art of speech. . . . So that one can hardly form tenable conjectures about this art of communicating thoughts and establishing inter-course between minds; a sublime art which is now very far from its origin. . . .

He holds that "general ideas can come into the mind only with the aid of words, and the understanding grasps them only through proposi-tions"—a fact which prevents animals, devoid of reason, from formulat-ing such ideas or ever acquiring "the perfectiblity which depends upon them." Thus he cannot conceive of the means by which "our new gram-marians began to extend their ideas and to generalize their words," or to develop the means "to express all the thoughts of men": "numbers, abstract words, aorists, and all the tenses of verbs, particles, syntax, the linking of propositions, reasoning, and the forming of all the logic of discourse." He does speculate about later stages of the perfection of the species, "when the ideas of men began to spread and multiply, and when closer communication was established among them, [and] they sought more numerous signs and a more extensive language." But he must, unhappily, abandon "the following difficult problem: which was most necessary, previously formed society for the institution of languages, or previously invented languages for the establishment of society?"

The Cartesians cut the Gordian knot by postulating the existence of a species-specific characteristic, a second substance that serves as what we might call a "creative principle" alongside the "mechanical principle" that determines totally the behavior of animals. There was, for them, no need to explain the origin of language in the course of historical evolution. Rather, man's nature is qualitatively distinct: there is no passage from body to mind. We might reinterpret this idea in more current terms by speculating that rather sudden and dramatic mutations might have led to qualities of intelligence that are, so far as we know, unique to humans, possession of language in the human sense being the most distinctive index of these qualities.[7] If this is correct, as at least a first approximation to the facts, the study of language might be expected to offer an entering wedge, or perhaps a model, for an investigation of human nature that would provide the grounding for a much broader theory of human nature.

To conclude these historical remarks, I would like to turn, as I have elsewhere,[8] to Wilhelm von Humboldt, one of the most stimulating and intriguing thinkers of the period. Humboldt was, on the one hand, one of the most profound theorists of general linguistics, and on the other, an early and forceful advocate of libertarian values. The basic concept of his philosophy is *Bildung,* by which, as J. W. Burrow expresses it, "he meant the fullest, richest and most harmonious development of the potentialities of the individual, the community or the human race."[9] His own thought might serve as an exemplary case. Though he does not, to my knowledge, explicitly relate his ideas about language to his libertarian social thought, there is quite clearly a common ground from which they develop, a concept of human nature that inspires each. Mill's essay *On Liberty* takes as its epigraph Humboldt's formulation of the "leading principle" of his thought: "the absolute and essential importance of human development in its richest diversity." Humboldt concludes his critique of the authoritarian state by saying: "I have felt myself animated throughout with a sense of the deepest respect for the inherent dignity of human nature, and for freedom, which alone befits that dignity." Briefly put, his concept of human nature is this:

> The true end of Man, or that which is prescribed by the eternal and immutable dictates of reason, and not suggested by vague and transient desires, is the highest and most harmonious development of his powers to a complete and consistent whole. Freedom is the first and indispensable condition which the possibility of such a development presupposes; but there is besides another essential—intimately connected with freedom, it is true—a variety of situations.[10]

Like Rousseau and Kant, he holds that

> nothing promotes this ripeness for freedom so much as freedom itself. This truth, perhaps, may not be acknowledged by those who have so often used this unripeness as an excuse for continuing repression. But it seems to me to follow unquestionably from the very nature of man. The incapacity for freedom can only arise from a want of moral and intellectual power; to heighten this power is the only way to supply this want; but to do this presupposes the exercise of the power, and this exercise presupposes the freedom which awakens spontaneous activity. Only it is clear we cannot call it giving freedom, when bonds are relaxed which are not felt as such by him who wears them. But of no man on earth—however neglected by nature, and however degraded by circumstances—is this true of all the bonds which oppress him. Let us undo them one by one, as the feeling of freedom awakens in men's hearts, and we shall hasten progress at every step.

Those who do not comprehend this "may justly be suspected of misunderstanding human nature, and of wishing to make men into machines."

Man is fundamentally a creative, searching, self-perfecting being: "To inquire and to create—these are the centres around which all human pursuits more or less directly revolve." But freedom of thought and enlightenment are not only for the elite. Once again echoing Rousseau, Humboldt states, "There is something degrading to human nature in the idea of refusing to any man the right to be a man." He is, then, optimistic about the effects on all of "the diffusion of scientific knowledge by freedom and enlightenment." But "all moral culture springs solely and immediately from the inner life of the soul, and can only be stimulated in human nature, and never produced by external and artificial contrivances." "The cultivation of the understanding, as of any of man's other faculties, is generally achieved by his own activity, his own ingenuity, or his own methods of using the discoveries of others. . . ." Education, then, must provide the opportunities for self-fulfillment; it can at best provide a rich and challenging environment for the individual to explore, in his own way. Even a language cannot, strictly speaking, be taught, but only "awakened in the mind: one can only provide the thread along which it will develop of itself." I think that Humboldt would have found congenial much of Dewey's thinking about education. And he might also have appreciated the recent revolutionary extension of such ideas, for example, by the radical Catholics of Latin America who are concerned with the "awakening of consciousness," referring to "the transformation of the passive exploited lower classes into conscious and critical masters of their own destinies"[11] much in the manner of Third World revolutionaries elsewhere. He would, I am sure, have approved of their criticism of schools that are

> more preoccupied with the transmission of knowledge than with the creation, among other values, of a critical spirit. From the social point of view, the educational systems are oriented to maintaining the existing social and economic structures instead of transforming them.[12]

But Humboldt's concern for spontaneity goes well beyond educational practice in the narrow sense. It touches also the question of labor and exploitation. The remarks, just quoted, about the cultivation of understanding through spontaneous action continue as follows:

> . . . man never regards what he possesses as so much his own, as what he does; and the labourer who tends a garden is perhaps in a truer sense its owner, than the listless voluptuary who enjoys its fruits. . . . In view of this consideration,[13] it seems as if all peasants

and craftsmen might be elevated into artists; that is, men who love their labour for its own sake, improve it by their own plastic genius and inventive skill, and thereby cultivate their intellect, ennoble their character, and exalt and refine their pleasures. And so humanity would be ennobled by the very things which now, though beautiful in themselves, so often serve to degrade it. . . . But, still, freedom is undoubtedly the indispensable condition, without which even the pursuits most congenial to individual human nature, can never succeed in producing such salutary influences. Whatever does not spring from a man's free choice, or is only the result of instruction and guidance, does not enter into his very being, but remains alien to his true nature; he does not perform it with truly human energies, but merely with mechanical exactness.

If a man acts in a purely mechanical way, reacting to external demands or instruction rather than in ways determined by his own interests and energies and power, "we may admire what he does, but we despise what he is."[14]

On such conceptions Humboldt grounds his ideas concerning the role of the state, which tends to "make man an instrument to serve its arbitrary ends, overlooking his individual purposes." His doctrine is classical liberal, strongly opposed to all but the most minimal forms of state intervention in personal or social life.

Writing in the 1790s, Humboldt had no conception of the forms that industrial capitalism would take. Hence he is not overly concerned with the dangers of private power.

> But when we reflect (still keeping theory distinct from practice) that the influence of a private person is liable to diminution and decay, from competition, dissipation of fortune, even death; and that clearly none of these contingencies can be applied to the State; we are still left with the principle that the latter is not to meddle in anything which does not refer exclusively to security. . . .

He speaks of the essential equality of the condition of private citizens, and of course has no idea of the ways in which the notion "private person" would come to be reinterpreted in the era of corporate capitalism. He did not foresee that "Democracy with its motto of *equality of all citizens before the law* and Liberalism with its *right of man over his own person* both [would be] wrecked on realities of capitalist economy."[15] He did not foresee that, in a predatory capitalist economy, state intervention would be an absolute necessity to preserve human existence and to prevent the destruction of the physical environment—I speak optimistically. As Karl Polanyi, for one, has pointed out, the self-adjusting market "could not exist for any length of time without annihilating the human and natural substance of society; it would have physically destroyed man and transformed his surroundings into a wilderness."[16] Humboldt did not foresee the consequences of the commodity character of labor, the doctrine (in Polanyi's words) that "it is not for the commodity to decide where it should be offered for sale, to what purpose it should be used, at what price it should be allowed to change hands, and in what manner it should be consumed or destroyed." But the commodity, in this case, is a human life, and social protection was therefore a minimal necessity to constrain the irrational and destructive workings of the classical free market. Nor did Humboldt understand that capitalist economic relations perpetuated a form of bondage which, as early as 1767, Simon Linguet had declared to be even worse than slavery.

> It is the impossibility of living by any other means that compels our farm laborers to till the soil whose fruits they will not eat, and our masons to construct buildings in which they will not live. It is want that drags them to those markets where they await masters who will do them the kindness of buying them. It is want that compels them to go down on their knees to the rich man in order to get from him permission to enrich him. . . . What effective gain has the suppression of slavery brought him? . . . He is free, you say. Ah! That is his misfortune. The slave was precious to his master because of the money he had cost him. But the handicraftsman costs nothing to the rich voluptuary who employs him. . . . These men, it is said, have no master—they have one, and the most terrible, the most imperious of masters, that is *need*. It is this that reduces them to the most cruel dependence.[17]

If there is something degrading to human nature in the idea of bondage, then a new emancipation must be awaited, Fourier's "third and last emancipatory phase of history," which will transform the proletariat to free men by eliminating the commodity character of labor, ending wage slavery, and bringing the commercial, industrial, and financial institutions under democratic control.[18]

Perhaps Humboldt might have accepted these conclusions. He does agree that state intervention in social life is legitimate if "freedom would destroy the very conditions without which not only freedom but even existence itself would be inconceivable"—precisely the circumstances that arise in an unconstrained capitalist economy. In any event, his criticism of bureaucracy and the autocratic state stands as an eloquent forewarning of some of the most dismal aspects of modern history, and the basis of his critique is applicable to a broader range of coercive institutions than he imagined.

Though expressing a classical liberal doctrine, Humboldt is no primitive individualist in the style of Rousseau. Rousseau extols the savage who "lives within himself"; he has little use for "the sociable man, always outside of himself, [who] knows how to live only in the opinion of others . . . from [whose] judgment alone . . . he draws the sentiment of his own existence."[19] Humboldt's vision is quite different:

> . . . the whole tenor of the ideas and arguments unfolded in this essay might fairly be reduced to this, that while they would break all fetters in human society, they would attempt to find as many new social bonds as possible. The isolated man is no more able to develop than the one who is fettered.

Thus he looks forward to a community of free association without coercion by the state or other authoritarian institutions, in which free men can create and inquire, and achieve the highest development of their powers—far ahead of his time, he presents an anarchist vision that is appropriate, perhaps, to the next stage of industrial society. We can perhaps look forward to a day when these various strands will be brought together within the framework of libertarian socialism, a social form that barely exists today though its elements can be perceived: in the guarantee of individual rights that has achieved its highest form—though still tragically flawed—in the Western democracies; in the Israeli *kibbutzim*; in the experiments with workers' councils in Yugoslavia; in the effort to awaken popular consciousness and create a new involvement in the social process which is a fundamental element in the Third World revolutions, coexisting uneasily with indefensible authoritarian practice.

A similar concept of human nature underlies Humboldt's work on language. Language is a process of free creation; its laws and principles are fixed, but the manner in which the principles of generation are used is free and infinitely varied. Even the interpretation and use of words involves a process of free creation. The normal use of language and the acquisition of language depend on what Humboldt calls the fixed form of language, a system of generative processes that is rooted in the nature of the human mind and constrains but does not determine the free creations of normal intelligence or, at a higher and more original level, of the great writer or thinker. Humboldt is, on the one hand, a Platonist who insists that learning is a kind of reminiscence, in which the mind, stimulated by experience, draws from its own internal resources and follows a path that it itself determines; and he is also a romantic, attuned to cultural variety, and the endless possibilities for the spiritual contributions of the creative genius. There is no contradiction in this, any more than there is a contradiction in the insistence of aesthetic theory that individual works of genius are constrained by principle and rule. The normal, creative use of language, which to the Cartesian rationalist is the best index of the existence of another mind, presupposes a system of rules and generative principles of a sort that the rationalist grammarians attempted, with some success, to determine and make explicit.

The many modern critics who sense an inconsistency in the belief that free creation takes place within—presupposes, in fact—a system of constraints and governing principles are quite mistaken; unless, of course, they speak of "contradiction" in the loose and metaphoric sense of Schelling, when he writes that "without the contradiction of necessity and freedom not only philosophy but every nobler ambition of the spirit would sink to that death which is peculiar to those sciences in which that contradiction serves no function." Without this tension between necessity and freedom, rule and choice, there can be no creativity, no communication, no meaningful acts at all.

I have discussed these traditional ideas at some length, not out of antiquarian interest, but because I think that they are valuable and essentially correct, and that they project a course we can follow with profit. Social action must be animated by a vision of a future society, and by explicit judgments of value concerning the character of this future society. These judgments must derive from some concept of human nature, and one may seek empirical foundations by investigating human nature as it is revealed by human behavior and human creations, material, intellectual, and social. We have, perhaps, reached a point in history when it is possible to think seriously about a society in which freely constituted social bonds replace the fetters of autocratic institutions, rather in the sense conveyed by the remarks of Humboldt that I quoted, and elaborated more fully in the tradition of libertarian socialism in the years that followed.

Predatory capitalism created a complex industrial system and an advanced technology; it permitted a considerable extension of democratic practice and fostered certain liberal values, but within limits that are now being pressed and must be overcome. It is not a fit system for the mid-twentieth century. It is incapable of meeting human needs that can be expressed only in collective terms, and its concept of competitive man who seeks only to maximize wealth and power, who subjects himself to market relationships, to exploitation and external authority, is antihuman and intolerable in the deepest sense. An autocratic state is no acceptable substitute; nor can the militarized state capitalism evolving in the United States or the bureaucratized, centralized welfare state be accepted as the goal of human existence. The only justification for repressive institutions is material and cultural deficit. But such institutions, at certain stages of history, perpetuate and produce such a deficit, and even threaten human survival. Modern science and technology can relieve people of the necessity for specialized, imbecile labor. They may, in principle, provide the basis for a rational social order based on free association and democratic control, if we have the will to create it.

A vision of a future social order is in turn based on a concept of human nature. If in fact humans are indefinitely malleable, completely plastic beings, with no innate structures of mind and no intrinsic needs of a cultural or social character, then they are fit subjects for the "shaping of behavior" by the state authority, the corporate manager, the technocrat, or the central committee. Those with some confidence in the human species will hope this is not so and will try to determine the intrinsic human characteristics that provide the framework for intellectual development, the growth of moral consciousness, cultural achievement, and participation in a free community. In a partly analogous way, a classical tradition spoke of artistic genius acting within and in some ways challenging a framework of rule. Here we touch on matters that are little understood. It seems to me that we must break away, sharply and radically, from much of modern social and behavioral science if we are to move toward a deeper understanding of these matters.

Here, too, I think that the tradition I have briefly reviewed has a contribution to offer. As I have already observed, those who were concerned with human distinctiveness and potential repeatedly were led to a consideration of the properties of language. I think that the study of language can provide some glimmerings of understanding of rule-governed behavior and the possibilities for free and creative action within the framework of a system of rules that in part, at least, reflect intrinsic properties of human mental organization. It seems to me fair to regard the contemporary study of language as in some ways a return to the Humboldtian concept of the form of language: a system of generative processes rooted in innate properties of mind but permitting, in Humboldt's phrase, an infinite use of finite means. Language cannot be described as a system of organization of behavior. Rather, to understand how language is used, we must discover the abstract Humboldtian form of language—its generative grammar, in modern terms. To learn a language is to construct for oneself this abstract system, of course unconsciously. The linguist and psychologist can proceed to study the use and acquisition of language only insofar as they have some grasp of the properties of the system that has been mastered by the person who knows the language. Furthermore, it seems to me that a good case can be made in support of the empirical claim that such a system can be acquired, under the given conditions of time and access, only by a mind that is endowed with certain specific properties that we can now tentatively describe in some detail. As long as we restrict ourselves, conceptually, to the investigation of behavior, its organization, its development through interaction with the environment, we are bound to miss these characteristics of language and mind. Other aspects of human psychology and culture might, in principle, be studied in a similar way.

Conceivably, we might in this way develop a social science based on empirically well-founded propositions concerning human nature. Just as we study the range of humanly attainable languages, with some success, we might also try to study the forms of artistic expression or, for that matter, scientific knowledge that humans can conceive, and perhaps even the range of ethical systems and social structures in which humans can live and function, given their intrinsic capacities and needs. Perhaps one might go on to project a concept of social organization that would—under given conditions of material and spiritual culture—best encourage and accommodate the fundamental human need—if such it is—for spontaneous initiative, creative work, solidarity, pursuit of social justice.

I do not want to exaggerate, as I no doubt have, the role of investigation of language. Language is the product of human intelligence that is, for the moment, most accessible to study. A rich tradition held language to be a mirror of mind. To some extent, there is surely truth and useful insight in this idea.

I am no less puzzled by the topic "language and freedom" than when I began—and no less intrigued. In these speculative and sketchy remarks there are gaps so vast that one might question what would remain, when metaphor and unsubstantiated guess are removed. It is sobering to realize—as I believe we must—how little we have progressed in our knowledge of human beings and society, or even in formulating clearly the problems that might be seriously studied. But there are, I think, a few footholds that seem fairly firm. I like to believe that the intensive study of one aspect of human psychology—human language—may contribute to a humanistic social science that will serve, as well, as an instrument for social action. It must, needless to say, be stressed that social action cannot await a firmly established theory of human nature and society, nor can the validity of the latter be determined by our hopes and moral judgments. The two—speculation and action—must progress as best they can, looking forward to the day when theoretical inquiry will provide a firm guide to the unending, often grim, but never hopeless struggle for freedom and social justice.

Psychology and Ideology

(1972)

CENTURY AGO, A VOICE OF BRITISH LIBERALISM DESCRIBED the "Chinaman" as "an inferior race of malleable orientals."[1] During the same years, anthropology became professionalized as a discipline, "intimately associated with the rise of raciology."[2] Presented with the claims of nineteenth-century racist anthropology, a rational person will ask two sorts of questions: what is the scientific status of the claims? and, what social or ideological needs do they serve? The questions are logically independent, but those of the second sort naturally come to the fore as scientific pretensions are undermined. In the case of nineteenth-century racist anthropology, the question of its scientific status is no longer seriously at issue, and it is not difficult to perceive its social function. If the Chinaman is malleable by nature, then what objection can there be to controls exercised by a superior race?

Consider now a generalization of the pseudoscience of the nineteenth century: it is not merely the heathen Chinese who are malleable by nature, but rather all people. Science has revealed that it is an illusion to speak of "freedom" and "dignity." What a person does is fully determined by his genetic endowment and history of reinforcement. Therefore we should make use of the best behavioral technology to shape and control behavior in the common interest.

Again, we may inquire into the exact meaning and scientific status of the claim, and the social functions it serves. Again, if the scientific status of whatever is clear is slight, then it is particularly interesting to consider the climate of opinion within which the claim is taken seriously.

In his speculations on human behavior, which are to be clearly distinguished from his experimental investigation of operant conditioning, B. F. Skinner offers a particular version of the theory of human malleability. The public reception is a matter of some interest. Skinner has been condemned as a trailblazer of totalitarian thinking and lauded for his advocacy of a tightly managed social environment. He is accused of immorality and praised as a spokesman for science and rationality in human affairs. He appears to be attacking fundamental human values, demanding control in place of the defense of freedom and dignity. There seems something scandalous in this, and since Skinner invokes the authority of science, some critics condemn science itself, or "the scientific view of man," for supporting such conclusions, while others assure us that science will "win out" over mysticism and irrational belief.

A close analysis shows that the appearance is misleading. Skinner is saying nothing about freedom and dignity, though he uses the words "freedom" and "dignity" in some odd and idiosyncratic sense. His speculations are devoid of scientific content and do not even hint at general outlines of a possible science of human behavior. Furthermore, Skinner imposes certain arbitrary limitations on scientific research which virtually guarantee continued failure.

As to its social implications, Skinner's science of human behavior, being quite vacuous, is as congenial to the libertarian as to the fascist. If certain of his remarks suggest one or another interpretation, it must be stressed that these do not follow from his "science" any more than their negations do. I think it would be more accurate to regard Skinner's *Beyond Freedom and Dignity* as a kind of Rorschach test. The fact that it is widely regarded as pointing the way to 1984 is, perhaps, a suggestive indication of certain tendencies in modern industrial society. There is little doubt that a theory of human malleability might be put to the service of totalitarian doctrine. If, indeed, freedom and dignity are merely the relics of outdated mystical beliefs, then what objection can there be to narrow and effective controls instituted to ensure "the survival of a culture"?

Given the prestige of science and the tendencies toward centralized authoritarian control that can easily be detected in modern industrial society, it is important to investigate seriously the claim that the science of behavior and a related technology provide the rationale and the means for control of behavior. What in fact has been demonstrated, or even plausibly suggested, in this regard?

Skinner assures us repeatedly that his science of behavior is advancing mightily and that there exists an effective technology of control. It is, he claims, a "fact that all control is exerted by the environment."[3] Consequently, "When we seem to turn control over to a person himself, we simply shift from one mode of control to another" (p. 97). The only serious task, then, is to design less "aversive" and more effective controls, an engineering problem. "The outlines of a technology are already clear" (p. 149). "We have the physical, biological, and behavioral technologies needed 'to save ourselves'; the problem is how to get people to use them" (p. 158).

It is a fact, Skinner maintains, that "behavior is shaped and maintained by its consequences" and that as the consequences contingent on behavior are investigated, more and more "they are taking over the explanatory functions previously assigned to personalities, states of mind, feelings, traits of character, purposes, and intentions" (p. 18).

> As a *science of behavior* adopts the strategy of physics and biology, the autonomous agent to which behavior has traditionally been attributed is replaced by the environment—the environment in which the species evolved and in which the behavior of the individual is shaped and maintained. [P. 184]

A "behavioral analysis" is thus replacing the "traditional appeal to states of mind, feelings, and other aspects of the autonomous man," and "is in fact much further advanced than its critics usually realize" (p. 160). Human behavior is a function of "conditions, environmental or genetic," and people should not object "when a scientific analysis traces their behavior to external conditions" (p. 75), or when a behavioral technology improves the system of control.

Not only has all of this been demonstrated; furthermore, it *must be* that as the science of behavior progresses, it will more fully establish these facts. "It is in the nature of scientific progress that the functions of autonomous man be taken over one by one as the role of the environment is better understood" (p. 58). This is the "scientific view," and "it is in the nature of scientific inquiry" that the evidence should shift in its favor (p. 101). "It is in the nature of an experimental analysis of human behavior that it should strip away the functions previously assigned to autonomous man and transfer them one by one to the controlling environment" (p. 198). Furthermore, physiology someday "will explain why behavior is indeed related to the antecedent events of which it can be shown to be a function" (p. 195).

These claims fall into two categories. In the first are claims about what has been discovered; in the second, assertions about what science must discover in its inexorable progress. It is likely that the hope or fear or resignation induced by Skinner's proclamations results, in part, from such assertions about the inevitability of scientific progress toward the demonstration that all control is exerted by the environment, that the ability of "autonomous man" to choose is an illusion.

Claims of the first sort must be evaluated in terms of the evidence presented for them. In the present instance, this is a simple task. No evidence is presented. In fact, as will become clear when we turn to more specific examples, the question of evidence is beside the point, since the claims dissolve into triviality or incoherence under analysis. Claims with regard to the inevitability of future discoveries are more ambiguous. Is Skinner saying that as a matter of necessity, science will show that behavior is completely determined by the environment? If so, his claim can be dismissed as pure dogmatism, foreign to the "nature of scientific inquiry." It is quite conceivable that as scientific understanding advances, it will reveal that even with full details about genetic endowment and personal history, a Laplacean omniscience could predict very little about what an organism will do. It is even possible that science may someday provide principled reasons for this conclusion (if indeed it is true). But perhaps Skinner is suggesting merely that the term "scientific understanding" be restricted to the prediction of behavior from environmental conditions. If so, then science may reveal, as it progresses, that "scientific understanding of human behavior," in this sense, is inherently limited. At the moment, we have virtually no scientific evidence and not the germs of an interesting hypothesis as to how human behavior is determined. Consequently we can only express our hopes and guesses as to what some future science may demonstrate. In any event, the claims that Skinner puts forth in this category are either dogmatic or uninteresting, depending on which interpretation we give to them.

The dogmatic element in Skinner's thinking is further revealed when he states that "the task of a scientific analysis is to explain how the behavior of a person as a physical system is related to the conditions under which the human species evolved and the conditions under which the individual lives" (p. 14). Surely the task of a scientific analysis is to discover the facts and explain them. Suppose that in fact the human brain operates by physical principles (perhaps now unknown) that provide for free choice, appropriate to situations but only marginally affected by environmental contingencies. The task of scientific analysis is not—as Skinner believes—to demonstrate that the conditions to which he restricts his attention fully determine human behavior, but rather to discover whether in fact they do (or whether they are at all significant), a very different matter. If they do not, as seems quite plausible, the "task of a scientific analysis" will be to clarify the issues and discover an intelligible explanatory theory that will deal with the actual facts. Surely no scientist would follow Skinner in insisting on the a priori necessity that scientific investigation will lead to a particular conclusion, specified in advance.

In support of his belief that science will demonstrate that behavior is entirely a function of antecedent events, Skinner notes that physics advanced only when it "stopped personifying things" and attributing to them "wills, impulses, feelings, purposes," and so on (p. 8). Therefore, he concludes, the science of behavior will progress only when it stops personifying people and avoids reference to "internal states." No doubt physics advanced by rejecting the view that a rock's wish to fall is a factor in its "behavior," because in fact a rock has no such wish. For Skinner's argument to have any force, he must show that people have wills, impulses, feelings, purposes, and the like no more than rocks do. If people differ from rocks in this respect, then a science of human behavior will have to take account of this fact.

Similarly Skinner is correct in asserting that "modern physics or most of biology" does not discuss such matters as "a crisis of belief" or "loss of confidence" (p. 10). Evidently, from this correct observation, nothing follows with regard to the science of human behavior. Physics and biology, Skinner observes, "did not advance by looking more closely at the jubilance of a falling body, or . . . the nature of vital spirits, and we do not need to try to discover what personalities, states of mind, feelings, traits of character, plans, purposes, intentions, or the other perquisites of autonomous man really are in order to get on with a scientific analysis of behavior"; and we must neglect "supposed mediating states of mind" (p. 15). This is true enough, if indeed there are no mediating states that can be characterized by an abstract theory of mind, and if personalities, etc., are no more real than the jubilance of a falling body. But if the factual assumptions are false, then we certainly do need to try to discover what the "perquisites of autonomous man" really are and to determine the "mediating states of mind"—at least this is so if we wish to develop a science of human behavior with any intellectual content and explanatory force. Skinner might argue, more rationally, that his "science" does not overlook these "perquisites" and inner states but rather accounts in other ways for the phenomena discussed in these terms. We shall see directly what substance there is to such a claim.

It is hardly possible to argue that science has advanced only by repudiating hypotheses concerning "internal states." By rejecting the study of postulated inner states, Skinner reveals his hostility not only to "the nature of scientific inquiry" but even to common engineering practice. For example, Skinner believes that "information theory" ran into a "problem when an inner 'processor' had to be invented to convert input into output" (p. 18). This is a strange way of describing the matter; "information theory" ran into no such "problem." Rather, the consideration of "inner processors" in the mathematical theory of communication or its applications to psychology followed normal scientific and engineering practice. Suppose that an investigator is presented with a device whose functioning he does not understand, and suppose that through experiment he can obtain information about input-output relations for this device. He would not hesitate, if rational, to construct a theory of the internal states of the device and to test it against further evidence. He might also go on to try to determine the mechanisms that function in the ways described by his theory of internal states, and the physical principles at work—leaving open the possibility that new and unknown physical principles might be involved, a particularly important matter in the study of the behavior of organisms. His theory of internal states might well be the only useful guide to further research. By objecting, a priori, to this commonplace research strategy, Skinner merely condemns his strange variety of "behavioral science" to continued ineptitude.

Skinner's antagonism to science is also revealed by his treatment of matters of fact. Psychologists concerned with the facts have argued that the child's acquisition of language and various concepts is in part a function of developmental age, that through maturational processes a child's language grows "like an embryo," and that isolation interferes with certain growth processes. Skinner rejects these hypotheses (pp. 139, 141, 221) and asserts rather that verbal and other environmental contingencies explain all of the observed phenomena. Neither here nor elsewhere does he provide any evidence or rational argument to this effect; nor does he show some other fault in the perfectly intelligible, though possibly incorrect, theories that he summarily rejects. (He does, however, give irrelevant objections that for some reason seem to him to be applicable—see pages cited above.) His dogmatism in this regard is particularly curious, since he would surely not deny that genetically determined maturational processes are involved in other aspects of development. But in this area he insists that the explanation must lie elsewhere. Though his conclusion might, by sheer accident, be correct, still it would be difficult to imagine an attitude more basically opposed to "the nature of scientific inquiry."

We cannot specify, a priori, what postulates and hypotheses are legitimate. Skinner's apriorism in this regard is no more legitimate than the claim that classical physics is not "science" because it appeals to the "occult force of gravity." If a concept or principle finds its place in an explanatory theory, it cannot be excluded on methodological grounds, as Skinner's discussion suggests. In general, Skinner's conception of science is very odd. Not only do his a priori methodological assumptions rule out all but the most trivial scientific theories; he is, furthermore, given to strange pronouncements such as the assertion that "the laws of science are descriptions of contingencies of reinforcement" (p. 189)—which I happily leave to others to decode.

It is important to bear in mind that Skinner's strictures do not define the practice of behavioral science. In fact, those who call themselves "behavioral scientists" or even "behaviorists" vary widely in the kinds of theoretical constructions that they are willing to admit. W. V. O. Quine, who on other occasions has attempted to work within the Skinnerian framework, goes so far as to define "behaviorism" simply as the insistence that conjectures and conclusions must eventually be verified in terms of observations.[4] As he points out, any reasonable person is a "behaviorist" in this sense. Quine's proposal signifies the demise of behaviorism as a substantive point of view, which is just as well. Whatever function "behaviorism" may have served in the past, it has become nothing more than a set of arbitrary restrictions on "legitimate" theory construction, and there is no reason why someone who investigates humans and society should accept the kind of intellectual shackles that physical scientists would surely not tolerate and that condemn any intellectual pursuit to insignificance.

Notice that what is at issue here is not "philosophical behaviorism," a set of ideas about legitimate claims to knowledge, but rather behaviorism as a set of conditions imposed on legitimate theory construction in the study of mental abilities and achievements and human social organization. Thus a person might accept Quine's version of "behaviorism" for scientific theory construction, thus in effect abandoning the doctrine, while still maintaining that the scientific theories constructed in accordance with the condition that hypotheses must eventually be verified in terms of observations do not truly constitute "knowledge." If consistent, such a person will also reject the natural sciences as not constituting "true knowledge." It is, of course, possible to impose conditions of arbitrary severity on the concept "knowledge." Whatever the interest of this enterprise may be, it is not what I am discussing here. Nor am I discussing the question whether the system of unconscious rules and principles that the mind constructs, or the innate schematism that provides the basis for such constructions, should properly be called "knowledge," or perhaps be given some other name. In my opinion, no investigation of the concept of "knowledge" in ordinary usage will provide an answer to these questions, since it is too vague and unclear at precisely the critical points. This, however, is not the question at issue in the present discussion, and I will pursue it no further here.

Let us consider more carefully what Skinner means when he asserts that all behavior is externally controlled and that behavior is a function of genetic and environmental conditions. Does he mean that full knowledge of such conditions would permit, in principle, specific predictions as to what a person will do? Surely not. Skinner means that genetic and environmental conditions determine "probability of response." But he is so vague about this notion that it is unclear whether his claims about determinism amount to anything at all. No one would doubt that the likelihood of my going to the beach depends on the temperature, or that the likelihood of my producing a sentence of English rather than Chinese is "determined" by my past experience, or that the likelihood of my producing a sentence of a human language rather than of some imaginable but humanly inaccessible system is "determined" by my genetic constitution. We hardly need behavioral science to tell us this. When we look for more specific predictions, however, we find virtually nothing. Worse, we discover that Skinner's a priori limitations on "scientific" inquiry make it impossible for him even to formulate the relevant concepts, let alone investigate them.

Consider, for example, the notion "likelihood of producing a sentence of English rather than Chinese." Given a characterization of "English" and "Chinese" by an abstract theory of postulated internal states (mental states, if you like), it is possible to give some meaning to this notion—though the probabilities, being negligible under any known characterization of determining factors, will be of no interest for the prediction of behavior.[5] But for Skinner, even this marginal achievement is impossible. For Skinner, what we call "knowledge of French" is a "repertoire acquired as a person learns to speak French" (p. 197). Therefore, probabilities will be defined over such "repertoires." But what does it mean to say that some utterance of English that I have never heard or produced belongs to my "repertoire," but not any utterance of Chinese (so that the former has a higher "probability")? Skinnerians, at this point in the discussion, appeal to "similarity" or "generalization," always without characterizing the ways in which a new expression is "similar" to familiar examples or "generalized" from them. The reason for this failure is simple. So far as is known, the relevant properties can be expressed only in terms of abstract theories which can be taken as descriptions of postulated internal states of the organism, and such theories are excluded, a priori, from Skinner's "science." The immediate consequence is that the Skinnerian must lapse into mysticism (unexplained "similarities" and "generalization" of a sort that cannot be specified) as soon as the discussion touches the world of fact. While the situation is perhaps clearer in the case of language, there is no reason to suppose that other aspects of human behavior will fall within the grasp of the "science" constrained by a priori Skinnerian restrictions.

It is interesting, incidentally, to see how Skinner's defenders respond to this inability to deal with concrete factual questions. Aubrey Yates, for example, refers to a criticism by Breger and McGaugh,[6] who argue that the Skinnerian approach to language learning and usage cannot handle facts that can be explained by postulating an abstract theory (a grammar) that is learned and used. Yates presents the following rebuttal, which he regards as "devastating": "the assertion that children learn and utilize a grammar is not . . . a 'fact' which Skinner has to explain, if his theory is to remain viable, but an *inference* or theoretical construct." "No one has ever observed a 'grammar' " and the child would be unable to specify it; "it is quite improper to set up a theoretical construct to account for complex verbal behavior and then demand that Skinner explain this theoretical construct by means of his own theory."[7]

But Breger and McGaugh do not insist that Skinner explain the theoretical construct "grammar" by means of his own theory (whatever this would mean); rather, they argue that by employing the theoretical construct "grammar" it is possible to account for important facts that escape the limits of Skinner's system. A proper answer would be that the proposed explanation fails, or that Skinner can explain these facts in some other way, or that the facts are not important for his particular purposes. But Yates' "devastating rebuttal," like Skinner's own refusal to face the problem, is merely an evasion. By similar logic, a mystic could argue that his account of planetary motion is not to be rejected on grounds of its inability to deal with the phenomena explained by Newtonian physics, which is, after all, merely a theory designed to account for the facts. As to the remark that the grammar cannot be "observed" or specified by the child, of course no theoretical construct is "observed," and the insistence that abstract characterizations of internal mental states be accessible to introspection, by the child or anyone else, is again (despite its distinguished ancestry) mere dogmatism, to be dismissed in serious inquiry. The explanatory theory that Berger and McGaugh discuss may be quite wrong, but it is irrelevant to remark that it cannot be observed or described by the person whose behavior is allegedly explained by use of this theory. Unfortunately, this kind of maneuver is all too typical.

Skinner's own response to criticism is no less illuminating. He believes that people attack him and argue against his "scientific picture of man" because "the scientific formulation has destroyed accustomed reinforcers" and causes "behavior previously reinforced by credit or admiration [to] undergo extinction," since "a person can no longer take credit or be admired for what he does." And extinction, he asserts, "often leads to aggressive attack" (p. 212). Elsewhere, he accuses his critics of "emotional instability," citing comments of Arthur Koestler and Peter Gay to the effect that behaviorism is "a monumental triviality" marked by "innate naïveté" and "intellectual bankruptcy" (p. 165). Skinner does not attempt to meet his criticism by presenting some relevant results that are not a monumental triviality. He is quite unable to perceive that objection to his "scientific picture of man" derives, not from extinction of certain behavior or opposition to science, but from an ability to distinguish science from triviality and obvious error. Skinner does not comprehend the basic criticism: when his formulations are interpreted literally, they are trivially true, unsupported by evidence, or clearly false; and when these assertions are interpreted in his characteristically vague and metaphorical way, they are merely a poor substitute for ordinary usage. Such criticisms cannot be overcome by verbal magic, by mere reiteration that his approach is scientific and that those who do not see this are opposed to science or deranged.

Similarly Skinner claims that Koestler's characterization of behaviorism is seventy years out of date, but does not indicate what great achievements of the past seventy years Koestler has neglected. In fact, the real achievements of behavioral science, so far as we know, in no way support Skinner's conclusions (insofar as these are nontrivial). It is for this reason, one must presume, that Skinner assures the reader that he has no "need to know the details of a scientific analysis of behavior" (p. 22), none of which are presented. It is not the depth or complexity of this theory that prevents Skinner from outlining it for the lay reader. For example, Jacques Monod, in his recent work on biology and human affairs,[8] gives a rather detailed presentation of achievements of modern biology that he believes to be relevant to his (clearly identified) speculations. I should add, to make myself clear, that I am not criticizing Skinner for the relative lack of significant achievement in the behavioral sciences as compared to, say, biology, but rather for his irresponsible claims regarding the "science of behavior" which the reader need not know but which has allegedly produced all sorts of remarkable results concerning the control of behavior.

Let us now turn to the evidence that Skinner provides for his extraordinary claims: as, that "an analysis of behavior" reveals that the achieve-

ments of artists, writers, statesmen, and scientists can be explained almost entirely in terms of environmental contingencies (p. 44); that it is
the environment that makes a person wise or compassionate (p. 171); that
"all these questions about purposes, feelings, knowledge, and so on, can
be restated in terms of the environment to which a person has been
exposed" and that "what a person 'intends to do' depends on what he
has done in the past and what has then happened" (p. 72); and so on.

According to Skinner, apart from genetic endowment, behavior is determined entirely by reinforcement. To a hungry organism, food is a
positive reinforcer. This means that "anything the organism does that is
followed by the receipt of food is more likely to be done again whenever
the organism is hungry" (p. 27); but "food is reinforcing only in a state
of deprivation" (p. 37). A negative reinforcer is a stimulus that increases
the probability of behavior that reduces the intensity of that stimulus; it
is "aversive" and, roughly speaking, constitutes a threat (p. 27). A stimulus can become a conditioned reinforcer by association with other reinforcers. Thus money is "reinforcing only after it has been exchanged for
reinforcing things" (p. 33). The same is generally true of approval and
affection. (The reader may attempt something that Skinner always avoids,
namely, to characterize the "stimuli" that constitute "approval"—for
example, why is the statement "This article ought to appear in journal
such-and-such" an instance of "approval" when made by one person and
of "disapproval" when made by another?) Behavior is shaped and maintained by the arrangement of such reinforcers. Thus "we change the
relative strengths of responses by differential reinforcement of alternative courses of action" (pp. 94–95); one's repertoire of behavior is determined by "the contingencies of reinforcement to which he is exposed as
an individual" (p. 127); "an organism will range between vigorous activity and complete quiescence depending upon the schedules on which it
has been reinforced" (p. 186). As Skinner realizes (though some of his
defenders do not),[9] meticulous control is necessary to shape behavior in
highly specific ways. Thus "the culture . . . teaches a person to make fine
discriminations by making differential reinforcement more precise" (p.
194), a fact which causes problems when "the verbal community cannot
arrange the subtle contingencies necessary to teach fine distinctions
among stimuli which are inaccessible to it"; "as a result the language of
emotion is not precise" (p. 106).

The problem in "design of a culture" is to "make the social environment as free as possible of aversive stimuli" (p. 42), "to make life less
punishing and in doing so to release for more reinforcing activities the
time and energy consumed in the avoidance of punishment" (p. 81). It
is an engineering problem, and we could get on with it if only we could
overcome the irrational concern for freedom and dignity. What we re-

quire is the more effective use of the available technology, more and better controls. In fact, "a technology of behavior is available which would more successfully reduce the aversive consequences of behavior, proximate or deferred, and maximize the achievements of which the human organism is capable" (p. 125). But "the defenders of freedom oppose its use," thus contributing to social malaise and human suffering. It is this irrationality that Skinner hopes to persuade us to overcome.

At this point, an annoying though obvious question intrudes. If Skinner's thesis is false, then there is no point in his having written the book or our reading it. But if his thesis is true, then there is also no point in his having written the book or our reading it. For the only point could be to modify behavior, and behavior, according to the thesis, is entirely controlled by arrangement of reinforcers. Therefore, reading the book can modify behavior only if it is a reinforcer, that is, if reading the book increases the probability of the behavior which led to reading the book (assuming an appropriate state of deprivation). At this point, we seem to be reduced to gibberish.

As a counterargument, it might be claimed that even if the thesis is false, there is a point to writing and reading the book, since certain false theses are illuminating and provocative. But this escape is hardly available. In this case, the thesis is elementary and not of much interest in itself. Its only value lies in its possible truth. But if the thesis is true, then reading or writing the book would appear to be an entire waste of time, since it reinforces no behavior.

Skinner would surely argue that reading the book, or perhaps the book itself, is a "reinforcer" in some other sense. He wants us to be persuaded by the book, and, not to our surprise, he refers to persuasion as a form of behavioral control, albeit a weak and ineffective form. Skinner hopes to persuade us to allow greater scope to the behavioral technologists, and apparently believes that reading this book will increase the probability of our behaving in such a way as to permit them greater scope (freedom?). Thus reading the book, he might claim, reinforces this behavior. It will change our behavior with respect to the "science of behavior" (p. 24).

Let us overlook the problem, insuperable in his terms, of specifying the notion "behavior that gives greater scope to behavioral technologists," and consider the claim that reading the book might reinforce such behavior. Unfortunately the claim is clearly false, if we use the term "reinforce" with anything like its technical meaning. Recall that reading the book reinforces the desired behavior only if it is a consequence of the behavior, and obviously putting our fate in the hands of behavioral technologists is not behavior that led to (and hence can be reinforced by) reading Skinner's book. Therefore, the claim can be true only if we deprive the term "reinforce" of its technical meaning. Combining these observations, we see that there can be some point to reading the book or to Skinner's having written it only if the thesis of the book is divorced from the "science of behavior" on which it allegedly rests.

Let us consider further the matter of "persuasion." According to Skinner, we persuade ("change minds") "by manipulating environmental contingencies," specifically "by pointing to stimuli associated with positive consequences" and "making a situation more favorable for action, as by describing likely reinforcing consequences" (pp. 91–93). Even if we overlook the fact that persuasion, so characterized, is a form of control (a variety of "reinforcement") unknown to Skinner's science, his argument is in no way advanced. Suppose Skinner were to claim that his book might persuade us by pointing to positive consequences of behavioral technology. But this will not do at all. It is not enough for him to point to those consequences (for example, to draw pictures of happy people); rather, he must show that these are indeed *consequences* of the recommended behavior. To persuade us, he must establish a connection between the recommended behavior and the pleasant situation he describes. The question is begged by use of the term "consequences."[10] It is not enough merely to conjoin a description of the desired behavior and a description of the "reinforcing" state of affairs (overlooking, again, that not even these notions are expressible in Skinner's terms). Were that sufficient for "persuasion," then we could "persuade" someone of the opposite by merely conjoining a description of an unpleasant state of affairs with a description of the behavior that Skinner hopes to produce.

If persuasion were merely a matter of pointing to reinforcing stimuli and the like, then any persuasive argument would retain its force if its steps were randomly interchanged, or if some of its steps were replaced by arbitrary descriptions of reinforcing stimuli. And the argument would lose its force if descriptions of unwelcome circumstances were randomly introduced. Of course, this is nonsense. For an argument to be persuasive, at least to a rational person, it must be coherent; its conclusions must follow from its premises. But these notions are entirely beyond the scope of Skinner's framework. When he states that "deriving new reasons from old, the process of deduction" merely "depends upon a much longer verbal history" (p. 96), he is indulging in hand-waving of a most pathetic sort. Neither Skinner nor anyone else has offered the faintest hint that "the process of deduction" can be characterized in his terms on the basis of "verbal history," however long. An approach that cannot even formulate properly, let alone solve, the problem of why some new expression is intelligible, but not, say, a permutation of its component elements (see above, p. 164), cannot even begin to consider the notions "coherent argument" or "process of deduction."

Consider Skinner's claim that "we sample and change verbal behavior, not opinions" (so a behavioral analysis reveals) (p. 95). Taken literally, this means that if, under a credible threat of torture, I force someone to say, repeatedly, that the Earth stands still, then I have changed his opinion. Comment is unnecessary, and we perceive at once the significance of the "behavioral analysis" that yields this conclusion.

Skinner claims that persuasion is a weak method of control, and he asserts that "changing a mind is condoned by the defenders of freedom and dignity because it is an ineffective way of changing behavior, and the changer of minds can therefore escape from the charge that he is controlling people" (p. 97). Suppose that your doctor gives you a powerful and rational argument to the effect that if you continue to smoke, you will die a horrible death from lung cancer. Is it necessarily the case that this argument will be less effective in modifying your behavior than any arrangement of true reinforcers? In fact, whether persuasion is effective or not depends on the content of the argument (for a rational person), a factor that Skinner cannot begin to describe. The problem becomes still worse if we consider other forms of "changing minds." Suppose that a description of a napalm raid on a Vietnamese village induces someone in an American audience to carry out an act of sabotage. In this case, the effective stimulus is not a reinforcer, the mode of changing behavior may be quite effective, and the act that is performed (the behavior "reinforced") is entirely new (not in the "repertoire") and may not even have been hinted at in the "stimulus" that induced the change of behavior. In every possible respect, then, Skinner's account is simply incoherent.

Since his William James lectures of 1947,[11] Skinner has been sparring with these and related problems. The results are nil. It remains impossible for Skinner to formulate the relevant notions in his terms, let alone investigate them. What is more, no nontrivial scientific hypotheses with supporting evidence have been produced to substantiate the extravagant claims to which he is addicted.[12] Furthermore, this record of failure was predictable from the start, from an analysis of the problems and the means proposed to deal with them. It must be stressed that "verbal behavior" is the only aspect of human behavior that Skinner has attempted to investigate in any detail. To his credit, he recognized quite early that only through a successful analysis of language could he hope to come to terms with human behavior. By comparing the results that have been achieved in this twenty-five-year period with the claims that are still advanced, we gain a good insight into the nature of Skinner's science of behavior. My impression is, in fact, that the claims are becoming more extreme and more strident as the inability to support them and the reasons for this failure become increasingly obvious.

It is unnecessary to labor the point any further. Evidently Skinner has no way of dealing with the factors that are involved in persuading someone or changing his mind. The attempt to invoke "reinforcement" merely leads to incoherence or pretense. The point is crucial. Skinner's discussion of persuasion and "changing minds" is one of the few instances in which he tries to come to terms with what he calls the "literature of freedom and dignity." The libertarian whom he condemns distinguishes between persuasion and certain forms of control. He advocates persuasion and objects to coercion. In response, Skinner claims that persuasion is itself a (weak) form of control and that by using weak methods of control we simply shift control to other environmental conditions, not to the person himself (pp. 97, 99). Thus, Skinner claims, the advocate of freedom and dignity is deluding himself in his belief that persuasion leaves the matter of choice to "autonomous man," and furthermore he poses a danger to society because he stands in the way of more effective controls. As we see, however, Skinner's argument against the "literature of freedom and dignity" is without force. Persuasion is no form of control at all, in Skinner's sense; in fact, he is quite unable to deal with the concept in his terms.

But there is little doubt that persuasion can "change minds" and affect behavior, on occasion, quite drastically. Since persuasion cannot be coherently described in terms of arrangement of reinforcers, it follows that behavior is not entirely determined by the specific contingencies to which Skinner arbitrarily restricts his attention, and that the major thesis of the book is false. Skinner can escape this conclusion only by claiming that persuasion *is* a matter of arranging reinforcing stimuli, but this claim is tenable only if the term "reinforcement" is deprived of its technical meaning and used as a mere substitute for the detailed and specific terminology of ordinary language (similarly the notion of "arrangement or scheduling of reinforcement"). In any event, Skinner's "science of behavior" is irrelevant; the thesis of the book is either false (if we use terminology in its technical sense) or empty (if we do not). And the argument against the libertarian collapses entirely.

Not only is Skinner unable to uphold his claim that persuasion is a form of control, but he also offers not a particle of evidence to support his claim that the use of "weak methods of control" simply shifts the mode of control to some obscure environmental factor rather than to the mind of autonomous man. Of course, from the thesis that all behavior is controlled by the environment, it follows that reliance on weak rather than strong controls shifts control to other aspects of the environment. But the thesis, insofar as it is at all clear, is without empirical support, and in fact may even be quite empty, as we have seen in discussing "probability of response" and persuasion. Skinner is left with no coherent criticism of the "literature of freedom and dignity."

The emptiness of Skinner's system is nicely illustrated in his treatment of more peripheral matters. He claims (p. 112) that the statement "You should (you ought to) read *David Copperfield*" may be translated "You will be reinforced if you read *David Copperfield.*" But what does this mean? Literally applying Skinner's definition (see above), it means that behavior that is followed by reading *David Copperfield* is more likely to be done again if you are in need of reading. Or perhaps it means that the act of reading *David Copperfield* will be followed by some stimulus that will increase the probability of this act. When I tell someone that he ought to read *David Copperfield,* then, I am telling him something of this sort. Suppose, say, I told you that you should read *David Copperfield* because this would disabuse you of the notion that Dickens is worth reading, or show you what true boredom really is. In fact, no matter how we try to interpret Skinner's suggestion, giving the term "reinforce" something like its literal sense, we fall into utter confusion.

Probably what Skinner has in mind in using the phrase "You will be reinforced if you read *David Copperfield*" is that you will like it, enjoy it, or learn something useful, and thus be "reinforced." But this gives the game away. We are now using "reinforce" in a sense quite different from that of the operant-conditioning paradigm. It would make no sense at all to try to apply results about scheduling of reinforcement, for example, to this situation. Furthermore, it is no wonder that we can "explain" behavior by using the nontechnical term "reinforce" with the full range of meaning of "like" or "enjoy" or "learn something from" or whatever. Similarly, when Skinner tells us that a fascinating hobby is "reinforcing" (p. 36), he is surely not claiming that the behavior that leads to indulging in this hobby will be increased in probability. Rather, he means that we enjoy the hobby. A literal interpretation of such remarks yields gibberish, and a metaphorical interpretation merely replaces an ordinary term by a homonym of a technical term, with no gain in precision.

The system of Skinnerian translation is quite readily available to anyone and can indeed be employed with no knowledge of the theory of operant conditioning and its results, and with no information, beyond normal observation, of the circumstances in which behavior takes place or the nature of the behavior itself. Recognizing this fact, we can appreciate the value of Skinner's "science of behavior" for the purposes at hand, and the insights it provides. But it is important to bear in mind that this system of translation leads to a significant loss of precision, for the simple reason that the full range of terms for the description and evaluation of behavior, attitude, opinion, and so on must be translated into the impoverished system of terminology borrowed from the laboratory (and deprived of its meaning in transition).[13] It is hardly surprising, then, that Skinnerian translation generally misses the point, even with the metaphorical use of such terms as "reinforce." Thus Skinner asserts that "a person wants something if he acts to get it when the occasion arises" (p. 37). It follows that it is impossible to act to get something, given the opportunity, but not to want it—say, to act thoughtlessly, or out of a sense of duty (we can, as usual, reduce Skinner's assertion to triviality by saying that what the person wants is to do his duty, and so on). It is clear from the context that Skinner means "if" as "if and only if." Thus it follows from his definition of "want" that it is impossible for a person to want something but not to act to get it when the occasion arises, say for reasons of conscience (again, we can escape to triviality by assigning such reasons to the "occasion"). Or consider the claim that "we are likely to admire behavior more as we understand it less" (p. 53). In a strong sense of "explain," it follows that we admire virtually all behavior, since we can explain virtually none. In a looser sense, Skinner is claiming that if Eichmann is incomprehensible to us but we understand why the Vietnamese fight on, then we are likely to admire Eichmann but not the Vietnamese resistance.

The real content of Skinner's system can be appreciated only by examining such cases, for example, as the following:

"Except when physically restrained, a person is least free or dignified when he is under threat of punishment" (p. 60). Thus someone who refuses to bend to authority in the face of severe threat has lost all dignity.

"We read books which help us say things we are on the verge of saying anyway but cannot quite say without help," and thus "we understand the author" (p. 86). Is the point supposed to be that we do not read books that we expect to disagree with, and would not be able to understand what they say? If not, the claim is empty. If so, it is absurd.

Things we call "good" are positive reinforcers and things we call "bad" are negative reinforcers (pp. 104, 107); we work to achieve positive reinforcers and avoid negative reinforcers (p. 107).[14] This explains why people, by definition, always seek good and avoid evil. Furthermore, "behavior is called good or bad . . . according to the way it is usually reinforced by others" (p. 109). As long as Hitler was being "reinforced" by events and by those around him, his behavior was good. On the other hand, the behavior of Dietrich Bonhoeffer and Martin Niemoeller was, by definition, bad. In the Biblical tale, it was self-contradictory to seek ten good men in Sodom. Recall that the study of operant reinforcement, the conclusions of which we are now reviewing, is "a science of values" (p. 104).

"A person acts intentionally . . . in the sense that his behavior has been strengthened by consequences" (p. 108)—as in the case of a person who intentionally commits suicide.

The hero who has killed a monster is reinforced by praise "precisely to induce him to take on other monsters" (p. 111)—and thus is never praised on his deathbed or at his funeral.

The statement "You should (you ought to) tell the truth" means, in this science of value, "If you are reinforced by the approval of your fellow men, you will be reinforced when you tell the truth" (p. 112). In a subculture so cynical that telling the truth is regarded as absurd and not approved, one who is reinforced by approval ought not to tell the truth. Or to be more precise, the statement "You ought to tell the truth" is false. Similarly, it is wrong to tell someone not to steal if he is almost certain to get away with it, since "You ought not to steal" can be translated "If you tend to avoid punishment, avoid stealing" (p. 114).

"Scientific discoveries and inventions are improbable; that is what is meant by discovery and invention" (p. 155). Thus by arranging mathematical formulas in some novel and improbable way, I succeed (by definition) in making a mathematical discovery.

Stimuli attract attention because they have been associated with important things and have figured in contingencies of reinforcement (p. 187). Thus if a cat with two heads walked into a room, only those to whom cats were important would notice it; others would pay no attention. An entirely new stimulus—new to the species or the individual—would be entirely ignored.

A person may derive his rules of behavior "from an analysis of punitive contingencies" (p. 69), and a person may be reinforced "by the fact that the culture will long survive him" (p. 210). Thus something imagined can be a "reinforcing stimulus." (Try to apply to this example the fanciful discussion of "conditioned reinforcers" that "usurp" the reinforcing effort of deferred consequences—pp. 120–22.)

A person "behaves bravely when environmental circumstances induce him to do so" (p. 197). Since, as noted earlier, we act to achieve positive reinforcers, we can conclude that no one behaves bravely when punishment or death is a likely consequence (unless he is "reinforced" by "stimuli" that impinge on him after his death).

A young man who is dissatisfied, discouraged, frustrated, has no sense of purpose, and so on is simply one who is not properly reinforced (pp. 146–47). Therefore, no one has such feelings if he can attain wealth and the positive reinforcers it can buy.

Notice that in most of these cases, perhaps all, we can convert error to tautology by relying on the vagueness of the Skinnerian terminology, for example, by using "reinforcement" as a cover term for whatever is liked, wanted, intended, and so on.

We can get a taste of the explanatory force of Skinner's theory from such (quite typical) examples as these: a pianist learns to play a scale smoothly because "smoothly played scales are reinforcing" (p. 204); "A person can know what it is to fight for a cause only after a long history during which he has learned to perceive and to know that state of affairs called fighting for a cause" (p. 190); and so on.

Similarly, we can perceive the power of Skinner's behavioral technology by considering the useful observations and advice he offers: "Punishable behavior can be minimized by creating circumstances in which it is not likely to occur" (p. 64); if a person "is strongly reinforced when he sees other people enjoying themselves . . . he will design an environment in which children are happy" (p. 150); if overpopulation, nuclear war, pollution, and depletion of resources are a problem, "we may then change practices to induce people to have fewer children, spend less on nuclear weapons, stop polluting the environment, and consume resources at a lower rate, respectively" (p. 152).

The reader may search for more profound thoughts than these. He may seek, but he will not find.

In this book, Skinner alludes more frequently to the role of genetic endowment than in his earlier speculations about human behavior and society. One would think that this would lead to some modification in his conclusions, or to new conclusions. It does not. The reason is that Skinner is as vague and uninformative about genetic endowment as he is about control by contingencies of reinforcement. Unfortunately zero plus zero still equals zero.

According to Skinner, "the ease with which mentalistic explanations can be invented on the spot is perhaps the best gauge of how little attention we should pay to them" (p. 160). We can turn this into a true statement by replacing "mentalistic" with "Skinnerian." In fact, a Skinnerian translation is always available for any description of behavior—we can always say that an act is performed because it is "reinforcing" or "reinforced" or because the contingencies of reinforcement shaped behavior in this way, and so on. There is a handy explanation for any eventuality, and given the vacuity of the system, we can never be proved wrong.

But Skinner's comment on "mentalistic explanations" is surely incorrect, given his usage of this term. Consider, for example, the expressions (1) through (4):

(1) The two men promised their wives to kill each other.
(2) The two men persuaded their wives to kill each other.
(3) The two men promised me to kill each other.
(4) The two men persuaded me to kill each other.

We understand these sentences (even if they are new in our experience) in the following way: (1) is a close paraphrase of "Each of the two men promised his wife to kill the other" and means that the men are to kill each other; (2) is a close paraphrase of "The two men persuaded their wives each to kill the other" and means that the wives are to kill each other; (3) is a close paraphrase of "Each of the two men promised me to kill the other"; but (4) cannot be paraphrased in any of these ways, and in fact is not a sentence of our "repertoire" at all. One can propose an explanation for such facts as these within an abstract theory of language, a theory that Skinner would (quite legitimately) call "mentalistic." It is, however, not at all easy to invent a satisfactory "mentalistic explanation" for these and many related facts,[15] that is, a system of general principles that will explain these facts and will not be refuted by other facts. To construct a theory of "internal (mental) states" is no easy task, contrary to what Skinner believes; though in this case too a Skinnerian explanation, employing the mystical notions "similar" and "generalize," can of course be invented on the spot, no matter what the facts may be. Skinner's failure to understand this results from his unwillingness to attempt to construct explanatory theories that have empirical content in the domain of human thought and action. Because of this unwillingness, there is also no discernible progress—today's formulations in this domain are hardly different from those of fifteen or twenty years ago—and no convincing refutation, for those who are untroubled by the fact that explanations can be invented on the spot, whatever the facts may be, within a system that is devoid of substance.

We have so far been considering the scientific status of Skinner's claims. Let us now turn to the matter of "design of a culture." The principles of Skinner's "science" tell us nothing about designing a culture (since they tell us virtually nothing), but that is not to say that Skinner leaves us completely in the dark as to what he has in mind. He believes that "the control of the population as a whole must be delegated to specialists—to police, priests, owners, teachers, therapists, and so on, with their specialized reinforcers and their codified contingencies" (p. 155). The controller and the designer of a culture should be members of the group that is controlled (p. 172). When the technology of behavior is "applied to the design of a culture, the survival of the culture functions as a value." If our culture "continues to take freedom or dignity, rather than its own survival, as its principal value, then it is possible that some other culture will make a greater contribution to the future." The refusal to exercise available controls may be "a lethal cultural mutation." "Life, liberty, and the pursuit of happiness are basic rights . . . [but] they have only a minor bearing on the survival of a culture" (pp. 180–83); one might wonder, then, what importance they have for the behavioral technologist who takes the survival of the culture as a value. These and similar observations, to which we turn directly, may be what led some readers to suspect that Skinner is advocating a form of totalitarian control.

There is no doubt that in his specific recommendations, vague though they are, Skinner succeeds in differentiating his position from the "literature of freedom." Skinner claims that the latter has "overlooked . . .

control which does not have aversive consequences at any time" (p. 41) and has encouraged opposition to all control, whereas he is proposing a much more extensive use of controls that have no aversive consequences. The most obvious form of control of this benign type is differential wages. It is, of course, incorrect to say that the "literature of freedom" has overlooked such controls. Since the industrial revolution, it has been much concerned with the problems of "wage slavery" and the "benign" forms of control that rely on deprivation and reward rather than direct punishment. This concern clearly distinguishes the literature of freedom from Skinner's social concepts. Or consider freedom of speech. Skinner's approach suggests that control of speech by direct punishment should be avoided, but that it is quite appropriate for speech to be controlled, say, by restricting good jobs to people who say what is approved by the designer of the culture. In accordance with Skinner's ideas, there would be no violation of academic freedom if promotions were granted only to those who conform, in their speech and writings, to the rules of the culture, though it would be wrong to go further and punish those who deviate by saying what they believe to be true. Such deviants will simply remain in a state of deprivation. In fact, by giving people strict rules to follow, so that they know just what to say to be "reinforced" by promotion, we will be "making the world safer" and thus achieving the ends of behavioral technology (pp. 74, 81). The literature of freedom would, quite properly, reject and abhor such controls.

In fact, there is nothing in Skinner's approach that is incompatible with a police state in which rigid laws are enforced by people who are themselves subject to them and the threat of dire punishment hangs over all. Skinner argues that the goal of a behavioral technology is to "design a world in which behavior likely to be punished seldom or never occurs"—a world of "automatic goodness" (p. 66). The "real issue," he explains, "is the effectiveness of techniques of control" which will "make the world safer." We make the world safer for "babies, retardates, or psychotics" by arranging matters so that punishable behavior rarely occurs. If only all people could be treated in this way, "much time and energy would be saved" (pp. 66, 74). Skinner even offers, perhaps unintentionally, some indications as to how this benign environment might be brought into being:

A state which converts all its citizens into spies or a religion which promotes the concept of an all-seeing God makes escape from the punisher practically impossible, and punitive contingencies are then maximally effective. People behave well although there is no visible supervision. [Pp. 67–68]

Elsewhere, we learn that "of course" freedom "waxes as visible control wanes" (p. 70). Therefore the situation just described is one of maximal freedom, since there is no visible control; for the same reason, it is a situation of maximal dignity. Furthermore, since "our task" is simply "to make life less punishing" (p. 81), the situation just described would seem ideal. Since people behave well, life will be minimally punishing. In this way, we can progress "toward an environment in which men are automatically good" (p. 73).

Extending these thoughts, consider a well-run concentration camp with inmates spying on one another and the gas ovens smoking in the distance, and perhaps an occasional verbal hint as a reminder of the meaning of this reinforcer. It would appear to be an almost perfect world. Skinner claims that a totalitarian state is morally wrong because of its deferred aversive consequences (p. 174). But in the delightful culture we have just designed, there should be no aversive consequences, immediate or deferred. Unwanted behavior will be eliminated from the start by the threat of the crematoria and the all-seeing spies. Thus all behavior would be automatically "good," as required. There would be no punishment. Everyone would be reinforced—differentially, of course, in accordance with ability to obey the rules. Within Skinner's scheme, there is no objection to this social order. Rather, it seems close to ideal. Perhaps we could improve it still further by noting that "the release from threat becomes more reinforcing the greater the threat" (as in mountain-climbing; p. 111). We can, then, enhance the total reinforcement and improve the culture by devising a still more intense threat, say, by introducing occasional screams, or by flashing pictures of hideous torture as we describe the crematoria to our fellow citizens. The culture might survive, perhaps for a thousand years.

Though Skinner's recommendations might be read in this way, nevertheless it would be improper to conclude that Skinner is advocating concentration camps and totalitarian rule (though he also offers no objection). Such a conclusion overlooks a fundamental property of Skinner's science, namely, its vacuity. Though Skinner seems to believe that "survival of a culture" is an important value for the behavioral technologist, he fails to consider the questions that arise at once. When the culture changes, has it survived, or died? Suppose that it changes in such a way as to extend the basic individual rights that Skinner personally regards as outdated (pp. 180–83). Is this survival, or death? Do we want the thousand-year Reich to survive? Why not, if survival of the culture functions as a value for the behavioral technologist? Suppose that in fact people are "reinforced" by (that is, prefer) reduction of both sanctions and differential reinforcement. Do we then design the culture so as to lead to this result, thus diminishing effective controls rather than extend-

ing them, as Skinner urges? Suppose that humans happen to be so constructed that they desire the opportunity for freely undertaken productive work. Suppose that they want to be free from the meddling of
technocrats and commissars, bankers and tycoons, mad bombers who
engage in psychological tests of will with peasants defending their homes,
behavioral scientists who can't tell a pigeon from a poet, or anyone else
who tries to wish freedom and dignity out of existence or beat them into
oblivion. Do we then "design our culture" to achieve these ends (which,
of course, can be given an appropriate Skinnerian translation)? There are
no answers to any of these questions in Skinner's science, despite his
claim that it accommodates (fully, it seems) consideration of "values." It
is for this reason that his approach is as congenial to an anarchist as to
a Nazi, as already noted.[16]

Skinner's treatment of the notions "leisure" and "work" gives an interesting insight into the behaviorist system of beliefs (insofar as an identifiable doctrine still exists—see p. 163 above). Recall his assertion that the
level of an organism's activity depends on its "environmental history of
reinforcement" and that "an organism will range between vigorous activity and complete quiescence depending upon the schedules on which it
has been reinforced" (p. 186). Weakening of controls, then, might induce
passivity or random behavior, particularly under conditions of affluence
(low deprivation). People are "at leisure," Skinner notes, if they "have
little to do," for example, people who "have enough power to force or
induce others to work for them," children, the retarded and mentally ill,
members of affluent and welfare societies, and so on. Such people "appear to be able to 'do as they please.' " This, Skinner continues, "is a
natural goal of the libertarian" (pp. 177–80). But leisure "is a condition
for which the human species has been badly prepared," and therefore a
dangerous condition.

Evidently, a distinction must be made between having nothing to do
and being able to do as one pleases. Both states presuppose lack of
compulsion, but being able to do as one pleases requires the availability
of opportunities as well. Under Skinnerian assumptions, it is difficult to
distinguish properly between having nothing to do and being able to do
as one pleases, since there is no reason to expect anyone to take the
opportunity to work without deprivation and reinforcement. Thus it is
not surprising that Skinner slips easily from the definition of "leisure" as
the state in which one appears to be able to do as one pleases, to the
assertion that leisure (that is, having nothing to do) is a dangerous condition, as in the case of a caged lion or an institutionalized person.

Being able to do as one pleases is a natural goal of the libertarian, but having nothing to do is not. While it may be correct to say that the human species is badly prepared for having nothing to do, it is quite a different matter to say that it is badly prepared for the freedom to do as one pleases. People who are able to do as they please may work very hard, given the opportunity to do interesting work. Similarly a child who is "at leisure" in Skinner's sense may not have to be "reinforced" to expend energy in creative activities, but may eagerly exploit the opportunity to do so. Skinner's loose usage of the term "leisure," while understandable under his assumptions, nevertheless, obscures the fundamental difference between freedom to do as one wishes (for Skinner, the appearance of this, since he believes there is no such thing) and having nothing to do, as in an institution or on welfare, when there is no interesting work available. Skinner's remarks thus convey the impression that it might be dangerous, perhaps another "lethal cultural mutation," to create social arrangements in which people are free to choose their work and to absorb themselves in satisfying work. A further comment that "specific cultural conditions" (not further specified) are necessary to enable those with leisure to engage in "artistic, literary, and scientific productivity" contributes as much to clarifying the issues as his other remarks about "contingencies of reinforcement."

Running through the discussion is a vague background assumption that unless "reinforcements" are provided, individuals will vegetate. That there may be an intrinsic human need to find productive work, that a free person may, given the opportunity, seek such work and pursue it with energy, is a possibility that is never faced—though of course the vacuous system of Skinnerian translation would permit us to say that such work is "reinforcing" (and undertaken for this reason), if we happen to enjoy tautologies.

We have noted that Skinner's "science" neither justifies nor provides any rational objection to a totalitarian state or even a well-run concentration camp. The libertarians and humanists whom Skinner scorns object to totalitarianism out of respect for freedom and dignity. But, Skinner argues, these notions are merely the residue of traditional mystical beliefs and must be replaced by the stern scientific concepts of behavioral analysis. However, there exists no behavioral science incorporating nontrivial, empirically supported propositions that apply to human affairs or support a behavioral technology. It is for this reason that Skinner's book contains no clearly formulated substantive hypotheses or proposals. We can at least begin to speculate coherently about the acquisition of certain systems of knowledge and belief on the basis of experience and genetic endowment, and can outline the general nature of some device that might duplicate aspects of this achievement. But as to how people who have acquired systems of knowledge and belief then proceed to use them in their daily life, we are entirely in the dark, at the level of scientific inquiry. If there were some science capable of treating such matters, it might well be concerned precisely with freedom and dignity and might suggest possibilities for enhancing them. Perhaps, as the classical literature of freedom and dignity sometimes suggests, there is an intrinsic human inclination toward free creative inquiry and productive work, and humans are not merely dull mechanisms shaped by a history of reinforcement and behaving predictably with no intrinsic needs apart from the need for physiological satiation. Then humans are not fit subjects for manipulation, and we will seek to design a social order accordingly. But we cannot, at present, turn to science for insight into these matters. To claim otherwise is pure fraud. For the moment, an honest scientist will admit at once that we understand virtually nothing, at the level of scientific inquiry, with regard to human freedom and dignity.

There is, of course, no doubt that behavior can be controlled, for example, by threat of violence or a pattern of deprivation and reward. This much is not at issue, and the conclusion is quite consistent with a belief in "autonomous man." If a tyrant has the power to demand certain acts, whether by threat of punishment or by allowing only those who perform these acts to escape from deprivation (e.g., by restricting employment to such people), his subjects may choose to obey—though some may have the dignity to refuse. They will be aware that they are submitting under compulsion. They will understand the difference between this compulsion and the laws that govern falling bodies. Of course, they are not free. Sanctions backed by force restrict freedom, as does differential reward. An increase in wages, in Marx's phrase, "would be nothing more than a better *remuneration of slaves,* and would not restore, either to the worker or to the work, their human significance and worth." But it would be absurd to conclude, merely from the fact that freedom is limited, that "autonomous man" is an illusion, or to overlook the distinction between a person who chooses to conform in the face of threat, or force, or deprivation and differential reward and a person who "chooses" to obey Newtonian principles as he falls from a high tower. The inference remains absurd even where it is possible to predict the course of action that most "autonomous men" would select, under conditions of duress and limited opportunity for survival. The absurdity merely becomes more obvious when we consider the real social world, in which determinable "probabilities of response" are so slight as to have virtually no predictive value. And it would be not absurd, but grotesque, to argue that since circumstances can be arranged under which behavior is quite predictable—as in a prison, for example, or the concentration-camp soci-

ety "designed" above—therefore there need be no concern for the freedom and dignity of "autonomous man." When such conclusions are
taken to be the result of a "scientific analysis," one can only be amazed
at human gullibility.

Skinner confuses science with terminology. He apparently believes that
if he rephrases commonplace "mentalistic" expressions with terminology
drawn from the laboratory study of behavior, but deprived of its precise
content, then he has achieved a scientific analysis of behavior. It would
be hard to conceive of a more striking failure to comprehend even the
rudiments of scientific thinking. The public may well be deceived, given
the prestige of science and technology. It may even choose to be misled
into agreeing that concern for freedom and dignity must be abandoned.
Perhaps it will choose this course out of fear and insecurity with regard
to the consequences of a serious concern for freedom and dignity. The
tendencies in our society that lead toward submission to authoritarian
rule may prepare individuals for a doctrine that can be interpreted as
justifying it.

The problems that Skinner discusses—it would be more proper to say
"circumvents"—are often real enough. Despite his curious belief to the
contrary, his libertarian and humanist opponents do not object to "design of a culture," that is, to creating social forms that will be more
conducive to the satisfaction of human needs, though they differ from
Skinner in the intuitive perception of what these needs truly are. They
would not, or at least should not, oppose scientific inquiry or, where
possible, its applications, though they will no doubt dismiss the travesty
that Skinner presents.

If a physical scientist were to assure us that we need not concern
ourselves over the world's sources of energy because he has demonstrated in his laboratory that windmills will surely suffice for all future
human needs, he would be expected to produce some evidence, or other
scientists would expose this pernicious nonsense. The situation is different in the behavioral sciences. A person who claims that he has a behavioral technology that will solve the world's problems and a science of
behavior that supports it and reveals the factors that determine human
behavior is required to demonstrate nothing. One waits in vain for psychologists to make clear to the general public the actual limits of what is
known. Given the prestige of science and technology, this is a most
unfortunate situation.

Equality

LANGUAGE DEVELOPMENT, HUMAN INTELLIGENCE, AND
SOCIAL ORGANIZATION
(1976)

―――――――――――――――――

*I*WOULD LIKE TO COMMENT ON THREE NOTIONS OF "EQUALITY": namely, equality of rights, equality of condition, and equality of endowment—and more generally, the nature of that endowment, or briefly, human nature and its variety. The last of these questions is essentially a matter of fact, poorly understood, but plainly in the domain of the natural sciences, to be answered, as best we can, by unprejudiced inquiry. The first two questions raise serious questions of value. All of these notions demand careful analysis, far beyond anything I can attempt here.

If the discussion of equality of rights and condition is to be at all serious—in particular, if it is to pertain to choice of action—then questions of fact inevitably intrude. Discussion becomes socially irrelevant, whatever interest it may retain as an intellectual exercise, to the extent that relevant facts are not accurately presented. In much current discussion of problems of equality, they are not accurately presented.

Consider, for example, a series of articles on "egalitarianism" by John Cobbs in *Business Week,* (December 1975), which is not untypical of current debate over these issues. Cobbs takes as his starting point the factual assumption that "in one way or another, all the government's social programs are equalizers" (although, he adds, federal programs do "not always achieve this result"). Does this factual premise even approximate the truth? A strong case can be made to the contrary. Subsidies to higher education, for example, tend to be roughly proportional to family income. The enormous federal highway program has been in large measure a subsidy to commercial trucking (and, arguably, has indirectly raised the cost of living) and to major corporations that make their profits from petroleum and from modes of transportation that carry a substantial social cost. Nor can the government housing programs of the past thirty years be readily described as "equalizers." For example, the programs that in my own city destroyed "a low-income, predominantly Italian neighborhood" on Beacon Hill and replaced it with "high-income apartment towers financed with government-insured loans"—I quote from MIT Professor of Architecture Robert Goodman in a review of federal housing programs that he describes as an "effective way of exploiting the poor."[1] Or consider the government subsidies to arms producers and agribusiness, the latter in part through subsidy of research into agricultural technology designed for the interests of large corporations, which is undertaken in government-supported universities. Or consider the vast government expenditures to insure a favorable international climate for business operations. In a highly inegalitarian society, it is most unlikely that government programs will be equalizers. Rather, it is to be expected that they will be designed and manipulated by private power for its own benefits; and to a significant degree the expectation is fulfilled. It is not very likely that matters could be otherwise in the absence of mass popular organizations that are prepared to struggle for their rights and interests. An effort to develop and implement government programs that really were equalizers would lead to a form of class war, and in the present state of popular organization and distribution of effective power, there can hardly be much doubt as to who would win—a fact that some "populists," who rightly deplore the government programs that benefit private economic power, sometimes tend to ignore.

Discussion of the role of the state in a society based on the principle of private power must not neglect the fact that "generally speaking, capitalism must be regarded as an economy of unpaid costs, 'unpaid' insofar as a substantial proportion of the actual costs of production remain unaccounted for in entrepreneurial outlays; instead they are shifted to, and ultimately borne by, third persons or by the community as a whole."[2] A serious analysis of the government's social programs—not to speak of its programs of economic intervention, military force, and the like—will assess the function of these programs in paying social costs that cannot realistically be relegated to a footnote. There may be a residual sense to the notion that the state serves as an equalizer, in that without its intervention the destructive forces of capitalism would demolish social existence and the physical environment, a fact that has been well understood by the masters of the private economy who have regularly called upon the state to restrain and organize these forces. But the common idea that the government acts as a social equalizer can hardly be put forth as a general principle.

As a second example, consider the widely held doctrine that moves toward equality of condition entail costs in efficiency and restrictions of freedom. The alleged inverse relation between attained equality and efficiency involves empirical claims that may or may not be true. If this relation holds, one would expect to find that worker-owned and -managed industry in egalitarian communities is less efficient than matched counterparts that are privately owned and managed and that rent labor in the so-called free market. Research on the matter is not extensive, but it tends to show that the opposite is true.[3] Harvard economist Stephen Marglin has argued that harsh measures were necessary in early stages of the industrial system to overcome the natural advantages of cooperative enterprise which left no room for masters, and there is a body of empirical evidence in support of the conclusion that "when workers are given control over decisions and goal setting, productivity rises dramatically."[4] From another point of view, Cambridge economist J. E. Meade has argued that efficiency and equitable distribution of income can be reconciled if measures are taken "to equalize the distribution of the ownership of private property and to increase the net amount of property which was in social ownership."[5] In general, the relation between equality and efficiency is hardly a simple or well-established one, despite many facile pronouncements on the matter.

Turning to the relation between equality and freedom, allegedly inverse, we also find nontrivial questions. Workers' control of production certainly increases freedom along some dimensions—extremely important ones, in my judgment—just as it eliminates the fundamental inequality between the person compelled to sell his labor power to survive and the person privileged to purchase it, if he so chooses. At the very least, we should bear in mind the familiar observation that freedom is illusion and mockery when conditions for the exercise of free choice do not exist. We only enter Marx's "realm of freedom" when labor is no longer "determined by necessity and mundane considerations,"[6] an insight that is hardly the precept of radicals and revolutionaries alone. Thus Vico observed that there is no liberty when people are "drowned . . . in a sea of usury" and must "pay off their debts by work and toil."[7] David Ellerman puts the issue well in an important essay:

> It is a veritable mainstay of capitalist thought (not to mention so-called "right-wing libertarianism") that the moral flaws of chattel slavery have not survived in capitalism since the workers, unlike the slaves, are free people making voluntary wage contracts. But it is only that, in the case of capitalism, the denial of natural rights is less complete so that the worker has a residual legal personality as a free "commodity-owner." He is thus allowed to voluntarily put his own working life to traffic. When a robber denies another person's right to make an infinite number of other choices besides losing his money or his life and the denial is backed up by a gun, then this is clearly robbery even though it might be said that the victim is making a "voluntary choice" between his remaining options. When the legal system itself denies the natural rights of working people in the name of the prerogatives of capital, and this denial is sanctioned by the legal violence of the state, then the theorists of 'libertarian' capitalism do not proclaim institutional robbery, but rather they celebrate the "natural liberty" of working people to choose between the remaining options of selling their labor as a commodity and being unemployed.[8]

Considering such questions as these, we can hardly rest comfortably with the assumption that freedom declines as equality—for example, in control over resources and means of production—increases. It may be true that equality is inversely related to the freedom to dispose of and make use of property under the social arrangements of capitalism, but the latter condition is not to be simply identified as "freedom."

I do not even consider here the immeasurable loss incurred when a person is converted to a tool of production, so that, as Adam Smith phrased it, he "has no occasion to exert his understanding, or to exercise his invention" and "he naturally loses, therefore, the habit of such exertion and generally becomes as stupid and ignorant as it is possible for a human creature to become," his mind falling "into that drowsy stupidity, which, in a civilized society, seems to benumb the understanding of almost all the inferior ranks of people."[9] What is the loss in "efficiency" and social product resulting from this enforced stupidity? What does it mean to say that a person driven to such "drowsy stupidity" by his conditions of work still remains "free"?

When we ask ourselves what would be a just and decent society, we are faced by conflicting intuitions, standards that are imprecise and poorly formulated, and significant questions of fact. Relying on some of these intuitions to the exclusion of others, we may seem to escape complexity and conflict, but at the risk of pursuing a mere logical exercise, and not a very interesting one at that. The hazards are well illustrated by some contemporary discussion. Consider, for example, the "entitlement theory of justice," now enjoying a certain vogue. According to this theory, a person has a right to whatever he has acquired by means that are just. If, by luck or labor or ingenuity, a person acquires such and such, then he is entitled to keep it and dispose of it as he wills, and a just society will not infringe on this right.

One can easily determine where such a principle might lead. It is entirely possible that by legitimate means—say, luck supplemented by contractual arrangements "freely undertaken" under pressure of need—one person might gain control of the necessities of life. Others are then free to sell themselves to this person as slaves, if he is willing to accept them. Otherwise, they are free to perish. Without extra question-begging conditions, the society is just.

The argument has all the merits of a proof that $2 + 2 = 5$. Presented with such a proof, we may be sufficiently intrigued to try to find the source of error in faulty reasoning or incorrect assumptions. Or, we may disregard it and proceed to more important matters. In a field with real intellectual substance, such as mathematics, it may be interesting, and has in the past really proven fruitful, to pursue such questions. In considering the problems of society and human life, the enterprise is of dubious value. Suppose that some concept of a "just society" is advanced that fails to characterize the situation just described as unjust, to an extreme (however the outcome may have come about). Then one of two conclusions is in order. We may conclude that the concept is simply unimportant and of no interest as a guide to thought or action, since it fails to apply properly even in such an elementary case as this. Or we may conclude that the concept advanced is to be dismissed in that it fails to correspond to the pretheoretical notion that it intends to capture in clear cases. If our intuitive concept of justice is clear enough to rule social arrangements of the sort described as grossly unjust, then the sole interest of a demonstration that this outcome might be "just" under a given "theory of justice" lies in the inference by *reductio ad absurdum* to the conclusion that the theory is hopelessly inadequate. While it may capture some partial intuition regarding justice, it evidently neglects others.

The real question to be raised about theories that fail so completely to capture the concept of justice in its significant and intuitive sense is why
not simply dismissed out of hand

on grounds of this failure, which is so striking in clear cases? Perhaps the answer is, in part, the one given by Edward Greenberg in a discussion of some recent work on the entitlement theory of justice. After reviewing empirical and conceptual shortcomings, he observes that such work "plays an important function in the process of . . . 'blaming the victim,' and of protecting property against egalitarian onslaughts by various non-propertied groups."[10] An ideological defense of privileges, exploitation, and private power will be welcomed, regardless of its merits.

These matters are of no small importance to poor and oppressed people here and elsewhere. Forms of social control that sufficed to ensure obedience in an expanding economy have lost their efficacy in times of stagnation. Ideas that circulate in the faculty club and executive suite can be transmuted into ideological instruments to confuse and demoralize. Furthermore, in 1976 we can hardly ignore the fact that the power of the American state has been employed, on a massive scale, to impose capitalist social forms and ideological principles on unwilling and resisting victims throughout the world. Academic ideologists and political commentators in the media may choose to interpret history in other terms, but the business press is considerably more accurate in observing that the "stable world order for business operations," "the international economic structure, under which U.S. companies have flourished since the end of World War II," has been dependent on the organized violence of the state: "No matter how negative a development, there was always the umbrella of American power to contain it," though in the world after Vietnam, they fear, this may no longer be so.[11]

I once visited a village in Laos in the midst of which there was a pleasant lake that had, at one time, served as the water supply for the village and a place where villagers could relax and enjoy themselves. One powerful individual had succeeded in gaining control of all access to the lake, now fenced off. To obtain water, villagers had to trudge several miles. They could see the lake beyond the fence, but it was no longer available to them. Suppose that ownership of that lake had been attained by means that were "just," as certainly might have been the case in principle.[12] Would we then conclude that the village was a "just society," in this respect? Would we seriously urge the villagers to accept this consequence as only right and just? The government backed—it would be more accurate to say imposed—by the United States implicitly took that position. The Pathet Lao organized the peasants of Laos to overcome such forms of "justice." So substantial was their success that the United States government undertook to demolish much of rural Laos in a war that was "secret," in that the free press in our free society freely chose to keep it secret for a long period while thousands of peasants were murdered and dispossessed. We now freely choose to forget what has happened and erase it from history, or to dismiss it as an unfortunate though minor incident, an example, of our "blundering efforts to do good," our "good intentions" mysteriously transmuted into "bad policy" through our ignorance, error, and naiveté.[13] In fact, the question of "justice," in crucial cases such as this one, is by no means abstract and remote, and we would do well to think seriously about it.

Similar questions arise in a stark form in our own society, one that has a substantial degree of freedom, by world standards. For example, we have free access to information, in principle. In the case of the secret war in Laos, it was possible to ascertain the facts—much too late—by visiting the country, speaking to people in refugee camps, reading reports in the foreign press and ultimately even our own. But freedom of that sort, though important for the privileged, is socially rather meaningless. For the mass of the population of the United States, there was no possibility, in the real world, to gain access to that information, let alone to comprehend its significance. The distribution of power and privilege effectively limits the access to information and the ability to escape the framework of doctrine imposed by ideological institutions: the mass media, the journals of opinion, the schools and universities. The same is true in every domain. In principle, we have a variety of important rights under the law. But we also know just how much these mean, in practice, to people who are unable to purchase them. We have the right of free expression, though some can shout louder than others, by reason of power, wealth, and privilege. We can defend our legal rights through the courts—insofar as we understand these rights and can afford the costs. All of this is obvious and hardly worth extended comment. In a perfectly functioning capitalist democracy, with no illegitimate abuse of power, freedom will be in effect a kind of commodity; effectively, a person will have as much of it as he can buy. We readily understand why the powerful and the privileged often rise to the defense of personal freedom, of which they are the chief beneficiaries in practice, though they manage to look the other way when, for example, the national political police become involved in political assassination and destruction of political groups that attempt to organize among the poor, as happened in Chicago not very long ago, to the resounding silence of the national press and journals of opinion.[14]

I have only barely touched on some of the questions that arise when we consider problems of equality and freedom. I have as yet said nothing at all about the third notion of equality, namely, "equality of endowment." Here, too, there is a widely held doctrine that deserves examination. Again, it is expressed clearly by John Cobbs. He poses what he takes to be "the great intellectual dilemma of the egalitarians," namely, that "a look at the real world demonstrates that some men are smarter than others." Is it fair to insist, he asks, that "the fast and slow . . . should all arrive at the same condition at the same time?" Is it fair to insist on equality of condition achieved, when natural endowment so plainly varies?

Presumably it is the case that in our "real world" some combination of attributes is conducive to success in responding to "the demands of the economic system." Let us agree, for the sake of discussion, that this combination of attributes is in part a matter of native endowment. Why does this (alleged) fact pose an "intellectual dilemma" to egalitarians? Note that we can hardly claim much insight into just what the relevant combination of attributes may be. I know of no reason to believe, and do not believe, that "being smart" has much to do with it. One might suppose that some mixture of avarice, selfishness, lack of concern for others, aggressiveness, and similar characteristics play a part in getting ahead and "making it" in a competitive society based on capitalist principles. Others may counter with their own prejudices. Whatever the correct collection of attributes may be, we may ask what follows from the fact, if it is a fact, that some partially inherited combination of attributes tends to lead to material success? All that follows, so far as I can see, is a comment on our particular social and economic arrangements. One can easily imagine a society in which physical prowess, willingness to murder, ability to cheat, and so on, would tend to bring success; we hardly need resort to imagination. The egalitarian might respond, in all such cases, that the social order should be changed so that the collection of attributes that tends to bring success will no longer do so. He might even argue that in a more decent society, the attributes that now lead to success would be recognized as pathological, and that gentle persuasion might be a proper means to help people to overcome their unfortunate malady. Again we return to the question: What is a just and decent social order? The "egalitarian" faces no special "intellectual dilemmas" distinct in character from those that confront the advocates of a different social order.

A standard response is that it is just "human nature" to pursue power and material interest by any means so long as one can get away with it. Let us suppose that human nature is such that under given social conditions these admirable traits manifest themselves, or more accurately, that people with such tendencies will prosper. Suppose further that wealth and power, once attained, can be employed to extend and protect such privilege, as has been the case under industrial capitalism. The obvious question, of course, is whether other social arrangements might be brought into being that would not encourage these tendencies but would rather be conducive to the flourishing of other traits that are no less part of our common nature: solidarity, concern, sympathy, and kindness, for example.

of such views is commonly directed against a straw-man opponent, as egalitarians have been quick to point out.[15] In fact, "equality of condition," much deplored by contemporary ideologists, has rarely been the express goal of reformers or revolutionaries, at least on the left. In Marx's utopia, "the development of human energy" is to be taken as "an end in itself" as humans escape the "realm of necessity" so that questions of freedom can be seriously raised. The guiding principle, reiterated to the point of cliché, is: "From each according to his abilities, to each according to his needs." The principle of "equality of condition" is nowhere invoked. If one person needs medical treatment and another is more fortunate, they are not to be granted an equal amount of medical care, and the same is true of other human needs.

Libertarian socialists who objected to the theory of proletarian dictatorship also saw little merit in "egalitarianism" as such and in fact condemned "authoritarian Socialism" for failing to comprehend that "Socialism will be free or it will not be at all":

> In the prison, in the cloister, or in the barracks one finds a fairly high degree of economic equality, as all the inmates are provided with the same dwelling, the same food, the same uniform, and the same tasks. The ancient Inca state in Peru and the Jesuit state in Paraguay had brought equal economic provision for every inhabitant to a fixed system, but in spite of this the vilest despotism prevailed there, and the human being was merely the automaton of a higher will on whose decisions he had not the slightest influence. It was not without reason that Proudhon saw in a "Socialism" without freedom the worst form of slavery. The urge for social justice can only develop properly and be effective when it grows out of a man's sense of freedom and responsibility, and is based upon it.[16]

For Rocker, anarchism was "voluntary socialism," and "freedom is not an abstract philosophical concept, but the vital concrete possibility for every human being to bring to full development all capacities and talents with which nature has endowed him, and turn them to social account." Marx would not have disagreed, and the basic conceptions can be traced back to earlier libertarian thought.[17] These ideas deserve close attention as the most serious expression, in my view, of a concept of a just and decent society that incorporates serious and critical principles while attending to significant social and historical facts.

Note that for such socialists as Marx, Bakunin, Rocker, and others of the left, there is no "intellectual dilemma" arising from inequality of endowment. Libertarian socialists, at least, looked forward to a "federation of free communities which shall be bound to one another by their common economic and social interests and arrange their affairs by mutual agreement and free contract," "a free association of all productive forces based upon co-operative labor, which would have for its sole purpose the satisfying of the necessary requirements of every member of society."[18] In such a society, there is no reason why rewards should be contingent on some collection of personal attributes, however selected. Inequality of endowment is simply the human condition—a fact for which we may be thankful; one vision of hell is a society of interchangeable parts. It carries with it no implications concerning social rewards.

In a socialist society, as envisioned by the authentic left,[19] a central purpose will be that the necessary requirements of every member of society be satisfied. We may assume that these "necessary requirements" will be historically conditioned in part, and will develop along with the expansion and enrichment of material and intellectual culture. But "equality of condition" is no desideratum, as we approach Marx's "realm of freedom." Individuals will differ in their aspirations, their abilities, and their personal goals. For some person, the opportunity to play the piano ten hours a day may be an overwhelming personal need; for another, not. As material circumstances permit, these differential needs should be satisfied in a decent society, as in healthy family life. In functioning socialist societies such as the Israeli kibbutzim, questions of this sort constantly arise. I cannot imagine that it is possible to formulate very strong general principles to resolve conflicts and measure individual opportunity against social demands. Honest people will differ in their assessments and will try to reach agreement through discussion and sympathetic consideration of the needs of others. The problems are not exotic ones; they arise constantly in functioning social groups, such as the family. We are not accustomed to think beyond such small groups, given the inhuman and pathological premises of competitive capitalism and its perverse ideology. It is no wonder that "fraternity" has traditionally been inscribed on the revolutionary banner alongside of "liberty" and "equality." Without bonds of solidarity, sympathy, and concern for others, a socialist society is unthinkable. We may only hope that human nature is so constituted that these elements of our essential nature may flourish and enrich our lives, once the social conditions that suppress them are overcome. Socialists are committed to the belief that we are not condemned to live in a society based on greed, envy, and hate. I know of no way to prove that they are right, but there are also no grounds for the common belief that they must be wrong.

The distinction between equality of condition and equality of rights loses its apparent sharpness when we attend to it more closely. Suppose that individuals, at each stage of their personal existence, are to be accorded their intrinsic human rights; in this sense, "equality of rights" is to be upheld. Then conditions must be such that they can enjoy these rights. To the extent that inequality of condition impairs the exercise of these rights, it is illegitimate and is to be overcome, in a decent society. What, then, are these rights? If they include the right to develop one's capacities to the fullest, to realize what Marx calls the "species character" of "free conscious activity" and "productive life" in free associations based on constructive, creative work, then conditions must be equalized at least to the rather considerable extent required to guarantee these rights, if equality of rights is to be maintained. The vision of the left, then, blurs the distinction between equality of rights and condition, denies that inequality of endowment merits or demands corresponding inequality of reward, rejects equality of condition as a principle in itself, and sees no intellectual dilemma in the conflict between egalitarian principles, properly understood, and variability of endowment. Rather we must face the problems of a repressive and unjust society, emerging with greater clarity as we progress beyond the realm of necessity.

Criticism of egalitarianism misfires when directed against at least this segment of the left. But one may legitimately raise other questions. Thus it might be argued that the intuitions that lead to this vision of a decent and just society conflict with others: for example, the belief that one must pay for one's sins or errors. Or it might be argued that all of this is utopian nonsense, and that wage slavery and authoritarian structures such as the modern business enterprise are an inescapable necessity in a complex society. Or one may consider a more limited time frame and work for "more equality" and "more justice," putting aside the question of further goals and the principles that inspire them. Here we enter the grounds of legitimate and useful controversy. For example, if an argument can be constructed that advanced industrial societies cannot survive unless some people rent themselves to others, some people give orders while others march to the beat of a drum, then it should be taken seriously. If correct, it undermines the socialist vision. But the burden of proof rests on those who insist that some fundamental conditions of repression, exploitation, or inequality are inescapable. To say merely that things have never been otherwise is not very convincing. On these grounds, one could have demonstrated, in the eighteenth century, that capitalist democracy is an impossible dream.

Can we seriously raise the question "What is human nature?" Can we make some progress toward the understanding of human nature? Can we develop a theory of intrinsic human needs, of the nature of human capacities and their variation in the species, of the forms these capacities will assume under varied social conditions, a theory that will have some consequences or at least be suggestive with regard to questions of human and social import? In principle, we enter at this point into the domain of scientific inquiry, though it is potential rather than actual science.

The proposition that humans differ in fundamental respects from other organisms in the natural world is hardly open to serious dispute. If a Martian scientist were to study earthly matters, he would have little doubt on this score. The conclusion would be particularly obvious if he were to observe changes in the life of organisms over an extended period. The humans of today are, with at most minor modifications, of the same genetic constitution as their forebears many millennia ago, but patterns of life have changed remarkably, particularly in the past few hundred years. This is not true of other organisms, except as a result of human intervention. A Martian observer would also be struck by the fact that at any moment of history there are remnants of earlier ways, even of Stone Age conditions, among humans who do not differ significantly in genetic constitution from those whose mode of life has changed most radically. He would note, in short, that humans are unique in the natural world in that they have a history, cultural diversity, and cultural evolution. In these respects, our hypothetical Martian might well be intrigued by the question, "Why is this so?"

The same question has, of course, been raised in one or another form since the earliest recorded origins of human thought. That is natural enough. Humans naturally seek to define their place in the world of nature. The question, "What is human nature?", the collection of attributes that so radically distinguish the human species from the rest of the organic world, is a profound and essentially unanswered question of science. It has been held to lie beyond the range of scientific inquiry, in that the specific difference of humans lies in their possession of an immortal soul that cannot be further understood by the methods of science. We might note that the inaccessibility of the soul to study is no essential conclusion of dualist theory. One might argue, say on Cartesian grounds, that humans and humans alone possess some nonmaterial quality— Cartesian mind; and yet one might maintain, as I think the Cartesians would have done, that there can be a science of mind. But putting this issue aside, there are quite unique properties of human intelligence, elements of distinctive human nature. Assuming no a priori limits to inquiry, it is an empirical question, a question of science, to determine what human nature may be.

The puzzlement of our hypothetical Martian observer, with regard to the uniqueness of the human species, would perhaps mount if he knew a little modern biology. Thus it seems to be the case that the quantity of DNA in the fertilized egg is not very different for a mouse, a cow, a chimpanzee, or a person. Structural differences revealed only at a more refined level of analysis are evidently responsible for the precise course and character of embryological development. In a complex and intricate system, small differences in initial condition may have major consequences for the form, size, structure, and function of the resulting organism and its components. The same phenomenon is a commonplace in the natural sciences. It can also be easily demonstrated in the investigation of a system of the intricacy of human language. Given a linguistic theory of sufficient range and complexity, it is easy to show that small modifications in general conditions imposed on rules may lead to very curious and varied changes among predicted phenomena, because of the complex interactions that take place as a sentence is generated by a system of rules operating under these conditions. Assuming that modern biology is essentially on the right track, it must be that natural selection gave rise somehow to a particular quality of genetic complexity, producing "a new force: the human mind," a "unique instrument [that] gave for the first time to a biological species the power to alter its relation to the environment . . . by conscious manipulation of the surrounding world," as well as the means for expression of thought and emotion, for creation of art and science, for planning actions and assessing their consequences over a hitherto inconceivable range. It is often assumed, quite plausibly, that in the development of this unique instrument, the human mind, "the critical step must have been the invention of language."[20] In some manner that is still poorly understood, genetic endowment was modified to produce a creature that grows a human language as part of a system of "mental organs," a creature that can then proceed to create the conditions under which it will live to an extent without significant analogue in the natural world, so far as we know.

The question "What is human nature?" has more than scientific interest. As we have noted, it lies at the core of social thought as well. What is a good society? Presumably, one that leads to the satisfaction of intrinsic human needs, insofar as material conditions allow. To command attention and respect, a social theory should be grounded on some concept of human needs and human rights, and in turn, on the human nature that must be presupposed in any serious account of the origin and character of these needs and rights. Correspondingly, the social structures and relations that a reformer or revolutionary seeks to bring into existence will be based on a concept of human nature, however vague and inarticulate.

Suppose that at the core of human nature lies the propensity to truck and barter, as Adam Smith alleged. Then we will work to achieve an early capitalist society of small traders, unhindered by monopoly, state intervention, or socially controlled production. Suppose, in contrast, that we take seriously the concepts of another classical liberal thinker, Wilhelm von Humboldt, who contends that "to inquire and to create—these are

the centers around which all human pursuits more or less directly revolve," and who further maintains that true creation can take place only
under conditions of free choice that goes beyond "instruction and guidance," in a society in which social fetters have been replaced by freely
created social bonds. Or suppose that we assume further with Marx that
"only in a state of community with others has each individual the means
to develop his predispositions in all directions; only in a state of community will personal freedom thus become possible"—where personal freedom presupposes abolition of the alienation of labor that Humboldt
condemned as well, the condition of labor that "casts some of the workers
back into barbarous kind of work and turns others into machines."[21] On
such assumptions about human needs we derive a very different conception of a social order that we should work to create.

Some Marxists have taken the view that "man has no essence apart
from his historical existence,"[22] that "human nature is not something *fixed
by nature,* but, on the contrary, a 'nature' which is *made by man* in his acts
of 'self-transcendence' as a natural being."[23] This interpretation derives
from Marx's dictum that "the nature which comes to be in human history—the genesis of human society—is man's real nature,"[24] and other
similar remarks. Even if we adopt this view, it still remains true that the
next step in social change should seek to provide the conditions for the
"real nature" that can be expressed at a given stage of historical and
cultural evolution.

Is it true that human nature is in no way "fixed by nature"? Evidently
it is not true of the physical components of human nature. When a
modern Marxist thinker such as Antonio Gramsci, for example, argues
that "the fundamental innovation introduced by Marxism into the science
of politics and history is the proof that there does not exist an abstract,
fixed and immutable 'human nature' . . . but that human nature is the
totality of historically determined social relations,"[25] he is referring, of
course, not to human physical organs in general but to one specific organ,
the human brain and its creations. The content of this doctrine must be
that at least so far as the higher mental functions are concerned, the
human brain is unique among the systems known to us in the natural
world in that it has no genetically determined structure, but is, in effect,
a *tabula rasa* on which the totality of historically determined social relations is then inscribed. For some segments of the left, there has been an
extraordinary compulsion to adopt some such view. In a report on a
recent discussion at the American Association for the Advancement of
Science, Walter Sullivan writes:

> The most extreme view, expressed by some members of the audi-
> ence, was that human brains were 'uncoupled' from any genetic

influences whatsoever—that, like computers built to a standard design, their relative levels of performance were completely determined by programming.[26]

As scientific hypotheses, these assumptions, which are familiar from radical behaviorism as well, seem to me to have little to recommend them. On these assumptions, it would be quite impossible to account for the richness and complexity of human cognitive systems and the uniformity of their growth, not to speak of the remarkable qualitative differences as compared with other species. Surely, no evidence or argument has been adduced in support of the belief that the human brain is so markedly distinct from every other structure known to us in the natural world, and it is perhaps a bit ironic that such views are proposed, not only on the left, as if they were an outgrowth of some kind of scientific naturalism. Exactly the contrary seems to me to be the case. The human brain is unique in many respects, and the mental structures that grow under the boundary conditions set by experience—the cognitive structures that are "learned," to employ the common and I think rather misleading locution—also provide humans with a "unique instrument." But it is difficult to imagine that this "uniqueness" resides in the total absence of structure, despite the antiquity of such a belief and its remarkable grip on the modern imagination. What little we know about the human brain and about human cognitive structures suggests a very different assumption: a highly constrained genetic program determines the basic structural properties of our "mental organs," thus making it possible for us to attain rich and intricate systems of knowledge and belief in a uniform manner on the basis of quite limited evidence. I might add that such a view comes as no surprise to biologists, particularly, as regards human language.[27] And I believe it would generally be regarded by neurophysiologists as entirely natural, if not almost obvious.

We need not rest with qualitative and vague remarks such as these. In the study of human language, at least, there are substantive hypotheses, which I believe have considerable force and explanatory power, as to the general character of the genetic program that provides for the growth of the capacity for language and the particular forms that it assumes. I see no reason to doubt that the same will prove true in other domains, as we come to understand the structure of human cognitive capacity. If so, we may think of human nature as a system of a sort familiar in the biological world: a system of "mental organs" based on physical mechanisms that are now largely unknown, though not beyond investigation in principle, a system that provides for a unique form of intelligence that manifests itself in human language; in our unique capacity to develop a concept of number and abstract space[28]; to construct scientific theories in certain domains; to create certain systems of art, myth, and ritual, to interpret human actions, to develop and comprehend certain systems of social institutions, and so on.

On an "empty organism" hypothesis, human beings are assuredly equal in intellectual endowments. More accurately, they are equal in their incapacity to develop complex cognitive structures of the characteristically human sort. If we assume, however, that this biologically given organism has its special capacities like any other, and that among them are the capacities to develop human cognitive structures with their specific properties, then the possibility arises that there are differences among individuals in their higher mental functions. Indeed, it would be surprising if there were not, if cognitive faculties such as the language faculty are really "mental organs." People obviously differ in their physical characteristics and capacities; why should there not be genetically determined differences in the character of their mental organs and the physical structures on which they are based?

Inquiry into specific cognitive capacities such as the language faculty leads to specific and I think significant hypotheses concerning the genetically programmed schematism for language, but gives us no evidence concerning variability. Perhaps this is a result of the inadequacy of our analytic tools. Or it may be that the basic capacities are truly invariant, apart from gross pathology. We find that over a very broad range, at least, there are no differences in the ability to acquire and make effective use of human language at some level of detail, although there may be differences in what is acquired, as there are evidently differences in facility of use. I see no reason for dogmatism on this score. So little is known concerning other cognitive capacities that we can hardly even speculate. Experience seems to support the belief that people do vary in their intellectual capacities and their specialization. It would hardly come as a surprise if this were so, assuming that we are dealing with biological structures, however intricate and remarkable, of known sorts.

Many people, particularly those who regard themselves as within the left-liberal political spectrum, find such conclusions repugnant. It may be that the empty organism hypothesis is so attractive to the left in part because it precludes these possibilities; there is no variability in a null endowment. But I find it difficult to understand why conclusions of this sort should be at all disturbing. I am personally quite convinced that no matter what training or education I might have received, I could never have run a four-minute mile, discovered Gödel's theorems, composed a Beethoven quartet, or risen to any of innumerable other heights of human achievement. I feel in no way demeaned by these inadequacies. It is quite enough that I am capable, as I think any person of normal endowments probably is, of appreciating and in part understanding what

others have accomplished, while making my own personal contributions
in whatever measure and manner I am able to do. Human talents vary
considerably, within a fixed framework that is characteristic of the species
and that permits ample scope for creative work, including the creative
work of appreciating the achievements of others. This should be a matter
for delight rather than a condition to be abhorred. Those who assume
otherwise must be adopting the tacit premise that people's rights or social
reward are somehow contingent on their abilities. As for human rights,
there is an element of plausibility in this assumption in the single respect
already noted: in a decent society, opportunities should conform as far
as possible to personal needs, and such needs may be specialized and
related to particular talents and capacities. My pleasure in life is enhanced
by the fact that others can do many things that I cannot, and I see no
reason to want to deny these people the opportunity to cultivate their
talents, consistent with general social needs. Difficult questions of practice are sure to arise in any functioning social group, but I see no problem
of principle.

As for social rewards, it is alleged that in our society remuneration
correlates in part with IQ. But insofar as that is true, it is simply a social
malady to be overcome much as slavery had to be eliminated at an earlier
stage of human history. It is sometimes argued that constructive and
creative work will cease unless it leads to material reward, so that all of
society gains when the talented receive special rewards. For the mass of
the population, then, the message is: "You're better off if you're poor."
One can see why this doctrine would appeal to the privileged, but it is
difficult to believe that it could be put forth seriously by anyone who has
had experience with creative work or workers in the arts, the sciences,
crafts, or whatever. The standard arguments for "meritocracy" have no
basis in fact or logic, to my knowledge; they rest on a priori beliefs, which,
furthermore, do not seem particularly plausible. I have discussed the
matter elsewhere and will not pursue it here.[29]

Suppose that inquiry into human nature reveals that human cognitive
capacities are highly structured by our genetic program and that there are
variations among individuals within a shared framework. This seems to
me an entirely reasonable expectation and a situation much to be desired.
It has no implications with regard to equality of rights or condition, so
far as I can see, beyond those already sketched.

Consider finally the question of race and intellectual endowments.
Notice again that in a decent society there would be no social consequences to any discovery that might be made about this question. Individuals are what they are; it is only on racist assumptions that they are
to be regarded as an instance of their race category, so that social consequences ensue from the discovery that the mean for a certain racial

category with respect to some capacity is such and such. Eliminating racist assumptions, the facts have no social consequences whatever they may be, and are therefore not worth knowing, from this point of view at least. If there is any purpose to investigation of the relation between race and some capacity, it must derive from the scientific significance of the question. It is difficult to be precise about questions of scientific merit. Roughly, an inquiry has scientific merit if its results might bear on some general principles of science. One doesn't conduct inquiries into the density of blades of grass on various lawns or innumerable other trivial and pointless questions. But inquiry into such questions as race and IQ appears to be of virtually no scientific interest. Conceivably, there might be some interest in correlations between partially heritable traits, but if someone were interested in this question, he would surely not select such characteristics as race and IQ, each an obscure amalgam of complex properties. Rather, he would ask whether there is a correlation between measurable and significant traits, say, eye color and length of the big toe. It is difficult to see how the study of race and IQ, for example, can be justified on any scientific grounds.

Since the inquiry has no scientific significance and no social significance, apart from the racist assumption that individuals must be regarded not as what they are but rather as standing at the mean of their race category, it follows that it has no merit at all. The question then arises, Why is it pursued with such zeal? Why is it taken seriously? Attention naturally turns to the racist assumptions that do confer some importance on the inquiry, if they are accepted.

In a racist society, inquiry into race and IQ can be expected to reinforce prejudice, pretty much independent of the outcome of the inquiry. Given such concepts as "race" and "IQ," it is to be expected that the results of any inquiry will be obscure and conflicting, the arguments complex and difficult for the layman to follow. For the racist, the judgment "Not proven" will be read, "Probably so." There will be ample scope for the racist to wallow in his prejudices. The very fact that the inquiry is undertaken suggests that its outcome is of some importance, and since it is important only on racist assumptions, these assumptions are insinuated even when they are not expressed. For such reasons as these, a scientific investigation of genetic characteristics of Jews would have been appalling in Nazi Germany. There can be no doubt that the investigation of race and IQ has been extremely harmful to the victims of American racism. I have heard black educators describe in vivid terms the suffering and injury imposed on children who are made to understand that "science" has demonstrated this or that about their race, or even finds it necessary to raise the question.

We cannot ignore the fact that we live in a profoundly racist society,

though we like to forget that this is so. When the *New York Times* editors
and U.N. Ambassador Moynihan castigate Idi Amin of Uganda as a "racist
murderer," perhaps correctly, there is a surge of pride throughout the
country and they are lauded for their courage and honesty. No one would
be so vulgar as to observe that the editors and the ambassador, in the not
very distant past, have supported racist murder on a scale that exceeds
Amin's wildest fantasies. The general failure to be appalled by their
hypocritical pronouncements reflects, in the first place, the extremely
powerful ideological controls that prevent us from coming to terms with
our acts and their significance and, in the second place, the nation's
profound commitment to racist principle. The victims of our Asian wars
were never regarded as fully human, a fact that can be demonstrated all
too easily, to our everlasting shame. As for domestic racism, I need hardly
comment.

The scientist, like anyone else, is responsible for the foreseeable consequences of his acts. The point is obvious and generally well understood;
consider the conditions on the use of human subjects in experiments. In
the present case, an inquiry into race and IQ, regardless of its outcome,
will have a severe social cost in a racist society, for the reasons just noted.
The scientist who undertakes this inquiry must therefore show that its
significance is so great as to outweigh these costs. If, for example, one
maintains that this inquiry is justified by the possibility that it may lead
to some refinement of social science methodology, as argued by Boston
University President John Silber (*Encounter,* August 1974), he provides an
insight into his moral calculus: the possible contribution to research
methodology outweighs the social cost of the study of race and IQ in a
racist society. Such advocates often seem to believe that they are defending academic freedom, but this is just a muddle. The issue of freedom of
research arises here in its conventional form: does the research in question carry costs, and if so, are they outweighed by its significance? The
scientist has no unique right to ignore the likely consequences of what
he does.

Once the issue of race and IQ is raised, people who perceive and are
concerned by its severe social cost are, in a sense, trapped. They may
quite properly dismiss the work on the grounds just sketched. But they
do so in a racist society in which, furthermore, people are trained to
consign questions of human and social importance to "technical experts," who often prove to be experts in obfuscation and defense of
privilege—"experts in legitimation," in Gramsci's phrase. The consequences are obvious. Or they may enter the arena of argument and
counterargument, thus implicitly reinforcing the belief that it makes a
difference how the research comes out, and thus tacitly supporting the
racist assumption on which this belief ultimately rests. Inevitably, then,

by refuting alleged correlations between race and IQ (or race and X, for any X one selects), one is reinforcing racist assumptions. The dilemma is not restricted to this issue. I have discussed it elsewhere in connection with debate over murder and aggression.[30] In a highly ideological society, matters can hardly be otherwise, a misfortune that we may deplore but cannot easily escape.

We exist and work in given historical conditions. We may try to change them but cannot ignore them, either in the work we undertake, the strategies for social change that we advocate, or the direct action in which we engage or from which we abstain. In discussion of freedom and equality, it is very difficult to disentangle questions of fact from judgments of value. We should try to do so, pursuing factual inquiry where it may lead without dogmatic preconception, but not ignoring the consequences of what we do. We must never forget that what we do is tainted and distorted, inevitably, by the awe of expertise that is induced by social institutions as one device for enforcing passivity and obedience. What we do as scientists, as scholars, as advocates, has consequences, just as our refusal to speak or act has definite consequences. We cannot escape this condition in a society based on concentration of power and privilege. There is a heavy responsibility that the scientist or scholar would not have to bear in a decent society, in which individuals would not relegate to authorities decisions over their lives or their beliefs. We may and should recommend the simple virtues: honesty and truthfulness, responsibility and concern. But to live by these precepts is often no simple matter.

the *U*NITED STATES *and the* *W*ORLD

THE COLD WAR

The Old and the New
Cold War

(1980)

*I*F THERE IS INDEED A RENEWAL OF SUPERPOWER CONFRON-
tation, it is likely to resemble the Old Cold War in certain
respects but to be crucially different in others. Consider first
some likely similarities. The Cold War is generally described as a "zero-
sum game" in which the gains of one antagonist equal the losses of the
other. But this is a highly questionable interpretation. It would be more
realistic to regard the Cold War system as a macabre dance of death in
which the rulers of the superpowers mobilize their own populations to
support harsh and brutal measures directed against victims within what
they take to be their respective domains, where they are "protecting their
legitimate interests." Appeal to the alleged threat of the powerful global
enemy has proven to be a useful device for this purpose. In this respect,

the Cold War has proven highly functional for the superpowers, which is one reason why it persists despite the prospect of mutual incineration if the system misbehaves, as sooner or later it very likely will. When the United States moves to overthrow the government of Iran or Guatemala or Chile, or to invade Cuba or Indochina or the Dominican Republic, or to bolster murderous dictatorships in Latin America or Asia, it does so in a noble effort to defend free peoples from the imminent Russian (or earlier, Chinese) threat. Similarly, when the USSR sends its tanks to East Berlin, Hungary, Czechoslovakia, or Afghanistan, it is acting from the purest of motives, defending socialism and freedom against the machinations of U.S. imperialism and its cohorts. The rhetoric employed on both sides is similar,[1] and is generally parroted by the intelligentsia in each camp. It has proven effective in organizing popular support, as even a totalitarian state must do. In this respect, the New Cold War promises to be no different, and can be understood in part as a natural outcome of the effort to overcome the "Vietnam syndrome."

Another typical gambit is the pretense that only a show of force will deter the superpower antagonist from its relentless marauding and subversion. The actual dynamics of the Cold War system suggest a rather different conclusion. Typically, acts of subversion, violence, and aggression, or development and deployment of new weapons systems, have had the predictable effect of reinforcing those elements of the antagonist state that are committed, for their own reasons, to similar practices, a recurrent pattern throughout the Cold War period. Examples that are cited in support of the standard thesis regularly collapse on examination, e.g., Angola, where the U.S.-backed South African intervention is generally disregarded in Western propaganda on the Cuban menace, and a more accurate assessment would take note of "the manner in which Kissinger tried to foment and sustain a civil war in Angola simply to convince the Russians that the American tiger could still bite."[2] It does not, of course, follow that a willingness to seek accommodation would mechanically lead to a relaxation of tensions and a reduction of international violence, but its role as a possible factor should not be discounted.

One persistent element of the Cold War system is the portrayal of the superpower antagonist in the most menacing terms. In Soviet propaganda, the United States is led by warmongers deterred from their limitless drive for expansion only by Russian power. In the West, it is now an article of faith that the Soviet Union is outspending its rivals in a race toward military domination of the planet. There is some basis of truth in these competing claims, as is usually the case even in the most vulgar propaganda exercises, but it is revealing to disentangle the element of truth from the web of distortion. The claim that the USSR is unrivaled in its commitment of resources to military production is based largely on

CIA analyses which estimate the dollar equivalent of the USSR military effort; thus the question asked is what it would cost the United States, in dollars, to duplicate the military force deployed by the USSR. As a number of commentators have observed,[3] these calculations have a built-in bias. The Soviet military force is labor-intensive, in contrast to the military system of the West with its superior technological level and higher cost of labor relative to capital. It would be highly inefficient, and extremely costly, for the United States to duplicate a technologically less advanced Soviet military machine that relies heavily on manpower. Hence calculations of dollar equivalents considerably exaggerate Russian power. For the United States to duplicate the Russian agricultural system, with its intensive use of human labor power and low level of technology, would also be extremely expensive. But we do not therefore conclude that the Russians are outmarching us in the field of agricultural production. For similar reasons, calculations of dollar equivalents give a highly misleading picture of relative military strength.

Suppose that we were to reverse the process and estimate a ruble-equivalent of the American military force. This would be a meaningless exercise. It is probable that the Soviet Union simply lacks the technological capacity to duplicate the American military machine, so the ruble-equivalent would be infinite. These observations simply point up the absurdity of the calculations that are used to frighten the populations of the West so that they will be induced to support the militarization of their own societies. The absurdity is heightened when we note that NATO, by any calculation, outspends the Warsaw Pact,[4] and when we bring into consideration such factors as the Sino-Soviet conflict and the strained relations between the Soviet Union and its Warsaw Pact allies. Franklyn Holzman notes that the American Joint Chiefs of Staff consistently conclude that the United States fields the world's most powerful military force, despite the insistent claims that the Russians are outspending us in their drive for world domination. The paradox is resolved when the analyses of relative military strength are dissected. No doubt an analysis of Soviet propaganda would reveal comparable duplicity.

The fact is that both of the superpowers—and many lesser powers as well—are ruining their economies and threatening world peace, indeed human survival, by a mindless commitment to military production for themselves and for export. Many factors contribute to the emphasis on military production, quite apart from the drive for global dominance. There has always been a temptation to resort to chauvinist appeals and militarization to deal with social and economic crises that appear unmanageable. The domestic power of the military-bureaucratic elite that rules the Soviet Union is enhanced by the diversion of resources to military production. In the 1950s, liberal economists in the United States denounced the Eisenhower administration for insufficient military spending, testifying before Congress that it was frittering away American affluence in "indulgences, luxuries, and frivolities" while the United States faced "the possibility of annihilation or humiliation" (Walter Heller), and calling for "accelerating and enlarging our defense effort" rather than diverting military resources to consumer goods for people who already have a "frivolous standard of living" (James Tobin).[5] When the Kennedy administration came to power, it followed their advice, using a faked "missile gap" as a propaganda device and relying on massive military expenditures as a mechanism for economic growth, thus setting off the arms race of the 1960s, accelerated by the needless humiliation of Khrushchev at the time of the Cuban missile crisis.[6] Without the benefit of Keynes, the fascist states of the 1930s also proved that the "new economics" works, as economies were stimulated by programs of rearmament. In principle, other methods are available, but a look at the class character of the major industrial powers helps to explain why governments have so commonly turned to production of waste (primarily, armaments) and bribes for the wealthy in their efforts to stimulate a sluggish economy. Unfortunately a great many factors—the drive for domestic and global power, the need to mobilize popular support for costly government programs, the concern to recycle petrodollars by exploiting the comparative advantage of the industrial powers in advanced technology (the arms trade), the requirement that state-induced production must not harm but rather must enhance the interests and power of the private empires that control the economy and largely staff the state executive in the state capitalist democracies—all converge on military production. Unless effective mass popular movements committed to different aims develop, the likely consequences are rather gloomy. In these respects, too, the New Cold War is likely to resemble its earlier phase, though the risks are now considerably more grave.

Focusing on Middle East oil production is still another respect in which the New Cold War is likely to resemble its earlier phase. Speaking to congressional leaders who were reluctant to return to military confrontation in February 1947, Secretary of State George Marshall warned them that "if Greece should dissolve into civil war" and Turkey should fall, then "Soviet domination might thus extend over the entire Middle East and Asia," an early version of the "domino theory." A more realistic concern was the question of how domination over the stupendous natural resources of the Middle East would be shared among the industrial capitalist states, with the United States gradually taking over positions that had long been held by Britain and France. According to James Forrestal, Marshall's first response to Britain's announcement that it was no longer capable of controlling Greece was that this was "tantamount to British abdication from the Middle East with obvious implications as to their successor,"[7] though the collapse of Britain's imperial position may well have been proceeding more rapidly than was anticipated in Grand Area planning at that point.

Joyce and Gabriel Kolko point out that the U.S. "dilemma . . . involved Western European capitalist nations rather than Russia" at that stage of planning, leading to the enunciation of the Truman Doctrine, with the Middle East one among a number of factors.[8] Nevertheless, the "Russian threat" was invoked, with adroitness and cynicism, in the style that became typical of subsequent Cold War interventionism, which, no doubt, learned a valuable lesson from this success. Dean Acheson, in his memoirs, takes credit for converting congressional leaders to the new doctrine in February 1947 with this rhetoric:[9]

> In the past eighteen months, I said, Soviet pressure on the Straits, on Iran, and on northern Greece had brought the Balkans to the point where a highly possible Soviet breakthrough might open three continents to Soviet penetration. Like apples in a barrel infected by one rotten one, the corruption of Greece would infect Iran and all to the east. It would also carry infection to Africa through Asia Minor and Egypt, and to Europe through Italy and France, already threatened by the strongest domestic Communist parties in Western Europe.

Acheson surely knew that the Soviet Union had already been rebuffed in its efforts to modify the Straits regime in its favor and gain a share in the exploitation of Iranian oil, and presumably was also aware that Stalin was urging restraint on the Greek guerrillas (recognizing that Greece was in the American sphere of influence) and instructing the Communist parties of the West to join in the reconstruction of capitalism. But the Russian threat served as a powerful device to mobilize support for intervention.

It is interesting that Acheson takes great pride in this exercise in deception. Acheson's concern over the dangers of democratic politics in the West is no less noteworthy. The New Cold War displays similar features once again, as is hardly necessary to document.

According to the "New Cold Warriors," the search for military bases in the Middle East and the general program of militarization of American society are "defensive measures" taken to protect potential victims of Russian aggression. Senator Church is more honest when he speaks of protecting "our interests," a fact that is well understood by those we are preparing to "protect." When the Islamic states met in Islamabad to condemn the Russian invasion of Afghanistan, they did not fail to warn against U.S. intervention as well, a fact that was hardly highlighted in the

U.S. press. A business-oriented review of economic and political news from the Middle East notes that the meeting "adopted a Saudi-inspired resolution to protect Iran from the effects of an American boycott," and reports that the Gulf countries "are more worried about the potential reaction of the United States to the crisis than they are about Soviet intervention itself." The Middle East is heading toward war, one official stated, "but towards a war which would mean the sharing by the super-powers of its oil and mineral wealth."[10] Subsequent indications confirm that these fears remain dominant.

When these facts are noted in the U.S. press, the phenomenon is often attributed to the mysterious process of "Finlandization," whereby states accommodate to Russian power because they recognize the weakness of the United States. Thus their expressed opposition to U.S. military intervention is neatly converted into an appeal that American military power be enhanced so that our "defensive umbrella" can be extended to states that would willingly take shelter under it if only they could place their trust in U.S. force.[11] This fanciful interpretation is easy enough to explain, given the commitments of its authors to U.S. interventionism and, in many instances, Israeli power. A more serious look at the facts shows quite clearly that the primary concern of the states in question is Israeli military power, which they regard as the primary threat as long as Israel continues with U.S. support to occupy territories conquered in 1967. Furthermore, they have repeatedly stated that they feel no less threatened by the U.S. intent to "defend its legitimate interests" than by the potential Russian menace.

A look at some of the American successes during the Old Cold War reveals that those we intend to "protect" have good reason for fear. The first major U.S. intervention in defense of freedom was in Greece, when Britain, which invaded and conquered Greece after the Nazis had withdrawn, could no longer maintain its position there in 1946–47 after its success in undermining the anti-Nazi resistance and restoring royalist elements and Nazi collaborators to state power, setting off a wave of violence and persecution that finally evoked armed resistance. Displacing the British, the American military mission (AMAG: American Mission for Aid to Greece) lent its fervent and uncompromising support to state violence, which included the imprisonment without trial of tens of thousands of people in concentration camps, where they were subjected to "reindoctrination" if they "were found to have affiliations which cast grave doubt upon their loyalty to the state," in the words of the AMAG chief. (It was only many years later, when the atrocity could be charged to an official enemy, that Westerners became exercised over "reeducation camps"; similarly, British and American reeducation camps for hundreds of thousands of German and Italian POWs up to three years after the war's end, where the victims were not only indoctrinated but also subjected to forced labor and severe mistreatment, are described in the West—if noted at all—as an amazing example of Western humanism, as contrasted with the atrocious behavior of the Vietnamese.)[12] Many thousands were executed and tens of thousands exiled, with the full support of the United States. U.S. chargé Karl Rankin warned in May 1948 that "there must . . . be no leniency toward the confirmed agents of an alien and subversive influence." Execution of political prisoners was legitimate, he argued, because even though when arrested they may not have been "hardened Communists, it is unlikely that they have been able to resist the influence of Communist indoctrination organizations existing within most prisons." Secretary of State George Marshall approved of the "administration of [Greek] justice." Meanwhile, U.S. intelligence engaged in extensive surveillance of Greek citizens and assisted the government in carrying out mass deportations of alleged subversives to concentration camps and reeducation centers, while forwarding to the FBI the names of U.S. citizens who wrote letters protesting executions; the FBI reciprocated by sending reports to the U.S. embassy on alleged Communist ties of Greek-American organizations.

The British protested some of these actions, but were rebuffed. When a British official objected that it was "unwise" to round up fourteen thousand people and exile them without trial to island concentration camps, American Ambassador Lincoln MacVeagh responded that the Greek government "had to throw their net very wide to catch the right people," whom he estimated at about "a dozen key men." This was the first major action undertaken after the United States took control under the aegis of the Truman Doctrine.

When the war was approaching its final stages, the United States insisted on the policy of systematic removal of population by force and backed renewed programs of mass arrest and executions, moderating these commitments only in the very last months of the war. Continued "screening and re-education" were recommended by the U.S. mission for the postwar period, while the State Department fought to block any substantive U.N. recommendations on amnesty, leniency, or an end to political executions.

Throughout, a prime concern of Washington and the U.S. mission in Greece was the unfavorable publicity resulting from the terror it advocated and organized. Measures were taken to control the flow of news. The State Department succeeded in preventing the *New York Times* from publishing stories on U.S. embassy support for repressive programs, and in convincing the United Press to appoint a "double-breasted

Americano" as UP representative in Greece in place of a *Christian Science Monitor* correspondent whom the department considered a leftist. The U.S. government also succeeded in aborting an investigation of the assassination of U.S. correspondent George Polk when evidence began to mount that it was a right-wing assassination rather than the responsibility of the Greek left, as had been claimed; the Pentagon withdrew the Air Force colonel who had been designated to investigate the murder by the Overseas Writers Association after he became convinced that the "extreme right" had committed the murder.

Meanwhile, the United States engaged in extensive psychological warfare operations, of which the ugliest example was fabrication of lies concerning the alleged "abduction" of children by the guerrillas (secretly, government officials conceded the fabrication); the Greek government was itself forcibly evacuating children from rebel-held territory. These allegations (whether there was some substance to them or not is, evidently, a question separate from the conscious fabrication) remained a staple of subsequent propaganda.

The long-term legacy of U.S. support for state terror in Greece was profound, culminating in the fascist coup of 1967, which was also welcomed and backed by the United States, sometimes with rhapsodic commentary on the opportunities it afforded for American business interests.[13]

The Greek experience reveals clearly the true meaning of President Truman's call "to support free peoples who are resisting attempted subjugation by armed minorities or by outside pressures."

The British economist Joan Robinson once described the American crusade against communism as a "crusade against development." It would be accurate to regard it as a crusade against independent development outside of the structure of the global system of exploitation organized under the umbrella of U.S. power after World War II. There is no dearth of documentary evidence on the planning behind this crusade; for example, the Grand Area planning, which remains under a taboo in American scholarship, discussed only far from the mainstream, despite —or perhaps because of—the fact that it provides a valuable insight into the reality that lies behind conventional rhetoric. This reality is remote from conventional ideology, but is lived every day by hundreds of millions of people whose torment is of little concern to Western moralists— unless, of course, they are aroused by "Communist agitators" and subjected to "alien influences." This reality is not a collection of strange coincidences or an indication of the limits of American power to do good, as is constantly proclaimed, but is in significant and deplorable measure a direct and predictable consequence of policy decisions based on the principles expressed in the cool and antiseptic rhetoric of the planners.

Until we come to appreciate these facts, we will understand very little about the contemporary world.

I have been discussing some features of the Old Cold War that one may expect, I believe, to persist if it is successfully resurrected. But there will also be differences. The world is not what it was a generation ago. It is doubtful that the United States, no longer in a position of overwhelming dominance, can devote its resources to the production of waste while maintaining its position in international trade—of course, apart from sales of military equipment, which continue to increase, not solely from the United States. Efforts to pressure U.S. allies to "bear their share of the burden" of military expenditures are not likely to prove too successful. Europe and Japan have shown little enthusiasm for the new crusade. East-West trade in Europe is now quite substantial, as traditional relationships are being reestablished, and it is unlikely that the European powers will be willing to sacrifice it. American allies may choose to take their own independent initiatives, not only toward the USSR but also toward the Middle East and other resource-rich areas, realizing long-term fears of American planners. It is worth recalling Henry Kissinger's warning, in explaining the thinking behind the "Year of Europe" in 1973, about "the prospect of a closed trading system embracing the European Community and a growing number of other nations in Europe, the Mediterranean, and Africa" from which the United States might be excluded. The proper organization of the world system, he explained, should be based on the recognition that "the United States has global interests and responsibilities," while our allies have "regional interests"; the United States must be "concerned more with the overall framework of order than with the management of every regional enterprise," these being accorded to our allies, as he elaborated elsewhere.[14] But this version of "trilateralism" is unlikely to survive for long.

The Trilateral Commission, which was formed in 1973 to come to terms with the problems of fragmentation within the First World of industrial capitalism, was quite correct in describing the international system that arose from World War II in these terms: "For a quarter century the United States was the hegemonic power in a system of world order"[15]—correct, at least, if we interpret the phrase "world order" with appropriate irony. It is true that in the system that arose from the ashes of World War II, the United States was in a position of quite considerable power, sufficient to materially influence historical developments though not to control them completely in its interests. It is hardly surprising, then, that it attempted to organize a global system, or at least a Grand Area, in the interests of those who held domestic power. The USSR created its own power bloc in Eastern Europe and to some degree China. This was the basic structure of the Old Cold War, but the world is now radically different. China is an American ally and a bitter enemy of the USSR, a major shift in the balance of world power in favor of the United States. And the capitalist world is drifting toward a kind of trilateralism which may eventuate in three partially closed trading blocks—a dollar bloc, a yen bloc, a European Currency Union bloc—as a recent OECD study suggests, with international consequences that are uncertain, and in many ways ominous. Those who recall the mood of 1914 and 1939 do so with some reason.

There is no doubt that U.S. power has waned as the bipolar system of the postwar years has gradually evolved to something more complex. The same is true of Soviet power. A recent study of the Center for Defense Information in Washington, tracing Russian influence on a country-by-country basis since World War II, concludes quite reasonably that it reached a peak in the late 1950s and has since declined to the point where by 1979, "the Soviets were influencing only 6% of the world's population and 5% of the world's GNP, exclusive of the Soviet Union."[16] For reasons already discussed, Cold War ideologists in both camps like to pretend that their adversary is marching from strength to strength, but the facts hardly support these conclusions. Though their capacity to destroy grows steadily, neither the United States nor the Soviet Union now has the power it once was able to wield in world affairs, and this process is not likely to be reversed.

Europe and Japan pose a greater potential threat to U.S. world power than the Soviet Union, if they move toward a more independent role. And a U.S.-sponsored New Cold War may press them in that direction, raising the possibility of new and unanticipated crises and alignments. In the shorter term, one may expect the superpowers to create new and more awesome forces of destruction and to try to subjugate those who stand in the way of their global ambitions, marching toward nuclear catastrophe.

The recent steps toward Armageddon have evoked little articulate protest in the United States, though there is a substantial groundswell of popular concern. This testifies again to the great success of the campaign to overcome the "Vietnam syndrome." A few recent examples will illustrate the astonishing achievements of the efforts to restore what Hans Morgenthau once called "our conformist subservience to those in power"—though the distance that had to be traveled was far less than is often supposed. First, some additional words of background.

The war against the world's poor and oppressed reached its peak under the liberal democratic administrations of the 1960s, with the considerable amplification of the doctrine and practice of counterinsurgency and counterrevolutionary subversion and violence. A plague of neofascist states spread through Latin America and elsewhere as well. Brazil, because of its size and power, was a particularly significant example. The U.S.-backed military coup of 1964 placed in power a repressive and murderous regime that carried out an "economic miracle" while keeping the great mass of the population in conditions of grinding poverty and actually lowering the already miserable standard of living for many of them. It also had a noticeable "domino effect," contributing to the spread of U.S.-backed military dictatorships committed to repression and violence. As always, U.S. support for the Brazilian coup was justified on the grounds that "the nation needed it in order to free itself of a corrupt government which was about to sell us out to international communism" (General Andrew O'Meara, commander of the U.S. Southern Command, testifying before Congress in 1965). President Kennedy's ambassador to Brazil, Lincoln Gordon, described the Brazilian "revolution" as the "the single most decisive victory for freedom in the mid-twentieth century."[17] Similarly the Indonesian coup a year later was welcomed in liberal circles as a vindication of the U.S. policy of standing firm in Indochina, while the resulting massacre of hundreds of thousands of landless peasants, if noted at all, was dismissed as an unfortunate reaction to Communist plotting. The revolution in Cuba, in contrast, was understood to pose such threats to human rights and civilized values that the leader of the Free World subjected Cuba to invasion, subversion, embargo, terrorism, poisoning of crops and livestock—and now, after this record, stands in judgment over Cuba for its violation of human rights.

The situation in Latin America has not gone unnoticed in establishment media. Richard Fagen writes in *Foreign Affairs* (Winter 1979) that the Linowitz Commission was accurate in describing the "plague of repression" that had settled over Latin America by 1976: "At no time in the recent history of the hemisphere had the incidence of military rule been so high, the gross violations of political and human rights so widespread, and the use of officially sponsored assassination, torture and brutality so systematic." But in journalistic or scholarly discussion, these facts are rarely related to U.S. initiatives; rather, these developments show that it is not within the power of the United States to eliminate inequality and poverty, as it has been striving so desperately to do for so many years in Brazil, Paraguay, Nicaragua, Guatemala, and elsewhere within the domains of its influence and control.

Actually, it is interesting to inquire into the relation between human rights violations and U.S. aid and support. There does, in fact, appear to be a correlation, which has been noted in several studies, one of them by Edward S. Herman and myself (see our *Political Economy of Human Rights*, vol. 1). We found, as did Michael Klare in an independent study, that the deterioration of the human rights climate in some Free World dependency tends to correlate rather closely with an increase in U.S. aid and support. Of course, one must be cautious with statistical correlations; the correlation in question should not be interpreted as implying that the U.S. government is rewarding some ruling group for the increase in torture, death squads, destruction of unions, elimination of democratic institutions, decline of living standards for much of the population, etc. These are not a positive priority for U.S. policy; rather, they are irrelevant to it. The correlation between abuse of human rights and U.S. support derives from deeper factors. The deterioration in human rights and the increase in U.S. aid and support each correlate, independently, with a third and crucial factor: namely, improvement of the investment climate, as measured by privileges granted foreign capital. The climate for business operations improves as unions and other popular organizations are destroyed, dissidents are tortured or eliminated, real wages are depressed, and the society as a whole is placed in the hands of a collection of thugs who are willing to sell out to the foreigner for a share of the loot—often too large a share, as business regularly complains. And as the climate for business operations improves, the society is welcomed into the Free World and offered the specific kind of "aid" that will further these favorable developments. If the consequences are, for example, that crops are produced for export by wealthy landowners or transnational agribusiness while the population starves, that is simply the price that must be paid for the survival of free institutions.

The correlation just cited, and the obvious explanation for it, reveal that there may well be a relation between U.S. foreign policy and human rights, though not precisely the one that is widely heralded throughout the international propaganda system. No less striking than the correlation is the general avoidance of all of these matters in respectable scholarship. In this context, it is possible for an American president to stand up and proclaim that concern for human rights is "the Soul of our foreign policy," and to be listened to with respect—even critics limit themselves to noting "contradictions," "inconsistencies," and "deviations," thus reinforcing the basic principle of the propaganda system, that the United States is committed to a program of freedom and human rights (as is the West in general), one of the great lies of modern history, and one of the most effective.

The spread of neofascist torture-and-corruption states in the Third World under U.S. sponsorship has in part been a response to "the lessons of Vietnam." General Maxwell Taylor, who has been described as the *éminence grise* of the Kennedy administration, explained that "the outstanding lesson [of the Indochina conflict] is that we should never let another Vietnam-type situation arise again. We were too late in recognizing the extent of the subversive threat. . . . We have learned the need for a strong police force and a strong police intelligence organization to assist in identifying early the symptoms of an incipient subversive situation."[18] This was in December 1965, after the Brazilian and Indonesian coups, after the invasion of the Dominican Republic, events that revealed how well the lessons of Vietnam had been absorbed by ruling groups that have a historical memory, a capacity to learn, and a high level of class consciousness, and that benefit by the absence of any substantial domestic critique. True, the "Vietnam syndrome" and the "crisis of democracy" impeded their programs for a time, but it is hoped that these maladies of our social order have now been overcome.

AT WAR WITH ASIA

The American Invasion of South Vietnam

Afghanistan and
South Vietnam

(1984)

*I*N MAY 1983, A REMARKABLE EVENT TOOK PLACE IN MOSCOW.
A courageous newscaster, Vladimir Danchev, denounced the
Russian invasion of Afghanistan in five successive radio broadcasts extending over five days, calling upon the rebels to resist. This
aroused great admiration in the West. The *New York Times* commented
accurately that this was a departure from the "official Soviet propaganda
line," that Danchev had "revolted against the standards of double-think
and newspeak." In Paris, a prize was established for "a journalist who
fights for the right to be informed." Danchev was taken off the air and
sent to a psychiatric hospital. He was returned to his position last December. A Russian official was quoted as saying that "he was not punished,
because a sick man cannot be punished."

In the West, all of this was understood as a glimpse into the world of 1984. Danchev was admired for his courage, for a triumph of the human will, for his refusal to be cowed by totalitarian violence. All of this is fair enough.

What was particularly remarkable about Danchev's radio broadcasts was not simply that he expressed opposition to the Soviet invasion and called for resistance to it, but that he called it an "invasion." In Soviet theology, there is no such event as the Russian invasion of Afghanistan; rather, there is a Russian *defense* of Afghanistan against bandits operating from Pakistani sanctuaries and supported by the CIA and other warmongers. The Russians claim that they were invited in, and in a certain technical sense this is correct. But as the London *Economist* grandly proclaimed, "An invader is an invader unless invited in by a government with a claim to legitimacy," and the government installed by the USSR to invite them in can hardly make such a claim, outside of the world of Orwellian Newspeak.

Implicit in the coverage of the Danchev affair in the West was a note of self-congratulation: it couldn't happen here; no American newscaster has been sent to a psychiatric hospital for calling an American invasion "an invasion" or for calling on the victims to resist. We might, however, inquire further into just why this has never happened. One possibility, at least an abstract possibility, is that the question has never arisen because no American journalist would ever mimic Danchev's courage, or could even perceive that an American invasion of the Afghan type is in fact an invasion or that a sane person might call on the victims to resist. If so, this would be a stage of indoctrination well beyond what has been achieved under Soviet terror, well beyond anything that Orwell imagined. Is this merely an abstract possibility, or is it an uncomfortably true portrayal of the actual circumstances in which we live?

Consider the following facts. In 1962, the United States attacked South Vietnam. In that year, President Kennedy sent the United States Air Force to attack rural South Vietnam, where more than 80 percent of the population lived, as part of a program intended to drive several million people to concentration camps (called "strategic hamlets"), where they would be surrounded by barbed wire and armed guards and "protected" from the guerrillas who, we conceded, they were willingly supporting. This was similar to what we are doing today in El Salvador, though in the Vietnamese case U.S. pilots were directly engaged in bombing of civilian targets and defoliation instead of merely guiding and coordinating air strikes against civilians and other military actions undertaken by the forces we train and arm. The direct U.S. invasion of South Vietnam followed our support for the French attempt to reconquer their former colony, our disruption of the 1954 "peace process," and a terrorist war against the South Vietnamese population that had already left some seventy-five thousand dead while evoking domestic resistance, supported from the northern half of the country after 1959, which threatened to bring down the terrorist regime that the United States had established. In the following years, the United States continued to resist every attempt at peaceful settlement and in 1964 began to plan the ground invasion of South Vietnam which took place in early 1965, accompanied by bombing of North Vietnam and an intensification of the bombing of the South, at triple the level of the more publicized bombing of the North. The United States also extended the war to Laos, then Cambodia.

The United States protested that it was invited in, but as the London *Economist* recognized in the case of Afghanistan (never, in the case of Vietnam), "an invader is an invader unless invited in by a government with a claim to legitimacy," and outside the world of Newspeak, the client regime established by the United States had no more legitimacy than the Afghan regime established by the USSR. Nor did the United States regard this government as having any legitimacy: in fact, it was regularly overthrown and replaced when its leaders appeared to be insufficiently enthusiastic about U.S. plans to escalate the terror, or when they were feared to be considering a peaceful settlement. The United States openly recognized throughout that a political settlement was impossible, for the simple reason that the "enemy" would win handily in a political competition, which was therefore unacceptable. The conflict had to be restricted to the military dimension, where the United States could hope to reign supreme. In the words of U.S. government scholar Douglas Pike, now head of the Indochina archives at Berkeley and much revered in mainstream journalism as one of a new breed of "nonideological" scholars, the South Vietnamese enemy "maintained that its contest with the [U.S.-installed government] and the United States should be fought out at the political level and that the use of massed military might was in itself illegitimate" until forced by the United States "to use counter-force to survive."

For the past twenty-two years, I have been searching to find some reference in mainstream journalism or scholarship to an American invasion of South Vietnam in 1962 (or ever), or an American attack against South Vietnam, or American aggression in Indochina—without success. There is no such event in history. Rather, there is an American *defense* of South Vietnam against terrorists supported from outside (namely, from Vietnam), a defense that was unwise, the doves maintain.

In short, there are no Danchevs here. Within the mainstream, there is no one who can call an invasion "an invasion," or even perceive the fact; it is unimaginable that any American journalist would have publicly called upon the South Vietnamese to resist the American invasion. Such a person would not have been sent to a psychiatric hospital, but he would surely not have retained his professional position and standing. Even today, those who refer to the U.S. invasion of South Vietnam in 1962, intensified in 1965, are regarded with disbelief: perhaps they are confused, or perhaps quite mad. Note that here it takes no courage to tell the truth, merely honesty. We cannot plead fear of state violence, as followers of the party line can in a totalitarian state.

Just to add a personal note, in a book I wrote shortly after the Russian invasion of Afghanistan, I compared it to the U.S. invasion of South Vietnam, and discussed more generally the responsibility of both superpowers for the Cold War system of conflict and intervention. American reviewers were unable to see the words, and complained that while there might be something to what I wrote, it would be more convincing if the story had been told "a little more evenhandedly" (Christopher Lehmann-Haupt in the *New York Times*) or that I was guilty of a "double moral standard" (James Fallows in the *Atlantic Monthly*). The same book was reviewed in the Communist press, which dismissed my "far-fetched and groundless concept that both powers have a vested interest in the Cold War" (James West of the American Communist Party Political Bureau, in the *World Marxist Review*), offering arguments that this was solely an American affair. What is of interest is that the Communist commentary, while incorrect, is at least rational, while the mainstream U.S. commentary reflects the kind of incapacity to perceive or think about simple issues that is sometimes found in the more fanatical religious cults.

It is common now to deride any analogy between the Soviet invasion of Afghanistan and the U.S. invasion of Grenada, and indeed they differ radically in scale and character. A comparison to the U.S. invasion of South Vietnam would be more appropriate, but is inconceivable within the mainstream.

Vietnam and United States Global Strategy

(1973)

WITH REGARD TO LONG-TERM UNITED STATES OBJECTIVES, the Pentagon Papers again add useful documentation, generally corroborating, I believe, analyses based on the public record that have been presented elsewhere.[1] In the early period, the documentary record presents a fairly explicit account of more or less rational pursuit of perceived self-interest. The primary argument was straightforward. The United States has strategic and economic interests in Southeast Asia that must be secured. Holding Indochina is essential to securing these interests. Therefore, we must hold Indochina. A critical consideration is Japan, which will eventually accommodate to the "Soviet bloc" if Southeast Asia is lost. In effect, then, the United States would have lost the Pacific phase of World War II, which was fought, in part,

to prevent Japan from constructing a closed "co-prosperity sphere" in
Asia from which the United States would be excluded. The theoretical
framework for these considerations was the domino theory, which was
formulated clearly before the Korean War, as was the decision to support
French colonialism. The goal: a new "co-prosperity sphere" congenial to
United States interests and incorporating Japan.

It is fashionable today to deride the domino theory, but in fact it
contains an important kernel of plausibility, perhaps truth. National independence and revolutionary social change, if successful, may very well be
contagious. The problem is what Walt Rostow and others sometimes call
the "ideological threat," specifically, "the possibility that the Chinese
Communists can prove to Asians by progress in China that Communist
methods are better and faster than democratic methods."[2] The State
Department feared that "a fundamental source of danger we face in the
Far East derives from Communist China's rate of economic growth which
will probably continue to outstrip that of free Asian countries, with the
possible exception of Japan," a matter of real as well as psychological
impact elsewhere.[3] The Joint Chiefs repeated the same wording two
weeks later (p. 1213), adding further that "the dramatic economic improvements realized by Communist China over the past ten years impress
the nations of the region greatly and offer a serious challenge to the Free
World" (p. 1226). State therefore urged that the United States do what
it can to retard the economic progress of the Communist Asian states (p.
1208),[4] a decision that is remarkable in its cruelty.

A few years later, in the midst of the fall 1964 planning to escalate the
war, Michael Forrestal argued that we must be concerned with Chinese
"ideological expansion," its need "to achieve ideological successes
abroad," and the danger that any such ideological success will stimulate
the need for further successes. Therefore "our objective should be to
'contain' China for the longest possible period";[5] or, as the analyst puts
it a bit more accurately, paraphrasing Forrestal, "the U.S. object should
be to 'contain' Chinese political and ideological influence" (III, 218).
William Sullivan picked up the same theme, viewing "Chinese political
and ideological aggressiveness . . . as a threat to the ability of these
peoples to determine their own futures, and hence to develop along ways
compatible with U.S. interests" (III, 218; analyst's paraphrase).

Note the typical assumption that self-determination is compatible with
United States interests, an assumption that is more than usually insipid
in the light of what the Pentagon Papers reveal about the actual American
response to Vietnamese efforts at self-determination. The same assumption, in effect, appeared much earlier in the important State Department
policy statement of September 1948, which took note of "our inability to
suggest any practicable solution of the Indochina problem." This inabil-

ity arose from the incompatibility of our long-term objectives with certain unpleasant facts. One long-term objective is to eliminate Communist influence so far as possible and to prevent Chinese influence, and "the unpleasant fact [is] that Communist Ho Chi Minh is the strongest and perhaps the ablest figure in Indochina and that any suggested solution which excludes him is an expedient of uncertain outcome." What is particularly interesting is the reason why we must "prevent undue Chinese penetration and subsequent influence in Indochina." The reason is "so that the peoples of Indochina will not be hampered in their natural developments by the pressure of an alien people and alien interests."

This laudable concern for the "natural developments" of the people of Indochina, free from alien interests, is coupled with the statement of another long-term objective of United States policy: "to see installed a self-governing nationalist state which will be friendly to the US and which . . . will be patterned upon our conception of a democratic state," and will be associated "with the western powers, particularly with France with whose customs, language and laws [the peoples of Indochina] are familiar, to the end that those peoples will prefer freely to coperate with the western powers culturally, economically and politically" and will "work productively and thus contribute to a better balanced world economy," while enjoying a rising standard of income *(DOD,* bk. 8, pp. 148, 144). The United States and France, in short, do not constitute "alien people and alien interests" so far as the peoples of Indochina are concerned, and association with them does not hamper "natural developments."

The National Security Council working group of November 1964, in discussing the domino theory, pointed out the danger that mainland Southeast Asia might fall to Communist domination if South Vietnam does, noting that "if either Thailand or Malaysia were lost, or went badly sour in any way, then the rot would be in real danger of spreading all over mainland Southeast Asia" (III, 627). The Joint Chiefs added that they were "convinced Thailand would indeed go." The NSC working group was further concerned with the "effects on Japan, where the set is clearly in the direction of closer ties with Communist China, with a clear threat of early recognition"; and with the possibility that "if the rest of Southeast Asia did in fact succumb over time," the effects might be "multiplied many times over" and might, "over time, tend to unravel the whole Pacific defense structure." The Joint Chiefs added that the loss of South Vietnam alone would have these effects, that the United States would not be able to prevent the rot from spreading, very likely, except through "general war," and that the time frame for the unraveling of the whole Pacific defense structure would be brief.

Shortly after, William Bundy and John McNaughton noted that the "most likely result" of the least aggressive option they were considering (option A) "would be a Vietnamese-negotiated deal, under which an eventually unified Communist Vietnam would reassert its traditional hostility to Communist China and limit its own ambitions to Laos and Cambodia." They added: "In such a case . . . whether the rot spread to Thailand would be hard to judge." It would, however, be likely that the Thai "would accommodate somehow to Communist China even without any marked military move by Communist China," because they would "conclude we simply could not be counted on" (III, 661).

Option A was unacceptable: the United States was unwilling to accept its "most likely result," a Vietnamese-negotiated deal leading to a unified Vietnam, Communist-led and hostile to China, its ambitions limited to Laos and Cambodia. Therefore, the planners quickly moved to heightened aggression. They are vague as to just how the rot will spread to Thailand or why they fear a Thai "accommodation" to China. This imprecision cannot be an oversight; these are, after all, the crucial issues, the issues that led the planners to recommend successive stages of aggression in Indochina, at immense risk and cost. But even internal documents, detailed analyses of options and possible consequences, refer to these central issues in loose and almost mystical terms. Occasionally, as in the document just cited, the planners make it clear that military conquest is not the mechanism by which the rot will spread. Surely they did not believe that Ho Chi Minh was going to conquer Thailand or Malaya or set sail for Jakarta or Tokyo. One must assume they were sufficiently in touch with reality to comprehend that Vietnamese support for guerrilla movements could hardly be very significant in Thailand or Malaya (and would be of no significance beyond). Such movements could succeed only if they had powerful roots and were capable of rallying the local population. If nothing else, repeated failures to incite resistance in North Vietnam would have sufficed to establish this fact. And it is difficult to believe that the planners, not ignorant men, feared Chinese aggression in Southeast Asia. As we see from the cited document, they regarded even a unified Vietnam that would be hostile to China as a danger to their plans, and anticipated that the mysterious Thai "accommodation" would take place even without any overt military moves by China.

In fact, the American political leadership desperately sought some indication that China had aggressive intentions. A case in point was their interpretation of Lin Piao's statement of September 1965, which emphasized that national liberation movements must be self-reliant and cannot count on China for meaningful support. To McNamara, Rusk, and others, this was a new *Mein Kampf.*[6] The response of the Kennedy intellectuals to Mao's talk about the East Wind prevailing over the West Wind,[7] or to Khrushchev's statements of support for wars of national liberation, was of the same order. It would be misleading to say that such statements inspired fear or concern in Washington; rather, ideologists eagerly seized upon them in an effort to justify programs that they wished to undertake or had already set in motion. As we shall see directly, United States intelligence agencies made determined (though unavailing) efforts to unearth evidence that would prove the Vietminh to be agents of "international communism," after having decided, with certain qualms, to support the reconquest of Indochina by France.

There is only one rational explanation for these and many similar incidents, and for the imprecision of the planners with regard to the spreading of the rot and the accommodation that they so feared. The "rot" is the Communist "ideological threat," which must be combatted by direct intervention against local Communist rebellion, whether or not armed attack is involved. The Thai elite, they fear, will "conclude we simply could not be counted on" to help them prevent internal social change in Thailand or to suppress a domestic insurgency. The only "threat" posed by a unified Vietnam, hostile to China and limiting its ambitions to Laos and Cambodia, is the threat of social and economic progress within a framework unacceptable to American imperial interests. This is the rot that may spread to Thailand, inspiring a Communist-led nationalist movement there. But no skillful ideologist would want to see the implications spelled out too clearly, to himself or others. Consequently the central factors noted are left a mystery, apart from occasional comments such as those just cited.

Recall that in this period there was much talk of competition between the Chinese and the Indian models of development. In this context, fear of Chinese "ideological expansion" gave substance to the domino theory, quite apart from any fantasies about Chinese troops roaming at will through northern Thailand or Kremlin-directed aggression by the Vietminh.

It is important to be clear about what is at stake in a discussion of the domino theory and related matters. The reality of perceived dangers is, of course, irrelevant to determining the motivation of policy-makers. The fact that threats were perceived and taken seriously suffices to establish motive. The question of the reality of the threats is nevertheless of interest, for a different reason. If, in fact, foolishness or ignorance led to the perception of imaginary dangers, as is often alleged, then policy could be "improved" (for whose benefit is another question) by replacing the policy-makers by others who are more intelligent and better informed. The issues are sometimes not kept separate, with much resulting confusion.

In Southeast Asia, the threat was heightened by a look at the allies of the United States. When Lyndon Johnson returned from Vietnam in May 1961, he spoke of the problem of reassuring our friends: in addition to

Diem, these were Chiang, Sarit, and Ayub (II, 56). Such friends as these—
the only ones mentioned—surely were endangered by the "ideological
threat" that Rostow and others perceived. The threat would be enhanced
if Vietnam were to be united under Communist leadership and successful
in mobilization of the population for social and economic development,
as might well have occurred had United States force not been introduced.

The comparison of development in South and North Vietnam was not
particularly encouraging to the United States in this regard. An intelligence estimate of May 1959 concluded that "development will lag behind
that in the North, and the GVN [Government of Vietnam] will continue
to rely heavily upon US support to close the gap between its own resources and its requirements" (*DOD*, bk. 10, p. 1191). In the North, the
standard of living is low and "life is grim and regimented," but "the
national effort is concentrated on building for the future." The South has
a higher standard of living (and "there is far more freedom and gaiety"—
for whom is not specified, nor is there discussion of the distribution of
wealth), but "basic economic growth has been slower than that of the
north." The alleged higher standard of living in the South was not unrelated to the more than $1 billion of American nonmilitary aid, the bulk
of which financed import of commodities (*DOD*, bk. 10, pp. 1191–93). In
a similar context a few years later, an NSC working group took note of
the discouragement in South Korea "at the failure to make as much
progress politically and economically as North Korea" (III, 627).

Perhaps the threat has now diminished, with the vast destruction in
South Vietnam and elsewhere and the hatreds and social disruption
caused by the American war. It may be that Vietnam can be lost to the
Vietnamese without the dire consequence of social and economic progress of a sort that might be meaningful to the Asian poor. Perhaps the
"second line of defense" of which American planners spoke can be held,
at least for a time. On such assumptions, the United States government
might be willing to reverse its long-standing opposition to a political
settlement among Vietnamese.

If our friends were toppled by popular movements, perhaps ultimately
leading Japan to realign, influencing India, affecting even the oil-rich
Middle East and then Europe, as the domino theory postulated, there
would be a serious impact on the global system dominated by the United
States and United States-based international corporations. Although
some of the formulations of the domino theory were indeed fantastic, the
underlying concept was not. Correspondingly it comes as no surprise to
discover that it is rarely challenged in this record. The analyst regards
support for the French against Ho Chi Minh as "the path of prudence
rather than the path of risk"; it "seemed the wiser choice," given the
likelihood that all of Southeast Asia might have fallen under Ho's leader-

ship (obviously not by military conquest, say, in Indonesia). This he regards as "only slightly less of a bad dream than what has happened to Vietnam since" (I, 52). The domino principle, he notes "was at the root of U.S. policy" since Chiang's defeat. It was also at the root of French policy, though the dominoes they were concerned with were in North Africa (I, 54). The domino theory was firmly reiterated by McGeorge Bundy in mid-1967 (IV, 159), and by many others.

In the years between, there is debate only over timing and probability. A CIA analysis of June 1964 has frequently been described as a challenge to the validity of the domino theory.[8] However, this analysis (III, 178) merely states that the surrounding nations probably would not *"quickly* succumb to communism as a result of the fall of Laos and South Vietnam" (my italics) and the spread of communism would not be "inexorable" and might be reversed, though the loss of South Vietnam and Laos "would be profoundly damaging to the U.S. position in the Far East," and might encourage the "militant policies" of Hanoi and Peking.

The documentation for the pre-Kennedy period gives substantial support to this interpretation of United States motives. By April 1945, the United States had publicly supported the reconstitution of French authority, somewhat evasively, while a "more liberal" pattern, specifically "liberalization of restrictive French economic policies," was recommended "for the protection of American interests" (*DOD*, bk. 8, pp. 6–10). The American interest in Indochina ("almost exclusively a French economic preserve, and a political morass") was considerably less than in Indonesia, where "extensive American and British investments . . . afforded common ground for intervention" (I, 29). It was urged that France move to grant autonomy to its colonies (or the people "may embrace ideologies contrary to our own or develop a Pan-Asiatic movement against all Western powers") and that open-door policies be pursued (*DOD*, bk. 8, p. 23). By December 1946, it was noted that "French appear to realize no longer possible maintain closed door here and non-French interests will have chance to participate in unquestioned rich economic possibilities" (p. 87). Although the resources of Indochina itself are repeatedly mentioned (e.g., p. 183), it was of course the whole region (on the hypothesis of the domino theory) that was the primary consideration: "if COMMIES gain control IC, THAI and rest SEA will be imperiled" (p. 220; June 1949).

A National Security Council report of December 1949 went into the situation in some detail (NSC 48/1; *DOD*, bk. 8, pp. 226–27). The problem is that now and for the foreseeable future, the Soviet Union threatens to dominate Asia, an area of significant political, economic, and military power. The "Stalinist bloc" might achieve global dominance if Japan, "the principal component of a Far Eastern war-making complex," were added to it. "Whether [Japan's] potential is developed and the way in which it is used will strongly influence the future patterns of politics in Asia." "In the power potential of Asia, Japan plays the most important part" by reason of its economic potential and strategic position. "The industrial plant of Japan would be the richest strategic prize in the Far East for the USSR." Communist pressure on Japan will mount, because of proximity, the indigenous Japanese Communist movement which might be able to exploit cultural factors and economic hardship, and "the potential of Communist China as a source of raw materials vital to Japan and a market for its goods." Japan requires Asian food, raw materials, and markets; the United States should encourage "a considerable increase in Southern Asiatic food and raw material exports" to avoid "preponderant dependence on Chinese sources." Analogous considerations hold for India. Furthermore, these markets and sources of raw materials should be developed for United States purposes. "Some kind of regional association . . . among the non-Communist countries of Asia might become an important means of developing a favorable atmosphere for such trade among themselves and with other parts of the world."

As John Dower, among others, has emphasized, "The United States has never intended to carry the burden of anti-Communist and anti-Chinese consolidation alone. It has always seen the end goal as a quasi-dependent Asian regionalism."[9] The Pentagon Papers enrich the available documentation on this matter in a rather interesting way.

Continuing with NSC 48/1, it is recommended that under certain restrictions trade with Communist China should be permitted, for the health of the Japanese and American economies. The industrial plant of Japan and such strategic materials as Indonesian oil must be denied to the Soviet Union and kept in the Western orbit. The particular problem in Southeast Asia is that it "is the target of a coordinated offensive directed by the Kremlin" (this is "now clear"), and has no responsible leaders, outside of Thailand[10] and the Philippines. If Southeast Asia "is swept by communism we shall have suffered a major political rout the repercussions of which will be felt throughout the rest of the world, especially in the Middle East and in a then critically exposed Australia."

The general lines of this analysis persist through the Truman and Eisenhower administrations. NSC 64 (I, 361–62) concluded that Thailand and Burma would "fall under Communist domination" and the rest of Southeast Asia would be "in grave hazard" if Indochina were "controlled by a Communist-dominated government." The Joint Chiefs urged "long-term measures to provide for Japan and the other offshore islands a secure source of food and other strategic materials from non-Communist held areas in the Far East" (I, 366; April 1950; they also recommended military aid and covert operations). A State Department policy committee interpreted NSC 64 as asserting that "the loss of Indochina to Communist forces would undoubtedly lead to the loss of Southeast Asia" (*DOD*, bk. 8, p. 351; October 1950). NSC 48/5 saw the Soviet Union as attempting to bring the mainland of East Asia and eventually Japan under Soviet control (pp. 425–26; May 1951). Given Asian population, military capacity, critical resources, and Japanese industrial capacity, it is essential to block this program. An NSC staff study of February 1952 warned:

> The fall of Southeast Asia would underline the apparent economic advantages to Japan of association with the communist-dominated Asian sphere. Exclusion of Japan from trade with Southeast Asia would seriously affect the Japanese economy, and increase Japan's dependence on United States aid. In the long run the loss of Southeast Asia, especially Malaya and Indonesia, could result in such economic and political pressures in Japan as to make it extremely difficult to prevent Japan's eventual accommodation to the Soviet Bloc. [I, 375]

It went on to speak of the importance of Southeast Asian raw materials (for example, Indonesian oil, and the significance of Malaya, the largest dollar earner of the United Kingdom, to Britain's economic recovery) and United States strategic interests, developing the domino theory in detail.

NSC 124/2 in June 1952 identified China as the main enemy and gave a clear formulation of the domino theory, emphasizing again the problem of raw materials and the threat of Japanese accommodation to communism (I, 83–84, 384–85). The same themes persist, with added and even clearer emphasis, under the Eisenhower administration. It was emphasized that Japan is the keystone of United States policy and that the loss of Southeast Asia (a likely consequence of the loss of Indochina, or even Tonkin) would drive Japan to accommodation with the Communist bloc, permitting Red China (now the main culprit, though some analyses still refer to "the Soviet Communist campaign in Southeast Asia"; cf. *DOD*, bk. 9, p. 214; January 1954) to construct a military bloc more formidable than that of Japan before World War II. The worldwide effects would be disastrous. Therefore, Indochina must be saved and its countries encouraged to integrate themselves into the "Free World" system and to stimulate the flow of raw-material resources to the Free World, Japan being the critical factor (see I, 436, 438, 450, 452). In June 1956, John F. Kennedy gave a clear formulation of the basic thesis:

> Vietnam represents the cornerstone of the Free World in Southeast Asia, the keystone to the arch, the finger in the dike. Burma, Thai-

land, India, Japan, the Philippines and, obviously, Laos and Cambodia are among those whose security would be threatened if the red tide of Communism overflowed into Vietnam. . . . Moreover, the independence of Free Vietnam is crucial to the free world in fields other than the military. Her economy is essential to the economy of all of Southeast Asia; and her political liberty is an inspiration to those seeking to obtain or maintain their liberty in all parts of Asia—and indeed the world. The fundamental tenets of this nation's foreign policy, in short, depend in considerable measure upon a strong and free Vietnamese nation.[11]

Intelligence estimates repeated, with various nuances, the general assumptions of the domino theory (see *DOD*, bk. 10, p. 999, September 1955, for a qualified statement). Memoranda of the NSC and of the Joint Chiefs of Staff also elaborate the same assumptions consistently, adding conventional recommendations that the investment climate for United States capital be improved (p. 1206) and that Southeast Asian countries be integrated into the Free World economic system (pp. 1206, 1228, 1234, 1288).

It is sometimes argued that at best, "citation of these views [which can now be documented extensively from internal documents as well as the public record] provides no more than conviction, and a mistaken conviction at that," and therefore the "radical argument" that Japanese relations with Southeast Asia were a dominant consideration in American planning can be discounted.[12] The argument is an obvious non sequitur, a particularly clear example of the fallacy noted earlier (p. 231 above). Documentation of the *conviction* suffices to establish motive; its *accuracy* is clearly irrelevant to the determination of motive. Robert W. Tucker compounds his logical fallacy with a factual error when he states that "the radical argument of Japanese dependence on Southeast Asia is difficult to take seriously." This is not a "radical argument" but rather the expressed conviction of United States policy-makers. By arguing merely the irrelevant question of the accuracy of the conviction, Tucker in effect concedes the actual "radical argument" while appearing to reject it. To make matters still worse, when he turns to the question whether the conviction was held, he hedges, claiming only that "at least after 1964" one cannot attribute Vietnam policy to this conviction. Again irrelevant, since what has actually been argued is that this was the operative factor through the 1950s, of diminishing importance in later years as deepening American involvement became self-motivating and increasingly irrational on imperialist grounds, leading finally to serious disenchantment on the part of rational imperialists and a "split in the ruling class." From every point of view, then, Tucker's discussion of this point is entirely inept, yet it is the only attempt I know of to respond seriously to what Tucker calls "the radical argument."[13]

In the 1960s, there is an increasing component of irrationalism and posturing, with much talk of psychological tests of will, humiliation, the American image, and so on. The insistence that the other fellow blink first is not without its ironic aspects. Thus the analyst regards 1961 as "a peculiarly difficult year" for the United States because of "the generally aggressive and confident posture of the Russians . . . and the generally defensive position of the Americans" (II, 21). It was therefore difficult to make concessions or to give ground to the Soviets, a matter which indirectly affected Vietnam. Anything, anywhere, that "was, or could be interpreted to be a weak U.S. response, only strengthened the pressure to hold on in Vietnam." Chester Cooper believes, however, that "Kennedy's foreign policy stance was given an added fillip in late 1962 following his dramatic success" in the Cuban missile crisis. Vietnam then provided an opportunity to prove to Peking and Moscow that their policy of "wars of liberation" was dangerous and unpromising, and also "provided both a challenge and an opportunity to test the new doctrines" of counterinsurgency.[14] Thus whether the United States stance with respect to its great-power rival is defensive or not, the determination to win in Indochina is fortified.

It is, I believe, reasonable to attribute the increasing irrationality of United States Indochina policy in the 1960s at least in part to the influx of technical intelligentsia into Washington and the expansion of the state role in the system of militarized state capitalism that has been evolving in the United States since World War II. The primary allegiance of the technical intelligentsia is to the state and its power, rather than to the specific interests of private capital, insofar as these interests can be distinguished. Furthermore, the claim of the technical intelligentsia to a share in power rests on their alleged expertise. For this reason, it is difficult for them to concede error or to shape state policy in terms of a pragmatic calculation of interests, once a commitment has been made to a particular policy. By admitting error, they concede that their claim to power was fraudulent. These problems are not faced in the same measure by someone whose authority is based on his role in controlling private empires or on an aristocratic heritage. If his policies founder and his judgments prove erroneous, his right to power is not correspondingly diminished and he is therefore somewhat more free to terminate an enterprise that is wasteful, failing, or indecisive.

By early 1964, concern over the effects of the "loss" of South Vietnam reached a peak of what can perhaps properly be called "hysteria." In the analyst's phrase, referring to the February deliberations, "Stopping Hanoi from aiding the Viet Cong virtually became equated with protecting U.S. interests against the threat of insurgency throughout the world" (III, 153). Ralph Stavins hardly exaggerates when he describes the "clouds on the horizon" as seen from Washington in the early 1960s: "Hanoi would overthrow Diem with a few guerrilla bands, and the United States, as a direct consequence, would be forced to retire from the arena of world politics."[15] Such fears were incorporated into the important NSAM 288 of March 1964, which presented what the analyst calls "a classic statement of the domino theory" (III, 3). Throughout the world, it held, "the South Vietnam conflict is regarded as a test case of U.S. capacity to help a nation to meet the Communist 'war of liberation.' Thus, purely in terms of foreign policy, the stakes are high. . . ." The memorandum stated in clear terms that "we seek an independent non-Communist South Vietnam" free to accept outside—meaning American—assistance, including "police and military help to root out and control insurgent elements." And it stated that unless we can achieve this objective, "almost all of Southeast Asia will probably fall under Communist dominance" or "accommodate to Communism," with an increased threat to India, Australia, and Japan and indeed throughout the world, given that the conflict is a "test case" (III, 50–51; II, 459–61). Although these views were modulated later on (cf. III, 220, 658), the essential idea of South Vietnam as a "test case" remained, and the commitment to a non-Communist South Vietnam was never modified.

Despite the hyperbole, the rational core of policy-making remained in the early 1960s, and in fact can even be detected in the exaggerated doctrine of Vietnam as a "test case." In one sense, Vietnam was indeed to serve as a test case. Developing countries were to be taught a harsh lesson. They must observe the rules of the international system as determined by the powerful—who, like many a stern disciplinarian, saw themselves as benign, even noble in intention. Developing countries must not undertake "national liberation" on the Chinese model, extricating themselves from the international system dominated by Western and Japanese state capitalism, with mass mobilization, a focus on internal needs, and exploitation of material and human resources for internal development. If they are so foolhardy as to disobey the international rules, they will be subjected to subversion, blockade, or even outright destruction by the global judge and executioner.

The problem of Japan continued to be a serious though much less central issue. In November 1964, an important NSC working group, considering the problem of escalation, discussed "the effect on Japanese attitudes through any development that appears to make Communist China and its allies a dominant force in Asia that must be lived with." They already perceived a danger that Japan would move toward closer ties with Communist China, and "the growing feeling that Communist

China must somehow be lived with might well be accentuated" if the United States were not to prevail in Indochina (III, 623, 627; William Bundy's draft). It is important, in short, that Japan not accommodate to China or drift toward a readiness to live with China. Again in June 1965, William Bundy warned of the importance of considering Japanese views in choosing policy, for fear that Japan may turn to "accommodation and really extensive relationships with Communist China" (IV, 614). We know from other sources that in the 1950s Japan was pressured to break trade relations with China, and that access to Southeast Asia was explicitly offered as an inducement.[16] Japan's need for markets was also an important consideration for President Kennedy.[17] It must, of course, be kept in mind that Japan in those years was not generally perceived as an immediate rival; in fact, until 1965 Japan always had an unfavorable trade balance with the United States.[18] Japan was perceived as a potential threat if it drifted from the United States global system and began to "live with" China.

Failure to appreciate the historical circumstances and the range of options actually available to policy-makers sometimes leads to superficial commentary on this matter. For example, Charles Kindleberger argues that Japan is a "difficult counterexample" to the theory that American economic foreign policy is motivated by self-interest,[19] specifically to the theory that "foreign aid to less developed countries is to keep these countries dependent" and that United States policies "are designed to use the dollar as a main instrument of control over the capitalist world." Putting aside the question whether the theory is defensible, consider the logic of Kindleberger's argument: why does he regard Japan as a "difficult counterexample"? His reason is that Japan has been assisted by the United States in various ways but is not "a puppet of the United States." By the same logic, we can prove that Soviet aid to China and Rumania was not granted out of self-interest. In fact, Kindleberger's argument holds only on the further assumption that the United States is omnipotent: on this assumption, if American aid is intended to induce some nation to remain within the American-dominated system, then that nation must be a puppet; and if the nation is not a puppet, it follows that American assistance cannot have been intended as a device to maintain control or influence.

In the real world, United States policy-makers faced a rather different problem. They had a variety of means at hand to influence postwar Japanese development toward integration into the "Free World" system. A possible alternative, which they successfully overcame, was that "the workshop of the Pacific" might undergo revolutionary social change or "accommodate" to the closed systems developing in East Asia (cf. NSC 48/1, discussed above). The option of guaranteeing that Japan would be "a puppet" was not available; whether it would have been chosen had it been feasible is another question.[20]

The results are a mixed blessing to American capital—bad for textiles and a bonanza for oil interests, to mention two examples—but surely preferable to the perceived alternatives. In any event, once Kindleberger's untenable implicit hypothesis is removed, the "difficult counterexample" becomes quite manageable. Reasonable discussion of the matter is impeded by a kind of paranoia that is developing about "Japan, Inc." For example, Zbigniew Brzezinski, in an article which is critical of such exaggeration, nevertheless predicts that Japan will seek to "exclude" computers from its liberalization policy on foreign investment, failing to mention that a wholly owned subsidiary of IBM, IBM Japan, has an estimated 40 percent share of the Japanese computer market (apart from other arrangements between American and Japanese companies in the computer fields).[21] In fact, Japanese liberalization is proceeding, and if the outcome of the competition between American and Japanese capital may be in doubt, it should not be forgotten that quite apart from questions of scale, the United States holds many cards—for example, control of most of Japan's sources of petroleum.[22] Prior to the full-scale United States invasion of South Vietnam, with its vast and unanticipated costs, it was quite reasonable to suppose that Japan would remain for some time a reasonably well-behaved junior partner in the American-dominated system.

Perhaps a word might be added with regard to the commonly heard argument that the costs of the Vietnam War prove that the United States has no imperial motives (as the costs of the Boer War prove that the British Empire was a figment of the radical imagination). The costs, of course, are profits for selected segments of the American economy, in large measure. It is senseless to describe government expenditures for petroleum, jet planes, cluster bombs, or computers for the automated air war simply as "costs of intervention." There are, to be sure, costs of empire that benefit no one: fifty thousand American corpses or the deterioration in the strength of the United States economy relative to its industrial rivals. The costs of empire to the imperial society as a whole may be considerable. These costs, however, are social costs, whereas, say, the profits from overseas investment guaranteed by military success are again highly concentrated in certain special segments of the society. The costs of empire are in general distributed over the society as a whole, while its profits revert to a few within. In this respect, the empire serves as a device for internal consolidation of power and privilege,[23] and it is quite irrelevant to observe that its social costs are often great or that as costs rise, differences may also arise among those who are in positions of power and influence. While serving as a device for internal consolidation of privilege, the empire also provides markets, guaranteed sources of inexpensive raw materials, a cheap labor market, opportunities for export of pollution (no small matter for Japan, for example), and investment opportunities. On the assumptions of the domino theory, even in its more rational versions, the stakes in Vietnam in this regard were considerable.

The same fallacy is one of several that undermine the familiar argument that our economic stake in the Third World is too slight a fraction of the gross national product to play any significant role in motivating Third World interventions.[24] The private interests that stand to gain from foreign intervention are undeterred by its social costs and will exert their often substantial influence to engage state power in support of their aims, irrespective of the percentage of GNP at stake. Quite apart from this, it is in general impossible to uncouple economic interests in the Third World from those in industrial societies, as the case of Vietnam clearly illustrates, with the long-standing concern of the policy-makers over the fate of the farther dominoes such as Japan, and in the early stages, the relationship to the critical problem of reconstructing Western European capitalism (cf. the matter of Malayan dollar-earning capacity, noted above, p. 235; or the matter of French unwillingness to accept West Germany as an unrestricted participant in a Western alliance prior to successful reconstruction of the French imperial system).

Still, it might very well be true that had the costs been anticipated, the Vietnam venture would not have been undertaken. But in the real world, policy-makers do not operate with a knowledge of ultimate costs and cannot begin all over again if plans go awry. At each point, they consider the costs and benefits of future acts. On these grounds, the Vietnam involvement might very well have seemed reasonable within the framework of imperialist motives, though by the 1960s, with the influx in Washington of ideologists and crisis managers, it can be argued that other and more irrational considerations came to predominate.

Furthermore, even now that the bill is in, the effort might be judged a moderate success for those segments of American society that have a major interest in preserving an "integrated global system" in which American capital can operate with reasonable freedom. Consider the assessment of the editor of the *Far Eastern Economic Review*, generally committed to economic liberalism. He speaks of "the ring of success stories in East and Southeast Asia," with the Japanese economy serving as "the main factor in pulling the region together and providing the shadowy outlines of a future co-prosperity sphere . . . and neatly complement[ing]" the economies of the rest of the region. "The U.S. presence in Vietnam," in his view, "has won time for Southeast Asia, allowing neighbouring countries to build up their economies and their sense of identity to a degree of stability which has equipped them to counter subversion, to provide a more attractive alternative to the peasant than the promises of the terrorist who steals down from the hills or from the jungles at night"—or on different ideological premises, allowing these countries to become more securely absorbed within the neocolonial global system. Whatever premises one adopts, the fact is that "American businessmen . . . are convinced of the potential of Asia and the Pacific Basin as the world's third largest and fastest growing market area," and are moving rapidly into the region, a process that is continuing "since the initiation of 'Vietnamisation.' " American investments now total nearly 70 percent of all foreign investments in the region.[25]

The imperial drive that is clearly expressed in many documents may have been blunted by the unexpected resilience and obstinacy of the Vietnamese resistance. Nevertheless, it has partially achieved its aims, though in retrospect it might be argued that other means would perhaps have been more efficacious.

To be sure, the imperial drive is often masked in defensive terms: it is not that we are seeking to dominate an integrated world system incorporating Western Europe and Japan, but rather that we must deny strategic areas to the Kremlin (or "Peiping"), thus protecting ourselves and others from their "aggression." The masters of the Russian empire affect a similar pose, no doubt with equal sincerity and with as much justification. The practice has respectable historical antecedents, and the term "security" is a conventional euphemism. The planners merely seek to guarantee the security of the nation, not the interests of dominant social classes.

There is, in fact, a sense in which the "defensive" rhetoric is appropriate. It is natural for the managers of the world's most advanced industrial superpower, organized more or less along capitalist lines, to seek free and open competition throughout the world in fair confidence that the interests they represent will tend to predominate. Thus they seek only to deny various areas to closed systems, national or imperial. The United States, like Britain in the period of its world dominance, tends toward the "imperialism of free trade," while maintaining the practice of state intervention for the benefit of special interests and demanding special rights (as in the Philippines) where they can be obtained.[26]

Many commentators deny that United States policy was determined or even influenced by long-term imperial objectives, and argue that the Pentagon Papers reveal no imperial drive. A case can be made for this view, specifically in the 1960s. Leslie Gelb makes the interesting point that "no systematic or serious examination of Vietnam's importance to the United States was ever undertaken within the government."[27] He attributes the persistence of the Vietnam venture, in the face of this oversight, to multiple factors: the stranglehold of Cold War assumptions;

bureaucratic judgments; anticommunism as a force in American politics, and other domestic pressures; and so on.[28] He points out that although the view that "Vietnam had intrinsic strategic military and economic importance" was argued, it never prevailed; properly, of course, since Vietnam has no such *intrinsic* importance. Rather, its importance derives from the assumptions of the domino theory, in his formulation the theory "by which the fall of Indochina would lead to the deterioration of American security around the globe." "It was ritualistic anticommunism and exaggerated power politics that got us into Vietnam," he maintains, noting that these "articles of faith" were never seriously debated *(New York Review of Books)*. Nor, we may add, is there any record of a debate or analysis of just how American "security" would be harmed by a victory of the Communist-led nationalist movement of Indochina, or just what components of "American security" would be harmed by the triumph of a nationalist movement which, it was expected, would be hostile to China and would limit its ambitions to Laos and Cambodia (see p. 230 above).

Hannah Arendt has discussed a variety of rather different irrational factors that impelled policy-makers in Vietnam.[29] "The ultimate aim," she concludes, "was neither power nor profit . . . [nor] particular tangible interests," but rather "image making," "something new in the huge arsenal of human follies." "American policy pursued no real aims, good or bad, that could limit and control sheer fantasy," in particular no imperial strategy. Ignorance, blind anticommunism, arrogance, and self-deception lie behind American policy. She is certainly correct in noting these elements in the Pentagon history. Thus in the face of all historical evidence, the American authorities persisted in the assumption, a point of rigid doctrine, that China was an agent of Moscow, the Vietcong an agency of North Vietnam, which was in turn the puppet of Moscow or "Peiping" or both, depending on the mood of the planners and propagandists, who surely had more than enough information at hand to refute these assumptions, or at the very least to shake their confidence in them. A kind of institutionalized stupidity seems a possible explanation.

There is ample material in the Pentagon Papers to support such interpretations, from the time when Dean Acheson, in a cable to Saigon, spoke of the need to aid the French and the Associated States of Indochina "to defend the territorial integrity of IC and prevent the incorporation of the ASSOC[iated] States within the COMMIE-dominated bloc of slave states" (I, 70; October 1950), and on to the present. One of the most remarkable revelations of the Pentagon study is that the analysts were able to discover only one staff paper, in a record of more than two decades, "which treats communist reactions primarily in terms of the separate national interests of Hanoi, Moscow, and Peiping, rather than primarily in terms of an overall communist strategy for which Hanoi is acting as an agent" (II,

107; an intelligence estimate of November 1961). Even in the "intelligence community," where they are paid to get the facts straight and not to rant about helping the French defend the territorial integrity of Indochina from its people and the Commie-dominated bloc of slave states, it was apparently next to impossible to perceive, or at least express the simple truth: that North Vietnam, like the Soviet Union, China, the United States, and the NLF, has its own interests, which are often decisive.

It is amusing to trace the efforts to establish that Ho Chi Minh was merely a Russian (or Chinese) puppet—as obviously must be the case. The State Department, in July 1948, could find "no evidence of direct link between Ho and Moscow" (but naturally "assumes it exists").[30] State Department intelligence, in the fall, found evidence of "Kremlin-directed conspiracy . . . in virtually all countries except Vietnam." Indochina appeared "an anomaly." How can this be explained? To Intelligence, the most likely explanation is that "no rigid directives have been issued by Moscow" or that "a special dispensation for the Vietnam government has been arranged in Moscow" (I, 5, 34). In September 1948, the State Department noted, "There continues to be no known communication between the USSR and Vietnam, although evidence is accumulating that a radio liaison may have been established through the Tass agency in Shanghai" (*DOD*, bk. 8, p. 148, grasping at straws). American officials in Saigon added, "No evidence has yet turned up that Ho Chi Minh is receiving current directives either from Moscow, China, or the Soviet Legation in Bangkok." "It may be assumed," they conclude from this, "that Moscow feels that Ho and his lieutenants have had sufficient training and experience and are sufficiently loyal to be trusted to determine their day-to-day policy without supervision" (p. 151). By February 1949, they were relieved to discover that "Moscow publications of fairly recent date are frequently seized by the French," indicating that "satisfactory communications exist," though the channel remains a mystery (p. 168); also, "there has been surprising[ly] little direct cooperation between local Chinese Communists and the Viet Minh."

"We are unable to determine whether Peiping or Moscow has ultimate responsibility for Viet Minh policy," an intelligence estimate of June 1953 relates (I, 396), but it must be one or the other—that is an axiom. In the context of a discussion of Chinese Communist strategy, intelligence concludes that the Communists are pursuing their present strategy in Indochina because it "diverts badly needed French and US resources from Europe at relatively small cost to the Communists" and "provides opportunities to advance international Communist interests while preserving the fiction of 'autonomous' national liberation movements, and it provides an instrument, the Viet Minh, with which Communist China and the

USSR can indirectly exert military and psychological pressures on the peoples and governments of Laos, Cambodia, and Thailand" (I, 399). Might there be another reason why the Vietminh fight on?

It is tempting to use such evidence to support the claim that ignorance, mythology, and institutionalized stupidity led United States policy-makers into a series of disastrous errors. If only they had realized that Stalin was lukewarm or negative toward Mao and the Greek guerrillas, that there was no "pattern of Communist conquest . . . manifest" in Guatemala in 1954,[31] that the Vietnamese were conducting their own struggle for national liberation. If only William Bundy had had a course in Vietnamese history at Yale. But ignorance and paranoia obscured the facts.

This theory, however, leaves too many questions unanswered. To mention only the simplest: Why were policy-makers always subject to the same form of ignorance and irrationality? Why was there such a systematic error in the delusional systems constructed by postwar ideologists? Mere ignorance or foolishness would lead to random error, not to a regular and systematic distortion: unwavering adherence[32] to the principle that whatever the facts may be, the cause of international conflict is the behavior of the Communist powers, and all revolutionary movements within the United States system are sponsored by the Soviet Union, China, or both.[33] Why was the latter assumption so far beyond challenge that no examination of Vietnam's importance was ever undertaken (Gelb)? Ignorance and stupidity can surely lead to error, but hardly to such systematic error or such certainty in error. And there is a second and even more obvious question: Why is the United States anti-Communist?

With respect to the first question, whether it is Acheson, Rostow, Stevenson, Kissinger, or whoever, one generally finds the same distortion as in the sorry record of the "intelligence community." From one or another such source, we hear that Stalin supported Mao and incited the Greek guerrillas and Ho Chi Minh, China attacked India, the Vietcong are agents of international Communist aggression, and so on. These are, indeed, articles of faith. The crisis managers do not argue these claims; they merely intone them. All are at best highly dubious and probably false, so the available record indicates, but questions of fact are beside the point in theological disputation.

What is not beside the point is that these articles of faith are highly functional. The fact is that anticommunism provides a convenient mythology to justify colonial wars, and to gain the popular support that is often hard to rally, given the grisly nature and substantial costs of such endeavors. But to explain the United States attack on Vietnam on grounds of anti-Communist delusions would be as superficial as explaining the Russian invasion of Czechoslovakia or Hungary merely on grounds of fear of West Germany or Wall Street. No doubt at some level the Soviet leadership believes what it says and is bewildered at the bitter reaction to its selfless and benevolent behavior. Perhaps Russian public opinion indeed "is proud of its country's armed power in Prague and speaks of Czechoslovak weakness, ingratitude, irresponsibility, etc."[34] Similarly Washington claims to be defending democracy and warding off "internal aggression" or subversion by agents of international communism when it helps to destroy a mass popular movement in Greece, supports an invasion of Guatemala, invades the Dominican Republic, and devastates the peasant societies of Indochina. Its defenders, and many critics as well, are at most willing to concede error if the costs mount too high, and cannot conceive that any "responsible" or "qualified" observer might have a rather different view. Some still insist that for the most part the United States pursues its foreign policy "for reformist, even utopian goals," and that this policy can be faulted only for being "callow, sentimental, savagely stupid . . . too little the work of an intellectually serious leadership."[35] It is remarkable how difficult it is, even for those who see themselves as critics, to interpret United States behavior by the standards of evaluation and analysis that would, properly, be applied to any other great power.

The fact that policy-makers may be caught up in the fantasies they spin to disguise imperial intervention, and may sometimes even find themselves trapped by them, should not prevent us from asking what function these ideological constructions fulfill—why *this* particular system of mystification is consistently expounded in place of some alternative. Similarly, one should not be misled by the fact that the delusional system presents a faint reflection of reality. It must, after all, carry some conviction. But this should not prevent us from proceeding to disentangle motive from myth.

The efforts of the "intelligence community" to establish the thesis that the Vietminh were agents of international communism reveal quite clearly the function of the "international Communist conspiracy" in postwar American foreign policy. There is no doubt that the Soviet Union, within the limits of its power, established its harsh and oppressive imperial rule. But it was not this fact that determined American policy in Southeast Asia. Contrary to the fantasies of Walt Rostow and others, the United States did not first discover that the Vietminh were agents of a Kremlin-directed conspiracy and then proceed to help France beat back Russian aggression against Southeast Asia. Rather, the United States merely applied in Indochina the general policy of establishing Western-oriented regimes that would cooperate ("freely") with the West and Japan, "culturally, economically, and politically," and "contribute to a better balanced world economy"—the "world economy" in question being, of course, that of the "free world" (cf. p. 229 above). In its essentials, the policy was not fundamentally different from, say, American policy in Italy in 1943, or in Greece and Korea shortly after.[36] To implement this policy in Vietnam, it was necessary to destroy the forces that had "captured the nationalist movement," since these forces had a different model of social and economic development in mind. But this would have appeared too cynical, if stated frankly. Therefore, it was necessary to recast the issue in "defensive" terms, and to establish that these nationalist forces were really the agents of aggression by an international conspiracy, aimed ultimately at destroying the freedom of the United States itself. The "intelligence community" thus was assigned the task of demonstrating the thesis that was required as the ideological underpinning of the American intervention. It is interesting, but not very surprising given the background, that the failure of intelligence to establish the needed link in no way impeded the ideologists, who simply continued to insist that the required thesis was correct, accepting and proclaiming it as an article of faith. The same pattern has appeared elsewhere, with predictable regularity.

Turning to the second question: why is the United States anti-Communist? A conventional answer is that the United States opposes communism because of its aggressive, expansionist character. Thus it is argued that we do not seek to overthrow communism where it represents the status quo, as in Eastern Europe; and that when President Kennedy, in an often-quoted remark, said that we would always prefer a Trujillo to a Castro,[37] he meant that "the power requirements of the struggle with the Soviet Union took precedence over the commitment to a 'decent democratic regime.' " As to China:

> The containment of China has not been pursued simply because China has a communist government, but because of China's outlook generally and her policy in Asia particularly. It is China's insistence upon changing the Asian status quo, and the methods she has used, that explain American hostility.[38]

Such proposals cannot withstand analysis. It is true, but irrelevant, that the United States will not risk nuclear destruction to roll back communism; again, one should not overlook the objective limits on American power. Tucker's interpretation of Kennedy's remark seems to presuppose that American hostility toward Castro was a consequence of his turn toward the Soviet Union, which is of course untrue. Perhaps one can argue that American hostility was not a determining factor in this move, but that it preceded it is beyond argument.[39] With respect to China, Tucker's argument is weaker still. What methods did China use in changing the status quo beyond its borders? In what respect were these methods "objectionable" in comparison with American methods in the Far East? In what sense was the forceful reimposition of French colonialism, in opposition to a Communist-led Vietnamese nationalist movement, an attempt to preserve the status quo after World War II? Why the effort to demonstrate that the Vietnamese revolutionaries—or the backers of Arbenz or Bosch—were Russian or Chinese agents, despite the evidence at hand, leading ultimately to the religious faith that this must be so? The answers to these questions entirely undermine Tucker's effort to "explain American hostility."

Tucker is in fact mistaken about what counts as an explanation of policy. He is nearer the mark when he points out that Castro "would refuse to do our bidding" and "would stand as a challenge to our otherwise undisputed hegemony in this hemisphere," but he does not pursue these observations to the degree of specificity that any serious discussion of policy must achieve. In what respects would Cuba refuse to do our bidding and challenge our hegemony? This question Tucker does not answer, or even pose. He says merely that "America's interventionist and counterrevolutionary policy . . . may be accounted for in terms of a reasonably well-grounded fear that the American example might become irrelevant to much of the world," along with the "will to exercise dominion over others." Tucker is in error when he states that "a radical critique cannot *consistently* accept this explanation."[40] It would, however, be quite accurate to say that no serious critique can accept such proposals *as an explanation of policy.* Rather, any serious critique will pursue the matter further, asking what elements of "the American example" a foreign society must adopt to allay these fears. Was it fear that Guatemala would choose soccer rather than baseball as its national sport that precipitated the 1954 intervention? Was the Bay of Pigs invasion rooted in the fear that Cuban intellectuals would prefer Continental phenomenology to American-style analytic philosophy? Is it our concern that the model of American political democracy might prove "irrelevant" that explains why the United States executive so prefers Brazil to Chile under Allende? Again, a serious look at real historical examples reveals at once the emptiness of Tucker's proposals. He believes himself to be offering a more cogent alternative to a "radical critique," whereas in fact he is offering no alternative at all, but merely abstracting away from the particular specific questions that must be faced by any serious effort, radical or not, to explain the American policy of counterrevolutionary intervention.

Tucker's failure to come to grips with the real problems follows a familiar pattern. It is commonly argued that American interventionism is not attributable to the normal workings of state capitalism, but to some deeper motive, such as the "drive for power." The reasoning is shoddy, and it is important to see why. The failure of the argument does not lie in the identification of the "power drive" as the cause of imperialist intervention; this premise is sufficiently vague so that we can grant it to be true without fear of refutation. Rather, the argument fails because it does not recognize that a generalization is not refuted by rephrasing it in terms that are logically equivalent, or even by tracing it to deeper theses from which it derives. Thus suppose one were to argue that the normal behavior of a businessman is not governed by the pursuit of profit (or, say, growth, assuming this to be an empirically distinguishable thesis), but rather by a "deeper" drive for power. Again, we may accept the claim that the normal behavior of the businessman is explained by a drive for power, which manifests itself in a capitalist society in the pursuit of profit. This claim merely restates, and does not contradict, the hypothesis that the behavior of a businessman in a capitalist society is governed by the pursuit of profit.

Much the same is true of the vague musings about a "generalized drive for power" which often appear in discussions of American foreign policy. It may well be true that any autocratic system of rule will support and intensify the "drive for power" and give it free rein. In a capitalist society, the operative form of autocratic rule is the private control of the means of production and resources, of commerce and finance, and further, the significant influence on state policy of those who rule the private economy, and who indeed largely staff the government. Elements of the private autocracy who have a specific concern with foreign affairs will naturally tend to use their power and influence to direct state policy for the benefit of the interests they represent. Where they succeed, we have imperialist intervention, quite commonly.

It might be argued that a healthy democracy would impede imperial planners, for two reasons: in the first place, considerations of self-interest would serve as a brake on imperial ventures with their often substantial social cost; and secondly, a functioning democracy might foster other values beyond domination and power—solidarity, sympathy, cooperative impulses, a concern for creative and useful work, and so on. The prevailing ideology tends to downgrade and scoff at such motives, often appealing to the alleged discoveries of the "behavioral sciences," but this farce need not detain us here. The important point is that the resort to a "power drive" as the explanation of imperial intervention is not false, but irrelevant, once its true character is laid bare. It is fair, I think, to suggest that this "alternative explanation" merely serves as a form of mystification, it serves to obscure the actual workings of power.

The question remains: Why is American ideology and policy anti-Communist? Or a further question: Why has the United States been antifascist (though selectively)? Why was fascist Japan evil in 1940, while fascist Greece and Portugal (preserving the status quo with American arms in Africa) are quite tolerable today? And why is the United States generally anticolonialist, as in Indonesia shortly after World War II, when the conservative nationalist leadership appeared at first to favor foreign investment, but (reluctantly) not in Indochina, where the alternative to a barely disguised French colonialism was an indigenous Communist resistance?

It is not too difficult to discern a criterion that serves rather well to determine which elements in foreign lands receive support and which are labeled enemies. It is surely not the humanitarian impulse (see p. 252 below); nor is it the prospects for development that determine the official United States response: China or Cuba might well have profited from capital grants for development—more so, at least, than from blockade, invasion, and harassment. Nor is it the fear of our great-power rivals that leads us to intervene halfway around the world, as is plainly shown by the determined effort to prove that Russia and China were responsible for the "internal aggression" in Vietnam, in the face of the evidence that they were not, and analogous efforts in the Caribbean and elsewhere. Nor do democratic or authoritarian rule, bloodthirstiness, aggressiveness, or a threat to United States security (in the proper sense of the term) provide a plausible criterion. Brazil and South Africa are as vicious as they come. The horrendous Indonesian massacre of 1965 was greeted with calm. China has been the least aggressive of the great powers. The Vietminh and the Pathet Lao are hardly a threat to United States security. Fascist Japan was no doubt an aggressive power—in some ways, not unlike the United States today[41]—but the United States was prepared to seek a modus vivendi in 1939 provided that its rights and interests on the mainland were guaranteed. And fascist Greece is quite all right today; it plays its NATO role, provides bases for American naval forces,[42] and as an added attraction there is—as Secretary of Commerce Maurice Stans put it so lyrically not long ago—"the welcome that is given here to American companies and the sense of security the Government of Greece is imparting to them."[43]

Friends and enemies can be identified, to a rather good first approximation, in terms of their role in maintaining an integrated global economy in which American capital can operate with relative freedom. The so-called "Communist" powers are particularly evil because their "do-it-yourself" model of development tends to extricate them from this system. For this reason, even European colonialism, which was bad enough, is preferable to indigenous communism. For the same reason, Washington will prefer a Trujillo to a Castro.

The study group of the Woodrow Wilson Foundation and the National Planning Association was perceptive, and more honest than many contemporary ideologists, when it described the primary threat of communism as the economic transformation of the Communist powers "in ways which reduce their willingness and ability to complement the industrial economies of the West,"[44] their refusal to play the game of comparative advantage and to rely primarily on foreign investment for development. If the "developing nations" choose to use their resources for their own purposes, or to carry out internal social change in ways which will reduce their contribution to the industrial economies of the state capitalist world, these powers must be prepared to employ sufficient force to prevent such unreasonable behavior, which will no doubt be described as aggression by agents of international communism. The Soviet Union reacts no differently when Czechoslovakia seeks a degree of independence or social change.

At a much different level of domination, British auto workers must not be permitted to demand too great economic benefits or a share in management in the Ford plant, and must remain subject to the threats that can be wielded quite effectively by an international corporation.[45] In East Asia, which many regard as a most promising region for the "internationalization of production" as well as for supplying raw materials, the problems will be particularly acute. Surely such considerations lie at the very core of American foreign policy. Though they are far from the sole operative factors in United States policy, and are often overwhelmed by the impact of ideological commitments which themselves grow out of such concerns, it is surely the beginning of wisdom to recognize their crucial role.

It is often maintained that United States policy is motivated by a commitment to political democracy. To test the force of this concern, we can consider how United States policy typically evolves when political democracy is destroyed, while American economic intervention is freed from constraints—and we can compare such policy with the typical United States reaction when an economy is closed to American economic penetration, whether or not political democracy is more or less maintained. Latin America provides an ample set of test cases. Considering American policy toward Brazil and Chile, Guatemala for the past two decades, the Dominican Republic in 1965, and so on, there can be little doubt as to the outcome of such an investigation. Gordon Connell-Smith puts the matter in terms that seem quite adequate:

> . . . United States concern for representative democracy in Latin America is a facet of her anti-communist policy. There has been no serious question of her intervening in the case of the many right-wing military coups, from which, of course, this policy generally has benefited. It is only when her own concept of democracy, closely

identified with private, capitalistic enterprise, is threatened by communism that she has felt impelled to demand collective action to defend it.[46]

Those who are called upon to implement and defend United States policy are often quite frank about the matter. The director of USAID (United States Agency for International Development) for Brazil, to take one recent and very important case, explains clearly that protection of a favorable investment climate for private business interests is a primary United States objective. To be sure, he mentions other objectives as well: our "humanitarian interests" and our "security objectives." As to our humanitarian interests, they seem a bit selective, and correlate remarkably well with "the protection and expansion, if possible, of our economic interests, trade and investment, in the hemisphere."[47] Thus our humanitarian interests in Brazil, as measured by the aid program, showed a marked upsurge after the April 1964 "revolution" which, among other achievements, overcame the "administrative obstacles to remittance of income developed under the Goulart regime" (pp. 185–87, 215). Another achievement that correlated with the vast flow of aid was the rise of private investment from 50 percent to 75 percent of total investment.[48]

Or perhaps our humanitarian interests, as measured by the aid flow, were stirred by the incidence of state violence and torture in Brazil under the new regime, or by the significant decline in the share of GNP of the bottom 80 percent of the population,[49] and the reported decline in wages for most workers that accompanied the significant rise in production under "a dictatorship, established to protect the privileges of a small property-owning class and to assure the growing control of the nation's economy by imperialistic interests."[50] As for the security objectives, the fear that Brazil under Goulart posed a security threat to the United States seems a bit farfetched; and as far as Brazil itself is concerned, the military perceive no external threat to the country,[51] so that the extensive American military aid is clearly either for "internal security"—that is, protection from its own population of the regime whose acts have so awakened our humanitarian concerns—or for threats against Brazil's neighbors, in particular those neighbors who might choose to jeopardize the closely related economic interests of the Brazilian privileged elite and American investors. We are, I am afraid, reduced to the first objective: the protection and expansion of "our" economic interests in the hemisphere.

Before we attribute this or that misadventure to "blind anticommunism," we would do well to distinguish several varieties of anticommunism. Opposition to indigenous movements that might pursue the so-called Communist model of development, extricating their societies from the international capitalist system, is not "blind anticommunism," strictly speaking. It may be "anticommunism," but it is far from blind. Rather, it is rational imperialism which seeks to prevent the erosion of the world system dominated by Western and Japanese capital. On the other hand, reference to a "coordinated offensive directed by the Kremlin" against Southeast Asia in 1949 (NSC 48/1) or to the "militant and aggressive expansionist policy advocated by the present rulers of Communist China" (George Carver of the CIA; IV, 82; April 1966) is indeed blind anticommunism—or to be more precise, it is perhaps blind, but it is not anticommunism at all. Rather, it is pure imperial ideology, beyond the reach of evidence or debate, a propaganda device to rally support for military intervention against indigenous Communist-led movements. (The device is no doubt useful for the self-image of the policy-makers themselves.) In Vietnam, the first form of anticommunism motivated United States intervention, while the second was called upon to justify it—as elsewhere, repeatedly.

It may be argued, with justice, that this view is no more than a first approximation to a general understanding of foreign policy, and that it omits many second-order considerations. Thus it would not be correct to claim that formation of foreign policy is in the interests of a monolithic corporate elite. On the contrary, there are conflicting interests. But we would expect to find—and do find—that those interests that are particularly concerned with foreign policy are well represented in its formation.[52] By similar dynamics, regulatory agencies tend to fall into the hands of industries that are particularly concerned with their decisions. It is, furthermore, no doubt true that at some point ideology takes on a motive force of its own. There are other interacting and for the most part mutually supportive factors: the interest of the "state management" in the Pentagon in enhancing its own power;[53] the role of government-induced production of rapidly obsolescing luxury goods (largely military) as a technique of economic management, with a resulting need to secure strategic raw materials; the usefulness of an external enemy as a device to whip the taxpayer into line, in support of the production of waste and the costs of empire; the heady sense of power, to which academic ideologues in particular seem to succumb so readily. Such factors as these produce a fairly stable system to support the basic imperial drive, which is second nature to the men of power in the state executive in any event.[54] There are many specific factors that must be considered in a detailed examination of particular decisions, such as those that led us ever more deeply into Indochina. Nevertheless, it seems reasonably clear that American policy, like that of any great power, is guided by the "national interest" as conceived by dominant social groups, in this case, the primary goal of maximizing the free access by American capital to the markets and human and material resources of the world, the goal of maintaining to the fullest possible extent its freedom of operation in a global economy. At the same time, ideologists labor to mask these endeavors in a functional system of beliefs.

It is interesting that such analyses of foreign policy, which incorporate the material interests of private or quasi-private capital as a central factor interacting with others, are often characterized as "vulgar economic determinism" or the like when put forth by opponents of the system of private control of resources and the means of production. On the other hand, similar formulations receive little attention when they appear, as they commonly do, in official explanations of state policy. What is more, explanations that emphasize, say, vague emotional states, or ideological elements, or error, are not similarly characterized as "vulgar emotional (ideological) determinism" or "vulgar fallibilism."

The term "vulgar economic determinism" is particularly surprising, given that those segments of (quasi-) private capital that are particularly affected by foreign-policy decisions are generally well represented in the formation of state policy. One would therefore expect that the view mislabeled "vulgar economic determinism" would serve as a kind of null hypothesis. Since it is, furthermore, quite plausible as an explanation for basic foreign-policy decisions (and not infrequently, the justification offered for them), the reaction becomes still more curious. The label too often serves to deflect attention from the proposed explanations, which are much easier to ignore when misrepresented. This is a standard reaction to analysis that raises questions about prevailing ideology. Compare much of the response to "revisionist" work on the Cold War several years ago.[55] Many illustrations can be given; in fact, there is an interesting literary genre, worthy of investigation in itself, devoted to the refutation of nonexistent arguments attributed to "radicals"—such as the argument that capitalism needs war to survive, or that the United States bears sole responsibility for the Cold War.

It is possible to give some useful advice to an aspiring political analyst who wants his work received as thoughtful and penetrating—advice which surely applies to any society, not merely to ours. This analyst should first of all determine as closely as possible the actual workings of power in his society. Having isolated certain primary elements and a number of peripheral and insignificant ones, he should then proceed to dismiss the primary factors as unimportant, the province of extremists and ideologues. He should rather concentrate on the minor and peripheral elements in decision-making. Better still, he should describe these in terms that appear to be quite general and independent of the social structure that he is discussing ("power drive," "fear of irrelevance," etc.). Where he considers policies that failed, he should attribute them to stupidity and ignorance, that is, to factors that are socially neutral. Or he may attribute the failures to noble impulses that led policy-makers astray ("tragic irony"), or to the venality, ingratitude, and barbarism of subject peoples. He can then be fairly confident that he will escape the criticism that his efforts at explanation are "simplistic" (the truth is often surprisingly simple). He will, in short, benefit from a natural tendency on the part of the privileged in any society to suppress—for themselves as well as others—knowledge and understanding of the nature of their privilege and its manifestations.

In the particular case of Vietnam, anticommunism served as a convenient device for mobilizing the American people to support imperial intervention. After a time, they were no longer willing to bear the costs or were appalled at the consequences. At this point, the propaganda device, no longer effective, is discarded. We now hear laments about the Cold War myths that led us to a "Greek tragedy" in Vietnam. But the war goes on.

The motive force for the American war in Indochina lies, it seems to me, where it was located in the earliest internal documents of the state executive: in the perceived significance of Southeast Asia for the integrated global system that was to be organized by American power—and, under reasonable assumptions, dominated by American power for the primary benefit of those who possess that power. Although in the 1960s other and more irrational considerations may have come to predominate, nevertheless the continuing effort by the United States to achieve a Korea-type solution in Indochina, whatever the cost to its people, can still be traced in part to the same fundamental objectives.[56]

Waging the War

After "Pinkville"

(1969)

*I*T IS IMPORTANT TO UNDERSTAND THAT THE MASSACRE OF the rural population of Vietnam and their forced evacuation is not an accidental by-product of the war. Rather it is of the very essence of American strategy. The theory behind it has been explained with great clarity and explicitness, for example by Professor Samuel Huntington, chairman of the Government Department at Harvard and at the time (1968) chairman of the Council on Vietnamese Studies of the Southeast Asia Development Advisory Group. Writing in *Foreign Affairs*, he explains that the Vietcong is "a powerful force which cannot be dislodged from its constituency so long as the constituency continues to exist." The conclusion is obvious, and he does not shrink from it. We can ensure that the constituency ceases to exist by " 'direct application of mechanical and conventional power' . . . on such a massive scale as to produce a massive migration from countryside to city," where the Vietcong constituency—the rural population—can, it is hoped, be controlled in refugee camps and suburban slums around Saigon.

Technically the process is known as "urbanization" or "modernization." It is described, with the proper contempt, by Daniel Ellsberg, a Department of Defense consultant on pacification in South Vietnam, who concludes, from his extensive on-the-spot observations, that "we have, of course, demolished the society of Vietnam," that "the bombing of the South has gone on long enough to disrupt the society of South Vietnam enormously and probably permanently"; he speaks of the "people who have been driven to Saigon by what Huntington regards as our 'modernizing instruments' in Vietnam, bombs and artillery."[1] Reporters have long been aware of the nature of these tactics, aware that "by now the sheer weight of years of firepower, massive sweeps, and grand forced population shifts have reduced the population base of the NLF,"[2] so that conceivably, by brute force, we may still hope to "win."

One thing is clear: so long as an organized social life can be maintained in South Vietnam, the NLF will be a powerful, probably dominant force. This is the dilemma which has always plagued American policy, and which has made it impossible for us to permit even the most rudimentary democratic institutions in South Vietnam. For these reasons we have been forced to the solution outlined by Professor Huntington: to crush the people's war, we must eliminate the people.

A second thing is tolerably clear: there has been no modification in this policy. Once again, as two years ago, there is mounting popular protest against the war. Once again, a tactical adjustment is being devised that will permit Washington to pursue its dual goal, to pacify the people of South Vietnam while pacifying the American people also. The first of these tasks has not been accomplished too well. The second, to our shame, has been managed quite successfully, for the most part. Now we hear that the burden of fighting the war is to be shifted away from the American infantry to the B-52s and fighter-bombers and a mercenary force of Vietnamese. Only a token force of between 200,000 and 300,000 men, backed by the Pacific Naval and Air Command, will be retained, indefinitely, to ensure that the Vietnamese have the right of self-determination.

And now there is Song My—"Pinkville." More than two decades of indoctrination and counterrevolutionary interventions have created the possibility of a name like "Pinkville"—and the acts that may be done in a place so named. Orville and Jonathan Schell have pointed out[3] what any literate person should realize, that this was no isolated atrocity but the logical consequence of a virtual war of extermination directed against helpless peasants: "enemies," "reds," "dinks." But there are, perhaps, still deeper roots. Some time ago, I read with a slight shock the statement by Eqbal Ahmad that "America has institutionalized even its genocide," referring to the fact that the extermination of the Indians "has become the object of public entertainment and children's games."[4] Shortly after, I was thumbing through my daughter's fourth-grade social science reader.[5] The protagonist, Robert, is told the story of the extermination of the Pequot tribe by Captain John Mason:

> His little army attacked in the morning before it was light and took the Pequots by surprise. The soldiers broke down the stockade with their axes, rushed inside, and set fire to the wigwams. They killed nearly all the braves, squaws, and children, and burned their corn and other food. There were no Pequots left to make more trouble. When the other Indian tribes saw what good fighters the white men were, they kept the peace for many years.
>
> "I wish I were a man and had been there," thought Robert.

Nowhere does Robert express, or hear, second thoughts about the matter. The text omits some other pertinent remarks: for example, by Cotton Mather, who said that "it was supposed that no less than six hundred Pequot souls were brought down to hell that day."[6] Is it an exaggeration to suggest that our history of extermination and racism is reaching its climax in Vietnam today? It is not a question that Americans can easily put aside.

The revelation of the Song My atrocity to a wide public appears to have been a by-product of the November mobilization. As Richard L. Strout wrote in the *Christian Science Monitor*:

> American press self-censorship thwarted Mr. Ridenhour's disclosures for a year. "No one wanted to go into it," his agent said of telegrams sent to Life, Look, and Newsweek magazines outlining allegations. . . . Except for the recent antiwar march in Washington the event might not have been publicized. In connection with the march a news offshoot (Dispatch News Service) of the left-wing Institute of Policy Studies of this city aggressively told and marketed the story to approximately 30 United States and Canadian newspapers.[7]

Apart from this, it probably would have disappeared from history, along with who knows what else.

The first investigation by the Pentagon "reported that the carnage was due to artillery fire. Civilian casualties by artillery fire among hostile villages are so common that this explanation ended the inquiry."[8] But the murdered Vietnamese were not the victims of artillery fire. Since the soldiers looked into the faces of their victims, the inquiry must continue, despite the difficulties. Henry Kamm reported in the *New York Times* that:

> The task of the investigators is complicated by the fact that last January, most of the inhabitants of the peninsula were forcibly evacuated by American and South Vietnamese troops in the course of a drive to clear the area of Vietcong. More than 12,000 persons were removed from Bantangan Peninsula by helicopters and taken to a processing camp near this provincial capital. Heavy American bombing and artillery and naval shelling had destroyed many of the houses and forced them to live in caves and bunkers for many months before the evacuation. . . . An elaborate interrogation and screening procedure, in which American intelligence agents were said to have taken an important part, yielded only a hundred or so active Vietcong suspects. Most of the people were sent to a newly established refugee camp. . . . Despite the extensive movement of the population and the military operation, the Vietcong remain active in the area.[9]

On November 22, Kamm adds the further information that "the number of refugees 'generated'—the term for the people forcibly dislocated in this process—exceeded intelligence estimates four-fold." "The 12,000, instead of being scattered in many hamlets where it would be difficult to keep out the Vietcong, are now concentrated in six guarded, camp-like settlements."

It is perhaps remarkable that none of this appears to occasion much concern. It is only the acts of a company of half-crazed GIs that are regarded as a scandal, a disgrace to America. It will, indeed, be a still greater national scandal—if we assume that to be possible—if they alone are subjected to criminal prosecution, but not those who have created and accepted the long-term atrocity to which they contributed one detail—merely a few hundred more murdered Vietnamese.

Recently, a study of American public opinion about Vietnam concluded with this speculation: ". . . little reaction to the war is based on humanitarian or moral considerations. Americans are not now rejecting 'war,' they merely wish to see this current conflict ended. To achieve this goal, most Americans would pursue a more militant policy and ignore resultant atrocities."[10] We may soon discover whether this speculation is correct. Of course, there is sure to be a segment of American society that will not "ignore resultant atrocities"—namely, the irresponsible, loudmouthed vocal minority, or those who are described so nicely by Colonel Joseph Bellas, commanding officer of a hospital in Vietnam where soldiers boycotted Thanksgiving dinner in protest against the war: "They're young, they're idealistic and don't like man's inhumanity to man. As they get older they will become wiser and more tolerant."[11] If a majority of the American people will, indeed, ignore resultant atrocities and support Nixon's policy of pursuing a war without discernible end, then this segment of American society may be subjected to domestic repression of a sort that is not without precedent in American history; we seem to be seeing the early signs today with the savage repression of the Panthers, the conspiracy trial in Chicago, and other incidents.

The fact that repression may be attempted does not imply that it must succeed. Surely the possibility exists, today, of creating a broad-based movement of opposition to war and repression that might stave off such an attack. It is now even imaginable, as a few years ago it was not, that a significant American left may emerge that will be a voice in national affairs, and even, perhaps, a potential force for radical social change. There has been a remarkable shift in popular attitudes over the past months, an openness to radical political thinking of a sort that I do not recall for many years. To let these opportunities pass is to condemn many others to the fate of Vietnam.

Laos

(1970)

───────────────────────

*I*T HAS BEEN CLAIMED THAT VIETNAM IS THE SECOND MOST heavily bombarded country in history. The most intensively bombarded, so it seems, is Laos. According to *Le Monde,* "North Vietnam was more heavily bombed than Korea; Laos is now being bombed even more than North Vietnam. And this battering has been going on for over five years. . . . The United States Air Force carries out more than 12,500 raids a month."[1] On the same day, October 1, 1969, the *New York Times* announced its discovery that in Laos "the rebel economy and social fabric" are now the main target of the American bombardment, which is claimed to be a success:

> Refugees from the Plaine des Jarres area say that during recent months most open spaces have been evacuated. Both civilians and soldiers have retreated into the forests or hills and frequently spend most of the daylight hours in caves or tunnels. Refugees said they could only plow their fields at night because they were unsafe during the day. "So long as the United States bombing continues at its new level," a European diplomat said here this week, "so-called Communist territory is little but a shooting range." The bombing, by creating refugees, deprives the Communists of their chief source of food and transport. The population of the Pathet Lao zone has been declining for several years and the Pathet Lao find it increasingly difficult to fight a "people's war" with fewer and fewer people.

The world's most advanced society has found the answer to people's war: eliminate the people.

It is, incidentally, remarkable that the *Times* can so blandly announce that the rebel economy and social fabric are the main target of the American bombardment. It is remarkable that this claim, which, if correct, sets American policy at the moral level of Nazi Germany, can be merely noted in a casual comment, with—so far as I know—no public reaction of horror and indignation.

Still, it is good that the American press has discovered that the rebel economy and social fabric are the target of the American bombardment of Laos. Perhaps we will be spared the pretense that our targets are steel and concrete, or that the bombing is "the most restrained in modern warfare" (as McGeorge Bundy so elegantly put it at the time when virtually every structure in North Vietnam, outside of the centers of Hanoi and Haiphong, was being demolished).

The discovery has been mysteriously delayed. For example, in July 1968 the Southeast Asia expert of *Le Monde*, Jacques Decornoy, published detailed reports of his visits to the liberated areas of Laos: ". . . a world without noise, for the surrounding villages have disappeared, the inhabitants themselves living hidden in the mountains . . . it is dangerous to lean out at any time of the night or day" because of the ceaseless bombardment which leads to "the scientific destruction of the areas held by the enemy." "The Americans are trying to 'break' the Laotian Left, both psychologically and, if possible, physically." The nature of their relentless attack "can only be explained if the target is the central administration of the Neo Lao Hak Sat"—the political organization that won handily in 1958 in the only unrigged election in Laos. This electoral victory inspired the American effort at subversion that led to the Laotian crisis of the early sixties, which still persists.

Decornoy describes "the motionless ruins and deserted houses" of the central town of Sam Neua district:

The first real raid against the population center itself was launched on February 19, 1965. Very serious attacks were made on it quite recently on March 17 and 19, 1968. . . . The two ends of the town were razed to the ground. The old ruins of 1965 have disappeared, those of March 1968 were still "smoking" when we visited them. Branches of trees lay all along the length of the river, houses were totally burned out (phosphorus had been used). At the other end of Sam Neua, the sight was even more painful. Everywhere enormous craters; the church and many houses were demolished. In order to reach the people who might be living there, the Americans dropped their all-too-famous fragmentation bombs. Here lay a "mother bomb" disembowelled, by the side of the road. All round, over a dozen meters, the earth was covered with "daughter bombs," little machines that the Vietnamese know well, unexploded and hiding hundreds of steel splinters. . . . One of the officials of Sam Neua district told us that between February 1965 and March 1968, 65 villages had been destroyed. A number impossible to verify in a short report, but it is a fact that between Sam Neua and a place about 30 kilometers away where we stayed, no house in the villages and hamlets had been spared. Bridges had been destroyed, fields up to the rivers were holed with bomb craters.

Decornoy reports that "American raids on 'liberated Laos' began in May 1964, therefore well before the Gulf of Tonkin incident (August 1964) and the policy of escalation to North Vietnam (spring 1965). Under these circumstances, Laos has, in some ways, served as a testing ground or experimental site." He describes the amazing persistence of the Laotians in maintaining and advancing the social revolution in the face of this attack, their "virulent nationalism" and refusal to follow foreign models, the schools and factories in caves, the prosperity of the rare villages that have still, for unknown reasons, escaped destruction. Finally he quotes an American diplomat in Vientiane who says: "To make progress in this country, it is necessary to level everything. It is necessary to reduce the inhabitants to zero, to eliminate their traditional culture, for it blocks everything." And Decornoy comments: "The Americans accuse the North Vietnamese of intervening militarily in the country. But it is they who talk of reducing Laos to zero, while the Pathet Lao exalts the national culture and national independence."

No doubt Laos is still serving as a testing ground or experimental site, for the next stage of the Vietnam War, for our new long-haul, low-cost policy. If the American people will only trust their leaders, perhaps there is still a chance to crush the people's war in South Vietnam in ways that will be as well concealed as have been those of the Laotian war.

The Mentality of the
Backroom Boys

(1973)

───────────────────────────

*P*ERHAPS THE MOST SIGNIFICANT CONTRIBUTION OF THE
Pentagon Papers is the insight it provides into the mentality of
the planners. Since there is no reason to expect changes in this
regard in coming years, it is particularly important to examine the attitudes that are revealed by their decisions and debate.

THE BOMBING OF NORTH VIETNAM

The callous disregard of the planners for the victims of American terror
is illustrated, in a fairly typical way, when one of the backroom boys
explains that a program of sustained bombing of the North "seems

cheap," despite its higher cost in American casualties—particularly since a reprisal policy "demonstrates U.S. willingness to employ this new norm in counter-insurgency." Thus it will "set a higher price for the future upon all adventures of guerrilla warfare, and it should therefore somewhat increase our ability to deter such adventures."[1] The importance of Operation Rolling Thunder (RT), the analyst explains, was that "breaking through the sanctuary barrier had been accomplished" (IV, 53). This was an important achievement, since the United States had previously been a staunch defender of the "sanctuary barrier," as when United Nations Ambassador Adlai Stevenson emphasized American disapproval of "retaliatory raids, wherever they occur and by whomever they are committed" after the British raids against Yemen in reprisal for Yemeni attacks.[2]

But, it is important to add, though the "sanctuary barrier" was effectively broken, the genocide barrier still remained,[3] for reasons that are most informative. A CIA analysis of March 1966 explicitly recommended intensification of RT, directed largely against "the will of the regime as a target system." But agriculture and manpower as target systems were "not recommended at this time"—the genocide barrier stands. The sole reason is, "the effects are debatable and are likely to provoke hostile reactions in world capitals."[4] And John McNaughton urged:

> Strikes at population targets (per se) are likely not only to create a counterproductive wave of revulsion abroad and at home, but greatly to increase the risk of enlarging the war with China and the Soviet Union. Destruction of locks and dams, however—if handled right—might (perhaps after the *next* Pause) offer promise. It should be studied. Such destruction does not kill or drown people. By shallow-flooding the rice, it leads after time to widespread starvation (more than a million?) unless food is provided—which we could offer to do "at the conference table." [IV, 43]

This was January 18, 1966. A report of the air war at that time states that only eight locks and dams were targeted as "significant to inland waterways, flood control, or irrigation," and one had been hit and heavily damaged (IV, 56). There is no further information here on the follow-up, if any, to McNaughton's proposal that the United States engage in explicit war crimes of the sort punished after World War II.[5] The DRV (Democratic Republic of Vietnam [North Vietnam]), however, reports attacks on dams in Thanh Hoa province (April 4, 1965; the Pentagon history reports only attacks on Thanh Hoa bridges from April 2–8; III, 285) and Nghe An province (June 26–28, 1965, and many later occasions) and elsewhere.[6] These attacks increased sharply after 1965.[7] Eyewitness reports have occasionally appeared in the American press, and bombing of the irrigation and hydraulic system in South Vietnam has been frequently reported.[8] The Pentagon Papers contain no information on the latter, as on most aspects of the American war in South Vietnam.

What is interesting, in the present connection, is McNaughton's reason for not breaching the genocide barrier in the North. Much the same considerations are stressed by McNamara when he argues that bombing of population centers in the North should be avoided because of the risk that it might precipitate Soviet or Chinese direct intervention and "appall allies and friends" (IV, 28–29), a most unfortunate consequence.

The analyst is under the illusion that "populated areas were scrupulously avoided" in the North (IV, 18). This is nonsense, as any visitor to the DRV quickly discovers as soon as he leaves Hanoi. The CIA estimated that by 1966, after 161,000 tons of bombs had fallen, there had been almost 30,000 civilian casualties (IV, 136). Note also that the figure of 1,000 killed or seriously wounded a week, cited below, refers to the bombing of North Vietnam. As early as December 1965, Bernard Fall reported that "at least one hospital [in North Vietnam] had been completely destroyed by bombers," as "verified by non-Communist outside observers," and that "Canadian officials who recently returned from North Vietnam also told me that the city of Vinh was 'flattened' "—a city of 60,000, he notes.[9] I myself have seen the ruins of towns and villages not far from Hanoi and the remains of the hospital in Thanh Hoa city, destroyed, according to the North Vietnamese, in June 1965.[10] Testimony on this matter is by now so voluminous that it is amazing, a real tribute to the power of government propaganda, that one can still read that the bombing of the North scrupulously kept to military targets. The appalling destruction in the North, which has suffered less than 10 percent of the total bombing through 1971 (and of course none of the still more destructive shelling, apart from naval bombardment), is small only in comparison with the accomplishments of our government elsewhere in Indochina.

United States government propaganda has tried to give the impression that aerial bombardment achieved near-surgical accuracy, so that military targets could be destroyed with minimal effect on civilians. Technical military documents give a different picture. For example, Captain C. O. Holmquist writes:

> One naturally wonders why so many bombing sorties are required in order to destroy a bridge or other pinpoint target. . . . However, with even the most sophisticated computer system, bombing by any mode remains an inherently inaccurate process, as is evident from our results to date in Vietnam. Aiming errors, boresight errors,

system computational errors and bomb dispersion errors all act to degrade the accuracy of the system. Unknown winds at altitudes below the release point and the "combat degradation" factor add more errors to the process. In short, it is impossible to hit a small target with bombs except by sheer luck. Bombing has proved most efficient for area targets such as supply dumps, built-up areas, and cities.[11]

The American government claim that the bombing of North Vietnam was directed against military targets does not withstand direct investigation. But even if one were to accept it, considerations such as those mentioned by Captain Holmquist indicate that this was to a large extent a distinction without a difference.

Later, McNaughton and McNamara were to raise other objections to bombing.

> The picture of the world's greatest superpower killing or seriously injuring 1000 non-combatants a week, while trying to pound a tiny backward nation into submission on an issue whose merits are hotly disputed, is not a pretty one. It could conceivably produce a costly distortion in the American national consciousness and in the world image of the United States—especially if the damage to North Vietnam is complete enough to be "successful." [IV, 172; 484]

The most important risk remains "the likely Soviet, Chinese and North Vietnamese reaction." The question whether there might conceivably be some other objection to killing or maiming 1,000 noncombatants a week, apart from its potential costs to us, is not raised.

The same logic underlies the CIA advocacy of an "unlimited campaign" as "the most promising" in January 1967 (IV, 139–40; analyst) but with the proviso that although "bombing the levee system which kept the Red River under control, if timed correctly, could cause large crop losses," nevertheless the military effects might be short-lived. A draft memo of the Clifford Group in March 1968 argued against "a change in our bombing policy to include deliberate strikes on population centers and attacks on the agricultural population through the destruction of dikes" on the sole grounds that this "would further alienate domestic and foreign sentiment" and might lose European and other support (IV, 251). For this reason, the genocide barrier must stand. Not that everyone agreed: see the proposals from CINCPAC (Commander in Chief, Pacific) and Air Force Secretary Harold Brown (IV, 261).

In an informative analysis of the management of the air war in the North, Ralph Stavins points out some differences, determined by interviews, among the planners. Paul Warnke "opposed the bombing to the hilt" and sought to restrict targets. According to Alvin Friedman of the Pentagon, he came "from a different geological age compared to the likes of McNaughton, M. Bundy, McNamara and Rusk." McNaughton, in particular, was quite uncritical in recommending targets. "Warnke himself said his disagreement with McNamara arose over the possibility that the bombing would draw the Communist superpowers into the war," throughout, a major factor in deterring all-out bombing of the major population centers.[12]

MILITARY OPERATIONS IN SOUTH VIETNAM

South Vietnam, of course, has borne the brunt of the American attack in Indochina. As noted above, the facts of the American war in South Vietnam are barely discussed in the thousands of pages of documents and analyses, and, the record suggests, were not a matter of great interest or concern to the backroom boys. For example, from the analysis of United States ground strategy, the reader can learn that "in the estimation of the MACV [(U.S.) Military Assistance Command, Vietnam] staff [Operation Cedar Falls] gained outstanding results, capturing large numbers of weapons, ammunition and other war materials, plus nearly a half-million pages of enemy documents" and destroying the Iron Triangle as a "secure base area."[13] But he will have to look elsewhere to discover that for over a week before this operation, the windows of Saigon were rattling from concentrated B-52 raids in this settled area, or to learn the fate of the inhabitants of Ben Suc, forcibly evacuated from their demolished village to barren camps surrounded by barbed wire, with a sign at the entrance saying "Welcome to Freedom."[14]

On the rare occasions when questions were raised about the United States attack on South Vietnam, the moral level of the analysis is on a par with the occasional qualms expressed about RT. For example, William Bundy (June 30, 1965) advocated that "our air actions against the South should be carried on a maximum effective rate," including "substantial use of B-52s against VC havens." He recognized only one problem: "We look silly and arouse criticism if these [B-52 raids] do not show significant results" (IV, 612). If the B-52 raids do show significant results, we may turn out to be mass murderers (since in the nature of the case, there could be at best partial information about the targets), but this appears to be no problem at all.[15]

As noted earlier, the Pentagon Papers contain virtually no record of the decision to bomb the South. Perhaps we are to infer that this, like the bombing of the North, was undertaken to raise the morale of the South

Vietnamese population. The reader who finds this remark overly cynical may turn to II, 546, where an MACV monthly evaluation appears for February 1965: "US/GVN *strikes against* DRV *and increased use of U.S. jet aircraft in* RVN [Republic of Vietnam (South Vietnam)] has had a salutary effect on both military and civilian morale which may result in a greater national effort and, *hopefully, reverse the downward trend*" (italics in original). Not a word on the character of the bombing, which was improving morale in South Vietnam by "literally pounding the place to bits," as Bernard Fall reported in October 1965. So effective was this pounding that McNamara, in a generally gloomy analysis of July 20, 1965, could at least point to the fact that "US/VNAF air strikes in-country have probably shaken VC morale somewhat" (IV, 620), an important matter given the high morale of the indigenous Vietcong and the civilian society in which they were embedded.

This is not the place to review once again the bloodbath for which the United States is directly responsible in South Vietnam. To appreciate the scale, recall the estimates presented by Bernard Fall in April 1965—prior to the outright American invasion, prior to the introduction of any regular units of the North Vietnamese so far as Washington was aware: 66,000 Vietcong killed between 1957 and 1961, that is, before the large-scale combat involvement of American air and helicopter forces; 89,000 between 1961 and April 1965.[16] McNamara estimated another 60,000 of the "enemy" killed by mid-1966 (IV, 348), overwhelmingly South Vietnamese and probably including many civilians. "The problem is that American machines are not equal to the task of killing communist soldiers except as part of a scorched-earth policy that destroys everything else as well," so that the task of United States technology must be "to 'bomb the hell out of Indochina,' as one airman put it."[17] Furthermore, it became necessary to demolish the rural society, for reasons to which we return. The consequences are indescribable, and entirely missing from the Pentagon Papers.

The facts, of course, will be denied, no matter how strong the evidence. For example, Brigadier General W. A. Tidwell, chief of the Reconnaissance and Photo Intelligence Division in Vietnam and director of the Target Research and Analysis Center in 1964–65, writes that he developed many of the bombing techniques (including B-52 bombardment), and assures the reader that there was virtually no possibility that villages were attacked, except during ground combat.[18] And no matter what the facts may be, there will always be a Sidney Hook to claim that Bertrand Russell "plays up as deliberate American atrocities the unfortunate accidental loss of life incurred by the efforts of American military forces to help the South Vietnamese repel the incursions of North Vietnam and its partisans."[19] One can imagine what the same commentator would write if the enemies of the state whose propaganda he so faithfully parrots[20] were to indulge in a small fraction of the savagery of the American attack on the population of South Vietnam.

In an era that has experienced good Germans and apologists for Stalinist terror, it is perhaps not surprising to find some who will depict the horrors inflicted by the United States on Indochina as "unintended consequences of military action." Still, even the most cynical might be somewhat taken aback when such apologetics are coupled with attacks on critics of the American war for overlooking the barbarism of the enemy. One can hear the voice of some party hack berating critics of the Russian intervention in Hungary because they fail to denounce the terror of the resistance. In fact, it was quite proper for Russell, whom Hook castigates for such an "omission," to concern himself with atrocities for which Americans bear responsibility, either by their own actions or through their local agents. Consider in contrast Hook's practice: denunciation of Communist atrocities, absolute silence with regard to the far greater GVN atrocities (for which the United States bears a large measure of responsibility), and miserable apologetics with regard to the United States attack on the civilian population, incomparably greater in scale as well as foreign in origin.

In the Pentagon study, the Vietnamese appear only marginally, and then only as items to be controlled by the American-instituted regime, never capable of performing its assigned task; or as infrastructure to be rooted out; or as people who must be permitted to "enjoy the inherent right to choose their own way of life and their own form of government" (John McNaughton, describing the "national commitment" of the United States; IV, 393) within the framework of a constitutional system that "opposes Communism in any form" and prohibits "every activity designed to publicize or carry out Communism" (Article 5 of the 1967 Constitution, the proclaimed legal basis of such monstrosities as the Phoenix program—see below, pp. 280–81).

There is occasional recognition that the creatures who inhabit Vietnam may be human, or at least animate. It is assumed, for example, that they have a threshold of pain that can perhaps be reached without too much danger to the United States—we have already noted the reasons why the bombing "was too light, gave too subdued and uncertain a signal, and exerted too little pain" (IV, 20). The bombing of the North, that is.

As for the South, the careful reader can determine from the Pentagon study that it was being bombed. There are scattered statements referring to the fact, side comments in the review of the extensive debate over the American ground invasion, or in the course of the elaborate and detailed discussion of the vicious though far milder bombing of the North, which was the real "attention getter" (III, 431). In comparison to this, the decision to land combat marines in March 1965 "created less than a ripple" (III, 433), although proposals for further buildup "were the center of much private debate in the spring and early summer of 1965" ("behind the scene while the American public was in ignorance of the proceedings"; III, 445), and therefore merit a lengthy chapter in the Pentagon study. The buildup of United States combat forces, like the bombing of the North, was expected to be costly to the United States and was uncertain and dangerous in its further consequences. Therefore, it was worthy of attention.

The decision to pound South Vietnam to bits was the subject of no internal debate, so far as the record indicates. In fact, the decision and its impact were so insignificant that even the lack of concern over it receives no comment (in contrast to the decision to land combat marines). A similar observation applies to "responsible" segments of the peace movement, in large measure. On July 30, 1965, McNamara pointed out to the president, not inaccurately, that the "hue and cry" over bombing relates primarily to the North (III, 387). There were, of course, those whom McGeorge Bundy called the "wild men in the wings,"[21] but their hue and cry over the destruction of the rural society of South Vietnam had not yet come to the attention of Washington, and would not, until it became considerably more strident and indecorous.*

The United States command found itself "fighting a war of attrition in Southeast Asia," in accordance with Westmoreland's concept of "a 'meat-grinder' "—"kill[ing] large numbers of the enemy but in the end do[ing] little better than hold[ing] our own" (IV, 442). "Essentially, we are fighting Vietnam's birth rate," states an official quoted in a "startlingly accurate" newspaper account (IV, 587). Specifically in North Vietnam, "the bombing was unable to beat the birth rate" (IV, 227). There is only one way to beat the birth rate, in North Vietnam but more crucially in the South, where the primary enemy of the United States, the South Vietnamese peasant, permits the NLF to "orient himself on the population." The method is that succinctly described by General Westmoreland's chief planner: "The solution in Vietnam is more bombs, more shells, more napalm . . . till the other side cracks and gives up."[22]

NATION BUILDING AND CRIMES OF WAR

In the South, the task faced by the United States was to build a nation while rooting out the infrastructure of the organization that had captured the nationalist movement. A difficult task, but perhaps not impossible,

---

*Following this paragraph, material has been deleted from the original essay.

given sufficient force and terror. Robert Komer, always an optimist, thought it could be done. He advocated "increasing erosion of southern VC strength" (IV, 391), and cheerily reported to the president (February 1967) that although "few of our programs—civil or military—are very efficient," still "we are grinding the enemy down by sheer weight and mass" (IV, 420). Later, Komer was to explain that "thanks to massive U.S. intervention at horrendous cost," a favorable military environment was created "in which the largely political competition for control and support of the key rural population could begin again" in this "revolutionary, largely political conflict."[23] The "constructive aims" of pacification, Komer explained, are to protect the rural population from the insurgents, "which also helps to deprive the insurgency of its rural popular base," and to generate support for the Saigon regime—not easy, given the character of this regime, as noted by McNamara and others. It was far easier to fulfill the constructive aim of depriving the insurgency of its rural popular base by stepping up the programs of deliberate refugee generation, as Komer proposed.

Komer finds it difficult to comprehend why some regard him as a possible candidate for a war-crimes trial. The issue was raised by Eqbal Ahmad, with reference to a speech in which Komer explained that Vietnam had proved the inefficacy of "gradual escalation" which permitted the "guerrillas to make adjustments"; the lesson of Vietnam, he said, is to escalate ruthlessly and rapidly, to "snow them under." In an outraged reply to Ahmad, Komer reviews his career as special assistant to the president from April 1966 and as "chief pacification adviser to the GVN" from May 1967 to November 1968. The charge, Komer claims, must seem strange to anyone familiar with the post-1966 program, which he helped develop, "one of the more sensible and constructive endeavors which the U.S. belatedly supported in Vietnam." Its first phase "was essentially a nation-building effort, an attempt to help build a viable socio-economic fabric in the middle of a shooting war." From May 1967, when CORDS ([U.S.] Civil Operations and Revolutionary Development Support) was set up under Komer's direction, the pacification program *"was wholly Vietnamese manned and commanded"* (his italics), his role being only "to provide advice and logistic/financial help" to the GVN effort. The program did not rely on "bombing, napalm, defoliation, and other technological means" and the "pacifiers" opposed and sought to minimize generation of refugees; "the stress was on local self-government, political checks and balances, and rule of law."[24]

In general, Komer explains, his task was clean, bloodless, and constructive: to help the Saigon regime "build a nation." Surely, then, only the ill-informed or malicious could possibly accuse him of complicity in criminal acts.

Noting Komer's laudable concern that "the record of U.S. pacification support and advice need not be hidden behind a classified screen," let us compare his presentation with the record that is available now that the classified screen has been partially lifted.

The "pacifiers," he tells us, did not seek "the displacement and dispossession of the rural population" and sought to minimize refugee generation. As already noted, Komer is one of the few administration officials on record with the explicit recommendation to *"step up refugee programs deliberately aimed at depriving the VC of a recruiting base"*(IV, 441; his italics).

Komer states that after the establishment of CORDS, the pacification program was *"wholly Vietnamese manned and commanded"*(his italics).

He fails to mention the fact, documented endlessly by the press, the Pentagon Papers, and others, that rooting out the Vietcong infrastructure and "denying the villages to the Viet Cong" was primarily an American responsibility. American armed force was to "provide the shield" behind which the ARVN (Army of the Republic of Vietnam) could undertake "pacification" (Westmoreland, August 1966; II, 588). Discussing the CORDS program, headed by Komer as deputy to COMUSMACV (United States Commander in Vietnam), the analyst remarks that the structure of CORDS was "so massive that the Vietnamese were in danger of being almost forgotten" (II, 622). McNamara proposed in September 1966 that COMUSMACV be assigned responsibility for pacification. Komer, supporting this proposal, noted that "the military are much better set up to manage a huge pacification effort," since 60 to 70 percent of the "real job of pacification is providing local security . . . [which] can only be done by the military" (II, 590). As Komer explains elsewhere,[25] "Given the massive military support required, it made good sense on the U.S. side to put the new unified U.S. advisory structure [CORDS] under military command."

In an announcement drafted by Komer in May 1967, Ambassador Ellsworth Bunker stated that support of Revolutionary Development is "to be neither exclusively a civilian nor exclusively a military function, but to be essentially civil-military in character," involving "both the provision of continuous local security in the countryside—necessarily a primarily military task [—] and the constructive programs conducted by the Ministry of Revolutionary Development [of the GVN], largely through its 59-member RD teams," trained by the CIA (II, 616–17; 567–68). Bunker reported that General Westmoreland would undertake "the responsibility for the performance of our U.S. Mission field programs in support of pacification or Revolutionary Development," with Komer serving as "the single manager for pacification" (II, 428). The Combined Campaign Plan for 1967 of the United States and Saigon military forces (MACV/JGS [Joint General Staff of the RVN Armed Forces]; II, 495–96) assigned to

ARVN regular forces the task of "operations to destroy VC guerrillas and infrastructure in specified hamlet or village areas" in conjunction with provincial military forces and civil intelligence and police. US-FW military forces were to conduct combined operations with the Saigon military and police forces "to destroy VC guerrillas and infrastructure in specified hamlet or village areas," though it was left to the provincial forces and the National Police to carry out "population and resources control" directly. US-FW military forces were also to conduct "military and civic action to help win the support of the people for the government with emphasis to ensure that credit is given to the GVN," a directive observed by Komer in the remarks cited in his "Epilogue."

Komer's remarks on the *"wholly Vietnamese manned and commanded"* program should also be read in the light of his recommendation that "leverage" must be applied "always in such manner as to keep the GVN foremost in the picture presented to its own people and the world at large" (II, 503–4). We are "applying more leverage in Pacification," he adds. His view was that "increased use of U.S. leverage . . . must be done discreetly" (II, 430; analyst). Perhaps it might be more accurate to say that the United States must pretend that the GVN exists, to ourselves, to the world at large, and to the population that we are trying to win for it.

Komer always emphasized the central military component in pacification: "We must dovetail the military's sweep operations and civil pacification" so as to "secure and hold the countryside cleared by military operations." Komer "put everyone politely on notice" that he had no hesitation in calling on "military resources, which are frequently the best and most readily available" (II, 570). Pacification "demands a multifaceted civil-military response" to provide security, for *"breaking the hold of the VC over the people,"* to *"systematize the flow of refugees,"* and so on (II, 572–3; his italics). The most important problem in pacification, in his constantly reiterated view, is security, a military-police problem. In comparison, his position on land reform, though he pressed for signs of progress and urged that it be accelerated "to consolidate rural support behind the GVN," was that "it was not an important issue in Vietnam." "Far more important was the matter of security in the countryside" (II, 400, 569, 392; IV, 441).

A CORDS report from Bien Hoa province for the period ending December 31, 1967, gives a bit more insight into the wholly Vietnamese programs that Komer and his American colleagues merely advised. Because of the corruption and inefficiency of the GVN officials (whose "primary interest . . . is money"), "CORDS has had to increasingly rely on the resources, skills and capabilities of resident US military units." "CORDS Bien Hoa (as well as the GVN itself) owes a great deal to these units and their commanders who have unselfishly devoted themselves to furthering pacification." The "disturbing truth" is that "it still remains for the government [of South Vietnam], with forceful and meaningful direction from above, to begin to assume the responsibility for prosecuting this war and the pacification effort" (II, 407). The Pentagon study terminates at this point, but we know from many other sources that in the following months the reliance on the United States military in preparing the ground for "pacification" increased, the My Lai massacre being only the best known and most grotesque example. Allan Goodman writes: "Whatever else the introduction of [American combat troops] may have achieved it is now clear that their participation in the conflict (particularly in the twelve months after the Tet offensive of 1968) seriously weakened the ability of the VC/NVA (North Vietnam Army) to conduct effective mobile warfare within South Vietnam."[26] Forced population removal and massive devastation intensified, laying the groundwork for Komer's program of constructive nation building.

The same period marked the implementation of another of Komer's important recommendations: *"Revamp and put new steam behind a coordinated US/GVN intelligence collation and action effort targeted on the VC infrastructure at the critical provincial, district, and village levels"* (IV, 441; his italics). The problem, he related, is that "we are just not getting enough payoff yet from the massive intelligence we are increasingly collecting. Police/military coordination is sadly lacking both in collection and in swift reaction."

Two months later, on June 14, 1967, in a memorandum for General Westmoreland entitled "Organization for Attack on V.C. Infrastructure," Komer recommended "consolidation, under his direction, of U.S. anti-infrastructure intelligence effort," and expressed his desire for a "unified GVN/US, civil/military 'management structure targeted on infrastructure.'" In response, the ICEX (Intelligence Coordination and Exploitation) structure was developed in July 1967, under Westmoreland and Komer (II, 429, 585). ICEX, involving CIA, American military and civilians, and the GVN military-police-intelligence apparatus, was the immediate predecessor of the Phoenix program, other sources indicate. Early internal directives describe the Phoenix program as an American program of advice, support, and assistance to the GVN *Phung Hoang* program. Later modifications delete reference to "Phoenix" and refer merely to the GVN *Phung Hoang* program, again in line with the approach of "keep[ing] the GVN foremost in the picture presented to its own people and the world at large."

On March 4, 1968, the secretary of defense recommended that "Operation Phoenix which is targetted against the Viet Cong must be pursued more vigorously in closer liaison with the US," while "Vietnamese armed forces should be devoted to anti-infrastructure activities on a priority basis" (IV, 578).

After Westmoreland and Komer's ICEX became Phoenix, the coordinated US-GVN intelligence-military-police programs succeeded in "neutralizing" some 84,000 "Viet Cong infrastructure" with 21,000 killed, according to reported "official figures."[27] According to the same UPI report, Komer is indeed correct when he states ("Epilogue") that United States advisers criticized excesses. One reports that local officials in the delta decided to kill 80 percent of the suspects, but American advisers were able to convince them that the proportion should be reduced below 50 percent. Another American adviser concedes that "naturally, we kill and torture many Vietcong. . . . The only way to combat these people who act like animals is to kill them." We treat them just as they treat us, he adds, failing, however, to list the American towns in which cadres assisted, trained, and paid by the NLF have conducted murder and torture missions. According to the same report, the actual assassinations are largely carried out by former criminals or former Communists recruited and paid by the CIA, which also organizes the provincial interrogation centers where prisoners are tortured. Other reports indicate that CIA-directed teams drawn from ethnic minorities are widely used; that American military men often conduct operations; and that the units often include Nationalist Chinese and Thai mercenaries. An American International Voluntary Service volunteer reports picking up two hitchhikers in the Mekong Delta, former criminals, who told him that by bringing in a few bodies now and then and collecting the bounty, they can live quite handsomely.[28]

The "pacification" program was reportedly accelerated substantially in March 1971, its "top priority" being neutralization of the political apparatus of the Vietcong, at a reported cost of considerably more than $1 billion to the United States and an undisclosed amount to the Saigon regime (hence indirectly, the United States).[29] A rare statistic for April 1971 reveals that in that month, of 2,000 "neutralized" more than 40 percent were assassinated,[30] possibly the first fruits of the accelerated terror program. A United States intelligence officer attached to the Phoenix program in the Mekong Delta states that when he arrived in his district, he was given a list of 200 names of people who were to be killed, and when he left six months later, 260 had been killed, but none of those on his list.[31]

As in other cases of "body count," the numbers given and the identity of the victims raise various questions. There is ample evidence that the operatives and intelligence collectors (heavily infiltrated, quite probably, by the NLF) often avoid the difficulties and hazards of trying to tangle with the NLF infrastructure, meeting their quotas in other ways.[32] As a device for terrorizing the political opposition, however, the Phoenix program may well be effective. Although the actual assassinations, torture, and imprisonment are conducted by operatives trained, advised, and paid by the United States, it would be "double think," Komer insists ("Epilogue"), to criticize the "GVN *Phung Hoang* program" too harshly.

We have noted Komer's insistence that his "pacifiers" are devoted to the rule of law. That may well be true, though the significance of this noble commitment only becomes clear when we explore the system of laws that they uphold. "Security offenses" can be tried by military field courts, and the laws are so severe that virtually any form of overt dissent might be regarded as a violation of national security: undermining public morale, or acts in furtherance of communism or pro-Communist neutralism, or acts to undermine the anti-Communist spirit of the country, all punishable by five years to death.[33]

The problem that Komer always regarded as the most important, namely, "security in the countryside," has been approached by the methods just indicated. Among the most savage were the programs of deliberate refugee generation and "swift reaction" by the military and police under the "coordinated US/GVN intelligence collation and action effort," as explicitly recommended in both cases by Komer, who tells us that he was concerned merely with the constructive tasks of nation-building, after United States military force had provided a "favorable military environment" for these benign activities. He is quite right, incidentally, in emphasizing that in the full spectrum of American activities in Vietnam, those that he directed are among the least criminal.

THE ASIAN MIND—THE AMERICAN MIND

So far as the bombing of the North was concerned, the analyst concludes that the idea was based "on a plausible assumption about the rationality of NVN's leaders," namely, that they would not want to bear its cost (IV, 57). But the guerrillas were "supplying themselves locally, in the main" (IV, 57), and, as McNamara rather prissily explained to a Senate committee, the North Vietnamese leaders' "regard for the comfort and even the lives of the people they control does not seem to be sufficiently high to lead them to bargain for settlement in order to stop a heightened level of attack" (IV, 202). Any Nazi could have said the same about Winston Churchill.

This line of thinking has been extended since by a number of thoughtful commentators. William Pfaff, liberal-in-residence at the Hudson Institute, explains that "ours has been a reasonable strategy," but it was "the strategy of those who are rich, who love life and fear 'costs.' "[34] For us, "death and suffering are irrational choices when alternatives exist." "We want life, happiness, wealth, power. . . ." But we failed to comprehend "the strategy of the weak," who "deal in absolutes, among them that man inevitably suffers and dies." The enemy "stoically accept[s] the destruction of wealth and the loss of lives"; "happiness, wealth, power—the very words in conjunction reveal a dimension of our experience beyond that of the Asian poor." The weak thus invite us to carry our "strategic logic to its conclusion, which is genocide,"[35] but we balk, unwilling to "destroy ourselves . . . by contradicting our own value system." As Townsend Hoopes formulated it, we hesitate because we realize "that genocide is a terrible burden to bear." Thus we fail. Neither Pfaff nor Hoopes tells us how he has determined that the Asian poor do not love life or fear costs or seek wealth and happiness. Perhaps this is demonstrated in a classified research study of the Hudson Institute.

Pfaff and Hoopes are rivaled in their understanding of the Asian mind by several secretaries of state. James Byrnes, in December 1946, alluded to the problems caused by the "almost childish Vietnamese attitude and knowledge of economic questions and vague groping for 'independence,'" which was causing all sorts of troubles, citing Abbot Moffat (*DOD*, bk. 8, p. 89). These childish attitudes and vague gropings were perhaps still more pronounced because the Vietnamese had "been thoroughly indoctrinated with the Atlantic Charter and other ideological pronouncements" and thus foolishly expected American help (Richard Sharp, reporting remarks of General Philip Gallagher; *DOD*, bk. 8, p. 56). Secretary George Marshall, more practical and realistic than the Vietnamese, understood the need for "a continued close association between newly-autonomous peoples and powers which have long been responsible for their welfare," as France had been responsible for the welfare of the Vietnamese;[36] and he recognized that "for an indefinite period" the Vietnamese would require not only French material and technical assistance but also "enlightened political guidance," under a voluntary association (DOD, bk. 8, pp. 100–101). Still another secretary of state commented that "as with most Orientals Diem must be highly suspicious of what is going on about him" (Dulles, April 1955; *DOD*, bk. 10, p. 909); though apparently Diem was not suspicious enough, as events were to prove in mid-1963.

The National Security Council, equally astute, explained the favorable prospects of the Soviet Union in Asia in part on the grounds that "its protégés deal with Asiatic peoples who are traditionally submissive to power when effectively applied" (*DOD*, bk. 8, p. 239; December 1949)—an insight that has been corroborated so conclusively by the effective application of force to the Vietnamese in the past quarter century.[37]

Similar perspicacity is exhibited by United States Ambassador Maxwell Taylor, who has been described elsewhere as the "chief adviser, if not *éminence grise*" of the Kennedy administration.[38] He bemoans the "national attribute" which "limits the development of a truly national spirit" among the South Vietnamese, perhaps "innate" or perhaps a residue of the colonial experience. And he then proceeds to speculate about "the ability of the Vietcong continuously to rebuild their units and to make good their losses"—"one of the mysteries of this guerrilla war"—and their remarkable morale and recuperative powers and continued strength, for which "we still find no plausible explanation" (III, 668; November 27, 1964). The only explanation he can conjure up is the dispatch to the South of "trained cadre and military equipment" and the flow of radio messages. Apparently it did not occur to him that US-GVN operations in North Vietnam somehow did not have a similar impact. It is, of course, completely beyond his comprehension that the true source of Vietcong resilience may be precisely a "national attribute," deeply rooted in the peasant society that we have systematically destroyed, an "attribute" that arouses the Vietnamese peasants to continued resistance to colonial domination—the attribute that is repeatedly characterized as "xenophobia" in these documents. The same remarkable foolishness is revealed when overflights for dropping leaflets in North Vietnam were recommended in May 1961 "to maintain morale of North Vietnamese population," as though the people of North Vietnam, enslaved by their Communist masters, were prayerfully awaiting salvation by American bombers, or perhaps by the "networks of resistance, covert bases and teams for sabotage and light harassment" to be formed in North Vietnam, "using the foundation established by intelligence operations" (II, 641).

It would perhaps be unfair to quote the various contributions of the Joint Chiefs—for example, their suggestion that a firm declaration of intent by the United States to block "aggression originating outside of Indochina . . . would in general raise the morale of all peoples in Southeast Asia and in particular would increase the determination of the Indochinese to fight the war to a successful conclusion" against the "Soviet Communist campaign in Southeast Asia" (January 15, 1954; *DOD*, bk. 9, pp. 214, 216).

In comparison, Eisenhower appears a model of profundity "in commenting philosophically" on the low morale among "democratic forces in Laos" and wondering aloud "why, in interventions of this kind, we always seem to find that the morale of the Communist forces was better than that of the democratic forces" (II, 637). "His explanation was that the Communist philosophy appeared to produce a sense of dedication" not matched among those "supporting the free forces." The problem had been noted much earlier, as in a national intelligence estimate of June 1953 pointing out the gloomy prospects for the "Vietnamese government" given "the failure of Vietnamese to rally to [it]," the effective

Vietminh "control," the fact that the population assist the Vietminh more than the French (making it difficult "to provide security for the Vietnamese population"), the inability of "the Vietnam leadership" to "overcome popular apathy and mobilize the energy and resources of the people," and so on (I, 391–92). With hardly more than a change of names, this analysis might be taken for the despairing report from pacification specialists (MACCORDS) on December 31, 1967, cited above, deploring the corruption of the GVN,[39] the "ever-widening gap of distrust, distaste and disillusionment between the people and the GVN," and its growing weakness. With these words, the record of US-GVN relations ends (II, 406–7). *Plus ça change . . .*

Somehow the United States never managed "to influence the GVN to do the things we believe they must do to save their own country" (II, 623). In October 1966, McNamara lamented "that the US had not yet found the formula for training and inspiring the Vietnamese" (II, 388; analyst): *"the discouraging truth is that, as was the case in 1961 and 1963 and 1965, we have not found the formula, the catalyst, for training and inspiring them into effective action* (IV, 349; McNamara's italics; Carver of the CIA disagreed, II, 598). All we seem to be able to do is kill, he adds.

Not that ideas were not put forth as to the proper formula, or catalyst. A memorandum of October 20, 1954, to the director of the CIA suggested that "a psychological operations concept entitled 'Militant liberty'" might do the trick. The concept was later endorsed by General Bonesteel of the NSC Planning Board (*DOD*, bk. 10, pp. 777, 975), but it then disappears from the record. The Joint Chiefs, in February 1964, while recommending increased crop destruction and other measures, added that it would be helpful to "create a 'cause' which can serve as a rallying point for the youth/students of Vietnam." A "National Psychological Operations Plan" might help, they thought (III, 45).

The technical intelligentsia were also rallied to the effort of finding the proper formula to inspire the Vietnamese to effective action. The journal *Army* (December 1966) discusses a meeting of

> a group of physicists in the so-called Jason division of the Institute for Defense Analyses (IDA), a think factory that works closely with the Department of Defense. . . . Although they concentrated upon such matters as night vision for detecting guerrillas, improved communications, and vulnerability of aircraft to guerrilla gunfire, the scientists finally concluded that the compelling research need was not in the "hard" sciences but in "softwares"—the social sciences.
>
> "We found that it was a very different problem from what we encountered in dealing with strategic weapons which are generally removed from human factors," said Dr. Jack Ruina, former presi-

dent of IDA and now a vice president at the Massachusetts Institute of Technology. "In nuclear weapons it's machine versus machine. When we started thinking about counterinsurgency we quickly realized that you cannot isolate these problems from people. What did we know about these people—the Viet Cong and the Vietnamese generally? We felt we needed to know a great deal more from the anthropologist, from the social scientists. The greatest insight we have obtained about the Vietnam situation comes from anthropologists who can speak Vietnamese.

"What we concluded at the Jason session was that social and political and cultural knowledge was very important. A systematic and scholarly study of these areas of the world was clearly necessary. There would be serious difficulties in this type of research, some false starts, and some obstacles, but it should be done."

The report goes on to cite some results, for example, a RAND study of the effects of American bombing, "finding that such raids in North Vietnam improved morale in South Vietnam; that raids in South Vietnam damaged Viet Cong morale and that hostility toward the U.S. did not grow materially in the bombed areas."

Another RAND study "showed Viet Cong recruits in the villages are lured by the promise of their own rifle and a uniform. As a result the Saigon government decided to try to attract youths with flashy uniforms, jaunty with red, yellow or other lively scarves and berets." This idea does not seem to have been quite the answer. Apparently some component is missing; further research is necessary.

Still another RAND study observed: "The communication of a charisma (miraculously acquired powers) or a set of sympathetic symbols has received attention as an effective leadership device to arouse responsiveness in populations of underdeveloped societies. Charisma or similar symbolism is parsimonious of administrative skill, but also unstable and difficult to use in accomplishing complex social cooperation." No doubt the Pentagon is still puzzling over how to translate this advice into an effective catalyst.

One should not laugh at this sort of inanity. When intelligence fails, there is plenty of force in reserve. As the insights from the social scientists proved inadequate, the United States simply extended and intensified its war of machines against people.

American ambassadors in Saigon were in no position to await the results of the research by government intellectuals, and therefore proposed programs of their own for creating a "cause" that would "accomplish complex social cooperation" on the part of the Vietnamese. Ambassador Bunker suggested that the United States should use its influence to get the GVN to "adopt a program and identify it with that of a former national hero"—in his words, "so as to give the new government an idealistic appeal or philosophy which will compete with that declared by the VC" (August 1967; II, 403). But this ingenious proposal met with no better results than the Ten Point Program for Success proposed by Ambassador Henry Cabot Lodge two years earlier. The first point: "Saturate the minds of the people with some socially conscious and attractive ideology, which is susceptible of being carried out" (II, 530). Apparently it didn't matter much what the ideology was. At least, nothing further is said. Somehow these far-reaching concepts never succeeded in overcoming the "idealistic appeal" of the Vietcong.

Since the United States never succeeded in "saturating the minds of the people" with a sufficiently attractive ideology, it turned to the easier task of saturating the country with troops and bombs and defoliants. A State Department paper observed: "Saturation bombing by artillery and air strikes . . . is an accepted tactic, and there is probably no province where this tactic has not been widely employed . . ." (IV, 398). The only objection raised is that it might be profitable to place greater emphasis on "unconventional war," specifically on winning popular support for the Saigon regime. That United States force should be devoted to winning support for its creation, the Saigon government, apparently seemed no more strange to the author than that the United States should be conducting saturation bombing of all provinces of South Vietnam.

Cambodia

(1985)

<hr>

*T*HE TORTURE OF CAMBODIA DURING THE "DECADE OF THE genocide" is one of the horror stories of the modern period, one that is far from ended. The Democratic Kampuchea (DK) coalition, based primarily on Pol Pot's Khmer Rouge forces, continues a border war against the Vietnamese troops who installed the Heng Samrin regime. The Khmer Rouge receive "massive support" from China, Nayan Chanda reports, while the United States has more than doubled its indirect support to the DK coalition. Deng Xiaoping, expressing the Chinese stand, states:

> I do not understand why some want to remove Pol Pot. It is true that he made some mistakes in the past but now he is leading the fight against the Vietnamese aggressors. [November 1984]

The State Department has meanwhile explained that the United States supports the DK coalition because of its "continuity" with the Pol Pot regime. The West refuses development aid, and while there has been some reconstruction from the devastation of the 1970s, immense tasks remain before the country regains a viable status.

The "decade of the genocide" had two phases: the 1970–75 war and the Khmer Rouge atrocities of 1975–78 (and the subsequent famine). The two are not unrelated. In 1970, correspondent Richard Dudman, then a Khmer Rouge captive, described how American bombs were mobilizing the Khmer Rouge, previously a marginal force. Few informed commentators would seriously question the assessment of David Chandler that:

> The bombing destroyed a good deal of the fabric of pre-war Cambodian society and provided the CPK (Khmer Rouge) with the psychological ingredients of a violent, vengeful and unrelenting social revolution. This was to be waged, in their words, by people with 'empty hands.' The party encouraged class warfare between the "base people," who had been bombed, and the "new people" who had taken refuge from the bombing, and thus had taken sides, in CPK thinking, with the United States. [*Pacific Affairs,* Summer 1983]

Merciless bombing and other atrocities have a way of making the victims angry, even brutal, a reaction not limited to peasants. People who had suffered far less than the peasants of Cambodia murdered thousands of alleged collaborators in France after liberation in 1944, when the country was under U.S. civil-military control.

When the Khmer Rouge peasant armies achieved victory in April 1975, the country was in ruins. A high American official estimated that one million would die from starvation and disease, and the final USAID report warned that:

> Slave labor and starvation rations for half the nation's people (probably heaviest among those who supported the republic) will be a cruel necessity for this year, and general deprivation and suffering will stretch over the next two or three years before Cambodia can get back to rice self-sufficiency.

Much of the population was surviving on U.S. aid, withdrawn with the Khmer Rouge victory. Even with it, 8,000 people starved to death in Phnom Penh in March 1975. Much of the countryside had been devastated. The prospects were appalling, even if there had been a benign regime receiving reparations and aid. The insistence of much Western commentary—in particular, the *Reader's Digest* study by John Barron and Anthony Paul—that events prior to April 1975 are irrelevant to what ensued cannot be taken seriously.

What was happening under Khmer Rouge rule was not easy to determine. The difficulties are illustrated by the population estimates offered for the end of the DK period by the *Far Eastern Economic Review* in January 1979 and a year later: the earlier figure, "mostly based on CIA estimates," is 8.2 million (the CIA estimates the Cambodian population at 7.1 million in 1975); the second is 4.2 million. The actual figure appears to have been 6.5 million or more. Meanwhile, the public was generally offered a version based on serious distortion of the evidence then available and on much outright fabrication.

Many felt that facts were unimportant, notably Jean Lacouture, who wrote in the *Nouvel Observateur* and the *New York Review of Books* that the Khmer Rouge had "boasted" of having "eliminated" 2 million people by mid-1976, adding a few weeks later (in the *New York Review* alone) that he had misread his source (François Ponchaud's *Cambodge année zéro*) and that the figure might be in the thousands or hundreds of thousands, while adding that a factor of 1,000 (thousands, millions) was of little moment; his figure of 2 million killed remained the standard one even after it was withdrawn, later to be replaced in much Western commentary by the Hanoi figure of 3 million. Lacouture's position was widely regarded as acceptable, even admirable. The reaction would hardly have been the same had he written that the United States "boasted" of the murder of 2 million people in the early 1970 bombings, later commenting that perhaps the actual number was in the thousands or hundreds of thousands, but that the distinction was unimportant. The example illustrates the casual attitude toward the facts often found when events can serve some ideological function. The books under review mark a major and salutary change in this respect.

The scale of casualties during the two phases of the terror appears to be in roughly the same range: half a million to a million deaths during the first phase and, according to Michael Vickery's estimate in his careful and detailed study, about 750,000 deaths "above the normal" during the second phase, including 200,000 to 300,000 outright executions. The Finnish Inquiry Commission reaches similar conclusions though it assumes far fewer executions, while endorsing figures for the decimation of the Chams that would merit the term "genocide." The CIA estimates 50,000 to 100,000 executions, which seems far too low, but as Vickery has shown, the CIA ignored the worst massacres, which were in 1978 (when the United States was beginning to "tilt" toward DK), while exaggerating deaths in the earlier period and apparently providing their figures to Barron and Paul, who presented them as their own.

To place these massacres in a broader context, by calculations similar to Vickery's, deaths caused by the U.S.-backed Indonesian aggression in Timor during the Pol Pot period would be in the neighborhood of 200,-000 to 300,000, in a country with one-tenth Cambodia's population. These deaths, like those of the first phase of the Cambodian terror, are primarily the responsibility of the United States. It is instructive to compare the Western response to these three major atrocities.

In their introduction to *Revolution and Its Aftermath,* Chandler and Kiernan observe that much more is known about the DK period than about Cambodia in earlier years. In fact, there has been little attention to what took place within Cambodia during the first phase of the "decade of the genocide." It was not a subject for much media attention at the time or for scholarship since, and though hundreds of thousands of refugees from the bombing were readily accessible in Phnom Penh, few were interested in what they had to relate. The Finnish study is unusual in extending the term "genocide" to this period, to which it devotes three pages.

Immediately after the Khmer Rouge victory in April 1975, there was a dramatic change. By July, the *New York Times* had denounced the Khmer Rouge actions as "genocide." Shortly after, the *Reader's Digest* (circulation 18 million) published Barron and Paul's "Murder in a Gentle Land" (where "murder" refers to the DK period), which became an international best-selling book. There were lurid accounts of Khmer Rouge genocide (or "autogenocide") in the popular press (e.g., in *TV Guide,* circulation 19 million) and intellectual journals (e.g., the *New York Review*), and throughout the media generally. The picture constructed forms what Vickery calls the "standard total view" of the DK period, which "has permeated most of the writing on Cambodia since 1975." It is unnecessary to comment on press coverage in the Communist states, which predictably reflected the varying demands of current policy.

There were skeptical voices at the time, primarily State Department intelligence, the most knowledgeable and in retrospect apparently the most accurate source. U.S. "Cambodia watchers" speculated that deaths from "brutal, rapid change" (not "mass genocide") might have reached hundreds of thousands by 1977. Their estimates were ignored in favor of the "standard total view," and are ignored today in favor of fables about "left-wing skepticism."

Vickery begins by demolishing the tales of the "gentle land" along with much of the work produced during the Khmer Rouge period, which he dismisses as propaganda efforts that were "immediately taken up by the press, pushed through large printings, excerpted and reviewed," and taken as "authoritative," "however unhistorical, uncritical, or dishonest" the work might have been. In a detailed and extremely valuable review, Vickery gives an area-by-area analysis of refugee reports, basing himself on his own extensive studies and others, and showing that in contrast to the "standard total view" (but as State Department intelligence and many Cambodia specialists had indicated), the picture was varied and complex. All the same, large parts of the country did approach the "standard total view" at the end, well after this account had been contrived and widely disseminated. One surprising conclusion is that the southwest area, "the power base of the Pol Pot central government," was relatively well-run and not particularly violent in the early years, though as Pol Pot's power extended, it brought enormous bloodshed.

Vickery explores the many factors that led to atrocities, including the policies of the central leadership and those rooted in earlier and recent history. He observes that "whatever else the (1970–75) conflict was, it was also, if not first of all, a war between town and countryside in which the town's battle was increasingly for the sole purpose of preserving its privileges while the rural areas suffered," one factor in the brutal treatment of the "new people," who were compelled to live the lives of poor peasants, or worse. The most terrible massacres, he concludes, took place as the central government purged the relatively tranquil eastern zone from mid-1978, in the context of the war with Vietnam and "intraparty factional conflict," which led to increased killings elsewhere as well. He notes that the Pol Pot faction had identified Vietnam as the "main enemy" as early as 1973. In the Chandler-Kiernan volume, Ben Kiernan gives a detailed account of the purges in the eastern zone, which he concludes led to over 100,000 killed. It was these massacres, covered up in the 1980 CIA demographic study, which produced "most of the mass graves and stacks of bones," according to Vickery.

Vickery's own conclusion is that DK was

> first of all, a victorious peasant revolution, perhaps the first real one in modern times, and it had at first considerable support; some of its policies were rational but carried out badly; and as a result it became at times and places a real chamber of horrors,

particularly as the power of the "Pol Pot faction" spread, with its violent purges and "strongly chauvinistic" streak of anti-Vietnamese hostility which led to border war and finally the Vietnamese invasion. He also argues that the sources of DK ideology may lie as much in the chauvinist-nationalism of Son Ngoc Thanh as in Marxism, and offers "a hypothetical sketch" of how the Paris-educated intellectuals who became the DK leadership "adopted poor-peasantism and anti-Vietnamese racism as their leading policies—policies which proved disastrous." It was "the victory of chauvinism over Marxism," he argues, that made the DK a "useful partner" for the United States by the end, and so it remains today.

Vickery also analyzes in detail the "standard total view" for 1979–80, finding it "so at variance with the truth that it must be based in part on deliberate lies," including the allegations of Vietnamese "genocide" and serious misrepresentation of the nature of the postwar famine, which he was one of the first to refute. He concludes that the policies of the current regime have been generally constructive.

The Finnish study covers much the same ground in less detail, arriving at rather similar conclusions, though not entirely. It suggests that by the end of 1978, DK "was finding solutions" to its basic problems and "creating the prerequisites for an economic revival," as was also reported in early 1979 by Nayan Chanda, and by Richard Dudman after a visit in late 1978. It is not clear that this conclusion is compatible with their view that

> in 1979, the very existence of Kampuchea was at stake; society was destroyed, and its people faced the risk of premature death as a result of starvation, diseases, violence and sheer exhaustion.

The study also contains an analysis of the international relief effort of 1979–80 (part of which went to Thai villagers who, it was discovered, were hardly better off than the Cambodian refugees, Vickery reports), noting also U.S. exploitation of the refugee problem to destabilize Vietnam and Cambodia. It concludes that the post-1979 aid program was generally successful, though apart from the Soviet bloc (which provided most of the aid in 1979–80), not directed to true development, for political reasons. A final section on the media is almost entirely limited to the Communist states, with unsurprising conclusions.

In the Chandler-Kiernan volume, Vickery summarizes some of the content of his book, noting also that Kiernan's early hypothesis about the special character of the northwest, from which horror stories were generalized incorrectly to the entire country, is supported by "all serious research efforts." Kiernan explores in much illuminating detail the history of the eastern zone. Serge Thion analyzes the ideology of the Khmer Rouge as "very close to Maoism," and very far from Marxism, with "an ideology which rationalizes the substitution of the radical intelligentsia" for the working classes; a similar (and quite accurate) critique of Leninism is familiar in left-Marxist and anarchist work. Thion holds that central authorities had little control over the economy or the "state power system." Anthony Barnett takes issue with this view, arguing against Thion and Vickery that "the Pol Pot group always managed to retain the initiative after 1975, and it used its power to impose and consolidate its rule," and that regional variations fell within centrally determined uniformities. It is not clear that much is at issue in this apparent disagreement. Chandler's analysis of the version of history presented by the DK leadership notes its nationalistic and presocialist aspects, its emphasis on the capacities of "ordinary people, when mobilized in vast numbers by the state," and the avoidance of standard Marxist themes or even references. Chanthou Boua gives a positive view (shared by most of those reviewed here) of the policies of the current regime, based on visits in 1980–81.

The other two papers are different in focus. Gareth Porter discusses Vietnamese Communist policies toward Cambodia from 1930 to 1970 emphasizing their "equivocal" and "ambivalent" attitude toward Vietnam's role, and their "decisions about Cambodia in the context of (the) struggle against more powerful outside foes." William Shawcross presents an account of Western reactions to DK and the subsequent famine, later expanded in a widely praised book concerned with the important topic of "Holocaust and modern conscience" and likely to become the "standard total view" of these aspects of the tragedy. Like earlier phases of the "standard total view," this one is marred by misrepresentation and considerable confusion. As for the latter, Shawcross notes that there was no "mass popular reaction" to atrocities in Cambodia until after the fall of DK, and erroneously concludes that there was little concern over these atrocities before. His analysis of the change in "mass popular reaction" after 1979 avoids the obvious reason: there was nothing to be done before and much after. Thus Shawcross did not use his ample access to the press to urge any "mass popular action" during the DK period, nor did he offer any suggestion as to how to mitigate the DK atrocities. This observation alone suffices to undermine his major thesis.

Shawcross' thesis that the West was unconcerned with the atrocities is demonstrably false, as documented in the references he cites and in Vickery's discussion; his further claim that this alleged failure was due to the "scepticism" of the left and its influence over Western media and opinion is simply ludicrous, and would be even if that skepticism had existed to any detectable extent (that is, apart from skepticism about fabrications and about the dismissal of such sources as U.S. intelligence). To support his thesis, Shawcross misrepresents the material he discusses, primarily a 1977 article by Edward Herman and me and a chapter in our 1979 study of U.S. global policies and propaganda. Thus he claims that we "were to believe for years" that "the refugees were unreliable, that the CIA was cooking up a bloodbath to say, 'We told you so.'" In fact, we barely mentioned the CIA (and recommended State Department intelligence as probably the most reliable source), and we accepted refugee reports as generally accurate. In our sole publication during the DK period, the 1977 article he cites, we recommended Ponchaud's French book as "serious and worth reading," with its "grisly account" of atrocities reported by refugees, and in our later book we began by emphasizing that refugee reports left no doubt that the record of Khmer Rouge atrocities was "substantial and often gruesome." We were concerned with an entirely different topic, namely, Vickery's "standard total view" and its origins; and we documented a remarkable record of deceit, by Shawcross in particular.

Shawcross' allegations are based on innuendo, not on fact or argument. Thus he cites our comment about the need to use care in analyzing refugee reports, falsely insinuating that we challenged these reports and concealing the fact that we are quoting Ponchaud, his primary source. He states his "own view, contrary to Chomsky and Herman," that the U.S. government was "remarkably inactive" in anti-Khmer Rouge propaganda; we proposed no U.S. government role in the record of deceit we documented. In commenting on the alleged failure of Western commentators to recognize that "the Khmer Rouge was a Marxist-Leninist government," he states that John Pilger "constantly compared" the Khmer Rouge with the Nazis, suppressing the fact that he compared their actions with "Stalin's terror." These examples are typical.

Shawcross concedes that coverage of the Pol Pot massacres was greater than that of the simultaneous U.S.-backed massacres in Timor; in fact, far greater and radically different in character, and crucially, in this case there was (and is) no problem as to how to bring them to a halt. He rejects the obvious explanation for the difference, offering instead a "more structurally serious explanation": "a comparative lack of sources" and lack of access to refugees. Lisbon and Australia are not harder to reach than the Thai-Cambodian border, but the many Timorese refugees there were ignored by the media, which preferred State Department handouts and Indonesian generals. Similarly the media ignored readily available refugee studies from sources at least as credible as those used as the basis for the Cambodian "standard total view," and disregarded highly credible witnesses of atrocities who reached New York and Washington, along with additional evidence from church sources and others. The coverage of Timor actually declined sharply as the massacres increased. The real reason for the difference in scope and character of coverage is not difficult to discern, though not very comfortable for Western opinion, and becomes still more obvious when a range of other cases is considered. While we now discuss the issue, the massacres continue, still evoking little concern in the countries that bear the major responsibility. Shawcross' "serious structural explanation" is hardly more than a form of apologetics for massacre and for submissiveness to the existing system of power and privilege, and sheds considerable light, though not of the sort intended, on "Holocaust and modern conscience."

The fate of Cambodia is tragic enough in itself; the horrors are simply compounded when they are exploited for political or opportunistic ends. This has happened far too often. These works for the most part represent a welcome change, an attempt to come to grips with the actual facts as far as they can be determined and to explore their significance. The authors leave no doubt that much remains uncertain, and make a creditable effort to distinguish fact from speculation and interpretation. Even their insistence that facts matter is a noteworthy departure from much that has come before, though only the naive would expect this position to become an influential one.

The books reviewed are: *Cambodia: 1975–82* by Michael Vickery (Boston: South End Press; London: George Allen & Unwin, 1983); *Revolution and Its Aftermath in Kampuchea: Eight Essays,* edited by David Chandler and Ben Kiernan (New Haven, Conn.: Yale University Press, 1983); and *Kampuchea: Decade of Genocide,* edited by Kimmo Kiljunen (London: Zed Books, 1984).

Punishing Vietnam

(1982)

<hr />

S INCE THE WAR'S END, THE UNITED STATES HAS DONE WHAT IT could to ensure that its partial victory would endure. "There is a great deal of evidence," Martin Woollacott writes, "that the foot-dragging policy of the United States on diplomatic relations and on aid, whether or not it was tagged with the humiliating label of reparations, helped to close off the Yugoslavia option for Vietnam."[1] That is quite correct. A World Bank official observes that "since 1977, the US has constantly refused to make any accommodation with Vietnam, forcing it further and further into the Soviet camp."[2] This is a typical procedure when some area is "lost" to the Free World; compare the case of China, Cuba, and now Nicaragua. It is a procedure that may be reversed (as in the case of China) if it is recognized that "rollback" is not in the cards.[3]

For the time being, however, the United States is committed to maximizing hardship and suffering in Vietnam. It has exerted effective pressure on the World Bank to withhold development aid,[4] and the Reagan administration "has launched a vigorous, behind-the-scenes campaign at UN headquarters to cut UN humanitarian and development aid to Vietnam."[5] The present moment is particularly opportune because of the starvation conditions in Vietnam and the fact that "refugees recently leaving Vietnam are reported to be citing economic reasons far more than any other for their flight from the hard-pressed Southeast Asian nation."[6] Thus cutting food aid has a double benefit: increasing misery, and increasing the refugee flow, so that Western humanitarians can then deplore the barbarian savagery of the Vietnamese leadership as illustrated by the tragic fate of the boat people. The United States and the European Economic Community have refused to respond to a UNICEF appeal for milk and food for the Vietnam emergency. The U.S. government also initially rejected an appeal from the Mennonite Central Committee to allow it to ship wheat to Vietnam, where, the committee's executive secretary for Asia points out, "drought in late 1979 and early 1980 was followed by typhoons and floods that caused heavy destruction to the rice crop in northern and central Vietnam."[7] At the same time, "prospects for loans from the Asian Development Bank and the World Bank are very bleak, since many donor countries, especially the US and Japan [which benefited substantially from the U.S. war as an offshore procurement base], are opposed to any assistance to Vietnam."[8]

The official reason for blocking international aid of any sort to Vietnam is to punish Vietnam for its illegal occupation of Cambodia. But this is pure fraud:

> One moderate third-world ambassador makes a point echoed by many of his colleagues: "By attempting to stop UN agencies from providing assistance and relief to Cambodia and to Vietnam, the United States is really trying to apply sanctions of sorts against Vietnam for its illegal occupation of Cambodia. How is it then that the United States is so reluctant to apply sanctions against South Africa for its illegal occupation of Namibia? If the US were consistent it would have a stronger case, morally and politically."[9]

Furthermore, the United States has not attempted to "punish Indonesia for its illegal occupation of East Timor"; rather, it has provided accelerating military aid to Indonesia since 1975 to assist in this aggression and the accompanying massacre (no one accuses Vietnam of conducting a massacre in Cambodia[10]—on the contrary, the invasion may have helped to avert further massacres—nor can it be claimed that Timorese border attacks in collusion with a powerful ally were a threat to Indonesia). And the United States never suggested sanctions against Israel to punish it for its attacks on Jordan and Lebanon or its occupation of the West Bank, Gaza Strip, Golan Heights, and Sinai, or for the settlement policy on the West Bank, which the Carter administration repeatedly described as "illegal." The true character of the U.S. stand is, furthermore, revealed with utter clarity by the U.S. refusal to provide more than a trickle of aid to help overcome the ravages of the U.S. war in Laos, where there has also been widespread starvation.[11]

In fact, the goal of U.S. policy is clear enough. Not content with a partial victory of the sort just described, the United States wants to ensure the maximum possible suffering in countries that have been so ignoble as to resist American aggression, in the hope that sooner or later "Vietnam will crack," and the partial victory can be extended to a total one. Perhaps analogues can be found in the gloomy history of great-power cynicism, but offhand none came to mind. Again, it is noteworthy that protest is next to nonexistent, providing further insights into "Western humanism" and the real significance of the wringing of hands over human rights violations committed by official enemies.

The United States did win a significant victory in Indochina, a fact that is crucial to the understanding of postwar events. True, it did not achieve the goal of retaining Indochina within the American system, so that its people could enjoy the happy life of the peasants, urban slum-dwellers, torture victims, and child slave laborers of Thailand, Indonesia, the Philippines, and Latin America. But that was always a secondary goal. The primary goal was to ensure that "the rot would not spread," in the terminology favored by the planners. In South Vietnam itself, the United States did win the war. The battering of the peasant society, particularly the murderous post-Tet accelerated pacification campaigns, virtually destroyed the indigenous resistance by eliminating its social base, setting the stage for the northern domination now deplored by Western hypocrites—exactly as had been predicted many years before. In Cambodia, the horrendous bombing campaign of 1973, which was directed primarily against the peasant society, was a significant factor in brutalizing the Khmer Rouge victors, a conclusion supported by U.S. government studies and other sources.[12] In Laos, the prospects for peaceful development in one of the world's poorest countries were destroyed by American subversion and military attack. North Vietnam, while not conquered, was left in ruins.

The terrible prospect of successful economic development has been overcome for a long time, perhaps permanently. No one knows when, or if, the land and people poisoned by chemical warfare and bombed to ruin will be restored to a viable social order. The postwar policy of refusing reparations, aid, or normal relations with Vietnam and blocking assistance from other sources where possible is perfectly rational, as a further contribution to ensuring maximal suffering. It also succeeded in driving Vietnam into alliance with the Soviet Union as the only alternative remaining, again a consequence eagerly exploited by the Western propaganda system. By systematically creating conditions under which existence is reduced to virtually the zero grade, Western power has attained its primary ends throughout Indochina. The West has once again taught the lesson that European civilization has offered to the world for centuries: those who try to resist the technologically advanced but morally primitive Western societies will pay a bitter price.

East Timor

(1985)

THE WESTERN-BACKED INVASION AND SUBSEQUENT MASSACRE IN East Timor, still in progress, reveals with much clarity the hypocrisy of Western posturing about human rights, the utter fraudulence of the show of anguish over a certain well-defined class of terrible atrocities (namely, those that are ideologically serviceable, since the perpetrators are official enemies), the casual acceptance of acts that would be described as genocidal were we not responsible for them, and the device of cloaking aggression in the guise of defense, almost too common to bear mention. The story is so revealing that it cannot be known, and indeed is not known except in tiny circles. Furthermore, the truth of the matter cannot be permitted to survive, and one can predict with some confidence that these events will find their way into Orwell's useful memory hole, and will be as well known in the United States and elsewhere in the West as the U.S. massacre of hundreds of thousands of Filipinos at the turn of the century, the genocidal destruction of Native Americans, and other matters not suitable to be enshrined in official history.

The background for the tragedy of East Timor lies in U.S. global planning in the post–World War II period. The political problems of Southeast Asia were to be solved in such a way as to enable the region "to fulfill its major function as a source of raw materials and a market for Japan and Western Europe," the State Department explained in 1949. Indonesia, with its wealth of raw materials, was to play a central role in the emerging global system, with Japanese and Western European capitalism reconstructed within a broader framework managed by the United States and ultimately subordinated to its interests. The Portuguese colony of East Timor, to which Indonesia laid no claim prior to its 1975 invasion, was also mentioned by the planners of the postwar world. Sumner Welles held that it should receive the right of self-determination, though with a slight delay: "It would certainly take a thousand years," he explained, expressing the familiar racist contempt for the lesser breeds. For Indonesia, self-determination—of a sort—would be permitted at once.

The United States supported the termination of Dutch colonialism, which, like other regional systems that the United States did not control, would be an impediment to U.S. plans for organizing the global system in a manner that would subordinate it to U.S. requirements. But unsatisfied with the outcome, the United States attempted to overthrow President Sukarno in 1958 through the means of a "rebellion" by Indonesian dissidents and mercenaries trained by the CIA in the Philippines. Even when a U.S. pilot (for an airline that was a CIA front) was shot down, the U.S. press was not sufficiently interested to inquire into charges that were dismissed by Bernard Kalb of the *New York Times* as "Communist propaganda." The attempt to overthrow the Indonesian government failed, but the efforts continued, along a different path, one that the United States has pursued with some regularity in overthrowing governments, including democratic governments, that it finds offensive to its taste: Chile under Allende is a well-known case. The United States maintained close contact with the Indonesian military and provided military aid while relations with the government became increasingly hostile. In 1965, six generals were murdered in what official doctrine (including much of scholarship) describes as a "Communist coup," which miraculously spared the pro-U.S. General Suharto while targeting elements of the military considered anti-American. Suharto then carried out an actual military coup, which led to the slaughter of some half a million people in a few months, mostly landless peasants, and crushed the popular-based Communist party, at the same time, incidentally, turning the country into a "paradise for investors."

The West observed all of this with much pleasure, even delight. Secretary of Defense Robert McNamara was asked in congressional hearings whether the military aid to Indonesia during a period of frosty U.S.-Indonesian relations had "paid dividends," and he agreed that it had. Congress agreed as well, as did the press, which welcomed the "gleam of light in Asia"; "the West's best news for years in Asia"; "Hope . . . where once there was none"; and so on. Western liberals hailed the "dramatic changes" that had taken place in Indonesia as justification for the U.S. attack against South Vietnam (called here "the defense of South Vietnam"), which had provided a "shield" behind which the Indonesian generals were encouraged to carry out their necessary work of purging the society and freeing it for Western exploitation. By now, respected journalists are able to write that the Communist party "subjected the country to a bloodbath" (George McArthur) and that "thousands were slaughtered" in 1965 "when the nation's military foiled a bloody attempt by President Sukarno and the Chinese-backed Communist party of Indonesia to replace the parliamentary government with a dictatorship" (Robert Toth). The victims have become the perpetrators of the massacre, and its level is reduced by a factor of 100 with its agency and the U.S. role suppressed, as is the norm in reference to atrocities committed by the "good guys" on our side, paying the dividends for our assistance.

A CIA study of the 1965 Indonesian operation remains secret. Former CIA agent Ralph McGehee, who was custodian of that study but is not permitted to discuss it, states that on the basis of the study "I know the specific steps the agency took to create the conditions that led to the massacre of at least half a million Indonesians."

With the political opposition demolished in one of the great massacres of the modern era and 750,000 arrested, many to remain safely in jails and concentration camps for fifteen years, Indonesia was welcomed into the Free World, where it continues to serve as a loyal outpost of liberty and democracy in the approved style, including impoverishment of much of the population in a potentially rich society, terror and torture, a political system that does not even merit the term "fraudulent," but, crucially, few barriers to foreign exploitation apart from the rapacity of the Indonesian generals and their local associates.

In 1974, with the overthrow of Portuguese fascism, steps toward independence were undertaken in the colony of East Timor. Indonesian-supported elements attempted a coup in August 1975, but the attempt was beaten back in a brief but bloody civil war in which some 2,000 to 3,000 people were killed. By early September, the country was in the hands of Fretilin, described by knowledgeable observers on the scene as "populist Catholic" in general orientation. International relief officials, journalists, and other observers praised the moderate and constructive efforts to move toward development and independence. But Indonesia had other ideas in mind, and the United States and its allies were happy to oblige, as long as the profits kept flowing.

Indonesian aggression began at once in the border areas, and there was little doubt that Indonesia would soon invade outright. Secret cables, leaked in Australia, reveal that the U.S. embassy in Jakarta was under instructions from Henry Kissinger not to involve itself in the matter and "to cut down its reporting on Timor" (Australian Ambassador Woolcott). The personal view of U.S. Ambassador David Newsom, as reported by the Australian ambassador, was that if Indonesia were to intervene they should do so "effectively, quickly and not use our equipment." The latter hope was mere deceit: its meaning was that Indonesia should not use our equipment too flamboyantly. Ninety percent of Indonesian military supplies were from the United States, granted under the condition that they be used only for self-defense; but the concept of "defense" can be construed quite broadly when necessary.

On December 7, Indonesia invaded outright, initiating a mass slaughter that may have cost the lives of some 200,000 people by 1979 while reducing the remnants to the level of existence in Biafra and on the Thai-Cambodian border. The United States, contrary to official lies, participated with enthusiasm. The U.S. government claimed to have initiated a secret six-month arms moratorium; as later exposed, the moratorium was so secret that Indonesia did not know about it, and during this period arms continued to flow and the United States even made new offers of equipment particularly useful for counterinsurgency operations. By 1977, Indonesia had actually begun to exhaust its military supplies in this war against a country of 700,000 people, so the Carter administration took some time off from its pieties and self-acclaim about its devotion to human rights—"the soul of our foreign policy"—to arrange a large-scale increase in the flow of arms to Indonesia, in the certain knowledge that they would be used to consummate a massacre that was approaching genocidal proportions.

As for the American media, they required no instructions from the State Department "to cut down reporting from Timor." Understanding their role, they virtually eliminated the topic from view. In the *New York Times,* for example, coverage of Timorese issues had been substantial in 1975, but declined as Indonesia invaded and reduced to zero as the atrocities reached their peak with the new equipment provided for that purpose by the Human Rights Administration in 1978. The occasional reports carefully avoided the many Timorese refugees in Portugal and

Australia, choosing to rely instead on Indonesian generals, who assured the reader, via the free press, that the Timorese who had been "forced" to the mountains by Fretilin were fleeing from its "control" to Indonesian protection. These "facts" were presented as facts by the free press, when it deigned to consider the slaughter. Later, the nature and scale of the atrocities were partially conceded, behind a curtain of deception and with the role of the U.S. government and the complicity of the press carefully excised.

While the United States was the major foreign participant in the slaughter, others tried to profit as they could and kept their silence. In Canada, the major Western investor in Indonesia, the government and the press were silent and the government now claims that "groups opposed to the Fretilin political faction requested the assistance of Indonesia and the Indonesian military intervened. Subsequently representatives of the anti-Fretilin factions submitted a formal request to the Indonesian government for the integration of East Timor and Timor is now an integral part of the Republic of Indonesia." That is all; Goebbels would have been impressed. *Le Monde* reported in September 1978 that the French government would sell arms to Indonesia while abstaining from any U.N. discussion of the invasion and in general doing nothing to "place Indonesia in an embarrassing position." The Paris intellectuals, much impressed at the time with their courage in denouncing Communist crimes in Indochina—which presumably washed clean a century of French atrocities there, in Africa, and elsewhere, which had elicited little protest, even during the French Indochina War—had no time to object to France's commitment to the ongoing massacre, and now haughtily inform us that Timor was too geographically and historically "marginal" to have merited concern (Gérard Chaliand). British journalists who were denouncing Cambodian autogenocide and even Vietnamese "genocide" in Cambodia present us with a "more structurally serious explanation" for the failure to cover what was happening in Timor: "there were not many refugees; there was no 'border' for journalists to visit," and "there has been a comparative lack of sources" (William Shawcross). We are thus being informed, with a straight face, that Lisbon, two hours by air from London, is harder to reach than the Thai-Cambodian border, and that the voluminous record provided by Church sources, smuggled letters, refugee studies by highly competent authorities that were ignored, etc., did not exist. Some 40,000 Timorese had died during World War II assisting Australian commandos fighting the Japanese; Australia registered its thanks by tacitly, now openly supporting the Indonesian aggression. The story is the same throughout the civilized world, with very rare exceptions, providing a certain insight into the nature of "civilization."

U.S. participation in the massacre extended beyond the level of crucial material support and complicity on the part of the ideological institutions. The U.S. government also lent diplomatic support to the Indonesian invasion. It was particularly important to block action at the United Nations to deter the aggression in the early days, when such action might have been effective. U.N. Ambassador Daniel Patrick Moynihan was assigned this task, and described his success in performing it with much pride. In a secret cable of January 23, 1976, to Secretary of State Kissinger, he cited his success in blocking U.N. action on Timor as part of the "considerable progress" he had achieved by arm-twisting tactics at the United Nations. In his memoirs, he explains the reasons why the U.N. was unable to act in a meaningful way:

> The United States wished things to turn out as they did and worked to bring this about. The Department of State desired that the United Nations prove utterly ineffective in whatever measures it undertook. This task was given to me, and I carried it forward with no inconsiderable success.

Moynihan also made it clear that he understood the nature of his accomplishment very well. He cites a February 1976 estimate by an Indonesian client in Timor "that some sixty thousand persons had been killed since the outbreak of the civil war" in August—recall that some 2,000 to 3,000 had been killed during the civil war, the remainder since the Indonesian invasion in December—"10 percent of the population, almost the proportion of casualties experienced by the Soviet Union during the Second World War." Thus Moynihan is taking credit for an achievement that he proudly compares to Hitler's in Eastern Europe.

Moynihan is highly admired for ridiculing Idi Amin and similar acts of heroism during his tenure at the United Nations, and he received much acclaim for his denunciation of the United Nations as "the scene of acts we regard as abominations," which the United States will "never forget"—these oratorical flourishes were issued exactly at the time he was working, with much success, to ensure that the United Nations would place no impediment in the path of the U.S.-backed Indonesian aggression. Moynihan is also much praised as a spokesman for the rule of law and for his criticism of the "the totalitarian left," with its "Orwellian" distortions that have "blunted . . . perceptions within the democracies." As he explained to an admiring audience at the National Humanities Center in April 1983 (reprinted by the American Academy of Arts and Sciences, much impressed with these insights), the "totalitarian left" has raised "peculiar difficulties" for the "liberal democracies" by such rhetorical devices. In December 1980, Moynihan was the main speaker at a conference of the Committee for United Nations Integrity which denounced the organization as "no longer the guardian of social justice, human rights and equality among nations" because it is "perverted by irrelevant political machinations" and "is in danger of becoming a force against peace itself"; the committee was concerned not with the success of its honored speaker in implementing a huge massacre in Timor by perverting the United Nations, but rather with the fact that that organization has supported Palestinian rights, a major crime in U.S. eyes.

More recently Moynihan explained that the Senate Select Committee on Intelligence, of which he was vice chairman, had approved administration requests for funding to support the contra attack on Nicaragua "on the grounds that international law not only authorized the United States" to support paramilitary operations in Central America "but even obligated it to do so, it being the case that the Government of Nicaragua was supporting efforts to subvert its neighbor, El Salvador." Moynihan has a subtle and discriminating sense of what constitutes "aggression": a trickle of aid to people being massacred by U.S. clients constitutes "aggression" obligating a foreign invasion by a proxy army (so that, *a fortiori*, the USSR has the right, even the obligation, to attack Pakistan, China, and the United States because of their support for efforts to "subvert" the legally recognized government of Afghanistan); but direct and outright aggression by a U.S. client with full and crucial U.S. support leading to one of the major massacres of the modern period does not constitute "aggression," and it is our right, even our obligation, to undermine international efforts to impede it, with much applause from liberal Western opinion.

On December 12, 1975, when Moynihan was carrying out his assigned task with much relish, he received the highest award from the International League for the Rights of Man (now the International League for Human Rights) in honor of his role as "one of the most forthright advocates of human rights on the national and international scene." On December 10, 1982, the league announced that it would bestow the same award to former President Jimmy Carter "in recognition of outstanding achievement in the field of human rights," one notable example being his dedication to ensuring that Indonesia would have the military means and diplomatic support to being its noble work in Timor to fruition. The league, incidentally, is well aware of the facts and the U.S. role, and indeed is one of the few groups with a respectable record of protest on the matter.

In 1977, when the death toll in Timor had perhaps reached 100,000 and Jimmy Carter authorized increased military aid to Indonesia to drive it still higher, the West was consumed with agony and outrage over atrocities in Cambodia under the Khmer Rouge. From mass-circulation journals such as the *Reader's Digest* and *TV Guide* to intellectual journals such as the *New York Review of Books,* the Khmer Rouge were condemned as the equals of Hitler and Stalin, perhaps worse, with their "boast" that they had "eliminated" one-fourth of the population, some 2 million people (Jean Lacouture, who conceded a few weeks later that the story was a fabrication and that the actual toll may have been in the thousands, but explained that a factor of 1,000 was of no significance: the 2 million figure remained orthodoxy in the West, despite this acknowledgment). Two years earlier, when the Khmer Rouge had killed perhaps thousands of people, it was accused of "genocide" by the *New York Times.* By mid-1977, according to U.S. intelligence, the death toll had reached "tens if not hundreds of thousands," mostly from disease, malnutrition, and overwork, the result primarily of "brutal, rapid change," not "mass genocide"; this assessment, ignored at the time since it did not satisfy the current propaganda requirements, is now quite generally confirmed by subsequent scholarship. This was in a country with ten times the population of East Timor, a country that had been ravaged by a U.S. attack that was responsible for the death of hundreds of thousands in the first half of the decade, and where people were dying from this attack at the rate of 100,000 a year in the city of Phnom Penh alone (no one knew, or cared to explore, what was happening in the countryside, subjected to one of the fiercest bombardments in history) just prior to the Khmer Rouge takeover. The outrage over the Khmer Rouge was not only extensive in scale, but also unprecedented in character, with some of the most astonishing fabrication and deceit on record, since the actual atrocities of the Khmer Rouge, gruesome enough as recognized with no question (apart from the qualifications of U.S. intelligence, the only people who knew anything about what was happening), were not deemed sufficient for the crucial purpose at the time: to shift the moral onus for the Indochina wars to the victim. The merits and nature of this outrage are revealed with much clarity by the reaction in the same circles to the simultaneous and quite comparable atrocities in Timor.

One must, however, take note of several crucial differences between these cases, the most important being that in the case of Cambodia, the outrage, while ideologically serviceable and hence intense, was quite impotent; no one suggested any way to bring the atrocities to an end, though later there was discussion about the legitimacy of intervention to protect the victims. In the case of Timor, the silence was crucial. It was of critical importance to ensure that the public was unaware of what was happening so that there would be no impediment to the ongoing slaughter. To bring the atrocities to an end required no intervention; it would have sufficed to call off the hounds. The example provides much insight into the nature of the Western conscience and its moral concerns, as does the fact that the Indonesian atrocities continue today, arousing no inter-

est in the West, which prefers farcical debates about what should have
been done in Cambodia.

When the truth about Timor finally became very partially known for a
brief period in 1980, then to be restored to its proper oblivion, the
comparison to Cambodia was raised in establishment circles, as it had
been before in the obscurity of protest. The *Wall Street Journal* was troubled by the comparison, which it quickly put to rest with reasoning that
need not detain us. But the *Journal* and others need no longer be concerned about the "inconsistency" between our opposition to Khmer
Rouge massacres and support for comparable Indonesian massacres.
The "inconsistency" has now been overcome, since the United States
now supports both Pol Pot and the Indonesian murderers. The United
States openly backs the Democratic Kampuchea coalition, based largely
on the Khmer Rouge, who are supported directly by the U.S. allies China
and Thailand. The reasons have been explained by John Holdridge of the
State Department in congressional hearings in September 1982. Asked
whether "the opposition in Cambodia [namely, the Khmer Rouge-based
Democratic Kampuchea coalition] is more representative of the Cambodian people than the Fretilin is of the Timorese people," Holdridge
replied: "Unquestionably because there has been this continuity since the
very beginning," namely, the continuity with the Pol Pot regime.

Those who prefer a more orderly world may now rest easy, "inconsistencies" having been resolved.

There is one bright spot in this sordid tale. Thanks to the efforts of a
handful of young people, some knowledge of the facts at last reached
parts of the population, members of Congress, and even—briefly—the
press. One result of these efforts was that the International Red Cross was
permitted intermittent access to Timor and some relief flowed, perhaps
saving tens of thousands of lives. This too teaches a lesson: there is a
great deal that can be done to mitigate and overcome state terror and
atrocities, if we are willing to escape the grip of the commissars and look
honestly at what is happening in the world. It remains possible, though
the likelihood diminishes with each passing year, that the Indonesian
aggression can be terminated by public pressure on the U.S. government
that provides it with the critically needed support; and that the people of
East Timor, those who have survived the onslaught, may yet enjoy the
right of self-determination that the United States professes to uphold,
perhaps even sooner than one thousand years hence.

CENTRAL AMERICA

Intervention in Vietnam and Central America: Parallels and Differences

(1985)

*I*F YOU TAKE ANY TWO HISTORICAL EVENTS AND ASK WHETHER there are similarities and differences, the answer is always going to be both yes and no. At some sufficiently fine level of detail, there will be differences, and at some sufficiently abstract level, there will be similarities. The question we want to ask in the two cases we are considering, Central America and Vietnam, is whether the level at which there are similarities is, in fact, a significant one. And I think the answer is that it is.

The level at which there are similarities is the level at which we consider U.S. intervention, its consequences, and, particularly, its sources in domestic institutions. At this level of discussion, I think we find quite substantial similarities. They are essentially the following:

(1) United States intervention was significant and decisive.

(2) The effects of intervention were horrifying.

(3) The roots of this intervention lie in a fixed geopolitical conception that has remained invariant over a long period and that is deeply rooted in U.S. institutions.

What I would like to sketch out, in the brief time I have, is what I think a full inquiry into this topic would reveal. I'll start by talking about the geopolitical conception. And I'd like to stress that, in my opinion, if you don't understand this geopolitical conception, the chances that you'll understand what is happening in the world are relatively slight; whereas if you do understand it, quite a lot of things fall into place, and you could even get a reputation as a good prophet. I will then consider what this geopolitical conception has entailed for Vietnam, and what it means today and in the likely future for Central America.

Before doing this, I would like to try to set this off against what one might call an official view, or maybe, less charitably, a party line, which pretty much dominates the interpretation of these issues. It's expressed, for example, with regard to Vietnam, when we read that the U.S. intervention in Vietnam began with "blundering efforts to do good," although it became a "disaster." That's Anthony Lewis in the *New York Times.* Or when we read that our involvement began from "an excess of righteousness and disinterested benevolence." That's John King Fairbank, the leading Asia specialist at Harvard, who points out further that what he calls our "defense" of South Vietnam was misconceived and not properly developed. Or, again, when we read that this "defense of South Vietnam" was a "failed crusade," "noble" but "illusory," and undertaken with the "loftiest intentions." That is Stanley Karnow in the best-selling companion volume to the Public Broadcasting System television series, which is highly acclaimed for its critical candor and is now under attack by the right wing for not having been sufficiently servile, only obedient.

Notice that these few comments are from the *critics,* from the doves. It would be hard, within the mainstream, to find people in scholarship or the media who were harsher critics of the war than Anthony Lewis, John Fairbank, or even Stanley Karnow, who is also considered dovish and critical.

The reason I picked those examples is because the rest follows *a fortiori.* The spectrum of debate within the mainstream extends from *that* position over to the position of Ronald Reagan and Norman Podhoretz, and in fact you can see a difference, but not much. That's the spectrum of discussion, and if you don't accept it, you're pretty much outside of civilized company. This official view is what I would like to contrast with what appears to be the real world.

In the real world, U.S. global planning has always been sophisticated and careful, as you'd expect from a major superpower with a highly centralized and class-conscious dominant social group. Their power, in turn, is rooted in their ownership and management of the economy, as is the norm in most societies. During World War II, American planners were well aware that the United States was going to emerge as a world-dominant power, in a position of hegemony that had few historical parallels, and they organized and met in order to deal with this situation.

From 1939 to 1945, extensive studies were conducted by the Council on Foreign Relations and the State Department. One group was called the War-Peace Studies Group, which met for six years and produced extensive geopolitical analyses and plans. The Council on Foreign Relations is essentially the business input to foreign-policy planning. These groups also involved every top planner in the State Department, with the exception of the secretary of state.

The conception that they developed is what they called "Grand Area" planning. The Grand Area was a region that was to be subordinated to the needs of the American economy. As one planner put it, it was to be the region that is "strategically necessary for world control." The geopolitical analysis held that the Grand Area had to include at least the Western Hemisphere, the Far East, and the former British Empire, which we were then in the process of dismantling and taking over ourselves. This is what is called "anti-imperialism" in American scholarship. The Grand Area was also to include western and southern Europe and the oil-producing regions of the Middle East; in fact, it was to include everything, if that were possible. Detailed plans were laid for particular regions of the Grand Area and also for international institutions that were to organize and police it, essentially in the interests of this subordination to U.S. domestic needs.

Of course, when we talk about the domestic economy, we don't necessarily mean the *people* of the United States; we mean whoever dominates and controls, owns and manages the American economy. In fact, the planners recognized that other arrangements, other forms of organization, involving much less extensive control over the world would indeed be possible, but only at what from their point of view was the "cost" of internal rearrangements toward a more egalitarian society in the United States, and obviously that is not contemplated.

With respect to the Far East, the plans were roughly as follows: Japan, it was understood, would sooner or later be the industrial heartland of Asia once again. Since Japan is a resource-poor area, it would need Southeast Asia and South Asia for resources and markets. All of this, of course, would be incorporated within the global system dominated by the United States.

With regard to Latin America, the matter was put most plainly by Secretary of War Henry Stimson in May 1945 when he was explaining how we must eliminate and dismantle regional systems dominated by any other power, particularly the British, while maintaining and extending our own system. He explained with regard to Latin America as follows: "I think that it's not asking too much to have our little region over here which never has bothered anybody."

The basic thinking behind all of this has been explained quite lucidly on a number of occasions. (This is a very open society and if one wants to learn what's going on, you can do it; it takes a little work, but the documents are there and the history is also there.) One of the clearest and most lucid accounts of the planning behind this was by George Kennan, who was one of the most thoughtful, humane, and liberal of the planners, and in fact was eliminated from the State Department largely for that reason. Kennan was the head of the State Department policy-planning staff in the late 1940s. In the following document, PPS23, February 1948, he outlined the basic thinking:

> We have about 50 percent of the world's wealth, but only 6.3 percent of its population. . . . In this situation, we cannot fail to be the object of envy and resentment. Our real task in the coming period is to devise a pattern of relationships which will permit us to maintain this position of disparity. . . . We need not deceive ourselves that we can afford today the luxury of altruism and world-benefaction. . . . We should cease to talk about vague and . . . unreal objectives such as human rights, the raising of the living standards, and democratization. The day is not far off when we are going to have to deal in straight power concepts. The less we are then hampered by idealistic slogans, the better.

Now, recall that this is a top secret document. The idealistic slogans are, of course, to be constantly trumpeted by scholarship, the schools, the media, and the rest of the ideological system in order to pacify the domestic population, giving rise to accounts such as those of the "official view" that I've already described. Recall again that this is a view from the dovish, liberal, humane end of the spectrum. But it *is* lucid and clear.

There are some questions that one can raise about Kennan's formulation, a number of them, but I'll keep to one: whether he is right in suggesting that "human rights, the raising of the living standards, and democratization" should be dismissed as irrelevant to U.S. foreign policy. Actually a review of the historical record suggests a different picture, namely that the United States has often opposed with tremendous ferocity, and even violence, these elements—human rights, democratization, and the raising of living standards.

This is particularly the case in Latin America and there are very good reasons for it. The commitment to these doctrines is inconsistent with the use of harsh measures to maintain the disparity, to ensure our control over 50 percent of the resources, and our exploitation of the world. In short, what we might call the "fifth freedom" (there were four freedoms, you remember, but there was one that was left out): the freedom to rob. That's really the only one that counts; the others were mostly for show. And in order to maintain the freedom to rob and exploit, we *do* have to consistently oppose democratization, the raising of living standards, and human rights. And we *do* consistently oppose them; that, of course, is in the real world.

These particular comments referred to the Far East, but Kennan applied the same ideas to Latin America in a briefing for Latin American ambassadors in which he explained that one of the main concerns of U.S. policy is the "protection of our raw materials." Who must we protect *our* raw materials from? Well, primarily, the domestic populations, the indigenous population, which may have ideas of their own about raising the living standards, democratization, and human rights. And that's inconsistent with maintaining the disparity. How will we protect our raw materials from the indigenous population? Well, the answer is the following:

> The final answer might be an unpleasant one, but . . . we should not hesitate before police repression by the local government. This is not shameful, since the Communists are essentially traitors. . . . It is better to have a strong regime in power than a liberal government if it is indulgent and relaxed and penetrated by Communists.

Well, who are the Communists? "Communists" is a term regularly used in American political theology to refer to people who are committed to the belief that "the government has direct responsibility for the welfare of the people." I'm quoting the words of a 1949 State Department intelligence report which warned about the spread of this grim and evil doctrine, which does, of course, threaten "our raw materials" if we can't abort it somehow.

So it is small wonder, with this kind of background, that John F. Kennedy should say that "governments of the civil-military type of El Salvador are the most effective in containing Communist penetration in Latin America." Kennedy said this at the time when he was organizing the basic structure of the death squads that have massacred tens of thousands of people since (all of this, incidentally, within the framework of the Alliance for Progress and, in fact, probably the only lasting effect of that program).

In the mid-1950s, these ideas were developed further. For example, one interesting case was an important study by a prestigious study group headed by William Yandell Eliot, who was Williams Professor of Government at Harvard. They were also concerned with what communism is and how it spreads. They concluded accurately that the primary threat of communism is the economic transformation of the Communist powers "in ways which reduce their willingness and ability to complement the industrial economies of the West." That is essentially correct and is a good operational definition of "communism" in American political discourse. Our government is committed to that view.

If a government is so evil or unwise as to undertake a course of action of this sort, it immediately becomes an enemy. It becomes a part of the "monolithic and ruthless conspiracy" to take over the world, as John F. Kennedy put it. It is postulated that it has been taken over by the Russians if that's the policy that it appears to be committed to.

On these grounds, one can predict American foreign policy rather well. So, for example, American policy toward Nicaragua after the 1979 revolution could have been predicted by simply observing that Nicaragua's health and education budget rose rapidly, that an effective land reform program was instituted, and that the infant mortality rate dropped very dramatically, to the point where Nicaragua won an award from the World Health Organization for health achievements (all of this despite horrifying conditions left by the Somoza dictatorship, which we had installed and supported, and continued to support to the very end, despite a lot of nonsense to the contrary that one hears). If a country is devoted to policies like those I've just described, it is obviously an enemy. It is part of the "monolithic and ruthless conspiracy"—the Russians are taking it over. And, in fact, it *is* part of a conspiracy. It is part of a conspiracy to take from us what is ours, namely "our raw materials," and a conspiracy to prevent us from "maintaining the disparity," which, of course, must be the fundamental element of our foreign policy.

If you want to know why we are committed to destroying Nicaragua, you can find the answer, for example, in a section of an Oxfam report that came out just a few weeks ago. It was written by Oxfam's Latin America desk officer Jethro Pettit, based on an interview with Esmilda Flores, a peasant woman, on a cooperative:

> "Before the revolution, we didn't participate in anything. We only learned to make tortillas and cook beans and do what our husbands told us. In only five years we've seen a lot of changes—and we're still working on it!" Esmilda Flores belongs to an agricultural cooperative in the mountains north of Esteli, Nicaragua. Together with seven other women and fifteen men, she works land that was formerly a coffee plantation owned by an absentee landlord. After the revolution in 1979, the families who had worked the land became

its owners. They have expanded production to include corn, beans, potatoes, cabbages, and dairy cows. "Before, we had to rent a small plot to grow any food," Flores said, "and we had to pay one-half of our crop to the landlord! Now we work just as hard as before—both in the fields and at home—but there's a difference, because we're working for ourselves." . . . There has been a profound shift in cultural attitudes [among women] as a result of their strong participation in Nicaragua's social reconstruction. Women have taken the lead in adult literacy programs, both as students and teachers. They have assumed key roles in rural health promotion and in vaccination campaigns.

Well, it is obvious that a country of this sort is an enemy—that is, part of the "monolithic and ruthless conspiracy"—and that we have to take drastic measures to ensure that the "rot does not spread," in the terminology constantly used by the planners. In fact, when one reads reports of this kind or looks at the health and education statistics—the nutritional level, land reform, and so on—one can understand very well why American hostility to Nicaragua has reached such fanatic, almost hysterical levels. It follows from the geopolitical conception previously outlined.

The people who are committed to these dangerous heresies, such as using their resources for their own purposes or believing that the government is committed to the welfare of its own people, may not be Soviet clients to begin with and, in fact, quite regularly they're not. In Latin America they are often members, to begin with, of Bible study groups that become self-help groups, of church organizations, peasant organizations, and so on and so forth. But by the time we get through with them, they will be Soviet clients. The reason they will be Soviet clients by the time we get through with them is that they will have nowhere else to turn for any minimal form of protection against the terror and the violence that we regularly unleash against them if they undertake programs of the kind described.

And this _is a net gain_ for American policy. One thing you'll notice, if you look over the years, is that the United States quite consistently tries to create enemies (I'm not being sarcastic) if a country _does_ escape from its grip. What we want to do is drive the country into being a base for the Russians because that justifies us in carrying out the violent attacks which we _must_ carry out, given the geopolitical conception under which we organize and control much of the world. So that's what we do, and then we "defend" ourselves. We engage in self-defense against the Great Satan or the Evil Empire or the "monolithic and ruthless conspiracy."

More generally, the Soviet Union plays the same kind of game within its own narrower domains, and that in fact explains a good bit of the structure of the Cold War.

Well, what has all of this meant for Indochina and Central America? Let's begin with Indochina.

Now remember I'm talking about the real world, not the one in the PBS television series and so on. In the real world, what happened was that by 1948 the U.S. State Department recognized, explicitly, that Ho Chi Minh was the sole significant leader of Vietnamese nationalism, but that if Vietnamese nationalism was successful, it could be a threat to the Grand Area, and therefore something had to be done about it. The threat was not so much in Vietnam itself, which is not terribly important for American purposes (the freedom to rob in Vietnam is not all that significant); the fear was that the "rot would spread," namely, the rot of successful social and economic development. In a very poor country which had suffered enormously under European colonialism, successful social and economic development could have a demonstration effect. Such development could be a model for people elsewhere and could lead them to try to duplicate it, and gradually the Grand Area would unravel.

This, incidentally, is the *rational* version of the domino theory. There's another version which is used to terrify the population. You know, Ho Chi Minh will get into a canoe and land in Boston and rape your sister and that sort of thing. That's the standard one used to terrify the population, and then people make fun of it afterward if something doesn't work out.

But there's also a rational version of the domino theory which is never questioned in planning documents because it's plausible, rational, and true. That is, successful social and economic development in one area may have a demonstration effect elsewhere, and the rot may spread. Incidentally, it is for this reason that the United States typically demonstrates what looks like such fanatic opposition to constructive developments in marginal countries. In fact, the smaller and less significant the country, the more dangerous it is. So, for example, as soon as the Bishop regime in Grenada began to take any constructive moves, it was immediately the target of enormous American hostility, not because that little speck in the Caribbean is any potential military threat or because we need its resources. It is a threat in other respects: if a tiny nothing-country with no natural resources can begin to extricate itself from the system of misery and oppression that we've helped to impose, then others who have more resources may be tempted to do likewise.

The same thinking explains the extraordinarily savage American attack on Laos in the 1960s. It was the heaviest bombing in history, up until the Cambodia bombing a few years later, and it was unrelated to the Vietnam War, as the State Department conceded. The bombing was in fact directed against a very mild sort of a revolution that was developing in northern Laos, and that had to be stamped out. Laos was barely a country. Many of the people there didn't even know they were in Laos. But when those things came from up above and started shooting at them, and when they had to hide in holes in the hills or caves for two years, they learned something about their country. They also learned something about the world, something that educated Westerners do not understand, or pretend not to understand. We had to destroy Laos because if a development can take place in such a marginal, backward country as this, then the demonstration effect would be even more significant. Again, that is predictable, and it follows from the geopolitical conception that I've described.

Well, we recognized that we had to prevent the rot from spreading, so we had to support France in its effort to reconquer its former colony, and we did so. By the time the French had given up, we were providing about 80 percent of the costs of the war and in fact we came close to using nuclear weapons toward the end, by 1954, in Indochina.

There was a political settlement, the Geneva Accords, in 1954, which the United States bitterly opposed. We immediately proceeded to undermine them, installing in South Vietiam a violent, terrorist regime, which of course rejected (with our support) the elections which were projected. Then the regime turned to a terrorist attack against the population, particularly against the anti-French resistance, which we called the Vietcong, in South Vietnam. The regime had probably killed about 80,000 people (that means we had killed, through our arms and mercenaries) by the time John F. Kennedy took over in 1961. This assault against the population, after several years, did arouse resistance—such acts have a way of doing that—and by 1959 the anti-French resistance received authorization from the Communist leadership, after several years and after tens of thousands of people were murdered, to use violence in self-defense. Then the government, which we had established, immediately began to collapse because it had no popular support, as the United States conceded.

By 1959 the resistance began to receive some support from the northern half of the country in retaliation against the violence unleashed by the American-organized attack against the population of the southern part. The government we had installed to carry out this attack and to block the political agreements quickly began to collapse as soon as resistance began. Then Kennedy had a problem. It's important to realize how he handled this. This is one of the *dis*similarities between Vietnam and Central America to which I'll return. In 1961 and 1962 Kennedy simply launched a war against South Vietnam. That is, in 1961 and 1962 the U.S. Air Force began extensive bombing and defoliation in South Vietnam, aimed primarily against the rural areas where 80 percent of the population lived. This was part of a program designed to drive several million people into concentration camps, which we called "strategic hamlets," where they would be surrounded by armed guards and barbed wire, "protected," as we put it, from the guerrillas whom, we conceded, they were willingly supporting. That's what we call "aggression" or "armed attack" when some other country does it. We call it "defense" when we do it.

This was when the "defense" of South Vietnam escalated, with this attack in 1961 and 1962. But that again failed. The resistance increased, and by 1965 the United States was compelled to move to an outright land invasion of South Vietnam, escalating the attack again. We also initiated the bombing of North Vietnam, which, as anticipated, brought North Vietnamese troops to the south several months later.

Throughout, however, the major American attack was against South Vietnam. When we began bombing North Vietnam in February 1965, we extended the bombing of South Vietnam which had already been going on for several years. We extended the bombing of South Vietnam to triple the scale of the bombing of North Vietnam, and, throughout, it was South Vietnam that bore the main brunt of the American war in Indochina. We later extended the war to Cambodia and Laos.

The result of all of this is often called a defeat for the United States, but I think that is misleading. The result was, in fact, a partial victory for the United States, a not insignificant victory. And we can see this if we look back at the reasons that explain why the war was fought. The United States did not achieve its maximal aims, that is, we did not succeed in bringing Vietnam to the happy state of Haiti or the Dominican Republic. But we did succeed in the major aims.

As far as the major aims were concerned, the American war was a smashing success. For one thing, there was a huge massacre. The first phase of the war, the French war, probably left about half a million dead. From 1954 to 1965, we succeeded in killing maybe another 160,000 to 170,000 South Vietnamese, mostly peasants. The war, from 1965 to 1975, left a death toll of maybe in the neighborhood of 3 million. There were also perhaps a million dead in Cambodia and Laos. So altogether about 4 to 5 million people were killed, which is a respectable achievement when you're trying to prevent any successful social and economic development. Furthermore, there were well over 10 million refugees created by the American bombardment, which was quite extraordinarily savage, not to mention the murderous ground operations.

The land was devastated. People can't farm because of the destruction and unexploded ordnance. And this is all a success. Vietnam is not going to be a model of social and economic development for anyone else. In fact, it will be lucky to survive. The rot will not spread. We also made sure of that by our actions in the surrounding areas, where we buttressed the American position.

American liberals, incidentally, supported the war almost throughout, contrary to current distortions. Look back to 1965, for example, when we backed a coup in Indonesia which led to the massacre of maybe 700,000 people, mostly landless peasants, within a few months turning the country into a "paradise for investors." This was called a "gleam of light in Asia" in one *New York Times* article, and in general was much applauded by American intellectuals, who explained that these wonderful events proved the wisdom of our policy in Vietnam, which encouraged the Indonesian generals to do their work.

Similarly, when we were supposedly reeling under the effects of the alleged Vietnam defeat, we still felt powerful enough to support a military coup in the Philippines, overthrowing Philippine "democracy," what there was of it, and installing a Latin American torture-and-terror-type regime, which we then massively supported. That again is complementary to destroying Vietnam: building a base of support in Indonesia, the Philippines, and elsewhere, where of course you massacre, you torture, and use terror and so on. But that does guarantee that the rot will not spread. There will be no domino effect of successful development emanating from Vietnam, and, in that sense, it is a very major victory for the United States.

The postwar U.S. policy has been designed to ensure that it stays that way. We follow a policy of what some conservative business circles outside the United States (for example, the *Far Eastern Economic Review*) call "bleeding Vietnam." That is, a policy of imposing maximum suffering and harshness in Vietnam in the hope of perpetuating the suffering, but also ensuring that only the most harsh and brutal elements will survive. Then you can use their brutality as a justification for having carried out the initial attack. This is done constantly and quite magnificently in our ideological system. We are now supporting the Pol Pot forces; we concede this incidentally. The State Department has stated that our reason for supporting the Democratic Kampuchea coalition, which is largely based on Khmer Rouge forces, is because of its "continuity" with the Pol Pot regime; therefore, we support it indirectly through China or through other means. This is part of the policy of "bleeding Vietnam." Also, of course, we offer no aid, no reparations, though we certainly owe them. We block aid from international institutions and we've succeeded in blocking aid from other countries.

For example, one of the side effects of the U.S. war against Indochina was that we pretty much destroyed the buffalo herds. This is a peasant society and buffalo are the equivalent of tractors, fertilizers, etc. The *Washington Post* published some pictures of peasants pulling plows in

Indochina—that's to prove the brutality of the Communists. The pictures they published in this case were probably fabrications of Thai intelligence, but they could have obtained accurate pictures because the buffalo were indeed destroyed.

India tried to send, in 1977, one hundred buffalo, a very small number, to Vietnam to try to replenish these losses. We tried to block it by threatening to cancel Food for Peace aid to India if they sent the hundred buffalo. The Mennonites in the United States tried to send pencils to Cambodia; again the State Department tried to block it. They also tried to send shovels to Laos to dig up the unexploded ordnance. Of course, we could do it easily with heavy equipment, but *that* we are plainly not going to do. We didn't even want to send them shovels.

In Laos the agricultural system was devastated—in fact, largely wiped out in many areas—by the intensive bombing. So, not surprisingly, there was massive starvation afterward, attributed, in the United States, to the evil nature of the Communists. The United States has diplomatic relations with Laos. We have an embassy there. And of all of the countries with food reserves that have diplomatic relations with Laos, we are the only nation that didn't send them food at the time of the worst period of starvation. We have the largest rice surplus in the world.

In fact, a protest began over this during the Carter administration. You'll recall that human rights was "the soul of our foreign policy" at that time, so something had to be done, since there was a certain amount of publicity over this. So it was announced with great fanfare and self-congratulation that we were sending a tiny quantity of rice; it was minuscule. Even that was a fraud. It turned out later that that amount of rice was simply deducted from a contribution to a United Nations program that was indirectly going to end up in Laos. So it ended up as a zero contribution. It's hard to imagine the degree of hypocrisy of these policies and the rhetoric used to surround them. You'd need a powerful imagination even to dream up examples like these.

Carter, incidentally, once explained in a news conference what he was up to. This was in 1977, when he was giving one of his sermons about human rights. He was asked, what about Vietnam? And he said that we owe Vietnam no debt because the "destruction was mutual." You can walk around the streets of Boston and see what he means. The fact that a president said this is not terribly surprising—one doesn't expect anything more. What *is* interesting and significant is that this statement aroused no comment. This statement is easily worthy of Hitler or Stalin, yet it aroused no comment in the United States among the articulate intelligentsia, press, or anyone else. It's just accepted that we owe Vietnam no debt because the "destruction was mutual."

Let's turn to Central America, that is, "our little region over here that never has bothered anybody," as Henry Stimson put it. Major U.S. military intervention in Central America began 131 years ago, in 1854, when the United States Navy bombarded and destroyed San Juan del Norte, a port town in Nicaragua. This town was in fact captured for a few days by contras from Costa Rica about a year ago. The press made a big fuss about it, but they failed to note the historical antecedents. Our bombing and destruction of the town was not a capricious act. It was an act of revenge. What had happened in 1854 was that a yacht owned by the American millionaire Cornelius Vanderbilt had sailed into the port and an official had attempted to levy port charges on it. So, in revenge, the navy burned the town down to the ground.

Well, that was our first military intervention in Nicaragua, and there have been many since. In the first third of this century, we sent military forces into Cuba, Panama, Mexico, and Honduras and occupied Haiti for nineteen years. There, under President Wilson, we reinstituted virtual slavery, burned villages, destroyed, tortured, and left a legacy which still remains, in one of the most miserable corners of one of the most miserable regions in the world. Woodrow Wilson, the great apostle of self-determination, celebrated this doctrine by invading Mexico and Haiti, and by launching a counterinsurgency war in the Dominican Republic, again with ample destruction and torture. This intervention led to a long-lasting military dictatorship, under Trujillo, one of the worst dictators we managed to establish in this region. The United States invaded Nicaragua repeatedly, finally leaving behind a brutal, corrupt, and long-lasting military dictatorship, the regular consequence of U.S. intervention.

In the post–World War II period, there have been military interventions in many places—in Guatemala, for example, several times. In Guatemala, in 1954, we managed to overthrow and destroy Guatemala's one attempt at democracy. There was a New Deal-style, reformist-capitalist democratic regime which we managed to overthrow, leaving a literal hell on earth, probably the country which comes closest in the contemporary world to Nazi Germany. And we repeatedly intervened to keep it that way.

In 1963, there was concern in Washington that there might be another election, and Kennedy therefore supported a military coup. By the late 1960s, the terrorism that we were supporting had aroused resistance, and so we sent Green Berets to lead a counterinsurgency campaign which left many thousands dead; maybe 8,000 to 10,000 people died. It was reported by the vice president of Guatemala that American planes based in Panama carried out napalm raids in Guatemala at that time. Well, that calmed things down for a while.

In the late 1970s, things erupted again. At that time, the United States was somewhat restricted in direct participation in the massacre by congressional human rights legislation. Incidentally you commonly read in the press and elsewhere that the United States stopped military aid to Guatemala in 1977. That's apparently false. Military aid continued at approximately the normal level—barely below the normal level. But we couldn't send the Green Berets. We couldn't participate as actively as we would have liked.

In the next stage of what the conservative Catholic hierarchy called "genocide," thousands of people were killed, mostly Indians. Since we couldn't do it ourselves, we used proxies, Argentine neo-Nazis, and particularly Israel, which was available for the purpose, and did a very effective job. Israel's role was widely praised in the West, I should say. The London *Economist,* for example, commented rather favorably on Israel's success in helping to organize major massacres, and contrasted it with the relative American failure in El Salvador at the same time. The scale is essentially unknown, but just to give you one figure, it's now estimated, from this period alone, that about 100,000 children have lost one or both parents.

That was Guatemala. There was also military intervention in Cuba, the Dominican Republic, El Salvador, and Grenada. A twenty-year war of terrorism was waged against Cuba. Cuba has probably been the target of more international terrorism than any other country, and, therefore, in the American ideological system it is regarded as the *source* of international terrorism, exactly as Orwell would have predicted. And now there's a war against Nicaragua.

The impact of all of this has been absolutely horrendous. There's vast starvation throughout the region while croplands are devoted to exports to the United States. There's slave labor, crushing poverty, torture, mass murder, every horror you can think of. In El Salvador alone, from October 1979 (a date to which I'll return) until December 1981—approximately two years—about 30,000 people were murdered and about 600,000 refugees created. Those figures have about doubled since. Most of the murders were carried out by U.S.-backed military forces, including so-called death squads. The efficiency of the massacre in El Salvador has recently increased with direct participation of American military forces. American planes based in Honduran and Panamanian sanctuaries, military aircraft, now coordinate bombing raids over El Salvador, which means that the Salvadoran air force can more effectively kill fleeing peasants and destroy villages, and, in fact, the kill rate has gone up corresponding to that.

At the same time, the war against Nicaragua has left unknown thousands killed, these added to the 50,000 or so killed in the last stages of the Somoza dictatorship. Since we overthrew the democratic government of Guatemala in 1954, according to a Guatemalan human rights group in Mexico (none can function in Guatemala), about 150,000 people have been murdered, again primarily by U.S.-backed forces and sometimes with direct U.S. military participation. These figures kind of lose their meaning when you just throw numbers around. You see what they mean when you look more closely at the refugees' reports: for example, a report by a few people who succeeded in escaping from a village in Quiché province where the government troops came in, rounded up the population, and put them in the town building. They took all the men out and decapitated them. Then they raped and killed the women. Then they took the children and killed them by bashing their heads with rocks. This is what our taxes have been paying for—sometimes by means of our proxies—since the successful overthrow of Guatemalan democracy, where we have effectively preserved order since.

I might mention that the 1954 American-instigated coup was referred to by John Foster Dulles, the secretary of state, as a "new and glorious chapter" in the "already glorious traditions of the American States."

Virtually every attempt to bring about any constructive change in this U.S.-constructed chamber of horrors has met with a new dose of U.S. violence. The historical record is one of the most shameful stories in modern history and naturally is very little known here, though in a free society it would be well understood and taught in elementary school in all of its sordid and gruesome detail.

Throughout this period, the public pose has always been that we are defending ourselves. So, in Vietnam, we were defending ourselves against the Vietnamese when we attacked South Vietnam. It's what Adlai Stevenson at the United Nations called "internal aggression," another phrase that Orwell would have admired and one that we use quite commonly. "Internal aggression," meaning aggression by the Vietnamese against us and our clients in Vietnam—and we've often had to defend ourselves against that kind of internal aggression. Nicaragua today is another case. So, for example, when our mercenary army attacks Nicaragua, we argue that this is defense—that we are defending Mexico, Central America, and ultimately ourselves from Russian imperialism or "internal aggression."

Well, it's interesting to look at that in the light of history. Virtually everything that is now happening has happened before, in corresponding or very similar forms. Our historical amnesia prevents us from seeing that. Everything looks new and therefore we don't understand it. It must just be a stupid error.

So, for example, in the late 1920s President Coolidge sent the marines once again to Nicaragua. At that time, we were defending Nicaragua against Mexico; now we are defending Mexico against Nicaragua. At that time, we were defending Nicaragua against Mexico, which was claimed to be a Bolshevik proxy, so we were defending Nicaragua against Russian imperialism when we sent the marines that time, eventually ending up with the establishment of the Somoza dictatorship. President Coolidge, in fact, said, "Mexico was on trial before the world," when we sent the marines into Nicaragua at that time. Notice that the bottom line remains the same as the cast of characters changes: Kill Nicaraguans.

What did we do before we had the Bolsheviks to defend ourselves against? For example, when Wilson sent the marines to Haiti and the Dominican Republic, that was before the Bolshevik revolution, so we couldn't be defending ourselves against Russian imperialism. Well, then we were defending ourselves against the Huns. The hand of the Huns was particularly obvious in Haiti. The marine commander there, a man named Thorpe, explained that "the handiwork of the German" was evident here because of the kind of resistance that the "niggers" were putting up. Obviously they couldn't be doing it on their own, so there must be German direction. The same sentiments were expressed throughout. So, for example, in the Dominican Republic the resistance was being carried out by the people whom Theodore Roosevelt had, during an earlier intervention, called "damned Dagoes," or by "spiks," "coons," "nigs" in the terms that are regularly used to describe the people against whom we're defending ourselves, the perpetrators of "internal aggression."

Well, let's go back a little further, because self-defense is deeply rooted in American history. In the nineteenth century, when we were wiping out the Native American population, we were defending ourselves against savage attacks from British and Spanish sanctuaries in Canada and Florida and therefore we had to take over Florida, and we had to take the West to defend ourselves from these attacks. In 1846, we were compelled to defend ourselves against Mexico. That aggression began deep inside Mexican territory, but again, it was self-defense against Mexican aggression. We had to take about a third of Mexico in the process, including California, where the explanation was that it was a preemptive strike. The British were about to take it over, and, in self-defense, we had to beat them to it. And so it goes, all the way back. The Evil Empire changes, but the truth of the matter remains about the same. And if American history were actually taught, people would know these things. This is the core of American history.

Let me return finally to Kennan's formula—"human rights, the raising of the living standards, and democratization"—considering now Latin America. I want to consider the question that I raised before: are they really irrelevant to our policy the way he suggested they ought to be? Let's take a closer look.

Take human rights. Now actually that's an empirical question. You can study how American foreign policy is related to human rights, and it has been studied for Latin America and elsewhere. The leading American specialist on human rights in Latin America, Lars Schoultz, has a study published in *Comparative Politics* (January 1981), in which he investigated exactly that question. He asked how the human rights climate in a country was correlated with American aid. He chose a very narrow conception of human rights, what he called "anti-torture rights," that is, the right to be free from torture by the government and so on. He found that there is a relationship between human rights and American foreign policy: namely, the more the human rights climate deteriorates, the more American aid increases. The correlation was strong. It does not result from a correlation between aid and need. This aid included military aid and it went on right through the Carter administration. To use his words, "Aid has tended to flow disproportionately to Latin American governments which torture their citizens," to the "hemisphere's relatively egregious violators of fundamental human rights." This might suggest that Kennan understated the case: human rights are not irrelevant; rather, we have a positive hatred of them. We send aid to precisely those governments which torture their citizens, and the more effectively they do so, the more we'll aid them. At least that's what the evidence shows in this and other studies.

A correlation isn't a theory. It's not an explanation. We still need an explanation, and a number of them come to mind. One possible explanation is that the American leadership just likes torture. So the more a government tortures its citizens, the more we will aid them. That's a possible explanation but it's an unlikely one. The real explanation is probably Kennan's: that is, human rights are irrelevant. What we like is something else. There have been other studies that suggest a theory to explain the correlation.

There's one by Edward Herman, who investigated the same sort of thing that Schoultz did but on a worldwide basis. Herman found the same correlation: the worse the human rights climate, the more American aid goes up. But he also carried out another study which gives you some insight into what's really happening. He compared American aid to changes in the investment climate, the climate for business operations, as measured, for example, by whether foreign firms can repatriate profits and that sort of thing. It turned out there was a very close correlation. The better the climate for business operations, the more American aid—the more we support the foreign government. That gives you a plausible theory. U.S. foreign policy is in fact based on the principle that human rights are irrelevant, but that improving the climate for foreign business operations is highly relevant. In fact, that flows from the central geopolitical conception.

Now how do you improve the business climate in a Third World country? Well, it's easy. You murder priests, you torture peasant organizers, you destroy popular organizations, you institute mass murder and repression to prevent any popular organization. And that improves the investment climate. So there's a secondary correlation between American aid and the deterioration of human rights. It's entirely natural that we should tend to aid countries that are egregious violators of fundamental human rights and that torture their citizens, and that's indeed what we find.

Well, so much for human rights. What about raising the living standards? In Latin America, there has been economic growth. If you look, the gross national product keeps going up, but at the same time, typically, there is increased suffering and starvation for a very large part of the population. So in one case, Brazil, the most important Latin American country, there has been what was called an "economic miracle" in the last couple of decades, ever since we destroyed Brazilian democracy by supporting a military coup in 1964. The support for the coup was initiated by Kennedy but finally carried to a conclusion by Johnson. The coup was called by Kennedy's ambassador, Lincoln Gordon, "the single most decisive victory for freedom in the mid-twentieth century." We installed the first really major national security state, Nazi-like state, in Latin America, with high-technology torture and so on. Gordon called it "totally democratic," "the best government Brazil ever had." And that, in turn, had a significant domino effect in Latin America; Brazil is an important country. Well, there was an economic miracle and there was an increase in the GNP. There was also an increase in suffering for much of the population. And that story is duplicated throughout much of Latin America, where the United States has succesfully intervened, from Haiti to the Dominican Republic, to Nicaragua and Guatemala and so on.

So much for the second element, raising of living standards. What about democratization? Well, we've repeatedly intervened to overthrow democratic governments. This is understandable. The more a country is democratic, the more it is likely to be responsive to the public, and hence committed to the dangerous doctrine that "the government has a direct responsibility for the welfare of the people," and therefore is not devoted to the transcendent needs of Big Brother. We have to do something about it. Democracy is okay, but only as long as we can control it and be sure that it comes out the way we want, just as the Russians permit what they call "democratic elections" in Poland. That is the typical history. In Guatemala the government was democratic but out of control, so we had to overthrow it. Similarly in Chile under Allende. Or take the Dominican Republic, which has long been the beneficiary of our solicitous care. Woodrow Wilson began a major counterinsurgency campaign which ended in the early 1920s and which led to the Trujillo dictatorship, one of the most brutal and vicious and corrupt dictatorships that we have supported in Latin America. In the early 1960s, it looked as though there was going to be a move toward democracy. There was, in fact, a democratic election in 1962. Juan Bosch, a liberal democrat, was elected. The Kennedy administration was very cool. The way it reacted is interesting. (You have to understand that the United States so totally dominates these countries that the U.S. embassy essentially runs them.) The American embassy blocked every effort that Bosch made to organize public support. So, for example, land reform, labor organizing, anything that could have developed public support against a military which was pretty certain to try another coup—any such effort was blocked by the Kennedy administration. As a result, the predicted military coup took place and Washington, which was essentially responsible for the success of the coup, shortly after it recognized the new government. A typical military dictatorship of the type we like was established. In 1965, there was a coup by liberal, reformist officers, a constitutionalist coup, which threatened to restore democracy in the Dominican Republic, so we intervened again. That time we simply sent troops. A bloody and destructive war took place, many thousands of people were killed, and we again succeeded in establishing a terror-and-torture regime. The country was also, incidentally, brought totally within the grip of the U.S. corporations. The Dominican Republic was virtually bought up by Gulf & Western and other corporations after the coup. The country was totally demoralized. It was, in fact, subjected to terror and suffering, crushing poverty, and so on. So then we could have elections, because it was guaranteed that nothing would happen. They can even elect social democrats for all we care, the basic results having been achieved. The government would never be able to accomplish anything for its population, that is, for that part of the population which had not been killed or fled. In this region, about 20 percent of the population has come to the United States, and in places where they have easier access, such as Puerto Rico, the figure is about 40 percent.

Well, let's turn to El Salvador in connection with our attitude toward democratization. There were democratic elections in El Salvador in 1972 and 1977. In both cases, the military intervened to abort them and installed military dictatorships. The people in Washington could not have cared less. There was no concern whatsoever. There were also the regular atrocities throughout this period, arousing little concern in Washington. However, there were developments, two in fact, that did elicit concern in the late 1970s. One was that the Somoza dictatorship fell in 1979. There is much mythology about this, but the fact of the matter is that Carter supported Somoza till the very end, even after the natural allies of the United States, the local business community, turned against him. That was a danger sign and it worried the United States with regard to El Salvador. There was another development that was even more dangerous. There were the beginnings of popular democratic organizations within El Salvador of the sort I mentioned earlier: Bible study groups turning into self-help groups, peasant cooperatives, unions, all sorts of organizations which seemed to be establishing the basis for a functioning democracy.

Now anybody who thinks, realizes that democracy doesn't mean much if people have to confront concentrated systems of economic power as isolated individuals. Democracy means something if people can organize to gain information, to have thoughts for that matter, to make plans, to enter into the political system in some active way, to put forth programs and so on. If organizations of that kind exist, then democracy can exist too. Otherwise it's a matter of pushing a lever every couple of years; it's like having the choice between Coca-Cola and Pepsi-Cola. In El Salvador, there were dangerous moves in this direction in the 1970s with the development of what were called "popular organizations," and therefore something had to be done about them because there might be real democracy. We plainly can't tolerate that.

These two developments did lead to some action on the part of the United States. In October 1979, the United States supported a reformist coup which overthrew the Romero dictatorship. There was in fact considerable fear that he was going to go the way of Somoza. What happened then? The United States insisted that some of the harshest and most brutal military elements be prominently placed in the junta. The killing rapidly increased right after the coup. By early 1980, the left-wing Christian Democrats, socialists, and reformist military elements had been eliminated from, or had simply fled from, the junta, and the country was in the hands of the usual thugs that we install in our domain. Duarte came in at that time as a useful cover, to preside over one of the great Central American massacres. The archbishop, Archbishop Oscar Romero, pleaded with Carter not to send military aid. The reasons were the following: he said that military aid would "sharpen the repression that has been unleashed against the people's organizations fighting to defend their most fundamental human rights." Therefore, he asked Carter not to send military aid.

Well, of course, that was the very essence of American policy: namely, to increase massacre and repression, to destroy the popular organizations, and prevent the achievement of human rights, so naturally the aid flowed and the war picked up steam. Archbishop Romero was assassinated shortly afterward. In May 1980, under Carter, remember, the war against the peasantry really took off, largely under the guise of land reform.

The first major action was a joint operation of the Honduran and

Salvadoran armies at the Sumpul River, where about 600 people were killed as they tried to flee into Honduras. That massacre was suppressed by the American press for about fifteen months, though it was published in the world press and the church press, right here in Cambridge, for example. In fact, U.S. press coverage during 1980 was unbelievably bad. In June 1980, the university in San Salvador was attacked and destroyed by the army. Many faculty and students were killed and much of the university facilities were simply demolished. In November, the political opposition was massacred. Meanwhile, the independent media were also destroyed.

We don't believe in censorship in the United States. We get very irate when governments like Nicaragua impose censorship on a paper that is supporting a military attack against Nicaragua. Of course, we would never do that. If some unimaginably huge superpower were attacking the United States and a newspaper here was supporting the attack, we would certainly not impose censorship (that is true: its employees and management would be in concentration camps). We don't like censorship. What we like is something different. What we like is what we did in El Salvador. That is, the way you get rid of the independent press is not by censorship—there isn't any censorship in El Salvador. Rather, you blow up the newspaper offices. You take the editor and murder him after hideous torture, and pretty soon you don't have any independent press to censor. Well, that's what happened under the Carter administration, so now there's no censorship.

This war had a number of significant successes. The popular organizations were destroyed; therefore we can now permit democratic elections—now that there is no concern anymore that they might mean something. These elections are carried out in "an atmosphere of terror and despair, of macabre rumor and grisly reality." That was the assessment by the head of the British Parliamentary Human Rights Group, Lord Chitnis, with regard to the 1984 elections in El Salvador—rather different from the media coverage here, as you may recall. The point is that once the basis for democracy has been destroyed, once state terrorism has been firmly established, then elections are entirely permissible, even worthwhile, for the sake of American public opinion. The contrast between our alleged concern for elections today and our actual concern for elections in the 1970s is, again, instructive. Well, that was a success—namely, destroying the popular organizations and so on. There was also, however, a failure.

The failure was that people began to join the guerrillas. There were only a few hundred guerrillas when all of this began. They grew to many thousands during this period. Of course, that's proof that the Russians are coming—anyone who understands the United States knows that. And, in fact, that is very similar to Vietnam in the 1950s. If you think through what I've just described, what happened in El Salvador under Carter and what happened in Vietnam under Eisenhower are very similar.

Well, meanwhile, we stepped up our war against Nicaragua, not because Nicaragua is brutal and oppressive. Even if you accept the harshest criticisms that have even a minimal basis in reality, by the standards of the governments that we support, Nicaragua is virtually a paradise. But we attack Nicaragua precisely because it is committed to a model of development that we cannot tolerate. Of course, this is presented as defense against the Russians, and as proof that it's defense against the Russians we note that the Nicaraguans receive weapons with which they can defend themselves against our attack. Foreign Minister d'Escoto pointed out that it's like "a torturer who pulls out the fingernails of his victim and then gets angry because the victim screams in pain." Actually, a closer analogy would be to a thug who hires a goon squad to beat up some kid in kindergarten whom the thug doesn't like, and then begins whining piteously if the child raises his arms to protect himself. That would be a pretty accurate analogy to what's happening there.

I should say at this point that this is nothing new. This shameful picture should remind us that our intellectual culture is really founded on the twin pillars of moral cowardice and hypocrisy. People like Reagan and Shultz are absolutely nothing new. This was recognized long ago, at the time when the Founding Fathers were expounding the doctrine of the natural rights granted by the Creator to every person, while they were bitterly deploring their own "enslavement" by the British tax collectors— "enslavement" is the term they commonly used. Samuel Johnson commented at the time, "Why is it that we hear the loudest yelps for freedom from the drivers of Negroes?" And Thomas Jefferson, a slave owner himself, added that "I tremble for my country when I reflect that God is just, that His justice will not sleep forever."

Reagan's problem in El Salvador was very similar to Kennedy's in South Vietnam twenty years ago. There was severe internal repression in both cases, which was very successful in destroying popular organizations, killing a lot of people, and so on. However, the internal repression did elicit resistance which the state that we had installed was unable to control. Kennedy simply attacked South Vietnam with bombardment and defoliation. And Reagan has been trying to do the same in El Salvador for the last couple of years, but he has not quite been able to. He has been blocked by domestic opposition. He has therefore been forced to use more indirect measures. These have certainly succeeded in killing many people and causing vast misery, but not yet in crushing the resistance. We are still short of air force bombings.

I've mentioned some of the similarities. What are the differences? Well, the main difference is that the United States has changed. The United States has changed a lot over the last twenty years. When Kennedy attacked South Vietnam, there was no protest, virtually none. That was in the early 1960s, when Kennedy began the direct military acts against South Vietnam. When Johnson escalated the attack against South Vietnam to a full-scale land invasion, there was also very little protest. In fact, protests reached a significant scale only when several hundred thousand American troops were directly engaged in the war against South Vietnam, a war which by then extended well beyond South Vietnam.

In contrast, Reagan's attempt to escalate the war in El Salvador has met with considerable popular opposition here. And that's significant. In fact, that's one of the most significant facts of contemporary history.

I quoted before some of the official views about the Vietnam War from the liberal doves: "excess of righteousness and disinterested benevolence," and so on and so forth. However, there was also a quite different view, a popular view. As recently as 1982, polls indicate that about 70 percent of the American population regarded the Vietnam War not as a "mistake," but as "fundamentally wrong and immoral." Many fewer "opinion leaders" expressed that view, and virtually none of the really educated class or articulate intelligentsia ever took that position. That, incidentally, is quite typical. It's typical for educated classes to be more effectively controlled by the indoctrination system to which they are directly exposed, and in which they play a social role as purveyors, hence coming to internalize it. So this degree of servility to the party line is not unique to this example. But the point is there's a split, a very substantial split, between much of the population and those who regard themselves as its natural leaders. That is even given a technical name—it's called the "Vietnam syndrome." Notice the term, "syndrome," as applied to disease. The disease is that a lot of people are opposed to massacre, aggression, and torture, and feel solidarity with the victims. Therefore, something has to be done about that. It was assumed in the early 1980s that the disease had been cured, and by reading the productions of the educated classes, you could certainly have believed that. But in fact the disease was never very widespread among the educated classes. However, among the population, it remains widespread and it's a problem—it impedes, it inhibits direct intervention and aggression.

Whether this opposition, which is quite real, can become sufficiently organized and effective to block further escalation, I don't know. It could be that the current level of attack on the population of Central America will suffice to achieve the major American policy ends. What is clear, however, is that we're living through another chapter in a sordid and shameful history of violence and terror and oppression.

Unless we can muster the moral courage and the honesty to understand all of this, and to act to change it, as we indeed can, then it's going to continue and there will be many millions of additional victims who will face starvation and torture, or outright massacre, in what we will call "a crusade for freedom."

El Salvador

(1982)

THE GENERAL PICTURE OF EL SALVADOR PRESENTED IN THE U.S. press as of early 1981 was that of the U.S. government: a moderate regime is attempting to carry out reforms in the face of left-wing violence ("a Pol Pot left," as Carter's Ambassador Robert White and others described the mixture of guerrillas, peasant organizations, unions, and church groups that stood in opposition to the government), unable to control the right-wing "death squads."[1] The picture presented by the foreign press was quite different.[2] Its coverage generally corresponds to the conclusions of church sources in El Salvador and of the Council on Hemispheric Affairs, whose 1980 Annual Human Rights Report found El Salvador and Guatemala to be the worst human rights violators in Latin America, replacing Argentina:

> More people have died in El Salvador during the past year, largely as the result of government-condoned right-wing "death squad" killings, than in all other nations of Latin America combined. . . . The death toll . . . reached almost 10,000, with the vast majority of the victims falling prey to the right-wing terrorism sanctioned by key government officials. . . . [T]hese countless killings have gone unpunished and even uninvestigated as the government's own military and police forces are almost always involved in them. . . .[3]

As the year ended, Professor Jeane Kirkpatrick of Georgetown University, now head of the U.S. delegation to the U.N., stated: "And I think it's a terrible injustice to the Government and the military when you suggest that they were somehow responsible for terrorism and assassination."[4] And the *Washington Post* chimed in that: "There is no real argument that most of the estimated 10,000 political fatalities in 1980 were victims of government forces or irregulars associated with them."[5]

If one wants to learn about what is happening in rural El Salvador, the best place to go is obviously to the Honduran border, where 35,000 refugees, mostly women and children, are living in misery, dreadful squalor, and starvation in remote areas, trying to escape the raids of the Salvadoran army and ORDEN (the paramilitary forces of the government of El Salvador), which cross the border to attack refugee camps to which they have driven the population, according to the U.N. High Commissioner for Refugees.[6] These refugees can tell the story of what is actually happening in the rural areas where reporters rarely can go except under government control.[7]

A U.S. congressional delegation visited the border areas on a fact-finding mission in January 1981 and submitted a report to Congress.[8] Members of the delegation interviewed many refugees along the border area, tape-recording the interviews. The refugees

> describe what appears to be a systematic campaign conducted by the security forces of El Salvador to deny any rural base for guerrilla operations in the north. By terrorizing and depopulating villages in the region, they have sought to isolate the guerrillas and create problems of logistics and food supply. . . . The Salvadoran method of "drying up the ocean" involves, according to those who have fled from its violence, a combination of murder, torture, rape, the burning of crops in order to create starvation conditions, and a program of general terrorism and harassment.

The report then presents sample interviews in which refugees describe bombing and burning of villages by the army, mass murder of fleeing civilians, shooting of defenseless peasants from helicopters, and extraordinary brutality (e.g.: mutilation; decapitation; "children around the age of 8 being raped, and then they would take their bayonets and make mincemeat of them"; "the army would cut people up and put soap and coffee in their stomachs as a mocking. They would slit the stomach of a pregnant woman and take the child out, as if they were taking eggs out of an iguana. That is what I saw"). With regard to the guerrillas, refugees report: "We don't complain about them at all," "they haven't done any of those kinds of things," "it's the military that is doing this. Only the military. The popular organization [i.e., the "Pol Pot left"] isn't doing any of this." As for the military: "They were killing everybody. They were looking for people to kill—that's what they were doing."[9] The delegation interviewed José Morales Ehrlich, the number-two civilian in the government, who informed them that "instead of putting military outlaws on trial, the worst of them have been assigned to desk jobs or given scholarships to study abroad"—these are the changes that have been made to correct "occasional mistakes from a human rights point of view" (summary of Ehrlich's remarks). The report concludes that the security forces of El Salvador, "operating independent of responsible civilian control . . . are conducting a systematic campaign of terrorism directed against segments of their own population." In fact, the government is effectively under right-wing military control, the reformist officers having been driven out of the governing junta.[10]

Several foreign journalists have visited the border areas. Édouard Bailby, in a lengthy report that appears to have received no coverage in the U.S. press, points out that journalists and international observers are not permitted to visit the regions where security forces operate, so that one must visit the Honduran border (as he did) to determine the facts from the refugees who have fled there since the Río Sumpul massacre in May 1980.[11] He found that refugees hide in the forest "in fear of the killer-commandos who come from El Salvador." He gives a detailed report of massacres, brutality, mutilation, and terror on the part of the armed forces that are "a true repetition of the methods utilized by the SS during the second world war," since the Sumpul River massacre, when "the genocide began," at times with the assistance of the Honduran army.[12]

David Blundy of the *Sunday Times* (London) spent ten days in the border area a few months later, interviewing doctors, priests, Honduran soldiers, Salvadoran refugees, and members of church aid groups, who "provided overwhelming evidence of atrocities of increasing brutality and repression by the Honduran army as well as the Salvadorans." The Salvadoran army, he writes, "is carrying out what can only be described as mass extermination of thousands of peasants living in the area" where the guerrillas are based in a "co-ordinated military campaign by the Salvadoran military, assisted by the Honduran army with—according to some Honduran sources—the support of the United States." Blundy reports refugee accounts of bombing, napalm attacks, destruction of villages, massacres, rape, torture by the Salvadoran and Honduran army forces, stories of "an existence of almost incomprehensible brutality." He also describes the Lempa River massacre of March 16, when thousands of refugees attempted to cross the river for two days under constant attack by the Salvadoran air force in cooperation with the Honduran army, who killed refugees with machetes and beat them to death with rifle butts, basing his account largely on the reports of priests who were present, attempting to save the victims.[13]

In the week before the Lempa River massacre (March 7–13), 798 people were killed, of whom 681 were peasants killed by bombing or helicopter gunships, according to the Legal Aid Office of the San Salvador Archdiocese.[14] Shortly after, the *New York Times* reported that "assassinations by government forces appear to be declining," a sign of President Duarte's success in curbing "extreme rightists" who are "losing influence" within the military.[15] On the day of the massacre, the *New York Times* story on El Salvador was headlined "For Salvador Peasants, Fruits of Change Seem Good," the second of a series on the great successes of the land reform program.[16] Shortly before, the *Times* reported the plight of the peasants, "vulnerable to both prowling guerrillas and trigger-happy soldiers"; only the depredations of the former are described, along with a description of "a small mob shouting for weapons with which to fight the guerrillas" and the testimony of "a paid vigilante in the service of the landowner" who explains that "here the terrorists do not come to propagandize. They attack and kill." "The exodus is greatest from rebel-controlled areas," Schumacher reports, "with the peasants leaving for either personal safety or political preference"—safety from the guerrillas, one must assume, given the evidence reported.[17]

Those reporting from areas not under the control of the army of El Salvador—though not in the *New York Times*—find a somewhat different picture, as noted, even sometimes in the U.S. press; for example, in the *Los Angeles Times,* where the director of the Honduran office of the U.N. High Commissioner for Refugees is quoted as saying, "The vast majority of these people are running from the armed forces."[18]

The reports from the Honduran border describe graphically the nature of the government that the United States is supporting, advising, training, and arming. There are other indications, also generally ignored by the U.S. media, though comparable sources are characteristically given wide and immediate publicity in the case of enemy crimes. The Legal Aid Office of the San Salvador Archdiocese (see note 14) provides a regular and detailed accounting of killings. According to its records, the killings are overwhelmingly the responsibility of the government security forces, secondarily the right-wing "death squads" that are closely tied to the military and probably commanded by them.[19] The situation is much the same in Guatemala, a more important domino. What the U.S. government has attempted to portray, with the general though not total collaboration of the media, is something quite different, as noted.

It may also be recalled that the government military forces that are conducting these massacre operations are U.S.-trained, as are many of those in the top positions of the military and security agencies, including the Treasury Police, who are sometimes accused of the worst atrocities. From 1957 to 1974, a U.S. public safety program was conducted under USAID to upgrade the "operational skills and effectiveness" of the Salvadoran security forces. Until 1963, it was directed mainly to the National Police, and afterward, to the National Guard. When the program terminated in 1974, USAID analysts concluded that "the National Police . . . has advanced from a non-descript, *cuartel*-bound group of poorly trained men to a well-disciplined, well-trained, and respected uniformed corps. It has good riot control capability, good investigative capability, good records and fair communications and mobility. It handles routine law enforcement well."[20] The impact of U.S. training in El Salvador— which is quite typical of the Latin American scene—is useful to bear in mind when we read that the United States is sending military advisers to train the military forces of El Salvador or some other client regime with the aim of "averting indiscriminate repression and creating a 'clean' counterinsurgency force" (*New York Times*, Feb. 23, 1980).

The major propaganda effort of the U.S. government was the State Department white paper released with great fanfare on February 23, 1981.[21] As noted earlier, the campaign to convince the world on the basis of this collection of documents that the USSR was engaged in aggression in El Salvador through the medium of its proxies from Cuba to Vietnam was met with derision or disregard. But in the United States, the press reported the conclusions of the white paper at face value, in accordance with the official interpretation, raising few serious questions. Many simply adopted the propaganda allegations as unchallengeable doctrine. *Business Week,* for example, stated flatly that "the most important question is whether Washington will deal with the ultimate source of aggression in the area—Cuba—because it is not only El Salvador that is under attack. . . . The decision in late February to send additional U.S. military advisers to El Salvador to help the junta repulse external aggression is likely to be only the first step in an escalation unless Washington persuades Fidel Castro and his Soviet sponsors to back off." A naval blockade is recommended, unless we want to relive the experience of Vietnam.[22]

Only one journalist, to my knowledge, immediately carried out a careful investigation of the actual documents, namely John Dinges. He discovered that the documents indicate that "only about 10 tons [of armaments] ever actually crossed the border," not the two hundred tons claimed in the accompanying government charges, and that the guerrilla representatives "encountered a cool reception in Moscow."[23] But his report was ignored, and the media generally just repeated what they were told. The conformism of the media did not go entirely unnoticed. Hodding Carter wrote that "the real story is that the administration's propaganda blitz went virtually unchallenged for several weeks" as the media "initially gave Washington's claims about the El Salvador civil war the kind of over-eager, over-credulous respect which warms the heart of every government flack," demonstrating "that big government sets the terms of public discussion about major issues far more often than the press likes to admit or the public understands."[24]

Carter claims that "many reporters did eventually start asking the hard questions." In fact, apart from Dinges, few "hard questions" were raised in the mainstream media[25] until June when the *Wall Street Journal* published an extensive critical commentary by Jonathan Kwitny that completely demolished the white paper, revealing—despite the understated tone—that it was a tissue of fabrications and distortions. Jon D. Glassman of the State Department, who bears primary responsibility for the report, conceded that the figure of two hundred tons of supplies does not come from the documents at all, but from alleged "intelligence." "The only concrete instance of Soviet aid delivered to the Salvadoran rebels reported in the 19 documents was an airplane ticket from Moscow to Vietnam for one guerrilla," Kwitny observes. Robert White, who was U.S. ambassador at the time that the documents were allegedly found, expressed "incredulity at Mr. Glassman's story of the discovery" of one batch of documents, and notes that the documents Glassman claimed were found in the dramatic manner he describes were already known to the embassy before he arrived in El Salvador. White does believe that the documents are genuine, however. He says, "The only thing that ever made me think that these documents were genuine was that they proved so little." Kwitny adds, "Mr. Glassman even expresses an opinion very close to that of Mr. White—that the shortcomings of the documents indicate that they are genuine 'and disprove the fabrication argument.' " Documents are misrepresented, misidentified, and used as the basis for "extrapolations" that are completely meaningless. In short, the whole story fell apart, though another column the same day informs us that the State Department will try again, with another white paper.[26]

The day after the *Wall Street Journal* critique appeared, the *Washington Post* published a skeptical article on the white paper, giving many additional examples of "factual errors, misleading statements and unresolved ambiguities that raise questions about the administration's interpretation of participation by communist countries in the Salvadoran civil war."[27] The *New York Times* held the line, however, restricting itself largely to government defense of the basic thrust of the white paper and to minor issues of detail.[28] With regard to arms shipments, the *Times* story conceded only that the documents "present a confusing picture" and "are even more unclear on the volume of arms reaching the rebels." The discussion by Dinges three months earlier is not mentioned (nor is it mentioned by the *Wall Street Journal* or the *Post*), nor the major discoveries of the *Journal* and *Post* investigations. On the timing of these critical studies, see note 46.

One intriguing element of Juan de Onis' State Department apologetics in the *Times* is his remark that "even" former Ambassador White, who has criticized the Reagan policies in El Salvador, "has not questioned the basic conclusion" of the white paper. Naturally, since as de Onis adds, "while still Ambassador, Mr. White said during the January guerrilla offensive that at least 100 insurgents had entered El Salvador by sea from Nicaragua to join the uprising." De Onis did not see fit to add that White opened his testimony before the Senate Foreign Relations Committee on April 9 by saying that "I have become increasingly skeptical of the reality of that invasion," in which "no one was captured and no battle took place."[29] De Onis does not even take note of the serious doubts expressed in the pages of the *New York Times* at the time.[30] This report notes that Ambassador White "gave credibility" to the "unconfirmed reports" of the guerrilla landing from Nicaragua. As for evidence, the junta offered none, apart from the claim that "the boats were made of wood not available in El Salvador" and "that a major battle had ensued in which 53 rebels had died." "Reporters who visited the area, however, were told that the local garrison had been attacked by guerrillas on successive nights, with seven soldiers and two guerrillas killed. Three small boats had also been found near La Unión several days before the landing was reported." The Nicaraguan government denied the charge, and "United States officials appeared to retract their initial claim, conceding that 'our rush to believe what we were told was not totally warranted' and 'there was some over-statement in the beginning.'" The "rush to believe" was evidently still overwhelming de Onis four months later.

Meanwhile, the U.S. government announced that it had shipped 343 tons of arms to El Salvador in 1981.[31] The press has been silent on the important question of other sources of arms for the junta. Press reports indicate that these must be extensive. "I doubt if there are better-equipped infantrymen anywhere in Central America," Philip Jacobson writes in the *Sunday Times* (London): "The troops one sees now all carry the latest automatic rifles and grenade-launchers; they have good steel helmets and sturdy boots; above all, they have so much small-arms ammunition that they are given to blazing away whole magazines at the slightest excuse." In contrast, guerrilla caches exhibited to journalists show only a variety of weapons ranging from U.S. M-16s to "bolt-action rifles, ancient shotguns and home-made bombs."[32] In addition, there is the crucial matter of air power and heavy artillery.

A careful reading of press reports, with their references to West German assault rifles, French helicopters, Israeli machine guns, etc., indicates that arms must be arriving from many sources, and sometimes there is even a more direct hint. For example, Kenneth Freed reports in the *Los Angeles Times* that "although Venezuelan President Luis Herrera Campins will not disclose amounts, he reportedly has poured hundreds of millions of dollars into El Salvador to help Duarte and the junta maintain control"[33]—the money, like U.S. "economic aid," is presumably used to purchase armaments from U.S. allies.

Hodding Carter's observation on how the government sets the terms of public discussion is much to the point. It is well illustrated by the case of the El Salvador white paper, and by many similar cases. The story is a very old one. A study of the first major government propaganda agency, the Committee on Public Information established during World War I, observes that "the CPI discovered in 1917–18 that one of the best means of controlling news was flooding news channels with 'facts,' or what amounted to official information."[34] While procedures may have become more sophisticated since that time, little of significance has changed, including the regular willingness of substantial segments of the articulate intelligentsia to accept the officially designated terms of public discussion, for example, with regard to U.S. aggression in South Vietnam from the early 1960s and other cases.

Suppose, in fact, that we do take the government's claims in the white paper at face value. Then it follows that from September 1980 the guerrillas began receiving supplies from the Communist countries—apparently the merest trickle. This was four months after the Sumpul River massacre when "the genocide began," according to Bailby, six months after the massive assault on the peasantry that coincided with the announcement of the land reform at a time when, according to President Duarte, "the masses were with the guerrillas."[35] How should we react to this momentous discovery?

One possible reaction is suggested by an account by T. D. Allman, one of the few U.S. reporters to have sought out people in the countryside apart from government guidance, describing his meeting with the remnants of a village near the town of Aguilares. The group had organized as a Catholic "grassroots congregation" *(comunidad de base),* devoted to

Bible study, prayer, and nonviolent methods of self-help. "At first only their leaders were harassed, beaten, and tortured," but later, as one put it, "the strict repression began." They were driven from their homes. Men who sought work or appeared in town were killed. Women were then sent to the town for food and medicine, but they were killed. They then sent children instead; an eight-year-old girl had just been killed. The murderers were government forces or ORDEN.[36] One of the men of the village told Allman that he "had heard that beyond the mountains where El Salvador becomes Honduras, beyond even the other sea on the other side of Honduras, there existed a country that might give them boots and uniforms and guns, called Cuba. But how could one get to that place? Even when one went to Aguilares to attend Mass, the Guardias took you, and tortured you, and killed you." An old man then asked Allman, "Can you tell us, please, sir, how we might contact these Cubans, to inform them of our need, so that they might help us?"[37]

But no such reaction as this to the white paper is or could be expressed in the conformist American press.

Allman reminds us that the origins of Reagan's policies lie in the Human Rights Administration: "Even in the good old hard-nosed days of *entente cordiale* between Washington and Batista and Trujillo and Papa Doc and all the rest, it would have been difficult to find an instance of an American president standing quite so resolutely behind a regime that quite so shamelessly tortured peasants and castrated doctors of philosophy and disemboweled little children and raped nuns and shot archbishops dead while they celebrated Mass." He also observes, with reason, that what is happening now in El Salvador is *Matanza,* Part II, a replay of the vast slaughter of peasants in 1932 when privilege had once before been seriously threatened by the poor, that time without our assistance, hence without the need to invoke the "Soviet drive for world domination."[38]

Something else that we are supposed to believe is that the land reform is marching from strength to strength in accordance with the plans of the "reformist junta," undermining the appeal of the guerrillas, as reported by Edward Schumacher in the *Times* while the army was massacring fleeing peasants at the Lempa River (see above, p. 342). One way to assess the success of the land reform would be to ask the opinion of the director of the agrarian reform program, José Rodolfo Viera. That possibility is excluded, however, because he was assassinated by right-wing elements on January 4, 1981. One can, however, inquire of his "former top assistant," Leonel Gómez, who "fled El Salvador after Mr. Viera's murder," the *New York Times* reports.[39] To say that Gómez fled after Viera's murder does not quite tell the whole story. In fact, we learn elsewhere, he fled when he "saw several dozen uniformed soldiers sealing off nearby streets" and realized that the "death squad" was coming for him, too, on January 13.[40] Gómez "thinks support for the terror and killings from within the officer corps is . . . virtually institutionalized," and that President Duarte has no real power. "The junta, he says, has virtually no support." "The Army is in control, according to Gómez, and the US is giving military aid to a 'killer government.' "[41]

Gómez, who comes from a landowning family and is quite critical of the civilians who resigned from the junta in January 1980 after a major outbreak of state terror, has had various things to say, in interviews and press conferences, about the land reform program for which he was a top adviser. He states that while the land reform program has seized large amounts of land from wealthy families, it "has distributed plots only to a relatively few peasants." The greatest success of the Salvadoran institute in charge of land reform (ISTA), of which he was a deputy, was in investigating the military: "We found huge amounts of corruption." "We were finding that ISTA was buying land already in government hands. They were buying land nobody wanted as a favor to rich friends. All of this piles up a debt that has to be paid by the peasants." He also believes that the left is nowhere near as strong militarily as the United States claims, and hopes "they will learn from experience and become like the Sandinistas in Nicaragua."[42] Gómez states further that the agrarian reform has become a "gravy train" for the military.[43]

A subsequent co-authored article expands on this interpretation of the land reform.[44] Gómez and Cameron believe that "Phase I of the program, which breaks up the country's largest estates, has worked" and that Phase III, the "Land to the Tiller plan" is supported by the peasants and "has the potential to improve dramatically the lives of those receiving the land where they had previously worked as sharecroppers" (Phase II, which was to break up middle-sized farm holdings, including the bulk of the coffee plantations, will not be enacted, it is generally assumed). The land reform, they believe, has broken the power of the traditional oligarchy, but is replacing it by a new military oligarchy. The Christian Democrats "have not achieved anything substantial for the people of El Salvador" and their presence in the junta "gives only a respectable facade to a military dictatorship." They believe that support for the guerrillas is not great, though "the government enjoys even less popularity," and the brutal killings by the army "have succeeded in traumatizing the Salvadoran people into fearful passivity." The army "is held together by a vast network of corruption," which now extends to the nationalized banks and 15 percent of the country's best farmland. "The vast majority of killings occur in sweeps of the countryside by the armed forces or by death squads operating under the formal direction or informal sanction of regional military commanders." The general picture they paint is of a shift of power from the traditional oligarchy to a military oligarchy of extraordinary brutality and corruption.

An Oxfam study of the land reform program takes a still dimmer view, concluding that "the majority of the rural population—landless and poorest—are excluded from any potential benefits under the present land reform" (close to two-thirds of the rural population, the authors estimate) and that it will be a disaster for most of the others, confining them for thirty years to tiny plots of marginal land that cannot provide even subsistence and that will be exhausted after a few years' planting. The reform was imposed by the United States without adequate planning and with no consultation with those who would allegedly benefit from it. Peasants in cooperatives believe "that they have simply changed *patronos,* that the agrarian reform does not represent a substantial change in their lives." Key Salvadoran officials regard its major component (Decree 207, the Land to the Tiller program) as a "misguided and U.S. imposed initiative" (in their own words). The land reform program "aggravates the most serious agrarian problems of El Salvador," the report concludes.

The authors also observe that the regions affected by Decree 207 "coincide almost identically with the areas of greatest repression against peasants by government security forces." Other reports strongly support their conclusion that the land reform had the effect of providing hard-line military with "the context in which they could pursue a counterinsurgency war," in the style already indicated.[45] The major repression against the peasantry was launched under the state of siege announced along with the land reform program.

As noted, the Reagan administration basically pursued and extended the Carter program of support for repression and massacre in El Salvador, while attempting to exploit the tragedy, in the manner of earlier years, for the purposes of their domestic programs of militarization and alms for the wealthy. It is interesting that in spite of the massive propaganda campaign and the generally willing cooperation of the media, the attempt was as much a failure domestically as it was internationally. The Carter-Reagan initiatives in El Salvador succeeded in revitalizing the peace movement, adding to the impetus already provided by Carter's evident turn toward a more militaristic posture in the latter part of his term. By early 1981, the level of opposition that had developed—spontaneously, without leadership, and with very little interaction for the most part—was reminiscent of the 1960s. The "Vietnam syndrome" has not been overcome as successfully as elite groups had hoped. In fact, the 1970s were by no means as quiescent as is widely believed, as a great many people know from their personal experience, though there was little activity on a national scale on major issues of peace and war (there was much local activity, and there were national actions on other issues).

The popular response to the U.S. support for a collection of murderers in El Salvador is of interest in two important respects. In the first place, there was a perceptible impact on the government and the press. By spring, the government had drawn back from its attempt to create an international confrontation over the El Salvador issue. The policies of support for repression and massacre continued, but the rhetoric was much muted.[46] There is little doubt that the policy shift was a result of the domestic reaction combined with the international opposition that had developed. For the tortured people of El Salvador, the difference is not great, and will not become significant unless the popular opposition to the U.S. support for the military junta continues and intensifies. But what seemed the easiest path to implement Reagan's long-term program in the context of a national mobilization has been blocked, a fact that may prove significant as the implications of this program become clear in practice. This does not mean that there is no danger of direct U.S. military intervention, either in El Salvador or, more likely, elsewhere. But perhaps a barrier has been placed on the road toward such actions.

Secondly, the response reveals serious flaws in the widely held argument that there has been a great "conservative shift" in the country in the past years. U.S. involvement in El Salvador in early 1981 was more or less comparable to Vietnam in about 1960, when the program of domestic repression in South Vietnam was recognized to be failing and plans were being laid for the outright aggression that began in 1962. But the public reaction is vastly different. In 1960 there was virtually no detectable opposition to the U.S. intervention in Indochina (primarily South Vietnam and Laos, where the United States succeeded in subverting the relatively free elections of 1958 and installed its own military client). The reaction to the current policies toward El Salvador is more similar to what was happening in the United States in 1965–67, when hundreds of thousands of American troops were invading South Vietnam and the United States had brought North Vietnam into the war (much as planners anticipated) by the bombing of the North.

Nicaragua

(1986)

━━

*T*HE REACTION OF U.S. ELITES TO THE SANDINISTA REVOLUTION is conveyed by Representative William Alexander, who describes "the lust members [of Congress] feel to strike out against Communism."[1] It is, in fact, notable that even congressional and media critics of the war against Nicaragua feel obliged, with only the rarest of exceptions, to make clear that they have nothing good to say about the Sandinistas; their position, rather, is that U.S. interests do not require such an attack, or that its means are inappropriate. "Only the bravest will say a word for the Sandinistas or question the president's premise that he has a perfect right to practice unlimited 'behavior modification' in a small, peasant nation," Mary McGrory writes.[2]

What is the reason for this "lust," this mood reminiscent of Khomeinist frenzy (but more extreme, since Iranians had sound historical reasons for hatred of their "Great Satan")? The official claims can hardly be taken seriously; even if all minimally credible charges are accepted, the Sandinista record compares favorably with that of U.S. clients in the region today, and in the past, and elsewhere, to put it rather mildly.[3] The conclusions that follow from comparisons within the region are too obvious for discussion among sane people, so let us consider the state that is by far the major recipient of U.S. aid, asking how it would fare under the charges brought against the Sandinistas. If the charges cannot withstand this test, then the level of hypocrisy is profound indeed.

U.S. propaganda regularly denounces the failure of the Sandinistas to meet their alleged "obligations" to the Organization of American States (OAS). The president claimed in July 1983 that they had "literally made a contract to establish a true democracy" with the OAS before taking power in July 1979. This claim is without foundation; Roy Gutman observes that this charge, constantly reiterated by apologists for U.S. atrocities, was concocted as part of a "successful U.S. disinformation campaign. . . . According to the OAS, in a July 16, 1979, telex to then General Secretary Alejandro Orfila the Sandinistas said they planned to convoke 'the first free elections in this century' but made no reference to timing and said nothing about creating a 'true democracy.' "[4] But although the charge has no merit with regard to the Sandinistas, it does apply to Israel; with considerably more force, in fact. Israel does have obligations, of a far more serious nature than those falsely attributed to the Sandinistas, which it has always rejected. Israel was admitted to the U.N. on the express condition that it would observe U.N. resolutions on return or compensation of refugees.[5] As would be expected in the age of Orwell, this charge against Nicaragua is featured prominently in Israeli propaganda journals, such as the *New Republic,* which naturally remain silent on Israel's obligations.

Another major charge against Nicaragua is censorship of *La Prensa.* A State Department official commented that the Sandinistas "know the censorship is the worst thing they can do, from the American point of view." Naturally if the United States were being attacked by a state of unimaginable power, we would not impose censorship on a journal that offered them support and that received a $100,000 grant from the aggressor;[6] that is, in fact, correct since the editors and anyone remotely connected to them would be in concentration camps; recall the fate of Japanese during World War II.

Censorship in Israel, however, is so severe that an Arab woman lecturing at the Hebrew University was denied permission even to publish an Arab-language social and political journal. The Arab press in East Jerusalem was seized by the authorities when it reported settler attacks against

Arabs after a prisoner exchange. An Arab bimonthly was shut down permanently in 1983, and the censor closed an Arab newspaper in Jerusalem for three days when it published an obituary of two young Arabs who died in a mysterious car explosion in 1985. Three hundred fifty books are officially banned in the occupied territories, along with others known to him personally, Knesset member Matti Peled (an Arabist and retired general) reports, including Hebrew translations of Theodore Herzl's diaries, Isaac Deutscher's *Non-Jewish Jew,* books on Israeli military and political history, a translation of "To Live with Arabs" by Elie Eliachar, the dovish president of the Council of the Sephardic Community in Israel, a book on the religious West Bank settlers (Gush Emunim) by the well-known Israeli journalist Danny Rubinstein, among others. Art exhibitions are censored; a Palestinian artist was given a six-month jail sentence on the charge that the colors of the Palestinian flag appeared in the corner of a painting. Arab plays have repeatedly been banned on political grounds, and a Hebrew play by an Israeli jailed for refusing military service was banned in September 1985 "on purely political grounds," Dan Fisher reports. The Hebrew press is also subject to censorship—as well as extensive self-censorship. Journalists are not permitted by the censor to publish abroad material that has appeared in the Hebrew press. All outgoing mail and packages are subject to censorship, and may be opened freely by the fifty-eight people assigned to this task. Surveillance of telephone conversations is so extensive that the censor has intervened directly in telephone conversation, Knesset member Michael Bar-Zohar reports.[7]

But we hear no cries that the U.S. must arm and direct terrorist forces to attack Israel. Nor does the U.S. Congress offer "humanitarian aid" (another Orwellism) to guerrilla forces resisting South African repression or opposing the illegal South African occupation of Namibia, or defending themselves against Israeli occupation in southern Lebanon; rather, they are all "terrorists," whose actions we deplore. The president, always quick to defend South Africa, even justified the murderous South African attack on Botswana on grounds that it may have been "retaliation" against the African National Congress (there is "no question," he said, about its "violence" and "murdering," but about South Africa we must withhold judgment).[8]

As for the "humanitarian aid" offered by Congress to the contras, the *Times* cites without comment the statement of rebel leader Adolfo Calero that it will be used for the purchase of "at least two helicopters."[9] No doubt Elliott Abrams will personally ensure that the helicopters are used solely for medical aid.

Another major charge against the Sandinistas has to do with their treatment of the Miskitos, surely the best-known American Indian group in the hemisphere and the only one whose travail merits agonized expressions of concern. That they were treated very badly by the Sandinistas is beyond question; they are also among the better treated Indians in the hemisphere. If an Indian group to their north were to put forth the demands for autonomy now being considered in Nicaragua, they would simply be slaughtered, if ridicule did not suffice. Miskito leader Armstrong Wiggins holds that the arrangement the Miskitos are demanding "has never been granted by any other country in the world to indigenous peoples, and goes beyond [their] status under the previous government" (which largely ignored the Atlantic coast); hitherto, he states, "the Sandinista policy towards indigenous people is just like the Mexican policy, just like the United States policy, just like Chilean policy."[10]

Sandinista abuses against the Miskitos were "more massive than any other human rights violations that I'm aware of in Central America," so Jeane Kirkpatrick testified before the Senate Foreign Relations Committee in March 1982—at a time when thousands of Indians were being slaughtered in Guatemala, and some 13,000 civilians had been murdered in El Salvador by U.S. clients in the preceding year alone, not to speak of torture, mutilation, starvation, semislave labor and other standard Free World amenities. The president chimed in with the news that the Sandinistas are conducting a "campaign of virtual genocide against the Miskito Indians" (June 6, 1985). In fact, some 10 percent of the Miskito population had been removed from war zones under a "policy [that] was clearly prompted by military considerations" and compares quite favorably with U.S. treatment of Japanese-Americans during World War II, an Americas Watch report comments, and twenty-one to twenty-four Miskitos had been killed three years earlier by government forces along with sixty-nine unresolved cases of "disappearance"; major atrocities, no doubt, but undetectable in the context of the behavior of the United States and its clients in the region.[11]

Reviewing the human rights situation in Nicaragua, the Americas Watch report finds that Nicaraguan government atrocities, which it believes it was able to review in full, are far slighter than those of the U.S.-organized terrorist army, and have sharply declined since 1982 in contrast to those of the contras, which can only be sampled given their scale and the lack of sources. Even in the case of the Miskitos, not the prime target of the U.S.-sponsored terrorists, Americas Watch finds that "the most serious abuses of Miskitos' rights have been committed by the *contra* groups," and "the *contras'* treatment of Miskitos and other Indians has become increasingly more violent" while that of the government has notably improved. Miskito leader Brooklyn Rivera comments that the FDN (Nicaraguan Democratic Front) "has been very hostile and aggressive toward us. They consider us an enemy because we maintain our independent positions and will not become soldiers in someone else's army." He alleges further "that the Reagan Administration was blocking Miskito unity because it wanted a group it could control" under Adolfo Calero of the FDN, whom the United States sees "as the future leader of Nicaragua," and states that the U.S.-controlled Honduran military kept him and other prominent Miskitos from entering Honduras to attend a Miskito conference, as part of this strategy.[12]

Again, it is pointless to compare the abuse of the Miskitos with the wholesale slaughter conducted by U.S. clients in Central America in the same years. So we might recall some moments of early U.S. history—for example, the Sullivan Expedition against the Iroquois in 1779, pursuant to General Washington's orders that the towns and territories of the Iroquois were "not to be merely overrun but destroyed." The orders were "fulfilled to the hilt," Fairfax Downey records in his upbeat account of "an outstanding feat in military annals," leading to "total destruction and devastation" of "cultivated fields and well-built towns," of "the North American Indian's finest civilization north of Mexico," with richly cultivated fields and orchards, stone houses, and log cabins beyond the level of most of the colonial farmers. Nothing was left but "smoking ruins and desolation"; "all this industry and plenty was doomed to be scorched earth." One column destroyed forty towns and 160,000 bushels of corn along with orchards and other crops, while a smaller one destroyed hundreds of houses and five hundred acres of corn. "The towns and field of the hostile Iroquois had been ruthlessly ravished," though one officer "sadly" observed that "the nests have been destroyed, but the birds are still on the wing." They survived in "miserable destitution" after "the wastage of their lands."[13]

Or we might consider one of the early exploits of our most favored client state, the massacre on October 28, 1948, at Doueimah, an un-defended town north of Hebron in an area where there had been no fighting. The massacre was conducted by a unit with tanks, leaving 580 civilians killed according to the accounting by its *mukhtar*—100 to 350, according to Israeli sources, 1,000 according to testimonies preserved in U.S. State Department records—including 75 old men praying in a mosque and 35 families, of whom only 3 people escaped, in a cave outside of the destroyed town where they took refuge. The conquest of the town—but not the massacre—was noted at once in Israel's major journal, *Ha'aretz,* in a report on the conquest of "historical sites" from the days of Bar Kochba and the Romans, "renewing again the connection between the people of Israel and the Land of Israel." Israeli military historians say that the affair is known, though not recorded. The first report appears to be in a letter in the Labor party journal *Davar* (September 4, 1979) by a kibbutz member who deplores the "ghetto mentality" of those who refrain from expelling Arabs. He cites eyewitness testimony by a participant who alleges that women and children were killed by crushing their skulls with sticks and that people were blown up in houses, among other atrocities, "not during the heat of battle" but "as a system of expulsion and elimination." The story was finally unearthed by a correspondent for *Hadashot* in 1984 and presented as newly discovered. Historian Yoram Nimrod writes that the background for this slaughter, and the general attitude of the time that "the Arabs and their possessions are fair game," can be traced to the attitudes of the leadership, who wanted the Galilee to be "free [literally, "clean"] of Arabs" and asserted that "for the Arabs of the Land of Israel there remains only one function: to flee" (David Ben-Gurion),[14] that the country must be "homogeneous" and hence with as few Arabs as possible (Moshe Dayan), and who insisted that the Arab civilians who had fled or had been expelled "cannot and need not return" (Chaim Weizmann), or even be settled nearby, even if this means rejecting peace overtures (Ben-Gurion).[15]

Nothing comparable to these early postindependence atrocities against the indigenous population in the U.S. and Israel can be charged to the Sandinistas.

Chaim Weizmann's principle was, incidentally, also followed in subsequent years, notably after the 1967 war when hundreds of thousands of Arabs fled or were expelled. A report by Eyal Ehrlich observes that "much was written, and with pride, about 'Operation Refugee,' which permitted 17,000 to return," but not about the fact, which he discovered in interviews with soldiers and officers, that the army was under orders, which it fulfilled, to kill returning refugees: "Civilians, women and children were killed. No one reported, no one counted the bodies, no one investigated and punished" these actions taken in pursuance of "policies established by such men as" Yitzhak Rabin (now minister of defense), Chaim Herzog (now president), and Uzi Narkis (commander of the Jordanian front, later head of the Department of Immigration and Absorption of the Jewish Agency, a bitter irony). Soldiers were ordered to shoot even if they heard "the crying of an infant."[16]

Other charges too have been leveled against the Sandinistas in the propaganda war. President Reagan, with a representative of the Anti-Defamation League of B'nai Brith (ADL) at his side, accused the Sandinistas of anti-Semitism on July 20, 1983—somehow overlooking a cable four days earlier from the U.S. embassy in Managua stating that it could find "no verifiable ground" to accuse the Sandinistas of anti-Semitism and that "the evidence fails to demonstrate that the Sandinistas have followed a policy of anti-Semitism or have persecuted Jews solely because of their religion."[17] The charges have been reiterated since, but are denied by human rights activists who are highly critical of the Sandinistas in Managua, by a delegation headed by a rabbi who had been a leader in the struggle against the anti-Semitism and terror of the Argentine neo-Nazis, and by a Panamanian rabbi (a former minister of the government who had been honored by the Latin American Jewish Congress) after a visit to Nicaragua. The Jewish Student Press Service reports that the ADL had "approached Presidential advisers with the idea of a deal" in an effort to "gain clout with the Reagan White House," accepted by the administration, who saw a way "to get the Jewish community to join the bandwagon" in the campaign to enlist public support for its Central American policies; the report cites officials in leading Jewish organizations, who denied the charges of anti-Semitism.[18]

Meanwhile, the White House, the media, and the ADL, while generally suppressing the cable from the ambassador that reached Reagan four days before the July 20 accusation, also have yet to report the homilies of their favorite, Nicaraguan Archbishop Obando y Bravo, who declaims that "the leaders of Israel . . . mistreated [the prophets], beat them, killed them. Finally as supreme proof of his love, God sent his Divine Son; but they . . . also killed him, crucifying him." "The Jews killed the prophets and finally the son of God. . . . Such idolatry calls forth the sky's vengeance."[19]

The Council on Hemispheric Affairs observes that "the White House keeps up a steady stream of calumny directed at Managua, charging the ruling Sandinistas with everything vile: drug-running, genocide, subverting their neighbors, and now international terrorism," charges that have not "been burdened with evidence" but are reported with only rare attempts at evaluation. The technique is the one pioneered during World War I, when the first major government propaganda agency, the Committee on Public Information, discovered "that one of the best means of controlling news was flooding news channels with 'facts,' or what amounted to official information."[20]

Few are willing to undertake the tedious task of refuting the regular flood of lies; they have little access to the public in any event, and they can always be dismissed by the charge that they are apologists for the enemy and its actual crimes. This standard device is sometimes used consciously as a technique to preserve the crucial right to lie in the service of the state; or, for the more deeply indoctrinated, it may simply be impossible to conceive of criticism of the Holy State as anything but support for its official enemies, principled criticism of the divine institution being unimaginable. In either case, the discussion shifts to the evil deeds of the official enemy and the critic can be dismissed as an apologist for these crimes, as having a "double standard," etc.: the Holy State and the Right to Lie in its service are secure. The device was, and still is, used with tiresome regularity with reference to the Indochina wars: a critic of the U.S. attack against South Vietnam must be a "supporter of Hanoi," so one can respond to the criticism by producing true or false charges against Hanoi, and if the critic refutes false charges, that just proves that he or she is an apologist for Hanoi as originally claimed and there is no need to consider the original criticism of the state one serves. The same device is now constantly used in the case of Central America.[21]

One would think that the transparent silliness of the procedure would embarrass its practitioners, but evidently this is not the case.

The irrelevance of government claims about the war against Nicaragua is evident from the way the motivation shifts as circumstances demand. At one point, the attack was justified by the need to prevent arms flow to El Salvador. By 1983, no significant arms flow having been detected despite massive efforts, the aim was to "bring the Sandinistas to the bargaining table" and force them to hold elections. In June 1984, the president told Congress that U.S. aid to the contras must continue, to pressure the Sandinistas to negotiate; unless we do, he said, "a regional settlement based on the Contadora principles will continue to elude us."[22] A few months later, elections had been held, the Sandinistas had accepted the Contadora principles, causing the administration to discover suddenly that they were a sham and a fraud, and they were continuing to request negotiations that the U.S. refuses. So the argument shifted again: we read in the news columns that "the Reagan Administration has demanded that Nicaragua demilitarize, reduce its ties with the Soviet Union and Cuba and change its form of government to a pluralistic democracy."[23] A moment's thought suffices to show that the best way to bring Nicaragua to demilitarize and cut its ties with the Soviet bloc would be to accept the Contadora agreements blocked by U.S. pressure and to call off the war, and that the commitment of the Reagan administration, or its predecessors, to "pluralistic democracy" in Central America is as believable as the Soviet commitment to "socialism" or "democracy" in its domains. But this drivel, for that is what it is, is blandly reported as "news" in the nation's press. Nothing could be more plain than the absurdity of the whole game, in which the media play their assigned role, earnestly reporting each pretense and occasionally commenting on the weakness of the argument or the "inconsistency" of the highly consistent and rational policy.

The real reasons for the "lust" to destroy the Sandinista regime have nothing to do with the charges that are raised, whether valid or simply concocted. That is obvious enough. The real reasons can readily be explained on other grounds: by fear of Nicaraguan success. Reports on Sandinista social successes inspire real fear; useless tanks do not. The real reasons are based on the argument that President Wilson regarded as "unanswerable": the interests of the people of Latin America are "an incident, not an end." What is paramount is a narrowly conceived American interest: "The protection of our raw materials," the fifth freedom. We must therefore become deeply concerned when some group becomes infected by the heresy detected by U.S. intelligence: "the idea that the government has direct responsibility for the welfare of the people," what U.S. political theology calls "communism" in our Third World domains, whatever the commitments of its advocates.

In the real world, as we shall see in more detail directly, the United States has consistently opposed "human rights, the raising of the living standards, and democratization," using harsh measures where necessary. These policies are natural concomitants of the geopolitical conceptions that have motivated planning and that are deeply rooted in American institutions. It is not surprising, for example, that the United States should react with extraordinary hostility to democracy in Laos or should overthrow the only democratic government in the history of Guatemala, keeping in power a series of mass murderers ever since. It is familiar to students of U.S. policy that "while paying lip-service to the encouragement of representative democracy in Latin America, the United States has a strong interest in just the reverse," apart from "procedural democracy, especially the holding of elections—which only too often have proved farcical." The reason is that democracies may tend to be responsive to popular needs, while "the United States has been concerned with fostering the most favourable conditions for her private overseas investment":[24]

> . . . United States concern for representative democracy in Latin America is a facet of her anti-communist policy. There has been no serious question of her intervening in the case of the many right-wing military coups, from which, of course, this policy generally has benefited. It is only when her own concept of democracy, closely identified with private, capitalistic enterprise, is threatened by communism [or to be more accurate, by independent development, whether capitalist, socialist, or whatever] that she has felt impelled to demand collective action to defend it.

It is only when some form of democracy contributes to maintaining the fifth freedom that the United States will tolerate it; otherwise, terror-and-torture states will have to do.

From these real-world considerations, one can come to understand the "lust" to strike out against Nicaragua—or Allende, or Cuba, or the National Liberation Front of South Vietnam. It is not because of the abuses of human rights and democratic principle, often real, sometimes despicable, but rarely approaching what we tolerate with equanimity, directly support, or carry out ourselves. Rather, U.S. policy toward Nicaragua is immediately predictable from the fact that the priorities of the new government "meant that Nicaragua's poor majority would have access to, and be the primary beneficiaries of, public programs;" the fact that infant mortality fell so dramatically that Nicaragua won an award from the World Health Organization for the best health achievement in a Third World nation; health standards and literacy sharply improved; a successful agrarian reform was carried out; GNP expanded by 5 percent in 1983 in contrast to other countries in the region; production and consumption of corn, beans, and rice rose dramatically; and Nicaragua came closer to self-sufficiency than any other Central American nation and made the most impressive gains of any Latin American nation in the Quality of Life Index of the Overseas Development Council, based on literacy, infant mortality, and life expectancy.[25] Burns comments that "Nicaragua should, in many ways, stand as an example for Central America, not its outcast. The grim social statistics from Honduras, a country in which the population is literally starving to death, stand in sharp contrast to the recent achievements of Nicaragua." That is just the point; the infection must be stopped before it spreads.

Similarly the crime of the Allende government was that it quickly raised production and real wages; conducted an effective agrarian reform and such programs as milk distribution for children, "measures that increased consumer demand and permitted industry to take advantage of unutilized capacity and idle labor"; and worse, did so under parliamentary democracy—though such dangerous progress could not long persist as the Nixon-Kissinger destabilization policy, designed to "make the economy scream," in Nixon's words, had its effects, along with other factors.[26]

Similarly U.S. policy toward Cuba is readily explained by the Quality of Life Index of the Overseas Development Council, which places Cuba well above any other Latin American country and approximately equal to the United States—actually better than the United States if we consider its more egalitarian character, thus with lower infant mortality rates than Chicago and far lower rates than the Navajo reservation. Tom Farer of the Rutgers Law School, member of the Inter-American Commission on Human Rights of the OAS and former State Department assistant for inter-American affairs, writes that

> there is a consensus among scholars of a wide variety of ideological positions that, on the level of life expectancy, education, and health, Cuban achievement is considerably greater than one would expect from its level of per capita income. A recent study of 113 Third World countries in terms of these basic indicators of popular welfare ranked Cuba first, ahead even of Taiwan—which is probably the

outstanding example of growth with equity within a capitalist economic framework. Data in the 1981 World Development Report of the International Bank for Reconstruction and Development also support the consensus. Cuba excelled according to all main indicators of human needs satisfaction. . . . What has changed remarkably is not so much the gross indicators as those that reflect the changed conditions of the poor, particularly the rural poor. In 1958, for example, the one rural hospital in the entire country represented about 2 percent of the hospital facilities in Cuba; by 1982 there were 117 hospitals, or about 35 percent of all hospitals in Cuba.

Furthermore, polio and malaria have been eliminated, and the causes of death have shifted from those associated with underdevelopment (diseases of early infancy, etc.) to those of the developed world (congenital abnormalities, diabetes, etc.).[27] These are the crimes for which Cuba must pay dearly; the real ones are of little interest to policy-makers, except for their propaganda effect.

As for the NLF in South Vietnam, its crime was explained ruefully by the bitterly anti-Communist journalist Denis Warner: "In hundreds of villages all over South-East Asia the only people working at the grass roots for an uplift in people's living standards are the Communists,"[28] the reason for the popular support that forced the United States to resort to violence and to undermine any political settlement.

Those who set their priorities in this way are evidently deficient in their understanding of U.S. needs and priorities. They have therefore joined the "monolithic and ruthless conspiracy," and must be driven into the hands of the Russians and subjected to aggression, terror, embargo, and other means, in accord with their status as "an incident, not an end."

Guatemala

(1986)

JUAN JOSÉ ARÉVALO WAS ELECTED PRESIDENT OF GUATEMALA in 1944, inaugurating a ten-year departure from military rule. His government, "favorably disposed initially toward the United States, was modeled in many ways after the Roosevelt New Deal." It quickly elicited U.S. hostility because of its commitment to democratic values (Communists were not repressed), a labor code that "sought to right the balance in a society where management had long dominated" and harmed the largest employer (United Fruit), hesitation about granting concessions to U.S. oil companies, and other similar crimes. When Arévalo's term ended in 1951, "the political rift between [the United States and Guatemala] was almost complete." As he left the presidency, Arévalo, recalling his belief in the noble words of President Roosevelt, commented sadly that "Roosevelt lost the war. The real winner was Hitler."[1]

The United States soon moved to prove the accuracy of these words. Arévalo's successor, Jacobo Arbenz, attempted to carry Arévalo's reforms forward, including a successful land reform that led to a rise in exports and a favorable balance of payments by 1954. The land reform not only increased productivity, but "also provided campesinos with their own food, even cash from sales, while involving them in the political system for the first time in 400 years." But this was not to be. Arbenz attempted to expropriate unused lands held by the United Fruit Company and to hand them over to landless peasants, offering compensation based on the company's fraudulent tax valuation. This and other reform measures enraged the United States further. Under Secretary of State Walter Bedell Smith, one of Eisenhower's closest advisers, reported to the president that "we have repeatedly expressed deep concern to the Guatemalan Government because it plays the Communist game," permitting Communist activists to enjoy civil rights and disturbing relations with the United States "because of the merciless hounding of American companies there by tax and labor demands, strikes, and, in the case of the United Fruit Company, inadequately compensated seizures of land under a Communist-administered Agrarian Reform Law." Exploiting the pretext of a Communist takeover, with the U.S. press loyally playing its part, the CIA engineered a coup in 1954, restoring military rule and turning the country into a literal hell on earth, which has been maintained by regular United States intervention until today. The land reform was repealed and its beneficiaries dispossessed, peasant cooperatives were dissolved, the literacy program was halted, the economy collapsed, the labor unions were destroyed, and the killings began.[2]

It is intriguing, in this context, to consider the interpretation of international law devised by advocates of the U.S. war against Nicaragua. Recall that the theory is that the United States is exercising the right of collective self-defense against Nicaragua's armed attack upon its ally, El Salvador. Suspending momentarily the reaction that any sane person would have to this farcical claim, consider the notion of "armed attack" that must be constructed to carry through the argument. Armed attack, in this conception, "includes assistance in organizing insurgency, training of insurgents, financing of the insurgency, use of facilities for command and control, ammunition and explosives supply, intelligence and communications assistance, logistics assistance, and political and propaganda support, as well as weapons supply"[3]; thus voicing support for the Afghan rebels constitutes "armed attack" against Afghanistan, to which the USSR is "obligated" to respond by military force, by bombing offices of the U.S. press, for example. In the light of this concept, consider the

CIA-engineered coup in Guatemala, the long U.S. terrorist war against Cuba, and innumerable other crimes. By the standards of apologists for U.S. atrocities, many an American leader should face the bar of justice for crimes against peace, and much of the world would be permitted under international law, indeed "obligated," to attack the United States in self-defense. The absurdity of this particular argument by apologists, now applied to their favored state, of course does not invalidate its conclusions, the first of which at least can be argued on rational grounds.

In 1963, Arévalo was permitted to return to take part in an election, after having been kept abroad "by an assortment of legal devices and physical threats."[4] A military coup, quickly recognized by the Kennedy administration and perhaps encouraged by it, prevented this danger. The new regime, guided by the Kennedy counterinsurgency doctrines, rapidly expanded the instruments of state terror with enthusiastic U.S. support.[5] Rising repression and impoverishment elicited insurgency and further U.S. intervention. A counterinsurgency campaign in 1966–68 led to the slaughter of perhaps 10,000 peasants with the help of American Green Berets, also to napalm bombing by US planes based in Panama, according to Guatemalan Vice President Rojas. In subsequent years, impoverishment of the mass of the population and indescribable terror increased, with constant U.S. assistance and occasional notice here. Thus in a brief report of the murder of yet another professor at the national university, the *Times* noted in passing that more than 40,000 people have disappeared and more than 95,000 "have died in political violence here since 1954" according to "the Mexican-based Guatemalan Human Rights Commission": to translate from Newspeak, some 140,000 have been eliminated by the governments *installed and kept in power by the United States since the United States overthrew Guatemalan democracy in 1954* (the crucial fact, regularly omitted in news reports and editorial comment), according to a Human Rights Commission which is Mexican-based because its members could not long survive in Guatemala. In May 1982, the conservative Guatemalan Conference of Bishops stated that "never in our history have such extremes been reached, with the assassinations now falling into the category of genocide." "A new study by two American anthropologists," Douglas Foster reports, "estimates that more than 50,000 Guatemalans—most of them Mayan Indians—have been killed since 1980"; one of the most powerful Guatemalan businessmen, not without reason, told him: "You Americans killed your Indians long ago, so don't lecture us." At the same time, U.S. military aid increased, along with renewed terror, as the country strides toward democracy, in official parlance.[6]

As in El Salvador, the national university has been a prime target of state terror for many years, and still is. The last two rectors were killed, in 1981 and 1983. Another fled into exile, in fear for his life. The current rector, who has received twenty death threats, narrowly escaped in 1983 when gunmen fired at his car. His possible successor was gunned down while walking to a class on campus. According to university records, thirty-six students and ten teachers were killed or have disappeared in two years, twelve in early 1985. The U.S. ambassador, Alberto Piedra, is coauthor of a 1980 book that dismisses the university as "a publicly financed echo chamber of revolutionary Communism." The rector, in contrast, "described the students of the university as members of a generation that had been wounded by state repression and political violence and that held little hope for the future," James LeMoyne reports. They do not disguise "their antipathy for the United States, which they hold responsible for supporting 30 years of repressive governments after a coup in 1954 supported by the Central Intelligence Agency."[7] LeMoyne deserves credit for departing from the norm with this reference to the U.S. coup; he might have added that the United States is not just *held* responsible, but *is* in large measure responsible for the thirty years of terror that followed.

As noted earlier, U.S. military aid to the mass murderers never ceased during the Carter years, contrary to what is commonly alleged, and in fact remained close to the norm. Furthermore, the U.S. military establishment maintained its close relations with the Guatemalan military, giving them a "convincing signal" that the human rights rhetoric was hardly to be taken seriously. In January 1980, top American military officials visited Guatemala, and the press noted the "particular satisfaction" the Guatemalan regime derived from the visits. Piero Gleijeses comments:

> . . . it is important to understand the rationale of those State Department "liberals." . . . They would have advocated military assistance for the regime had they believed that it was necessary for its survival. But in their eyes [military dictator] Lucas was not yet seriously threatened—hence the United States could afford to wait (while military assistance was provided by Argentina, Israel and other countries). In this fashion, the Carter administration would avoid dirtying its hands and would preserve the facade of its human rights policy as long as possible.

In fact, military assistance also was provided by the United States, and distancing from the regime was only a public posture.[8]

In short, another fine example of how "the overall effect of American power on other societies was to further liberty, pluralism, and democracy" (Samuel Huntington).

While overcoming the threat of democracy in the Dominican Republic and Guatemala, the United States also succeeded, not surprisingly, in thoroughly alienating its leading advocates, who were to write bitterly about the U.S. role, thus demonstrating to the faithful that they were really Communists at heart all along.[9]

These are only a few cases. The record is shameful and appalling. The Central America–Caribbean region has been turned into a horror chamber, with regular U.S. intervention serving to keep matters on course.

THE MIDDLE EAST

Rejectionism and Accommodation

(1983)

A FRAMEWORK FOR DISCUSSION

*W*HAT HAVE BEEN THE ATTITUDES AND POLICIES OF THE major participants in the Arab-Israeli conflict, and those concerned with it, during the period since 1967, when the U.S.-Israel relationship became established in something like its present form? To approach this question sensibly, we should begin by clarifying what we take to be the valid claims of those who regard the former Palestine as their home. Attitudes toward this question vary widely. I will simply state certain assumptions that I will adopt as a framework for discussion. The first of these is the principle that Israeli Jews and Palestinian Arabs are human beings with human rights, equal rights; more specifically, they have essentially equal rights within the territory of the former Palestine. Each group has a valid right to national self-determination in this territory. Furthermore, I will assume that the State of Israel within its pre-June 1967 borders had, and retains, whatever one regards as the valid rights of any state within the existing international system. One may formulate these principles in various ways, but let us take them to be clear enough to serve at least as a point of departure.

The Concept of Rejectionism

The term "rejectionism" is standardly used in the United States to refer to the position of those who deny the right of existence of the State of Israel, or who deny that Jews have the right of national self-determination within the former Palestine; the two positions are not exactly the same because of the question of the status of Israeli Arabs and of Jews outside of Israel, but let us put these questions aside temporarily. Unless we adopt the racist assumption that Jews have certain intrinsic rights that Arabs lack, the term "rejectionism" should be extended beyond its standard usage to include also the position of those who deny the right of national self-determination to Palestinian Arabs, the community that constituted nine-tenths of the population at the time of the First World War, when Great Britain committed itself to the establishment of a "national home for the Jewish people" in Palestine. I will use the term "rejectionism" in this nonracist sense. By "accommodation," I will mean the position that accepts the basic assumptions of the preceding paragraph. Each position can take various forms, as regards the manner in which national rights are realized, boundaries, etc.

The doctrine of self-styled "supporters of Israel," which has largely dominated discussion here, holds that the PLO and the Arab states have been undeviatingly rejectionist (apart from Egypt since 1977), while the United States and Israel have sought a peaceful settlement that will recognize the valid claims of all. A more recent version is that the "beautiful Israel" of earlier years, which was realizing the dream of democratic socialism and becoming "a light unto the nations," has been betrayed by Begin and his cohorts, a consequence of the refusal of the Arabs to accept the existence of Israel and the unwavering commitment of the PLO—a collection of thugs and gangsters—to the destruction of Israel, the murder of innocents, and the intimidation of all "moderate" opinion in the occupied territories.[1] Like virtually all propaganda systems, this one contains elements of truth. But the real world is rather different, as will quickly be discovered if the historical record is rescued from the oblivion to which it has been consigned.

The International Consensus

Since 1967, a broad international consensus has taken shape, including Europe, the USSR and most of the nonaligned nations. This consensus initially advocated a political settlement along approximately the pre-June 1967 borders, with security guarantees, recognized borders, and various devices to help assure peace and tranquillity; it envisioned the gradual integration of Israel into the region while it would remain, in essence, a Western European society. This is the way the basic international document, U.N. Security Council Resolution 242, has been understood throughout most of the world, though its actual wording was left vague so that agreement on it could be achieved. As Jon Kimche comments: "Everybody subscribed to it and no one believed in it, since neither Arabs nor Israelis, Russians or Americans could agree on what the Resolution meant."[2] This is not quite accurate, since in fact there was substantial agreement along the lines of the consensus just described.* The official position of the United States, for example, was that only "insubstantial alterations" of the pre-June 1967 borders would be allowed.[4]

Note that this consensus was rejectionist, in that it denied the national rights of Palestinian Arabs, referring to them solely in the context of a refugee problem. For this reason, the PLO has refused to accept the resolution. This refusal may be a tactical error, but it is easy to understand its motivation. One would hardly have expected the World Zionist Organization, in 1947, to have accepted a U.N. resolution concerning Palestine that referred to Jewish interests only in terms of a refugee problem, denying any claim to national rights and any status to the Zionist movement or its organizations.

The United States has refused any direct contacts with the PLO on the grounds of its unwillingness to accept U.N. 242 and to recognize the existence of the State of Israel, basing this refusal on a "Memorandum of Agreement" concluded with Israel by Secretary of State Kissinger in September 1975. This policy raises two questions. The narrower one is that the status of the memorandum is dubious. In testimony before the Senate Foreign Relations Committee, Kissinger specified that its terms are not "binding commitments" of the United States and warned against creating such commitments. Furthermore, "Congress specifically dissociated itself from the related memoranda of agreement," including this one.[5] More broadly, whatever one thinks about the attitude of the PLO toward U.N. 242, it is quite clear, as we shall see, that it has been far more

---

*The resolution was accepted by Israel, Egypt, Jordan and Lebanon, and in 1972 by Syria with the condition that Palestinian "rights" must be recognized.[3]

forthcoming than either Israel or the United States with regard to an accommodationist settlement. Nevertheless, the refusal of Israel to recognize the PLO, or to accept Palestinian national rights in any meaningful form, is not invoked as a reason to refuse contacts with Israel. Unless we adopt rejectionist assumptions, then, the argument supporting the American refusal to enter into direct contacts with the PLO has no force.

From the mid-1970s, the terms of the international consensus have been modified in one significant respect: the right of the Palestinians to national self-determination has been recognized, and the consensus now includes the concept of a Palestinian state in the West Bank and Gaza Strip, with perhaps some minor border rectifications. The newer form of the international consensus overcomes the earlier rejectionism and falls under the rubric of "accommodation" in the sense of this term described above. Within the international consensus, there has been little discussion of whether such a settlement—henceforth, a "two-state settlement"—reflects higher demands of abstract justice; rather, it has been taken to be a politically realistic solution that would maximize the chances for peace and security for the inhabitants of the former Palestine, for the region, and for the world, and that satisfies the valid claims of the two major parties as well as is possible under existing conditions. One can imagine various subsequent developments through peaceful means and mutual consent toward a form of federation or other arrangements.

The existence of this international consensus, and the nature of the rejectionist forces that block its realization, are well-understood outside of the United States, and are also recognized by knowledgeable observers here. For example, Seth Tillman concludes his recent study of U.S. policies in the Middle East by noting "the emergence of a *consensus* among moderates in the Arab world, the United States, and Europe—with some minority support in Israel as well—on the approximate terms of a viable and equitable comprehensive settlement in the Middle East," namely, along the lines just sketched. He notes that "the essentials of the consensus of moderates are well known, approximating in most respects the *official* policy of the United States" since 1967. "Outside of Israel, the United States, a few 'rejectionist' Arab states, and certain groups within the PLO, support for a settlement along these lines approaches worldwide unanimity," he observes.[6] A simpler but quite accurate formulation would be that U.S.-Israeli rejectionism has consistently blocked the achievement of "a viable and equitable comprehensive settlement."

I will assume the international consensus, as just sketched, to be reasonable in essence. Let us consider, then, three basic positions as points of reference: the international consensus in its more recent form, and the two varieties of rejectionism. Note that I do not mean to imply that these are the only possible solutions that merit consideration. In fact, in my view, they are not optimal. Furthermore, from 1967 to the October 1973 war, there were realistic alternatives that would have been far preferable for all concerned, I believe. These were rejected at the time, and after the 1973 war the short-term possibilities narrowed to essentially those sketched, within the framework of accommodation.[7]

Perhaps I should qualify these remarks, saying rather that I will assume the international consensus to *have been* reasonable in essence during the period under review here. It might be argued that as a result of U.S.-Israeli rejectionism, a peaceful political settlement is no longer possible, that the U.S.-financed program of Israeli settlement in the occupied territories has "created facts" that cannot be changed short of war. If persistent U.S. rejectionism brings about this state of affairs, as sooner or later it will if U.S. policy does not change course, the primary objective for Americans concerned with peace and justice will no longer be to try to bring the United States in line with the international consensus, now irrelevant, but to block American support for the next step: expulsion of a substantial part of the Arab population on some pretext, and conversion of Israel into a society on the South African model with some form of Bantustans, committed to regional disruption, etc.

THE STANDS OF THE MAJOR ACTORS

Adopting this as the basic framework for discussion, we can turn to consideration of the attitudes and policies of the major actors since 1967, considering in turn the United States, Israel, the Palestinians under Israeli occupation, and the Arab states and the PLO. I will intersperse this historical account with some comment on the ways in which the history has been interpreted in the United States, an important matter bearing on the ideological support for Israel discussed earlier, and thus bearing crucially on the development of policy and the prospects for the future.

The United States

As far as the United States is concerned, there has been internal conflict over the issue throughout the period. At one extreme, the Rogers Plan, announced by Secretary of State William Rogers in December 1969, reflected the international consensus of the time. At the other extreme, Henry Kissinger advocated the rejectionist position: a "Greater Israel" should refuse any accommodation, and should maintain control over the occupied territories. This position was never explicitly formulated, at least in publicly available documents, but the policies pursued conform to it quite closely and it even emerges with relative clarity from the murky rhetoric of Kissinger's memoirs, as we shall see directly. Kissinger succeeded in taking control over Middle East affairs by 1970, and the rejectionist "Greater Israel" position became U.S. policy in practice. It has remained so in essence ever since, with post-1973 modifications to which we return. Echoes of these conflicting positions remain today.

Major sectors of American corporate capitalism, including powerful elements with interests in the Middle East, have supported the international consensus, as have others. But this position has lost out in the internal policy debate in favor of the concept of an Israeli Sparta serving as a "strategic asset." The persistent policy debate concerns the question of whether the fundamental U.S. interests are better served by this rejectionism, or by a move toward the international consensus, with a peaceful resolution of the conflict. In the latter view, the radical nationalist tendencies that are inflamed by the unsettled Palestinian problem would be reduced by the establishment of a Palestinian ministate that would be contained within a Jordanian-Israeli military alliance (perhaps tacit), surviving at the pleasure of its far more powerful neighbors and subsidized by the most conservative and pro-American forces in the Arab world, in the oil-producing monarchies, which have been pressing for such a settlement for some years. This would, in fact, be the likely outcome of a two-state settlement. The internal policy debate has certainly been influenced, at the congressional level substantially so, by highly effective pressure groups.

A number of prominent supporters of Israel, particularly in left-liberal circles, have adduced the fact that oil companies tend to favor the international consensus as support for their own rejectionism.[8] This makes about as much sense as the fringe right-wing argument that if Soviet leaders happen to advocate some proposal for their own purposes (say, ratification of Salt II), then we should oppose it. The further claim that Israel is being "sold out" for oil is hardly consistent with the plain facts. The levels of U.S. aid to Israel, apart from all else, tell us just to what extent Israel has been "sold out." In fact, it is the Palestinians who have consistently been "sold out" in the United States, with no objection from left-liberal proponents of such arguments, in favor of a militarized Israel that will serve the U.S. interest of controlling the petroleum reserves of the Middle East. The policy debate in elite circles takes for granted, on all sides, the goal of maintaining U.S. control over Middle East petroleum resources and the flow of petrodollars. The question is a tactical one: how best to realize this goal.

U.S. policy, then, has in practice been consistently rejectionist, and still is, despite continuing internal conflict that is barely reflected in public discourse, with its overwhelmingly rejectionist commitments and assumptions.

Israel

Within Israel, the policy debate has been much narrower in scope. There are two major political groupings in Israel, the coalition dominated by the Labor party (the Labor Alignment, *Ma'arach*), and the Likud coalition dominated by Menachem Begin's Herut party. The Labor party governed with various partners until 1977, the Likud coalition since then.

The Rejectionist Stands of Labor and Likud

Contrary to illusions fostered here, the two major political groupings in Israel do not differ in a fundamental way with regard to the occupied territories. Both agree that Israel should effectively control them; both insistently reject any expression of Palestinian national rights west of the Jordan, though the Labor Alignment contains a margin of dissidents. Thus both groupings have been consistently rejectionist. Furthermore, both have departed from the accommodationist assumptions sketched above in another respect as well. The State of Israel, as the courts have determined, is not the state of its citizens. Rather, it is "the sovereign State of the Jewish people," where "the Jewish people consists not only of the people residing in Israel but also of the Jews in the Diaspora." Thus "there is no Israeli nation apart from the Jewish people," in this sense.[9] Almost one-sixth of the citizens of the State of Israel are not Jews.

The professed reason for the rejectionism of the two major political groupings is security, but from this fact we learn nothing, since every action of every state is justified in these terms. Nevertheless, there is no doubt that Israel faces a serious security problem. As the matter is posed and discussed in the United States, Israel's security problem is the paramount issue. This presupposed framework of discussion again reflects the profound racism of the American approach to the topic. Evidently, the indigenous population also has a "security problem"; in fact, the Palestinians have already suffered the catastrophe that Israelis justly fear. The familiar rhetoric concerning the issue only reveals more clearly the underlying racism. Thus it is argued that the Arabs already have twenty-two states, so the Palestinians have no valid claim to self-determination, no claim comparable to that of the European Jews who established the State of Israel in 1948; at a similar moral level, a fanatic anti-Semite could have argued in 1947 that there are, after all, many European states, and Palestinians of the Mosaic persuasion could settle there if they were not satisfied with minority status in an Arab region. Another argument is that there are numerous Palestinians in Jordan, even in the government, so *that* should be the Palestinian state—and by similar logic, the problem could be solved by settling Israeli Jews in New York, where there are many Jews, even the mayor and city officials, not to speak of their role in economic and cultural life. Or it is argued against the Palestinians that the Arab states have not supported their nationalist efforts, a stand that contrasts so markedly with the loving attitude that Europeans have shown toward one another during the centuries of state-formation there. Other familiar arguments are at about the same moral and intellectual level.

Dropping racist assumptions, there are two security problems to be dealt with. The international consensus in fact provides the most satisfactory, if quite imperfect, response to this dual problem in the contemporary period. In the unlikely event that it is realized, a major security problem will remain—namely, for the Palestinian state, confronted with one of the world's major military powers and dependent on the most conservative elements in the Arab world for survival. Whatever security problems Israel would then face do not compare with those it has been in the process of creating for itself by its commitment to expansionism and confrontation, which guarantees endless turmoil and war, and sooner or later, probable destruction.

Though Israel's security concerns—by now, in large part self-generated—are not to be dismissed, they do not provide an impressive basis for U.S.-Israeli rejectionism, even if we were to accept the familiar tacit assumption that the security of the Palestinians is of null import. In fact, there are other motives for Israel's rejectionism that appear to be more compelling. The territories provide Israel with a substantial unorganized labor force, similar to the "guest workers" in Europe or migrant workers in the United States. They now play a significant role in the Israeli economy, performing its "dirty work" at low pay and without rights (it might be noted that child labor among Arabs, particularly those from the occupied territories, has caused something of a scandal in Israel, though without affecting the practice, but not here). The process of proletarianization of Arab labor in the territories, in part through land restrictions, mimics what happened in Israel itself. Shai Feldman of the Center for Strategic Studies of Tel Aviv University comments accurately that "at present, important sectors of Israel's economy cannot function without manpower provided by the West Bank and the Gaza Strip," including tourism, construction, and to some extent, agriculture.[10]

The territories are also a controlled market for Israeli goods, with export sales of about $600 million per year according to the military

government. These sales are paid for in hard currency, since the territo-
ries in turn export about $100 million a year in agricultural products to
Jordan and the Gulf states and receive hard currencies from them from
various payments and remittances. Income to Israel from West Bank
tourism may amount to about $500 million, so that the potential loss to
Israel of abandoning the territories may come to over $1 billion per year.
Noting these facts, Thomas Stauffer of the Harvard Center of Middle East
Studies observed that there is a crucial difference between Israel's interest in these territories and in the Sinai, which had little economic value
once the oil fields had been returned.[11] In addition, there was of course
a major gain for Israel in the Sinai settlement, in that the most powerful
state in the Arab world was removed from the Arab-Israeli conflict, so
that Israel could pursue its programs in the occupied territories and
Lebanon without undue concern over any military deterrence. It is, then,
extremely misleading to think of the withdrawal from occupied Sinai as
providing any sort of precedent for the West Bank; as for the Gaza Strip
and the Golan Heights, they have been virtually excluded from the discussion of potential political settlement, within Israel or the United
States.

Furthermore, Israel is now heavily dependent on the West Bank for
water, a more significant commodity than oil in the Middle East. Its own
water supplies are exploited to the maximum limit, and it is now estimated that about one-third of Israel's water is from West Bank sources.[12] An Israeli technical expert writes that "cutting Judea and Samaria
[the West Bank, in Israeli parlance] off from the rest of the country" will
lead to serious consequences with regard to water management. "There
is no solution in sight for the water deficiency problem from the natural
water resources of the area," he writes, so that "the eventual solution
must be sought in the import of water from external, still unutilized
resources, and in brackish and seawater desalination on a large scale"
(which to date, has not proven feasible). The only unexploited source
nearby is the Litani River in southern Lebanon, which Israel has long
coveted and will sooner or later place under its control, quite probably,
if the United States supports Israel's steps to impose the political arrangements of its choice in southern Lebanon.[13]

One consequence of the Lebanon war was that Israel's national water
company took over "total control of the scarce and disputed water resources in the West Bank," an important move toward further integration
of the territories. Zvi Barel comments that the decision contradicts the
Camp David principle that control over water should fall under the autonomy provisions, and that knowledgeable sources attributed the decision
to political factors, not technical considerations as was claimed.[14] It may
be that this step was taken in defiance after the announcement of an

unwelcome U.S. "peace plan" on September 1, 1982, to which we return. It is, incidentally, noteworthy that the September 1982 U.S. peace plan makes special mention of Israel's rights to "fair safeguards" with regard to West Bank water, the only exception specifically noted to the "real authority" that is to be granted the Palestinian inhabitants.[15]

In the past, there has been considerable conflict over utilization of the waters of the Jordan and its tributaries, and it is likely that this will continue. One potential point of conflict has to do with the Yarmuk River, a tributary of the Jordan. The Israeli press reports that current Jordanian projects will decrease the flow of Yarmuk waters to the Jordan, where they are utilized by the Israeli water system. Chief of Staff Rafael Eitan "travelled yesterday along the border with Jordan near the Yarmuk, opposite the Jordanian water project. It was not possible to learn his reaction to the Jordanian project."[16] It is unlikely that Israel will permit such a project within Jordan on any significant scale.

While the two major political groupings, Labor and Likud, agree in their overall rejectionism, they do differ in the arrangements they prefer for the occupied territories. The Labor governments pursued what has been called the "Allon Plan," proposed by Minister Yigal Allon. Its basic principles were that Israel should maintain control of the Golan Heights, the Gaza Strip, parts of the eastern Sinai, and much of the West Bank including the Jordan Valley, a considerably expanded area around Jerusalem (Arab East Jerusalem was annexed outright by the Labor government over virtually unanimous international protest, including in this case the U.S.), and various corridors that would break up the Arab West Bank and ensure Israeli control over it. In his study of this period, Israeli journalist Amnon Kapeliouk writes that the Allon Plan was "rendered operational" in 1970, and envisioned the annexation of about one-third of the West Bank—actually about 40 percent. The centers of dense Arab settlement, however, would be excluded, with the population remaining under Jordanian control or stateless so as to avoid what is called "the demographic problem," that is, the problem of absorbing too many non-Jews within the Jewish state. To the present, this remains essentially the position of the Labor party. Thus former Prime Minister Rabin, interviewed in the Trilateral Commission journal in January 1983, states that "speaking for myself, I say now that we are ready to give back roughly 65% of the territory of the West Bank and the Gaza Strip where over 80% of the population now resides,"[17] a formulation that is less extreme than most. We return to other expressions of this unchanging commitment.

The Allon Plan was designed to enable Israel to maintain the advantages of the occupation while avoiding the problem of dealing with the domestic population. It was felt that there would be no major problem of administrative control or support by Western liberal opinion (an important matter for a state that survives largely on gifts and grants from the West) as long as the second-class Arab citizens remained a minority, though such problems might arise if their numbers approached half the population. As Anthony Lewis writes, actual annexation "will change the very nature of the Jewish state, incorporating within it a large, subservient and resentful Arab population"[18]—in contrast to the 15 percent minority of today, to which the same terms apply.

In contrast, Begin's Likud coalition has been moving toward extension of Israeli sovereignty over the West Bank and Gaza and has virtually annexed the Golan Heights, though it was willing to return the Sinai in full to Egypt—over strong objections from leading segments of the Labor party—in the context of the Camp David accords.* Like Labor, Likud also apparently intends to keep the Gaza Strip. Contrary to what is often assumed, Likud has not called for annexation of the West Bank and does not appear to be aiming for this, at least in the short run. Extension of Israeli sovereignty—the actual announced intent—is a more subtle device, which will allow Israel to take what it wants while confining the Arab population to ever narrower ghettoes, seeking ways to remove at least the leadership and possibly much of the population, apart from those needed as the beasts of burden for Israeli society. Outright annexation would raise the problem of citizenship for the Arabs, while extension of sovereignty, while achieving the purposes of annexation, will not, as long as liberal opinion in the West is willing to tolerate the fraud.

The logic of the Likud position does, however, appear to be that the Arab population must somehow be reduced, and it has been alleged that then Defense Minister Ariel Sharon "hopes to evict all Palestinians from the West Bank and Gaza and drive them into Jordan."[20] Sharon is not entirely alone in this view, though his position, if correctly reported, is extreme. The idea that the solution to the problem is for the Palestinians to leave—go far away—has deep roots in liberal and socialist Zionism, and has recently been reiterated by American "democratic socialists" as well as by Israeli leaders sometimes regarded as doves.

While the two major political groupings do differ in the ways in which they formulate their rejectionist positions, neither has been explicit about

---

*Former Prime Minister Golda Meir "assailed Prime Minister Begin's government yesterday, calling his peace plan 'a concrete, terrible danger' for Israel," and "accused" Begin of "agreeing to concessions she would never stand for"; "Labor Knesset Member [former Chief of Staff] Mordechai Gur today sharply opposed the continuation of the peace process with Egypt" on the grounds that Sadat would demand return to the 1967 borders. Many Labor leaders were particularly opposed to the return of the northeast Sinai settlements that they had established.[19]

the matter—which is easy enough to understand, given Israel's dependence on liberal opinion in the West—and it is therefore not easy to formulate this difference clearly. Thus as noted, while the policies of the Likud government have regularly been interpreted as leading to annexation by the Labor opposition and others, in fact, Begin calls for the establishment of Israeli "sovereignty" over the currently occupied territories. Under this Israeli sovereignty, those Arabs who remain would have some form of local autonomy. Presumably they and their descendants would not receive Israeli citizenship under this arrangement, so that the "demographic problem" would not arise. Or, perhaps, if their numbers are sufficiently restricted they might opt for either Israeli or Jordanian citizenship, while Israeli sovereignty remains in force over the entire territory in question. Surely it is intended by both Labor and Likud that the Jewish settlers will retain Israeli citizenship. Under the Labor Alignment plan, the inhabitants would be Jordanian citizens or stateless, but effectively under Israeli control.

In essence, then, the two programs are not very different. Their difference lies primarily in style. Labor is, basically, the party of the educated, Europe-oriented elite—managers, bureaucrats, intellectuals, etc. Its historical practice has been to "build facts" while maintaining a low-keyed rhetoric with conciliatory tones, at least in public. In private, the position has been that "it does not matter what the Gentiles say, what matters is what the Jews do" (Ben-Gurion) and that "the borders [of Israel] are where Jews live, not where there is a line on a map" (Golda Meir).[21] This has been an effective method for obtaining the ends sought without alienating Western opinion—indeed, while mobilizing Western (particularly American) support.

In contrast, the mass base of the Likud coalition is largely the underclass, the lower middle class, and the work force, the Sephardic population of Arab origin, along with religious-chauvinist elements, including many recent immigrants from the United States and the USSR; it also includes industrialists and many professionals. Its leadership is not so attuned to Western styles of discourse and has frequently been willing to flaunt its disregard for the hypocritical Gentile world, often in a manner regarded as openly insulting in the West, including the United States. For example, in response to Reagan's September 1982 call for a settlement freeze, the Likud leadership simply announced plans for ten new settlements while Begin sent a "Dear Ron" letter with a lesson on "simple historic truth."[22] Under somewhat similar circumstances in the past, Labor responded not by establishing new settlements but by "thickening" existing ones or by establishing military outposts which soon became settlements, meanwhile keeping to conciliatory rhetoric. The more devious Labor approach is much more welcome to the West, and raises fewer problems for "supporters of Israel."

In the case of Reagan's September 1982 proposals, Labor's response was one of qualified interest. In part, the reason was the traditional difference in style; in part, it reflected the fact that Reagan's proposals, while vague in essentials, could be interpreted as compatible with Labor's ideas in part, though they certainly were not consistent with the Likud demand for total "sovereignty." Furthermore, Labor's show of states-manlike interest might, it was hoped, strengthen its dismal electoral pros-pects by discrediting the government. Labor speaks of "territorial compromise" or "trading peace for territory," terms that have a pleasant sound to American ears, though the reality they disguise is not very different from Likud's "sovereignty." In fact, the "compromise" and "trade" are explicitly rejectionist positions. There have already been two "territorial compromises" in Mandatory Palestine: the 1947 U.N. Gen-eral Assembly resolution that recommended partitioning Palestine into a Palestinian and a Jewish state, and the 1949 armistice agreement that divided the Palestinian state, with about half annexed by Israel and the rest annexed by Jordan or administered by Egypt. A further "compro-mise," in terms of some version of the Allon Plan, simply eliminates the right of Palestinian self-determination.

It is often alleged that there was, in fact, an earlier "territorial compro-mise," namely, in 1922, when Transjordan was excised from the pro-mised "national home for the Jewish people." In fact, in 1922 "the Council of the League of Nations accepted a British proposal that Trans-jordan should be exempted from all clauses in the mandate providing for . . . the development of a Jewish National Home in Palestine," a decision that is difficult to criticize in the light of the fact that "the number of Jews living there permanently in 1921 has been reliably estimated at two, or according to some authorities, three persons."[23]

The Legacy of the Founding Fathers

Both political groupings, then, have been consistently rejectionist, willing to grant no national rights to the indigenous Arab population. Israel's consistent rejectionism is founded on the attitudes expressed by the long-time leader of the Labor party, David Ben-Gurion, when he stated that the Palestinian Arab shows no "emotional involvement" in this coun-try:

> Why should he? He is equally at ease whether in Jordan, Lebanon or a variety of places. They are as much his country as this is. And as little.[24]

Elsewhere, "Ben-Gurion followed Weizmann's line when he stated that: 'there is no conflict between Jewish and Palestinian nationalism because the Jewish Nation is not in Palestine and the Palestinians are not a nation'."[25] Essentially the same view was expressed by Moshe Dayan at a time when he was a principal spokesman for the Labor party. The cause of the Palestinians (which he professed to understand and appreciate) is "hopeless," he intimated, so they should establish themselves "in one of the Arab countries. . . . I do not think," he added, "that a Palestinian should have difficulties in regarding Jordan, Syria or Iraq as his homeland."[26] Like Ben-Gurion, Dayan was asserting that the Palestinians, including the peasantry, had no particular attachment to their homes, to the land where they had lived and worked for many generations, surely nothing like the attachment to the land of the Jews who had been exiled from it two thousand years ago.

Similar views were expressed by Prime Minister Golda Meir of the Labor party, much admired here as a grandmotherly humanitarian figure, in her remark that:

> It was not as though there was a Palestinian people in Palestine considering itself as a Palestinian people and we came and threw them out and took their country away from them. They did not exist.[27]

Elsewhere, she describes the Palestinian problem as merely an "invention of some Jews with distorted minds."[28]

In accordance with these dominant views concerning the Palestinians, an Israeli court ruled in 1969 that the Palestinians "are not a party to the conflict between Israel and the Arab States," and Foreign Minister Abba Eban of the Labor party (a well-known dove) insisted that the Palestinians "have no role to play" in any peace settlement,[29] a position that received no major challenge within the Labor party when it governed or in opposition. Simha Flapan concludes his study of this question with the observation that "the Palestinians were never regarded as an integral part of the country for whom long-term plans had to be made, either in the Mandatory period or since the establishment of the state." This was the most "lasting impact" of "Weizmann's legacy."[30] This appears to be quite a realistic judgment, as far as the mainstream of the Zionist movement was concerned.

These positions, which have been consistently maintained, amount to rejectionism in its clearest form, though the matter is rarely seen in this light in the United States. Both major political groupings in Israel have taken the position that Jordan is a Palestinian state, and that Israel will accept no third state between Israel and Jordan—the "Jordanian-Pales-

tinian Arab State" in the official words of the Labor party,[31] the "Palestinian State" in Likud rhetoric.

The Disguise

The consistent rejectionism of both major political groupings in Israel
is disguised in the United States by two main devices. First, as already noted, the concept of "rejectionism" is restricted to the denial of
Jewish national rights, on the implicit racist assumption that the indigenous inhabitants of Palestine do not have the human rights that
we naturally accord to Jews. Second, it is observed—quite accurately—
that Israel has always been more than willing to negotiate with the
Arab *states,* while those states have not reciprocated this willingness.
It requires barely a moment's thought to perceive that Israel's willingness in this regard is strictly rejectionist, since the Palestinians are excluded. When a framework for negotiations has been proposed that
includes the Palestinians, Israel has always refused to participate. Thus
Israel's apparently forthcoming position with regard to negotiations,
much heralded in the United States, is simply part and parcel of its
commitment to the rejection of Palestinian rights, an elementary point
that is regularly suppressed in discussion of the issue in the United States.
Like the term "territorial compromise," so also the appealing phrase
"negotiated settlement" has become a disguise for outright rejectionism
in American discourse.

When these simple points are understood, we can interpret properly
the pronouncements of Israel's American propagandists. For example,
the general counsel to the Anti-Defamation League of B'nai Brith, Arnold
Forster, condemns current U.S. government policy because he sees the
United States as insisting that an Israel-Lebanon peace must be part of
a more "comprehensive" settlement:

> Absurdly, the Israelis are made to appear dreadful simply because
> they ask of Lebanon open borders, tourism both ways, trade rela-
> tions, negotiations in their respective capitals[32] and regular political
> contacts—all the stuff of a healthy, peaceful relationship between
> countries. Our Government argues that if genuine peace is achieved
> only between Israel and Lebanon, the pressure would then be off
> the Jewish state to resolve the West Bank Palestinian problem along
> the lines of President Reagan's fading peace plan. Secretary Shultz's
> clever tactic is therefore to deny Israel the peace with Lebanon it

hungers for—unless Israel simultaneously withdraws from the West Bank.[33]

This argument will no doubt seem impressive to those who share the assumptions of this well-known civil rights group, specifically, the assumption that Palestinians do not have the same rights as Jews. Dropping these assumptions, we see at once that Israel's proposals, which Forster advocates, would simply take another long step toward the extension of Israeli sovereignty over the occupied territories. In short, Forster is simply presenting a brief for a "Greater Israel" and for the denial of elementary human rights to the Arabs of Palestine. Furthermore, the "healthy, peaceful relationship" that Israel seeks to impose on Lebanon by force would be one that subordinates Lebanon—at the very least, southern Lebanon—to Israeli interests, as a market for Israeli goods, a potential source of cheap labor and water, etc., a fact that is plain when we consider the relations of economic and military power and that was well on its way toward realization as Forster wrote. This "healthy, peaceful relationship," then, would be of the sort imposed by many other "peace-loving states" during the colonial era—for example, the relationship imposed on India by benevolent Britain (after the destruction of native Indian enterprise) or on China at the time of the Opium Wars, to mention two of many classic examples. All of this is so transparent that it might be surprising that the general counsel of an alleged human rights organization would be willing to make such statements publicly—until one recalls that this is the *New York Times,* with an audience of educated readers for whom the underlying racist assumptions are so firmly implanted that the obvious conclusions will generally not be drawn. As to whether Forster is correct in his belief that the U.S. government is really dropping its rejectionist stance, that is another matter; the increase in aid to Israel, passed by Congress at exactly that time, surely belies this assumption, as already noted.

The Population of the Occupied Territories

The third party to be considered is the population of the occupied territories, the Gaza Strip and the West Bank—the latter, called "Judea and Samaria" by both the Labor government and Likud, though the U.S. press regularly attributes this usage, which is taken to imply a biblically endorsed right of possession, to Menachem Begin.* In fact, reference to

---

*The same error is made by commentators who should know better, for example,

biblical rights is common in both political groupings. Thus Shimon Peres, the socialist leader of the Labor party, accepted Begin's rationale for retaining the West Bank, writing: "There is no argument in Israel about our historic rights in the land of Israel. The past is immutable and the Bible is the decisive document in determining the fate of our land." This doctrine apparently causes few raised eyebrows in the Socialist International, in which Peres and his Labor party are honored members.[35] Nevertheless, Peres advocates "territorial compromise" in accordance with the Allon Plan, to free Israel of an unwanted Arab population which "would eventually endanger the Jewish character of Israel. . . ."[36]

Attitudes under Occupation

The attitudes of the indigenous population are generally ignored in the United States, on the assumption—racist in essence—that they simply do not count. In the early years of the occupation, the Labor government refused to permit any independent political expression on the part of the population, even rejecting the request of pro-Jordanian "notables" to form an anti-PLO grouping, a fact revealed in 1974 by the former military commander of the West Bank, General (now president) Chaim Herzog (breaking government censorship), and arousing no concern among American liberals and democratic socialists, firm supporters of the Labor Alignment.[37]

In 1976, relatively free elections were permitted for municipalities in the West Bank. The elected candidates soon made it clear that they regarded the PLO as their sole legitimate representative. In recent years, the Begin government and others have attributed this outcome to PLO pressure and intimidation. No such claims were made at the time. On the contrary, the elections were regarded as a crowning achievement of the "benign occupation." There was, in fact, interference in the electoral process, namely, by Israel, in favor of more conservative elements. Two nationalist candidates were expelled in violation of the governing military regulations, to ensure the election of more acceptable opponents. The PLO took no position with regard to the elections, Amnon Kapeliouk

---

Rabbi Arthur Hertzberg, who describes the terms "Judea" and "Samaria" as those that "the Likud and its sympathizers prefer," in an interchange that exhausts the usual range of tolerable opinion: Hertzberg (with the assent of Irving Howe) representing the position of "Jewish moderates, headed by the Labor Party," and Ivan Novick, president of the Zionist Organization of America, representing the Likud position.[34]

observes in a detailed commentary on them.[38] He also points out that a significant political structure arose in the territories at the time, regarding the PLO as its representative and prepared to reach a political settlement with Israel. Instead of recognizing the Palestinian right to self-determination alongside of Israel, however, "the Rabin [Labor] government opened the door to Gush Emunim," the fanatic religious-chauvinist settlers in the occupied territories.

Since that time, the inhabitants of the occupied territories have made known their support for the PLO, and for an independent Palestinian state, on every possible occasion. To cite only two of many examples, the mayors of West Bank towns sent a letter to Secretary of State Cyrus Vance when he toured the area in 1977, stating that the Palestinian people had chosen as "its sole legal representative, irrespective of the place . . . the PLO under the leadership of Mr. Arafat,"[39] an act of no small courage given the nature of the occupation—people generally regarded as moderates had been expelled for much less. Turning to the present, after the PLO had been evacuated from Beirut in September 1982 (so that alleged PLO intimidation was now a thing of the past), a group of "Palestinian personalities" in the occupied territories were asked for their evaluation of the outlook, among them Elias Freij (the last remaining mayor of a major town, the others having been dismissed by Israel) and Rashad Shawa (the conservative and pro-Jordanian dismissed mayor of Gaza); Freij and Shawa are represented here as leading figures of the "moderate" nationalist alternative to the PLO. They were uniform, including Freij and Shawa, in their support for the PLO, some holding that support for the PLO had in fact increased as a result of the Lebanon invasion (Shawa).[40]

An indication of current opinion in the West Bank (no one doubts that the results would be similar in the Gaza Strip) is given by the results of a poll undertaken by the PORI Institute, a leading public opinion research organization in Israel, in March 1982.[41] The results will come as no surprise to people who have been following developments in the occupied territories since 1967.* Ninety-eight percent were in favor of an

---

*The actual wording of the questions is not given. Therefore, one does not know exactly how to interpret the *Time* paraphrase: "As might be expected, 98% of the respondents said that they favored the creation of a Palestinian state. Yet only 59% agree with the P.L.O. that such a state should encompass 'all of Palestine' (*i.e.*, including Israel); 27% seem ready to accept a Palestinian state made up only of the West Bank and Gaza Strip" (the actual PLO position, for several years). Surely, however, no sensible person can have much doubt that whatever the preferences of the population, as expressed in the Israeli poll, they would be more than willing to be relieved of Israeli or Jordanian occupation and to exercise their right of self-determination in an independent state—for the large majority

independent Palestinian state, and 86 percent said that they wanted this state to be run solely by the PLO. Of other figures, the most popular (68 percent support) was Nablus Mayor Bassam Shak'a, dismissed shortly before by West Bank "Civilian Administrator" Menachem Milson as part of his general attack on free political expression. Other pro-PLO figures on the West Bank received various degrees of support. At the very bottom was Mustafa Dudin, who received the support of 0.2 percent of the population. Among Arab leaders, King Hussein of Jordan ranked low, admired by 4 percent. King Hussein is the U.S. choice for representative of the inhabitants of the West Bank, while Dudin is the choice of the government of Israel and its supporters here. He is the head of the "Village Leagues" created by Israel in an effort to replace the elected leadership, and is claimed to represent the rural majority of the population—the "silent majority." He is regularly described in the United States press as a "moderate," and it is claimed that only PLO terror prevents the population from supporting him openly; evidently, fear of the PLO is so great that close to 100 percent of the population were afraid to state their support for Dudin secretly and anonymously in an Israeli-run poll.

The "Peace Process"

Also of interest were the attitudes expressed toward the two Israeli political groupings: 0.9 percent preferred to see Begin's Likud in power, while 2 percent preferred the Labor Party; 93 percent registered complete indifference. As for Camp David, 2 percent felt it helped the Palestinian cause, while 88 percent regarded it as a hindrance.

In news reporting as in editorial commentary in the United States, the arrangements set in motion by the Camp David accords are known simply as "the peace process." Evidently those whose lives are at stake do not share the assumptions that underlie this usage, which simply reflects a tacit acceptance of the U.S. propaganda system by the media and scholarship.

It is also quite likely that the inhabitants of the occupied territories understand some facts about "the peace process" that are little noted here. Specifically it is plain, on the ground, that the government of Israel never had the slightest intention of joining "the peace process" in anything other than a rhetorical sense, beyond the Sinai agreements, which had the merit of giving Israel a free hand elsewhere by effectively excluding Egypt from the conflict. Not only is this obvious from the settlement·

---

of them, a state organized by the PLO—set up alongside of Israel and coexisting with it.

program and the internal repression, but it is even clear from the official record, a fact that Abba Eban has pointed out. He cites the official "Government policy guidelines" adopted by the Knesset (by a single vote), which state that "after the transition period laid down in the Camp David accords, Israel will raise its claim and *will act to fulfill its rights* to sovereignty over Judea, Samaria and the Gaza district" (Eban's italics). "There is no resource of language," he notes, "that can possibly bridge the gulf" between this decision and the Camp David accords, which leaves the status of the territories to be determined after the transition period by negotiations between Israel, Jordan, Egypt, and elected representatives of the inhabitants of the territories, not by Israeli actions. Eban states that he is unable to find any precedent "in the jurisprudence of any government for such a total contradiction between an international engagement and a national statement of policy." Surely an exaggeration,* but nevertheless an understandable reaction to the immediate announcement by the government of Israel that it intended to disregard the Camp David accords, to which it pledges (and demands of others) total fidelity.[42]

The poll results reflect the attitudes of those who have learned about the occupation, as conducted by the Labor party and then Likud, from their own lives. They are deprived of *New York Times* editorials, and therefore—as their low regard for the Labor party indicates—they are unaware that under the Labor party the occupation was a "model of future cooperation" and a "nine-year experiment in Arab-Israeli coexistence," or that the Labor party in 1980 "has taken a giant step toward compromise with the West Bank Palestinians and thus challenged the Arab world to reciprocate with acts of restraint and conciliation"[43]; the "giant step" was a reiteration, once again, of the rejectionist Allon Plan put into effect by the Labor party ten years earlier.

The Arab States and the PLO

We have reviewed the international consensus and the positions of the United States, Israel, and the Palestinians in the occupied territories.

---

*To mention only one obvious case, consider the statement of U.S. government policy by Kissinger and Nixon in January 1973 as they announced the signing of the Paris peace agreements concerning Vietnam, adding in the clearest and most explicit terms that the United States intended to violate every obligation to which it had just committed itself. For details concerning the facts, the consequences, and the U.S. reactions, see *Towards a New Cold War* (henceforth referred to as *TNCW*), chap. 3.

What about the Arab states and the PLO? The historical record is rather different from what is generally believed in the United States.

The Erosion of Rejectionism and the U.S.-Israeli Response

In the immediate post-1967 period, the Arab states and the PLO took a rejectionist position comparable to the stand that has been consistently maintained by Israel and the United States. Not long after, this rejectionism began to erode. In February 1970, President Nasser of Egypt declared that "it will be possible to institute a durable peace between Israel and the Arab states, not excluding economic and diplomatic relations, if Israel evacuates the occupied territories and accepts a settlement of the problem of the Palestinian refugees." Amnon Kapeliouk observes that "this declaration received no response at the time in Israel."[44] Note that settlement of the refugee problem within the context of a negotiated peace has been the official position of the United States, along with virtually the entire world apart from Israel, since 1949, and is regularly endorsed in U.N. resolutions. Note also that Nasser made no reference to a Palestinian state, in accordance with the international consensus of the time. Nasser also "accepted the [Secretary of State William] Rogers [June 1970] proposals for a cease-fire and subsequent negotiations," a "brave and constructive step" in the words of Zionist historian Jon Kimche.[45]

After Nasser's death, the new president, Anwar Sadat, moved at once to implement two policies: peace with Israel and conversion of Egypt to an American client state. In February 1971, he offered Israel a full peace treaty on the pre-June 1967 borders, with security guarantees, recognized borders, and so on. This offer caused much distress in Israel (it caused "panic," in the words of the well-known Israeli writer Amos Elon),[46] and was promptly rejected with the statement that Israel would not return to the internationally recognized pre-1967 borders. Note that Sadat's offer of February 1971 was more favorable to Israel than what he proposed in November 1977 on the trip to Jerusalem that officially established him as "a man of peace," since he made no mention of Palestinian rights, allegedly the stumbling block in the Camp David "peace process." Sadat's offer was in line with the international consensus of the period, in particular, with the Rogers Plan, which had been angrily rejected by Israel.[47] In internal discussion in Israel, Labor party doves recognized that a peace settlement was within reach, but recommended against it on the grounds that territorial gains would be possible if they held out.[48]

Israel's only reaction to Sadat's offer, apart from the immediate flat rejection, was to increase settlement in the occupied territories. On the same day that Sadat's offer was officially rejected, the Labor government authorized plans for settlement in the hills surrounding the Arab portion of Jerusalem, well beyond the earlier borders of the city, as part of the process of "thickening Jerusalem." Noting this fact, Edward Witten comments on the similarity to Begin's response to the Reagan plan in 1982: new settlements in response to a request for a settlement freeze. Witten also points out that Sadat clearly expressed his desire for "coexistence" with Israel at the same time in a *Newsweek* interview, and that Foreign Minister Abdullah Salah of Jordan announced that Jordan, too, was ready to recognize Israel, if it returned to the internationally recognized pre-June 1967 borders (February 23, 1971). There appears to have been no Israeli response.[49] In 1972, Israel's Labor government angrily rejected the proposal of King Hussein of Jordan to establish a confederation of Jordan and the West Bank (again, a rejectionist position, denying Palestinian national rights). In response, the Israeli Knesset "determined," for the first time officially, "that the historic right of the Jewish people to the Land of Israel [including the West Bank] is beyond challenge," while Prime Minister Golda Meir stated that "Israel will continue to pursue her enlightened policy in Judea and Samaria. . . ." Her political adviser Israel Galili, who was in charge of settlement in the occupied territories, stated that the Jordan River should become Israel's "agreed border—a frontier, not just a security border," the latter term implying the possibility of some form of self-government, however limited, for the indigenous population.[50]

Returning to Sadat's February 1971 offer of a full peace treaty, Israel was backed in its rejection by the United States. Unfortunately for Sadat, his efforts came just at the time when Israel had established in Washington its thesis that it was a "strategic asset" for the United States. Kissinger assumed that Israel's power was unchallengeable, and takes considerable pride, in his memoirs, in his steadfastness in blocking the efforts of his primary enemy—the State Department—toward some peaceful resolution of the conflict. His aim, he writes, "was to produce a stalemate until Moscow urged compromise or until, even better, some moderate Arab regime decided that the route to progress was through Washington. . . . Until some Arab state showed a willingness to separate from the Soviets, or the Soviets were prepared to dissociate from the maximum Arab program, we had no reason to modify our policy" of stalemate, in opposition to the State Department.[51]

Kissinger's account is remarkable for its ignorance and geopolitical fantasies, even by Kissingerian standards.* Sadat had explicitly decided that "the route to progress was through Washington," joining Saudi Arabia and others (even when Sadat expelled Soviet advisers in 1972,

Kissinger did not see the light). Saudi Arabia was not only willing "to separate from the Soviets" but in fact did not even have diplomatic relations with them. The USSR backed the international consensus including the existence of Israel within recognized (pre-June 1967) borders and with security guarantees.[52]

Apparently under Kissinger's influence, the Nixon administration decided to suspend State Department efforts aimed at a peaceful settlement in accordance with the international consensus and the explicit proposals of Egypt. An envoy was sent to a conference of U.S. ambassadors in the Mideast to announce the suspension of these efforts. "To a man, the U.S. ambassadors replied that if the countries in the Mideast concluded that the process itself had ended, there would be a disastrous war."[53] Sadat also repeatedly warned that he would be forced to resort to war if his efforts at a peaceful settlement were rebuffed, but he was dismissed with contempt, apparently because of the widespread belief in Israel's military supremacy. Warnings from American oil companies operating in the Arabian peninsula concerning threats to U.S. interests were also disregarded.[54] Nahum Goldmann, long a leading figure in the Zionist movement, observed that Sadat had conducted a "daring" policy by "declaring himself ready to recognize Israel, despite the opposition," and that "if he cannot show that he can obtain results, the army will be compelled to launch a war." Israel listened no more than Kissinger did, and on the same assumptions. After Israel shot down 13 Syrian planes with one Israeli plane lost in September 1973, the editor of one major Israeli journal wrote: "This battle will remind our Arab neighbors that they cannot manage their affairs without taking into consideration who is the true master of this region."[55]

In October 1973, Sadat made good his threat. As a group of Israeli and American-Israeli scholars observe, "After the Egyptian Ra'is [Sadat] had realized that all diplomatic efforts would lead to a dead end, he decided to try a limited military option which, combined with an oil embargo, would lead to a significant Israeli withdrawal from Arab territories."[56] To

---

*Kissinger's inability to comprehend what was happening in the Middle East was almost monumental in its proportions. The second volume of his memoirs extends the story. See the review by James E. Akins (U.S. ambassador to Saudi Arabia from 1973 to 1976), who argues that "the truly tragic consequence of Watergate is that President Nixon was not in a strong enough position to dominate his secretary of state. Weakened and distracted by domestic issues, he allowed Kissinger to frustrate his own Middle East design. Had it not been for Watergate, it is possible, even probable, that Nixon would have achieved a just and lasting peace in the area and that the world would be much safer today." See note 51.

the great surprise of Israel, the United States, and virtually everyone else, Egypt and Syria were remarkably successful in the early stages of the war and Saudi Arabia was compelled (reluctantly, it seems) to join in an oil boycott, the first major use of the "oil weapon," a move with considerable long-term implications in international affairs. Primary responsibility for these developments is attributable to Henry Kissinger's ignorance and blind reliance on force.

At that point, U.S. policy shifted, reflecting the understanding that Egypt and the oil-producing states could not be so easily dismissed or controlled. Kissinger undertook his shuttle diplomacy and other diplomatic efforts. Concealed behind the razzle-dazzle was the easily discernible intent, now surely clear in retrospect even to those who could not perceive it at the time, to accept Egypt as a U.S. client state while effectively removing it from the Middle East conflict with a Sinai agreement. Then Israel would be free to continue its policies of integrating the occupied territories—and to concentrate its forces for war on the northern border without concern for the major Arab military force, as when Israel invaded Lebanon in 1978 and again in 1982.

Egypt continued to press for a full-scale peace settlement, now joined by other Arab states. In January 1976, the United States was compelled to veto a U.N. Security Council resolution calling for a settlement in terms of the international consensus, which now included a Palestinian state alongside of Israel. The resolution called for a settlement on the 1967 borders, with "appropriate arrangements . . . to guarantee . . . the sovereignty, territorial integrity and political independence of all states in the area and their right to live in peace within secure and recognized boundaries," including Israel and a new Palestinian state in the occupied territories. The resolution was backed by the "confrontation states" (Egypt, Syria, Jordan), the PLO, and the USSR. President Chaim Herzog, who was Israel's U.N. ambassador at the time, writes that the PLO not only backed this peace plan but in fact "prepared" it; the PLO then condemned "the tyranny of the veto" (in the words of the PLO representative) by which the United States blocked this important effort to bring about a peaceful two-state settlement. The occasion for Herzog's remarks was the Saudi Arabian peace proposal that had just been announced, which Israel was right to reject, Herzog asserts, just as it correctly rejected the "more moderate" PLO plan of January 1976. According to Herzog, the "real author" of the 1981 Saudi Arabian (Fahd) peace plan was also the PLO, who never seem to cease their machinations.[57]

Israel refused to attend the January 1976 Security Council session, which had been called at Syrian initiative. The Rabin government—a Labor party government regarded as dovish—announced that it would not negotiate with any Palestinians on any political issue and would not negotiate with the PLO even if the latter were to renounce terrorism and recognize Israel, thus adopting a position comparable to that of the minority Rejection Front within the PLO.[58] The main elements of the PLO had been moving toward acceptance of a two-state settlement, and continued to do so, at times with various ambiguities, at times quite clearly, as in this case.

The Arab states and the PLO continued to press for a two-state settlement, and Israel continued to react with alarm and rejection. In November 1976, the *Jerusalem Post* noted that Egyptian Prime Minister Ismail Fahmy had offered four conditions for a Middle East peace settlement: "Israel's withdrawal to the pre-1967 war frontiers; the establishment of a Palestinian state in the West Bank and the Gaza Strip; the ban on nuclear weapons in the region; and the inspection of nuclear installations in the area." It noted further President Sadat's statement to a group of U.S. senators "that he was prepared to sign a peace treaty with Israel if it withdrew from all Arab territories captured in the 1967 war, and if a Palestinian state was created on the West Bank and in the Gaza Strip." The Labor party journal *Davar* quoted Prime Minister Rabin's response to this disturbing "peace offensive":

> But there is nothing new in all of this, in the objectives that the Arabs wish to obtain, stressed the Prime Minister when recalling that back in 1971 Sadat told Dr. Jarring of his willingness to reach a peace settlement as he understood it. On the contrary, he has even made the conditions harder, since then, as opposed to now, he did not link an Israeli-Egyptian agreement with agreements with other Arab countries and did not raise, in such a pronounced manner [in fact, at all], his demand for a Palestinian state in the West Bank and the Gaza Strip.[59]

Thus no Israeli reaction was in order.

The following year, Egypt, Syria, and Jordan "informed the United States that they would sign peace treaties with Israel as part of an overall Middle East settlement."[60] The Palestinian National Council, the governing body of the PLO, issued a declaration on March 20, 1977, calling for the establishment of "an independent national state" in Palestine— rather than a secular democratic state *of* Palestine—and authorizing Palestinian attendance at an Arab-Israeli peace conference. Prime Minister Rabin of Israel responded "that the only place the Israelis could meet the Palestinian guerrillas was on the field of battle."[61] The same session of the National Council elected a new PLO Executive Committee excluding representatives of the Rejection Front.[62]

Shortly after, the PLO leaked a "peace plan" in Beirut which stated that the famous Palestinian National Covenant would not serve as the basis for relations between Israel and a Palestinian state, just as the founding principles of the World Zionist Organization were not understood as the basis for interstate relations, and that any evolution beyond a two-state settlement "would be achieved by peaceful means."[63]

Supporters of Israel have long treasured the Covenant as the last line of defense for their rejectionism when all else fails. Israeli doves, in contrast, have always dismissed this last-ditch effort. For example, Elie Eliachar, former president of the Council of the Sephardic Community in Israel and the first person from Jerusalem to represent it at the Zionist congresses, made the following statement in a lecture at the Hebrew University in 1980:

> On the basis of personal contacts I have had with leaders of the PLO, in London and elsewhere [in] meetings that were held openly, and that interested people know all about, I can say categorically that the idea that the PLO covenant is an obstacle to negotiations is utter nonsense. . . . There is no Arab organization in existence today which can bring about a durable peace in our region, except the PLO, including its extremist factions.

Mattityahu Peled, asked why the PLO does not abandon the Covenant, responded:

> For the same reason that the Government of Israel has never renounced the decisions of the Basle Zionist Congress, which supported the establishment of a Jewish state in the historic land of Israel—including Transjordan. No political body would do this. Similarly Herut and the Irgun [its terrorist forerunner] never abandoned their map [which includes Transjordan, contemporary Jordan; the official slogan of Begin's Herut Party still calls for an Israel on both banks of the Jordan]. We demand a ritual abandonment of the Covenant—a kind of ceremony of humiliation—instead of concerning ourselves with the decisions that were accepted by the PLO from 1974, which support the establishment of a Palestinian state in the territories evacuated by Israel.

It is, in fact, interesting to see how Israeli propoganda has focused on the Covenant with increasing intensity as it is deemphasized by the PLO in favor of subsequent resolutions which drastically modify its terms, for reasons that are hardly obscure.[64] We should note that the Covenant holds a rejectionist view comparable to that of the Labor party and Likud.

A few months after releasing the 1977 peace plan, the PLO endorsed the Soviet-American statement of October 1977, which called for the "termination of the state of war and establishment of normal peaceful relations" between Israel and its neighbors, as well as for internationally guaranteed borders and demilitarized zones to enhance security. "The United States had, however, quickly backed away from the joint statement under Israeli protest," Seth Tillman observes, adding that "without exception," proposals for superpower collaboration to bring about a settlement and to guarantee it "have been shot down by Israeli leaders and supporters of Israel in the United States, who have perceived in them the bugbear of an 'imposed' settlement"—that is to say, a settlement that is unacceptable (otherwise, no sane person would care whether it was "imposed" or not) because it departs from their rejectionist principles. There were "a few dissenters from the prevailing consensus," Tillman points out, among them Nahum Goldmann, who described the Soviet-American agreement of October 1977 as "a piece of real statesmanship," adding that "it is regrettable that Israel's opposition and that of the pro-Israel lobby in America rendered the agreement ineffective" (Goldmann's words), another piece in the familiar pattern.[65]

Sadat's Trip to Jerusalem and the Rewriting of History

The failure of many such efforts as these led Sadat to undertake his November 1977 trip to Jerusalem, motivated by a desire to convene a Geneva conference of major powers to settle the conflict, according to Hermann Eilts, who was U.S. ambassador to Egypt at the time.[66] It is also likely that Sadat was motivated by concern over the escalating conflict across the Israel-Lebanon border, initiated by Israeli-Maronite bombing of Nabatiya and culminating in Israeli air raids that killed some seventy people, mostly Lebanese.[67]

The United States has generally been opposed to a Geneva conference, which would include the USSR and the European powers. As Kissinger had explained, his diplomatic efforts were designed "to keep the Soviets out of the diplomatic arena" and "to ensure that the Europeans and Japanese did not get involved in the diplomacy" concerning the Middle East, where the U.S. role is to remain predominant. Israel has also consistently opposed the idea, adamantly so if the PLO participates. The reason was explained by Prime Minister Rabin of the Labor party after the Knesset had approved a resolution to this effect. If Israel agrees to negotiate "with any Palestinian element," he stated, this will provide "a basis for the possibility of creating a third state between Israel and Jordan."

But Israel will never accept such a state: "I repeat firmly, clearly, categorically: it will not be created."[68] The Labor party's rejection of the right of the Palestinians to any meaningful form of self-determination has been consistent and exceptionless.

Sadat's dramatic visit to Jerusalem did not open the way to negotiations for a comprehensive political settlement involving true accommodation in the sense of the earlier discussion and the international consensus. Rather, the resulting Camp David "peace process," as the U.S. government and the press designate it, consummated Kissinger's earlier efforts. Egypt has, temporarily at least, been incorporated within the U.S. system and excluded from the Arab-Israeli conflict, allowing Israel to continue its creeping takeover of the occupied territories, apart from the Sinai, now returned to Egypt and serving as a buffer zone. Diplomatic efforts remain largely in the hands of the United States, excluding both the USSR and the rivals/allies of Europe and Japan.

From 1977, the Begin government rapidly extended land expropriation and settlement in the occupied territories while instituting a considerably more brutal repression there, particularly from the fall of 1981, with the Milson-Sharon administration. The U.S. government signaled its approval by increasing the massive aid which, in effect, funded these projects—while also emitting occasional peeps of protest. As noted earlier, the Begin government indicated from the start its rejection of the "peace process," so it is not surprising that it moved at once to "fulfill its rights to sovereignty" by large-scale development projects designed to ensure that the West Bank could not be separated from Israel.

Evidently the actual historical record—here briefly reviewed up to Sadat's November 1977 trip to Jerusalem—is not exactly in accord with the familiar picture of U.S.-Israel-Arab diplomatic interactions in this period. The preferred story is one of Arab intransigence and U.S.-Israeli efforts at accommodation. Sadat, for example, is regularly portrayed as a typical Arab warmonger who tried to destroy Israel by force in 1973, then learned the error of his ways and became a man of peace under the kindly tutelage of Henry Kissinger and Jimmy Carter. As the *New Republic* puts the matter, Sadat's "decision to make peace" came *after* the 1973 war: "Finally, after the enormous destructiveness of the 1973 war, Anwar Sadat realized that the time had come to replace the conflict of war with law and rights."[69] The other Arabs—particularly the PLO—persist in their evil ways.* Endless references can be cited from the press to illustrate this version of history.[70]

---

*The *New Republic* goes on to explain that one of the great achievements of the Israeli war in Lebanon is that the destruction of the PLO and "its elimination as

To reconcile the actual history with the preferred picture has been a relatively simple matter. It has only been necessary to resort to Orwell's useful memory hole. The historical record has been so effectively sanitized that even as well-informed a person as Harold Saunders (former assistant secretary of state for Near Eastern and South Asian affairs) can write that "as long as no Arab government but Egypt would make peace, Israel saw no alternative to maintaining its security by the force of its own arms."[71]

Sadat's pre-1977 peace efforts have been conveniently expunged from the record, like the January 1976 Security Council resolution and much else. In Israel and Egypt, Sadat's 1971 offer is described as his "famous" attempt to establish a genuine peace with Israel.[72] Similarly, Amnon Kapeliouk describes Sadat's expression of willingness "to enter into a peace agreement with Israel" (the words of the official English text of Israel's recognition of Sadat's offer) as a "historic event in Israel-Arab relations."[73]

Consider, in contrast, the two-page encomium to Sadat by Eric Pace, Middle East specialist of the *New York Times,* after Sadat's assassination.[74] There is no mention here of the real history, as briefly sketched above; indeed, in the *New York Times* version, the well-documented facts are explicitly denied. Thus referring to Sadat's trip to Jerusalem in 1977, Pace writes:

> Reversing Egypt's longstanding policy, he proclaimed his willingness to accept Israel's existence as a sovereign state. Then, where so many Middle East negotiators had failed, he succeeded, along with Presidents Carter and Reagan and Prime Minister Menachem Begin of Israel, in keeping the improbable rapprochement alive.

An elegant example of what has sometimes been called "historical engineering,"[75] that is, redesigning the facts of history in the interests of established power and ideology, a crime of which we justly accuse our enemies.

---

an independent *political* force [will] allow those on the Arab side who have no designs on Haifa or Tel Aviv to negotiate free from intimidation" (my italics). Prior to 1982, this leading journal of American liberalism would have us believe, no Arabs were "allowed" to consider a settlement that would include the existence of Israel. Compare the record sampled here.

THE CONTINUING THREAT OF PEACE

The well-known Israeli writer Amos Elon has written of the "panic and unease among our political leadership" caused by Arab peace proposals. "The most extreme instance," he adds, "though not the only one, was in early 1971, when Sadat threw Israel off balance with his announcement, for the first time, that he was willing to enter into a peace agreement with Israel, and to respect its independence and sovereignty in 'secure and recognized borders.' " Elon describes the harshly negative reaction of the government, the silence of most of the press, and the convoluted efforts of most Orientalists to prove that Sadat's offer did not mean what it said—rather like Mark Helprin's insight into the devious "verbal trick" of the Arabs when they speak of a settlement in which the occupied territories will be turned over to their inhabitants.[76] The occasion for Elon's article was the "emotional and angry" reaction of the government to the just announced Saudi (Fahd) peace plan of August 1981, a response which he found "shocking, frightening, if not downright despair-producing."*

Elon had good reason for his despair. The Labor party journal *Davar* found Israel's reaction—including military flights over Saudi Arabia—to be so "irrational" as to cause foreign intelligence services to be concerned over Israeli bombing of Saudi oil fields.[78] Another well-known journalist described "the frightened, almost hysterical response of the Israeli government to the Saudi plan" as "a grave mistake," adding that if the PLO offered to negotiate with Israel, "the government would undoubtedly declare a national day of mourning."[79] In fact, the PLO had repeatedly expressed a willingness to accept a negotiated settlement and to participate in general peace negotiations, but no call for a day of mourning was necessary, since the denial of the facts was still effectively in force.

A few months later, in February 1982, Uri Avneri criticized a similar Israeli reaction to a Syrian proposal calling for "termination of the state of war between the Arabs and Israel . . ." along with confirmation of the right of the Palestinians to an independent state alongside of Israel in the

---

*Israeli Foreign Minister Yitzhak Shamir stated that "even the suggestion of Saudi recognition of Israel is not new."[77] The Saudi plan called for a two-state settlement on the 1967 borders, with recognition of the right of all states in the region to exist in peace. It should be noted that many Labor leaders denounced the Saudi peace plan, e.g., Chaim Herzog, who warned that it was prepared by the PLO (see p. 394), and party chairman Shimon Peres, who "remarked today that the Saudi peace proposal threatened Israel's very existence" (*Ha'aretz*, August 10, 1981; *Israeli Mirror*).

occupied territories.[80] B. Michael made a similar observation in *Ha'aretz.*
Noting the immediate efforts to dismiss the statement of the Syrian minister of information that a peace agreement would be possible if Israel were
to withdraw to its 1967 borders, he commented sardonically that "we
must therefore be careful not to underestimate the danger posed by the
Syrian plot, and we must do our best to kill it while it is still small."[81]

In the same month (February 1982), Saudi Arabia's state radio twice
"called for direct peace negotiations between the Arabs and Israel, on
condition that Israel recognize the PLO as the negotiating partner."
These initiatives, too, were ignored, as was a subsequent Iraqi initiative.[82]

Israeli propaganda beamed to an American audience, however, regularly speaks of the willingness of "socialist Zionism" to make peace if
only some Arab leader would show some sign that Israel may exist in
the region,[83] ignoring—in fact, denying—the actual extreme rejectionism of mainstream socialist Zionism and the halting and sometimes ambiguous steps of the PLO and the Arab states over the past years
toward a political settlement, which, whatever one thinks of them,
clearly go far beyond anything that the Israeli Labor party has been
willing to consider and in fact go beyond what the Israeli "Peace Now"
group has proposed. American commentators are still more extreme in
their rejection of the historical record, as in the sample of cases cited.
In earlier years, the PLO was no less rejectionist than Israel, and its call
for a "democratic secular state" was not what it appeared to be on the
surface (see *TNCW,* p. 430). But it simply cannot be denied that from
the mid-1970s the PLO has moved increasingly toward an accommodationist position. While concealing this record, propagandists search
desperately for statements by PLO spokesmen that reveal their unremitting hostility to Israel and unwillingness to accept it. Israeli doves
have regarded such efforts with contempt, pointing out that the same
logic would lead to the conclusion that no one should have any dealings
with the Zionist movement or the State of Israel, since its leaders have
consistently rejected any Palestinian rights and have repeatedly indicated that they regard any political settlement as a temporary stage
leading to further expansion. What is more, they have acted on these
principles. We return to the record, which is not without interest and is
generally concealed here. That outright propagandists should resort to
these deceptive practices is not very surprising; that, after all, is their
vocation. It is more interesting that the practice is common across a
broad spectrum of Western opinion, particularly in the United States,
as one aspect of the ideological support for Israel.

There have been other examples of missed chances, before and since.
Mattityahu Peled alleges that "a historic opportunity was missed to start
a dialogue between Israel and the PLO" in 1976, when plans were de-

vised for mutual conciliatory gestures, leading to further peaceful contacts. He states that the plan collapsed because of Israeli military actions in Lebanon. Just at the time when Arafat was scheduled to make a conciliatory statement, as part of the plan, the Israeli navy began capturing boats belonging to Lebanese Moslems, turning the passengers over to Israel's Lebanese Christian allies, who then killed them.[84]

In the light of American beliefs about the history of terrorism, it should perhaps be observed that along with acts of piracy such as these, Israel has also resorted to hijacking airplanes, and may indeed have initiated this practice. In December 1954, a Syrian civilian airliner was captured by Israeli military aircraft to obtain hostages for exchange with Israeli soldiers who had been captured within Syria. The prime minister of Israel, Moshe Sharett, states in his diary that he was informed by the State Department that "our action was without precedent in the history of international practice." Note that this Israeli action is a direct precedent for much later PLO actions to capture hostages for exchange with captured guerrillas, as in the major terrorist incidents that were widely and properly denounced in the West—at Ma'alot in 1974, for example.[85]

Returning to PLO initatives, by the late 1970s, Seth Tillman concludes, "the evidence seemed persuasive . . . that Arafat and al-Fatah [the PLO mainstream] were prepared to make peace on the basis of the West Bank–Gaza state and to accept Israel within its approximate borders of 1967," though not to "concede the moral legitimacy of Israel." In November 1978, requesting a dialogue with the United States in a discussion with Representative Paul Findley, "Arafat issued the following statement: 'The PLO will accept an independent Palestinian state consisting of the West Bank and Gaza, with connecting corridor, and in that circumstance will renounce any and all violent means to enlarge the territory of that state. I would reserve the right, of course, to use nonviolent means, that is to say, diplomatic and democratic means, to bring about the eventual unification of all of Palestine.' " Tillman reports further that he promised: "We will give de facto recognition to the State of Israel." Neither these statements, nor others of a similar nature that were conveyed directly to the State Department, "elicited a response from the Carter administration."[86]

In its April 1981 session, the PLO National Council unanimously passed a resolution endorsing a February proposal of Soviet President Brezhnev for peace in the Middle East in which Brezhnev—in accordance with what has been consistent Soviet policy—enunciated the following principles:

> The inalienable rights of the Arab people of Palestine must be secured up to, and including, the establishment of their own state.

It is essential to ensure the security and sovereignty of all states of the region including those of Israel. These are the basic principles.[87]

Citing the unanimous PLO endorsement of the Brezhnev proposal at a Paris press conference on July 14, 1982, Issam Sartawi of the PLO National Council* stated that

from this it follows that the PLO has formally conceded to Israel, in the most unequivocal manner, the right to exist on a reciprocal basis. This eliminates automatically the obstacle placed by Secretary of State Kissinger in the way of U.S. recognition of the PLO and the establishment of U.S.-PLO dialogue.

See page 373. The statement was welcomed by the British and French governments (with qualifications in the former case) as a recognition of the right of Israel to exist on a reciprocal basis. A joint communiqué issued by Sartawi and Mattityahu Peled on July 20 noted that "the PLO has made its willingness to accept and recognize the state of Israel on the basis of mutual recognition of each nation's legitimate right of self-determination crystal clear in various resolutions since 1977."[88]

---

*On April 10, 1983, Sartawi was assassinated at a meeting of the Socialist International in Portugal. Responsibility for the assassination was announced by the Abu Nidal group, which has been at war with the PLO for a decade. In October 1973 Abu Nidal was condemned to death by a Fatah military tribunal. He is assumed to have been responsible for the assassination of several PLO figures in Europe, among them the leading PLO moderate Said Hammami in London in 1978, Naim Khader in Brussels in 1981, and others, and also for murderous attacks on synagogues and Jewish establishments in Vienna and probably in France. He was also responsible for the attempted assassination of Israeli Ambassador Shlomo Argov in London in June 1982, the event that sparked the Israeli invasion of Lebanon. In an effort to piece together his murky and bloody history, Philippe Boggio describes him as "a dangerous fomentor of antagonisms, an expert agitator who can do a better job than any army of demolishing the PLO's naturally ambiguous relations with a good part of the world," and whose activities have consistently been directed to undermining PLO efforts from the early 1970s "to get all its factions to abandon the terrorist tactics discrediting the organisation." The PLO has charged that he is an Israeli agent, noting that his operations "frequently serve Israeli interests indirectly," a charge that is "one of the assumptions you bear in mind" according to a French secret service specialist. It is generally assumed that he is supported by Iraq, sometimes Syria, where his offices are located and where he appears to have access to considerable funding. (Philippe Boggio, *Le Monde*, October 13, 14, 1982; *Manchester Guardian Weekly*, Oct. 31, 1982.)

One might argue that this exaggerates the clarity of these declarations, but there is no doubt about the general drift of policy of the PLO and the Arab states, the "panic" that this has regularly inspired in Israel, and the reaction of dismissal or simply denial of the facts in the United States.

To cite one last example, *Ha'aretz* published an interview with Shafiq el-Hout, official PLO spokesman in Beirut, who stated that "the PLO is prepared to offer peace to Israel on the condition that the Israelis will obey the UN resolutions and will recognize the national rights of the Palestinian people. . . . We are prepared to participate in any official effort aimed at bringing a just and comprehensive peace settlement in the Middle East."[89] Again, perhaps not what Israel is prepared to accept, but hardly consistent with the incessant charge that the PLO is adamant in its refusal to accept the existence of Israel on any terms, that "the backbone of its existence is the philosophy of destruction of Israel, and the road to this is the use of terror" (Yitzhak Rabin).[90]

The concern over evidence of Arab moderation, illustrated repeatedly above, can be traced to the early days of the Zionist movement. Simha Flapan discusses "Weizmann's opposition to negotiations with the Palestinians themselves for a political solution" from the early 1920s, and his concern that the Arabs might be "moderate enough to be likely to agree to [a constitutional settlement] and thereby preclude forever the possibility of a Jewish state." This concern grew when "the moderate trend gained the upper hand among the Palestinians," a "new and moderate trend in Palestinian nationalism" that Weizmann viewed "with grave suspicion."[91] One can understand the reasons. Arab moderation might have stood in the way of Zionist goals at the time, and therefore had to be resisted. Comparable remarks hold today.

In fact, it was not only the Saudi Arabian peace plan and other conciliatory gestures of the Arab states that were causing the familiar "panic" by 1981–82. A still more serious problem was the increasing difficulty in portraying the PLO as merely a gang of terrorists, particularly in the light of its observance of the U.S.-arranged cease-fire on the Lebanon-Israel border despite much Israeli provocation. There is good reason to believe that this threat was one prime factor impelling Israel to invade Lebanon, as we shall see.

Putting such considerations to the side for the moment, the historical record seems plain enough. It strongly confirms the conclusion that the United States and Israel have headed the rejectionist camp, increasingly so as the 1970s progressed. The Arab states that are directly involved in the conflict have approached or joined the international accommodationist consensus, as has the mainstream of the PLO. Irrelevantly to these considerations, it should perhaps be remarked, given the climate of irrationality on this matter in the United States, that this historical record does not show that the Arab states are decent regimes—they most definitely are not—nor does it bear on one's judgments about the merits of the PLO.* It is simply a matter of fact.

As for the matter of principle, it seems to me that rejectionist programs are unacceptable, for the reasons already indicated. Furthermore, whatever one's views about these matters may be, there surely is no justification for maintaining the illusions and misrepresentations that are so characteristic of the American literature on this subject.

---

*Though the matter is of no relevance here, for the record, my own judgments have been consistently harsh, both with regard to their actions and programs. See, e.g., *Peace in the Middle East?*, pp. 99ff., 108; *TNCW*, pp. 262, 430; *Socialist Revolution*, April–June 1976.

NOTES

The Responsibility of Intellectuals

This is a revised version of a talk given at Harvard University and published in *Mosaic,* June 1966. It appeared in substantially this form in the *New York Review of Books,* February 23, 1967. The present version is reprinted from my *American Power and the New Mandarins* (New York: Pantheon Books, 1969).
1. Such a research project has now been undertaken and published as a "Citizens' White Paper": F. Schurmann, P. D. Scott, and R. Zelnik, *The Politics of Escalation in Vietnam* (New York: Fawcett World Library, and Boston: Beacon Press, 1966). For further evidence of American rejection of United Nations initiatives for diplomatic settlement, just prior to the major escalation of February 1965, see Mario Rossi, "The US Rebuff to U Thant," *New York Review of Books,* November 17, 1966. See also Theodore Draper, "How Not To Negotiate," *New York Review of Books,* May 4, 1967. There is further documentary evidence of NLF attempts to

establish a coalition government and to neutralize the area, all rejected by the United States and its Saigon ally, in Douglas Pike, *Viet Cong* (Cambridge, Mass.: MIT Press, 1966). In reading material of this latter sort, one must be especially careful to distinguish between the evidence presented and the "conclusions" that are asserted, for reasons noted briefly below (see note 33).

It is interesting to see the first, somewhat oblique published reactions to *The Politics of Escalation* by those who defend our right to conquer South Vietnam and institute a government of our choice. For example, Robert Scalapino (*New York Times Magazine,* December 11, 1966) argues that the thesis of the book implies that our leaders are "diabolical." Since no right-thinking person can believe this, the thesis is refuted. To assume otherwise would betray "irresponsibility," in a unique sense of this term—a sense that gives an ironic twist to the title of this chapter. He goes on to point out the alleged central weakness in the argument of the book, namely, the failure to perceive that a serious attempt on our part to pursue the possibilities for a diplomatic settlement would have been interpreted by our adversaries as a sign of weakness.

2. *New York Times,* October 14, 1965.

3. *Ibid.,* February 6, 1966.

4. *Boston Globe,* November 19, 1965.

5. At other times, Schlesinger does indeed display admirable scholarly caution. For example, in his introduction to *The Politics of Escalation,* he admits that there may have been "flickers of interest in negotiations" on the part of Hanoi. As to the administration's lies about negotiations and its repeated actions undercutting tentative initiatives toward negotiations, he comments only that the authors may have underestimated military necessity and that future historians may prove them wrong. This caution and detachment must be compared with Schlesinger's attitude toward renewed study of the origins of the Cold War: in a letter to the *New York Review of Books,* October 20, 1966, he remarks that it is time to "blow the whistle" on revisionist attempts to show that the Cold War may have been the consequence of something more than mere Communist belligerence. We are to believe, then, that the relatively straightforward matter of the origins of the Cold War is settled beyond discussion, whereas the much more complex issue of why the United States shies away from a negotiated settlement in Vietnam must be left to future historians to ponder.

It is useful to bear in mind that the United States government itself is on occasion much less diffident in explaining why it refuses to contemplate a meaningful negotiated settlement. As is freely admitted, this solution would leave it without power to control the situation. See, for example, note 37.

6. Arthur M. Schlesinger, Jr., *A Thousand Days: John F. Kennedy in the White House* (Boston: Houghton Mifflin Co., 1965), p. 421.

7. Walt W. Rostow, *The View from the Seventh Floor* (New York: Harper & Row, Publishers, 1964), p. 149. See also his *United States in the World Arena* (New York: Harper & Row, Publishers, 1960), p. 244: "Stalin, exploiting the disruption and

weakness of the postwar world, pressed out from the expanded base he had won during the Second World War in an effort to gain the balance of power in Eurasia . . . turning to the East, to back Mao and to enflame the North Korean and Indochinese Communists. . . ."

8. For example, the article by CIA analyst George Carver, "The Faceless Viet Cong," in *Foreign Affairs*, vol. 44 (April 1966), pp. 347–72. See also note 33.

9. Cf. Jean Lacouture, *Vietnam: Between Two Truces* (New York: Random House, 1966), p. 21. Diem's analysis of the situation was shared by Western observers at the time. See, for example, the comments of William Henderson, Far Eastern specialist and executive, Council on Foreign Relations, in Richard W. Lindholm, ed., *Vietnam: The First Five Years* (East Lansing: Michigan State University Press, 1959). He notes "the growing alienation of the intelligentsia," "the renewal of armed dissidence in the South," the fact that "security has noticeably deteriorated in the last two years," all as a result of Diem's "grim dictatorship," and predicts "a steady worsening of the political climate in free Vietnam, culminating in unforeseen disasters."

10. See Bernard Fall, "Vietnam in the Balance," *Foreign Affairs*, vol. 45 (October 1966), pp. 1–18.

11. Stalin was pleased neither by the Titoist tendencies inside the Greek Communist party nor by the possibility that a Balkan federation might develop under Titoist leadership. It is nevertheless conceivable that Stalin supported the Greek guerrillas at some stage of the rebellion, in spite of the difficulty in obtaining firm documentary evidence. Needless to say, no elaborate study is necessary to document the British or American role in this civil conflict, from late 1944. See D. G. Kousoulas, *The Price of Freedom* (Syracuse, N.Y.: Syracuse University Press, 1953), and *Revolution and Defeat* (New York: Oxford University Press, 1965), for serious study of these events from a strongly anti-Communist point of view.

12. For a detailed account, see James Warburg, *Germany: Key to Peace* (Cambridge, Mass.: Harvard University Press, 1953), pp. 189ff. Warburg concludes that apparently "the Kremlin was now prepared to accept the creation of an All-German democracy in the Western sense of that word," whereas the Western powers, in their response, "frankly admitted their plan 'to secure the participation of Germany in a purely defensive European community'" (i.e., NATO).

13. *The United States in the World Arena*, pp. 344–45. Incidently, those who quite rightly deplore the brutal suppression of the East German and Hungarian revolutions would do well to remember that these scandalous events might have been avoided had the United States been willing to consider proposals for neutralization of Central Europe. Some of George Kennan's recent statements provide interesting commentary on this matter, for example, his comments on the falsity, from the outset, of the assumption that the USSR intended to attack or intimidate by force the Western half of the continent and that it was deterred by American force, and his remarks on the sterility and general absurdity of the demand for unilateral Soviet withdrawal from East Germany together with "the inclusion of

a united Germany as a major component in a Western defense system based primarily on nuclear weaponry" (Edward Reed, ed., *Peace on Earth* [New York: Pocket Books, 1965]).

It is worth noting that historical fantasy of the sort illustrated in Rostow's remarks has become a regular State Department specialty. Thus we have Thomas Mann justifying our Dominican intervention as a response to actions of the "Sino-Soviet military bloc." Or, to take a more considered statement, we have William Bundy's analysis of stages of development of Communist ideology in his Pomona College address, February 12, 1966, in which he characterizes the Soviet Union in the 1920s and early 1930s as "in a highly militant and aggressive phase." What is frightening about fantasy, as distinct from outright falsification, is the possibility that it may be sincere and may actually serve as the basis for formation of policy.

14. *New York Times,* February 6, 1966.

15. *United States Policy Toward Asia,* Hearings Before the Subcommittee on the Far East and the Pacific of the Committee on Foreign Affairs, U.S. House of Representatives (Washington D.C.: Government Printing Office, 1966), p. 89.

16. *New York Times Book Review,* November 20, 1966. Such comments call to mind the remarkable spectacle of President Kennedy counseling Cheddi Jagan on the dangers of entering into a trading relationship "which brought a country into a condition of economic dependence." The reference, of course, is to the dangers in commercial relations with the Soviet Union. See Schlesinger, *A Thousand Days,* p. 776.

17. *A Thousand Days,* p. 252.

18. *Ibid.,* p. 769.

19. Though this too is imprecise. One must recall the real character of the Trujillo regime to appreciate the full cynicism of Kennedy's "realistic" analysis.

20. Walt W. Rostow and R. W. Hatch, *An American Policy in Asia* (New York, Technology Press and John Wiley & Sons, 1955).

21. "End of Either/Or," *Foreign Affairs,* vol. 45 (January 1967), pp. 189–201.

22. *Christian Science Monitor,* November 26, 1966.

23. *Ibid.,* December 5, 1966.

24. Although, to maintain perspective, we should recall that in his wildest moments, Alfred Rosenberg spoke of the elimination of thirty million Slavs, not the imposition of mass starvation on a quarter of the human race. Incidentally, the analogy drawn here is highly "irresponsible," in the technical sense of this neologism discussed earlier. That is, it is based on the assumption that statements and actions of Americans are subject to the same standards and open to the same interpretations as those of anyone else.

25. *New York Times,* February 6, 1966. What is more, Goldberg continues, the United States is not certain that all of these are voluntary adherents. This is not the first such demonstration of Communist duplicity. Another example was seen in the year 1962, when according to United States government sources 15,000

guerrillas suffered 30,000 casualties. See Arthur Schlesinger, *A Thousand Days*, p. 982.

26. Reprinted in a collection of essays entitled *The End of Ideology: On the Exhaustion of Political Ideas in the Fifties* (New York: Free Press, 1960), pp. 369–75. I have no intention here of entering into the full range of issues that have been raised in the discussion of the "end of ideology" for the past dozen years. It is difficult to see how a rational person could quarrel with many of the theses that have been put forth, e.g., that at a certain historical moment the "politics of civility" is appropriate, and perhaps efficacious; that one who advocates action (or inaction—a matter less frequently noted) has a responsibility to assess its social cost; that dogmatic fanaticism and "secular religions" should be combated (or if possible ignored); that technical solutions to problems should be implemented, where possible; that *"le dogmatisme idéologique devait disparaître pour que les idées reprissent vie"* (Aron); and so on. Since this is sometimes taken to be an expression of an "anti-Marxist" position, it is worth keeping in mind that such sentiments as these have no bearing on non-Bolshevik Marxism, as represented, for example, by such figures as Luxemburg, Pannekoek, Korsch, Arthur Rosenberg, and many others.

27. Rostow and Hatch, *op. cit.*, p. 10.

28. The extent to which this "technology" is value-free is hardly very important, given the clear commitments of those who apply it. The problems with which research is concerned are those posed by the Pentagon or the great corporations, not, say, by the revolutionaries of northeast Brazil or by SNCC. Nor am I aware of a research project devoted to the problem of how poorly armed guerrillas might more effectively resist a brutal and devastating military technology—surely the kind of problem that would have interested the free-floating intellectual who is now hopelessly out of date.

29. In view of the unremitting propaganda barrage on "Chinese expansionism," perhaps a word of comment is in order. Typical of American propaganda on this subject is Adlai Stevenson's assessment, shortly before his death (cf. *New York Times Magazine,* March 13, 1966): "So far, the new Communist 'dynasty' has been very aggressive. Tibet was swallowed, India attacked, the Malays had to fight 12 years to resist a 'national liberation' they could receive from the British by a more peaceful route. Today, the apparatus of infiltration and aggression is already at work in North Thailand."

As to Malaya, Stevenson is probably confusing ethnic Chinese with the government of China. Those concerned with the actual events would agree with Harry Miller, in *Communist Menace in Malaya* (New York: Frederick A. Praeger, 1954), p. 230, that "Communist China continues to show little interest in the Malayan affair beyond its usual fulminations via Peking Radio." There are various harsh things that one might say about Chinese behavior in what the Sino-Indian Treaty of 1954 refers to as "the Tibet region of China," but it is no more proof of a tendency toward expansionism than is the behavior of the Indian government with regard to the Naga and Mizo tribesmen. As to North Thailand, "the apparatus of infiltration" may well be at work, though there is little reason to suppose it to be Chinese—and it is surely not unrelated to the American use of Thailand as a base for its attack on Vietnam. This reference is the sheerest hypocrisy.

The "attack on India" grew out of a border dispute that began several years after the Chinese had completed a road from Tibet to Sinkiang in an area so remote from Indian control that the Indians learned about this operation only from the Chinese press. According to American air force maps, the disputed area is in Chinese territory. Cf. Alastair Lamb, *China Quarterly*, no. 23 (July–September 1965), pp. 202–7. To this distinguished authority, "it seems unlikely that the Chinese have been working out some master plan . . . to take over the Indian sub-continent lock, stock and overpopulated barrel." Rather, he thinks it likely that the Chinese were probably unaware that India even claimed the territory through which the road passed. After the Chinese military victory, Chinese troops were, in most areas, withdrawn beyond the McMahon Line, a border which the British had attempted to impose on China in 1914 but which has never been recognized by China (Nationalist or Communist), the United States, or any other government.

It is remarkable that a person in a responsible position could describe all of this as Chinese expansionism. In fact, it is absurd to debate the hypothetical aggressiveness of a China surrounded by American missiles and a still expanding network of military bases backed by an enormous American expeditionary force in Southeast Asia. It is conceivable that at some future time a powerful China may be expansionist. We may speculate about such possibilities if we wish, but it is American aggressiveness that is the central fact of current politics.

30. W. S. Churchill, *The Second World War*, vol. 5, *Closing the Ring* (Boston: Houghton Mifflin Co., 1951), p. 382.

31. *United States Policy Toward Asia*, p. 104. See note 15.

32. *Ibid.*, p. 105.

33. Douglas Pike, *op. cit.*, p. 110. This book, written by a foreign service officer working at the Center for International Studies, MIT, poses a contrast between our side, which sympathizes with "the usual revolutionary stirrings . . . around the world because they reflect inadequate living standards or oppressive and corrupt governments," and the backers of "revolutionary guerrilla warfare," which "opposes the aspirations of people while apparently furthering them, manipulates the individual by persuading him to manipulate himself." Revolutionary guerrilla warfare is "an imported product, revolution from the outside" (other examples besides the Vietcong are "Stalin's exportation of armed revolution," the Haganah in Palestine, and the Irish Republican Army—see pp. 32–33). The Vietcong could not be an indigenous movement since it has "a social construction program of such scope and ambition that of necessity it must have been created in Hanoi" (p. 76—but on pp. 77–79 we read that "organizational activity had gone on intensively and systematically for several years" before the Lao Dong party in Hanoi had made its decision "to begin building an organization"). On p. 80 we find that "such an

effort had to be the child of the North," even though elsewhere we read of the prominent role of the Cao Dai (p. 74), "the first major social group to begin actively opposing the Diem government" (p. 222), and of the Hoa Hao sect, "another early and major participant in the NLF" (p. 69). Pike takes it as proof of Communist duplicity that in the South the party insisted it was "Marxist-Leninist," thus "indicating philosophic but not political allegiance," whereas in the North it described itself as a "Marxist-Leninist organization," thus "indicating that it was in the main-stream of the world-wide Communist movement" (p. 150). And so on. Also revealing is the contempt for "Cinderella and all the other fools [who] could still believe there was magic in the mature world if one mumbled the secret incantation: solidarity, union, concord"; for the "gullible, misled people" who were "turning the countryside into a bedlam, toppling one Saigon government after another, confounding the Americans"; for the "mighty force of people" who in their mindless innocence thought that "the meek, at last, were to inherit the earth," that "riches would be theirs and all in the name of justice and virtue." One can appreciate the chagrin with which a sophisticated Western political scientist must view this "sad and awesome spectacle."

34. Lacouture, *op. cit.,* p. 188. The same military spokesman goes on, ominously, to say that this is the problem confronting us throughout Asia, Africa, and Latin America, and that we must find the "proper response."

35. Charles Mohr, *New York Times,* February 11, 1966. My italics.

36. *New York Times,* February 18, 1966.

37. William Bundy, "The United States and Asia," in Alastair Buchan, ed., *China and the Peace of Asia* (New York: Frederick A. Praeger, 1965), pp. 29–30.

38. *Op. cit.,* p. 80.

39. *United States Policy Toward Asia,* pp. 191–201 *passim.*

40. Rostow and Hatch, *op. cit.,* p. 10.

41. *United States Policy Toward Asia,* p. 128.

42. Lindholm, *op. cit.,* p. 322.

Objectivity and Liberal Scholarship

Parts of this essay were delivered as a lecture at New York University in March 1968, as part of the Albert Schweitzer Lecture Series, and appeared in *Power and Consciousness in Society,* edited by Conor Cruise O'Brien and William D. Vanech (New York: New York University Press, 1969). This essay is excerpted from the version published in *American Power and the New Mandarins* (New York: Pantheon Books, 1969).

1. Cited in Paul Avrich, *The Russian Anarchists* (Princeton, N.J., Princeton University Press, 1967), pp. 93–94. A recent reformulation of this view is given by Anton Pannekoek, the Dutch scientist and spokesman for libertarian communism, in his *Workers Councils* (Melbourne, 1950), pp. 36–37:

It is not for the first time that a ruling class tries to explain, and so to perpetuate, its rule as the consequences of an inborn difference between two kinds of people, one destined by nature to ride, the other to be ridden. The landowning aristocracy of former centuries defended their privileged position by boasting their extraction from a nobler race of conquerors that had subdued the lower race of common people. Big capitalists explain their dominating place by the assertion that they have brains and other people have none. In the same way now especially the intellectuals, considering themselves the rightful rulers of to-morrow, claim their spiritual superiority. They form the rapidly increasing class of university-trained officials and free professions, specialized in mental work, in study of books and of science, and they consider themselves as the people most gifted with intellect. Hence they are destined to be leaders of the production, whereas the ungifted mass shall execute the manual work, for which no brains are needed. They are no defenders of capitalism; not capital, but intellect should direct labor. The more so, since now society is such a complicated structure, based on abstract and difficult science, that only the highest intellectual acumen is capable of embracing, grasping and handling it. Should the working masses, from lack of insight, fail to acknowledge this need of superior intellectual lead, should they stupidly try to take the direction into their own hands, chaos and ruin will be the inevitable consequence.

2. Albert Parry has suggested that there are important similarities between the emergence of a scientific elite in the Soviet Union and the United States, in their growing role in decision-making, citing Bell's thesis in support. See the *New York Times*, March 27, 1966, reporting on the Midwest Slavic Conference.

3. Letter to Herzen and Ogareff, 1866, cited in Daniel Guérin, *Jeunesse du socialisme libertaire* (Paris: Librairie Marcel Rivière, 1959), p. 119.

4. Rosa Luxemburg, *The Russian Revolution,* trans. Bertram D. Wolfe (Ann Arbor: University of Michigan Press, 1961), p. 71.

5. Luxemburg, cited by Guérin, *Jeunesse du socialisme libertaire,* pp. 106–7.

6. *Leninism or Marxism,* in Luxemburg, *op. cit.,* p. 102.

7. For a very enlightening study of this matter, emphasizing domestic issues, see Michael Paul Rogin, *The Intellectuals and McCarthy: The Radical Specter* (Cambridge, Mass.: MIT Press, 1967).

8. *The Spanish Republic and the Civil War: 1931–1939* (Princeton, N.J.: Princeton University Press, 1965).

9. Respectively, president of the Republic, prime minister from May until the Franco insurrection, and member of the conservative wing of the Popular Front selected by Azaña to try to set up a compromise government after the insurrection.

10. It is interesting that Douglas Pike's very hostile account of the National

Liberation Front, cited earlier, emphasizes the popular and voluntary element in its striking organizational successes. What he describes, whether accurately or not one cannot tell, is a structure of interlocking self-help organizations, loosely coordinated and developed through persuasion rather than force—in certain respects, of a character that would have appealed to anarchist thinkers. Those who speak so freely of the "authoritarian Vietcong" may be correct, but they have presented little evidence to support their judgment. Of course, it must be understood that Pike regards the element of voluntary mass participation in self-help associations as the most dangerous and insidious feature of the NLF organizational structure.

Also relevant is the history of collectivization in China, which, as compared with the Soviet Union, shows a much higher reliance on persuasion and mutual aid than on force and terror, and appears to have been more successful. See Thomas P. Bernstein, "Leadership and Mass Mobilisation in the Soviet and Chinese Collectivization Campaigns of 1929–30 and 1955–56: A Comparison," *China Quarterly*, no. 31 (July–September 1967), pp. 1–47, for some interesting and suggestive comments and analysis.

The scale of the Chinese Revolution is so great and reports in depth are so fragmentary that it would no doubt be foolhardy to attempt a general evaluation. Still, all the reports I have been able to study suggest that insofar as real successes were achieved in the several stages of land reform, mutual aid, collectivization, and formation of communes, they were traceable in large part to the complex interaction of the Communist party cadres and the gradually evolving peasant associations, a relation which seems to stray far from the Leninist model of organization. This is particularly evident in William Hinton's magnificent study *Fanshen* (New York: Monthly Review Press, 1966), which is unparalleled, to my knowledge, as an analysis of a moment of profound revolutionary change. What seems to me particularly striking in his account of the early stages of revolution in one Chinese village is not only the extent to which party cadres submitted themselves to popular control, but also, and more significant, the ways in which exercise of control over steps of the revolutionary process was a factor in developing the consciousness and insight of those who took part in the revolution, not only from a political and social point of view, but also with respect to the human relationships that were created. It is interesting, in this connection, to note the strong populist element in early Chinese Marxism. For some very illuminating observations about this general matter, see Maurice Meisner, *Li Ta-chao and the Origins of Chinese Marxism* (Cambridge, Mass.: Harvard University Press, 1967).

I am not suggesting that the anarchist revolution in Spain—with its background of more than thirty years of education and struggle—is being relived in Asia, but rather that the spontaneous and voluntary elements in popular mass movements have probably been seriously misunderstood because of the instinctive antipathy toward such phenomena among intellectuals, and more recently, because of the insistence on interpreting them in terms of Cold War mythology.

11. "The Spanish Background," *New Left Review*, no. 40 (November–December 1966), pp. 85–90.

12. José Peirats, *La C.N.T. en la revolución española*, 3 vols. (Toulouse: Ediciones C.N.T., 1951–52). Jackson makes one passing reference to it. Peirats has since published a general history of the period, *Los anarquistas en la crisis política española* (Buenos Aires: Editorial Alfa-Argentina, 1964). This highly informative book should certainly be made available to an English-speaking audience.

13. An exception to the rather general failure to deal with the anarchist revolution is Hugh Thomas' "Anarchist Agrarian Collectives in the Spanish Civil War," in Martin Gilbert, ed., *A Century of Conflict, 1850–1950: Essays for A. J. P. Taylor* (New York: Atheneum Publishers, 1967), pp. 245–63. See note 60 below for some discussion. There is also much useful information in what to my mind is the best general history of the Civil War, *La Révolution et la guerre d'Espagne*, by Pierre Broué and Émile Témime (Paris: Les Éditions de Minuit, 1961). A concise and informative recent account is contained in Daniel Guérin, *L'Anarchisme* (Paris: Gallimard, 1965). In his extensive study *The Spanish Civil War* (New York: Harper & Row, Publishers, 1961; paperback ed. 1963), Hugh Thomas barely refers to the popular revolution, and some of the major events are not mentioned at all—see, for example, note 51 below.

14. *Collectivisations: l'oeuvre constructive de la Révolution espagnole*, 2nd ed. (Toulouse: Éditions C.N.T., 1965). The first edition was published in Barcelona (Éditions C.N.T.-F.A.I., 1937). There is an excellent and sympathetic summary by the Marxist scholar Karl Korsch, "Collectivization in Spain," in *Living Marxism*, vol. 4 (April 1939), pp. 179–82. In the same issue (pp. 170–71), the liberal-Communist reaction to the Spanish Civil War is summarized succinctly, and I believe accurately, as follows: "With their empty chatter as to the wonders of Bolshevik discipline, the geniality of Caballero, and the passions of the Pasionaria, the 'modern liberals' merely covered up their real desire for the destruction of all revolutionary possibilities in the Civil War, and their preparation for the possible war over the Spanish issue in the interest of their diverse fatherlands . . . what was truly revolutionary in the Spanish Civil War resulted from the direct actions of the workers and pauperized peasants, and not because of a specific form of labor organization nor an especially gifted leadership." I think that the record bears out this analysis, and I also think that it is this fact that accounts for the distaste for the revolutionary phase of the Civil War and its neglect in historical scholarship.

15. An illuminating eyewitness account of this period is that of Franz Borkenau, *The Spanish Cockpit* (1938; reprinted Ann Arbor: University of Michigan Press, 1963).

16. Figures from Guérin, *L'Anarchisme*, p. 154.

17. A useful account of this period is given by Felix Morrow, *Revolution and Counter-Revolution in Spain* (1938; reprinted London, New Park Publications, 1963).

18. Cited by Camillo Berneri in his "Lettre ouverte à la camarade Frederica [*sic*] Montseny," *Guerre de classes en Espagne* (Paris: 1946), a collection of items translated from his journal *Guerra di Classe*. Berneri was the outstanding anarchist intellectual in Spain. He opposed the policy of joining the government and argued for an alternative, more typically anarchist strategy to which I will return below. His own view toward joining the government was stated succinctly by a Catalan worker whom he quotes, with reference to the Republic of 1931: "It is always the old dog with a new collar." Events were to prove the accuracy of this analysis.

Berneri had been a leading spokesman of Italian anarchism. He left Italy after Mussolini's rise to power, and came to Barcelona on July 19, 1936. He formed the first Italian units for the antifascist war, according to anarchist historian Rudolf Rocker (*The Tragedy of Spain* [New York: Freie Arbeiter Stimme, 1937], p. 44). He was murdered, along with his older comrade Barbieri, during the May Days of 1937. (Arrested on May 5 by the Communist-controlled police, he was shot during the following night.) Hugh Thomas, in *The Spanish Civil War*, p. 428, suggests that "the assassins may have been Italian Communists" rather than the police. Thomas' book, which is largely devoted to military history, mentions Berneri's murder but makes no other reference to his ideas or role.

Berneri's name does not appear in Jackson's history.

19. Burnett Bolloten, *The Grand Camouflage: The Communist Conspiracy in the Spanish Civil War* (New York: Frederick A. Praeger, 1961), p. 86. This book, by a UP correspondent in Spain during the Civil War, contains a great deal of important documentary evidence bearing on the questions considered here. The attitude of the wealthy farmers of this area, most of them former supporters of the right-wing organizations that had now disappeared, is well described by the general secretary of the Peasant Federation, Julio Mateu: "Such is the sympathy for us [that is, the Communist party] in the Valencia countryside that hundreds and thousands of farmers would join our party if we were to let them. These farmers . . . love our party like a sacred thing . . . they [say] 'The Communist Party is our party.' Comrades, what emotion the peasants display when they utter these words" (cited in Bolloten, p. 86). There is some interesting speculation about the backgrounds for the writing of this very important book in H. R. Southworth, *Le mythe de la croisade de Franco* (Paris: Ruedo Ibérico, 1964; Spanish edition, same publisher, 1963).

The Communist headquarters in Valencia had on the wall two posters: "Respect the property of the small peasant" and "Respect the property of the small industrialist" (Borkenau, *op cit.*, p. 117). Actually, it was the rich farmer as well who sought protection from the Communists, whom Borkenau describes as constituting the extreme right wing of the Republican forces. By early 1937, according to Borkenau, the Communist party was "to a large extent . . . the party of the military and administrative personnel, in the second place the party of the petty bourgeoisie and certain well-to-do peasant groups, in the third place the party of the employees, and only in the fourth place the party of the industrial workers" (p. 192). The party also attracted many police and army officers. The police chief in Madrid and the chief of intelligence, for example, were party members. In general, the party, which had been insignificant before the revolution, "gave the urban and rural middle classes a powerful access of life and vigour" as it defended them from the revolutionary forces (Bolloten, *op. cit.,* p. 86). Gerald Brenan describes the situation as follows, in *The Spanish Labyrinth* (1943; reprinted Cambridge: Cambridge University Press, 1960), p. 325:

> Unable to draw to themselves the manual workers, who remained firmly fixed in their unions, the Communists found themselves the refuge for all those who had suffered from the excesses of the Revolution or who feared where it might lead them. Well-to-do Catholic orange-growers in Valencia, peasants in Catalonia, small shopkeepers and business men, Army officers and Government officials enrolled in their ranks. . . . Thus [in Catalonia] one had a strange and novel situation: on the one side stood the huge compact proletariat of Barcelona with its long revolutionary tradition, and on the other the white-collar workers and *petite bourgeoisie* of the city, organized and armed by the Communist party against it.

Actually the situation that Brenan describes is not as strange a one as he suggests. It is, rather, a natural consequence of Bolshevik elitism that the "Red bureaucracy" should act as a counterrevolutionary force except under the conditions where its present or future representatives are attempting to seize power for themselves, in the name of the masses whom they pretend to represent.

20. Bolloten, *op. cit.,* p. 189. The legalization of revolutionary actions already undertaken and completed recalls the behavior of the "revolutionary vanguard" in the Soviet Union in 1918. Cf. Arthur Rosenberg, *A History of Bolshevism* (1932; republished in translation from the original German, New York: Russell & Russell, Publishers, 1965), chap. 6. He describes how the expropriations, "accomplished as the result of spontaneous action on the part of workers and against the will of the Bolsheviks," were reluctantly legalized by Lenin months later and then placed under central party control. On the relation of the Bolsheviks to the anarchists in postrevolutionary Russia, interpreted from a proanarchist point of view, see Guérin, *L'Anarchisme,* pp. 96–125. See also Avrich, *op. cit.,* pt. 2, pp. 123–254.

21. Bolloten, *op. cit.,* p. 191.

22. *Ibid.,* p. 194.

23. For some details, see Vernon Richards, *Lessons of the Spanish Revolution* (London: Freedom Press, 1953), pp. 83–88.

24. For a moving eyewitness account, see George Orwell, *Homage to Catalonia* (1938; reprinted New York: Harcourt, Brace & World, 1952, and Boston:

Beacon Press, 1955; quotations in this book from Beacon Press edition). This brilliant book received little notice at the time of its first publication, no doubt because the picture Orwell drew was in sharp conflict with established liberal dogma. The attention that it has received as a Cold War document since its republication in 1952 would, I suspect, have been of little comfort to the author.

25. Cited by Rocker, *The Tragedy of Spain,* p. 28.

26. See *ibid.* for a brief review. It was a great annoyance to Hitler that these interests were, to a large extent, protected by Franco.

27. *Ibid.,* p. 35.

28. *Op. cit.,* pp. 324.

29. Borkenau, *op. cit.,* pp. 289–92. It is because of the essential accuracy of Borkenau's account that I think Hobsbawm (*op. cit.*) is quite mistaken in believing that the Communist policy "was undoubtedly the only one which could have won the Civil War." In fact, the Communist policy was bound to fail, because it was predicated on the assumption that the Western democracies would join the antifascist effort if only Spain could be preserved as, in effect, a Western colony. Once the Communist leaders saw the futility of this hope, they abandoned the struggle, which was not in their eyes an effort to win the Civil War, but only to serve the interests of Russian foreign policy. I also disagree with Hobsbawm's analysis of the anarchist revolution, cited earlier, for reasons that are implicit in this entire discussion.

30. *Op. cit.,* pp. 143–44.

31. Cited by Rosenberg, *op. cit.,* pp. 168–69.

32. Bolloten, *op. cit.,* p. 84.

33. *Ibid.,* p. 85. As noted earlier, the "small farmer" included the prosperous orange growers, etc. (see note 19).

34. Brenan, *op. cit.,* p. 321.

35. Correspondence from Companys to Prieto, 1939. While Companys, as a Catalonian with separatist impulses, would naturally be inclined to defend Catalonian achievements, he was surely not sympathetic to collectivization, despite his cooperative attitude during the period when the anarchists, with real power in their hands, permitted him to retain nominal authority. I know of no attempt to challenge the accuracy of his assessment. Morrow (*op. cit.,* p. 77) quotes the Catalonian premier, the entrepreneur Juan Tarradellas, as defending the administration of the collectivized war industries against a Communist (PSUC) attack, which he termed the "most arbitrary falsehoods." There are many other reports commenting on the functioning of the collectivized industries by nonanarchist firsthand observers, that tend to support Companys. For example, the Swiss socialist Andres Oltmares is quoted by Rocker (*op. cit.,* p. 24) as saying that after the revolution the Catalonian workers' syndicates "in seven weeks accomplished fully as much as France did in fourteen months after the outbreak of the World War." Continuing, he says:

> In the midst of the civil war the Anarchists have proved themselves to be political organizers of the first rank. They kindled in everyone the required sense of responsibility, and knew how by eloquent appeals to keep alive the spirit of sacrifice for the general welfare of the people.
>
> As a Social Democrat I speak here with inner joy and sincere admiration of my experience in Catalonia. The anti-capitalist transformation took place here without their having to resort to a dictatorship. The members of the syndicates are their own masters, and carry on production and the distribution of the products of labor under their own management with the advice of technical experts in whom they have confidence. The enthusiasm of the workers is so great that they scorn any personal advantage and are concerned only for the welfare of all.

Even Borkenau concludes, rather grudgingly, that industry was functioning fairly well, as far as he could see. The matter deserves a serious study.

36. Quoted in Richards, *op. cit.,* pp. 46–47.

37. *Ibid.* Richards suggests that the refusal of the central government to support the Aragon front may have been motivated in part by the general policy of counterrevolution. "This front, largely manned by members of the C.N.T.-F.A.I., was considered of great strategic importance by the anarchists, having as its ultimate objective the linking of Catalonia with the Basque country and Asturias, i.e., a linking of the industrial region [of Catalonia] with an important source of raw materials." Again, it would be interesting to undertake a detailed investigation of this topic.

That the Communists withheld arms from the Aragon front seems established beyond question, and it can hardly be doubted that the motivation was political. See, for example, D. T. Cattell, *Communism and the Spanish Civil War* (1955; reprinted New York: Russell and Russell, Publishers, 1965), p. 110. Cattell, who in general bends over backward to try to justify the behavior of the central government, concludes that in this case there is little doubt that the refusal of aid was politically motivated. Brenan takes the same view, claiming that the Communists "kept the Aragon front without arms to spite the Anarchists." The Communists resorted to some of the most grotesque slanders to explain the lack of arms on the Aragon front; for example, the *Daily Worker* attributed the arms shortage to the fact that "the Trotskyist General Kopp had been carting enormous supplies of arms and ammunition across no-man's land to the fascists" (cited by Morrow, *op. cit.,* p. 145). As Morrow points out, George Kopp is a particularly bad choice as a target for such accusations. His record is well known, for example, from the account given by Orwell, who served under his command (see Orwell, *op. cit.,* pp. 209ff.). Orwell was also able to refute, from firsthand observation, many of the other absurdities that were appearing in the liberal press about the Aragon front, for example, the statement by Ralph Bates in the *New Republic* that the POUM troops were "playing football with the Fascists in no man's land." At that moment, as Orwell observes, "the P.O.U.M. troops were suffering heavy casualties and a number of my personal friends were killed and wounded."

38. Cited in *Living Marxism*, p. 172.

39. Bolloten, *op. cit.*, p. 49, comments on the collectivization of the dairy trade in Barcelona as follows: "The Anarchosyndicalists eliminated as unhygienic over forty pasteurizing plants, pasteurized all the milk in the remaining nine, and proceeded to displace all dealers by establishing their own dairies. Many of the retailers entered the collective, but some refused to do so: 'They asked for a much higher wage than that paid to the workers . . . , claiming that they could not manage on the one allotted to them' [*Tierra y Libertad*, August 21, 1937—the newspaper of the FAI, the anarchist activists]." His information is primarily from anarchist sources, which he uses much more extensively than any historian other than Peirats. He does not present any evaluation of these sources, which—like all others—must be used critically.

40. Morrow, *op. cit.*, p. 136.

41. Borkenau, *op. cit.*, p. 182.

42. *Ibid.*, p. 183.

43. *Ibid.*, p. 184. According to Borkenau, "it is doubtful whether Comorera is personally responsible for this scarcity; it might have arisen anyway, in pace with the consumption of the harvest." This speculation may or may not be correct. Like Borkenau, we can only speculate as to whether the village and workers' committees would have been able to continue to provision Barcelona, with or without central administration, had it not been for the policy of "abstract liberalism," which was of a piece with the general Communist-directed attempts to destroy the revolutionary organizations and the structures developed in the revolutionary period.

44. Orwell, *op. cit.*, pp. 109–11. Orwell's description of Barcelona in December (pp. 4–5), when he arrived for the first time, deserves more extensive quotation:

> It was the first time that I had ever been in a town where the working class was in the saddle. Practically every building of any size had been seized by the workers and was draped with red flags or with the red and black flag of the Anarchists; every wall was scrawled with the hammer and sickle and with the initials of the revolutionary parties; almost every church had been gutted and its images burnt. Churches here and there were being systematically demolished by gangs of workmen. Every shop and café had an inscription saying that it had been collectivized; even the bootblacks had been collectivized and their boxes painted red and black. Waiters and shopwalkers looked you in the face and treated you as an equal. Servile and even ceremonial forms of speech had temporarily disappeared. Nobody said "Señor" or "Don" or even "Usted"; everyone called everyone else "Comrade" and "Thou," and said "Salud!" instead of "Buenos dias." Tipping had been forbidden by law since the time of Primo de Rivera; almost my

first experience was receiving a lecture from an hotel manager for trying
to tip a lift-boy. There were no private motor cars, they had all been
commandeered, and all the trams and taxis and much of the other transport
were painted red and black. The revolutionary posters were everywhere,
flaming from the walls in clean reds and blues that made the few remaining
advertisements look like daubs of mud. Down the Ramblas, the wide central
artery of the town where crowds of people streamed constantly to and fro,
the loud-speakers were bellowing revolutionary songs all day and far into
the night. And it was the aspect of the crowds that was the queerest thing
of all. In outward appearance it was a town in which the wealthy classes had
practically ceased to exist. Except for a small number of women and fo-
reigners there were no "well-dressed" people at all. Practically everyone
wore rough working-class clothes, or blue overalls or some variant of the
militia uniform. All this was queer and moving. There was much in it that
I did not understand, in some ways I did not even like it, but I recognized
it immediately as a state of affairs worth fighting for. Also I believed that
things were as they appeared, that this was really a workers' State and that
the entire bourgeoisie had either fled, been killed, or voluntarily come over
to the workers' side; I did not realize that great numbers of well-to-do
bourgeois were simply lying low and disguising themselves as proletarians
for the time being . . .

. . . waiting for that happy day when Communist power would reintroduce the old
state of society and destroy popular involvement in the war.

In December 1936, however, the situation was still as described in the following
remarks (p. 6):

Yet so far as one can judge the people were contented and hopeful. There
was no unemployment, and the price of living was still extremely low; you
saw very few conspicuously destitute people, and no beggars except the
gipsies. Above all, there was a belief in the revolution and the future, a
feeling of having suddenly emerged into an era of equality and freedom.
Human beings were trying to behave as human beings and not as cogs in
the capitalist machine. In the barbers' shops were Anarchist notices (the
barbers were mostly Anarchists) solemnly explaining that barbers were no
longer slaves. In the streets were coloured posters appealing to prostitutes
to stop being prostitutes. To anyone from the hard-boiled, sneering civilization of the English-speaking races there was something rather pathetic in
the literalness with which these idealistic Spaniards took the hackneyed
phrases of revolution. At that time revolutionary ballads of the naïvest kind,
all about proletarian brotherhood and the wickedness of Mussolini, were
being sold on the streets for a few centimes each. I have often seen an
illiterate militiaman buy one of these ballads, laboriously spell out the

words, and then, when he had got the hang of it, begin singing it to an appropriate tune.

Recall the dates. Orwell arrived in Barcelona in late December 1936. Comorera's decree abolishing the workers' supply committees and the bread committees was on January 7. Borkenau returned to Barcelona in mid-January; Orwell, in April.
45. See Bolloten, *op. cit.*, p. 74, citing the anarchist spokesman Juan Peiró, in September 1936. Like other anarchists and left-wing Socialists, Peiró sharply condemns the use of force to introduce collectivization, taking the position that was expressed by most anarchists, as well as by left-wing socialists such as Ricardo Zabalza, general secretary of the Federation of Land Workers, who stated on January 8, 1937: "I prefer a small, enthusiastic collective, formed by a group of active and honest workers, to a large collective set up by force and composed of peasants without enthusiasm, who would sabotage it until it failed. Voluntary collectivization may seem the longer course, but the example of the small, well-managed collective will attract the entire peasantry, who are profoundly realistic and practical, whereas forced collectivization would end by discrediting socialized agriculture" (cited by Bolloten *op. cit.*, p. 59). However, there seems no doubt that the precepts of the anarchist and left-socialist spokesmen were often violated in practice.
46. Borkenau, *op. cit.*, pp. 219–20. Of this officer, Jackson says only that he was "a dependable professional officer." After the fall of Málaga, Lieutenant Colonel Villalba was tried for treason, for having deserted the headquarters and abandoned his troops. Broué and Témime remark that it is difficult to determine what justice there was in the charge.
47. Jesús Hernández and Juan Comorera, *Spain Organises for Victory: The Policy of the Communist Party of Spain Explained* (London: Communist Party of Great Britain, n.d.), cited by Richards, *op. cit.*, pp. 99–100. There was no accusation that the phone service was restricted, but only that the revolutionary workers could maintain "a close check on the conversations that took place between the politicians." As Richards further observes, "It is, of course, a quite different matter when the 'indiscreet ear' is that of the O.G.P.U."
48. Broué and Témime, *op. cit.*, p. 266.
49. Jackson, *op. cit.*, p. 370. Thomas suggests that Sesé was probably killed accidentally (*The Spanish Civil War*, p. 428).
50. The anarchist mayor of the border town of Puigcerdá had been assassinated in April, after Negrín's carabineros had taken over the border posts. That same day a prominent UGT member, Roldán Cortada, was murdered in Barcelona, it is presumed by CNT militants. This presumption is disputed by Peirats (*Los Anarquistas:* see note 12), who argues, with some evidence, that the murder may have been a Stalinist provocation. In reprisal, a CNT man was killed. Orwell, whose eyewitness account of the May Days is unforgettable, points out that "one can gauge the attitude of the foreign capitalist Press towards the Communist-

Anarchist feud by the fact that Roldán's murder was given wide publicity, while the answering murder was carefully unmentioned" (*op. cit.*, p. 119). Similarly one can gauge Jackson's attitude toward this struggle by his citation of Sesé's murder as a critical event, while the murder of Berneri goes unmentioned (cf. notes 18 and 49). Orwell remarks elsewhere that "in the English press, in particular, you would have to search for a long time before finding any favourable reference, at any period of the war, to the Spanish Anarchists. They have been systematically denigrated, and, as I know by my own experience, it is almost impossible to get anyone to print anything in their defence" (p. 159). Little has changed since.

51. According to Orwell (*op. cit.*, pp. 153–54), "A British cruiser and two British destroyers had closed in upon the harbour, and no doubt there were other warships not far away. The English newspapers gave it out that these ships were proceeding to Barcelona 'to protect British interests,' but in fact they made no move to do so; that is, they did not land any men or take off any refugees. There can be no certainty about this, but it was at least inherently likely that the British Government, which had not raised a finger to save the Spanish Government from Franco, would intervene quickly enough to save it from its own working class." This assumption may well have influenced the left-wing leadership to restrain the Barcelona workers from simply taking control of the whole city, as apparently they could easily have done in the initial stages of the May Days.

Hugh Thomas comments (*The Spanish Civil War,* p. 428) that there was "no reason" for Orwell's "apprehension" on this matter. In the light of the British record with regard to Spain, it seems to me that Thomas is simply unrealistic, as compared with Orwell, in this respect.

52. Orwell, *op. cit.*, pp. 143–44.

53. *Controversy,* August 1937, cited by Morrow, p. 173. The prediction was incorrect, though not unreasonable. Had the Western powers and the Soviet Union wished, compromise would have been possible, it appears, and Spain might have been saved the terrible consequences of a Franco victory. See Brenan, *op. cit.*, p. 331. He attributes the British failure to support an armistice and possible reconciliation to the fact that Chamberlain "saw nothing disturbing in the prospect of an Italian and German victory." It would be interesting to explore more fully the attitude of Winston Churchill. In April 1937 he stated that a Franco victory would not harm British interests. Rather, the danger was a "success of the trotskyists and anarchists" (cited by Broué and Témime, *op. cit.*, p. 172). Of some interest, in this connection, is the recent discovery of an unpublished Churchill essay written in March 1939—six months after Munich—in which he said that England "would welcome and aid a genuine Hitler of peace and toleration" (see *New York Times,* December 12, 1965).

54. I find no mention at all in Hugh Thomas, *The Spanish Civil War.* The account here is largely taken from Broué and Témime, pp. 279–80.

55. *Op cit.*, p. 405. A footnote comments on the "leniency" of the government

to those arrested. Jackson has nothing to say about the charges against Ascaso and others, or the manner in which the old order was restored in Aragon.

To appreciate these events more fully, one should consider, by comparison, the concern for civil liberties shown by Negrín on the second, antifascist front. In an interview after the war, he explained to John Whitaker (*We Cannot Escape History* [New York: Macmillan Publishing Co., 1943], pp. 116–18) why his government had been so ineffective in coping with the fifth column, even in the case of known fascist agents. Negrín explained that "we couldn't arrest a man on suspicion; we couldn't break with the rules of evidence. You can't risk arresting an innocent man because you are positive in your own mind that he is guilty. You prosecute a war, yes; but you also live with your conscience." Evidently, these scruples did not pertain when it was the rights of anarchist and socialist workers, rather than fascist agents, that were at stake.

56. Cf. Broué and Témime, *op. cit.*, p. 262. Ironically, the government forces included some anarchist troops, the only ones to enter Barcelona.

57. See Bolloten, *op. cit.*, p. 55, n. 1, for an extensive list of sources.

58. Broué and Témime cite the socialists Alardo Prats, Fenner Brockway, and Carlo Rosselli. Borkenau, on the other hand, suspected that the role of terror was great in collectivization. He cites very little to substantiate his feeling, though some evidence is available from anarchist sources. See note 45 above.

Some general remarks on collectivization by Rosselli and Brockway are cited by Rudolf Rocker in his essay "Anarchism and Anarchosyndicalism," n. 1, in Paul Eltzbacher, ed., *Anarchism* (London, Freedom Press, 1960), p. 266:

> Rosselli: In three months Catalonia has been able to set up a new social order on the ruins of an ancient system. This is chiefly due to the Anarchists, who have revealed a quite remarkable sense of proportion, realistic understanding, and organizing ability. . . . All the revolutionary forces of Catalonia have united in a program of Syndicalist-Socialist character . . . Anarcho-Syndicalism, hitherto so despised, has revealed itself as a great constructive force. I am no Anarchist, but I regard it as my duty to express here my opinion of the Anarchists of Catalonia, who have all too often been represented as a destructive if not a criminal element.
>
> Brockway: I was impressed by the strength of the C.N.T. It was unnecessary to tell me that it is the largest and most vital of the working class organizations in Spain. That was evident on all sides. The large industries were clearly in the main in the hands of the C.N.T.—railways, road transport, shipping, engineering, textiles, electricity, building, agriculture. . . . I was immensely impressed by the constructive revolutionary work which is being done by the C.N.T. Their achievements of workers' control in industry is an inspiration. . . . There are still some Britishers and Americans who regard the Anarchists of Spain as impossible, undisciplined uncontrollables. This is poles away from the truth. The Anarchists of Spain, through

the C.N.T., are doing one of the biggest constructive jobs ever done by the working class. At the front they are fighting Fascism. Behind the front they are actually constructing the new workers' society. They see that the war against Fascism and the carrying through of the social revolution are inseparable. Those who have seen them and understood what they are doing must honor them and be grateful to them. . . . That is surely the biggest thing which has hitherto been done by the workers in any part of the world.

59. Cited by Richards, *op. cit.*, pp. 76–81, where long descriptive quotations are given.

60. See Hugh Thomas, "Anarchist Agrarian Collectives in the Spanish Civil War" (note 13). He cites figures showing that agricultural production went up in Aragon and Castile, where collectivization was extensive, and down in Catalonia and the Levante, where peasant proprietors were the dominant element.

Thomas' is, to my knowledge, the only attempt by a professional historian to assess the data on agricultural collectivization in Spain in a systematic way. He concludes that the collectives were probably "a considerable social success" and must have had strong popular support, but he is more doubtful about their economic viability. His suggestion that "Communist pressure on the collectives may have given them the necessary urge to survive" seems quite unwarranted, as does his suggestion that "the very existence of the war . . . may have been responsible for some of the success the collectives had." On the contrary, their success and spontaneous creation throughout Republican Spain suggest that they answered to deeply felt popular sentiments, and both the war and Communist pressure appear to have been highly disruptive factors—ultimately, of course, destructive factors.

Other dubious conclusions are that "in respect of redistribution of wealth, anarchist collectives were hardly much improvement over capitalism" since "no effective way of limiting consumption in richer collectives was devised to help poorer ones," and that there was no possibility of developing large-scale planning. On the contrary, Bolloten (*op. cit.*, pp. 176–79) points out that "in order to remedy the defects of collectivization, as well as to iron out discrepancies in the living standards of the workers in flourishing and impoverished enterprises, the Anarchosyndicalists, although rootedly opposed to nationalization, advocated the centralization—or, socialization, as they called it—under trade union control, of entire branches of production." He mentions a number of examples of partial socialization that had some success, citing as the major difficulty that prevented still greater progress the insistence of the Communist party and the UGT leadership—though apparently not all of the rank-and-file members of the UGT—on government ownership and control. According to Richards (*op. cit.*, p. 82): "In June, 1937 . . . a National Plenum of Regional Federations of Peasants was held in Valencia to discuss the formation of a National Federation of Peasants for the co-ordination and extension of the collectivist movement and also to ensure an equitable distribution of the produce of the land, not only between the collectives but for the whole country. Again in Castille in October 1937, a merging of the 100,000 members of the Regional Federation of Peasants and the 13,000 members in the food distributive trades took place. It represented a logical step in ensuring better co-ordination, and was accepted for the whole of Spain at the National Congress of Collectives held in Valencia in November 1937." Still other plans were under consideration for regional and national coordination—see, for example, D. A. de Santillan, *After the Revolution* (New York: Greenberg Publisher, 1937), for some ideas.

Thomas feels that collectives could not have survived more than "a few years while primitive misery was being overcome." I see nothing in his data to support this conclusion. The Palestinian-Israeli experience has shown that collectives can remain both a social and an economic success over a long period. The success of Spanish collectivization, under war conditions, seems amazing. One can obviously not be certain whether these successes could have been secured and extended had it not been for the combined fascist, Communist, and liberal attack, but I can find no objective basis for the almost universal skepticism. Again, this seems to me merely a matter of irrational prejudice.

61. The following is a brief description by the anarchist writer Gaston Leval, *Né Franco, Né Stalin, le collettività anarchiche spagnole nella lotta contro Franco e la reazione staliniana* (Milan: Istituto Editoriale Italiano, 1952), pp. 303ff.; sections reprinted in *Collectivités anarchistes en Espagne révolutionnaire, Noir et Rouge,* undated.

> In the middle of the month of June, the attack began in Aragon on a grand scale and with hitherto unknown methods. The harvest was approaching. Rifles in hand, treasury guards under Communist orders stopped trucks loaded with provisions on the highways and brought them to their offices. A little later, the same guards poured into the collectives and confiscated great quantities of wheat under the authority of the general staff with headquarters in Barbastro. . . . Later open attacks began, under the command of Lister with troops withdrawn from the front at Belchite more than 50 kilometers away, in the month of August. . . . The final result was that 30 percent of the collectives were completely destroyed. In Alcolea, the municipal council that governed the collective was arrested; the people who lived in the Home for the Aged . . . were thrown out on the street. In Mas de las Matas, in Monzon, in Barbastro, on all sides, there were arrests. Plundering took place everywhere. The stores of the cooperatives and their grain supplies were rifled; furnishings were destroyed. The governor of Aragon, who was appointed by the central government after the dissolution of the Council of Aragon—which appears to have been the signal for the armed attack against the collectives—protested. He was told to go to the devil.
>
> On October 22, at the National Congress of Peasants, the delegation of

the Regional Committee of Aragon presented a report of which the following is the summary:

"More than 600 organizers of collectives have been arrested. The government has appointed management committees that seized the warehouses and distributed their contents at random. Land, draught animals, and tools were given to individual families or to the fascists who had been spared by the revolution. The harvest was distributed in the same way. The animals raised by the collectives suffered the same fate. A great number of collectivized pig farms, stables, and dairies were destroyed. In certain communes, such as Bordon and Calaceite, even seed was confiscated and the peasants are now unable to work the land."

The estimate that 30 percent of the collectives were destroyed is consistent with figures reported by Peirats (*Los anarquistas en la crisis politica española*, p. 300). He points out that only two hundred delegates attended the congress of collectives of Aragon in September 1937 ("held under the shadow of the bayonets of the Eleventh Division" of Lister) as compared with five hundred delegates at the congress of the preceding February. Peirats states that an army division of Catalan separatists and another division of the PSUC also occupied parts of Aragon during this operation, while three anarchist divisions remained at the front, under orders from the CNT-FAI leadership. Compare Jackson's explanation of the occupation of Aragon: "The peasants were known to hate the Consejo, *the anarchists had deserted the front during the Barcelona fighting,* and the very existence of the Consejo was a standing challenge to the authority of the central government" (my italics).

62. Regarding Bolloten's work, Jackson has this to say: "Throughout the present chapter, I have drawn heavily on this carefully documented study of the Communist Party in 1936–37. It is unrivaled in its coverage of the wartime press, of which Bolloten, himself a UP correspondent in Spain, made a large collection" (p. 363 n.).

63. See note 18. A number of citations from Berneri's writings are given by Broué and Témime. Morrow also presents several passages from his journal, *Guerra di Classe.* A collection of his works would be a very useful contribution to our understanding of the Spanish Civil War and to the problems of revolutionary war in general.

64. Cattell, *op. cit.,* p. 208. See also the remarks by Borkenau, Brenan, and Bolloten cited earlier. Neither Cattell nor Borkenau regards this decline of fighting spirit as a major factor, however.

65. *Op. cit.,* p. 195, n. 7.

66. To this extent, Trotsky took a similar position. See his *Lesson of Spain* (London: Workers' International Press, 1937).

67. Cited in Richards, *op. cit.,* p. 23.

68. H. E. Kaminski, *Ceux de Barcelone* (Paris: Les Éditions Denoël, 1937), p. 181.

This book contains very interesting observations on anarchist Spain by a skeptical though sympathetic eyewitness.

69. May 15, 1937. Cited by Richards, *op. cit.*, p. 106.

70. Cited by Broué and Témime, *op. cit.*, p. 258, n. 34. The conquest of Saragossa was the goal, never realized, of the anarchist militia in Aragon.

71. *Ibid.*, p. 175.

72. *Ibid.*, p. 193.

73. The fact was not lost on foreign journalists. Morrow (*op. cit.*, p. 68) quotes James Minifie in the *New York Herald Tribune*, April 28, 1937: "A reliable police force is being built up quietly but surely. The Valencia government discovered an ideal instrument for this purpose in the Carabineros. These were formerly customs officers and guards, and always had a good reputation for loyalty. It is reported on good authority that 40,000 have been recruited for this force, and that 20,000 have already been armed and equipped. . . . The anarchists have already noticed and complained about the increased strength of this force at a time when we all know there's little enough traffic coming over the frontiers, land or sea. They realize that it will be used against them." Consider what these soldiers, as well as Lister's division or the *asaltos* described by Orwell, might have accomplished on the Aragon front, for example. Consider also the effect on the militiamen, deprived of arms by the central government, of the knowledge that these well-armed, highly trained troops were liquidating the accomplishments of their revolution.

74. Cited in Rocker, *The Tragedy of Spain*, p. 37.

75. For references, see Bolloten, *op. cit.*, p. 192, n. 12.

76. Cited in Rocker, *The Tragedy of Spain*, p. 37.

77. Liston M. Oak, "Balance Sheet of the Spanish Revolution," *Socialist Review*, vol. 6 (September 1937), pp. 7–9, 26. This reference was brought to my attention by William B. Watson. A striking example of the distortion introduced by the propaganda efforts of the 1930s is the strange story of the influential film *The Spanish Earth*, filmed in 1937 by Joris Ivens with a text (written afterward) by Hemingway—a project that was apparently initiated by Dos Passos. A very revealing account of this matter, and of the perception of the Civil War by Hemingway and Dos Passos, is given in W. B. Watson and Barton Whaley, "The Spanish Earth of Dos Passos and Hemingway," unpublished, 1967. The film dealt with the collectivized village of Fuentidueña in Valencia (a village collectivized by the UGT, incidentally). For the libertarian Dos Passos, the revolution was the dominant theme; it was the antifascist war, however, that was to preoccupy Hemingway. The role of Dos Passos was quickly forgotten, because of the fact (as Watson and Whaley point out) that "Dos Passos had become anathema to the Left for his criticisms of communist policies in Spain."

78. As far as the East is concerned, Rocker (*The Tragedy of Spain*, p. 25) claims that "the Russian press, for reasons that are easily understood, never uttered one least little word about the efforts of the Spanish workers and peasants at social recon-

struction." I cannot check the accuracy of this claim, but it would hardly be surprising if it were correct.

79. See Patricia A. M. Van der Esch, *Prelude to War: The International Repercussions of the Spanish Civil War (1935–1939)* (The Hague: Martinus Nijhoff, 1951), p. 47; and Brenan, *op. cit.,* p. 329, n. 1. The conservative character of the Basque government was also, apparently, largely a result of French pressure. See Broué and Témime, *op. cit.,* p. 172, no. 8.

80. See Dante A. Puzzo, *Spain and the Great Powers: 1936–1941* (New York: Columbia University Press, 1962), pp. 86 ff. This book gives a detailed and very insightful analysis of the international background of the Civil War.

81. Jules Sauerwein, dispatch to the *New York Times* dated July 26. Cited by Puzzo, *op. cit.,* p. 84.

82. Cf., for example, Jackson, *op. cit.,* pp. 248 ff.

83. As reported by Herschel V. Johnson of the American embassy in London; cited by Puzzo, *op. cit.,* p. 100.

84. See Broué and Témime, *op. cit.,* pp. 288–89.

85. Cited by Thomas, *The Spanish Civil War,* p. 531, no. 3. Rocker, *The Tragedy of Spain,* p. 14, quotes (without reference) a proposal by Churchill for a five-year "neutral dictatorship" to "tranquilize" the country, after which they could "perhaps look for a revival of parliamentary institutions."

86. Puzzo, *op. cit.,* p. 116.

87. *Ibid.,* p. 147. Eden is referring, of course, to the Soviet Union. For an analysis of Russian assistance to the Spanish Republic, see Cattell, *op. cit.,* chap. 8.

88. Cf. Puzzo, *op. cit.,* pp. 147–48.

89. *Ibid.,* p. 212.

90. *Ibid.,* p. 93.

91. *Op. cit.,* p. 248.

92. Puzzo, *op. cit.,* pp. 151 ff.

93. *Ibid.,* pp. 154–55 and n. 27.

94. For some references, see Allen Guttmann, *The Wound in the Heart: America and the Spanish Civil War* (New York: Free Press, 1962), pp. 137–38. The earliest quasi-official reference that I know of is in Herbert Feis, *The Spanish Story,* (New York: Alfred A. Knopf, 1948), where data are given in an appendix. Jackson (*op. cit.,* p. 256) refers to this matter, without noting that Texaco was violating a prior agreement with the Republic. He states that the American government could do nothing about this, since "oil was not considered a war material under the Neutrality Act." He does not point out, however, that Robert Cuse, the Martin Company, and the Mexican government were put under heavy pressure to withhold supplies from the Republic, although this, too, was quite legal. As noted, the Texas Company was never even branded "unethical" or "unpatriotic," these epithets of Roosevelt's being reserved for those who tried to assist the Republic. The cynic might ask just why oil was excluded from the Neutrality Act of January 1937, noting that while Germany and Italy were capable of supplying arms to Franco, they could not meet his demands for oil.

The Texas Company continued to act upon the pro-Nazi sympathies of its head, Captain Thorkild Rieber, until August 1940, when the publicity began to be a threat to business. See Feis, *op. cit.,* for further details. For more on these matters, see Richard P. Traina, *American Diplomacy and the Spanish Civil War* (Bloomington: Indiana University Press, 1968), pp. 166 ff.

95. Puzzo, *op. cit.,* p. 160. He remarks: "A government in Madrid in which Socialists, Communists, and anarchists sat was not without menace to American business interests both in Spain and Latin America" (p. 165). Hull, incidentally, was in error about the acts of the Spanish government. The irresponsible left-wing elements had not been given arms but had seized them, thus preventing an immediate Franco victory.

96. See Jackson, *op. cit.,* p. 458.

97. Cf. Guttmann, *op. cit.,* p. 197. Of course, American liberalism was always proloyalist, and opposed both to Franco and to the revolution. The attitude toward the latter is indicated with accuracy by this comparison, noted by Guttmann, p. 165: "300 people met in Union Square to hear Liston Oak [see note 77] expose the Stalinists' role in Spain; 20,000 met in Madison Square Garden to help Earl Browder and Norman Thomas celebrate the preservation of bourgeois democracy," in July 1937.

98. *Ibid.,* p. 198.

99. To conclude these observations about the international reaction, it should be noted that the Vatican recognized the Franco government *de facto* in August 1937 and *de jure* in May 1938. Immediately upon Franco's final victory, Pope Pius XII made the following statement: "Peace and victory have been willed by God to Spain . . . which has now given to proselytes of the materialistic atheism of our age the highest proof that above all things stands the eternal value of religion and of the Spirit." Of course, the position of the Catholic Church has since undergone important shifts—something that cannot be said of the American government.

100. See note 14.

101. See, for example, the reference to Machajski in Harold D. Lasswell, *The World Revolution of Our Time: A Framework for Basic Policy Research* (Hoover Institute Studies; Palo Alto, Calif.: Stanford University Press, 1951); reprinted, with extensions, in Harold D. Lasswell and Daniel Lerner, eds., *World Revolutionary Elites: Studies in Coercive Ideological Movements* (Cambridge, Mass.: MIT Press, 1965), pp. 29–96. Daniel Bell has a more extensive discussion of Machajski's critique of socialism as the ideology of a new system of exploitation in which the "intellectual workers" will dominate, in a very informative essay that bears directly on a number of the topics that have been mentioned here: "Two Roads from Marx: The Themes of Alienation and Exploitation, and Workers' Control in Socialist Thought," in *The End of Ideology,* pp. 335–68.

102. Lasswell and Lerner, *op. cit.,* p. 85. In this respect, Lasswell's prognosis resembles that of Bell in the essays cited earlier.

103. Summarized in the *Christian Science Monitor,* March 15, 1968. I have not seen the text and therefore cannot judge the accuracy of the report.

104. To mention just the most recent example: on January 22, 1968, McNamara testified before the Senate Armed Services Committee that "the evidence appears overwhelming that beginning in 1966 Communist local and guerrilla forces have sustained substantial attrition. As a result, there has been a drop in combat efficiency and morale. . . ." The Tet offensive was launched within a week of this testimony. See *I. F. Stone's Weekly*, February 19, 1968, for some highly appropriate commentary.

105. See the first section of the original essay, omitted here. The reality behind the rhetoric has been amply reported. A particularly revealing description is given by Katsuichi Honda, a reporter for *Asahi Shimbun*, in *Vietnam—A Voice from the Villages*, 1967.

The Manufacture of Consent

This essay is excerpted from an address by the same title given at the Community Church of Boston on December 9, 1984.

Language and Freedom

This essay was presented as a lecture at the University Freedom and the Human Sciences Symposium, Loyola University, Chicago, January 8–9, 1970. It is to appear in the Proceedings of the Symposium, edited by Thomas R. Gorman. It also was published in *Abraxas*, vol. 1, no. 1 (1970), and in *TriQuarterly*, nos. 23–24 (1972). A number of the topics mentioned here are discussed further in my *Problems of Knowledge and Freedom* (New York: Pantheon Books, 1971).

1. F. W. J. Schelling, *Philosophical Inquiries into the Nature of Human Freedom*, trans. and ed. James Gutmann (Chicago: Open Court Publishing Co., 1936).

2. R. D. Masters, introduction to his edition of Jean-Jacques Rousseau, *First and Second Discourses*, (New York: St. Martin's Press, 1964).

3. Compare Proudhon, a century later: "No long discussion is necessary to demonstrate that the power of denying a man his thought, his will, his personality, is a power of life and death, and that to make a man a slave is to assassinate him."

4. Cited in A. Lehning, ed., Bakunin, *Etatisme et anarchie* (Leiden: E. J. Brill, 1967), editor's note 50, from P. Schrecker, "Kant et la révolution française," *Revue philosophique*, September–December 1939.

5. I have discussed this matter in *Cartesian Linguistics* (New York: Harper & Row, 1966) and *Language and Mind* (New York: Harcourt Brace Jovanovich, extended ed., 1972).

6. See the references of note 5, and also my *Aspects of the Theory of Syntax*, (Cambridge, Mass.: MIT Press, 1969), chap. 1, sec. 8.

7. I need hardly add that this is not the prevailing view. For discussion, see E. H. Lenneberg, *Biological Foundations of Language* (New York: John Wiley & Sons,

1967); my *Language and Mind;* E. A. Drewe *et al.,* "A Comparative Review of the Results of Behavioral Research on Man and Monkey," (London; Institute of Psychiatry, unpublished draft, 1969); P. H. Lieberman, D. H. Klatt, and W. H. Wilson, "Vocal Tract Limitations on the Vowel Repertoires of Rhesus Monkeys and other Nonhuman Primates," *Science,* June 6, 1969; and P. H. Lieberman, "Primate Vocalizations and Human Linguistic Ability," *Journal of the Acoustical Society of America,* vol. 44, no. 6 (1968).

8. In the books cited above, and in *Current Issues in Linguistic Theory* (New York: Humanities Press, 1964).

9. J. W. Burrow, introduction to his edition of Wilhelm von Humboldt, *The Limits of State Action* (London: Cambridge University Press, 1969), from which most of the following quotes are taken.

10. Compare the remarks of Kant, quoted above. Kant's essay appeared in 1793; Humboldt's was written in 1791–92. Parts appeared, but it did not appear in full during his lifetime. See Burrow, introduction to Humboldt, *Limits of State Action.*

11. Thomas G. Sanders, "The Church in Latin America," *Foreign Affairs,* vol. 48, no. 2 (1970).

12. *Ibid.,* The source is said to be the ideas of Paulo Freire. Similar criticism is widespread in the student movement in the West. See, for example, Mitchell Cohen and Dennis Hale, eds., *The New Student Left* rev. ed. (Boston: Beacon Press, 1967), chap. 3.

13. Namely, that a man "only attains the most matured and graceful consummation of his activity, when his way of life is harmoniously in keeping with his character"—that is, when his actions flow from inner impulse.

14. The latter quote is from Humboldt's comments on the French Constitution, 1791—parts translated in Marianne Cowan, ed., *Humanist Without Portfolio: An Anthology* (Detroit: Wayne State University Press, 1963).

15. Rudolf Rocker, "Anarchism and Anarcho-syndicalism," in Paul Eltzbacher, *Anarchism* (London: Freedom Press, 1960). In his book *Nationalism and Culture* (London: Freedom Press, 1937), Rocker describes Humboldt as "the most prominent representative in Germany" of the doctrine of natural rights and of the opposition to the authoritarian state. Rousseau he regards as a precursor of authoritarian doctrine, but he considers only the *Social Contract,* not the far more libertarian *Discourse on Inequality.* Burrow observes that Humboldt's essay anticipates "much nineteenth century political theory of a populist, anarchist and syndicalist kind" and notes the hints of the early Marx. See also my *Cartesian Linguistics,* n. 51, for some comments.

16. Karl Polanyi, *The Great Transformation: The Political and Economic Origins of Our Time* (Boston: Beacon Press, 1957).

17. Cited by Paul Mattick, "Workers' Control," in Priscilla Long, ed., *The New Left* (Boston: Porter Sargent, 1969), p. 377.

18. Cited in Martin Buber, *Paths in Utopia* (Boston: Beacon Press, 1958). p. 19.

19. Yet Rousseau dedicates himself, as a man who has lost his "original simplicity" and can no longer "do without laws and chiefs," to "respect the sacred

bonds" of his society and "scrupulously obey the laws, and the men who are their authors and ministers," while scorning "a constitution that can be maintained only with the help of so many respectable people . . . and from which, despite all their care, always arise more real calamities than apparent advantages."

Psychology and Ideology

The essay from which this excerpt is taken was expanded from one published in *Cognition,* vol. 1, no. 1 (1972). Parts appeared, in a slightly different form, as a review of B. F. Skinner, *Beyond Freedom and Dignity,* in the *New York Review of Books,* December 30, 1971. The original essay deals also with the investigation of race and IQ.

1. *The Economist,* October 31, 1862. Cited by Frederick F. Clairmonte in his review of *The Race War,* by Ronald Segal, *Journal of Modern African Studies,* vol. 8, no. 3 (October 1970).

2. Marvin Harris, *The Rise of Anthropological Theory* (New York: Thomas Y. Crowell Co., 1968), pp. 100–101. By the 1860s, he writes, "anthropology and racial determinism had become almost synonyms."

3. B. F. Skinner, *Beyond Freedom and Dignity* (New York: Alfred A. Knopf, 1971), p. 82. Subsequent references will be to page number only.

4. W. V. O. Quine, "Linguistics and Philosophy," in Sidney Hook, ed., *Language and Philosophy* (New York: New York University Press, 1969), p. 97.

5. We can, of course, design circumstances under which behavior can be predicted quite closely, as any military interrogator in the field is aware. And we can reduce the issue to triviality by regarding a person's wishes, intentions, purposes, and so on as part of the circumstances that elicit behavior. If we are really intent on deluding ourselves, we might go on to "translate" wishes, intentions, and purposes into the terminology of operant-conditioning theory, along the lines that we will explore in a moment.

6. L. Breger and J. L. McGaugh, "Critique and Reformulation of 'Learning-Theory' Approaches to Psychotherapy and Neurosis," *Psychological Bulletin,* May 1965.

7. Aubrey J. Yates, *Behavior Therapy* (New York: John Wiley & Sons, 1970), p. 396. Skinner also points out, irrelevantly to any rational consideration, that "the speaker does not feel the *grammatical rules* he is said to apply in composing sentences, and men spoke grammatically for thousands of years before anyone knew there were rules" (p. 16).

8. Jacques Monod, *Choice and Necessity: An Essay on the Natural Philosophy of Modern Biology* (New York: Alfred A. Knopf, 1971).

9. See, e.g., Kenneth MacCorquodale, "On Chomsky's Review of Skinner's *Verbal Behavior,*" *Journal of the Experimental Analysis of Behavior,* vol. 13, no. 1 (1970).

10. As Koestler points out, in remarks Skinner quotes, Skinner's approach repre-

sents "question-begging on a heroic scale" (p. 165). It will not do to respond, as Skinner does, by claiming that this is "name-calling" and a sign of emotional instability. Rather it will be necessary to show that this is not the literal and obvious truth (as indeed it is).

11. See his *Verbal Behavior* (New York: Appleton-Century-Crofts, 1957), which incorporates and extends these lectures.

12. In reviewing Skinner's *Verbal Behavior* (*Language*, vol. 35, no. 1 [1959], pp. 26–58), I stated that there did appear to be one result, namely, with regard to modifying certain aspects of the speaker's behavior (say, production of plural nouns) by "reinforcement" with such expressions as "right" and "good," without the speaker's awareness. The result is at best of marginal interest, since evidently the speaker's behavior in such respects could be far more "effectively" modified by a simple instruction, a fact that cannot be incorporated into the Skinnerian system, if the latter is interpreted at all strictly. Of course, if the subject is aware of what the experimenter is doing, the result is of no interest at all. It turns out that this may very well be the case. See D. Dulany, "Awareness, Rules and Propositional Control: A Confrontation with S-R Behavior Theory," in Theodore R. Dixon and David Horton, eds., *Verbal Behavior and General Behavior Theory* (New York: Prentice-Hall, 1968). Therefore, it seems that there are no clear nontrivial results that have been achieved in the study of normal human speech by application of the operant-conditioning paradigm.

Interesting reading, in this connection, is MacCorquodale, "On Chomsky's Review of Skinner." I cannot take the space here to correct the many errors (such as his misunderstanding of the notion of "function," which leads to much confusion). The major confusion in the article is this: MacCorquodale assumes that I was attempting to disprove Skinner's theses, and he points out that I present no data to disprove them. But my point was, rather, to demonstrate that when Skinner's assertions are taken literally, they are false on the face of it (MacCorquodale discusses none of these examples accurately) or else quite vacuous (as when we say that the response "Mozart" is under the control of a subtle stimulus), and that many of his false statements can be converted into uninteresting truths by employing such terms as "reinforce" with the full imprecision of "like," "want," "enjoy," and so on (with a loss of accuracy in transition, of course, since a rich and detailed terminology is replaced by a few terms that are divorced entirely from the setting in which they have some precision). Failing to understand this, MacCorquodale "defends" Skinner by showing that quite often it is possible to give a vacuous interpretation to his pronouncements; exactly my point. The article is useful, once errors are eliminated, in revealing the bankruptcy of the operant-conditioning approach to the study of verbal behavior.

13. See MacCorquodale, "On Chomsky's Review of Skinner," for a revealing example of complete inability to understand this point.

14. Note the shift in Skinner's account from the discussion of things that taste good to value judgments about things that we call good (pp. 103–5).

15. One way out would be to deny that these are facts. This is the approach taken by Patrick Suppes, in remarks that MacCorquodale quotes. Suppes refers to several books that contain a variety of facts such as these and explore the problem of accounting for them by an explanatory theory, and he asserts simply that these books contain no data. Apparently Suppes would have us believe that these facts become "data" only when someone conducts an experiment in which he "proves" that the facts are what we know them to be, on a moment's thought. It would, of course, be a straightforward matter to devise such experiments (adjusting them, in the typical fashion of such experimental work, until they give what we antecedently know to be the right results), were anyone willing to waste his time in such ways. Then the books would contain "data," in Suppes' sense.

16. Libertarian thinkers have often been "radical environmentalists," mistakenly so, in my opinion, for reasons discussed elsewhere (see my *Problems of Knowledge and Freedom* [New York: Pantheon Books, 1971]).

Equality: Language Development, Human Intelligence, and Social Organization

This paper was first presented at the "Conference on the Promise and Problems of Human Equality" held at the University of Illinois (Urbana) in March 1976. The version given here is reprinted from *Equality and Social Policy*, edited by Walter Feinberg (Champaign: University of Illinois Press, 1978).

1. Robert Goodman, *After the Planners* (New York: Simon & Schuster, 1971).

2. K. William Kapp, *The Social Cost of Private Enterprise, 1950* (New York: Schocken Books, 1971), p. 231.

3. Cf. Seymour Melman, "Industrial Efficiency Under Managerial Versus Cooperative Decision-making," *Review of Radical Political Economics*, Spring 1970; reprinted in B. Horvat, M. Markovic, and R. Supek, eds., *Self-Governing Socialism*, vol. 2 (White Plains, N.Y.: International Arts and Sciences Press, 1975). See also Melman, *Decision-Making and Productivity* (Oxford; Blackwell, 1958); and Paul Blumberg, *Industrial Democracy: The Sociology of Participation* (New York: Schocken Books, 1969).

4. Stephen A. Marglin, "What Do Bosses Do?," *Review of Radical Political Economics*, Summer 1974; Herbert Gintis, "Alienation in Capitalist Society," in R. C. Edwards, M. Reich, and T. E. Weiskopf, *The Capitalist System* (Englewood Cliffs, N.J.: Prentice-Hall, 1972).

5. J. E. Meade, *Efficiency, Equality and the Ownership of Property* (Cambridge, Mass.: Harvard University Press, 1965).

6. Karl Marx, *Capital,* vol. 3 (Moscow: Foreign Languages Publishing House, 1959).

7. Giambattista Vico, *The New Science,* trans. T. G. Bergin and M. H. Fisch (Garden City, N.Y.: Anchor Books, 1961).

8. David Ellerman, "Capitalism and Workers' Self-Management," in G. Hunnius, G. D. Garson, and J. Case, eds., *Workers' Control* (New York: Random House, 1973), pp. 10–11.

9. Adam Smith, *Wealth of Nations,* cited by Marglin, "What Do Bosses Do?"

10. Edward S. Greenberg, "In Defense of Avarice," *Social Policy,* January–February 1976, p. 63.

11. "The Fearful Drift of Foreign Policy," Commentary, *Business Week,* April 7, 1975.

12. In fact, in this case, sheer robbery backed by state power is a more likely explanation.

13. On the interpretation of the "lessons of Vietnam" by academic scholars and liberal commentators as the war ended, see my "Remaking of History," *Ramparts,* September 1975 (reprinted in *Towards a New Cold War* [New York: Pantheon Books, 1982]), and "The United States and Vietnam," *Vietnam Quarterly,* no. 1, (Winter 1976).

14. For a discussion of this topic, see my introduction to N. Blackstock, ed., *Cointelpro* (New York: Vintage Books, 1976).

15. See, for example, Herbert J. Gans, "About the Equalitarians," *Columbia Forum,* Spring 1975.

16. Rudolf Rocker, "Anarchism and Anarcho-Syndicalism," in P. Eltzbacher, ed., *Anarchism* (London: Freedom Press, 1960), pp. 234–35.

17. I have discussed some of the roots of these doctrines elsewhere: e.g., *For Reasons of State* (New York: Pantheon Books, 1973). See the two preceding chapters.

18. Rocker, *op. cit.*, p. 228. Rocker is characterizing the "ideology of anarchism." Whether Marx would have welcomed such a conception is a matter of conjecture. As a theoretician of capitalism, he did not have very much to say about the nature of a socialist society. Anarchists, who tended to the view that the workers' organizations must create "not only the ideas but also the facts of the future itself" within capitalist society (Bakunin), correspondingly provided a more extensive theory of postrevolutionary society. For a left-Marxist view of these questions, see Karl Korsch, "On Socialization," in Horvat *et al., op. cit.,* vol. 1.

19. Evidently there is a value judgement here, for which I do not apologize.

20. Quotes are from Salvador E. Luria, *Life: The Unfinished Experiment* (New York: Scribner's Sons, 1973).

21. For references and discussions, see note 17; also, Frank E. Manuel, "In Memoriam: Critique of the Gotha Program, 1875–1975," *Daedalus,* Winter 1976.

22. Fredy Perlman, *Essay on Commodity Fetishism,* 1968, reprinted from *Telos,* no. 6 (Somerville, Mass.: New England Free Press, 1968).

23. István Mészáros, *Marx's Theory of Alienation* (London: Merlin Press, 1970).

24. Cited by Mészáros, *Marx's Theory of Alienation*.

25. See my *Reflections on Language* (New York: Pantheon Books, 1975) for reference and discussion.

26. Walter Sullivan, "Scientists Debate Question of Race and Intelligence," *New York Times*, February 23, 1976, p. 23. His account may well be accurate; I have often heard and read similar comments from left-wing scientists.

27. Cf., for example, the remarks on language in Luria, *op. cit.;* Jacques Monod, *Chance and Necessity* (New York: Alfred A. Knopf, 1971); and François Jacob, *The Logic of Life,* (New York; Pantheon Books, 1973). For some recent discussion of this issue, see my *Reflections on Language.*

28. It is extremely misleading to argue, as some do, that certain birds have an elementary "concept of number" as revealed by their ability to employ ordinal and visually presented systems up to some finite limit (about 7). The concepts one, two . . . seven are not to be confused with the concept of natural number, as formally captured, e.g., by the Dedekind-Peano axioms and intuitively understood, without difficulty, by normal humans, as an infinite system.

29. Cf. my *For Reasons of State,* chap. 7.

30. *American Power and the New Mandarins* (New York: Pantheon Books, 1969), introduction.

The Old and the New Cold War

This essay is excerpted from "Towards a New Cold War," in *Towards a New Cold War: Essays on the Current Crisis and How We Got There* (New York: Pantheon Books, 1982).

1. See Thomas M. Franck and Edward Weisband, *Word Politics: Verbal Strategy Among the Superpowers* (New York: Oxford University Press, 1971) for discussion of how the Khrushchev and Brezhnev doctrines mirrored, respectively, the earlier Eisenhower and Johnson doctrines in the rhetoric adopted to justify military intervention in satellite states.

2. Thomas Powers, *The Man Who Kept the Secrets* (New York: Alfred A. Knopf, 1979), p. 306. Cf. also Basil Davidson, "South Africa's Border Wars," *New Society*, March 19, 1981, and for the general background, John Marcum, *The Angolan Revolution*, vol. 2 (Cambridge, Mass.: MIT Press, 1978). Also John Stockwell, *In Search of Enemies* (New York: W. W. Norton & Co., 1978). The French role in Africa is also consistently underplayed in U.S. commentary. See Daniel Volman, "Gendarme of Africa," *Progressive* (March 1981), for a rare exception. Attention in the United States is generally focused not on intervention by France or South Africa, or Belgium, Egypt, and Morocco (in Zaire, as U.S. proxies), or Zaire (in Angola), etc., but rather on the Cuban role, interpreted as Kremlin-inspired aggression. Whatever one thinks of Cuba's activities in Africa, it is well to recall that in Angola, Cuba's intervention in support of the MPLA (whose government is now recognized by black Africa and the West apart from the United States) "followed upon substantial intervention by others, including Zaire and South Africa . . . there is no question that Cuba's intervention was partly an improvised response to South Africa's" (Marcum, *op. cit.*). Furthermore, the country remains

under regular attack by South African forces and mercenaries. On this matter, see Jonathan Steele's report from Angola (*Manchester Guardian Weekly*, February 8, 1981), concluding that "it is clear that South Africa is conducting a systematic policy of striking economic and military targets in Angola" and that "there can be no more doubt that the broad thrust of Angola's complaints that it is facing South African aggression is true, despite South African denials." Steele also gives a detailed account of the savagery and brutality of South African mercenaries (and their contempt for Savimbi's UNITA guerrillas, described as "a lot of crap"; Savimbi, widely touted as a freedom fighter in the United States, had made his peace with South Africa by mid-1975, shortly before he began receiving U.S. arms; see Marcum, *op. cit.*, who notes that American arms also "poured in on C130s from Zaire to the FNLA's staging areas," while this group, too, was being helped by South Africa). The latter account is based on an interview with a British mercenary who explains how his colleagues "love killing," particularly "killing women, hanging them and things." "They don't see them as people, just as things that are there."

As for Cuba serving as a Soviet proxy, while it is obvious that the USSR foots the bill, Cuba has its own reasons for involvement in Angola. The majority of the population of Cuba is African in origin, many from what is now Angola, and relations would no doubt be close even apart from South African aggression and terror, motivated in large part by South African efforts to defy U.N. decisions on independence for mineral-rich Namibia.

Angola has stated publicly that Cuban forces will withdraw when South African aggression ceases and Namibia gains independence, in accordance with U.N. resolutions (*Washington Post*, April 25, 1981).

For detailed analysis of the U.S. press on Angola and its close adherence to official doctrine, see Marsha Coleman's Ph.D. dissertation, "American Prestigious Newspapers' Coverage of African Crises Events," MIT, 1982.

3. See, for example, Franklyn Holzman, "Are the Soviets Really Outspending the U.S. on Defense?", *International Security*, Spring 1980).

4. Holzman estimates this gap at perhaps $400 billion in the past decade; "The Military Expenditure Gap—Fact or Fiction," manuscript, Tufts University, 1981.

5. See Richard B. Duboff and Edward S. Herman, "The New Economics: Handmaiden of Inspired Truth," *Review of Radical Political Economics*, August 1972. See also their review of James Tobin, *The New Economics One Decade Older* (Princeton) in *Commonweal*, December 20, 1974.

6. These events, and the way they are commonly treated here, merit careful consideration. It will be recalled that at a crucial stage of the missile crisis, the Kennedy administration was faced with what it regarded as a serious dilemma: whether to accept Khrushchev's offer to arrange a mutual withdrawal of Soviet missiles from Cuba and American missiles from Turkey (obsolete missiles, for which a withdrawal order had already been given since they were being replaced by Polaris submarines), or to reject this offer and face a probability of nuclear war that top-level Kennedy advisers estimated at 1:3 to 1:2. The latter course was

chosen, so as to establish the principle that we have the right to maintain missiles at their borders (but not conversely), and to ensure that there would be no challenge to the machismo image that the Kennedy administration endeavored so desperately to project. On the general character of Kennedy's much admired statesmanship during this period, see Richard J. Walton, *Cold War and Counter-Revolution* (Baltimore: Penguin Books, 1972). The memoirs of the participants make sufficiently chilling reading.

7. Cited from the *Forrestal Diaries* in Joyce and Gabriel Kolko, *The Limits of Power* (New York: Harper & Row, 1972), which remains the most important analytic study of evolving U.S. policy in this period, though there has been much useful work since.

8. *Ibid.*, p. 341. The all too common incapacity of mainstream scholarship even to comprehend what is being said in work that departs too far from the chauvinist consensus is evident in the discussion of the Anglo-American conflict during this period. Consider, for example, John C. Campbell's review in *Foreign Affairs*, Spring 1981, of Barry Rubin's *The Great Powers in the Middle East, 1941–1947* (London: Frank Cass, 1980), a book that provides documentation generally supporting the account by the Kolkos and other "revisionists," while typically disparaging the revisionist literature without serious argument. Campbell writes that the message of Rubin's book "brings no comfort to the revisionist school of cold-war historians" because it shows that U.S. policy was anti-imperialist ("Wilsonian") and "anti-British, and only anti-Soviet after the Russians began to subvert the independence of Middle East states." The anti-British element in U.S. policy and its "anti-imperialism" (i.e., opposition to imperial prerogatives that blocked the expansion of U.S.-based economic interests) is a major thesis of the revisionist literature—apart from the fact that Rubin's book hardly demonstrates any great success of the Russians in subverting the independence of Middle East states, a task that was then and subsequently a prerogative of the West, primarily.

9. Dean Acheson, *Present at the Creation* (New York: W. W. Norton & Co., 1969), p. 219.

10. *An-Nahar Arab Report & Memo*, Beirut, February 4, 1980.

11. See, for example, Bernard Lewis, *New York Times*, March 29, 1980.

12. For documentation and discussion, see Noam Chomsky and Edward S. Herman, *The Political Economy of Human Rights*, 2 vols. (Boston: South End Press, 1979), vol. 2, chap. 2.

13. The material just reviewed is from Lawrence S. Wittner, "The Truman Doctrine and the Defense of Freedom," *Diplomatic History*, vol. 4 (Spring 1980), largely drawn from government documents. See also Secretary of Commerce Maurice Stans, quoted in the *New York Times*, April 24, 1971, on "the welcome that is given here to American companies and the sense of security the Government of Greece is imparting to them" under the fascist regime of the U.S.-trained colonels.

14. Henry Kissinger, *American Foreign Policy,* expanded ed. (New York: W. W. Norton & Co., 1974).

15. Samuel P. Huntington, in his contribution to M. J. Crozier, S. P. Huntington, and J. Watanuki, *The Crisis of Democracy* (New York: New York University Press, 1975).

16. *Defense Monitor,* January 1980.

17. This and the preceding quote are cited in the important study by Jan K. Black, *United States Penetration of Brazil* (Philadelphia: University of Pennsylvania Press, 1977).

18. Cited in *ibid.*

Afghanistan and South Vietnam

This essay is an excerpt from "The Manufacture of Consent," an address given at the Community Church of Boston on December 9, 1984.

Vietnam and United States Global Strategy

This essay is excerpted from "The Backroom Boys," in *For Reasons of State* (New York: Pantheon Books, 1973).

1. Cf. in particular Gabriel Kolko, *The Roots of American Foreign Policy,* (Boston: Beacon Press, 1969); the discussion in Gabriel and Joyce Kolko, *The Limits of Power: The World and United States Foreign Policy, 1945–1954* (New York: Harper & Row, 1972); my *At War with Asia* (New York: Pantheon Books, 1970), chap. 1; and Committee of Concerned Asian Scholars, *The Indochina Story* (New York: Pantheon Books, 1970), pt. 3. See also the articles by John Dower, Richard Du Boff, and Gabriel Kolko in Noam Chomsky and Howard Zinn, eds., *Critical Essays* (Boston: Beacon Press, 1972), vol. 5 of the *Pentagon Papers*; see note 5, below.

2. See Walt W. Rostow and Richard W. Hatch, *An American Policy in Asia,* (Cambridge, Mass.: MIT Press, 1955), p. 7. In Rostow's view, this "ideological threat to our interest . . . is as great as the military threat" posed by Communist China and the Soviet Union. It is essential, Rostow notes, "to emphasize . . . especially the close link between Japan's dangerous foreign trade problem and the requirements of growth in Southeast Asia" (p. 12), and to remove the "illusory glamor" of trade with the Communist bloc, which "represent[s] a powerful attraction" (though an unreal one), particularly to Japan (pp. 46–47). Furthermore, "The relative performance of India and Communist China over the course of their respective First Five Year Plans may very well determine the outcome of the ideological struggle in Asia" (p. 37). "India and Asia could be won to Communism without a Chinese Communist soldier crossing Chinese borders," if "the

Communist bid to win Asia by demonstrating rapid industrialization" is more successful than development in "Free Asian societies" (pp. 51–52). It is also necessary "to learn to deal effectively with subversion and insurrection . . . as now in Southern Vietnam" (p. 7). The book is interesting as the ideological expression of an influential planner of the 1960s, with its emphasis on our fundamental interest in preserving open societies with no "concentrated power" in the state (pp. 4–5, 14; other forms of "concentrated power" go unmentioned). For further discussion, see my *American Power and the New Mandarins,* (New York: Pantheon Books, 1969), p. 332 (p. 69, above).

3. U.S., Department of Defense, *United States-Vietnam Relations. 1945–67* (Washington, D. C.: Government Printing Office, 1971), bk. 10, p. 1198; June 1959. This work is the government offset edition of the Pentagon Papers, censored but including valuable documents unavailable elsewhere, referred to throughout this book as *DOD.*

4. These fears were reevaluated shortly, when it appeared that China was undergoing an economic crisis, but may well be voiced again in the future.

5. *The Pentagon Papers,* Senator Gravel Edition, 5 vols. (Boston: Beacon Press, 1971), vol. 3, p. 592 [III, 592]; November 4, 1964. References throughout this book are to this edition, in the style indicated in brackets, except where otherwise noted.

6. For some discussion, see Donald Zagoria, "The Strategic Debate in Peking," in Tang Tsou, ed., *China in Crisis,* vol. 2 (Chicago: University of Chicago Press, 1968), pp. 249ff.

7. See, for example, Roger Hilsman's discussion of this speech in his *to Move a Nation* (Garden City, N.Y.: Doubleday & Co., 1967). For comments, see my *American Power and the New Mandarins,* chap. 3, pp. 262–66.

8. For example, by Chester Cooper, "The CIA and Decision-making," *Foreign Affairs,* vol. 50, no. 2 (1972).

9. John Dower, "The Superdomino in Postwar Asia: Japan In and Out of the *Pentagon Papers,"* in Chomsky and Zinn, *Critical Essays.*

10. Compare Ho Chi Minh and Phibun Songkhram, the Japanese collaborator who had overthrown the government of Thailand in April 1948 after his poor showing in the elections, "the first pro-Axis dictator to regain power after the war" (Frank C. Darling, *Thailand and the United States* [Washington, D.C.: Public Affairs Press, 1965], p. 65). Support from the United States was immediate, one of the measures taken "to deter Communist aggression in Southeast Asia" (p. 67).

11. Cited in Chester Cooper, *The Lost Crusade: America in Vietnam* (New York: Dodd, Mead & Co., 1970) p. 168. A bit "melodramatic," Cooper feels, but otherwise unexceptionable.

12. Robert W. Tucker, *The Radical Left and American Foreign Policy* (Baltimore: Johns Hopkins University Press, 1971), pp. 116–17.

13. On Japanese-Southeast Asian relations and their significance, see Jon Halli-

day and Gavan McCormack, *Japanese Imperialism Today* (New York: Monthly Review Press, 1972).

14. Cooper, *Lost Crusade*, pp. 410–11.

15. Ralph Stavins, Richard J. Barnet, and Marcus G. Raskin, *Washington Plans an Aggressive War* (New York: Random House, 1972), p. 20.

16. See my *At War with Asia*, chap. 1, for references. For general background, see Dower, "The Superdomino in Postwar Asia."

17. See C. Fred Bergsten, "Crisis in U.S. Trade Policy," *Foreign Affairs*, vol. 49, no. 4 (1971).

18. For data, see Yasuo Takeyama, "Don't Take Japan for Granted," *Foreign Policy*, vol. 1, no. 2 (1971–72).

19. Or as Kindleberger puts it in his caricature, the theory that "United States economic foreign policy is unrelievedly evil." Review article on *The Age of Imperialism* by Harry Magdoff, *Public Policy*, Summer 1971.

20. On the evolution of United States policy in the crucial 1945–50 period, see John Dower, "Occupied Japan and the American Lake," in Edward Friedman and Mark Selden, eds., *America's Asia* (New York: Pantheon Books, 1971). On the limits of American power in the real world, see Kolko and Kolko, *Limits of Power*.

21. Zbigniew Brzezinski, "Japan's Global Engagement," *Foreign Affairs*, vol. 50, no. 2 (1972); Takeyama, "Don't Take Japan for Granted." For comparison, American firms control about 40 percent of the British computer industry (Raymond Vernon, *Sovereignty at Bay* (New York: Basic Books, 1971), p. 240. Excluding tabletop machines, IBM has about 70 percent of Japan's computer market (Koji Nakamura, "The Okinawa Payoff," *Far Eastern Economic Review*, August 21, 1971).

22. On this and related matters, see Malcolm Caldwell, "Oil and Imperialism in East Asia," *Journal of Contemporary Asia*, vol. 1, no. 3 (1971).

23. Thus the director of USAID for Brazil finds it quite natural that "we have spent $2 billion [since 1964] on a program one objective of which is the protection of a favorable investment climate for private business interests in this country," while the total investment is about $1.7 billion. Senator Frank Church, in Hearings Before the [Church] Subcommittee on Western Hemisphere Affairs, U.S. Senate, May 1971, pp. 165–66.

24. This is argued, with reference to Vietnam, by Arthur Schlesinger, Jr., in testimony before the Senate Foreign Relations Committee, May 10, 1972; and commonly by others. Schlesinger considers the "more sophisticated" economic argument that defeat in Vietnam would jeopardize American economic interests throughout the Third World, failing to notice that this is only part of the argument offered by those he hopes to refute. Rather, they have generally pointed out that United States policy in Indochina was closely related to its efforts to consolidate Japanese and Western European capitalism. Schlesinger also remarks that the Pentagon Papers seem to record "no instances of business intervention in American Vietnam policy." The relevance of this observation is not apparent, given the fact that the state executive is largely staffed by representatives of corporate

interests, as has often been noted (see note 52). It is hardly necessary for business to "intervene" in an enterprise that it largely controls. Schlesinger also urges that "stupidity" should not be underestimated as a factor in shaping policy.

25. Derek Davies, "The Region," *Far Eastern Economic Review Yearbook,* 1971, p. 38; 1972, pp. 37–40. Although Davies refers to the domino theory as "a flight of fantasy," he unwittingly expresses a moderate version of it in such assessments as these. The economic and strategic significance of Southeast Asia is stressed by many observers. Few would go so far as Peter Lyon, who argues that if some enemy monopolized the region and exploited its resources fully (as Japan could not, in World War II), "then plainly the world balance of power very probably would have swung already in favour of South-east Asia's new hegemon" *(War and Peace in South-east Asia,* (Oxford: Royal Institute of International Affairs, 1969), p. 106). But, with qualifications, the point of view is not uncommon.

26. On the British precedent, see Michael Barratt Brown, *After Imperialism,* rev. ed. (New York: Humanities Press, 1970); and Eric Hobsbawm, *Industry and Empire: The Making of Modern English Society,* vol. 2 (New York: Pantheon Books, 1968).

27. Leslie H. Gelb, "Vietnam: The System Worked," *Foreign Policy,* vol. 1, no. 3 (1971). See also his comments in "On Schlesinger and Ellsberg: A Reply," *New York Review of Books,* December 2, 1971, and in "Lessons of the Pentagon Papers," *Life,* September 17, 1971.

28. Daniel Ellsberg explores in detail the hypothesis that domestic factors, in particular the effect of anticommunism on electoral success, predominated in decision-making. "The Quagmire Myth and the Stalemate Machine," *Public Policy,* Spring 1971. See his *Papers on the War* (New York: Simon & Schuster, 1972) for an extended version. Emphasis on these factors is not inconsistent with the imperialist interpretation, if we inquire further into the origins of domestic anticommunism, though an important question of emphasis remains (see note 40). Notice also that by 1965, questions of long-term motive were of diminished importance. We were there. Period. See the remarks of John McNaughton (IV, 47).

29. Hannah Arendt, "Lying in Politics: Reflections on the Pentagon Papers," *New York Review of Books,* November 18, 1971.

30. Similarly the analyst, discussing the origins of the insurgency, notes that no direct links had been established between Hanoi and the Southern insurgents in the 1956–59 period. Still he tends, rather cautiously, toward the view that "some form of DRV apparatus" may have "originated and controlled the insurgency" in those years (though "it can only be inferred"—the reader is invited to sample the evidence presented for the inference; I, 243).

31. Senate Concurrent Resolution 91 of June 25, 1954, found "strong evidence of intervention by the international Communist movement in the State of Guatemala, whereby government institutions have been infiltrated by Communist agents, weapons of war have been secretly shipped into that country, and the pattern of Communist conquest has become manifest" (cited by Thomas M. Franck and Edward Weisband, *Word Politics* [Oxford: Oxford University Press, 1971], p. 52).

32. It is sometimes argued that United States policy revealed its freedom from counterrevolutionary imperatives in Bolivia and Yugoslavia. In Bolivia, Eisenhower supported the most right-wing group that had any base of power—successfully, as it turned out, from the viewpoint of American economic interests. For a succinct review, see Rebecca Scott, "Economic Aid and Imperialism in Bolivia," *Monthly Review,* May 1972. As for Tito, Acheson explained in connection with the possibility of a "Titoist outcome" in Indochina that "U.S. attitude [could] take [account] such possibility only if every other possible avenue closed to preservation area from Kremlin control" (*DOD*, bk. 8, p. 197; May 1949). Recall that Acheson had no evidence of Kremlin control in Indochina, nicely illustrating the point at issue. In general, United States policy toward Yugoslavia in the context of the Cold War hardly serves as a counterexample to the thesis that it is guided by the principle of maintaining a "stable" system of societies open to American economic penetration.

33. On this matter, see John Gittings, "The Great Asian Conspiracy," in Friedman and Selden, *America's Asia.* He shows how easily China replaced Russia as the master plotter in official and academic interpretation of Far Eastern affairs, when reliance on the alleged Russian role became too far-fetched. It now appears that the official demonology is being reconstructed once again, with the Soviet Union as the chief villain, surely a wise move by state propagandists. It would, for example, be difficult in the long run to gain taxpayer support for an immense military budget on the basis of the "Chinese threat," but it is considerably easier to whip up hysteria over the alleged Soviet menace, along the lines of the "bomber gap" and "missile gap" of earlier years. Precisely what we see today. The United States lead in deliverable warheads and strategic weapons technology (e.g., MIRV) notwithstanding, the Alsop brothers and the like would have us believe that we are now virtually at the mercy of the Kremlin.

34. Peter Wiles, "The Declining Self-confidence of the Super-powers," *International Affairs*, vol. 47, no. 2 (1971).

35. William Pfaff, *Condemned to Freedom*, (New York: Random House, 1971), p. 80. A variant is the view expressed by Michael Howard: "The suspicion, clumsiness, and brutality of the Russians; the inexperience and confusion of the Americans; the weariness, impotence and nostalgia of the British"—these were the major factors in preventing a postwar settlement. "The Americans, bless them, still found it hard to believe that natural processes would not everywhere throw up regimes which would docilely accept their leadership" ("Realists and Romantics: On Maintaining an International Order," *Encounter,* April 1972). This particular form of sentimentality finds little support in the historical record, which reveals fairly systematic policies designed to take over British positions of power and influence and to create a global capitalist order in which the United States, given its enormous advantages, would be likely to predominate. The United States did not believe that "natural processes" would lead to subservient regimes in Southern Europe, France, East Asia, and the Caribbean, nor did it await such processes; rather, it acted directly and forcefully to undermine popular forces it opposed or

to institute regimes of the sort it preferred. While not uniformly successful, these policies and their execution revealed no more inexperience or confusion than might be expected, given the unavoidable uncertainties of global planning. See Kolko and Kolko, *Limits of Power.*

36. On Italy, see Gabriel Kolko, *The Politics of War* (New York: Random House, 1969). On Greece, see Kolko, *The Politics of War;* Kolko and Kolko, *The Limits of Power;* and Richard Barnet, *Intervention and Revolution* (New York: World Publishing Co., 1968). On Korea, see Jon Halliday, "The Korean Revolution," *Socialist Revolution,* vol. 1, no. 6 (1970); also Soon Sung Cho, *Korea in World Politics,* 1940–1950 (Berkeley: University of California Press, 1967); and Gregory Henderson, *Korea: The Politics of the Vortex,* (Cambridge, Mass.: Harvard University Press, 1968), chaps. 5–6. Though Cho and Henderson do not accept Halliday's interpretation of these events, what they describe is the destruction of indigenous Korean political and social structures by force and terror and the imposition of a right-wing regime. Their explanation in terms of "blunders," "ignorance and policy weakness," and so on becomes much less persuasive if we consider United States Korean policy, not in isolation, as in common academic practice, but rather in its global context, where remarkable similarities appear to American intervention and its effects elsewhere, as in Greece at exactly the same time.

Halliday's openly and clearly expressed sympathies for socialist revolution may be compared with the conservative bias implicit—but, typically, never explicitly recognized—in Henderson and Cho. Consider such observations as these: though under the People's Republic that the United States destroyed in South Korea there were occasional acts such as "interventions, usually against landlords in landlord-tenant disputes," nevertheless "people were generally well-behaved" (Henderson, p. 119); ". . . the Americans in the South took steps to encourage democratization by establishing an effective Korean administration under the military government, and by stamping out what they felt were irresponsible leftist political movements" (Cho, p. 131), beginning with the outright suppression of the Communist party in late 1946.

In fact, the Korean policy of the United States from 1945 presents suggestive analogies, in some interesting respects, to its policy in Vietnam, a matter that might be further explored.

37. Arthur M. Schlesinger, Jr., *A Thousand Days: John F. Kennedy in the White House* (Boston: Houghton Mifflin Co., 1965), p. 769.

38. Robert W. Tucker, *The Radical Left and American Foreign Policy* (Baltimore: Johns Hopkins University Press, 1971), p. 112; *Nation or Empire? The Debate over American Foreign Policy* (Baltimore: Johns Hopkins University Press, 1968), p. 117.

39. This is admitted even by those who deny that "Castro was unwillingly pushed into the Soviet camp by American blunders or malevolence" (Ernst Halperin, characterizing the position of Andrés Suárez, *Cuba: Castroism and Communism,* [Cambridge, Mass.: MIT Press, 1967], in the foreword). Thus Suárez points out

that Cuba was attacked "by airplanes based along the U.S. coastline" at the time when the United States was using its influence to prevent the Cubans from buying jets in Great Britain (October 1959), and adds, "I think this makes it sufficiently clear why, and for what, Soviet aid was sought" (p. 74). Though the matter is not relevant to refuting Tucker's contention, a good case can be made that American hostility was a factor of some importance in Castro's shift to the Soviet camp. See Maurice Zeitlin and Robert Scheer, *Cuba: Tragedy in Our Hemisphere*, (New York: Grove Press, 1963). For a general discussion of the background, see Gordon Connell-Smith, *The Inter-American System* (New York: Oxford University Press, 1966). He draws the quite reasonable conclusion that "the Cuban government's intention to implement a policy aimed at ending the privileged position hitherto enjoyed by the United States in the island's affairs" made the clash as inevitable as "the growing links between Cuba and international communism" (p. 170); and this intention also lies behind the fact that "the United States infinitely preferred Trujillo to Castro" (p. 169). Given the vagueness of his discussion, it is unclear whether Tucker would agree with this conclusion. If he would, then his objection to the "radical critique" is of vanishing empirical content.

40. Tucker, *The Radical Left*, pp. 111–12. My italics. Tucker refers to a third consideration underlying Kennedy's observation on supporting a Trujillo as long as there is a risk of a Castro, namely, concern for domestic anticommunism. This overlooks the crucial question of the origins and function of this domestic anticommunism, in particular the role and purpose of state propaganda. On this matter, see Richard M. Freeland, *The Truman Doctrine and the Origins of McCarthyism*, (New York: Alfred A. Knopf, 1972), and several essays in David Horowitz, ed., *Corporations and the Cold War*, (New York: Bertrand Russell Peace Foundation and Monthly Review Press, 1968).

41. On certain similarities, see my *American Power and the New Mandarins*, chap. 2; also Hilary Conroy, "Japan's War in China: Historical Parallel to Vietnam?" *Pacific Affairs*, vol. 43, no. 2 (1970).

42. Supporting what might misleadingly be called a United States security interest. On the relation between Greece and American interests in the Middle East, see Kolko and Kolko, *Limits of Power*, chap. 8.

43. M. S. Modiano, "Stans, in Athens, Hails the Regime," *New York Times*, April 24, 1971. It may be recalled that the Truman Doctrine was, in the first instance, specifically directed to Greece and Turkey. Greece required United States assistance "to become a self-supporting and self-respecting democracy" and "the future of Turkey as an independent and economically sound state is clearly no less important to the freedom-loving peoples of the world than the future of Greece" (Harry S. Truman, March 12, 1947). A look at the state of freedom in Greece and Turkey twenty-five years later gives a certain insight into the "policy of the United States," as formulated by President Truman on that occasion: "to support free peoples who are resisting attempted subjugation by armed minorities or by outside pressures."

44. William Y. Elliot, ed., *The Political Economy of American Foreign Policy*, (New York: Holt, Rinehart & Winston, 1955), p. 42. For quotations from this interesting document, and some discussion, see my *At War with Asia*, pp. 5, 17, 35–38. See Barratt Brown, *After Imperialism*, for a historical discussion of this matter.

45. Raymond Vernon *(Sovereignty at Bay)* concludes that the multinational corporations are "seen as posing a threat [in the host countries] for government leaders bent on control, for local businessmen who aspire to compete, and for intellectuals who are hoping to challenge the status quo" (pp. 249, 265). But he makes no mention of workers who are concerned, say, that management can break a strike by threatening to transfer operations to another country. Unions and others concerned with workers' interests take a different view. See, e.g., Hugh Scanlon, "International Combines Versus the Unions," *Bulletin of the Institute for Workers' Control*, vol. 1, no. 4 (1969); and several articles in the preceding special issue on the motor industry. These articles, incidentally, deal with concrete examples, not merely hypothetical concerns. See also John Gennard, *Multinational Corporations and British Labour*, (London: British–North American Committee, 1972), again with several concrete examples. Vernon's failure to consider this matter cannot be attributed to his (likely) belief that the concern is irrational, since he does not seem overly impressed with the "psychic needs" of the "élite groups" he does consider.

It is, furthermore, disturbing to see how myths are perpetuated in such work. Consider Vernon's reference to the "extraordinary concept of aid to less-developed countries"—a look at the facts would show that this concept is something less than extraordinary; see, e.g., Michael Hudson, "The Political Economy of Foreign Aid," in Denis Goulet and Michael Hudson, *The Myth of Aid* (New York: Orbis Books and IDOC, North America, 1971)—or his speculation that nations will "continue to emphasize such goals as the redistribution of personal income" (pp. 213, 257). Which nations will "continue" to emphasize such goals? The United States?

46. Connell-Smith, *The Inter-American System*, pp. 343–44.

47. Church Subcommittee Hearings, p. 165. See note 23 above.

48. *Ibid.*, p. 208. See, in this connection, "The Hanna Industrial Complex, Part I," *NACLA Newsletter*, vol. 2, no. 3 (May 1968). Hanna was one of the major beneficiaries of the 1964 coup.

49. *Washington Post*, December 6, 1971: some "awkward points" for visiting dictator Medici. Christopher Roper reports in the finance section of the *Manchester Guardian Weekly*, May 13, 1972: "Wages have been deliberately held down, and statistical evidence shows that real wages of factory workers in São Paulo—the largest industrial centre in the southern hemisphere of the world—have been almost halved over the past 10 years. Family incomes have only kept pace by workers working longer hours and wives going out to work." But, "foreign capital has been given a warm welcome"; "Volkswagen operates one of the largest integrated car manufacturing plants in the world; Ford is about to man-

ufacture Pinto engines for Detroit in São Paulo [the ones Henry Ford decided not to make in Britain? cf. note 45]; and Nippon Steel from Japan is thinking about building one of the world's largest steel mills." Notice that while United States policy is quite clearly determined, as stated, by "the protection and expansion . . . of our economic interests," the rules of the international capitalist game, if more or less followed, lead to certain problems even for the strongest player.

50. Marcio Moreira Alves, "Brazil: What Terror Is Like," *The Nation,* March 15, 1971. Alves is a former member of Parliament, a leader of the Catholic left, now in exile in Paris. He cites figures indicating that the average wage for 70 percent of workers has declined by almost 20 percent since 1964, while production has increased by more than 20 percent. He also describes the concentration of wealth, "the hunger and misery that drive millions of landless peasants to the cities"; the destruction of peasant leagues by the army, the police, and the private paramilitary forces of landlords; the banning in many places of the Catholic basic-education movement which promoted peasant organization; the destruction of schools for peasants established by foreign missionaries, "the incredible violence that the state itself must use to keep the masses quiet while the privileged squander the nation's riches"; the torture and murder; the anti-Semitism of the military officers; and so on.

51. Church Subcommittee Hearings, p. 149.

52. On this matter, see Kolko, *The Roots of American Foreign Policy,* chap. 1; Richard Barnet, *The Economy of Death,* (New York: Atheneum Publishers, 1969), pt. 2, and *Roots of War,* (New York: Atheneum Publishers, 1972), chap. 3 and pt. 2; G. William Domhoff, *The Higher Circles: The Governing Class in America.* (New York: Random House, 1970), chap. 5; David Horowitz, "The Foundations," *Ramparts,* April 1969, and "The Making of America's China Policy," *Ramparts,* October 1971. See also Peter Dale Scott, *The War Conspiracy* (Indianapolis: Bobbs-Merrill Co., 1972), introduction and chap. 8, on interconnections between the CIA and important business interests.

53. See p. 237, above. This particular factor is explored by Seymour Melman in his *Pentagon Capitalism* (New York: McGraw-Hill Book Co., 1970).

54. See *At War with Asia,* chap. 1, for some further discussion of the multiplicity of mutually supportive factors and the stable system they tend to produce.

55. For instance, Herbert Feis ridicules the view, which he attributes without specific reference to Gar Alperovitz, that "the Soviet government . . . was merely the hapless object of our vicious diplomacy." The view that Alperovitz actually develops is that "the Cold War cannot be understood simply as an American response to a Soviet challenge, but rather as the insidious interaction of mutual suspicions, blame for which must be shared by all." Cf. Alperovitz, *Cold War Essays,* (Garden City, N.Y.: Anchor Books, 1970), pp. 135, 31; also Christopher Lasch's comments, in the introduction, on "the general failure of orthodox historians to engage the revisionist argument."

56. On the substance of the "Nixon Doctrine," see John Dower's essay in Virginia Brodine and Mark Selden, eds., *Open Secret: The Kissinger-Nixon Doctrine in Asia* (New York: Harper & Row, 1972).

After "Pinkville"

This is an excerpt from "After Pinkville," in *At War with Asia: Essays on Indochina* (New York: Pantheon Books, 1970).
1. Richard M. Pfeffer, ed. *No More Vietnams?: The War and the Future of American Foreign Policy* (New York: Harper & Row, 1968), p. 212. For further discussion, see chap. 1, sec. 3, and my article in *The New York Review of Books*, January 2, 1969.
2. Elizabeth Pond, *Christian Science Monitor*, November 8, 1969.
3. *New York Times*, November 26, 1969.
4. In Pfeffer, ed., *No More Vietnams?*, p. 18. On the widely noted analogy between Vietnam and the Indian wars, see my *American Power and the New Mandarins*, pp. 279–80, n. 42.
5. Harold B. Clifford, *Exploring New England* (New Unified Social Studies; Chicago: Follett Publishing Co., 1961).
6. See Howard Zinn, "Violence and Social Change," Boston University *Graduate Journal*, Fall 1968. When disease decimated the Indians, Mather said: "The woods were almost cleared of those pernicious creatures, to make room for a better growth."
7. On November 24, 1969. Attention, Mr. Agnew.
8. *Christian Science Monitor*, November 29, 1969.
9. Henry Kamm, *New York Times*, November 15, 1969.
10. J. Robinson and S. G. Jacobson, in Walter Isard, ed., *Vietnam: Some Basic Issues and Alternatives* (Cambridge, Mass.: Schenkman Publishing Co., 1968), a symposium of the Peace Research Society (International). This organization, following a script by Orwell, is concerned with a special kind of peace research: the question of "how pacification can be achieved in turbulent village societies," along lines that we have been pioneering in Vietnam, for example. But even the Peace Research Society (International) is not monolithic. It would be unfair to assume that the conclusion of the cited study is mere wishful thinking. It has to be taken seriously.
11. Reuters, *Boston Globe*, November 27, 1969.

Laos

This is an excerpt from "Laos," in *At War with Asia: Essays on Indochina* (New York: Pantheon Books, 1970).
1. *Le Monde Weekly Selection*, October 1, 1969.

The Mentality of the Backroom Boys

This essay is excerpted from "The Backroom Boys," in *For Reasons of State* (New York: Pantheon Books, 1973).

1. McGeorge Bundy, February 7, 1965; III, 687–91. The reprisals against North Vietnam are for *"any* VC act of violence to persons or property," as in the case of the Pleiku attack used as a pretext for initiating the bombing of the North, where there was not even a pretense that North Vietnamese were involved. This is quite in accord with NSC 5429/2, more than ten years before. See my *For Reasons of State* (New York: Pantheon Books, 1973), pp. 100f.

2. April 6, 1964. The Security Council then proceeded to adopt a resolution condemning reprisals as "incompatible with the purposes and principles of the United Nations." For this and other references to the illegality of reprisal, see Lawyers Committee on American Policy Toward Vietnam, *Vietnam and International Law* (Flanders, N.J.; O'Hare Books, 1967), pp. 53–54, 98–101.

3. In the North, at least. In the South, and under Nixon-Kissinger in Laos and Cambodia, the question arises in a different form. With memories of gas chambers, some may be reluctant (as I have been personally) to use such terms as "genocide." The question whether the term is technically appropriate, in the light of the United Nations Convention of 1948, is a different matter. It was considered by the Russell Tribunal well before the significant escalation of the technological war in 1968 and on the basis of a small fraction of the evidence now available. See John Duffett, ed., *Against the Crime of Silence* (Flanders, N.J.; O'Hare Books, 1968), pp. 612–43.

4. IV, 71–74. Discussing the plans to destroy North Vietnamese petroleum reserves, the analyst notes that "neither in OSD nor the White House had anyone opposed these measures on other than prudential grounds—the risk of alienating allies or provoking Chinese or Russian intervention or uncertainty that results would justify either the risks or the costs" (IV, 74–75).

5. See Gabriel Kolko in Duffett, *Against the Crime of Silence*, p. 224.

6. See *Chronology of the Vietnam War*, bk. 1, distributed by Association d'Amitié Franco-Vietnamienne, 5, rue Las Cases, 75-Paris (7).

7. Note that RT in 1965 amounted to 33,000 tons of bombs, of a total of about 530,000 dropped on North Vietnam by the end of 1968. See Rafael Littauer *et al., The Air War in Indochina* (Preliminary Report, Cornell University Center for International Studies, October 1971), p. SS-14.

8. See my *American Power and the New Mandarins*, p. 15. See also Barry Weisberg, ed., *Ecocide in Indochina* (San Francisco: Canfield Press, 1970), in particular the eyewitness report by Orville Schell and Barry Weisberg, p. 24. Attacks on the "dams and waterways in the crucial Red River Delta" were reported during the first monsoon season following the initiation of RT ("The 'Enemy': 20,000 Missions Later," *Newsweek*, October 11, 1965). The planes struck in August, according to this report. On the logic of such attacks, see the staff study "The Attack

on the Irrigation Dams in North Korea," *Air University Quarterly Review,* Winter 1953–54. Gloating over the USAF attack on dams which caused a flash flood that "scooped clean 27 miles of valley below," constituting "one of the most significant air operations of the Korean War," the study explains that the smashing of the dams means "the destruction of their chief sustenance—rice": "The Westerner can little conceive the awesome meaning which the loss of this staple food commodity has for the Asian—starvation and slow death . . . more feared than the deadliest plague. Hence the show of rage, the flare of violent tempers. . . ."

9. Bernard Fall, "This Isn't Munich, It's Spain," *Ramparts,* December 1965; reprinted in *Last Reflections on a War* (Garden City, N.Y.: Doubleday & Co., 1967), pp. 232–33.

10. The hospital compound that replaced it was bombed on December 26, 1971. See the eyewitness report by Banning Garrett, who visited a few days later, in *The Guardian* (New York), February 16, 1972; the *New York Times,* February 10, 1972, contains a briefer report. The hospital was visited by George Wald on February 19; see his "Our Bombs Fall on People," *Washington Monthly,* May 1972. See also the report of Joel Henri of AFP, *New York Times,* May 9, 1972: "In the bomb-scarred provinces of Thanhhoa and Namha, where no military target could be seen, this correspondent today visited a hospital and school struck by American bombs. . . . It was hard for the visitors to believe that the destruction [of the Thanh Hoa hospital], which was considerable, could have been the result of a mistake. The buildings, surrounded by rice fields, were also attacked last December, according to the North Vietnamese." Henri is describing the raid of April 27, 1972. This final destruction of the hospital caused it to be evacuated to the mountains. Henri also visited a village where the primary school was bombed during morning classes, leaving twenty dead and twenty-five wounded: "We looked for the military targets that might have justified the raid, but there was nothing—just mud and straw huts."

11. C. O. Holmquist, "Developments and Problems in Carrier-Based Attack Aircraft," *Naval Review,* 1969, p. 214. Laser-controlled bombs and other innovations now give pinpoint accuracy, it is claimed. Therefore, the extensive destruction of civilian targets cannot be attributed to "error." Cf. Claude Julien, reporting from Hanoi on the "remarkable precision of American bombings" of "hospitals, dikes, villages," in *Le Monde,* May 20, 1972.

12. Ralph Stavins, Richard J. Barnet, and Marcus G. Raskin, *Washington Plans an Aggressive War* (New York: Random House, 1972), pp. 182–83. Stavins' analysis is also interesting with regard to the "conspiracy" in the field against Washington. Pilots have complained that interservice rivalries led to dangerous missions with high loss rate. See also Colonel James Donovan, *Militarism, U.S.A.* (New York: Charles Scribner's Sons, 1970), pp. 180–81.

13. IV, 408–9. Shortly after the Iron Triangle was "destroyed" in Operation Cedar Falls, "basically the same area" was invaded again in Operation Junction City. The reader will find a brief description of the latter, but not the official map

indicating the areas, including many villages, scheduled for destruction by preliminary air and artillery bombardment.

14. Philip Jones Griffiths, *Vietnam Inc.* (New York: Macmillan Publishing Co.,
1971), p. 89. Bernard Fall, *Last Reflections on a War* (Garden City, N.Y.: Doubleday
& Co., 1967), p. 248. See also Jonathan Schell, *The Village of Ben Suc* (New York:
Alfred A. Knopf, 1968), and my *American Power and the New Mandarins*, chap. 3,
n. 19, pp. 276–78.

15. B-52 raids in 1965 in the densely populated Mekong Delta were reported by
Bernard Fall, "Vietnam Blitz," *New Republic*, October 9, 1965. Takashi Oka
reported B-52 raids in "the populous delta" on December 4, 1965 (*Christian
Science Monitor;* Seymour Melman, ed., *In the Name of America* (Annandale, Va.:
Turnpike Press, 1968), p. 248), noting the civilian casualties and the refugees
fleeing to government-controlled areas "because they could no longer bear the
continuous bombings." Fall also flew on bombing attacks on undefended villages, at about the same time ("This Isn't Munich, It's Spain," *Ramparts*, December 1965, reprinted in his *Last Reflections on a War* [Garden City, N.Y.:
Doubleday & Co., 1967]), as have many others. George Smith, a special forces
sergeant captured by the NLF, reports B-52 raids (in Cambodia, he believes),
along with constant and heavy bombing with napalm and high explosives in the
free-fire zone where his camp was located, the latter from December 1964
(*P.O.W.: Two Years with the Viet Cong* [Berkeley, Calif.: Ramparts Press, 1971]).
Of course, the bombers were no more able to avoid villages than his POW
camp. See also Anthony Russo, "Inside the RAND Corporation and Out: My
Story," *Ramparts*, April 1972, on the effects of B-52 raids, as determined from
refugee interviews.

16. Bernard Fall, "Vietcong—the Unseen Enemy in Vietnam," *New Society*, April
22, 1965, reprinted in Bernard Fall and Marcus G. Raskin, eds., *The Vietnam Reader*
(New York: Vintage Books, 1965), p. 261.

17. T. D. Allman, "The Blind Bombers," *Far Eastern Economic Review*, January 29,
1972.

18. *New York Times*, letter, January 12, 1972.

19. Sidney Hook, "Lord Russell and the War Crimes 'Trial,' " *New Leader*, October 24, 1966. The reader who suspects that Hook may have learned something
since may turn to *The Humanist*, January 1971, where he describes the destruction
in Vietnam as "the unintended consequences of military action."

20. Rather consistently. In the same (1966) article, Hook refers to the United
States' Dominican intervention of 1965 as an "error" traceable to "mistaken
appraisal of the involvement of foreign Communist regimes."

21. McGeorge Bundy, "End of Either/Or," *Foreign Affairs*, vol. 45, no. 2 (1967).
My reference is inexact, since Bundy seemed to regard anyone who disagreed on
more than tactical matters as a wild man. Earlier, "the McGeorge Bundy group"
(which included McNaughton, Cooper, and Unger) drafted a memorandum (February 7, 1965; III, 309) which "represents a highly personal Bundy assessment

and point of view," and which notes that "none of the special solutions or criticisms put forward with zeal by individual reformers in government or in the press is of major importance." The Americans in Vietnam are the "first team," and though some of their tactical decisions may not have been perfect, clearly only a wild man in the wings would dare to question the first team in any more fundamental way.

22. General DePuy; cf. Ellsberg, "Bombing and Other Crimes," in *Papers on the War* (New York: Simon & Schuster, 1972).

23. Robert Komer, "Impact of Pacification on Insurgency in South Vietnam," *Journal of International Affairs*, vol. 25, no. 1 (1971).

24. Komer, "Epilogue," *ibid.*, no. 2; Eqbal Ahmad, "Revolutionary War and Counter-insurgency," *ibid.*, no. 1, p. 44.

25. Komer, "Pacification: A Look Back," *Army*, June 1970, p. 23.

26. Allan Goodman, "The Ending of the War as a Setting for the Future Development of South Vietnam," *Asian Survey*, vol. 11, no. 4 (1971), p. 342 n.

27. UPI, *Le Monde*, November 5, 1971. Quotes are retranslated, since I have not come across this UPI report in the American press, apart from a reference by Richard Ward in *The Guardian*, November 17, 1971. For information on Operation Phoenix in 1968–69, see my *At War with Asia*, pp. 301–2, and Edward S. Herman, *Atrocities in Vietnam* (Boston: Pilgrim Press, 1970), p. 47. On American programs in earlier years to develop "assassination teams" and "prosecutors-executors," see William A. Nighwsonger, *Rural Pacification in Vietnam* (New York: Frederick A. Praeger, 1967), pp. 136–37.

For more recent reports, see also Seymour Hersh, *Cover-up* (New York: Random House, 1972); Jeffrey Race, *War Comes to Long An* (Berkeley: University of California Press, 1971); and Frances Fitzgerald, *Fire in the Lake: The Vietnamese and the Americans in Vietnam* (Boston: Little, Brown & Co., 1972). For a general review of the Phoenix program, see Jon Cooper, "Operation Phoenix," Department of History, Dartmouth College.

The official figures cited in the UPI report are far more conservative than those cited in other sources. An official publication of the Saigon Ministry of Information gives the figure 40,994 killed in the Phoenix program of a total of 81,039 convicted, killed, rallied. The period covered is August 1, 1968, given as the date of the launching of the Phoenix program, through mid-1971 (*Vietnam 1967–71*, p. 52). Senator Kennedy refers to "the estimated 48,000 civilians of the Vietcong infrastructure who have been killed by American-sponsored assassination teams" (*Problems of War Victims in Indochina*, Hearings before the [Kennedy] Subcommittee on Refugees and Escapees, U.S. Senate, May 9, 1972, p. 9). The killing of 40,000 of the "communist infrastructure" is reported by the Saigon Ministry of Information under the heading "Programme Defending People Against Terrorism."

28. Reported in Jon Cooper, "Operation Phoenix." The informant is Don Luce.

29. Tad Szulc, *New York Times*, April 7, 1971.

30. Frances Starner, "I'll Do It My Way," *Far Eastern Economic Review,* November 6, 1971.

31. Richard West, "Vietnam: The Year of the Rat," *New Statesman,* February 25, 1972.

32. Former American participants report that United States intelligence nets were also penetrated by right-wing Vietnamese groups who fed reports to fuel the "bloodbath theory," knowing that these would be transmitted to Washington and would leak to industrious reporters. To explain the absence of predicted uprisings and bloodbaths, the same right-wing agents point to the success of the Phoenix program in weakening the NLF infrastructure. Thus while inciting bloodbath fears to gain United States support, these agents are also attempting to increase support for terror programs which may well succeed in providing such sects as the VNQDD with a degree of political control under the American aegis. See the report by Jeffrey Stein, an agent handler in 1968–69, "Bloodbath over the Rainbow," *The Phoenix* [Boston], May 10, 1972. As he notes, the bloodbath argument conveniently overlooks the absence of a bloodbath in areas under long NLF control—apart from the bloodbath caused by United States air and artillery.

33. See Jon Cooper, "Operation Phoenix," mimeographed (Department of History, Dartmouth College) for details. Also George McT. Kahin and John W. Lewis, *The United States in Vietnam,* rev. ed. (New York: Dial Press, 1969), app. 15.

34. William Pfaff, *Condemned to Freedom* (New York: Random House, 1971), pp. 75–77, a close paraphrase (with no acknowledgment) of some remarkable passages in Townsend Hoopes's *Limits of Intervention* (New York: David McKay Co., 1969), on which I have commented elsewhere (*At War with Asia,* pp. 297–300). Since Hoopes mentions Pfaff in this earlier book, it is unclear who deserves the credit for these insights.

35. Pfaff adds at this point that "it is not clear that [the Chinese Communists] understand the significance of the claim which Mao Tse-tung has made that China can 'win' a nuclear war in which 300 million Chinese would die." This "claim" has been frequently attributed to Mao in anticommunist propaganda, but no source has been discovered. Chang Hsin-hai concludes that it is "an outrageous and unmitigated falsehood, which everybody has accepted as gospel truth" (*America and China* [New York: Simon & Schuster, 1965], p. 227).

36. On the welfare of the Vietnamese under French rule, see Ngo Vinh Long, *Before the Revolution* (Cambridge, Mass.: MIT Press, 1973).

37. On the earlier period, see Truong Buu Lam, *Patterns of Vietnamese Response to Foreign Intervention: 1858–1900* (New Haven, Conn.: Yale University Press, 1967); Tam Vu and Nguyen Khac Vien, *A Century of National Struggle: 1847–1945* (Hanoi, 1970); David G. Marr, *Vietnamese Anti-colonialism: 1885–1925* (Berkeley: University of California Press, 1971); and Long, *Before the Revolution.*

38. Colin S. Gray, "What RAND Hath Wrought," *Foreign Policy,* vol. 1, no. 4 (1971).

39. "The lucrative US presence . . . created a virtual gold mine of wealth which

is directly or indirectly syphoned off and pocketed by the officials." Compare the situation since. From 1966 through 1971, United States economic assistance to South Vietnam averaged over $600 million per year; the capital flow from South Vietnam is about one-third of this. The recent fiscal reforms (heralded as the "autumn revolution"—fall 1971) raised the price of rice, sugar, milk powder, and pharmaceuticals while lowering prices for refrigerators and air conditioners. Rotten rice still sells at black-market prices. Phi Bang, "South Vietnam: A Hand-to-Mouth Economy," *Far Eastern Economic Review*, January 15, 1972. For more examples, see *Thoi-Bao Ga*, December 1971.

Cambodia

This essay originally appeared in the magazine *Inside Asia*, February-March 1985, under the title "Decade of Genocide in Review."

Punishing Vietnam

This is an excerpt from the introduction and the chapter "Towards a New Cold War," in *Towards a New Cold War: Essays On The Current Crisis and How We Got There* (New York: Pantheon Books, 1982).
1. Martin Woollacott, *Manchester Guardian Weekly*, June 15, 1980. It is not clear why it should be "humiliating" to offer reparations for criminal destruction. Was it humiliating for the postwar German government to offer reparations to Jews for Nazi crimes? Would it have been humiliating for the Nazi government itself to have done so, had it survived?
2. In an interview with the *Far Eastern Economic Review*, May 9, 1980.
3. As late as the late 1960s, high State Department officials appear to have been hoping that China would break up into warring constituencies under the impact of the cultural revolution, leaving the way open to a more direct assertion of U.S. control. It is not unlikely that such thinking played some part in the decision to hold on in Indochina, giving the United States a base for the projection of its power onward. On the debates over policy toward China in the mid-1950s between those whom Michael Klare was later to label "the Prussians" and "the traders," see my *At War with Asia*, chap. 1.
4. John Pilger reports that an official from the Asian Development Bank informed him that "the Americans have told us to lose the file on Vietnam" (*New Statesman*, May 22, 1981).
5. Louis Wiznitzer, "US Tries to Punish Vietnam by Paring UN Assistance," *Christian Science Monitor*, May 26, 1981. This U.S. effort failed, however. See Ted Morello, "The U.S. Loses a Vietnam Battle," *Far Eastern Economic Review*, July 10, 1981.

6. Daniel Southerland, "US Squeezes Vietnam's Economy," *Christian Science Monitor,* May 14, 1981; also UPI, *Christian Science Monitor,* May 13.

7. Southerland, "US Blocks Private Shipment of Wheat to Vietnam," *Christian Science Monitor,* May 13, 1981. According to Elizabeth Becker, this decision was reversed after lobbying by religious groups. She also alleges that the EEC decision to withhold food from UNICEF for Vietnam was taken under strong U.S. pressure ("Milk for Vietnam," *New York Times,* Op-Ed, July 3, 1981).

8. François Nivolon, "Debt Shackles Vietnam," *Far Eastern Economic Review,* May 22, 1981. See also Ted Morello, "Reagan's Aid Weapon: The Axe Hangs over UN Agencies as Washington Seeks Revenge over Kampuchea," *Far Eastern Economic Review,* May 1, 1981; and Murray Hiebert, "The Food Weapon: Can Vietnam Be Broken?," *Indochina Issues,* April 1981.

9. Wiznitzer (see note 5). He also notes that UNICEF adopted a relief plan for Cambodia "despite an attempt by the US to restrict it."

10. There have, however, been repeated accusations that "the Vietnamese are now conducting a subtle 'genocide' in Cambodia," François Ponchaud's charge as presented by William Shawcross, "The End of Cambodia?" *New York Review of Books,* January 24, 1980. For analysis and refutation of charges by Shawcross and Ponchaud, see Michael Vickery, "Ending Cambodia," manuscript, Australian National University (June 1981), submitted to the *New York Review* but not published.

11. On the remarkable cynicism of the Human Rights Administration in this regard, see Noam Chomsky and Edward S. Herman, *The Political Economy of Human Rights,* 2 vols. (Boston: South End Press, 1979), vol. 2, chap. 5.

12. See Chomsky and Herman, *The Political Economy of Human Rights,* vol. 2, chap. 6, for references and discussion.

East Timor

This is an excerpt from the Introduction to José Ramos-Horta, *East Timor Debacle: Indonesian Intervention, Repression, and Western Compliance* (Trenton, N.J.: Red Sea Press, 1986).

Intervention in Vietnam and Central America: Parallels and Differences

This is the edited transcript of a talk given at Harvard University on March 19, 1985. A shorter version appeared in *Radical America,* vol. 19, no. 1 (1985), in an issue entitled "Questions for the Peace Movement: Anti-Interventionism and Anti-Militarism."

El Salvador

This essay is excerpted from the Introduction to *Towards a New Cold War: Essays on the Current Crisis and How We Got There* (New York: Pantheon Books, 1982).

1. On the success of land reform adviser Roy Prosterman and former U.S. ambassador to El Salvador Robert White in using the "Pol Pot left" comparison in lobbying Congress for economic and military aid for the military junta that was massacring the peasantry, see Laurence R. Simon and James C. Stephens, Jr., *El Salvador Land Reform 1980–1981*, Impact Audit, Oxfam America (February 1981), p. 51.

2. See Cynthia Brown and Fernando Moreno, "Force-Feeding the Press on El Salvador," *The Nation*, April 25, 1981; and *Latin America Weekly Report*, February 20, 1981, for discussion of studies comparing U.S. and foreign press coverage. Also the interview with a Panamanian reporter who worked with UPI (Alexander Cockburn, *Village Voice*, April 8, 1981), who describes home-office manipulation of his reports and the practices of U.S. correspondents; and William Wipfler, "El Salvador: Reform as Cover for Repression," *Christianity and Crisis*, May 12, 1980, also describing editorial manipulation in the *New York Times* as described by a wire service correspondent.

3. Cited from the report and the January 5, 1981, press release of the Council on Hemispheric Affairs, in *Human Rights Internet Reporter*, February–March 1981.

4. *New York Times*, December 7, 1980; interview moderated by Juan de Onis.

5. Editorial, "Reform in El Salvador," reprinted in the *Manchester Guardian Weekly*, February 22, 1981.

6. "Salvador Rightists Accused of Raiding Honduran Sites," *Christian Science Monitor*, March 23, 1981, a ninety-word item. This report only refers to ORDEN raids; others, cited below, to attacks by the military forces themselves.

7. Again, there are exceptions; e.g., T. D. Allman, "Rising to Rebellion," *Harper's*, March 1981.

8. Representative Gerry E. Studds (Mass.), *Central America, 1981*, Report to the Committee on Foreign Affairs, U.S. House of Representatives, March 1981 (Washington, D.C.: Government Printing Office, 1981).

9. Transcripts of some of the interviews were played on WMUA radio, Amherst, Massachusetts, February 22, 1981; Robbie Leppzer, producer. Virtually nothing of this appeared in the press, to my knowledge.

Cf. W. Scott Thompson, professor of international politics at the Fletcher School of Law and Diplomacy, Tufts University, "Choosing to Win," *Foreign Policy*, Summer 1981: "True, right-wing forces strike back, often without government sanction. In the past year they have perhaps caused even more than the 6,000 deaths the left takes credit for—but not with weapons supplied by an international power overtly hostile to the United States and not to overthrow an established government."

The "6,000" figure appears regularly in U.S. government propaganda, but with no source cited, to my knowledge. If a source exists, it probably refers to guerrilla claims concerning soldiers killed in combat, but in the absence of any reference, one can only speculate. On assessments by the Catholic Church of responsibility for massacres, see below.

In general, caution is in order with regard to statements attributed to enemies of the state, given the tendency of many foreign correspondents to rely on U.S. government handouts. For example, the U.S. press regularly referred to the "final offensive" announced by the guerrillas in January 1981. Since the government still stands, that proves that the guerrillas failed because of lack of popular support. The generally well-informed *Latin America Weekly Report,* however, maintains that although "the US press has been full of stories about a supposed 'final offensive' by the FDR at the beginning of January, launched in the hope of achieving victory before President Reagan's inauguration on 20 January," in fact there was no such announcement; rather, "opposition spokesmen are cautiously describing the wave of attacks, launched on 10 January, as a 'general offensive in preparation for the final onslaught' " (*Latin America Weekly Report,* January 16, 23, 1981).

10. "Col. Arnoldo Majano, an outspoken liberal who has been in hiding since he was ousted as head of the ruling junta here two months ago, has been held under arrest by Government authorities since last Wednesday, according to informed sources. The Government has refused to release any details of the arrest or the charges against the colonel, who, until an assembly of army officers voted him out of the junta, had been the symbol of American policy in this country. Colonel Majano was the leader of a group of young army officers who overthrew a right-wing military dictatorship 16 months ago and began to institute land and economic changes. . . . He had been releasing statements, for example, that were harshly critical of the continued assassinations of leftists and moderates by right-wing and corrupt elements in the armed forces, which neither he nor the present junta has been able to control [the reporter's conclusion, not Majano's]. His successor, however, José Napoleón Duarte, a civilian Christian Democrat who is equally liberal, says that the number of such incidents is declining" ("Salvadoran Liberal Ousted by Junta Is Under Arrest," *New York Times,* February 22, 1981). The report assures us that despite Majano's ouster, the government "has continued with most of the changes."

11. This massacre of six hundred peasants in a joint operation of the armies of El Salvador and Honduras was reported by AFP in June 1980, and in *Overview Latin America* (9 Sacramento Street, Cambridge, MA 02138, a church-based group) in midsummer 1980, on the basis of a communiqué from the Diocese of Santa Rosa de Copan in Honduras. It was also reported in *Inquiry,* November 10, 1980, by Anne Nelson. There is a detailed study by David Blundy, "Victims of the Massacre That the World Ignored," *Sunday Times* (London), February 22, 1981. It was apparently not mentioned by the mainstream U.S. press. I found no reference in the *New York Times* prior to an article by Warren Hoge, *New York*

Times, June 8, 1981, reporting a similar massacre on March 17 at the Lempa River.
12. Édouard Bailby, "Terreur dans les campagnes d'El Salvador," *Le Monde diplomatique,* January 1981. Similar reports of Pol Pot massacres in the French press were immediately given wide publicity in the U.S. press, side by side with the accounts of American journalists on the Thai-Cambodian border. See Chomsky and Herman, *The Political Economy of Human Rights,* vol. 2, chap. 6, and Michael Vickery ("Ending Cambodia—Some Revisions," manuscript, Australian National University, June 1981), who discusses apparent collusion of the CIA and "independent journalists" (John Barron and Anthony Paul) in fabricating statistics, among other related matters; see his *Cambodia 1975–1982* (Boston: South End Press, 1983) for much further detail.
13. David Blundy, "The Innocents Caught in Lempa River Massacre," *Sunday Times* (London), April 26, 1981. See also Alex W. Drehsler, *Boston Globe,* March 26, 1981; Hoge, *op.cit.;* and *Latin America Weekly Report,* April 3, 1981. A March 25 letter to journalist Anne Nelson from an American who participated in the rescue of some of the thousands of fleeing peasants gives a vivid picture of this mid-March massacre which made it to the *New York Times* by June. Refugees had been hiding in caves for three days under daily bombardment before fleeing to the river. The river was deep; there were few swimmers; the refugees, including many women and children, had been without food for three days; many were seriously wounded; helicopters of the Salvadoran army machine-gunned and bombed the river trying "to systematically massacre us all." Only a little more than half of the announced seven thousand refugees were able to cross the river to Honduras, where they remain in "heartrending" misery in an area sealed off by the Honduran army. Many of the surviving children are seriously ill, many with pneumonia, as a result of the harsh crossing and lack of care.
14. "Central American Watch," *The Nation,* April 18, 1981. The Legal Aid Office of the San Salvador Archdiocese was established by twelve Catholic lawyers and invited to become part of the archdiocesan services by the assassinated Archbishop Oscar Romero.
15. Edward Schumacher, "Duarte, Three Months in Power, Bringing Change to El Salvador," *New York Times,* March 30, 1981. Schumacher notes that assassinations "continue," despite the alleged decline.
16. Schumacher, "Program in Salvador to Redistribute Land Prospers in First Year," *New York Times,* March 15, 1981; "For Salvador Peasants, Fruits of Change Seem Good," *New York Times,* March 16, 1981.
17. Schumacher, "Salvadoran Peasants Flee War-Ravaged Villages," *New York Times,* February 19, 1981. Some light on the "killing from both sides" is given by a "conservative priest" who states: "The difference in the violence is that the left kills selectively—members of ORDEN and Government security forces. Killing by the right and the army is more indiscriminate. When they sweep through a village looking for leaders and leftist sympathizers, they kill a lot of innocent peasants" (Raymond Bonner, "The Agony of El Salvador," *New York Times Magazine,* February 22, 1981). If this is an accurate statement of general tendencies,

as numerous other reports indicate, then what it means is that the guerrillas are at war with the army that is seeking to destroy them and what peasants and independent scholars refer to as "the popular organizations," while the government is at war with the people.

18. "U.N. Official Claims Refugees Fleeing Government Forces," *Los Angeles Times,* April 2, 1981. The same report, from the Honduran border, states that 99 percent of the refugees in Honduras were farm laborers who fled the government soldiers: "This is the answer that virtually all the refugees give when they are asked who is behind the violence that drove them out of their country." See also Al Kamen, "Question in El Salvador: Who Kills Noncombatants?," *Washington Post,* April 9, reporting that in private conversations peasants in urban slums and rural cooperatives blame the army for the killings, and quoting a businessman who "scoffed at the suggestion that the government could not stop the random killing" by the paramilitary organization ORDEN, which theoretically no longer exists: " 'Are you kidding?' he asked rhetorically. 'ORDEN *is* the government.' " Also Kamen, "Land Reform and Repression," *Washington Post,* April 5, 1981, reporting that board members of an agricultural cooperative blamed the left for the murders, but: "In a pattern repeated again and again, a resident who was not on the board of directors later approached a group of visitors as they were leaving and whispered that he and everyone else knew that the killings were almost all the work of the government security forces," an allegation with which "many U.S. officials and AFL-CIO advisers here agree." Cited from CISPES *Central America Monitor,* May 11, 1981. Apparently the *New York Times* correspondent picked up no such whispers.

19. For a detailed accounting, see "Documents of Repression in El Salvador," *Overview Latin America,* February 1981; Vicente Navarro, "Genocide in El Salvador," *Monthly Review,* April 1981. Also James Petras, "The Junta's War Against the People," *Inquiry,* December 20, 1980.

It would be a useful exercise to compare these regular reports of the Archdiocese Legal Aid Office with reports at the same time in the U.S. press. These reports are certainly known to the press, and one finds an occasional mention; e.g., "Salvadorans Fear Revenge Attacks After 5 Leftist Leaders Are Killed," UPI, *New York Times,* November 29, 1980, the last paragraph: "The Roman Catholic Church has blamed the right-wing paramilitary groups for 80 percent of the 9,000 political killings reported in El Salvador since Jan. 1 and has accused the junta of covertly backing them"; see also Alan Riding, "Rightist Offensive Seen in Latin Region," *New York Times,* November 30, 1980, in the latter part of a column: "But United States officials believe much of the right-wing violence is carried out by two special forces, the National Guard and the National Police." But in general, the press kept to the official picture of a centrist government unable to constrain right-wing "death squads" or soldiers out of control, with responsibility for the killings shared by left and right. The press generally mirrors the U.S. government, which is "incapable of grasping [a charitable interpretation] that in El Salvador, as in Nicaragua before it, the centrist forces which the United States perceives as its natural allies have joined with the very forces which the United States perceives as its natural enemy—the radical Left" (William M. LeoGrande and Carla Anne Robbins, "Oligarchs and Officers: the Crisis in El Salvador," *Foreign Affairs,* Summer 1980). Alan Riding alleges that "under the Carter Administration, United States officials said security forces were responsible for 90 percent of the atrocities," not " 'uncontrollable' right-wing bands" (*New York Times,* September 27, 1981). If this is correct, it provides an enlightening commentary on the behavior of the media at the time.

A good place to begin such a comparison would be with the accounts of the killings of the five "leftist" leaders on November 27, 1980, aborting the possibility for a negotiated settlement. The most prominent of these "leftist" leaders was Enrique Alvarez, "a certified member of the country's long dominant economic oligarchy," "a millionaire cattle rancher" who "had served in previous governments," as the *New York Times* noted in an editorial (November 29) condemning the killings. The UPI story, describing the dilemmas of the junta ("besieged by leftist guerrillas and rightist paramilitary groups"), reports that the "five leftists" were abducted "from a Jesuit-run high school three blocks from the United States Embassy by a band of nearly 200 men who raided the school"; the Legal Aid Office, whose offices are in the school, issued a statement reporting that "some 200 *soldiers and police* had surrounded the high school" (my italics). The same statement notes that the high school watchman was kidnapped and taken "to the premises of the Salvadoran Institute for Social Security" and that the vehicles that surrounded the school had license plates identifying them "as belonging to official organizations." "Another revealing piece of information," the statement continues, "is the total immunity with which the operation was carried out: in full daylight, at the largest secondary school in the country, along one of the most heavily-traveled roads of the capital, and three blocks from the most guarded building, the Embassy of the United States. Given these elements, it seems incredible that no authority came to the scene of the events during the operation," which lasted for more than twenty-five minutes. It also cites an AP cable sent "moments after the events" from San Salvador, which appeared in the local press on the front page, stating: "The authorities today announced that they had captured the highest leaders of the FDR, who were offering political leadership for leftist organizations."

Little reference to these facts (and, to my knowledge, no reference to the Legal Aid Office statement) is found in the national press, though the facts were known; e.g., in the Riding column cited above, the quote given is followed by this comment: "Witnesses said uniformed troops had surrounded the Jesuit-run San José High School Thursday before plainclothed gunmen seized the opposition leaders" (gunmen who were in radio communication with the Salvadoran Institute for Social Security, according to witnesses reported by the Legal Aid Office statement).

This pattern of general suppression, stories framed in accordance with state propaganda, and occasional glimpses of the facts, is quite typical.

20. U.S. Agency for International Development, *Phaseout Study of the Public Safety Program in El Salvador* (Washington, D.C.: Government Printing Office, 1974); cited by Cynthia Arnson, "Background Information on the Security Forces in El Salvador and U.S. Military Assistance," Institute for Policy Studies *Resource,* March 1980.

21. *Communist Interference in El Salvador,* Special Report no. 80, February 23, 1981, United States Department of State, Bureau of Public Affairs, Washington, D.C.

22. Sol W. Sanders, "The Vietnam Shadow over Policy for El Salvador," International Outlook, *Business Week,* March 16, 1981. Sanders deftly refutes "the Communist line," which is "that Central American revolutionary movements are local, indigenous, and as one Soviet spokesman in Washington puts it—ideologically Roman Catholic rather than Communist-oriented. This argument parallels the argument used in Vietnam that the revolt against President Ngo Dinh Diem in the early 1960s was a local South Vietnamese movement. The conquest of Saigon in 1975 by northern forces never dissipated this canard."

On the press response to the white paper, see Jonathan Evan Maslow and Ana Arana, "Operation El Salvador: The administration dusted off the domino theory. The pushover press fell into line," *Columbia Journalism Review,* June 1981.

23. John Dinges, "White Paper or Blank Paper?," *Los Angeles Times,* March 17, 1981; also *In These Times,* April 1, 1981.

24. Hodding Carter III, "The El Salvador Crusade," *Wall Street Journal,* March 19, 1981. Carter was assistant secretary of state for public affairs, department spokesman for the press, under the Carter administration.

25. Elsewhere, hard questions were raised, for example, by James Petras, "White Paper on the White Paper," *The Nation,* March 1981; reprinted in *El Salvador: The Roots of Intervention,* by the Nation Associates. See also the detailed analysis by Philip Agee in *White Paper? Whitewash!: Philip Agee on the CIA in El Salvador,* Werner Poelchau, ed., (New York: Deep Cover Publications, 1981). Also Maslow and Arana, *op.cit.,* and Konrad Ege, "El Salvador White Paper?," *Counterspy,* May 1981.

26. Jonathan Kwitny, "Apparent Errors Cloud U.S. 'White Paper' on Reds in El Salvador," *Wall Street Journal,* June 8, 1981. An accompanying story indicates that the next attempt will implicate religious and charitable organizations as supporters of "the Communist war effort in El Salvador, with or without the charities' knowledge" ("A New White Paper Is Expected Soon; Leaks of Its Contents Distress Churches"). Subsequently the U.S. embassy in Honduras "sharply criticized" Catholic and Protestant relief organizations, accusing them "of delivering more than 50 percent of their assistance to the Salvadoran guerrillas" ("El Salvador Says 30,000 Refugees May Be Moved from Its Border," *New York Times,* June 27, 1981). The latter *Times* report speaks coyly of "several alleged massacres of refugees by Government troops as the refugees attempted to cross the border into Honduras," presumably referring to the Sumpul and Lempa river massacres, which are still only "alleged."

According to the *Latin America Weekly Report,* June 19, 1981, Agee's then forthcoming book (see note 25) was an unacknowledged source for the *Wall Street Journal* story.

27. Robert G. Kaiser, "White Paper on El Salvador Is Faulty," *Washington Post,* June 9, 1981.

28. Juan de Onis, "State Dept. Defends Report on Salvador," June 9, 1981; "U.S. Officials Concede Flaws in Salvador White Paper but Defend Its Conclusions," June 10, 1981. See also Juan de Onis, "U.S. Defends Report on Salvador Arms," *New York Times,* June 19, 1981; Robert G. Kaiser, "U.S. Issues Rebuttal to Critics in Press of Salvador Aid Report," *Washington Post* Service, *International Herald Tribune,* June 20–21, 1981.

29. Cynthia Arnson, "El Salvador: There's More to the Disturbing Story," *Boston Globe,* April 23, 1981; also Arnson, "White Papers," *The Nation,* May 9, 1981.

30. "Leftists' Offensive in El Salvador Stalls," *New York Times,* January 26, 1981.

31. AP, *Boston Globe,* April 15, 1981.

32. Philip Jacobson, "Why El Salvador's Civil War Raises Ghosts of Vietnam— Whatever Washington Says," *Sunday Times* (London), March 8, 1981. There were many similar reports in the foreign press at the time. See, *inter alia, Latin America Weekly Report,* February 27, March 20, 1981.

33. Kenneth Freed, "Venezuela Now Leads Opposition to Leftists," *Los Angeles Times–Boston Globe,* February 18, 1981. The same page of the *Globe* carries a story by Tom Fiedler, "US Aides Lay Ground for Hike in Military Aid to El Salvador," Knight-Ridder Service, describing the Reagan administration efforts "laying the groundwork to request that the embattled government of El Salvador be given a big increase in US military aid to defeat leftist revolutionaries"—efforts that reached their peak with the issuance of the white paper a few days later. Fiedler reports that Congress was "given documents showing that Salvadoran guerrilla leaders were given money by Cuba to carry on their revolution." This shows that Cuba is engaged in Soviet-sponsored aggression. Hundreds of millions of dollars given to the junta by a U.S. ally, however, do not imply that it is engaged in a U.S.-sponsored massacre of the peasant population.

34. Stephen L. Vaughn, *Holding Fast the Inner Lines* (Chapel Hill: University of North Carolina Press, 1980), p. 194.

35. Schumacher, "From Washington and Salvador, Differing Views on Fighting Rebels," *New York Times,* February 21, 1981.

36. On the backgrounds of ORDEN, "in essence . . . an irregular militia enjoying government patronage and local privilege," often drawn from the poorest sectors and commanded by the army, see *'Disappearances': A Workbook* (Amnesty International USA, 1981). For more extensive discussion of the historical background for the development of the popular organizations and ORDEN, and for the present crisis, see Federico G. Gil, Enrique A. Baloyra, and Lars Schoultz, *The Failure of Democratic Transition in Latin America: El Salvador* (December 1980); draft submitted to the State Department under contract. This study alone suffices to make nonsense of State Department claims about the origins of the current crisis. It re-

ceived some notice in the press; see Robert Parry, "Study Hits US Path in Salvador," AP, *Boston Globe,* February 22, 1981.

37. T. D. Allman, "Rising to Rebellion," *Harper's,* March 1981.

38. On the peasant uprising of 1932 and its bloody suppression, see Thomas P. Anderson, *Matanza: El Salvador's Communist Revolt of 1932* (Lincoln: University of Nebraska Press, 1971). Anderson estimates that about one hundred people were killed by the rebels, about half of them soldiers and police. His rather conservative estimate is that about ten thousand people were then killed in the *matanza,* which "means that the government exacted reprisals at the rate of about one hundred to one." Anderson concludes that "the whole political labyrinth of El Salvador can be explained only in reference to the traumatic experience of the uprising and the *matanza.*"

39. AP, *New York Times,* March 13, 1981, a fifteen-line report of Gómez' press conference under the general heading: "Salvador Leftists Accused of Raid." In this press conference, Gómez stated that promises of free elections are worthless, since "all meaningful opposition is either dead or outside the country."

40. Steven Kinzer, "Salvador activist Gómez Finds It Pays to Stay One Step Ahead," *Boston Globe,* February 25, 1981, a lengthy interview with Gómez.

41. Daniel Southerland, "New Allegations Against Rightists in El Salvador," *Christian Science Monitor,* March 4, 1981.

42. Kinzer, *op.cit.*

43. *Latin America Weekly Report,* February 13, 1981.

44. Leonel Gómez and Bruce Cameron, "El Salvador: The Current Danger: American Myths," *Foreign Policy,* Summer 1981.

45. Simon and Stephens, *op.cit.* (see note 1). See also Mac Chapin, "A Few Comments on Land Tenure and the Course of Agrarian Reform in El Salvador," June 1980 (Chapin is an AID official). On the role of the U.S. labor movement's AIFLD, see Carolyn Forché and Philip Wheaton, *History and Motivations of U.S. Involvement in the Control of the Peasant Movement in El Salvador* (Ecumenical Program for Interamerican Communication and Action [EPICA], n.d.).

46. Correspondingly the media too began to decide that there might be reason for a diagnosis of the El Salvador affair that differs from the standard government line that a centrist regime is being attacked from the left and is unable to control the right. See, among other articles, Philip Geyelin, "Time for a Second Opinion on El Salvador," *Washington Post–Boston Globe,* May 17, 1981, discussing the opinions of a Christian Democrat economist who quit his position in the agrarian reform program and fled the country in January when he noticed armed men parked in front of his apartment, drawing the obvious conclusions. According to Geyelin, who regards him as "rather more like a rising young banker than, say, Che Guevara," he "sees a harshly repressive right-wing military government, under the tight thumb of a rich and ruthless oligarchy, with only the thin facade of Christian Democracy in Duarte's presence as its nominal leader," and "he sees the guerrilla forces as the home-honed military cutting edge of a political opposi-

tion movement whose representation—peasant organizations, labor unions, the clergy, businessmen, technocrats—reflects a wider consensus and a tighter cohesion than that of any comparable movement in Latin America." Not unlike a rather standard interpretation outside of the United States, though credence might be given to the Gómez view that a brutal and corrupt military is to some degree replacing the traditional oligarchy.

A few months earlier, Geyelin had been writing that "the so-called central [*sic*] government, a coalition of Christian Democrats and the military, remains perilously threatened by extremists from the far right and the far left" ("El Salvador: Proving Ground," *Washington Post*, February 10, 1981).

I believe that one can plausibly account for a detectable shift in the character of media coverage of El Salvador in spring 1981, in part indicated above, as a reflection of the partial abandonment of a militant public posture by the government, in response to domestic and international failures. See note 19.

Nicaragua

This essay is excerpted from *Turning the Tide: U.S. Intervention in Central America and the Struggle for Peace* (Boston: South End Press, 1986).

1. *New York Times*, May 5, 1985.
2. *Washington Post Weekly*, April 22, 1985.
3. For the government case as presented by a respected advocate, see John Norton Moore, "Legal Issues in the Central America Conflict," *Journal of Contemporary Studies*, Winter–Spring 1985; also my comments, "Law and Imperialism in the Central American Conflict," Spring–Summer 1985, and Moore's response, "Tripping Through Wonderland with Noam Chomsky," in the same issue, which is quite revealing: e.g., his claim that we may discount statements of intent by the president, high government officials, the contra leaders, etc., as well as the pattern of actual events, because "as anyone with a twelfth-grade education understands," U.S. policy requires congressional approval. The impossibility of executive wars and intervention should come as a great comfort to their victims in Guatemala, Laos, Cambodia, Cuba, etc. In fact, what every sane twelfth-grader understands is that civics textbooks are one thing, the real world quite another. Another typical example is his proof that the United States did not attack South Vietnam by bombing it from 1962, later invading outright; the proof is that North Vietnam invaded the South thirteen years later, and according to the US government, controlled the southern insurgency. Putting the first argument aside out of charity, Moore's Communist counterparts could demonstrate by similar logic that the USSR did not invade Afghanistan, since the insurgency is controlled from Pakistan and the guerrilla groups have been attacking from Pakistan with Pakistani support since 1973 (*Far Eastern Economic Review*, June 9, 1983). A few similar examples appear below, along with examples of gross misrepresentation. Alto-

gether, not a very impressive performance by "the staff of the Center for Law and National Security," whom he thanks for their "substantial research assistance." I am, however, indebted to Moore for pointing out that the full statement by FDN leader Calero is even more awful than the part I quoted. The editors of this right-wing journal demonstrate their standards, e.g., in attributing to me the view that "U.S. actions in Grenada and Central America are no different from actions in Afghanistan"—their paraphrase of my statement: "There are, of course, numerous respects in which Soviet aggression in Afghanistan is not comparable to U.S. intervention in El Salvador [Grenada is nowhere mentioned]; a closer comparison would be to the U.S. attack against South Vietnam. . . ." The latter comparison cannot even be heard in these circles, so offensive is it to jingoist sensibilities. This material is worth reading for its insight into the intellectual bankruptcy of these "conservative" circles and the curious incapacity to understand that chanting of government slogans does not constitute argument.

4. Roy Gutman, "America's Diplomatic Charade," *Foreign Policy*, Fall 1984.

5. General Assembly Resolutions 194 and 273; reprinted in John Norton Moore, ed., *The Arab-Israeli Conflict*, vol. 3 (Princeton, N.J.: Princeton University Press, 1974).

6. "La Prensa's editors have lobbied for continued U.S. funding of the contras, never acknowledging their human-rights violations" (Council on Hemispheric Affairs and Newspaper Guild [AFL-CIO, CLC], *Press Freedom in Latin America 1984–85*, 51, discussing the "inexcusable" government harassment of *La Prensa*); Joel Brinkley, *New York Times*, March 26, 1985, reporting the grant, through a federally financed foundation.

7. Noam Chomsky, *The Fateful Triangle* (Boston: South End Press, 1983), p. 139; *Hadashot*, May 23, 1985; *Al Fajr* (Jerusalem), August 9, 1985; Matti Peled, *Koteret Rashit*, August 14, 1985; *Hadashot*, May 16, 1984; Dan Fisher, *Los Angeles Times*, October 5, 1985; *Ha'aretz*, July 10, 1985; Moshe Negbi, April 5, 1985, excerpted from a forthcoming book. On the mechanisms of self-censorship, see also Moshe Negbi, *Koteret Rashit*, June 19, 1985.

8. News conference, *New York Times*, June 19, 1985.

9. Stephen Kinzer, *New York Times*, September 9, 1985.

10. Interview, COHA's *Washington Report on the Hemisphere*, July 9, 1985. See Penny Lernoux, *The Nation*, September 28, 1985, for a reasoned discussion of the current situation. The United States secured British recognition of the sovereignty of Nicaragua over the Miskitos, which the United States regarded as "unquestionable" in 1895; Dexter Perkins, *The Monroe Doctrine*, 3 vols. (1927, 1933, 1937; reprinted ed., Gloucester, Mass.: Peter Smith, 1965–66), 3:40ff.

11. *Human Rights in Nicaragua: Reagan, Rhetoric and Reality*, Americas Watch, July 1985; *Violations of the Laws of War by Both Sides in Nicaragua: 1981–1985*, Americas Watch, March 1985. The former is a detailed critique of Reagan administration lies concerning Nicaragua. On administration lies, see also *In Contempt of Congress* (Institute for Policy Studies, 1985) and the bipartisan congressional report "U.S.

Aid to El Salvador," discussing the record of the administration in providing "insufficient, misleading and in some cases false information to Congress." Its lies to the public have become notorious.

12. Stephen Kinzer, *New York Times,* September 17, 1985; Shirley Christian, *New York Times,* October 8, 1985.

13. Fairfax Downey, *Indian Wars of the U.S. Army* (Garden City, N.Y.: Doubleday & Co., 1963), pp. 32ff.

14. The preferred version is that Ben-Gurion "opposed only the return of Arabs who had joined the enemy" (Marie Syrkin, *New Republic,* Oct. 21, 1985).

15. Yoela Har-Shefi, *Hadashot,* August 24, 1984; Yoram Nimrod, *Al Hamishmar,* June 7, 1985; see my *Towards a New Cold War* (New York: Pantheon Books, 1982), pp. 464–65, on the earlier 1979 report. An AP report on the *Hadashot* story appeared in the *Boston Globe,* without details and with an apologetic commentary (August 26, 1984), but not elsewhere, to my knowledge. For more on the background, including the rejection of Arab peace overtures, see Tom Segev, *1949* (Jerusalem: Domino, 1984; Hebrew). This and other recent work based on newly available archival material will substantially revise the conventional picture.

16. Eyal Ehrlich, "Ambush on the Jordan," *Koteret Rashit,* August 14, 1985. Commenting on this material, a group of dissident Israeli journalists note that contrary to what Ehrlich states, "it isn't true that no one knew about what was going on," citing protests by tiny left-wing groups and writers at the time, adding that others preferred not to disturb the victory celebrations (Report no. 19, Alternative Information Center, 14E Koresh St., Jerusalem).

17. AP, *Boston Globe,* September 21, 1983.

18. Rabbi Morton Rosenthal of ADL, letter, *New York Times,* September 27, 1983, responding to an op-ed piece of September 13 by Ilana DeBare; Walter Ruby, *Jerusalem Post,* August 21, 1984; *Genesis 2,* September 1984; Americas Watch, *Human Rights in Nicaragua;* Ignacio Klich, *Le Monde diplomatique* December 1983; Stan Steinreich, Jewish Student Press Service, *Genesis 2* September–October 1983. For Rabbi Rosenthal's reiteration of the ADL charges, see *Jewish Post,* September· 5, 1984; *Le Monde diplomatique,* June 1984.

19. *Human Rights in Nicaragua.*

20. COHA press release, August 1985; Stephen Vaughn, *Holding Fast the Inner Lines* (Chapel Hill, N.C.: University of North Carolina Press, 1980), p. 194. For discussion and the broader context, see my *Towards a New Cold War,* chap. 1.

21. E.g., Moore, "Tripping through Wonderland," who attributes to me the claim that "progressive" forces such as Cuba, Nicaragua, and the Salvador guerrillas, have an "exemplary human rights record"—what I wrote is that their "abuses of human rights and democratic principle, often real," are not the cause of U.S. opposition to Cuba and Nicaragua, as is obvious from U.S. support for far more violent regimes; the Salvador guerrillas are not mentioned; the word "progressive," which he repeatedly gives in quotes, is his invention. Moore also speaks of my "commitment to the radical regime," nonexistent of course, but Moore would

have no other way of interpreting heretical views with regard to the Holy State.
22. 1983 Report of the House Permanent Select Committee on Intelligence, cited by Joanne Omang and Edward Cody, *Washington Post,* March 11, 1985; Wayne Smith, *Los Angeles Times,* August 25, 1985.
23. Joel Brinkley, *New York Times,* June 5, 1985.
24. Gordon Connell-Smith, *The Inter-American System* (Oxford: Royal Institute of International Affairs, 1966), pp. 23ff., 343.
25. *The Electoral Process in Nicaragua,* Latin American Studies Association (LASA) official publication, November 19, 1984, report of a delegation of LASA to observe the November 1984 elections; Colman McCarthy, *Washington Post, MG Weekly,* March 17, 1985; Joseph Collins *et al., What Difference Could a Revolution Make?* (Institute for Food and Development Policy, 1982); John Booth, *The End and the Beginning* (Boulder, Colo.: Westview Press, 1985); and UCLA historian E. Bradford Burns, *In These Times,* January 25, 1984.
26. Karen Remmer, in Jan Black, ed., *Latin America: Its Problems and Its Promise* (Boulder, Colo.: Westview Press, 1984). See also, among others, Morton Halperin *et al., The Lawless State* (New York: Penguin Books, 1976); and Seymour Hersh, *The Price of Power* (New York: Summit Books, 1983).
27. Council on Hemispheric Affairs, April 2, 1985; also June 26, 1983; Jan Black in Black, *Latin America;* Tom Farer, "Human Rights and Human Welfare in Latin America," *Daedalus,* Fall 1983.
28. Denis Warner, *The Last Confucian* (New York: Macmillan Publishing Co., 1963), p. 312.

Guatemala

This essay is excerpted from *Turning the Tide: U.S. Intervention in Central America and the Struggle for Peace* (Boston: South End Press, 1986).
1. Cole Blasier, *The Hovering Giant* (Pittsburgh: University of Pittsburgh Press, 1976), pp. 57ff.
2. Walter LaFeber, *Inevitable Revolutions* (New York: W. W. Norton & Co., 1983), pp. 112ff.; Lars Schoultz, in Martin Diskin, ed., *Trouble in Our Backyard* (New York: Pantheon Books, 1983); Smith quoted in Blanche Wiesen Cook, *The Declassified Eisenhower* (Garden City, N.Y.: Doubleday & Co., 1981), p. 253. On the CIA coup, see Cook, *op. cit.*; Stephen Kinzer and Stephen Schlesinger, *Bitter Fruit* (Garden City, N.Y.: Doubleday & Co., 1981); and Richard Immerman, *The CIA in Guatemala* (Austin: University of Texas Press, 1982).
3. John Norton Moore, "Tripping Through Wonderland with Noam Chomsky," *Journal of Contemporary Studies,* Spring–Summer 1985. The same intriguing conception of our "obligation" to attack Nicaragua under international law is advanced by Senator Daniel Patrick Moynihan in a speech applauding the increase of the budget for intelligence (meaning, e.g., war against Nicaragua) to the high-

est level "by any country at any point in history." The *Times* heading for this disgraceful performance is "Required Reading," October 15, 1984.

4. Edwin Lieuwen, *Generals vs. Presidents* (New York: Frederick A. Praeger, 1964), p. 39.

5. For details, see Michael McClintock, *The American Connection*, 2 vols. (London: Zed Press, 1985), vol. 2, pp. 51ff.

6. LaFeber, *op. cit.*, p. 165; Hugh O'Shaughnessy, *New Statesman*, December 1, 1967, and Marcel Niedergang, *Le Monde*, January 19, 1968; AP, *New York Times*, November 27, 1983; Schoultz, in Diskin, *op. cit.;* Douglas Foster, *Mother Jones*, November-December 1985. Like Blasier, Schoultz attributes to U.S. planners "the best of all intentions." See also Julia Preston, *Boston Globe*, November 2 and 3, 1985.

7. James LeMoyne, *New York Times*, August 24, 1985.

8. McClintock, *op. cit.*, vol. 2, pp. 216–17, citing an unpublished manuscript by Piero Gleijeses, Johns Hopkins University (SAIS), 1982.

9. See Juan José Arévalo, *The Shark and the Sardines* (New York: Lyle Stuart, 1981); and Juan Bosch, *Pentagonism* (New York: Grove Press, 1968).

Rejectionism and Accommodation

This essay is excerpted from *The Fateful Triangle: The United States, Israel, and the Palestinians* (Boston: South End Press, 1983).

1. For examples, see virtually any article or editorial on the topic in the *New Republic*; e.g., for various aspects of the picture, Michael Walzer, "The New Terrorists," August 30, 1975; David Pryce-Jones, "The Palestinian Pattern," November 8, 1982.

2. Jon Kimche, *There Could Have Been Peace* (New York: Dial Press, 1973), p. 306.

3. For discussion, see Fred J. Khouri, "The Arab-Israeli conflict," in P. Edward Haley and Lewis W. Snider, eds., *Lebanon in Crisis* (Syracuse, N.Y.: Syracuse University Press, 1979).

4. *U.S. Department of State Bulletin*, January 5, 1970, cited by Khouri, *op. cit.*, p. 299.

5. Seth Tillman, *The United States in the Middle East* (Bloomington: University of Indiana Press, 1982), pp. 223ff.

6. *Ibid.*, pp. 276–77; italics in original.

7. For discussion of these matters, see my *Peace in the Middle East?* and *Towards a New Cold War* (*TNCW*).

8. See, for example, Tom Hayden, *The American Future* (Boston: South End Press, 1980), for argument in support of his rejectionist position on the Arab-Israeli conflict (roughly, that of the Israeli Labor party), in essentially the terms described.

9. For references, see *TNCW*, pp. 249, 438.

10. *Foreign Affairs*, Spring 1981.

11. Thomas R. Stauffer, *Christian Science Monitor*, January 13 1982.

12. For a detailed analysis of technical aspects of the problem, see Jehoshua Schwarz, "Water Resources in Judea, Samaria, and the Gaza Strip," in Daniel J. Elazar, ed., *Judea, Samaria, and Gaza: Views on the Present and Future* (Washington, D.C.: American Enterprise Institute, 1982). Also Thomas R. Stauffer, *Christian Science Monitor*, January 20, 1982. For further references, see *TNCW*, p. 447. See also David Elstein and Sharon Goulds, *New Statesman*, July 10, 1981, and *Middle East International*, July 31, 1981; *Business Week*, December 20, 1982, citing an Israeli estimate that by the year 2000 demand will outrun expected supply.

13. Schwarz, *op. cit.* See Thomas R. Stauffer, *Christian Science Monitor*, January 20, 1982, and *Middle East International*, July 30, 1982, on what he calls "the lure of the Litani."

14. *The Economist*, September 11, 1982; Zvi Barel, *Ha'aretz*, September 9, 1982.

15. See "Talking Points," *New York Times*, September 9, 1982.

16. Shaya Segal, *Ma'ariv*, December 7, 1982.

17. Amnon Kapeliouk, *Israël: la fin des mythes* (Paris: Albin Michel, 1975), p. 23; Yitzhak Rabin, interview ("1983: New Opportunities for Peace"), *Trialogue*, Winter 1983.

18. *New York Times*, November 1, 1982. Lewis, who has been one of the most outspoken critics of recent Israeli policies in U.S. journalism, basically supports the Labor party position, it appears.

19. *Boston Globe*, June 1, 1978; *Ma'ariv*, October 11, 1981; *Israeli Mirror*, London.

20. Amos Perlmutter, *New York Times*, May 17, 1982.

21. Kapeliouk, *Israël*, pp. 220,21. Ben-Gurion's statement is "known to every child in Israel," according to Kapeliouk.

22. *New York Times*, September 6, 1982.

23. Christopher Sykes, *Crossroads to Israel: 1917–1948* (Bloomington: University of Indiana Press, 1965), p. 48.

24. David Ben-Gurion, *Memoirs* (New York: World Publishing Co., 1970), p. 118.

25. Simha Flapan, *Zionism and the Palestinians* (New York: Barnes & Noble, 1979), p. 134, citing a speech of October 12, 1936. For the actual record of Palestinian nationalism, see the outstanding two-volume study by Yehoshua Porath, *The Emergence of the Palestinian-Arab National Movement*, (London: Frank Cass, 1974, 1977).

26. Kapeliouk, *Israël*, p. 32.

27. *Sunday Times*, (London), June 15, 1969. For a longer excerpt, see John K. Cooley, *Green March, Black September* (London: Frank Cass, 1973), pp. 196–97. See Porath, *op. cit.*, for a serious discussion of the facts concerning Palestinian nationalism.

28. Kapeliouk, *Israël*, p. 32.

29. Cooley, *Green March, Black September*, p. 197.

30. Flapan, *Zionism and the Palestinians*, p. 83.

31. See *TNCW*, p. 231, citing an official government document. As noted, this

state is to incorporate parts of the West Bank, according to Labor party doctrine.

32. The reference is to Israel's demand, later abandoned, that the negotiations take place in Jerusalem, recognized by virtually no one (specifically, not by the U.S.) as Israel's capital.

33. Arnold Forster, letter, *New York Times,* December 20, 1982.

34. *New York Review of Books,* November 18, 1982.

35. The Socialist International has been unusual, outside of the United States and Israel, in often taking a rejectionist stand, denying Palestinian rights, leading to sharp condemnation by Israeli doves. See *TNCW,* pp. 270–71.

36. Cited by Tillman, *The United States in the Middle East,* p. 143, from the *New York Times,* August 6, 1978.

37. See *TNCW,* p. 442, citing the Israeli journal *Emda,* December 1974.

38. K. Amnon (Amnon Kapeliouk), "The 1976 Elections in the Territories," *Al Hamishmar,* April 16, 1982.

39. See *TNCW,* p. 269.

40. See *The Dawn (Al Fajr),* Jerusalem, Sept. 3, 1982.

41. The results appear in *Time,* May 24, 1982.

42. Abba Eban, "Obstacles to Autonomy," *New Outlook* (Tel Aviv), June–July 1982.

43. *New York Times,* May 19, 1976, and December 21, 1980; see *TNCW,* pp. 281ff., for fuller discussion.

44. Kapeliouk, *Israël,* p. 281, citing an interview with Eric Rouleau, *Le Monde,* February 19, 1970.

45. Kimche, *There Could Have Been Peace,* pp. 288ff.

46. Amos Elon, *Ha'aretz,* November 13, 1981; reprinted in *Israleft News Service* (Jerusalem), November 17, 1981.

47. See Kimche, *There Could Have Been Peace,* pp. 286ff.

48. See the comments by General Haim Bar-Lev, a cabinet member in the Meir and Rabin governments, in the Labor party journal *Ot,* March 9, 1972, quoted in *TNCW,* p. 460.

49. Edward Witten, "Cold Silence," *Ha'aretz,* January 6, 1983.

50. See my *Peace in the Middle East?* (New York: Pantheon Books, 1974), pp. 120–22.

51. Henry Kissinger, *The White House Years* (Boston; Little, Brown & Co., 1976), pp. 1279, 1291; for further discussion of this curious document, see *TNCW,* chap. 6; James Akins, review of *Years of Upheaval* (Boston: Little, Brown & Co., 1982), in *American-Arab Affairs,* Summer 1982. For some further examples of Kissinger's astonishing inanities, which much impressed many journalists and academics, see *TNCW,* p. 406.

52. See Tillman, *The United States in the Middle East,* chap. 6, on Soviet policies. He observes that "the official Soviet position has been consistent since 1948 in support of Israel's right to exist and consistent since 1967 in support of Israel's right to a secure national existence, as called for in Security Council Resolution

242, within its 1967 borders." The USSR has even offered to provide security guarantees (p. 246).

53. Charles William Maynes (editor of *Foreign Policy*), *Boston Globe*, June 15, 1982.

54. For some examples, see *Multinational Oil Corporations and U.S. Foreign Policy*, Report to the Committee on Foreign Relations, U.S. Senate, January 2, 1975 (Washington, D.C.: Government Printing Office, 1975), pt. 3, sect. 6.

55. *Ha'aretz*, June 25, 1973; *Yediot Ahronot*, September 16, 1973. Cited by Kapeliouk, *Israël*, pp. 49–50, along with a range of similar evaluations by Israeli generals (among them, Sharon), intelligence specialists, Orientalists, and others.

56. Amos Perlmutter, Michael Handel, and Uri Bar-Joseph, *Two Minutes Over Baghdad* (London: Vallentine, Mitchel & Co., 1982), p. 33–34. They argue that Sadat's war aims were limited because of the threat of nuclear retaliation by Israel, and also allege that Israel's threat to use nuclear weapons impelled the U.S. to provide a massive shipment of conventional weapons to Israel. For more on this topic, see *TNCW*, pp. 321, 458. As for the USSR, "Evidence that the Soviet Union did not support President Sadat's decision to go to war is persuasive" (Barry M. Blechman and Douglas M. Hart, "The Political Utility of Nuclear Weapons," *International Security*, vol. 7, no. 1, 1982).

57. *Jerusalem Post*, November 13, 1981. On the January 1976 Arab initiative, which has virtually disappeared from history in the United States (it is not even mentioned in the unusually careful review in Tillman, *The United States and the Middle East*, for example), see *TNCW*, pp. 267, 300, 461.

58. For references and discussion, see *TNCW*, p. 268.

59. *Jerusalem Post*, November 15, 1976; *Davar*, November 21, 1976; *Israleft News Service*, December 1, 1976.

60. Bernard Gwertzman, *New York Times*, August 21, 1977.

61. *New York Times*, March 21, 1977.

62. Tillman, *The United States and the Middle East*, p. 213. Tillman gives an extensive (though incomplete) record of PLO moves toward accommodation, some of them fairly explicit. See also my articles in *New Politics*, Winter 1975–76 and Winter 1978–79, reviewing many of these developments. See also *TNCW*, chaps. 9, 13.

63. David Hirst, *Manchester Guardian Weekly*, August 7, 1977.

64. Elie Eliachar, quoted by Merle Thorpe (president, Foundation for Middle East Peace), in Hearings Before the Subcommittee on Europe and the Middle East of the Committee on Foreign Affairs, U.S. House of Representatives, December 16, 1981 (Washington, D.C.: Government Printing Office, 1982); Mattityahu Peled, interview, *Hotam*, January 28, 1983; the Basel program did not actually refer to a "Jewish state" but rather to the vaguer concept of a national "home." The history of the exploitation of the Covenant would make an interesting research project, which might contain some surprises.

65. Tillman, *The United States in the Middle East*, pp. 217, 271–72, 238.

66. Letter, *New York Times*, January 12, 1982.

67. See *TNCW*, p. 321; also John K. Cooley, "The Palestinians," in Haley and Snider, eds., *Lebanon in Crisis*, pp. 28–29, citing Sadat directly to this effect.

68. Cited by Amnon Kapeliouk, *Le Monde diplomatique*, August 1982, from *Ma'ariv*, December 5, 1975. On Kissinger, see *Fateful Triangle*, p. 20.

69. Editorial, *New Republic*, November 29, 1982.

70. For example, Theodore Draper writes that "even Mr. Sadat admittedly did not accept [Israel's] existence until he decided to come to Jerusalem" in 1977, and even then his "program called for peace on the most extreme Arab terms, except for those Arab extremists who would be satisfied with nothing but the total destruction of the state of Israel" (*New York Times Book Review*, May 17, 1981; for a longer quote, see *TNCW*, p. 460). Or Mitchell Cohen, professor of political science at CUNY: "We must also note the historical persistence of the Palestinian national movement's insistence on no compromise and no partition, which helped lead it to destruction in 1948 and to Beirut in 1982" (*New Republic*, October 25, 1982). Or Arthur P. Mendel, professor of history at the University of Michigan: It is now likely "that Hussein will follow Sadat's example and negotiate with Israel the compromise that most Israelis and Palestinians (in contrast to the P.L.O.) have long wanted" (letter, *New York Times*, October 10, 1982). Or Kenneth Jacobson, director of Middle Eastern Affairs for the Anti-Defamation League: "In fact, the PLO is the major obstacle to Arab-Israeli peace, ideologically committed to Israel's destruction, never moving an iota from that commitment. . . ." (*Christian Science Monitor*, July 13, 1982). Or Ivan Novick, who, with innumerable others, explains that "the core problem of the Arab-Israeli dispute is the failure of the Arab nations to come to terms with the existence of the permanence of the Jewish State" (*New York Review of Books*, November 18, 1982). Or Yitzhak Rabin: "The facts speak for themselves"; "the main reason—the heart of the Arab-Israeli conflict—was, and still is, the fact that except for Egypt, there has been no readiness on the part of the Arab leaders to reconcile themselves with the existence of Israel as a viable, Jewish, independent state—regardless of its boundaries"; and as for Egypt, "for 28 years [i.e., until 1977], no one believed that Egypt would make peace with Israel" (*Harvard International Review*, September–October 1982; recall his statement in *Davar*, November 1976, referring to Sadat's willingness to make peace in 1971, p. 395 above, though in that case to an Israeli audience, who could be expected to know the facts). Or, to cite one of a thousand editorials: "The unexpected conquest of the land in 1967 and the Arabs' refusal to reclaim it with a peace treaty have left the Begin-Sharon bulldozers in charge of policy" (Max Frankel, editor, *New York Times*, November 15, 1982). See also note 83. And so on, in an almost endless litany.

71. *New York Times*, June 20, 1982, referring to the situation as of 1982. Note that as in the case of many of the references of the preceding note, this was written well after numerous other Arab initiatives, beyond the pre-1977 ones just reviewed.

72. ". . . Sadat was the first Arab leader who, a year after coming to power, declared his willingness to make peace with Israel in his famous reply [February

1971] to [UN negotiator] Dr. Jarring's memorandum" (editorial, *Ha'aretz*, October 8, 1981); four days after Sadat's "initiative, later known by his own name, for solving the Middle East problem," Gunnar Jarring presented his "famous report of 8 February 1971 . . . to which Egypt gave a positive reply" (Ghali Shoukri, *Egypt: Portrait of a President*, [London; Zed Press, 1981], pp. 50–51). See also Mordechai Gur (*Ma'ariv*, October 11 1981; *Israeli Mirror*) "In February 1971 [Sadat] said that he was prepared to make peace with Israel." Also Rabin, p. 395 above, and many others.

73. Kapeliouk, *Israël*, pp. 59–60.

74. Eric Pace, "Anwar el-Sadat, the Daring Arab Pioneer of Peace with Israel," *New York Times*, October 7, 1981.

75. Frederic L. Paxson, one of a group of American historians who offered their services to the state for this purpose during World War I; see *TNCW*, p. 70.

76. See note 46, above. Helprin, *New York Times Magazine*, Nov. 7, 1982.

77. On Israel's immediate rejection of the Fahd plan, see Norman Kempster, *Los Angeles Times—Boston Globe*, August 10, 1981, and the brief story in the *New York Times* on the same day.

78. Daniel Bloch, *Davar*, November 13, 1981. See *Fateful Triangle*, chap. 7, for a fuller discussion.

79. Yoel Marcus, *Yediot Ahronot*, November 6, 1981.

80. See *Palestine/Israel Bulletin*, April 1982, citing *Haolam Haze*, February 3, and the *Jerusalem Post*, February 1, 1982.

81. "How Syria's Peace Plan Was Swept Under the Carpet," *Ha'aretz*, February 12, 1982; *Israeli Mirror*.

82. *Jerusalem Post*, International Edition, February 14–20, 1982; cited in *Palestine/Israel Bulletin*, April 1982. See *Fateful Triangle*, note on p. 203.

83. For example, Amos Oz, "Has Israel Altered its Visions?," *New York Times Magazine*, July 11, 1982. Compare the picture portrayed by Mark Helprin in the same journal, "American Jews and Israel: Seizing a New Opportunity," November 7, 1982. See also note 70. See also Amos Oz, "From Jerusalem to Cairo," *Encounter*, April 1982, for an intriguing method of evading the historical record. Oz claims that "there is no symmetry" between Israel and the PLO, because "the PLO resembles the *militant* position in Israel," namely, the position that "disregard[s] the identity of the Palestinian problem" (note that this "militant position," contrary to what he asserts, is the mainstream position in Israel, adopted by both political groupings, and has been such since the days of Weizmann and Ben-Gurion). How does he conclude that the PLO resembles this position? By totally ignoring the record of their actual proposals, as reviewed briefly above, and restricting himself to their unwillingness to recognize the legitimacy of Zionism or to support partition "as a fundamental and right solution," rather than a compromise imposed by circumstances (a stand in which they mimic Ben-Gurion and others, contrary to Oz's claims). He also grossly misrepresents Sadat, claiming that his "visit to Jerusalem" represented "a conceptual revolution." With this technique of presenting a completely false picture of the history of socialist

Zionism including the stand of the Labor governments and the current position of the Labor Alignment, and ignoring the diplomatic efforts of the Arabs including the PLO in favor of irrelevant commentary about the PLO attitude toward the "legitimacy" of Zionism, Oz is able to maintain the pose of the tragic victim, so willing to make peace if only the Arabs were not committed to their militancy. This pose has been a great success among Western intellectuals, though Israeli doves naturally find it extremely offensive—and pernicious, in that it makes a major contribution to reinforcing attitudes and policies in the West (primarily the U.S.) that contribute directly to settlement and oppression in the occupied territories, aggression in Lebanon, and so on.

84. *Jerusalem Post*, March 6, 1981. Rabin, who was prime minister at the time, conceded the facts but said that the boats were captured before the proposed gesture, and that this was simply an excuse for the PLO to back out of the agreement. Shimon Peres, who was defense minister at the time, declined to comment.

85. See *TNCW*, p. 458, citing Livia Rokach's very important study, *Israel's Sacred Terrorism* (AAUG, Belmont, 1980), based largely on Sharett's *Personal Diary*, (*Yoman Ishi*, Hebrew, *Ma'ariv*, 1979).

86. Tillman, *The United States in the Middle East*, pp. 215–18. Congressman Findley was the senior Republican member of the House Middle East Subcommittee. See *New York Times*, November 27, 1978, for a brief report; there is no further mention of the matter in the *Times*. Tillman cites Arafat's statement to Findley with no qualifications, making no mention of the allegation that Findley transmitted it inaccurately or that the PLO retracted it. According to Tillman, "Thwarted by the lack of American response to its signals of willingness to compromise and angered by the Camp David agreement and Egypt's separate peace with Israel, the PLO reverted to bluster and threat and stepped up acts of terror" (p. 218).

87. *Israel & Palestine* (Paris), July–August 1982; Brezhnev's statement is cited from his address to the 26th Congress of the Soviet Communist Party in February 1981. See also Shmuel Segev, *Ma'ariv*, March 2, 1983, noting the reendorsement of this position at the PLO National Council meeting in Algiers in February 1983. I noticed no reference to these facts (or much else reported here) in the U.S. press, apart from quotes from Arafat and Sartawi in an article from Tunis by Lally Weymouth, special to the *Boston Globe*, December 21, 1982. There is an oblique and inaccurate reference to the facts in the *New York Times* at the end of a story on a different topic by Thomas Friedman, who writes that the Brezhnev plan "indirectly recognized the right of Israel to live in peace," and was endorsed by the PLO; there was nothing "indirect" about it. It is doubtful that even this reference would have appeared in the *Times* had it not been for the context, a story worth emphasis as illustrating PLO intransigence; see note 88.

88. *Israel & Palestine*, July–August 1982. Sartawi's relations with the PLO had been stormy. While he was regularly defended by Arafat against the "radicals" and rejectionists, his conflicts with them were sufficiently harsh so that he occasionally

resigned from the National Council, with varying interpretations as to what had in fact occurred. See *TNCW*, pp. 443–44 for a mid-1981 example. See also Thomas L. Friedman, "A P.L.O. Moderate Resigns in Protest," *New York Times*, February 21, 1983, reporting at length Sartawi's resignation from the National Council once again after he was prevented from addressing the group (the resignation was not accepted; see Trudy Rubin, *Christian Science Monitor*, March 11, 1983; it is also worth noting that Labor party leader Shimon Peres had succeeded in preventing him from speaking at the Socialist International meeting, just prior to his assassination). Some PLO officials stated that Arafat did not object "to the substance of his ideas but that the P.L.O. leader feared it would lead to a dispute that could upset the entire conference and scuttle his own quiet maneuvering to gain approval for more meetings with Israelis," but Friedman questions this interpretation in the light of the statement by the official PLO representative that Sartawi "did not represent the views of the Palestinian leadership." Peled is far more marginal in Israeli politics than Sartawi was within the PLO. Peled had been associated with the tiny Sheli party, a dovish Zionist party that has no current members in the Knesset, but broke relations with it after the Lebanon war when some of its leaders denounced his meetings with Arafat and gave their support to "crimes against humanity" in Lebanon (Peled, interview; see note 64). These facts are suppressed by those who point to Sartawi's troubled relationship with the central PLO decision-making body as proof of PLO iniquity.

89. *Ha'aretz*, July 10, 1981, cited in a July 1982 publication (*Who Will Stop Them?*, Hebrew), of the Committee Against the War in Lebanon, Jerusalem.

90. *Migvan*, Labor Party Monthly, August 1982. For further discussion of these matters, see *TNCW*; Tillman, *The United States in the Middle East*; and the regular reporting in such journals as the *New Outlook, Israel & Palestine*, and *Palestine/Israel Bulletin*.

91. Flapan, *Zionism and the Palestinians*, pp. 70ff. Within the mainstream, he notes, Moshe Sharett (then Shertok) disagreed with this view, arguing that it was pointless to deny that the leadership is the "legal representative" of the Palestinians and to refuse to negotiate with them (pp. 149–50).

Index